CHARL[ES]

...erhaps the greatest novelist in the English language, he was the creator of characters who live immortally in the English imagination: Mr Pickwick, the Artful Dodger, Mrs Gamp, Mr Micawber, Pip, Miss Havisham and many more. He was also a demonically hard-work[ing jo]urnalist, father of ten children, indefatigable walker and [travel]ler, and tireless in his support of liberal social causes.

At th[e age o]f twelve he was sent by his affectionate but feckless parents to wo[rk in] a blacking factory. By the time of his death in 1870 he drew [adorin]g crowds to his public appearances, had met princes and presi[dents,] and had amassed a fortune. He was truly 'the inimitable', as he ha[d teasi]ngly described himself. When he died, the world mourned, and h[e was] buried – against his wishes – in Westminster Abbey.

The [energ]y and brilliance concealed a complex and divided character. A re[publica]n, he took strongly against America when he visited the coun[try; se]ntimental about the family in his writings, he cast his wife into o[uter d]arkness after taking up with a young actress; often generous with [his tim]e and money, he cut off his more impecunious children and siblin[gs. Aft]er his death his own daughter wrote to Bernard Shaw, 'If you c[ould m]ake the public understand that my father was not a joyous, jocos[e gentl]eman walking about the world with a plum pudding and a bowl [of pun]ch, you would greatly oblige me.'

Cha[rles Dic]kens: A Life is the examination of Dickens we deserve. It gives full m[easu]re to his heroic stature – his huge virtues both as a writer and as a [huma]n being – while observing his failings in both respects with an under[sta]nding but unblinking eye. Twenty years ago Claire Tomalin's award-winning *The Invisible Woman* convincingly traced the relationship between Dickens and Nelly Ternan in a triumph of sympathetic scholarship. Now she has written a full-scale biography worthy of Dickens's own pen: a comedy that turns to tragedy as the very qualities that made him great – his indomitable energy, boldness, imagination, showmanship and enjoyment of fame – finally destroyed him.

Charles Dickens

Charles Dickens

A Life

CLAIRE TOMALIN

VIKING
an imprint of
PENGUIN BOOKS

VIKING

Published by the Penguin Group
Penguin Books Ltd, 80 Strand, London WC2R 0RL, England
Penguin Group (USA) Inc., 375 Hudson Street, New York, New York 10014, USA
Penguin Group (Canada), 90 Eglinton Avenue East, Suite 700, Toronto, Ontario, Canada M4P 2Y3
(a division of Pearson Penguin Canada Inc.)
Penguin Ireland, 25 St Stephen's Green, Dublin 2, Ireland (a division of Penguin Books Ltd)
Penguin Group (Australia), 250 Camberwell Road, Camberwell, Victoria 3124, Australia
(a division of Pearson Australia Group Pty Ltd)
Penguin Books India Pvt Ltd, 11 Community Centre, Panchsheel Park, New Delhi – 110 017, India
Penguin Group (NZ), 67 Apollo Drive, Rosedale, Auckland 0632, New Zealand
(a division of Pearson New Zealand Ltd)
Penguin Books (South Africa) (Pty) Ltd, 24 Sturdee Avenue, Rosebank,
Johannesburg 2196, South Africa

Penguin Books Ltd, Registered Offices: 80 Strand, London WC2R 0RL, England

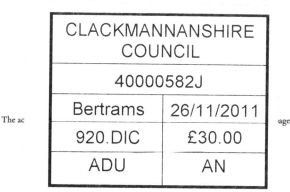

The ac   age

Set in Bembo Book MT Std 12/14.75 pt
Typeset by Palimpsest Book Production Limited, Falkirk, Stirlingshire
Printed in Great Britain by Clays Ltd, St Ives plc

A CIP catalogue record for this book is available from the British Library

HARDBACK ISBN: 978–0–670–91767–9
TRADE PAPERBACK ISBN: 978–0–670–92048–8

www.greenpenguin.co.uk

I dedicate this book to the memory of two remarkable women:
my mother, the composer Muriel Emily Herbert, 1897–1984,
who shared with me her enjoyment of Dickens when I was a child;
and my French grandmother, a schoolteacher, Franceline Jennaton
Delavenay, 1873–1963, who in about 1888, when she was at boarding
school in Grenoble, read *David Copperfield* in its entirety in English,
and loved Dickens ever afterwards.

My sister and I first realised Mr Dickens himself . . . as a sort of brilliance in the room, mysteriously dominant and formless. I remember how everybody lighted up when he entered.

– Annie Thackeray writing in 1913

I suppose that for at least five-and-twenty years of his life, there was not an English-speaking household in the world . . . where his name was not as familiar as that of any personal acquaintance, and where an allusion to characters of his creating could fail to be understood.

– George Gissing in 1898

The life of almost any man possessing great gifts, would be a sad book to himself.

– Charles Dickens in 1869

It will not do to draw round any part of such a man too hard a line.

– John Forster, friend of Dickens, in his biography

Contents

14   A Home   202

15   A Personal History   211

16   Fathers and Sons   226

17   Children at Work   238

18   Little Dorrit and Friends   252

19   Wayward and Unsettled   270

     PART THREE

20   Stormy Weather   289

21   Secrets, Mysteries and Lies   305

22   The Bebelle Life   324

23   Wise Daughters   339

24   The Chief   353

25   'Things look like work again'   371

26   Pickswick, Pecknicks, Pickwicks   384

27   The Remembrance of My Friends   401

     Notes   418

     Select Bibliography   489

     Acknowledgements   493

     Index   496

Illustrations

All illustrations are reproduced courtesy of the Charles Dickens Museum except where indicated.

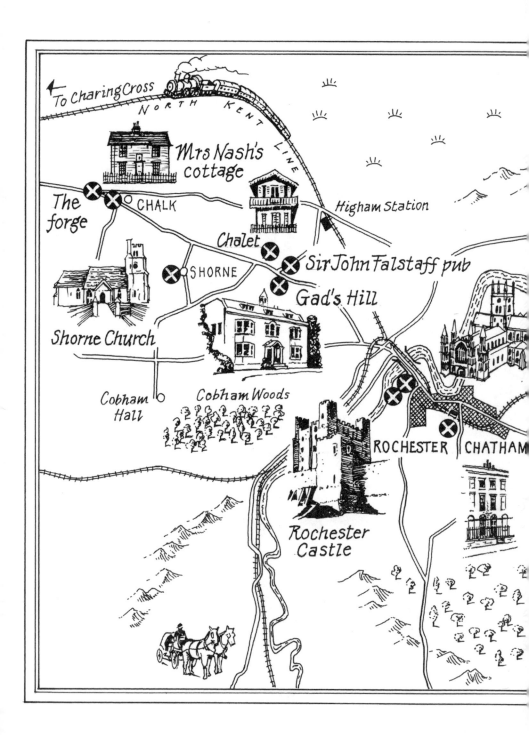

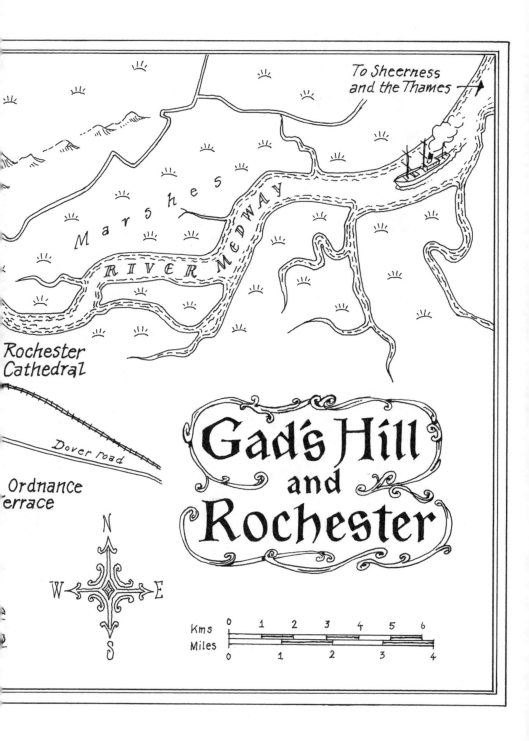

To Sheerness
and the Thames

Marshes

RIVER MEDWAY

Rochester
Cathedral

Dover road

Ordnance
Terrace

Gad's Hill
and
Rochester

N
W E
S

Kms 0 1 2 3 4 5 6
Miles 0   1   2   3   4

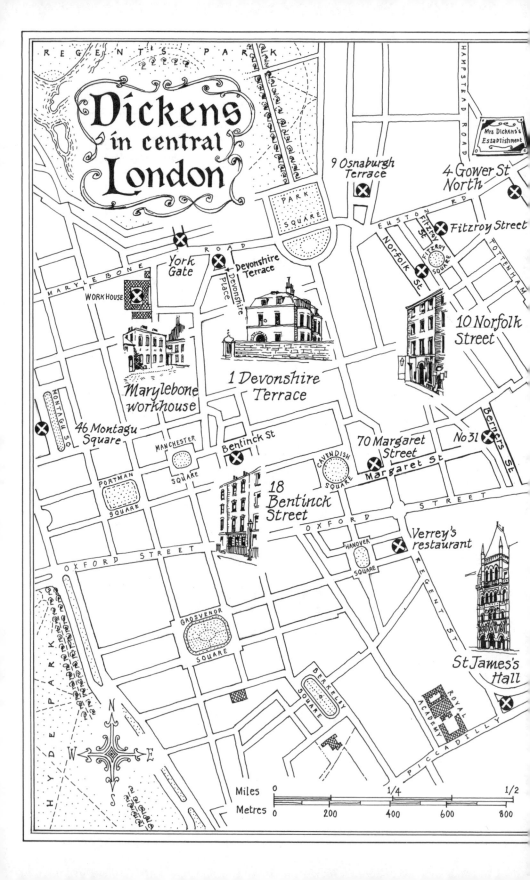

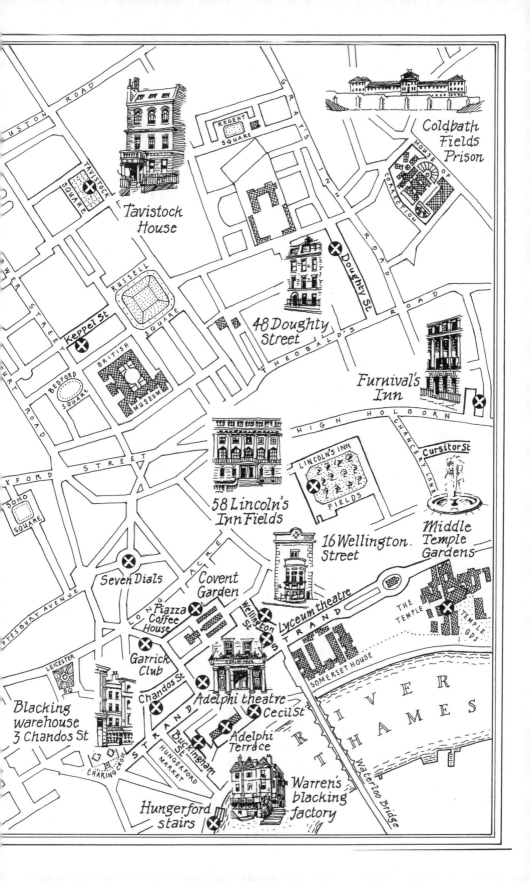

Coldbath Fields Prison

Tavistock House

48 Doughty Street

Furnival's Inn

Cursitor St

58 Lincoln's Inn Fields

16 Wellington Street

Middle Temple Gardens

Seven Dials

Covent Garden

Piazza Coffee House

Lyceum theatre

THE TEMPLE

Garrick Club

Chandos St

Adelphi theatre

Cecil St

RIVER THAMES

Blacking warehouse 3 Chandos St

Buckingham St

Adelphi Terrace

Warren's blacking factory

Hungerford stairs

Waterloo Bridge

SOMERSET HOUSE

REGENT SQUARE

TAVISTOCK SQUARE

RUSSELL SQUARE

BRITISH MUSEUM

Keppel St

BEDFORD SQUARE

GRAYS INN

HIGH HOLBORN

LINCOLN'S INN FIELDS

CHANCERY LANE

Doughty St

THEOBALD'S

HOUSE OF CORRECTION

EUSTON ROAD

GOWER STREET

COURT ROAD

OXFORD STREET

SOHO SQUARE

SHAFTESBURY AVENUE

LEICESTER SQ

CHARING CROSS

HUNGERFORD MARKET

LONG ACRE

Wellington St

STRAND

TEMPLE GDS

Key to Maps

Gad's Hill and Rochester

John Dickens and his young family lived in **Rochester** and **Chatham** from 1817 to 1822, first at **No. 2 Ordnance Terrace** above Rochester, then from 1821 at No. 18 St Mary's Place, near the dockyards. Dickens was sometimes taken by his father up the **Medway** in the naval yacht. He went to school here from the age of nine.

Chalk village: Dickens spent his honeymoon here in 1836 in **Mrs Nash's cottage**, working on *The Pickwick Papers*.

Gad's Hill: Dickens saw the house as a child, purchased it in 1856, made it his country home thereafter and died there. He loved walking in **Cobham Woods**, showing friends the beauties of the Kentish countryside and Rochester, and taking a boat on the Medway. He wished to be buried in the country, and the family first chose **Shorne Churchyard** and then **Rochester Cathedral**, but were persuaded that Westminster Abbey was the appropriate place. His body was taken on a special train from **Higham Station** to Charing Cross early in the morning of 14 June, accompanied by the family mourners.

Dickens in Central London

Adelphi Theatre, Strand: Dickens was inspired by the character acting of Charles Mathews, who was the star here in the 1820s and 1830s. Many dramatizations of Dickens's early novels and Christmas stories were played here from 1834 on.

Buckingham Street: Dickens lodged here in 1834, and put David Copperfield into lodgings here.

No. 18 Bentinck Street: Dickens lodged here in 1833.

No. 31 Berners Street: Maria and Nelly Ternan lived in lodgings here autumn 1858 to spring 1859, when they moved to Houghton Place (see North London map).

Cecil Street: Dickens lodged here briefly in 1832. The street has disappeared under the Shell building.

No. 3 Chandos Street: Dickens was set to work in the window of the blacking warehouse here, where he was noticed by Charles Dilke, who gave him half-a-crown.

Coldbath Fields Prison: Dickens was an obsessive visitor of prisons and this was a favourite, the governor Augustus Tracey a close friend. It was built on Mount Pleasant, where the Post Office now has a sorting office.

No. 1 Devonshire Terrace: home of Dickens from December 1839 until December 1851, let out when he went abroad.

No. 48 Doughty Street: Dickens bought lease in 1837, lived here until December 1839. Now the Charles Dickens Museum.

No. 13 Fitzroy Street: Dickens lodged here occasionally with his parents in 1832.

Furnival's Inn: Dickens moved to chambers here in 1834, and to better rooms on his marriage in 1836. His first child, Charley, was born here January 1837. They moved out March 1837.

Garrick Club: Dickens a member from 1837, resigning and rejoining frequently.

No. 4 Gower Street North: Dickens lived here with parents in 1823, his mother hoping to establish a school.

Hungerford Stairs, Warren's blacking factory: the factory, set beside the river stairs before the Embankment was built, was reached through the old Hungerford Market, over which Charing Cross Station was built in 1864.

No. 34 Keppel Street: Dickens installed John Dickens in a doctor's house here, and was present at his father's death in 1851.

No. 58 Lincoln's Inn Fields: John Forster lodged here from

1834, expanding steadily into more rooms to take his growing book collection. He left on his marriage in 1856.

Lyceum Theatre, Strand: theatre well known to Dickens. *A Tale of Two Cities* played here in 1860, Dickens's friend Fechter was the lessee in 1864, Mrs Ternan made her last stage appearance here in 1866.

No. 70 Margaret Street: Dickens lodged here with parents early in 1831.

Marylebone Workhouse: a very large group of buildings, where Dickens served on a jury in 1840.

No. 46 Montagu Square: John Forster lived here after his marriage in 1856.

No. 10 Norfolk Street (now Cleveland Street): Dickens lodged here with parents 1815–16 and again in 1829.

No. 9 Osnaburgh Terrace: Dickens rented a house briefly here in 1844 when Devonshire Terrace was let to a tenant. His children were moved to No. 25 Osnaburgh Street during his American trip in 1842.

Piazza Coffee House in Covent Garden: meeting place for Dickens, Forster and friends. Dickens also put up here, e.g., in December 1844.

St James's Hall: Dickens did most of his London readings here. He started in St Martin's Hall in Longacre, which burnt down in 1860, and also gave readings in Hanover Square rooms.

Somerset House: John Dickens worked here in the Navy Pay Office 1805–9 and 1822–5.

Strand: the *Morning Chronicle*, for which Dickens wrote, was at No. 332, and his publishers Chapman & Hall at No. 186.

Tavistock House: bought by Dickens in 1851, intending to remain for life, but he sold it in 1860.

Verrey's Restaurant: Dickens's favourite London restaurant from the 1850s.

No. 16 Wellington Street: Dickens's office for *Household Words* from 1850, with private rooms for himself above. It was handy for theatres, and he entertained here a good deal. In 1858, when he started *All the Year Round*, he moved along the street to the larger No. 26, furnishing the private rooms comfortably and employing a housekeeper

Dickens in North London

Ampthill Square: Dickens found a house for his widowed mother here in 1851.

No. 16 Bayham Street: John and Elizabeth Dickens moved here from Rochester with their family in 1822.

Euston Station was built in 1837, **King's Cross** in 1852, **St Pancras** in 1868.

No. 70 Gloucester Crescent: Catherine Dickens lived here after the separation until her death.

No. 4 Grafton Terrace: Dickens installed his widowed sister-in-law, Helen, with her children in 1860, and then his mother, who remained here until her death.

No. 2 Houghton Place (Ampthill Square): the house bought for Fanny and Maria Ternan in 1859 and transferred to Ellen (Nelly) Ternan on her majority in 1860. There can be little doubt that it was paid for by Dickens.

No. 29 Johnson Street: John and Elizabeth Dickens and family lived here from December 1824 to March 1827.

No. 27 Little College Street: John and Elizabeth Dickens and family lived in lodgings here in 1824.

No. 17 The Polygon: John and Elizabeth Dickens lived here from March 1827 to 1829.

Wellington House Academy: Charles Dickens went to school here 1825 to 1827.

Dickens rode and walked regularly for years in the countryside north of London, and he stayed in Collins's Farm (now Wylds) on Hampstead Heath in 1837. In 1843 he rented a 'lonely Farm House', Cobley's Farm, in rural Finchley, for three months: it is all built over now. He also thought of buying a house in Highgate; and in Highgate Cemetery he buried his sister Fanny and her eight-year-old son, Harry, his father, his own baby daughter, Dora, and his mother.

Immediately north of this map are Highgate and Hampstead, where John Dickens occasionally moved to escape his creditors and also took his family in the summer, to No. 32 North End in May 1832.

Cast List

Abbreviations

AYR	*All the Year Round*
Catherine D	Catherine Dickens
D	Charles Dickens
F	John Forster
GH	Georgina Hogarth
HW	*Household Words*

The Dickens Family

D's grandmother **Elizabeth Dickens**, *née* Ball (1745–1824), a ladies' maid, then housekeeper to Crewe family at Crewe Hall and Mayfair (John Crewe raised to peerage 1806).

D's grandfather **William Dickens** (*c.* 1720–85), butler to the Crewe family.

Their son **William** (1782–1825), London coffee-stallkeeper, was D's uncle, married, childless.

Their second son was D's father, **John Dickens** (1785–1851), Navy Pay Office clerk, married 1809 **Elizabeth** *née* **Barrow** (1789–1863), D's mother, one of ten children of Charles Barrow (1759–1826), also employed by the Navy Pay Office, and his wife Mary (1771–1851). For significant **Barrow children**, D's uncles and aunts, see below.

Of the eight children of John and Elizabeth Dickens, two died in infancy (Alfred Allen and Harriet), the others being:

Frances Elizabeth (Fanny) (1810–48), musician, married 1837 singer Henry Burnett, two sons.

Charles John Huffam (1812–70), married 1836 Catherine Hogarth *q.v.*, ten children.

Letitia Mary (1816–93), married 1837 Henry Austin *q.v.*

Frederick William (1820–68), clerk, married 1848 Anna Weller *q.v.*

Alfred Lamert (1822–60), engineer, married 1846 Helen Dobson (1823–1915), three sons, including Edmund (1849–1910), two daughters.

Augustus Newnham (1827–66), accountant, married 1848 Harriet Lovell, one child, abandoned 1858 for Bertha Phillips, Bertram and five other illegitimate children in Chicago.

⁂

Catherine Thomson Hogarth, later Dickens (1815–79), eldest of the ten children of **George Hogarth** (1783–1870), Edinburgh lawyer and musician turned journalist, and his wife **Georgina** *née* **Thomson** (1793–1863), married in 1814. Younger children included **Mary Scott** (1819–37), **Georgina** (1827–1917), Helen, George, Robert, William.

The Children of Dickens and Catherine *née* Hogarth

Charles Culliford Boz (Charley) (1837–96), businessman, married 1861 Bessie Evans (1838–1907), six daughters one son, Ethel, Charles Walter, Sydney Margaret, Dorothy, Beatrice, Cecil Mary, Evelyn.

Mary (Mamie) (1838–96).

Kate Macready (Katey) (1839–1929), artist, married [1] 1860 Charles Collins *q.v.* [2] 1874 Carlo Perugini (1839–1918), one son died in infancy.

Walter Landor (1841–63), Indian Army 1857.

Francis Jeffrey (Frank) (1844–86), to India 1863, Bengal Mounted Police, to Canada 1871, North West Mounted Police.

Alfred D'Orsay Tennyson (1845–1912), to Australia 1865, station manager, etc., married 1873 Augusta Jessie Devlin (1849–78), two daughters.

Sydney Smith Haldimand (1847–72), naval officer.

Henry Fielding (1849–1933), lawyer, married 1876 Marie-Thérèse Roche, seven children.

Dora Annie (1850–51).

Edward Bulwer Lytton (Plorn) (1852–1902), to Australia 1868, married 1880 Constance Desailly.

The Ternan Family

Mrs Frances *née* Jarman (1802–73), admired actress, married actor Thomas Teman 1834, widowed 1846, three daughters.

Ternan, Frances Eleanor (1835–1913), child actress, opera singer, married T. A. Trollope *q.v.* 1866, lived in Italy, first novel published by D, wrote many more.

Ternan, Maria Susanna (1837–1904), child actress, singer, married Rowland Taylor 1863, left him 1873, became artist, journalist, traveller, writer.

Ternan, Ellen Lawless (Nelly) (1839–1914), child actress, gave up career, married George Wharton Robinson 1876, son Geoffrey born 1879, daughter Gladys 1884.

❧

Ainsworth, William Harrison (1805–82), novelist, met D 1835, introduced him to publisher Macrone, illustrator Cruikshank. Friendship dwindled by 1850.

Andersen, Hans Christian (1805–75), writer, admirer of D, stayed at Gad's Hill 1857.

Austin, Henry (?1812–61), architect, engineer, good friend of D from early 1830s, married D's sister Letitia 1837, became Secretary to London Sanitary Commission.

Barrow, Mary (?1792–1822), D's aunt, known as Fanny, married [1] naval officer Allen [2] army surgeon Matthew Lamert, father of **James Lamert**, who finds job for D in blacking factory.

Barrow, Thomas Culliford (?1793–1857), D's uncle, employed by

Navy Pay Office from age of eleven, leg amputated 1823, Head of
Prize Branch, married 1824, son John Wylie Barrow (1828–85),
settled New York.

Barrow, John Henry (1796–1858), D's uncle, married Kitty Collins
1817, left her to live with Lucina Pocock from 1828, ten children.
Novelist, reporter, employed young D, who in 1845 sent him to
India for *Daily News*. Daughter Emily known to D.

Barrow, Edward (1798–1869), D's uncle, parliamentary reporter,
joined in theatricals with D, artist wife Janet Ross painted D.
Member of Newspaper Press Fund from Jan. 1859.

Barrow, Frederick, D's uncle, daughter Rebecca born 1817, known
to D, other Barrow daughters Jane, Sarah, Maria.

Beadnell, Maria (1810–86), third daughter of George Beadnell, senior
clerk in City bank, met D 1830, romance ended 1832, married
Henry Winter 1845, renewed friendship with D 1855. Model for
Dora in *David Copperfield* and Flora Finching in *Little Dorrit*.

Beard brothers: Sussex born. **Thomas** (1807–91), journalist, met D
1834, best man at his wedding, godfather to Charley, lifelong
friend; **Francis** (1814–93), physician, became D's doctor 1859.

Bentley, Richard (1794–1871), printer then publisher, magazine
proprietor, D was editor of *Bentley's Miscellany* in which *Oliver
Twist* was serialized, disputes over contracts for various books
throughout 1838, parted company.

Berger, Francesco (1834–1933), Charley's Leipzig friend, wrote
music for *The Frozen Deep*.

Berry, Mary (1763–1852), and her sister Agnes, learned ladies and
protégées of Horace Walpole, entertained D at their Twickenham house, Little Strawberry Hill, 1 July 1839.

Black, John (1783–1855), editor *Morning Chronicle*, Liberal paper,
employed D 1834, appreciated his outstanding gifts.

Blanchard, Samuel Laman (1804–45), Liberal journalist, early
friend, committed suicide.

Blessington, Marguerite, Countess of (Marguerite Gardiner)
(1789–1849), beauty, novelist, journalist, companion of Count
D'Orsay *q.v.*, D met 1840. Her niece Marguerite Power protégée
of D.

Boyle, Mary (1810–90), well-connected literary lady, amateur actress, devoted to D from first meeting in 1850.

Bradbury, William (1800–1869), with partner Frederick Evans *q.v.*, known to D from 1830s as printers for Chapman & Hall, became publishers of *Punch* 1842, *Daily News* 1846, D's publishers 1844 to 1858 (Christmas books and novels) and part-owners of *HW*.

Brown, Mrs William, *née* Hannah Meredith (?1805–78), companion to Miss Coutts *q.v.*, married Dr Brown 1844 (he died 1855), continued as Miss C's companion.

Browne, Hablot Knight ('Phiz') (1815–82), artist, fine illustrator of D's work from 1836 to 1859, after which he was dropped and the friendship ended.

Buckstone, John (1802–79), comic actor, playwright, lifelong friend of D, manager of Haymarket Theatre 1853–77, employed Ternans.

Bulwer Lytton, Edward George Earle Lytton, first Baron Lytton (1803–73), hugely successful, prolific novelist, playwright, known to D from 1837, worked with him and F to set up Guild of Literature and Art to assist writers. Changed his name from 'Bulwer' to 'Bulwer Lytton' 1844.

Burgess, Eliza (1816–?), servant girl, brought up in workhouse, accused of infanticide, helped by D, tried at Old Bailey June 1840 and freed.

Carlyle, Thomas (1795–1881), D met 1840, revered, dedicatee of *Hard Times*. Also his wife, **Jane Welsh Carlyle** (1801–66), cheerfully attended D's Christmas parties.

Cattermole, George (1800–1868), Norfolk squire's son, antiquarian painter, illustrated *The Old Curiosity Shop*, lost touch with D in the 1850s, son Leonardo remembered D as the best of storytellers.

Céleste, Madame (?1814–82), French actress, dancer, manager of Adelphi Theatre from 1844, well known to D, put on dramatized *A Tale of Two Cities*. (See **Webster**)

Cerjat, W. W. F. de (?–1869), Swiss friend of D from 1846, to whom he sent informative annual letters.

Chapman, Edward (1804–80), publisher and bookseller with William Hall *q.v.*, published *Pickwick Papers*, bought back copyright of *Oliver*

Twist from Bentley, continued with D until 1844, when D broke with firm, returning 1859.

Chapman, Frederic (1823–95), cousin of Edward, knew D from 1845, took over Chapman & Hall in 1864 when Edward retired.

Charlton, Charles William, and his wife **Elizabeth Culliford** (1781–1853), she D's great-aunt, lodging-house keeper, he clerk at Doctors' Commons, both helpful to D in youth.

Chateaubriand, François-René de (1768–1848), writer, diplomat, visited by D in Paris 1847.

Chesterton, George Laval (?–1868), Army officer, then reforming Governor Coldbath Fields Prison in Clerkenwell 1829–54. D met him in 1835, respected, later worked with.

Chorley, Henry (1808–72), music critic, general reviewer, wrote for *AYR*, became family friend.

Church, Mary Anne (1832–?), robbed employers 1850, sent by Tracey *q.v.* from Tothill Fields Prison to Miss Coutts's Home 1851, caused 'consistent botheration', ejected April 1852; in 1855 she was well known as a prostitute, charged with stealing from a brothel.

Collins brothers: **Wilkie** (1824–89), writer, from 1851 collaborated, acted, travelled with D; **Charles** (1828–73), artist, invalid, married Katey Dickens 1860.

Compton, Emmeline, *née* Montague (?–1910), actress, D saw her debut as Juliet 1839, friend for many years, acted with him, left recollections.

Cooper, Louisa, enters Miss Coutts's Home from Magdalen Asylum April 1853, stayed two years, sent to Cape, returned 1856, bringing D ostrich egg, engaged to be married to an English gardener.

Coutts, Angela Burdett (1814–1906), heiress, philanthropist, dear friend of D, who advised her on many charitable projects from early 1840s until 1858, when her disapproval of his treatment of Catherine ended their close association. *Martin Chuzzlewit* dedicated to her. Created Baroness 1871.

Cowden-Clarke, Mary, *née* Novello (1809–98), Shakespeare scholar, writer, met D 1848, acted with and adored him, moved abroad 1856.

Cranstone, Frances (1836–58), entered Miss Coutts's Home 1853, expelled for trouble-making April 1854, died in Shoreditch Workhouse.

Cruikshank, George (1792–1878), artist, friend of D, superb illustrator of *Sketches by Boz* and of *Oliver Twist*, the plot of which he later claimed to have originated, without any justification.

De La Rue, Emile, Swiss banker working in Genoa, and his English wife, **Augusta**, née Granet, friends of D in Genoa in 1844. De La Rue invited D to treat his wife for psychological disorders, and he agreed to do so by mesmerism, with only partial success.

Dilke, Charles Wentworth (1789–1864), colleague of John Dickens at Navy Pay Office, saw D working blacking factory circa 1824. Editor *Athenaeum* 1830s, D sent him *Sketches by Boz* for review.

Dolby, George (1831–1900), managed D's reading tours from 1866, true friend.

D'Orsay, Count Gédéon Gaspard Alfred de Grimaud (1801–52), artist, gambler, dandy, illegitimate son of Napoleonic general, while living in London with his mother-in-law, Lady Blessington *q.v.*, met D 1836, to mutual delight. D's fourth son named for him (and Tennyson). Debts obliged him to move to Paris 1849.

Dostoevsky, Fyodor (1821–81), visited D in London 1862, recalled conversation in 1878.

Dumas, Alexandre (1802–70), novelist, playwright, D supped with in Paris 1847, kept in contact.

Egg, Augustus Leopold (1816–63), son of Piccadilly gun-maker, studied Royal Academy School, fine genre and historical painter. Friend of D from late 1840s, acted in theatricals, travelled abroad with him. Died in Algiers.

Eliot, George (Marian Evans) (1819–80), novelist, admired from very first by D, cordial contact although she never wrote for his magazines.

Elliot, Frances, née Dickinson (1820–98), heiress with rackety marital history introduced to D by Collins, persuaded D to intervene in her difficulties in 1860s, questioned him in vain about his private life.

Elliotson, John (1791–1868), physician, a founder of University College Hospital, forced to resign 1838 after mesmerism displays, known to D from 1837, became his doctor, godfather to his son Walter.

Elton, Edward William (1794–1843), actor, chairman Theatrical Fund, widower, drowned, leaving seven children. D raised large sums for their education and training, particularly impressed by eldest, Esther, who became teacher.

Evans, Frederick (?1803–70), printing partner of Bradbury *q.v.* from 1830. Family friendship broken by D 1858. Daughter Bessie married Charley Dickens 1861, to D's disapproval.

Fechter, Charles Albert (1822–79), actor in France, then London from 1860, D praised him as 'Anti-Humbug', formed intimate friendship, assisted in his career.

Felton, Cornelius (1807–62), Professor of Greek, later President of Harvard, D's firmest American friend in 1842 – he rated D with Shakespeare – then regular correspondent.

Fields, James T. (1817–81), Boston publisher, met D 1842, became friend 1860 on London visit with wife Annie, entertained him on US reading tour, saw much of him in England 1869.

Fitzgerald, Percy (1834–1925), Irish lawyer turned jobbing writer, contributor to *AYR*, D protégé.

Fletcher, Angus (1799–1862), eccentric Scottish sculptor, met D 1830s through Macrone, made marble bust of D 1839, with him Scotland, Broadstairs, Italy.

Fonblanque, Albany (1793–1872), radical journalist, editor of the *Examiner* 1830, friend of Carlyle, Macready, D'Orsay, early admirer of D, wrote political leaders for his *Daily News*.

Forster, John (1812–76), D's closest and most trusted friend, adviser and negotiator from 1837, and his chosen biographer. Journalist, historian, man of letters, married 1856 Elizabeth Colburn, published *Life of Charles Dickens* in three volumes, 1872, 1873, 1874.

Fortescue, Julia (1817–99), actress, reared for stage by mother, breeches parts, admired for beauty by D, Maclise, Macready, who gave her work; distracted by Lord Gardner, a married aristocrat to whom she bore five children. Played in D's theatricals 1845, 1848.

Frith, William Powell (1819–1909), artist commissioned by F to paint portrait of D in 1854, friend.

Gaskell, Elizabeth (1810–65), novelist, D thought highly of her *Mary Barton* (1849), she became frequent, favoured contributor to *HW* and *AYR*, resisted his attempts to change or cut her copy.

Gautier, Théophile (1811–72), poet visited by D in Paris 1847.

Goldsmith, Martha (1829–84), Berkshire girl, London prostitute, wanting to reform, taken into Miss Coutts's Home 1848, sent to Australia 1849, married carpenter Geo. Hamilton in Melbourne 1851, settled life thereafter.

Gordon, Isabella, lively girl arrived at Miss Coutts's Home early 1849, liked by D but ejected after nine months for trouble-making.

Graves, Caroline (?1830–95), widow, mistress of Wilkie Collins from 1858, and her daughter born 1851, known to D as 'the Butler'.

Haldimand, William (1784–1862), wealthy philanthropist living Lausanne, met D 1846.

Hall, William (1800–1847), partner of Edward Chapman *q.v.* in bookselling and publishing business from 1830, signed up D in 1836 to write *Pickwick*. His tough financial dealings in 1844 led to D's break with the firm.

Harley, John Pritt (1786–1858), 'Fat Jack', skinny London-born comic actor best known for Shakespearean clowns, in D's *The Strange Gentleman* 1836, remained friend.

Holland, Baroness (Elizabeth Fox) (1771–1845), Whig hostess of Holland House, wife of Charles James Fox's nephew; summoned D to her salon early in his career, late in hers. They appreciated one another, corresponded.

Hollingshead, John (1827–1904), journalist, wrote for D's magazines from 1857, went on to theatre management.

Huffam, Christopher, Limehouse naval rigger, served in Napoleonic wars, godfather to D.

Hugo, Victor (1802–85), complimented D, who visited him at home in Paris 1846.

Hullah, John (1812–84), musician, composer, teacher, known to D

through his sister Fanny, a fellow student at Royal College of
Music. Wrote score for D's *The Village Coquettes*.

Hunt, Leigh (1784–1859), poet, essayist, editor, imprisoned for
insulting Prince Regent, D met 1839, friend, but satirized in *Bleak
House* as Skimpole.

Irving, Washington (1783–1859), American writer, influenced D,
friendship made during D's visit to US withdrawn after he read
American Notes and *Martin Chuzzlewit*.

Jeffrey, Francis, Lord (1773–1850), Scottish judge, critic, a founder
and editor of the *Edinburgh Review*, lover of D's work, friendship
established 1841, third son named for him.

Jerrold, Douglas William (1803–57), playwright, humorist,
journalist, friend from 1836. At Jerrold's death D raised money
for his family.

Joachim, Joseph (1831–1907), great Austrian violinist, played at
Gad's and at D's last reception in 1870. D particularly liked his
Tartini's 'Devil's Trill' Sonata.

Keeley, Robert (1793–1869), comic actor, gave D lessons 1832,
managed Lyceum 1844–7, played Mrs Gamp, actress wife **Mary
Anne** (1806–99) played Smike; son-in-law, Albert Smith, theatrical entrepreneur, *q.v.*, also friend of D.

Kemble, Charles (1775–1854), actor, well known to D, as were his
daughters, actress Fanny Kemble and singer Adelaide Kemble,
later Sartoris.

Kent, Charles (1823–1902), writer and journalist, editor of liberal
paper the *Sun*, devotee of D, contributor to his magazines from
1850.

Knowles, James Sheridan (1784–1862), playwright, D aimed to
make him curator of Shakespeare House, Stratford. Used two of
his play plots in writing *Our Mutual Friend*.

Kolle, Henry (?1808–81), bank clerk, friend of D from 1830 (also
brother **John**), joined in early theatricals, D best man at wedding
to Anne Beadnell. Friendship lapsed.

Lamartine, Alphonse de (1790–1869), writer, diplomat, liberal
politician, briefly head of French government in 1848. D visited
him in Paris 1847, 1856.

Landor, Walter Savage (1775–1864), poet, essayist, met D 1840, immediate rapport, D named second son for him.

Landseer, Edwin (1802–73), artist, known to D from the 1830s, as were his brothers Thomas, the engraver, and Charles, also an artist.

Layard, A. H. (1817–94), archaeologist, excavated Nineveh 1847, Liberal MP, D supported his Association for Administrative Reform 1855, well-established friendship.

Leech, John (1817–64), Londoner, Charterhouse, medical student, became painter, radical, associated with *Punch*. D met through Cruikshank 1836, close friendship, jaunts, family holidays together.

Lemon, Mark (1809–70), playwright, editor of *Punch* from 1841, acted with D, close family friend until 1858, when he negotiated for Catherine D's settlement.

Lewes, G. H. (1817–78), writer, partner of George Eliot *q.v.*, visited D 1838, thereafter occasional exchanges, contact, wrote critical obituary essay.

Linton, Eliza Lynn (1828–98), novelist, journalist, contributor from 1853 to *HW* and *AYR*, first met D at Landor's 1849, sold him Gad's Hill.

Longfellow, Henry Wadsworth (1807–82), poet, met D in Boston 1842, immediate liking, visited D in London, 1842, and at Gad's Hill 1868.

Maclise, Daniel (1806–70), Irish artist working in London, successful historical painter, ladies' man, met D 1837, enthusiastic friendship but depressive, drifted apart during 1840s.

Macready, William Charles (1793–1883), intimate, much loved friend of D from 1837, leading actor, dedicatee *Nicholas Nickleby*, married [1] 1824 Catherine Atkins (1805–52), many children [2] 1860 Cecile Spencer (1837–?), one son. Acted with and assisted Mrs Ternan *q.v.*

Macrone, John (1809–37), D's first publisher, friendship and contracts broken by D, but when Macrone died D raised money for widow and children.

Marryat, Captain Frederick (1792–1848), naval-officer-turned-author of novels, naval and children's stories, including *The Children of the New Forest*.

Mathews, Charles (1776–1835), actor who inspired young D with his one-man shows, or monopolylogues, in which he impersonated a series of characters. D studied and imitated him, showing his influence in later readings.

Millais, John Everett (1829–96), artist attacked by D in 1850 in *HW* article, became friend 1855. Drew D's face after his death.

Milnes, Richard Monckton, first Baron Houghton (1809–85), genial man of letters, politician, host, traveller, *bon viveur*, known to D from 1840. Married 1851 Annabella Crewe, granddaughter of Lord and Lady Crewe whose housekeeper was D's grandmother.

Mitton, Thomas (1812–78), solicitor, son of Somers Town publican, met D 1827, did his legal business for many years, replaced by Ouvry *q.v.*

Molloy, Charles (?1796–1852), solicitor for whom D clerked in 1828, acted for D in negotiations with publisher Bentley 1837–8. Cut his own throat.

Morley, Henry (1822–94), writer on medical subjects, staff post on *HW* 1851–9, *AYR* 1859–68, sacked by D, became academic, taught English at University College London.

Morson, Mrs Georgiana (?–1880), doctor's widow, matron of Miss Coutt's Home from 1849 to 1854 when she remarried. A pearl. Other matrons were Mrs Holdsworth, Mrs Marchmont.

Mosley, Julia (1828–56), Gloucestershire tailor's daughter, pickpocket, Tothill Fields prisoner taken into Miss Coutts's Home 1847, to Australia 1848, married 1853 in Adelaide, one son died infancy.

Normanby, first Marquess (Constantine Henry Phipps) (1797–1863), Liberal politician, protégé of Melbourne, travel writer, novelist, dandy, D knew from 1840, British Ambassador Paris 1846–52, career in decline. *Dombey* is dedicated to his marchioness, Maria (1798–1882), portrayed by Disraeli in *Endymion* as Lady Montfort.

Norton, Mrs Caroline, *née* Sheridan (1808–77), poet, novelist, writer on legal position of married women, involved in scandal when husband accused her of adultery with Lord Melbourne; she and sisters, Lady Seymour, Lady Dufferin, famous beauties, granddaughters of Richard Brinsley Sheridan. Known to D from 1836. He also knew their brother Charles in 1847 at British Embassy in Paris.

Norton, Charles Eliot (1827–1908), critic, met D in Boston 1868, visited Gad's same year.

Olliffe, Joseph (1808–69), Irish friend of Maclise, studied medicine in Paris, became physician to British Embassy, knew D from mid-1840s.

Ouvry, Frederic (1814–81), D's solicitor from 1856, partner at Farrer's at No. 66 Lincoln's Inn Fields.

Overs, John (1808–44), London cabinet-maker and writer, advised and helped by Dickens from 1839.

Phelps, Samuel (1804–78), actor, theatre manager, ran Sadler's Wells 1844–62, playing Shakespeare repertory, D knew from 1840s, wrote in praise of Sadler's Wells 1851. Mrs Ternan acted with him 1850s.

Picken, Eleanor (1820–98), through Smithson family connection made friends with D at Broadstairs in 1840, wrote vivid account of experiences. Married naval officer Edward Christian 1842.

Pollard, Rhena (1836–99), Sussex girl, workhouse, prison at sixteen, entered Miss Coutts's Home Aug. 1853, wanted to leave, persuaded to stay by D, doing well Feb. 1855, sent to Canada, wrote 1856 that she was married, settled life thereafter, children.

Régnier, François (1807–85), distinguished French actor, friend, correspondent of D.

Rogers, Samuel (1763–1855), poet, son of banker, generous, hospitable, from 1839 knew, admired, entertained D, who dedicated *The Old Curiosity Shop* to him.

Russell, Lord John, first Earl (1792–1878), Whig politician, introduced Reform Act 1832, reduced number of capital offences, Prime Minister 1846–52, 1865–6. D reported his early speeches, friend from 1846, dedicated *A Tale of Two Cities* to him.

Sala, George (1828–96), journalist, one of D's circle of young men, working for *HW* from 1851. Wrote short biography of D.

Scribe, Eugène (1791–1861), writer of comedies and farces, D met in Paris 1847, entertained in London 1850, friendly exchanges again Paris 1856.

Shaftesbury, seventh Earl (Anthony Ashley Cooper) (1801–85), Whig philanthropist, put through reforms relating to causes also taken up by D, whom he met 1848.

Smith brothers: Albert (1816–60), theatrical entertainer, worked with D material from 1844; and **Arthur** (1825–61), D's tour manager 1858, 1861.

Smith, Revd Sydney (1771–1845), wit, D visited, entertained, corresponded with from 1839, Smith admired *Martin Chuzzlewit* particularly. D's fifth son named after him (and William Haldimand) 1847.

Smithson, Charles (1804–44), lawyer, partner of Mitton, acted for D 1838, married to sister of T. J. Thompson *q.v.*, D godfather to daughter.

Stanfield, Clarkson (1793–1867), Catholic, child actor, pressed into Navy, became scene painter, admired marine artist. D met 1837, loved with unbroken affection, provided scenery for theatricals, *Little Dorrit* dedicated to him.

Stone, Frank (1800–1859), Manchester-born artist, close friend of D from 1838, walks, dinners, jaunts, acting together. Many Stone children liked and helped by D.

Stonnell, Mary Ann (?1832–?), worked with gang of thieves, prison sentence Coldbath Fields, one of first intake into Miss Coutts's Home, left of her own accord, soon in prison again. D considered her incurable.

Talfourd, Sir Thomas Noon (1795–1854), radical lawyer, MP, playwright, friend of D from 1837, dedicatee of *Pickwick Papers*.

Tennent, Sir James, first Baronet (1804–69), politician, travel writer, fought in Greece 1824, met Byron, knew D through F, Macready. *Our Mutual Friend* dedicated to him.

Tennyson, Alfred, first Baron (1809–92), poet, in 1842 D wrote to him of 'the love I bear you as a man whose writings enlist my whole heart and nature', named fourth son for him (and D'Orsay), reciprocal affection, but Tennyson troubled by D's sentimentality.

Thackeray, William Makepeace (1811–63), first met D 1836 when he applied to illustrate *Pickwick Papers*. Praised D's work generously, but said his behaviour in 1858 was 'a fatal story for our trade'. Edginess, fallings out, always underlying friendship. Daughter **Annie Thackeray** (1837–1919), friend of Mamie, Katey Dickens, frequent visitor to D's home until 1858, left vivid reminiscences of him.

Thompson (or Maynard), Caroline (age unknown but born late 1820s), worked as prostitute to support herself and child, helped by D in 1854 when her brother approached him, emigrated 1856.

Thompson, John (1826–?70s), employed aged fourteen by D as coachman, remained as general servant twenty-six years. Married Hannah Manton 1852, two daughters, Emily, born 1854, Matilda Dorrit, born 1857, dismissed for theft 1866, D continued to assist financially.

Thompson, T. J. (1812–81), wealthy clubman, collector, traveller, friend of D from 1838, widower, married Christiana Weller *q.v.*, settled in Italy.

Townshend, Chauncey Hare (1798–1868), rich, Cambridge-educated hypochondriac, met D 1840 through Elliotson, mesmerism; travelled abroad, dedicated poems to D, who dedicated *Great Expectations* to him, gave him manuscript – huge reward for foolish friend.

Tracey, Augustus (1798–1878), naval officer, then Governor of Tothill Fields Prison 1834–55, friend of D from 1841, worked with him from 1847 for Miss Coutts's Home, recommending young women prisoners.

Trollope brothers: **Thomas Adolphus** (1810–92), writer, settled Florence 1834 with writer mother Frances, earned living by his pen, very much liked D, married [1] Theodosia Garrow (1825–65) [2] Frances Ternan *q.v.*, who was introduced to him by D; **Anthony** (1815–82), novelist, friend, disliked D's style, placed

Thackeray, George Eliot above him, described him as a man 'powerful, clever, humorous . . . very ignorant, and thick-skinned, who had taught himself to be his own God'.

Watson, Hon. Richard (1800–1852), and wife **Lavinia** (1816–88), met D Switzerland 1846, entertained him at Rockingham Castle, enthusiastic friends, dedicatees of _David Copperfield_.

Webster, Benjamin (1798–1882), actor, dramatist, manager, ran Adelphi Theatre from 1844, adapted and appeared in _Cricket on the Hearth_, lifelong friend; business partner and lover of Céline Céleste _q.v._

Weller, Christiana (1825–1910), pianist, met D 1844, married T. J. Thompson _q.v._ 1845, settled in Italy (daughter was Alice Meynell). Her sister **Anna**, born 1830, married Fred Dickens in 1848, divorced him 1859.

Wiggin, Kate Douglas (1856–1923), American writer, met D on train in 1868, aged twelve, engaged him in conversation, charmed him, published her account 1912.

Wills, William Henry (1810–80), diligent assistant to D on _Daily News_, _HW_, _AYR_.

Yates, Edmund (1831–94), son of actors, journalist, met D 1854, friend, contributor, companion, at the circus with him two months before his death.

Prologue: The Inimitable

1840

14 January 1840, London. An inquest is being held at Marylebone Workhouse, a muddled complex of buildings spread over a large area between the Marylebone Road and Paddington Street. The Beadle, a parish officer responsible for persuading householders to do their duty as jurors at such inquests, has assembled twelve men. Most of them are middle-aged local tradesmen, but one stands out among them as different. He is young and slight, smartly dressed and good-looking, neither tall nor short at five foot nine inches, with dark hair falling in curls over his forehead and collar. He is a new resident who has just moved into a fine airy house with a large garden, close to Regent's Park at York Gate: it is No. 1 Devonshire Terrace, from which the Beadle has made haste to summon him to his duty.

It is only a short walk from Devonshire Terrace to the workhouse, but it is a different world he has entered through its gates. He is directed to a room in which the other jurors are talking among themselves as they wait for the inquest to begin. They have come to pronounce on a case of suspected infanticide, a servant girl accused of killing her newborn baby in the kitchen of her employers' house. One of the jurors immediately declares himself in favour of the utmost rigour of the law being applied to the young woman. The new young juror recognizes him as a furniture-dealer he suspects of cheating him over the recent purchase of a pair of card tables. Another solid parishioner presses his card into his hand, murmuring that he hopes to be of service to him in the future: he is an undertaker.

Before they can settle down for the inquest the jurors must be taken downstairs to the workhouse mortuary in the basement to be shown the body of the baby. It is lying on a box set upon a clean white cloth, with a surgical instrument beside it that has been used to open it up for examination. The baby has been sewn up again. The new juror, who has a two-month-old baby daughter of his own at home – Katey – reflects that it looks as though the cloth were laid and the Giant coming to dinner, but he does not share this thought with his fellow jurors. They agree among themselves that the mortuary is clean and well whitewashed, the foreman says, 'All right, gentlemen? Back again, Mr Beadle,' and they troop upstairs. The coroner is Thomas Wakley, a surgeon and until recently a Member of Parliament. The new juror is Charles Dickens.

Now the young woman accused of murder is brought in by one of the workhouse nurses. She looks weak, ill and frightened. She is allowed to sit in one of the horsehair chairs and tries to hide her face on the shoulder of the unsympathetic nurse. Eliza Burgess is twenty-four or five years old, a maid of all work and an orphan, which may be why there is uncertainty about her age. It is likely that she grew up in a workhouse, quite possibly this one. Her story is that on Sunday, 5 January, she went into labour in the kitchen of her employers' house, No. 65 Edgware Road, where she was the only servant. When the front doorbell rang, she hurried upstairs to let in two lady visitors, and by the time she got back to the kitchen the baby – a boy – had been born under her skirts and appeared to be dead. It is not clear whether the birth took place on the stairs, but she delivered him herself, and must have cut the umbilical cord and cleaned up as best she could. Then she found a box, or a pot, in which she placed the dead newborn child and hid him under the dresser. Her mistress, Mrs Mary Symmons, sent her up to scrub the front-door steps in the cold after her guests left, and then, seeing how ill and thin she looked, taxed her with having given birth. At first she denied it, but then, being threatened with a medical examination, confessed and showed Mrs Symmons where she had put the baby. Mrs Symmons sent for a hackney coach to remove Eliza and her dead child from her house to the Marylebone Workhouse infirmary.

Mrs Symmons appears as an unsympathetic witness and resists questions from Dickens, who hopes to give a favourable turn to the case. The coroner gives a look of encouragement to the juror and the accused girl wails. The next witness is the house surgeon, Mr Boyd, who reports that the accused told him she was seized with labour in the kitchen when the bell was rung by two ladies. She hurried to let them in, and 'in the act of doing so the child was born, and on her return it was dead'. He is not able to say positively whether it was born alive or dead. Afterwards, in private conversation, Mr Wakley tells Dickens that it is very unlikely that the child could have drawn more than a few breaths, if indeed any, since there was foreign matter in his windpipe.

Miss Burgess is led away while the jurors discuss the case. Dickens resolves to take on those who are ready to find her guilty of killing her child, and, with some encouragement from Mr Wakley, he argues against them, so firmly and forcefully that he wins the argument. When Miss Burgess is brought back the verdict is given: 'Found Dead'. She falls on her knees to thank the jurors, 'with protestations that we were right – protestations among the most affecting that I have ever heard in my life'.[1] Then she faints, and is carried away. She will still have to be held in prison and appear at the Old Bailey in due course, but the threat of the death penalty has now been taken from her. Dickens, who is without doubt the busiest man of the twelve, goes home and makes arrangements for her to be sent food and other comforts in prison. He also finds an excellent barrister – Richard Doane of the Inner Temple, a friend and amanuensis of the late Jeremy Bentham – to defend her at the Old Bailey trial.

That night he cannot sleep. He is overcome with sickness and indigestion, does not want to be alone and asks his wife, Catherine, to sit up with him. The dead baby in the workhouse, the thought of prison and the terrified, ignorant, unhappy young woman prisoner have upset him. In the morning he writes to his closest friend, John Forster, 'Whether it was the poor baby, or its poor mother, or the coffin, or my fellow-jurymen, or what not, I can't say . . .'[2] He already knows a good deal about prisons, since he has seen his father held in one for debt. Also about babies dying, since two of his younger siblings perished early – happily his own three little ones are stout and healthy. And he knows about maids of all work, or 'slaveys', well remembering the one who served his family when he was a boy, straight out of the workhouse where she grew up. He recovers from his sickness, and in the evening he and Forster meet at the Adelphi Theatre to see *Jack Sheppard* – the highwayman – played *en travesti* by Mary Anne Keeley, an actress well known to Dickens, since he had taken lessons in acting from her husband eight years earlier.

☙❧

Charles Dickens had been observing the world about him since he was a child, and reporting on what he saw for the past six years, as a journalist and then as a novelist. Much of it amused him, but more of it upset him: the poverty, the hunger, the ignorance and squalor he saw in London, and the indifference of the rich and powerful to the condition of the poor and ignorant. Through his own energy and exceptional gifts he had raised himself out of poverty. But he neither forgot it, nor turned aside from the poverty about him. He drew attention to it in his books, and he was personally generous with his time and his money, and not only in the case of Eliza Burgess.

Her case came up at the Old Bailey on 9 March and was reported in *The Times* the next day. She was indicted for unlawfully concealing the birth of a male child delivered on the 5th of January. Her barrister, Mr Doane, pleaded that she was of weak intellect. He was also able to produce a crucial witness to her character, Mr Clarkson, a tradesman in Great Russell Street; she had previously worked for his family, and he was willing to do his best for her. Mr Clarkson said his wife was greatly interested in Eliza and had got her a promise of a place in the Magdalen Asylum, an institution that looked after young women who strayed from the path of virtue, and did its best to restore them to it. The Clarksons were willing to take her back into their service until she could be admitted there. The willingness of these respectable people to help Eliza was good for her case. The jury found her guilty of concealment but strongly recommended her to mercy. The judge, Mr Serjeant Arabin, said that under the circumstances he would respite judgment till next session, and that meanwhile she was free. Nothing more is heard of her except a brief word by Dickens that her sentence had been lenient, and that 'her history and conduct proved it right.' This was written twenty-three years later, in 1863: Dickens had stored up the memory of the sad young woman.[3]

This is a very small episode in the life of Dickens, but it allows us to see him in action, going to the workhouse just along the road from his own home, and deciding to help a young woman whose character and history are quite without interest or colour, and who comes from the very bottom of the social heap, a workhouse child, a servant and a victim – a victim of ignorance, of gullibility, of an unknown seducer and a harsh employer, and of the assumptions made by respectable jurors. He is at his best as a man, determined in argument, generous in giving help, following through the case, motivated purely by his profound sense that it was wrong that she should be victimized further.

What makes his behaviour the more remarkable is that he was himself living under intense pressure at this time in 1840. He was very successful, and also exhausted. He had spent the past four years in the hard labour of writing three long novels in monthly instalments, huge efforts of imagination and penmanship that had lifted him from obscurity to fame and comfort. Their publication as serials established a new style in publishing and reached a new public, because the paper numbers were cheap to buy and could be passed round, collected and preserved; and they found readers who were for the first time buying fiction to keep on a shelf at home. The names of his characters passed into the language: Pickwick, Sam Weller, Fagin, Oliver, Squeers, Smike. The voice of Dickens, offering fun and jokes, then switching to pathos, with a good peppering of indignation, seemed like the voice of a friend. His stories were dramatized and played in theatres all over the country – Mary Anne Keeley took the part of Smike at the Adelphi. His success was unprecedented and thrilling, but he felt the strain, because his income and standard of living depended on keeping up the pace. He had no savings, lived from month to month, and worried about money; yet he had just vowed not to commit himself to another serial novel, having convinced himself that he could earn as much for less work by becoming editor of a new weekly journal. In January 1840, in the very month of the inquest, he was starting work on the first numbers.

He was able to keep many servants, a horse for himself, and a coach, with a fourteen-year-old lad to drive it, John Thompson, who would remain in his service in different capacities for the next twenty-six years. He took his family out of town for a month in June and again in September, and also made short pleasure trips with his wife – 'my missis' or 'my better half'. At the same time he was being lionized, invited by the ultra-respectable and rich Miss Coutts (court dress required when royalty present), by the less respectable but very clever Lady Holland, and by the wholly unrespectable, brilliant and charming Lady Blessington and her companion Count D'Orsay. His missis did not go with him to these ladies' houses, or to the breakfast given by Richard Monckton Milnes, man of letters and Tory Member of Parliament. Lord Northampton, President of the Royal Society, invited him to a reception at his house in Piccadilly. Thomas Carlyle got him to attend an early meeting about the establishment of the London Library, and Dickens became a supporter and subscriber. There was a great demand for engravings of his portrait, and his head was being modelled by an admiring sculptor.

This was Dickens nearly halfway through his life: he was twenty-eight in February 1840, and had another thirty years ahead of him. He was living in a country that had been at peace for a quarter of a century. There had been no foreign wars, and no revolution at home, partly thanks to the Reform Bill of 1832, passed under the old King, William IV, in which parliamentary constituencies were redrawn and the electorate widened, cautiously. But the courts and alleys of London remained squalid with poverty, overcrowding and disease, and the rich in their great houses were unshaken. Railways were changing the habits of the nation more than votes, and railway stations at Euston and Paddington already connected London to the north and the West Country. New Oxford Street had just been cut, and the Finchley Road, the Caledonian and Camden Road, and Charles Barry was designing Trafalgar Square. In January the penny post was established, covering the whole country: in its first year it would double the volume of letters written. London was preparing for a royal wedding on 10 February, when the young Queen Victoria was to be married to a German prince, Albert of Saxe-Coburg-Gotha. In parliament there was a debate over what allowance should be paid to the foreign Prince. It was settled at £30,000, and in the streets people sang, 'Prince Hallbert he vill alvays be/My own dear Fancy Man' – at any rate according to Dickens.[4] The novelist pretended to fall in love with the Queen, went to Windsor and lay down on the ground outside the castle to show his passion, to the considerable surprise of passers-by.

Dickens was still a young man. His grammar could be shaky, his clothes too flamboyant – 'geraniums and ringlets' mocked Thackeray – his hospitality too splendid, his temper fierce, but his friends – mostly artists, writers and actors – loved him, and their love was reciprocated. When he went out of London in order to have peace to write, he would within days summon troops of friends to join him. He was a giver of celebratory parties, a player of charades, a dancer of quadrilles and Sir Roger de Coverleys. He suffered from terrible colds and made them into jokes: 'Bisery, bisery,' he complained, or 'I have been crying all day . . . my nose is an inch shorter than it was last Tuesday, from constant friction.'[5] He worked furiously fast to give himself free time. He lived hard and took hard exercise. His day began with a cold shower, and he walked or rode every day if he could, arduous expeditions of twelve, fifteen or twenty miles out of town, often summoning a friend to go with him. He might be in his study from ten at night until one in the morning, or up early to be at his desk by 8.30, writing with a quill pen he sharpened himself and favouring dark blue ink. He was taking French lessons from a serious teacher.[6] He was also doing his best to help a poor carpenter with literary ambitions, reading what he had written and finding him work.[7]

He was an obsessive organizer of his surroundings, even rearranging the furniture in hotel rooms: he wrote to Catherine from a hotel in Bath, 'of course I *arranged* both the room and my luggage before going to bed'; and, from lodgings in Broadstairs, to an old friend, 'the furniture in all the rooms has been entirely re-arranged by the same extraordinary character' – he meant himself.[8] He smoked cigars, and often mentions his wine-dealers in letters, and the brandy, gin, port, sherry, champagne, claret and Sauternes delivered and enjoyed;

and although he was very rarely the worse for drink, he sometimes confessed to feeling bad in the mornings after overindulging the night before. Raspberries were his favourite fruit, served without cream, and he was very fond of dates in boxes.[9] He belonged to the Garrick Club and the Athenaeum, and he knew and frequented all the theatres in London and could ask any of their managers for a box when he wanted one. Eating out, going to the theatre, adventuring through the rough areas of London with a friend or two were habitual ways of spending his evening. He also walked the streets by himself, observing and thinking. He was passionately interested in prisons and in asylums, the places where society's rejects are kept.

He revisited the Marylebone Workhouse ten years later, in May 1850,[10] when it held 2,000 inmates of all ages from newborn to dying, and wrote a painfully vivid account of the place: the smell of so many people kept in wards together, the listlessness, the dreary diet, the sullen lethargy of the old who had nothing to look forward to except death. He found then that it was redeemed by one thing – the good care given to the pauper children, who were kept in large, light, airy rooms at the top of one of the buildings, and who impressed him as lively and cheerful as they ate their potatoes, with 'two mangy pauper rocking-horses rampant in the corner'. But what struck him most was the grief of one of the pauper nurses, a 'flabby, raw-boned, untidy' woman of coarse aspect, who had been tending a 'dropped child' – one found in the street – and was now sobbing bitterly because the child had died. Once again he did his best to help: 'If anything useful can be done for her, I should like to do it,' he wrote, 'if you can put me in the way of helping her, do me the kindness of telling me how it can be best done?' he wrote to Jacob Bell, the philanthropist and MP.[11] Once again, it was a poor woman and a dead child who spoke to him.

He saw the world more vividly than other people, and reacted to what he saw with laughter, horror, indignation – and sometimes sobs. He stored up his experiences and reactions as raw material to transform and use in his novels, and was so charged with imaginative energy that he rendered nineteenth-century England crackling, full of truth and life, with his laughter, horror and indignation – and sentimentality. Even one of his most hostile critics acknowledged that he described London 'like a special correspondent for posterity'.[12] Early in his writing career he started to call himself 'the inimitable': it was partly a joke with him, but not entirely, because he could see that there was no other writer at work who could surpass him, and that no one among his friends or family could even begin to match his energy and ambition.[13] He could make people laugh and cry, and arouse anger, and he meant to amuse and to make the world a better place. And wherever he went he produced what, much later, an observant girl described as 'a sort of brilliance in the room, mysteriously dominant and formless. I remember how everyone lighted up when he entered.'[14]

Part One

I

The Sins of the Fathers

1784–1822

Charles Dickens was born on Friday, 7 February 1812, just outside the old town of Portsmouth in the new suburb of Landport, built in the 1790s. The small terraced house is still standing in a landscape so altered by time, bombing and rebuilding that it is a wonder the inside is so well preserved. The address has changed too: in 1812 it was No. 13 Mile End Terrace, Landport; today it is No. 393 Old Commercial Road, Portsmouth.[1] There is a patch of front garden, a small flight of steps up to the entrance, two storeys, attic and basement, good plain Georgian windows, and in 1812 there was a view over Cherry Garden Field. The terrace had no running water then, and the privy was outside. It was a modest house, but big enough for a young family. The new Dickens baby was announced in the press, 'On Friday, at Mile-end-Terrace, the lady of John Dickens, Esq., a son', and christened two months later on 4 March at St Mary's Church. The name decided upon was 'Charles John Huffham' – Charles for his maternal grand-father, John for his father and Huffham (misspelt by the parish clerk) for a London friend of his father, Christopher Huffam of Limehouse, oar-maker and rigger of ships to the Royal Navy.[2] His mother, Eliza-beth, was twenty-two, his father twenty-seven, and they already had one child, a daughter, Fanny, aged two. John Dickens walked daily into the dockyard where he had a steady job in the Navy Pay Office, handling payroll accounts at an annual salary of £110, which was set to rise.

His father, John, is the most mysterious figure in Dickens's back-ground. Nothing is known of John's education and nothing certain of his first twenty years. His mother, born Elizabeth Ball in Shrop-shire in 1745, was a servant, and at the age of thirty-six, when she was working as a maid to Lady Blandford in London, she married

William Dickens, a manservant in the household of John Crewe, a landowning gentleman with estates in Cheshire and a town house in Lower Grosvenor Street, Mayfair. This was in November 1781. Her husband was a good bit older than her, probably in his sixties. With her marriage she too came to work in the Crewe household. A son, also named William, was born to them in 1782. By 1785 William Dickens senior had been promoted to the position of butler, but in October of the same year he died, in London. A second son, John, was born to Elizabeth Dickens in the same year, not in London, and was said to have been a posthumous child, and this boy was to be the father of Charles Dickens. She remained in service with the Crewes, and moved with them between Crewe Hall and Mayfair. In 1798, for instance, when John Dickens was thirteen, she was in London – 'Paid Mrs Dickens Servant in your town house 8.8.0' reads the Crewe household accounts book.[3]

John did not follow his parents into service: he was going to do better. Many years later the Crewes' granddaughter said she remembered 'old Mrs Dickens' grumbling about 'that lazy fellow John . . . who used to come hanging about the house' and how she had given him 'many a sound cuff on the ear'.[4] Someone came to the rescue, and his next appearance is in April 1805 when he is twenty, and appointed to the Navy Pay Office in London at five shillings a day. The Treasurer of the Navy at this point was George Canning, a friend of the Crewe family, and the job undoubtedly came to John Dickens through Canning's patronage, on which all such appointments depended. The Navy needed staff to keep the war against France running effectively, and young Dickens proved bright enough to give satisfaction. Two years later, on 23 June 1807, he was promoted to 15th Assistant Clerk at £70 a year with two shillings extra for every day of actual attendance. This was a fortune compared with anything his father had ever earned.

Why was John Dickens favoured in this way? The assumption is that the Crewes put forward his name to Canning in gratitude to his mother for being a loyal servant. His elder brother, William, however, made his own way, running a coffee shop in Oxford Street. What made the difference between Mrs Dickens's two sons? John saw himself as a man of taste, with cultural interests. Another thing we know about him is that he acquired quite a large collection of books, essays, plays and novels of the eighteenth century: was he given them?[5] Books were expensive. Living in a grand household, where he could observe and hear brilliant people, appears to have had an effect on him, and the Crewe household was where you might overhear some of the best conversation in the land. John Crewe's wife, Frances, was well read, well informed and witty, as well as a noted beauty, and around the Crewes a remarkable circle of politicians and writers gathered, the most eminent being Charles James Fox, Edmund Burke and Richard Brinsley Sheridan, the playwright, theatre-owner and politician who became the darling of society. During the election of 1784 Frances Crewe led a canvassing party, and when victory was celebrated at her house, the Prince of Wales made the toast 'True blue and Mrs Crewe' and she replied 'True blue and all of you', expressing her sense of the fellowship among the Whig group. She conducted a long love-affair with Sheridan, who had dedicated his play *The School for Scandal* to her in 1777. In 1785 the affair was still causing distress to Sheridan's wife, Elizabeth, who wrote to her friend Mrs Canning, 'S is in Town – and so is Mrs Crewe. I am in the country and so is Mr Crewe – a very convenient Arrangement, is it not?'[6] Both Sheridans were nonetheless regular visitors to Crewe Hall, and in 1790 Mrs Sheridan had another story to tell, of how her husband was found locked in a bedroom in an unfrequented part of the house with the governess. He was notoriously promiscuous, but his behaviour was far from unusual in the circles in which he mixed. He also became Treasurer of the Navy in 1807, the year John Dickens got his promotion.

John Dickens may have been the son of the elderly butler, but it is also possible that he had a different father – perhaps John Crewe, exercising his *droit de seigneur*, cheering himself up for his wife's infidelities, or another of the gentlemen who were regular guests at the Crewe residences. Or he may have believed that he was. His silence about his first twenty years, his habit of spending and borrowing and enjoying good things as though he were somehow entitled to do so, all suggest something of the kind, and harks back to the sort of behaviour he would have observed with dazzled eyes at Crewe Hall and in Mayfair. This was the style of Sheridan, and also Fox, who gambled away several fortunes and borrowed from all his friends without a thought of ever repaying any of them. What is worth noting is that he can be presumed to have grown up with a group of men as models who were, as well as gamblers and drinkers, the most eloquent of their time. The housekeeper's boy developed his own elaborate turns of phrase, which his son found entertaining enough to record, and to turn to comic use in his writing; he described, for instance, a letter from his father in which he wrote that 'he has reason to believe that he will be in town with the pheasants, on or about the first of October', and went on to observe that his father has discovered on the Isle of Man 'troops of friends, and every sort of continental luxury at a cheap rate'. Another of his grand pronouncements, putting down a boastful friend, was 'The Supreme Being must be a very different individual from what I have every reason to believe him to be, if He would care in the least for the society of your relations.'[7] John Dickens also developed his own habits of extravagance and debt, which nearly wrecked his son's life and drove him to rage and despair.[8]

John Dickens was a character – he was the model for his son's most famous character, Micawber. He was also lucky. In 1806 John Crewe was raised to the peerage by Fox, who died that year. George Canning, no Whig but a liberal Tory, and the cleverest of the younger generation of politicians, had become a friend of the Crewes, and since he was Treasurer of the Navy from 1804 to 1806, he was in a position to hand out a job to the son of their housekeeper.[9] She was now an elderly woman and delighted the Crewe grandchildren with her storytelling. And when Sheridan followed Canning as Treasurer, he was also in a position to have John Dickens promoted. Two years later John's salary was up to £110 and he was able to marry, in June 1809, just before his transfer to the Portsmouth dockyard. Sheridan died in 1816, Lady Crewe in 1818 and her onetime housekeeper in 1824: old Mrs Dickens left enough money to help her son John out of the trouble he had got into, but she died too soon to see the achievements of her grandson Charles, or to tell him tales of life at Crewe Hall and Lower Grosvenor Street.

So much for the background of John Dickens, something he seems not to have spoken about to his son Charles, who in turn never said anything about it. The Navy Pay Office was a good employer and the interminable wars with the French, now almost in their twentieth year, meant there was plenty of work for him in Portsmouth. Elizabeth Dickens's brother Thomas Barrow worked alongside her husband – this was how the couple had met – and her father, Charles Barrow, was also employed at Somerset House in London under the impressive title of 'Chief Conductor of Monies in Town'. But little Charles never knew the grandfather for whom he was named because Mr Barrow had to leave England suddenly in 1810 when it was discovered that he had been defrauding the Navy Pay Office for seven years. Life was hard with ten children, he pleaded, and he had been driven to it by need, but criminal proceedings were started and he fled across the Channel. This was only a few months after witnessing the marriage of his daughter to John Dickens at the church of St Mary-le-Strand in June 1809. She was in Portsmouth when he was disgraced and made his secret escape abroad, and, while the subject would surely not have been mentioned at Mile End Terrace, it meant there was a secret hanging in the air, a story that could not be told. Both Charles Dickens's grandfathers were unknown and unmentioned figures.

As daughters often do, Elizabeth had chosen a husband who shared some of her father's traits, and in particular the taste for living above his income. John Dickens was expansive by nature, with a tendency to speak in loose, grand terms, and an easy way with money. When required to describe himself he wrote 'gentleman' on documents and announced himself as 'Esquire' in the newspaper announcement of his first son's birth.[10] He liked to dress well, as young Regency bucks did, he bought expensive books and enjoyed entertaining friends, from whom he might later ask for a loan. His voice had a slight thickness, as though his tongue was a little too large for his mouth, but he was likeable, plump and full of fun, and he and Elizabeth made a cheerful couple.

She was a slim, energetic young woman, and she allegedly spent the evening before the birth of her son out dancing.[11] She also appreciated music and books, and knew some Latin. Her father, before he went to work for the Navy Pay Office, had been an instrument-maker and music teacher, and also ran a circulating library in London. The Barrows were better educated than the Dickenses, and she had talented brothers. Thomas, her husband's colleague, overcame the matter of his father's fraud by his own trustworthiness and diligence, and rose high in the Navy Pay Office. John Barrow published poetry and a historical novel, and started his own newspaper, and Edward Barrow was a good amateur musician with artistic tastes – he married a painter of miniatures from a family of artists – and he worked as a parliamentary reporter. They were all helpful to their sister and brother-in-law, and became significant figures in Charles's young life.

When he was only five months old the family was obliged to move to a smaller house on a poor street, with no front garden.[12] They were already short of money, and the house would have matched the one described by Jane Austen in *Mansfield Park* at exactly this time, where Fanny Price visited her parents in Portsmouth, and found the passage and stairs so narrow and the walls so thin that you could hear all the noises from room to room.[13] Here a third child, Alfred, was born, and died at six months in September 1814. The family moved again, to a better house in Portsea, at No. 39 Wish Street, and a nurse cared for Fanny and Charles; he claimed to remember her carrying him out to see the soldiers exercising. That winter their father was summoned to work at Somerset House, and the family went with him to London. They left Portsmouth under snow, according to Dickens's own recollection, and did not return.[14]

They found lodgings in Norfolk Street (Cleveland Street today), only recently paved over and transformed from one of the old 'Green Lanes' out to the country into a residential road that took you to the new suburbs of Somers Town and Camden Town. This was the north edge of London, where big town houses were under construction in Fitzroy Square, while to the east of Tottenham Court Road there were still farms and fields. John Dickens's brother, William, was still running his coffee shop in Oxford Street, and in 1815 he married; but John, in spite of his steady employment with the Navy Pay Office, where he was now earning £200 a year, found it as hard to manage as ever and took to asking their mother for money, as she noted when she came to write her will. Whether old Mrs Dickens ever sat with Fanny and Charles while their mother was busy, or told them stories, is not recorded. In April 1816 a fourth Dickens child was born – Letitia, who was to outlive all the others.[15]

While the younger Dickenses were in London the war against Napoleon and the French finally came to an end in 1815. Now that the Navy needed fewer officers, the work of the Pay Office was changing, and in December 1816 John Dickens was sent out of town again. This time it was only thirty miles away, to Kent. He went first for a few weeks to Sheerness dockyard, where the River Medway runs into the Thames estuary through the salt marshes, and then on to Chatham, where Rochester Castle stands above the bridge over the Medway, and Chatham and Rochester are effectively one town folded around the spectacular double curve of the river, with the Kentish hills rising sharply above. The Romans settled there, and it had a great castle and a cathedral, a medieval bridge, ancient streets, inns and houses, fine dwellings for the naval officers and great industrial buildings in the dockyards. The newest construction was Fort Clarence, a gigantic brick-built defence meant to deter Napoleon, put up in 1812 and named for the Lord High Admiral of the Navy, Prince William, Duke of Clarence, destined to become King in 1830. Landscape and buildings are dramatic, and they imprinted themselves strongly on the imagination of the small boy. Here Dickens became fully aware of the world around him and began to store up impressions.

He arrived round about his fifth birthday, with his two sisters, seven-year-old Fanny and baby Letitia. Their father was busily engaged, in and out of the vast Chatham dockyard, often aboard the old Navy yacht *Chatham*, sailing up the Medway to Sheerness and back. He installed his family in another small, neat, Georgian terraced house at the top of the steep hill rising above Chatham and Rochester, with views down to the river. No. 2 Ordnance Terrace is still there, battered by time and neglect, and you can see it was one of a group of modest terraces built near the large houses in the New Road laid out along the hilltop in the 1790s. The town was prosperous, rough and lively, crammed with working people serving the needs of the Navy, and the Army too, since Chatham was also a recruiting centre for soldiers. There were many blacksmiths and rope-makers there, and their apprentices had their own songs and celebrations when they paraded with bands, wearing masks and collecting money.

Up the hill at Ordnance Terrace things were quieter. There was plenty of open space, with farmland at the back and the grassy expanse of a hay field in front, where the children could play safely, picnic under the hawthorn trees and make friends with their neighbours. George and Lucy, children of Mr Stroughill, the plumber next door, became their playmates, and Charles fell in love with Lucy, whom he claimed to remember afterwards as 'peach-coloured, with a blue sash'. The grass on which they sat eating sweets together has long since gone, sliced off by a Victorian railway cutting, and large trees along its edge obscure the view, but you can still get a sense of how agreeable it must have been. Each house has a few steps up to its narrow front door, with a small fanlight above; below, a basement; one front window on the ground floor, two each on the first and second floors. Into this simple box went Mr and Mrs Dickens, her sister Mary Allen, known as 'Aunt Fanny', widow of a naval officer, the three children, their nurse Mary Weller and the maid Jane Bonny.

By now the boy could just about read, although not yet the splendid and expensive volume his father brought home, *The History and Antiquities of Rochester and Its Environs*, newly published with a folding map and five plates. It was his mother who gave him daily lessons in reading over a period of time, and taught him 'thoroughly well', he told his friend John Forster. Forster says Dickens used almost exactly the words he gave to David Copperfield, 'I faintly remember her teaching me the alphabet; and when I look upon the fat black letters in the primer, the puzzling novelty of their shapes and the easy good nature of O and S, always seem to present themselves before me as they used to do.'[16] This makes Elizabeth Dickens sound like a mother who cherished her son through careful teaching which sparked his imagination, and from then on words were associated with pleasure and he was set on his path. Without her he might not have embarked on his own crash course of literary studies through the library of books left by his father in the little room next to his bedroom at the top of the stairs. They were hefty eighteenth-century travel books and novels: Defoe's *Robinson Crusoe*, Fielding's *Tom Jones*, Goldsmith's *The Vicar of Wakefield*, Smollett's *Roderick Random*, *Peregrine Pickle* and *Humphry Clinker*; also Mrs Inchbald's collection of farces, some volumes of the *Tatler* and the *Spectator*, and fairy stories, the *Arabian Nights* and *The Tales of the Genii*. Catching the light of the long summer evenings as he sat alone at the top of the house, he travelled, suffered and triumphed with the heroes of the small print, his imagination free of constraint.

According to one account, his nurse Mary Weller described him as 'a terrible boy to read'. She also remembered him coming downstairs and asking for the kitchen to be cleared for a game. Then George from next door would bring his magic lantern and Charles and Fanny would sing, recite and perform, a favourite piece for him being Dr Watts's 'The Voice of the Sluggard', with gestures and actions. She found him 'a lively boy, of a good, genial, open disposition', and Mrs Dickens was 'a dear, good mother'.[17] He himself kept a vivid memory of his mother taking him out to see a royal carriage passing through town. Years later he told the son of a friend, as they walked together up a street in Chatham where there was a low wall with an iron railing on the top, 'I remember my poor mother, God forgive her, put me up on the ledge of that wall, so that I might wave my hat and cheer George IV – the Prince Regent – who was driving by.' The 'poor mother, God forgive her' was from the adult Dickens, who had a low opinion of George IV, but as a boy small enough to be lifted up on to the wall he would without doubt have taken innocent pleasure in waving his hat at the Prince, richly dressed and bloated, as he went past in his magnificent carriage.

Looking back on those years, he remembered himself as a delicate and sometimes lonely child, unable to join in the games of the local boys, neighbours and sons of naval officers, who spent the summer playing cricket and Prisoner's Base. He had begun to suffer from spasms in his side, so painful they kept him from running about, and he would lie in the grass to see the other boys playing their games, or sit near them with a book in his hand, his left wrist clasped in his right hand, swaying slightly as he read.[18] So he grew used to watching, and being set apart from those he watched. At night he was in thrall to his nurse's bedtime stories of a Captain Murderer who cooked and ate his brides in pies, and a shipwright Chips haunted by rats: they terrified and delighted him in equal measure. On other nights his aunt Fanny 'hummed the evening hymn to me, and I cried on my pillow'.[19]

The pains in his side came and went, and he was not always passive. His singing of comic songs was encouraged by his family, who hoisted him up on to chairs and tables to perform. His father made a friend of the landlord of the Mitre Tavern in Chatham High Street, John Tribe, and Fanny and Charles were both taken there to show off their singing skills in comic solos and duets.[20] Once you have enjoyed performance and applause, you want to try again, and Dickens's life-long passion for both began here. He was the junior partner for the moment, since Fanny's musical skills were so advanced, and she was two years ahead of him in everything. Both were sent to a dame school above a shop to be put through the standard lessons, where the discipline consisted of a rap or a blow and not much was learnt.

They were also taken to the theatre, the Rochester Theatre Royal built by the great Mrs Baker, once a puppeteer and married to a clown, who became a formidable businesswoman and ran the Kent circuit with a mixture of Shakespeare, pantomime and variety. Mrs Baker died in 1816, but the theatre continued with the mixture as before and there the children enjoyed *Richard III* and *Macbeth* – alarming yet also instructive in the way of the theatre, as it let them see that the witches and King Duncan all reappeared as other characters. And twice, in 1819 and 1820, when he was seven and eight, there were expeditions to London during the pantomime season, to see the great Grimaldi clowning his way through song and dance and comic impersonations.[21] More theatre enthusiasts were introduced into the family circle by aunt Fanny, who was courted by a Dr Lamert working at the Ordnance Hospital, with a teenage son, James, both lovers of the drama. As well as taking the children to the theatre in town, the doctor and his son got up their own productions and put them on in an empty room in the hospital. It was easy to see that it could be even more fun building sets and putting on greasepaint and costumes than watching other people doing it. Soon Charles was writing his own tragedy, *Misnar, the Sultan of India*. The manuscript did not survive, but he remembered his pride in writing it. 'I was a great writer at eight years old or so,' he joked later, and 'an actor and a speaker from a baby.'[22]

Another treat for Fanny and Charles was to be taken by their father aboard the *Chatham*, the small naval yacht in which he sailed on Pay Office business to Sheerness and back. They had to be punctually at the dockyard to catch the tide, there was the bustle of the sailors handling ropes and sails as they moved through a mass of shipping, Upnor Castle on the far side of the river with its grey towers, the slop and splash of brown water as the Medway widened between its mud banks, a few churches in sight, low islands and ancient forts, Hoo Ness and Darnet Ness, rebuilt to guard against Napoleon. After hours of sailing, as they approached Sheerness and the Thames estuary, the far Essex bank came into view five miles away across a world of water. This landscape and the sludge-coloured tidal rivers haunted him all his life and became part of the fabric of his late novels. His father also pointed out, when they were walking together, the house set on the top of Gad's Hill, on the Rochester to Gravesend road, where Sir John Falstaff held up the travellers and was commemorated by an inn named for him. Gad's Hill Place was a plain, solid brick house with wide views over the countryside stretching away below, and it immediately appealed to the child. He decided he would like to live in it, his father told him that if he worked very hard he might one day do so, and a version of this exchange was repeated whenever they passed it, as they did many times during the years in Kent. Years later he summed up what he liked about its situation to a friend: 'Cobham Woods and Park are behind the house; the distant Thames in front; the Medway, with Rochester, and its old castle and cathedral on one side. The whole stupendous property is on the old Dover Road.'[23]

Their parents' closest friends among the neighbours were the Newnhams, a retired tailor and his genteel and kindly wife, with a comfortable income. Newnham lent John Dickens money and, unlike most of his creditors, who were disappointed by his failure to repay loans, kept in friendly touch with the family even after they left Chatham. The youngest Dickens was given the name 'Augustus

Newnham' in their honour, but the Newnhams were more interested in the daughters, and in due course left small legacies to Letitia and Fanny. Although John Dickens was now earning a substantial salary of more than £350 a year, he was getting into difficulties again. In the summer of 1819 he borrowed £200 from a man he knew in London, at Kennington Green, which he agreed to pay back at £26 a year; it should have taken a little more than eight years, but his financial incompetence was such that he was still paying it off thirty years later. Worse, he asked his brother-in-law Thomas Barrow to guarantee a deal that brought him £200 in cash, and then failed to make the required payments to the third party involved. Barrow was obliged to pay back the £200 and more, and he was so angry that he told Dickens he would not have him under his roof again.

In 1821 they were obliged to leave Ordnance Terrace and move down the hill to a house in a less salubrious street: No. 18 St Mary's Place, next to a Baptist chapel and close to the dockyard. There were two more children in the family by now: Harriet born in the summer of 1819, and Frederick a year later. Money was tight, John Dickens was not popular with his relations in London, and there were no more trips to the metropolitan pantomime. A big fire in Chatham gave him a chance to earn something by his pen, and he wrote it up for *The Times*, which printed the story and paid him. He gave two guineas to the fund for the victims of the fire, probably more than his fee for writing the piece, but it showed the world that he was a gentleman.

That winter of 1821 their aunt married Dr Lamert and left with him for Cork in Ireland, where he had a new appointment. They took the Dickenses' maid Jane Bonny with them, and left James Lamert to lodge with them. He was fond of Charles, and kept up the visits to the theatre. And now Fanny and Charles were sent to a proper school, Mr Giles's 'classical, mathematical and commercial' establishment. William Giles was the son of a local minister, had himself been to Oxford, was a good teacher and ran his school well. He recognized that he had an unusual pupil and Charles responded to his encouragement and worked hard. He also had fun. When asked to recite, he gave a piece out of *The Humourist's Miscellany*, and the other children applauded enough for two encores. He was liked by teachers and fellow pupils, and gaining confidence in his abilities. Mr Giles served him ill in one way, by teaching him to take snuff, a kind known as 'Irish blackguard', and although Charles gave up the habit after a few years and did not resume it, he had got the taste for tobacco, and he became a serious smoker at the age of fifteen.[24]

Dickens looked back on the years in Chatham as the idyll of his life. He had the blessings of secure family love, ideal landscape, river and town, good teaching, and his small world was beginning to expand pleasurably around him. When he reached his tenth birthday in February 1822, he was happy at school, encouraged and favoured by his teacher and enjoying his studies. At home, his mother was about to give birth to another child, who arrived on 3 April and was given the name of the baby who had died in 1814, Alfred, and of her sister's husband, Lamert. He thrived, and they could all look forward to summer and long days out on the river or in the open country. Then they heard that their father was being taken back to London and they would have to leave with him. The pantomime visits were all the elder children remembered of London, but their mother was a Londoner by birth and her brothers were there, so she may have been pleased to be returning to town.

They began to prepare. The children's nurse, Mary Weller, wanted to stay in Chatham and to marry her sweetheart, who worked in the docks, and she put in an offer for the Dickenses' chairs, which was accepted. They would take with them only a little maid they had acquired from the Chatham Workhouse, an orphan of no known parentage and seemingly no name – or at least Dickens never gives her one.[25] Mr Giles offered to keep Charles until the end of the half and invited him to lodge with his family, and this was agreed to. He saw the house packed up and waved goodbye to his parents, sisters and brothers. The Giles family made a fuss of him, with Miss Giles admiring his long curly hair, and for a few weeks the routine of school continued to absorb him.

The ten-year-old boy made his memories of the years in Kent into a treasure trove in his mind. For the rest of his life he enjoyed bringing them out, and taking friends to walk over the territory he had known and loved so well. In 1857 he described the seven miles between Maidstone and Rochester as 'one of the most beautiful walks in England'.[26] Kent was always a place of delight and pleasure, a paradise of woods and orchards, sea coast, marshes and rivers. Here he chose to spend his honeymoon, here he would go roaming alone or with chosen companions, here he took his children for long summer months, and here he bought his dream house, and died in it. Here he wished to be buried. The landscape and towns of Kent gave him settings for many of his books. His first novel, *The Pickwick Papers*, is partly set in Rochester and round about, and his last, the unfinished *Mystery of Edwin Drood*, centres on its streets and assigns real houses to its characters. David Copperfield tramps across its bridge on his way to find his aunt, who will save him from the cruelty of his stepfather, believe in him and cherish him. *Great Expectations* inhabits the streets and houses of Rochester and the Medway marshes and estuary. The pattern, structure and setting of human lives was the stuff of his novels, and he saw the structure and pattern of his own life as closely related to place. Journeys in and out of London make crucial turning points in his novels, for good or ill, and in July 1822 he made just such a crucial journey, aged ten, and alone. At the end of term Mr Giles gave him a copy of Goldsmith's *The Bee*[27] to remember him by, his few clothes were packed up, he was given sandwiches for the journey and put into the London coach. It happened to be empty, and he travelled with no one at his side through the Kentish countryside on a rainy summer's day, and into the heart of London. He remembered it as a damp and sorrowful journey.

2

A London Education

1822–1827

The Dover-to-London mail coach, known as the Commodore, stopped in Rochester to pick up passengers at half past two in the afternoon, and three hours later arrived at the end of its route outside the Golden Cross Inn, Charing Cross, close to the Navy Pay Office in Somerset House, where John Dickens worked. It was a summer evening, and a hackney cab cost money, so father and son are likely to have walked north together to their new home in Camden Town, through streets now observed for the first time by a child eager to learn his surroundings.[1] What he saw would become the backdrop to much of his life as well as provide scenes for his novels; and he always kept an allegiance to those districts that were his parents' chosen territory, extending north-west from the Strand, across Oxford Street, into Bloomsbury, Marylebone and Regent's Park, and up the Hampstead Road to St Pancras, Somers Town and Camden Town.

The streets through which he walked beside his father were crowded, noisy and dirty. There was smoke in the air and filth on the ground, but also excitement and bustle. Carts, horses and pigs were part of the scene, men on horseback, pony traps, carriages, and among the throng of men and women there were a great many children, mostly poor, ragged and barefoot. The streets were their playground, where there was always something to look at and someone to talk to, and their workplace too, because they could earn pennies by running errands, or beg, or steal. There were food and coffee stalls on wheels, rattling hackney cabs and large hackney coaches, and street-sellers shouting their various wares – brooms, baskets and flowers. At this time there was a good deal of builders' chaos to be got round, and scaffolding to be wondered at, where new roads were being cut and new houses built, since King George IV and his architect John Nash had set about improving London: Regent Street was under construction, as were the terraces round Regent's Park.

A new church of St Pancras, built of white Portland stone, with great eye-catching caryatids in imitation of ancient Greek statues, had just appeared on the south side of the New Road – it was not renamed the Euston Road until 1838, after the building of Euston Station. When his parents were children the New Road had divided London from the fields to the north, but as the population grew streets and housing spread over the farmland and market gardens. In the parish of St Pancras alone the population grew between 1811 and 1831 from 46,000 to 100,000.

Camden Town, where the Dickens family had installed itself, was one of the areas of expansion. They fitted tightly into a narrow terraced house, No. 16 Bayham Street: three floors, basement, ground and first, an exiguous garret above and a wash house out at the back. Into this small space went the six children, including the new baby, Alfred, their nameless maid and their lodger James Lamert. Where and how they slept is hard to work out, and a further mystery is that, when two-year-old Harriet fell ill with smallpox later that year and died, the others escaped infection.[2] Bayham Street had been cut through the gardens of the Mother Red Cap Inn on the Hampstead Road and the houses were built during the last years of the war, so they were quite new. There was no sense of community, as there had been in Chatham, and afterwards Dickens could recall only two neighbours, the washerwoman next door and a Bow Street officer across the road. As he began to get his bearings, he failed to find other children to make friends with, and although there were still hay fields behind the house he had no memory of playing there; but he did remember walking alone to the almshouses along the road, from which there was a view through the smoky air and over some great dust heaps to the dome of St Paul's, a sight that caught his imagination. Inside the house there was always plenty to do in the way of keeping the four little ones amused and giving his mother and the maid a hand. Fanny managed to work at her music – a piano must somehow have been squeezed in for her – and so effectively that a family friend noticed how gifted she was, and within a year recommended her as a pupil to the newly established Royal Academy of Music.

What Charles most enjoyed was being taken into town by one or the other of his parents. It could only have been his mother who took him to see his uncle Thomas Barrow, her eldest brother, who had not allowed John Dickens under his roof since he had fleeced him of his £200. Barrow had started working for the Navy Pay Office at the age of eleven, when he and John Dickens first met, and he was currently living in lodgings in Gerrard Street in Soho, recovering from a major operation: he had broken a thigh at fifteen, the leg failed to mend properly and now at last it had to be amputated. The amputation succeeded so well that he was able to get on with his life better than before, and indeed married the following year, had a family, and was further promoted at the Pay Office. In spite of his difficult early years he was a man of some culture, and one of his visitors at Gerrard Street, seen and remembered by Charles, was Charles Dilke, a fellow worker at the Pay Office and later editor of the *Athenaeum* magazine: Dilke was also a friend of Keats, who had just died. Barrow's willpower and determination to succeed against the odds, so different from John Dickens's lackadaisical incompetence, must have impressed itself on his nephew. Charles grew fond of him, and visited him often over a period of a few months, becoming his 'little companion and nurse', which suggests that he learnt to make his way to Soho on his own; and his conduct over the next decade showed a stoicism and perseverance that might have been modelled on Thomas Barrow's.[3]

Below his uncle's lodgings in Gerrard Street lived the widow of a bookseller, a Mrs Manson, who was keeping up her late husband's business. Meeting Charles on the stairs, she took a liking to him and offered to lend him books. They could not have found a more appreciative reader. *Broad Grins*, a popular miscellany of comic verse by the playwright George Colman, became a favourite, and Charles was so impressed by the description of Covent Garden in one of the pieces that he took himself – again, on his own – to the real Covent Garden, where he snuffed up the smell of cabbage leaves 'as if it were the very breath of comic fiction'.[4] Another was Holbein's *Dance of Death*, a series of black-and-white prints showing death as a grinning skeleton collecting his victims among rich and poor, old people and children, kings, queens, priests and lawyers. Holbein shows naked bodies as well as clothed, life as well as death, and the prints caught the boy's attention and stayed in his mind.

During his early months in London a family friend from Kent offered to take him out for the day, set off with him and failed to keep an eye on him, so that Charles was lost in the Strand, somewhere near Northumberland House as he remembered. He spent a long day wandering by himself into the City, past the Guildhall, the Mansion House, Austin Friars and India House in Leadenhall Street; then, having a shilling in his pocket, he took himself into a theatre in Goodman's Fields, off the Whitechapel Road. Coming out at the end of the performance into darkness and rain, he very sensibly found a watchman who took him to the watchhouse, where he fell asleep, waking up to find his father had arrived to fetch him home. He had shed some tears, been frightened by a chimney sweep and tormented by several boys but, by his own account, had not thought of his mother, and had made up his mind that he would never be found. Yet he remained remarkably composed and fatalistic about what might happen to him next.

His Dickens grandmother was now approaching eighty and living in Oxford Street with his uncle William, and although it is not known whether he visited her, it is certain that he received from her, as eldest grandson, a large silver watch that had belonged to her husband, which he then carried about in his pocket.[5] He did remember being taken to see his godfather Christopher Huffam in Church Row at Limehouse. There Huffam ran his business as a ship rigger, dealing in whatever was needed for sailing ships. He was a cheerful, kindly man, who tipped Charles half-a-crown on his birthday and invited him to sing his comic songs, which led a fellow guest to declare that the boy was a prodigy.[6] The praise was important to him, because the last praise he had been given was at Mr Giles's school, and he was anxious to continue his education. As the summer ended and holiday time was over, he could not understand why he was not sent to school, but kept at home with nothing to do but run errands, clean his father's boots before he set off for Somerset House each morning and look after the younger children. His parents could have seen to it, he believed, and could have afforded it had they only organized their spending better: 'something might have been spared, *as certainly it might have been*, to place me at any common school.'⁷

James Lamert tried to cheer him up by making him a toy theatre. His other occupation was writing descriptions of people he observed. These men and women were not glamorous or heroic, but odd, and old: one was the talkative barber who came to shave his uncle Barrow in Gerrard Street, and knew a great deal about the late wars and the mistakes made by Napoleon. The other was the deaf woman who helped in the kitchen at Bayham Street and prepared 'delicate hashes with walnut-ketchup', which he liked. Few children of ten or eleven write character sketches of old people without any prompting, and this was a more certain pointer to his prodigious future than his singing of comic songs. He was proud of his writing, but privately, showing it to no one, and so was given no encouragement to write more. His parents were preoccupied with their many young children and with money troubles. There were sorrows too: in September they heard from Ireland of the death of the children's aunt Fanny, their mother's sister, who had been a much loved part of their lives throughout the years at Chatham. She had been married for less than a year, and now she was gone, carried off like one of the figures in the Holbein prints.

The winter went by, with no change, except that James Lamert moved out, perhaps because there was really not room for him, and also because he had found a job in a cousin's business. In the spring of 1823 Fanny was awarded a place at the Royal Academy of Music, newly established in Tenterden Street off Hanover Square, and she was to be one of the first boarders, starting in April. She was twelve, and she would be studying the piano with Ignaz Moscheles, a pupil of Beethoven, as well as harmony with the principal, Dr Crotch, and singing. The fees were thirty-eight guineas a year, and although Dickens maintained that he never felt any jealousy of what was done for her, he could not help but be aware of the contrast between his position and hers, and of their parents' readiness to pay handsome fees for her education, and nothing for his. It is such a reversal of the usual family situation, where only the education of the boys is taken seriously, that the Dickens parents at least deserve some credit for making sure Fanny had a professional training, although none for their neglect of her brother. For the next six months he continued without formal education of any kind, but instead was free to wander about London, learning the layout and character of districts and streets, and observing the contrast between Regent Street, which was opened this year, so wide and fine with its colonnade, and the narrow lanes not far from it, around Seven Dials for instance, where second-hand clothes for sale were hung outside the shops, and he was inspired to imagine the life stories of those who had last worn them and been reduced to selling them.

The shortage of money in his own family led his mother to think how she could put her talents to use now that her husband's salary was not growing fast enough to keep pace with the needs of the children. It was after all the very problem that had driven her father to embezzle, and after consulting with friends she decided on a bold plan. She would run a school, on the principle that she was able to teach her own children and therefore might as well teach others. In the autumn of 1823 she took a lease on a large house in Gower Street North and put up a brass plate announcing: 'Mrs Dickens's Establishment'. She was encouraged by Huffam, who had contacts in the east, and who thought she would be sure to get pupils from among the many British children sent home by their parents from India. Bayham Street was abandoned, along with a pile of unpaid bills, and the family moved down the hill to take up their abode in the much more spacious house in Gower Street North.[8] Charles was sent out with circulars advertising the school, and began to hope it might lead to his being sent to school himself. His hopes did not last long. No pupils arrived and no inquiries were made. All that happened was that they were pursued by creditors with increasing ferocity, their furious knockings and shoutings at the front door driving his father to ignominious hiding places upstairs. Finally he could hide no more and he was arrested for debt in February 1824.

John Dickens was taken first to a sponging house, kept by a bailiff as a preliminary place for holding debtors. Here Charles was sent by his mother to attend on him, and used by his father as a messenger to carry his various apologies and requests for help to family and friends. No help came from his brother William in Oxford Street, or from Mrs Dickens senior, or from his Barrow brothers-in-law. They had all had enough. Charles was frightened. He loved his father, for all his failings, and now saw him about to be taken to the Marshalsea debtors' prison, across the river in Southwark. Before he was escorted away he made a dramatic statement to his son, to the effect that the sun was setting on him for ever. Whatever he meant to convey, the child was reduced to despair.

Yet when his mother sent him to the Marshalsea the next day, he found his father had cheered up. He offered Charles the sound advice Dickens later credited to Mr Micawber: that with an income of £20 a year an expenditure of £19.19s.6d. meant happiness, but an expenditure of one shilling more meant unhappiness.[9] Then he sent his little son to borrow a knife and fork from Captain Porter in the room above, and prepared to settle in comfortably, since he would continue to receive his salary and no longer be pestered by his creditors. There was after all something to be said for prison, even though the buildings were old and shabby and there was only a small fire in the grate of his room.

In Gower Street things got worse from day to day. Charles, as the man of the family, just twelve years old, was sent out to a pawnbroker in the Hampstead Road, first with the books he loved, then with items of furniture, until after a few weeks the house was almost empty and the family was camping out in two bare rooms in the cold weather. All these experiences – of debt, fear, angry creditors, bailiffs, pawnbrokers, prison, living in freezing empty rooms and managing on what can be borrowed or begged – were impressed on his mind and used again and again in his stories and novels, sometimes grimly, sometimes with humour.

Now James Lamert came to see Mrs Dickens with a helpful proposal. He was currently managing a small but steady business in a warehouse belonging to his cousin George, at Hungerford Stairs between the Strand and the river bank, where boot and shoe blacking was manufactured and put into pots to be sold. Seeing the situation of the Dickens family, he suggested that Charles might help out by coming to work at Warren's factory, a light job, covering and labelling the pots of blacking. He would be paid six shillings a week, and Lamert promised that he personally would give him lessons during his lunch hour to keep up his education. When Dickens came to write his account of this, twenty-five years later, he dwelt with horror and indignation on such a proposal being made for a young, sensitive and promising child, and on his parents' indifference to what it meant for him: 'No one made any sign. My father and mother were quite satisfied. They could hardly have been more so, if I had been twenty years of age, distinguished at a grammar-school, and going to Cambridge.'[10] The contrast between the blacking-factory job and the idea of Cambridge University is startling, because it suggests how strong his hopes and self-belief had been, even though no one in his family had attended a university, or would do so for another forty years.

He was small for his age, and still subject to the attacks of pain in his side that had stopped him joining in boys' games in Kent; and he wore a child's pale suit of trousers and jacket to go to work. On the first day Lamert must have walked with him to Charing Cross, through the Hungerford Market and on to the Hungerford Stairs, where the dirty, tidal Thames rose and fell dramatically each day. The Embankment was not yet made, and the river bank was broken ground and ditches, with working boats and barges constantly passing. The warehouse was set up in a half-ruined building above the river, and Dickens particularly remembered that there were rats in the basement, so many of them that you could hear their squeaking when you were in the rooms upstairs. A small staff worked there, of men and boys. Of the boys he got to know, an older one, Bob Fagin, was an orphan living with his brother-in-law, a waterman; and Poll Green was the son of a fireman with a Drury Lane connection – and his sister 'did imps in pantomimes', a detail that interested Charles enough to fix itself in his mind. At first he was put to work apart from them in the counting house, but soon it was found easier for them to work together and he moved downstairs. The lunchtime lessons lapsed. He was known to them all as 'the young gentleman', and they were kind to him, Bob Fagin in particular, who looked after him with much tenderness when he was taken ill with the sharp pain in his side one day. All the same, 'No words can express the secret agony of my soul as I sank into this companionship . . . the sense I had of being utterly neglected and hopeless; of the shame I felt in my position . . . My whole nature was penetrated with grief and humiliation.'[11]

What is most remarkable is the strength of the image he had of himself, his belief in his own capacities and potential, justified by everything that came after, but quite uncertain then. Looking back, he lays stress on the pathos of his situation, and on his vulnerability, and to be sure he was lonely and often hungry, and desperately missed his father and mother; and the misery was made worse by the knowledge that they had willingly put him into this situation. To begin with he walked from Gower Street each day, but soon Mrs Dickens decided she must give up the house there and join her husband in the Marshalsea Prison with the smaller children. The little servant was put into lodgings in Southwark, Fanny remained at the Academy, and Charles was lodged with a woman he disliked, a Mrs Roylance in Little College Street in Camden Town, who took in children cheaply and treated them accordingly. He had to share a room with two other boys, and his walk to and from work was considerably lengthened. On Sundays he collected Fanny from the Academy and they went together to the Marshalsea to spend the day with their parents.

One Sunday night he told his father how much he hated being separated from the family all week, with nothing to return to each evening but 'a miserable blank'. It was the first time he had said anything about what he felt, and tears came into his eyes as he spoke. Seeing his distress, his father responded, and another lodging was found for him close to the prison, in Lant Street, where a kindly landlord with a gentle wife gave him a room. His window looked over a timber yard, which pleased him, and now he was able to breakfast and take his supper in the prison with his own family, and life seemed much better. He still wandered in his spare time, exploring the Adelphi arches, Piranesi-like structures beneath the Adam houses and the Strand, where the land sloped down to the river; he looked into the shops in the Blackfriars Road, and occasionally watched a travelling puppet-show van at the corner of a street; and when, waiting on London Bridge for the gates to be opened, he sometimes met the little nameless maid who served his parents, he would entertain her with stories he made up about the Tower of London and the wharves. There were even days when he played on the coal barges in the Thames with Bob and Poll.

Dickens details the life of the small boy he was with apparently good recall and sureness of touch, and his narrative is as painful as anything in his novels. It immediately links him with the many children who endure suffering in their pages: Oliver, Smike, Nell, Paul, Florence, Esther, Jo, David and Little Dorrit – who is of course the 'child of the Marshalsea', created more than thirty years later, when the prison had long been closed. As his friend and biographer John Forster wrote of these fictional children after Dickens's death, 'They were not his clients whose cause he pleaded with such pathos and humour, and on whose side he got the laughter and tears of all the world, but in some sense his very self.'[12] Yet Dickens's own account also shows him to have been resourceful, careful, well organized and with a sense of his own dignity even at that tender age. He did after all succeed in making his father change the living arrangements he disliked. He was able to work out his own budget and make sure his earnings would last until the next pay day by dividing the coins and wrapping them up into seven little parcels, each labelled with a day of the week, and not to be touched in advance. He maintained his dignity at his workplace, never expressing what he felt about it, never letting anyone know his father was in prison, never allowing anyone to see his distress. He even kept a sense of occasion, and allowed himself, on his birthday, to go into a public house in Westminster and order a glass of the 'very best ale . . . with a good head to it', to the considerable surprise of the landlord and his wife. And he became conscious of his own powers of observation and memory after watching a group of prisoners one evening at the Marshalsea, when they had gathered to sign a petition that they should be allowed to drink a toast to the King on his birthday. He saw that it was a scene of comedy and pathos, made a mental note of the different manner of each of the men, and thought about them over and over again when he was at work, re-creating them in his mind.

At the end of April old Mrs Dickens died. Her elder son, William, arranged for her funeral service to be held at St George's, Hanover Square, where she had been married, and she was buried in its graveyard in the Bayswater Road, without a memorial stone. John Dickens could not attend, and William was clearly aware of his plight because he immediately paid off his brother's outstanding debt of £40, long before any inheritance could come through.[13] This allowed John Dickens to petition for release from prison, and at the end of May he was discharged from the Marshalsea as an 'insolvent debtor'. He had already prepared a request to the Navy Pay Office to be retired early with an invalid's pension, although he was not yet forty, and he had obtained a certificate from a doctor to say that he was suffering from a bladder complaint. For the moment, while the Admiralty considered his request, he went back to work at Somerset House.

The whole family lodged briefly with Mrs Roylance until they found a house to rent in Somers Town, at No. 29 Johnson Street. The movements of the Dickens family from house to house, lodging to lodging, are so many that they are confusing to anyone reading about them, and indeed anyone writing about or researching them. But, as already indicated, they remained in what can roughly be called North London – Camden Town, Somers Town, the areas round Fitzroy Square and Manchester Square, with excursions to Islington, Hampstead and North End. They did not go south of the Thames – apart from the Marshalsea – or venture west into Paddington or north into Holloway. William Dickens continued to live in Oxford Street with his wife until he died in December of the following year, aged only forty-three, and childless.

By the time John Dickens returned to Somerset House the blacking business had moved from Hungerford Stairs to premises in Covent Garden, a place well known to Charles, and which, in other circumstances, he particularly liked. Now he walked from Somers Town, and sometimes was given some 'cold hotch potch in a small basin tied up with a handkerchief' for his lunch, which he carried with him. Nobody suggested he might leave the blacking business. He and Bob, who were the quickest of the boys, were positioned in a window of the house where they worked, on the corner of Chandos Street and Bedford Street, and passers-by sometimes stopped to admire their dexterity as they closed and labelled the jars of blacking.[14] One day Charles saw his father walk in 'when we were very busy, and I wondered how he could bear it'. Somerset House was not far from Covent Garden, and on another occasion John Dickens walked past with a colleague from his office, the same Charles Dilke his son had met at Thomas Barrow's, and this time the two men stopped to watch the boys at work. Either Dilke recognized Charles or John Dickens explained that the smaller boy was his son: and Dilke, a sensitive and kindly man, went in and gave him half a crown, and received in return a very low bow.[15] This scene, described by Dilke, not Dickens, does more to suggest the humiliation he felt in being put in such a position than anything else: pitied and tipped, while his father stood simpering by.

Meanwhile Fanny was redeeming the family pride at the Academy, winning a prize and a silver medal. On 29 June 1824 she performed at a public concert at which Princess Augusta, the King's sister, presented the prizes. The Dickens family was in the audience, and Charles's reaction was painful, though silent. 'I could not bear to think of myself – beyond the reach of all such honourable emulation and success. The tears ran down my face. I felt as if my heart were rent. I prayed, when I went to bed that night, to be lifted out of the humiliation and neglect in which I was. I had never suffered so much before.' He went on, 'There was no envy in this.' It seems more likely that the envy was sternly repressed, adding to his pain.[16]

How long he remained pasting and labelling is unsure, not least because he could not remember himself. It seems to have lasted for a little over a year, from February 1824, when he was twelve, to March 1825, when he was thirteen.[17] It was in March that his father was granted his pension and retired from the Pay Office. The Admiralty lords chose to be generous and ordered that he should be given £145.16s.8d. a year; they were also keen to be rid of a recent bankrupt. The payments he had to make on his existing debts took a bite

out of the pension, but he was now free to find other work, the bladder complaint having no effect on his ability to do so.

John Dickens's next action was to quarrel with James Lamert.
Charles was asked to take a letter from his father to Covent Garden
when he went to work, and he watched Lamert grow angry as he
read it. The subject of the letter was his own position at the blacking
warehouse, and Charles suspected it might be something to do with
his sitting in the window and being noticed by passers-by, but
whether it was that or something else, he was upset when Lamert
accused his father of insulting him. Lamert did not vent his anger on
Charles; he remained gentle with him but told him he had better go
home. An old soldier who worked with him said reassuringly that it
would be for the best, and, 'with a relief so strange that it was like
oppression, I went home.'[18]

His mother immediately offered to make up the quarrel with
Lamert. She wanted Charles to go back to his job; she may no doubt
have remembered how her brother Tom had started work at eleven,
and made a good thing of it, and she went to see Lamert the next
morning, returning with an invitation to her son to return to the
blacking factory. It seems extraordinary and incomprehensible to us
now, and it was intolerable to him then. 'I do not write resentfully or
angrily: for I know how all these things have worked together to
make me what I am: but I never afterwards forgot, I never shall forget, I never can forget, that my mother was warm for my being sent
back.'[19] His father now suddenly woke from his long trance, remembered that his son needed to be educated and said he must after all go
to school. Charles was sent round with a card asking for terms to
Wellington House Academy, a nearby boys' school said to be good,
where Latin, mathematics and English were taught, together with
dancing.

The most surprising part of this whole affair is also told by Dickens: that neither his father nor his mother ever mentioned the
blacking factory or Charles's year as a child labourer again in their
lives – not a word, not a hint. 'From that hour . . . my father and
mother have been stricken dumb upon it. I have never heard the least
allusion to it, however far off or remote, from either of them.'[20] It

was as though it had not happened. John Forster, who was the first to be told the whole story more than twenty years later, believed that it had given Dickens his exceptional determination and energy to ride over obstacles, with 'a sense that everything was possible to the will that would make it so', and also a cold, fierce aggression that burst out occasionally, quite at odds with his normal generosity and warmth. And Dickens himself invoked the unhappy time during his childhood to explain, during the great crisis in his life, the reappearance of 'the character formed in me then'.[21] Well, perhaps, but if the experience did some damage it strengthened his character too. It also gave him a subject he used again and again in his books, where a vulnerable and suffering child is shown either succumbing to ill-treatment and dying, as Nell, Paul and Jo do, or enduring and triumphing over it, as Oliver, the Marchioness, Florence, Esther, Sissy and Little Dorrit do in their different ways. In some cases there is ambiguity. Tiny Tim is allotted alternative possible fates. Louisa Gradgrind grows through the disastrous course of life she has embarked on, emerging wiser but scarcely happy. Pip too remains unresolved: he has survived, but he is damaged; he has done some good and some harm to those around him, and the best he can hope for is to end his days with a measure of self-knowledge – and in this way it is the truest of the novels. In the same book Estella is allowed to survive and understand the reason for the mistakes she has made, but not rewarded for her understanding.[22]

Wellington House Academy seemingly turned him into an ordinary boy again, although it proved to be an indifferent school. The proprietor and headmaster, William Jones, was an ignorant man who carried a large mahogany ruler used chiefly for caning boys, something he enjoyed doing. His habit was to draw their trousers tight with one hand while he thrashed them as hard as he could with the other. Dickens seems to have escaped his attentions, perhaps because he was a day boy who might complain at home. Most of the pupils were boarders, which underlined his own happiness at having a home again. He did not distinguish himself as a scholar, but one teacher gave him decent courses in mathematics, English and a little Latin. The first known examples of his handwriting, which date from this time, show that it was clear, well formed and bold, and that he was already experimenting with a line beneath his signature for emphasis, which he elaborated later and made his trademark. Like most of the boys he read penny magazines and enjoyed speaking a 'lingo', which involved adding letters to the end of each word to make it sound like a foreign language. He needed to play after his working year, and throughout his life he continued to take huge pleasure in games, charades, conjuring tricks, cricket, races, quoits and other boyish amusements. At school he was also a leading spirit in putting on theatrical performances; and he wrote and circulated stories, and got up 'Our Newspaper' with another boy, hiring it out to readers who paid in marbles for the privilege. It is a relief to learn that those of his schoolmates who remembered him described him as a cheerful and mischievous boy, joining in pranks such as keeping bees and mice in their desks, and constructing miniature coaches and pumps for the mice to set in motion; and sometimes, as a joke, pretending to be one of the many poor children of the streets and begging from the old ladies of Camden Town.

3

Becoming Boz

1827–1834

In February 1827 Dickens was fifteen, and within a few weeks of his birthday his formal education came to an end. The reason was simple: his father could no longer pay the fees. John Dickens had been supplementing his pension by writing articles on marine insurance, as City correspondent for a newspaper grandly named the *British Press*, but when a recession hit England at the end of 1826 the paper collapsed. He had no money put by against misfortune and, as usual, many debts. Now he was unable to pay the rates, and the family was evicted from the house in Johnson Street. To add to their problems, Mrs Dickens found she was pregnant again. She was only thirty-eight, yet it came as a surprise after a gap of five years. Fanny's fees at the Royal Academy of Music were so badly in arrears that she had to leave; but she showed such promise and determination that she was able to make an arrangement which allowed her to return and pay for her studies by taking on part-time teaching. The younger boys, Alfred, aged five, and seven-year-old Fred, remained at their school in Brunswick Square. Eleven-year-old Letitia came into a small inheritance from their old neighbour, Mr Newnham at Ordnance Terrace, who had wisely left the bequest in trust, which saved it from being swallowed up by her father.[1] She seems to have stayed at home to be taught by their mother. But for Charles there was only one possible course: he must go out and earn his living.

Whatever he felt about having his education stopped short again, he was prepared to take his place in the adult world, and also to accept his mother's help in finding him work, in spite of her bad behaviour over the blacking-factory job. One of her aunts, a Mrs Charles Charlton, was married to a senior clerk in Doctors' Commons, and they kept a lodging house in Berners Street, letting out rooms to lawyers.

Elizabeth Dickens had met a young partner in a law firm there, Edward Blackmore, and she thought he might give Charles a job with Ellis & Blackmore, and took him along to be inspected. Blackmore judged Charles a very presentable boy, with a fresh intelligent face, neat clothes and good manners, and offered him ten shillings and sixpence a week. For this he would be working six days a week in an office in Gray's Inn, called a clerk but really no more than an office boy. He would not be acquiring any formal qualifications, but it was a start.

The Dickens family found new lodgings four streets south of Johnson Street, at No. 17 The Polygon. The Polygon had been an architectural innovation of the 1790s: a ring of four-storey houses built round a central garden, intended as the first part of the builder's plan for a superior suburb, next to the green meadows rising towards Hampstead, while still within walking distance of central London. The plan failed when money ran low during the war years, and streets of small terraced houses were put up, hemming in The Polygon, and Somers Town became shabby-genteel. William Wills, who worked with Dickens later, also moved there in the 1820s when his father, a Plymouth shipowner, lost his money, and walked daily to work in the Strand. When the Dickens family arrived, there were still a few artists and writers living in The Polygon, giving it a touch of distinction, and years later Charles chose to install a character, the artistic and improvident Harold Skimpole (of *Bleak House*), in one of its decaying dwellings. Skimpole camped out in a single prettily furnished room while his wife and daughters managed as best they could in the rest of the house, and the local tradesmen's bills went unpaid, a situation Dickens understood perfectly.[2] His father too had a vision of a life of culture and comfort which was always just out of his reach.

In May, Fanny, currently the most successful member of the family, sang in a benefit concert at Drury Lane for the singer and comedian John Pritt Harley, and in the same month Charles started work. His daily walk to Gray's Inn took him half an hour. It was all familiar territory, and if memories of the unhappiness of three years earlier came into his mind as he made his way over some of the same ground, he put them aside. Now he was eager to live the life of a young Londoner.[3] He was always well turned out, kept his hair carefully combed, and he had a distinctive way of dressing: an Army cap with a strap going round his chin, more straps holding his trousers over his boots and a tight dark blue jacket, with a black neckerchief concealing the shirt beneath. The dandy of the late 1830s was already forming.

The other clerks took to him. He was such a good mimic that he had them laughing with his imitations of everyone who amused him – people he listened to in the streets, the old woman who swept the offices, clients and lawyers. He could do comic songs and turn himself into various well-known singers of the day. Soon he was spending his earnings on going to the theatre with his new companions, discussing actors and plays, and always ready to give them long passages of Shakespeare. In the summer of 1828 the veteran comedian Charles Mathews was at Drury Lane doing his hugely popular one-man shows in which he played multiple parts, calling them 'monopolylogues', and Mathews became the actor Dickens admired above all others. For the next six years he appeared at the Adelphi Theatre every season, and Dickens went as often as he could, learning his performances by heart, words, songs, movements and gestures.[4] It was just as well he was soon given a rise to thirteen shillings a week. There was an occasional dinner with a friend, and on special occasions a brandy or whisky grog and a mild Havana cigar. He found out what it was like to be drunk and to feel ill in the morning. When their boss Blackmore got married he gave the whole office dinner, and one clerk stayed away sick the next day, insisting on his return that it was not the drink that had made him ill, 'It was the *salmon!*' Dickens laughed, stored it up and used it in his first novel, where the respectable Mr Pickwick makes the same excuse after getting drunk: 'It was the *salmon!*' There was no disapproval in Dickens's joking, because wine and spirits were among the legitimate pleasures of life for him, along with cigars, and he was always ready to mock the temperance movement.

He soon knew his way around all the streets, courts, alleys, inns, chambers and gardens of the legal district. When the firm moved to

upstairs premises with a view over Holborn, the clerks amused themselves by dropping cherry stones from the windows on passers-by,
and those who came up to complain were met by Dickens acting
injured innocence to perfection, and went away baffled. If office life
was dull, outside in the streets there was everything to learn. This is
the least documented time in his life, but the sketches he wrote in the
1830s tell us what he observed, what interested him and what sort of
young man he was. The law did not impress him, then or ever, except
for the particular eccentricities and general obduracy of its practitioners, although he understood that it was a respectable way to make
money. He was exploring the world in which he found himself, and
gathering himself together to make some sort of assault upon it, but
had not yet discovered what his line of attack would be.

In November 1828 he left Ellis & Blackmore and went to work for
another solicitor, Charles Molloy, in Chancery Lane, where he knew
one of the clerks, Thomas Mitton, whose family also lived in The
Polygon, his father keeping a pub near by. Mitton was serving his
articles with Molloy in order to become a lawyer himself. The two
young men made friends and Mitton went on to act as Dickens's
solicitor. Dickens thought about getting a legal qualification himself,
not as a solicitor but at the Bar, and continued to think about it on
and off for years. He went so far as to enter his name at the Middle
Temple in 1839, without going any further; but the law in its many
ramifications fascinated him, and lawyers figure in almost all his
novels. They are not heroes: Dodson & Fogg in *The Pickwick Papers*,
Sampson Brass in *The Old Curiosity Shop*, Mr Tulkinghorn and Mr
Vholes in *Bleak House* all display varieties of evil behaviour; Mr Jaggers in *Great Expectations* does something to redeem the profession but
remains sinister. Mr Wickfield is a feeble country solicitor who takes
to drink, and his ambitious clerk Heep is an out-and-out villain.
Only Traddles, who is about to become a judge at the end of *David
Copperfield*, is an honourable man, and Grewgious, in *The Mystery of
Edwin Drood*, preserves his virtue by performing no legal function
beyond acting as Receiver and Agent to two estates, and deputing
any work involved to a solicitor.

The law struck Dickens as a murky business that thrived on delay, complication and confusion, whereas he had a passion for order. If he was born with it, it must have been strengthened in response to the chaotic conditions of his youth, and his father's inability to keep control of things. Yet, determined as he was to set his own life in perfect order, the next ten years were ones of continuous confusion in his affairs as he worked through a series of self-imposed tasks, mastering different skills and experimenting to find out what suited him best. Whether it was paid work or self-education, whatever he took on was done with energy and determination. There were many distractions and he never ceased to do his best to be a helpful son and brother, however intensely he was pursuing his various goals. During these same years, while still a boy himself, he also made up his mind to get a wife in the hope of setting up a home of his own. Eighteen was much too young to be thinking about marriage, but as soon as he fell in love he sought commitment, determined to have everything put in order. All about him in London was the sexual chaos of the streets and the theatres, where he could see how prostitution thrived. If it was a temptation, it was one he wanted to shut off.

Shut off, but also observe. He was always looking, listening to the voices and reacting to the dramas, absurdities and tragedies of London life. From these early observations he built up a store of knowledge that would nourish his art for the rest of his life. In his early writings, sketches written for papers and magazines, he describes, for instance, exactly how the men of North London walked to work, six days a week, in their thousands, setting off early from the suburbs of Somers Town and Camden Town, Islington and Pentonville, where the bakers opened an hour earlier than those in town, so that the vast population of clerks pouring into the City, Chancery Lane, Gray's Inn, Lincoln's Inn and all the other Inns of Court could get their morning rolls before they started walking. He noticed the middle-aged men, 'whose salaries have by no means increased in the same proportion as their families', plodding steadily along, knowing almost everybody by sight after twenty years' walking, but not wasting their energy in stopping to shake hands or speak; and in *A Christmas Carol* he would make Bob Cratchit walk, and sometimes run, the three miles from Camden Town to the City every day, to earn his fifteen shillings a week, not much more than Dickens was paid for his first office job. He saw the small office lads 'who are made men before they are boys', and alongside them the girls, milliners' and stay-makers' apprentices, 'the hardest worked, the worst paid, and too often, the worst used class of the community'.[5]

Another picture: two sisters coming out of a prisoners' van, handcuffed together, thirteen and sixteen, the younger hiding her face and crying into her handkerchief. A woman in the crowd that has gathered shouts, 'How long are you for, Emily?' The elder girl shouts back, 'Six weeks and hard labour . . . and here's Bella a-going too for the first time. Hold up your head, you chicken . . . Hold up your head, and show 'em your face. I an't jealous, but I'm blessed if I an't game!' Dickens thinks the girls have been put to work as prostitutes by a vicious mother, and sympathizes with little Bella's shame and horror, but he also enjoys Emily's bold defiance and her readiness to play to the crowd. In this she is just like the thirteen-year-old boy in court who defies the judge, telling him he has witnesses to his character 'fifteen gen'lm'n is a vaten outside, and vos a vaten all day yesterday; vich they told me the night afore my trial vos a'comin' on.' No witnesses are found, and the boy will be re-created as the Artful Dodger, whose act of defiance in the dock, from which he threatens to have his friends ask questions in parliament about his case, is one of the high points of *Oliver Twist*, where Dickens invites his readers to approve of such wit and total lack of contrition.[6]

And here is a pale, bony little girl with a necklace of blue glass beads, being trained up by her mother for the stage in a small private theatre off the Strand, where one of Dickens's colleagues made an appearance or two, and just possibly Dickens himself also.[7] The little girl will dance her first hornpipe on stage 'after the tragedy'. She is a forerunner of the gin-fed Infant Phenomenon in *Nicholas Nickleby*.[8] He takes us inside a smart new Gin Shop, all plate glass, Turkey carpets, royal arms, stucco, mahogany and varnish to please the poor and get their money, where girls of fourteen or fifteen, with matted hair, are seen 'walking about barefoot, and in white greatcoats, almost their only covering'. And also to the Eagle pleasure gardens between Pentonville and the City, where courting couples go on summer

Sundays to enjoy tea and a concert at the Rotunda. Jemima Evans of Camden Town is there, wearing 'a white muslin gown carefully hooked and eyed, a little red shawl, plentifully pinned, a large white straw bonnet trimmed with red ribbons, a small necklace, a large pair of bracelets, Denmark satin shoes, and open-worked stockings; white cotton gloves on her fingers, and a cambric pocket handkerchief, carefully folded up, in her hand'. She is so closely observed she could be painted, and we can hear her voice too: she pronounces Evans 'Ivins', finds the gardens 'ev'nly' and calls for an 'Horficer!' when there is a brawl.[9]

The young Dickens wanted to laugh, and to make others laugh, and he took his own impoverished and uncertain background, its anxieties over etiquette, entertaining, wooing and marriage, money problems, inheritances and culture, and poked fun at every aspect of it. Two stories are set in a boarding house, such as the one his great-aunt Charlton ran. Another is about the difficulty of finding a husband for daughters over twenty-five, and the humiliation of discovering that the young man who seemed like a desirable suitor is nothing better than a shop assistant. The farce has an edge of contempt when he deals with a wealthy hypochondriac, or a doctor who grows rich on telling women what they want to hear, or a man who makes money on the stock exchange and immediately aspires to break into a higher level of society. The same broker's man who tells a funny story about agreeing to serve at the dinner table of a temporarily embarrassed rich man, pretending to be a servant to allow him time to raise the money he needs, has other stories of destitution and dying wives. And the comic tale of the inoffensive Mr Watkins Tottle, persuaded by a smart friend to stave off impending bankruptcy by proposing to a rich spinster, turns grim when she refuses him, and he kills himself rather than be taken to the sponging house. The young Dickens can pull jokes out of misery and pitch harmless decent people into disaster. Watching his father's manoeuvres gave an edge to many of his observations. Was his father a gentleman or a fraud? A victim or a swindler?

Dickens was a loyal family member, and although he suffered from his father's inability to stay out of debt, the idea of the large family as a force for good, convivial and energizing, remained powerful for him. Some of his earliest surviving letters are notes to friends summoning them to parties, music or dancing at home, and show how easy he felt there. A Christmas sketch published in 1835 suggests that the gathering of children, cousins and old people round the turkey and pudding does more to perpetuate good feeling than any number of religious homilies penned or spoken.[10] In November 1827 a new brother made his appearance, and was named for an emperor, Augustus. Charles took to calling him Moses by the time he was a toddler, nicknaming him after the son of the Vicar of Wakefield in Goldsmith's story, a favourite book. 'Moses' became 'Boses' when spoken through the nose, and Charles was prone to colds in the head, so 'Boses' became 'Boz', which in turn became the pen name adopted by him for his first published writing, in 1834. Dickens liked to keep hold of every part of his life, and relate each to the others. Years later, when he had his own family, he would take John Forster out with him to walk about the streets of Somers Town and Kentish Town on Christmas mornings, past the shabby-genteel houses, to watch the dinners preparing or coming in. This is the behaviour of a man who treasures the past and seeks to recapture and relive it.[11]

⚜

It is not easy to follow his day-to-day activities during the late 1820s and early 1830s because he was doing so much, taking in so much, spreading himself over so many activities, feeling everything with such intensity; and when he talked about those years afterwards he crammed too much into his accounts. He was living mostly with his parents, who moved in dizzying fashion from one lodging to another. In 1829 they left The Polygon for Norfolk Street, off Fitzroy Square.[12] Sometime in 1830 they had lodgings in George Street, off the Strand – this was the year of the death of George IV and accession of his brother William IV. In 1831 they were in Margaret Street, near Cavendish Square, but in the later part of the year John Dickens tried to put a distance between himself and his creditors by moving up to Hampstead and even further to North End. They were all there with him in the spring of 1832, except that Charles deserted them for a while and took a lodging in Cecil Street, one of many such small streets running south of the Strand to the river, and discovered he could take healthy plunges into the Roman bath in nearby Strand Lane, where a spring of fresh water ran through a pool.[13] This was when the Reform Bill was going through, to become law in June. He rejoined the family when they moved back to town – Fitzroy Street – later in the year and went with them to Highgate in August for a fortnight of fresh air. There, he told a friend, he 'discovered a green lane which looks as if nature had intended it for a Smoking place'.[14] He took up riding and became what was known as a Cockney rider, hiring horses to get as many miles out of town as he could. By the end of 1832 the whole family was in Bentinck Street, near Manchester Square.

For all John Dickens's shortcomings, he led a good example to his eldest son in one important respect: by setting himself to learn shorthand and making a success of it. In 1828 he went to work as a parliamentary reporter for a brother-in-law who was still prepared to speak to him, the enterprising John Barrow, who was just starting up a newspaper, the *Mirror of Parliament*. Barrow's intention was to rival Hansard by offering a complete record of what went on at the House of Commons, and he needed a team of reliable reporters to make a success of it. A fourth Barrow brother, Edward, also joined the paper as a reporter, and Charles was inspired to learn shorthand too. He gave a fictional account of the struggle to master it in *David Copperfield*, in which David learns to write it down only to find he cannot read it back and has to start all over again; he also gave David swift success in becoming a parliamentary reporter.[15]

This was not quite what happened in reality. Charles left Molloy's office sometime in 1829, when he had mastered shorthand well enough to find work as a reporter in the ecclesiastical courts at Doctors' Commons, close to St Paul's Cathedral, where his great-aunt Charlton's husband was a senior clerk. The courts held at Doctors' Commons dealt mostly with marriage, divorce and wills, and were held in a great pillared room decorated with the coats of arms of judges who had sat there over the centuries, a place of arcane practices where proctors argued in wigs and furred and scarlet gowns.

Dickens found it fusty and even sinister, as he made clear in a descriptive piece he published in 1836.[16] It was his first view of such outworn rituals kept creakily going, and convinced him that they would be better swept away.

The work he was able to get there was in any case irregular. He had to wait in a box to be chosen by one of the proctors to provide his shorthand services, and outside of the law terms there was none. But he was not idle. On reaching eighteen in 1830 he applied to the British Museum for a ticket to the Reading Room. Once again the Charltons proved helpful, and Mr Charlton was his sponsor. The ticket was renewed at least four times and for several years he read in the Reading Room when he could. A few of his book slips survive and show that he looked at Shakespeare's plays, at Goldsmith's *History of England* and at some Roman history, and returned to the Hollar engravings of Holbein's *Dance of Death*; also an eighteenth-century medical book on male midwives, perhaps seeking information about the mysterious anatomy of the other sex.

Even in the Reading Room his eyes were not always on the books. One of his early descriptive pieces describes a fellow reader, a man in a threadbare suit with a steadily diminishing number of buttons. His shabbiness fascinated Dickens and when he disappeared for a week he assumed he had died. But he was wrong, and the man reappeared, looking different, in a bright black suit. Slowly Dickens realized it was the original suit, 'revived' by being painted over in glossy black paint. Soon the pale seams, knees and elbows reappeared, and a rainy day entirely removed the 'reviver'. Dickens leaves the story there. It is one of several pieces in which he gives a deadpan account of respectable failures and victims of London, lonely men who never rise to any success. Another is a clerk he sees in St James's Park, who eats and lodges alone: 'Poor, harmless creatures such men are; contented but not happy; broken-spirited and humbled, they feel no pain but they never know pleasure.' The tone is dispassionate, but these men are emblematic warnings of what can easily happen to young men who fail to seize and make the most of their chances.[17]

How did he appear to other people at this stage of his life? There is a miniature portrait of him at eighteen, by his uncle Edward Barrow's wife, Janet, a professional painter, who shows him as a self-conscious clever boy, wide-eyed, with a half-smile, a large black stock round his neck, his thick, dark curly hair cut short. He looks promising, interesting, but not yet ready to play a romantic lead. This did not stop him attempting the role, because this was the year he met and fell in love with Maria Beadnell. She seemed enchantingly pretty to him, even with eyebrows that almost met in the middle. She had a small pet dog, and an album in which he wrote an acrostic on her name; she had been to Paris, and she played the harp. He remembered afterwards that she wore blue gloves, and particularly entranced him in a raspberry-coloured dress with black velvet trimming at the top, cut into vandykes. She was capricious and, to judge by what she later became, silly. His account of falling in love in *David Copperfield* used his memories of her, making her into a doll-like creature with the mentality of a six-year-old, who screams and sobs in terror when he suggests she might learn to cook and keep accounts before their marriage. Maria was in fact two years older than him, and they met in May 1830, when he was eighteen to her twenty: he was smitten at once and remained obsessed by her for three years.

Working at Doctors' Commons in the City was convenient for visiting her since she lived in Lombard Street. Her father was a City bank official and she had grown up in this comfortable home, the third and youngest daughter, and so the pet of the household; there was also an elder brother, Alfred, away in India, a lieutenant in the Army.[18] The Beadnells entertained a good deal, and Dickens met there Henry Kolle, an admirer of Maria's elder sister Anne. Dickens and Kolle both enjoyed singing, Anne played the lute and Maria the harp, and there was music. He made no attempt to hide what he felt for Maria, and in the early stages of his devotion she responded to his energetic wooing and seemed happy to believe they might one day be married. Looking back at that time, he described how, one day when they were caught in the rain as they walked together in the City, evidently unchaperoned, he took her into a church in Huggin Lane, near Mansion House, and said, 'Let the blessed event . . . occur at no altar but this!' and she consented that it should be so.[19] But the tenderness of this moment passed, and the Beadnell parents decided he would not do as a suitor for their daughter. Although Mr Beadnell was only a clerk at the bank at Mansion House, he was evidently a senior clerk, and his brother was the manager of the bank, raising him well above the Dickens family financially. Kolle and Anne became formally engaged, but Kolle was a bank clerk with a steady income and a respectable father in business, whereas Dickens had no financial security and a barely presentable father. Mrs Beadnell did not even bother to get his name right, always addressing him as 'Mr Dickin'.

He saw that to have any hope of impressing her parents and winning her hand he must become something more than a reporter in Doctors' Commons. He began to turn up at the editorial office of his uncle John Barrow's *Mirror of Parliament*, where his father and his uncle Edward were already employed, offered his help informally, and so managed to make a start on parliamentary reporting. He soon showed he could match their skills and was tried out among the reporters at the House of Commons. The House was another fusty old place, but more alive than Doctors' Commons, and once he had proved himself he did not have to wait around to be offered work. Instead he had to be available for debates which might go on into the small hours, sitting in the cramped gallery, straining to hear the exchanges below in the thick atmosphere of the chamber and writing on his knees by the light of the gas chandeliers. He quickly made a reputation for speed and accuracy, and may have contributed to the full report of the first major debate on the proposed Reform Act, in March 1831, given in the *Mirror of Parliament*. After a time he was given a staff job, and in 1832 he was also reporting for another newly established paper, the *True Sun*.[20]

The early 1830s were a dramatic time in politics, and Dickens's sympathies were all on the side of reform; but, although the Reform Act of 1832 was followed by bills against slavery and for the protection of factory workers and miners and other causes which certainly appealed to him, no sign of his interest or enthusiasm remains in letters or other writing. He did not learn to respect the House of Commons

as a place, or its procedures. He described it, when full, as 'a conglom-
eration of noise and confusion', worse than Smithfield cattle market,
with all the 'talking, laughing, lounging, coughing, oh-ing, questioning or groaning'.[21] He was not gripped by the excitement of the debates,
and may well have taken against its atmosphere of a club where most of
the members spoke in much the same way, a style learnt at their public
schools and colleges, the better ones rising to occasional wit, the
majority dull, the worst fatuous. Of two striking outsiders among the
new MPs, the radical William Cobbett and the Irish leader Daniel
O'Connell, Dickens afterwards admired Cobbett's writing, and accused
O'Connell of making 'fretty, boastful, frothy' speeches.[22] Others
whose speeches he took down became known to him personally later:
they included Lord Ashley, many of whose reforming ideas he
shared; Edward Stanley, afterwards fourteenth Earl of Derby, and
Prime Minister in the 1850s, who singled him out for his excellence
as a reporter, and was surprised by his youthful appearance when
they met;[23] and Lord John (later Earl) Russell, with whom a true
friendship developed. But if he had anything to say about them and
the words he heard them speak and took down at the time, it has not
survived. His only known mention of Earl Grey, who pushed
through the Reform Act with determination and skill, was a joke:
that the shape of his head 'weighed down my youth'.[24]

From the day he stopped reporting the doings of the House, he
chose never to return to it and never had a good word for it. He felt it
had little connection with what he saw going on in the world outside,
the poverty, ignorance and degradation of so many men, women and
children who lived without hope or comfort, and who needed to be
noticed and helped; and he came to endorse the view of his contemporary, the historian Henry Thomas Buckle, who believed lawgivers
were more likely to get in the way of what needed to be done than to
help society. Dickens thought he could do more good as a writer who
drew attention to abuses than in any other way, and he turned down
several invitations to stand for parliament himself, and attacked the
bombastic and cliché-ridden style of the typical MP with contempt.
Nothing ever thrilled him about the Commons or the Lords, not the
oratory, not the causes, not the personalities of the politicians.

Reporting kept him busy, but not too busy to keep up his studies in the Reading Room. When parliament was sitting, it was hard to visit the Beadnells or have any social life, since he had to be at the House in the afternoon and evening. He could read at the Museum in the mornings and, when parliament was in recess, all through the day, but earn nothing unless he could find other work. During 1832 the Beadnells took action to end their daughter's flirtation by sending her to Paris again, and when she returned it was clear that she had lost interest in him. She came to his twenty-first birthday party – 'the important occasion of my coming of age', celebrated with dancing of quadrilles – and used the occasion to make it plain she did not take his suit seriously.[25] 'Our meetings of late have been little more than so many displays of heartless indifference on the one hand while on the other they have never failed to prove a fertile soil of wretchedness in a pursuit which has long since been worse than hopeless,' he wrote to her, returning her letters and a present she had given him in happier times. He decided she had been playing a game, toying with his admiration, and that it meant nothing to her. He was left with 'a feeling of utter desolation and wretchedness'.[26] Her sister Anne wrote to him saying she did not understand Maria, or know what she felt, and counselling patience; while his sister Fanny failed to pass on something Maria had said, at which Charles raged, 'if I were to live a hundred years I would never forgive it.'[27]

He told Maria later that 'When we were falling off each other I came from the House of Commons many a night at two or three o'clock in the morning only to wander past the place she was asleep in.'[28] This meant walking from Westminster into the City, and, having patrolled Lombard Street, setting off back to Bentinck Street. It must have taken two hours and got him home not much before morning. Still in the grip of his obsession, he did nothing half-heartedly, and night-walking was a sort of tribute to her – although she had no idea he was doing it – and a way of dealing with his pain. In May he was still writing tormented letters, telling her, 'I never have loved and I never can love any human creature breathing but yourself.'[29] Three days later, on 22 May, he saw her at her sister's wedding to Henry Kolle, where he acted as best man, and that was the end. Maria remained unmarried until, at the age of thirty-five, she became the bride of a saw-mill manager in Finsbury, at which time Dickens was travelling in Italy and already the father of five children. Ten years after that, in 1855, he wrote to her again to say that the 'wasted tenderness of those hard years' made him suppress emotion, 'which I know is no part of my original nature, but which makes me chary of showing my affections, even to my children, except when they are very young'.[30] He blamed the coldness he was aware of in himself on the pain of that young experience, when love had seemed a matter of life and death, overwhelming and unrepeatable. He believed that he had felt more intensely then than at any time since, so that even the memory of those intense feelings became precious to him, a gold standard for love. At the same time, in writing about it in *David Copperfield*, he allowed David the best of all worlds, letting him marry Dora and then sending her into a decline to die young, leaving her husband heartbroken but also relieved that he has been rescued from his mistake. There was a web of ironies here that only he understood.

Throughout all this time of work, and love, and study, and constant moving from place to place, he was pursuing another, completely different and overpowering passion: for the theatre. Amazing as it seems, according to his own sober account it filled his life. He said that he went to a play almost every night for at least three years, 'really studying the bills first, and going to where there was the best acting'; and, on top of this, practising 'often four, five, six hours a day: shut up in my own room, or walking about in the fields'. This account is hard to square with his many other activities in 1829, 1830 and 1831, especially once he had started reporting parliamentary debates.[31] But, whether literally true or not, early in 1832 he made up his mind to explore a possible career as an actor. He asked Robert Keeley, a popular comedian specializing in low-life parts, to coach him. He had already memorized many of Charles Mathews's 'At Homes', practising in front of a mirror to perfect his performances. His sister Fanny helped him rehearse and accompanied his songs on the piano. When he felt ready, he wrote to the stage manager at Covent Garden, George Bartley, asking for an audition. A day was fixed when he was to appear before Bartley and the actor Charles Kemble. Just before the appointed day he was struck down by one of his incapacitating colds: his face was inflamed, his voice gone, and an ear was giving trouble too. He wrote to cancel the audition, saying he would reapply during the next season. 'See how near I may have been, to another sort of life,' he told Forster as he looked back years later.[32]

He never did reapply, but he also never lost the feeling that the theatre was in some sense his true destiny, what he understood best, what he did best and enjoyed best. All his writing is theatrical, his characters are largely created through their voices, and in due course he re-created them for public performance and spoke their lines on stage himself. His plots tend towards the theatrical and melodramatic. He devoted much time and energy to amateur acting. William Macready, the great actor, on first hearing him read as a young man, wrote in his diary, 'He reads as well as an experienced actor would – he is a surprising man.'[33] And in the last month of his life he told a friend that his most cherished daydream was ' "To settle down now for the remainder of my life within easy distance of a great theatre, in the direction of which I should hold supreme authority. It should be a house, of course, having a skilled and noble company, and one in every way magnificently appointed. The pieces acted should be dealt with according to my pleasure, and touched up here and there in obedience to my own judgment; the players as well as the plays being absolutely under my command. There," said he, laughingly, and in a glow at the mere fancy, "*that's* my daydream!" '[34] The confession underlines the strength and consistency of his feeling that he and the theatre were meant for one another, even though he turned his back on the possibility of becoming a professional actor in 1832.

He was soon putting on a private theatrical performance of his own, in April 1833, in the family's upstairs lodgings at No. 18 Bentinck Street, with himself as stage manager, actor, singer, prologue writer, scenery-builder and accordionist in the band. He organized friends to paint the scenery and do the lighting, and rehearsed the actors for weeks, every Wednesday evening, sending them strict summonses.

As was normal in the theatre then, there were to be three pieces played. They were all up-to-date works, the principal one, *Clari; or, The Maid of Milan*, an English opera first performed at Covent Garden only ten years before – the tale of a peasant girl abducted by a nobleman, who sang the immensely popular song, 'Home, Sweet Home'.[35] Fanny Dickens naturally took the lead, with Letitia and Charles playing her mother and father. One of the two farces was *The Married Bachelor*, in which servants pitted their wits against their employers, while the other, *Amateurs and Actors*, featured a half-starved orphan boy from the workhouse, part comic and part pathetic.[36] Uncle Edward Barrow took this interesting role, and also directed the band. Family and friends were all pressed into performing: John Dickens, Tom Mitton, John Kolle and two new friends, Tom Beard, a fellow reporter recently arrived in London, and Henry Austin, a young architect and engineer.

During the June parliamentary recess Dickens set about trying to find more work. In July he dined with his uncle John Barrow to meet John Payne Collier, a journalist and man of letters on the staff of the *Morning Chronicle*, the leading Liberal newspaper, who was in a position to recommend him for a job there. When Collier asked Barrow about his nephew's education, he was given a vague answer, with a reference to his having assisted Warren, the blacking man. The dinner was a success to the extent that it culminated in Charles singing one of his favourite popular songs, 'The Dog's Meat Man', and one of his own, 'Sweet Betsy Ogle'. It sounds as though everybody drank a good deal, and although Collier later said he liked Charles and had recommended him for a job, none was offered. Barrow was living in the outer suburb of Norwood, having left his wife and set up house with another woman, Lucina Pocock, whose black eyes appealed to Charles, and this autumn he often stayed with them. In October he got up more theatricals, this time writing his own comic play, 'O'thello'.

He was also working on stories and sketches and, released from love and serious theatrical ambition, finding his voice. Kolle and his wife, Maria's sister, remained friends he trusted and relied on, and in December he wrote to Henry Kolle asking for 'Mrs K's criticism of a little paper of mine (the first of a Series) in *the Monthly* (not the New

Monthly) Magazine of this month'. The *Monthly* was a very small circulation magazine run from premises in Johnson's Court, off Fleet Street, and Dickens had dropped his first offering 'stealthily one evening at twilight, with fear and trembling, into a dark letter box in a dark office up a dark court', after they had closed.[37] A postscript to his letter to Kolle confessed, 'I am so dreadfully nervous, that my hand shakes to such an extent as to prevent my writing a word legibly.'[38] He was not paid for his work, and it appeared anonymously, but there it was, as he had written it, in print. He bought a copy of the *Monthly* magazine from a shop in the Strand and walked with it to Westminster Hall 'and turned into it for half an hour, because my eyes were so dimmed with joy and pride, that they could not bear the street, and were not fit to be seen there'.[39] It was a moment never to be forgotten, and by coincidence the man who served him in the bookshop in the Strand was William Hall, whom he met and recognized two years later when the publishers Chapman & Hall approached him with a commission.[40]

The sketch was 'A Dinner at Poplar Walk', only nine pages, but a remarkable first effort. It cuts a sharp slice through London and suburban life as Dickens observed them in 1833, and presents a small dramatic episode. It is played out between two cousins and two views of life: a forty-year-old bachelor clerk with precise habits, lodged in town, and his cheerful younger cousin who lives in the suburbs with a wife and son. Hoping to coax a legacy, the younger cousin calls on the elder with an invitation to dinner, bringing his dog with him, which turns out to be a mistake. Dickens had already mastered comic dialogue: '. . . damn the dog! he's spoiling your curtains,' points out the cheerful owner of the dog to the sour owner of the curtains. The detail of each man's domestic surroundings, and the agony of the bachelor cousin travelling on unreliable transport – the coach from Bishopsgate Street, every half-hour to the Swan at Stamford Hill – to a social event he has no wish to attend, are unsparingly laid out, and very funny. Both cousins are absurd but neither is wholly unsympathetic, and the drama bites, without villain, hero, moral or sentimentality.[41] Order and muddle are set against each other, a theme that would run through his writing, and through his life.

In January 1834 the second sketch appeared, about a family putting on a play, again drawn loosely from his home theatricals. The *Monthly* was keen to have more of his work, and Dickens, who was revolving an idea for a novel in his head, told Kolle that he might cut his 'proposed Novel up into little Magazine Sketches'.[42] Whether he did or not, he was launched, modestly but surely. Sketch followed sketch, and in August 1834 he signed himself for the first time 'Boz', and under this name rose to fame.

He had spent seven years applying himself to master a series of different skills, always seeking to find a congenial way to earn a good income. He had served in lawyers' offices, taught himself shorthand, taken down law cases, reported the procedures of the House of Commons and the House of Lords, prepared himself for the acting profession and turned to writing about what he saw around him for magazines. All were demanding activities and one by one he tried them, rejecting some, persevering with others. Even when he did find the right path, there was still a long way to go before he could hope to establish himself professionally. But his pursuit of various goals was so energetic, and he demonstrated such an ability to do many different things at once, and fast, that even his search for a career had an aspect of genius.

4

The Journalist

1834–1836

He had a foot on the path to success, but he was still poor, at twenty-two still living with his parents, still a freelance. Even the excitement of his sketches coming out each month was clouded by their being unpaid work, especially when one was taken over by a well-known playwright, John Buckstone, and made into a farce, produced and published without acknowledgement. Dickens remained good-tempered, acknowledged that Buckstone had put in material of his own and realized that more good than harm would come of his piracy. At home, life was not always easy. His sister Fanny left the Royal Academy this year, was honoured with an associate honorary membership, was a true musician and admired when she sang at public concerts, but she was not going to be a star; there was no question of her becoming an opera singer, and she cannot have earned much. Letitia was often ill, and John Dickens was no longer working for his brother-in-law's *Mirror of Parliament*, and falling into debt yet again. Of the three younger boys, Augustus was six, Alfred twelve and Fred fourteen, and their future needed to be thought of. Charles must have doubted that their father would be capable of planning for his brothers. Here was another cause for anxiety.

John Barrow continued to welcome Charles at home in Norwood, and he was often out at his uncle's house. He had also built up a group of friends with whom he took long tramps and rides, the occasional river trip, evening parties – 'having a flare', as he put it – and companionable smoking and drinking. There were Kolle and Mitton, and now Tom Beard, a fellow reporter, five years older than Dickens, a quiet, steady Sussex man, dullish, and always ready to help when asked. Another new friend was Henry Austin, architect and engineer, a pupil of Robert Stephenson, and soon to work with him on the building of the London and Blackwall railway through the East End.[1] Austin was up to date, intelligent and concerned with social issues, and Dickens liked him so much that when he moved into a place of his own at the end of the year, he invited him to share with him. Austin declined – he was living comfortably with his mother – but they remained close, and their friendship was strengthened when Austin married Letitia Dickens in 1837.

For the moment Dickens was in the House reporting for the *True Sun* and the *Mirror*. The most important debates that summer were on proposed amendments to the Poor Law. Conditions were very bad all over the country, half-starved agricultural workers protesting, burning ricks and attempting to form trade unions. When a group of Dorset labourers was sentenced to transportation for this last offence, they were called the 'Tolpuddle Martyrs' by other trade unionists and a protest march was held in London on their behalf. The view of most parliamentarians was that the poor needed tough treatment, and if they could not support themselves, through old age, misfortune or having too many children to feed, or were laid off by their usual employers, rather than being given piecemeal payments by the parish to keep them going in their cottages, they should be forced into enlarged workhouses. Here they would be housed, scantily fed and humiliated by being made to wear uniforms, and their families would be broken up, husbands and wives, mothers and children, put into separate dormitories. To most landowners and middle-class members of parliament this made good sense, but not to all, and many expressed revulsion at what they saw as punishing the poor for being poor. The strongest speaker in the House against the harsh proposed amendments to the Poor Law was William Cobbett, who attacked them day after day, asking for an inquiry into the causes of the present conditions of the poor before any new bill should be passed, warning the legislators that 'they were about to dissolve the bonds of society' and that to pass their law would be 'a violation of the contract upon which all the real property of the kingdom was held'.[2] He particularly objected to the separation of families, and to workhouse inmates being obliged to wear badges or distinctive clothing. Other MPs predicted that the workhouses would become 'prisons for the purpose of terrifying applicants from seeking relief'. One simply called the bill 'absurd'. A country landowner pointed out that there were petitions from all over the country against it, and pleaded especially that the aged poor should not be taken from their cottages and sent away to workhouses.[3] In the last debate Daniel O'Connell said that although, as an Irishman, he would not say much, he objected to the bill on the grounds that it 'did away with personal feelings and connections'. This was a view to which Dickens would certainly have subscribed. As a parliamentary reporter he must have attended many of the debates, and taken away enough from them to give impetus to one of the themes of his second novel, *Oliver Twist*. The passing of the amended bill must also have made him doubt the effectiveness of parliament, where informed and intelligent voices lost the argument; the evil consequences they predicted were felt all over England for many decades.[4]

�֍

Through the recommendation of Tom Beard, Dickens was at last offered a permanent job by the *Morning Chronicle* in August, with a salary of five guineas a week, giving him financial security for the first time, and allowing him to begin to plan how best to put his life in order. The offices of the *Morning Chronicle* were on familiar territory in the Strand, at No. 332, and the editor, John Black, had a high opinion of the talents of his new employee. Black was a Scot, a friend of James Mill and follower of Jeremy Bentham, and he ran the *Chronicle* as a reforming paper, and set out to rival *The Times*, encouraged by a tough new owner, John Easthope, a Liberal politician who had made a fortune on the stock exchange. Dickens would be a key member of the team taking on *The Times*. Black was also delighted to publish more of his sketches of London life: Dickens called him 'my first hearty out-and-out appreciator'.[5] From now on he signed his sketches 'Boz', and under that name, and with a wider readership, he began to attract more attention.

For his first reporting job Black sent him to Edinburgh to cover a celebratory banquet for Earl Grey, who was being given the freedom of the city. It was work, but also a treat, and Beard went with him. The two reporters travelled up by steamboat and put in a good account of the bands, the flags and especially the dinner, where they made it clear that the guests fell so greedily on the lobsters, roast beef and other luxury foods provided that they had polished off almost everything on the tables before the Earl arrived.

More sardonic amusement in October, when a fire burnt down the House of Commons. No life was lost, and Dickens observed that the cause was the belated burning of old wooden tallies used for accounting through the centuries until the 1820s, which he saw as symbolic of the disastrous consequences of English attachment to worn-out practices and traditions. In November the aged Prime Minister, Lord Melbourne, was asked to resign by the King, who invited the still older Wellington to take over; when Wellington sensibly refused, the King was obliged to summon the liberal Conservative Robert Peel. Attentive as he had to be to these political manoeuvres, Dickens was now distracted by problems of his own at home, where his father had again been arrested and removed to a sponging house, in imminent danger of prison for paying neither his wine merchant nor his rent. Their landlord refused to wait any longer, and Charles feared that he might be taken too, since he was living at the same address. This would provide 'the next act in this "domestic tragedy"', he joked, or half joked. It happened just as he was looking at chambers in Furnival's Inn on Holborn, with the intention of separating himself from the family, but had not yet fixed a date. So now a flurry of letters went out to Tom Mitton and Tom Beard, asking for loans and begging them to visit his father. Both obliged, Charles raised five pounds 'from my French employer' – an unexplained reference suggesting he had taken on more freelance work – and there was enough cash to release the elder Dickens before the younger had to leave for Birmingham, where he was due to report on a Liberal congress.[6]

When he got back to London his father had taken 'to the winds', as he himself put it, in fact to North End, beyond Hampstead, which he thought remote enough to be out of reach of creditors. The rest of the family moved into rooms in George Street, near the Adelphi, to be close to Fanny's singing engagements, and Charles now established himself in his own rented, unfurnished chambers in Furnival's Inn.[7] He was paying £35 for a year's lease, for which he had three rooms on the third floor, with use of a cellar and a lumber room in the roof. Since Henry Austin had turned down his invitation, he invited his brother Fred (Frederick, not Alfred) to join him. Although he was establishing his independence, Dickens always wanted people about him. He entirely lacked the romantic writer's need to be alone, and instead of being glad to be rid of younger brothers he was eager to have Fred, who had a ready laugh and a wish to please.[8] They had to do their own housekeeping, and living without their mother they were soon in difficulties about their laundry. Everyone in the family was short of money, and their younger brother Alfred was forced to walk to Hampstead and back in his dancing pumps, carrying messages to and from their father, as Charles had done before him. Charles's current shoes were also in holes, and he had nothing left to pay for repairs after moving house. Tom Beard stumped up with another loan, and Charles invited his friends to George Street to celebrate his mother's birthday on 21 December, when she would be forty-five. There was to be another party of his own – 'a flare' – in his chambers, in spite of the fact that he had no dishes, no curtains and no money. No matter, 'I have got some really *extraordinary* french brandy.'[9]

In January 1835 he was covering election meetings in Chelmsford, 'the dullest and most stupid place on earth', where he could not even find a newspaper on Sunday.[10] Sometimes driving a hired gig with an unpredictable horse, and sometimes taking the stagecoach, he got round Braintree, Sudbury, Colchester and Bury St Edmunds and came away with no better opinion of any of them, or of the part played by electioneering in the political process. There would be more travelling into the provinces to report on political meetings, long, damp and freezing coach journeys and dashes back to London to get his copy in before the reporter for *The Times*. Meanwhile another invitation came to write more of his London sketches or stories for a new sister evening paper to the *Chronicle*. Its co-editor was

George Hogarth, like John Black a Scotsman, and both saw that Dickens was the most gifted of the young journalists on the staff. When he asked if he might be paid for his contributions to the *Evening Chronicle*, his salary was raised to seven guineas a week.

Hogarth, a fatherly fifty-year-old, invited Dickens to visit him at his home in Kensington. He was a man of wide cultural interests, had recently written and published *Musical History, Biography and Criticism*, and his career was worth hearing about: he had been a lawyer in Edinburgh, and a friend of Lockhart and Walter Scott, for whom he had acted professionally. In 1830 he decided to move south, using his knowledge of music and literature to help him find work as a journalist and critic, and made a success of his second profession. Dickens would not have been told that he had to leave Scotland for financial reasons, but he did learn that Mrs Hogarth came of a prosperous and hard-working family, and that her father had been a collector and publisher of songs, and an intimate of Robert Burns. Their recollections of such friendships with great men were important to the Hogarths, and impressed Dickens.

They had a large and still growing family, and when he made his first visit to their house on the Fulham Road, surrounded by gardens and orchards, he met their eldest daughter, nineteen-year-old Catherine. Her unaffectedness appealed to him at once, and her being different from the young women he had known, not only in being Scottish but in coming from an educated family background with literary connections. The Hogarths, like the Beadnells, were a cut above the Dickens family, but they welcomed Dickens warmly as an equal, and George Hogarth's enthusiasm for his work was flattering.[11] Catherine was slim, shapely and pleasant-looking, with a gentle manner and without any of Maria Beadnell's sparkling beauty; but his experience with Maria's beauty and unpredictable behaviour had marked him as a burn marks, and left its scar. Better less sparkle and no wound.

His decision to marry her was quickly made, and he never afterwards gave any account of what had led him to it, perhaps because he came to regard it as the worst mistake in his life. We can see that the Hogarth family admired him and approved of his suit, and that

Catherine was a nicely brought-up and uncomplicated young woman. She wrote to a cousin soon after meeting him, 'Mamma and I were at a Ball on Saturday last and where do you think at Mr Dicken's [*sic*]. It was in honour of his birthday. It was a batchelors party at his own chambers. His Mother and sisters presided. one of them a very pretty girl who sings beautifully . . . Mr Dickens improves very much on acquaintance he is very gentlemanly and pleasant.'[12] Soon she was evidently in thrall to him. He saw in her the offer of affection, compliance and physical pleasure, and he believed he was in love with her. That was enough for him to ask her to be his wife. There were many protestations of enduring love in his letters. She was not clever or accomplished like his sister Fanny and could never be his intellectual equal, which may have been part of her charm: foolish little women are more often presented as sexually desirable in his writing than clever, competent ones. He wanted to be married. He did not want a wife who would compel his imagination.

For the three summer months of 1835 he took rooms close to the Hogarth house, in Selwood Terrace, to be near Catherine, and you can feel the pressure of his need for her: 'dear Mouse', 'darling Tatie', 'my own dearest darling Pig' he calls her, and urges her to come round and make a late breakfast for him, after he has been working at the House into the small hours: 'It's a childish wish my dear love; but I am anxious to hear and see you the moment I wake – Will you indulge me by making breakfast for me this Morning? . . . it will be excellent practice for you against next Christmas,' when he hoped they would be married, although he had to wait a few months more.[13]

Like all young men, he needed sexual excitement and comfort, and the London prostitutes so freely available were not what he wanted. He knew enough of them to pity them: the children put on the streets by their mothers, the girls driven by poverty to sell themselves, the young women who gave passionate loyalty to their criminal lovers, the theatrical ladies who stooped to frailty, the defiant young street sinners who refused to be ashamed of themselves. He admired some for their spirit, and if he was tempted and succumbed on occasion – something we don't know – he was still against the system. He wanted to think well of women, and he wanted them to be good, not to be degraded, or to degrade their users. Marriage was the solution, for reasons of sexual hygiene, for domestic comfort, for companionship, and so within less than six months of meeting Catherine Hogarth he was engaged to her. One of his earliest letters tells her not to be capricious or trifle with him, warning her that although he is 'warmly and deeply attached' to her, he will give her up at once if her show of coldness means she has wearied of him.[14] There is never any doubt who is running the relationship. He was putting his life in order, and he would always be the one responsible for keeping it in order.

❦

The year of 1835 was even busier than the one before. If he was not at the House, which sat until 1.30 a.m., he was away covering the provinces, by-elections, Liberal dinners, the Home Secretary Lord John Russell's speech in Exeter in May, when he strained every nerve to get his report in ahead of *The Times*, bribing post boys and taking dictation in pelting rain. He arrived back in London with rheumatism, deaf, worn out, without his bag or a clean shirt, but Beard sent him round a shirt, and he found the competition exhilarating. Writing his sketches had to be squeezed into odd moments, and was more than once put off in order to give him time with Catherine. She had to be introduced to his people, now reunited in lodgings in Bloomsbury. When Black decided he should be reviewing plays as well as reporting, he was suddenly in the theatre in the evenings again, and he had to sit down to finish his own writing when he got home afterwards, or start early the next morning with an editor waiting impatiently. Sometimes the strain was too much. He described to Catherine being 'taken so extremely unwell when we got to Knightsbridge last night, that I really thought I should have been unable to proceed; my head was so extremely bad, and the dizziness affected my sight so much that I could scarcely see at all, in addition to which cheerful symptoms my tottering legs gave me the appearance of being particularly drunk'. He treated himself with a large pill of calomel, a purgative made from mercury which acted on the liver and produced 'such singular evolutions in my interior that I am unable to leave home'.[15] But he threw off illness when he had to, and the next day he was keeping an appointment to visit Newgate Prison.

In November he was looking at houses in Pentonville, finding them pretty but extremely dear at £55 a year. He was sent to Hatfield in December, where a fire had destroyed part of the great house and incinerated the Dowager Marchioness: 'Here I am, waiting until the remains of the Marchioness of Salisbury are dug from the remains of her Ancestor's Castle.' A week later he was in Kettering, where 'we had a slight flare here yesterday morning, just stopping short of murder and riot' – this was a by-election. Catherine – often Kate or Katie now – was treated to an account of the Tories, 'a ruthless set of bloody-minded villains ... perfect savages ... superlative blackguards ... Would you believe that a large body of horsemen, mounted and armed, who galloped on a defenceless crowd yesterday, striking about them in all directions, and protecting a man who cocked a loaded pistol, were *led* by Clergymen, and Magistrates?'[16] Two days later he described the dinner he had ordered for himself and four fellow journalists: 'cod and oyster sauce, Roast beef, and a pair of ducks, plum pudding, and Mince Pies'. Having survived this he was cheerful about returning to London, even though he had to end his letter with a P.S., 'Damn the Tories – They'll win here I am afraid' – and they did.[17]

Before the year was out, he was writing the libretto for a comic opera on an English theme, *The Village Coquettes*, with music by Fanny's friend from her student days, John Hullah. He was also overseeing the proofs of his first book. It had come about through another new friend, the novelist Harrison Ainsworth, who was growing rich from his historical and low-life fiction, *Rookwood*, about Dick Turpin, and *Jack Sheppard*, another criminal hero. He was seven years older than Dickens, good-looking, well dressed and sophisticated. He lived with a lady not his wife, the formidable Eliza Touchet, who made clever conversation; she was older than him, the widow of a cousin, and since he had separated from his wife she had taken charge of him, at Kensal Lodge, where they entertained in style. Ainsworth saw how good Boz's work was, set out to discover his true identity, introduced himself and urged Dickens to publish a collection of his sketches. Nothing could be easier: here was his own publisher, John Macrone, and here was another friend, George Cruikshank, the most admired artist in the country, to provide the illustrations. Ainsworth knew how to do things.

In October, Dickens was negotiating with Macrone, inviting him to Furnival's for 'Scotch Whiskey and Cigars' and setting up a sensational new piece to crown the first collection of his sketches, an account of Newgate Prison. A day-long visit was arranged through Black, who persuaded a radical MP to take Dickens inside: this was the occasion for which he rose from his sick bed.[18] In the prison school he saw young boys awaiting trial for picking pockets. They appeared pleased with their own importance and they shocked him: 'fourteen such terrible little faces we never beheld. – There was not one redeeming feature among them – not a glance of honesty – not a wink expressive of any thing but the gallows and the hulks . . .' The resulting sketch, 'A Visit to Newgate', ended with the condemned cell, plainly described, where he allowed himself to imagine the dreams of a prisoner who is to be hanged in the morning.

The name of Dickens was not to appear – he was to remain 'Boz', and the title he suggested was *Sketches by 'Boz', Illustrative of Every-day Life, and Every-day People*, chosen because 'it is both unaffected and unassuming – two requisites which it is very desirable for a young author not to lose sight of.' This is at any rate what he meant to write, although he slipped up and left out the 'not'.[19] It was to be published in two volumes on 8 February 1836, the day after his twenty-fourth birthday.

5

Four Publishers and a Wedding

1836

For Dickens, 1836 was to be an *annus mirabilis*, but it did not feel like it in January. 'I am so ill this morning that I am unable to work,' he wrote to Catherine. 'I wrote till 3 oclock this morning (I had not done for the paper till 8) and passed the whole night . . . in a state of exquisite torture from the spasm in my side far exceeding anything I ever felt. It still continues exceedingly painful and my head is aching so from pain and want of rest, that I can hardly hold it up . . . I have not had so severe an attack since I was a child.' Stoically he was up and working again after writing to her, and the following day he described how he had 'dragged on as well as I could 'till a little after One in the morning, and got up at eight'.[1] On most evenings he was either at the House, taking down debates into the small hours, or at the theatre, with a review to write afterwards. Deadlines loomed perpetually for stories or sketches promised to other papers, and he was under pressure to get on with his libretto for the planned opera, *The Village Coquettes*. At the office he was arguing about his terms of engagement. He gave time to teach Catherine's younger brother shorthand, and worried about finding a job for his own brother Fred. No wonder he sometimes collapsed.

With *Sketches by Boz* about to appear on 8 February, he had to send out review copies to people who might have an influence on its reception: Lord Stanley, who knew him as a reporter, Charles Dilke, now editor of the *Athenaeum* (who had noticed him at the blacking factory), and John Easthope, his imperious boss. Dickens and Macrone prepared for publication together harmoniously and were on increasingly close and friendly terms: Macrone was 'My dear Sir' until publication day, thereafter 'My Dear Macrone'. Dickens wrote a consoling letter when Macrone's baby son died, and invited him to be best man at his wedding. Macrone supplied Dickens with a copy of *Hints on Etiquette*, which he had asked for, no doubt in preparation for married life; and obligingly took Fred Dickens into his accounts department in the summer. Macrone was ambitious and enterprising. He had arrived in London from unknown parts – possibly the Isle of Man – cut a few corners by borrowing money from an older woman, enough to set himself up in an office in St James's Square, and ditched her to marry another woman, an American.[2] He was full of ideas: he commissioned busts of famous men to set up around his office, made by an eccentric Scottish sculptor, Angus Fletcher, who became a friend of Dickens and made the first bust of him in 1839.[3] He got Turner to illustrate *Paradise Lost*, and he ran over to Paris to try to sign up Victor Hugo. He and Dickens worked hard together to get the *Sketches* noticed and puffed in advance, with triumphant results. It was well reviewed: George Hogarth praised Dickens in the *Chronicle*

Dickens smoking in the office of his publisher Macrone: Thackeray's sketch, showing himself and another writer, Mahoney, standing.

as 'a close and acute observer of character and manners', and for showing 'the vices and wretchedness' of London life, and there was praise everywhere for its wit, truth and descriptive powers. It sold well and went into a second edition in the summer. Both Macrone and Dickens had every reason to be pleased with their collaboration.

While this was going on, a second publisher appeared at Dickens's door one evening in February with a proposal. This was William Hall, who had set up in business with his friend Edward Chapman in the Strand, at No. 186, in 1830. Hall asked Dickens if he would write sketches to go with drawings by a young artist, Robert Seymour, who specialized in sporting scenes, and was keen to make a series of plates showing the adventures of a fishing club. Dickens recognized Hall as the man who, in December 1833, had sold him a copy of his own first story, just published in his *Monthly* magazine, and both felt that this was a good omen.[4] Dickens said he was interested, but hoped for a slightly wider brief. Hall was a good businessman and agreed to this at once, offered £14 for each monthly episode and added that the fee might rise if the series did well. With this Dickens was happy. There was no formal agreement, just a letter. In such an easy-going way began a relationship that made Chapman & Hall rich and helped to establish Dickens's supremacy among the novelists of the nineteenth century.

Dickens saw that the money offered would allow him to keep a wife and live comfortably. He already had an idea for a comic character, Mr Pickwick, a rich, retired businessman with a taste for good food and a tendency to drink too much, an innocent, playful and benevolent – he would be well described by W. H. Auden as 'a pagan god wandering through the world imperviously' – and with a group of younger friends with whom he sets off on modest travels through southern England. He also thought he would vary the narrative of his adventures by inserting separate, unconnected short stories at intervals. He began to write at once. While he was about it, he offered Chapman & Hall *The Strange Gentleman*, a farce he had adapted from one of his stories, which would be put on later in the year, and they agreed to publish that too.

The wedding date was now fixed for 2 April. Before it arrived a third publisher appeared on the scene, introduced to Dickens by his future father-in-law. This was the gentlemanly Richard Bentley, also remembered as the man who brought out the first reprints of Jane Austen in 1833, with fine illustrations, and persuaded her brother Henry to write an introductory note. Bentley had begun his career as a high-quality printer, turned to publishing and produced handsome editions of standard novels, and now he was keen to sign up new writers. Dickens was interested, but for the moment too preoccupied to attend to any proposals Bentley had in mind. He was busy ordering furniture – rosewood for the drawing room, mahogany for the dining room – and shopping, for a sideboard, decanters, jugs, china jars; also having a workbox inscribed 'from Chas. Dickens to Kate' as a wedding present to his bride. His sister Letitia fell ill, so ill that their father thought she was dying and needed support. Happily she recovered, but Dickens was busier than ever, embarked on his new project. '"Pickwick" must be attended to,' he told Catherine.[5] On 20 March he apologized for not seeing her: 'I am tired and worn out today, mind and body; and have that to do, which will certainly occupy me till 1 or 2 o'Clock. I did not get to bed till 3 oClock this morning; and consequently could not begin to write until nearly one ... forced to deny myself the least recreation, and to sit chained to my table.'[6]

The wedding plans had to be changed when Mrs Macrone insisted that the best man must be a bachelor, and Dickens was obliged to ask Tom Beard instead of Macrone. Shortly before the day he wrote to his uncle Thomas Barrow, wishing he could invite him, and explaining that Barrow's refusal to have John Dickens under his roof made it impossible; he recalled his own visits to him as a child, and thanked him for his interest and affection.[7] It is clear that the Barrow side of the family was the one he was proud of, and yet he remained loyal to his father, feeling the strain, and unhappy about the division in the family.

His mother arranged the honeymoon lodgings for him, in a cottage belonging to a Mrs Nash in Chalk, a small pretty village on the marshes of north Kent, between Rochester and Gravesend. They would not have much more than a week there, and he would be working on *Pickwick* during that time. On 2 April a simple ceremony at St Luke's Church in Chelsea married Charles and Catherine in the presence of their immediate families, the only other guests being Tom Beard as best man and John Macrone. After a wedding breakfast at the Hogarths', the bride and groom set off for Kent, a journey of about two hours by public coach. Dickens wanted to show Catherine the country of his childhood and no doubt hoped to walk with her to favourite spots – Cobham Woods, Gad's Hill, Rochester – in the April sunshine. Catherine was never a great walker, while his idea of enjoyment was to stride far and fast across country, and here perhaps the pattern of their life was set, since he was also obliged to work at *Pickwick* during their few days away. Writing was necessarily his primary occupation, and hers must be to please him as best she could within the limitations of her energy: writing desk and walking boots for him, sofa and domesticity for her.[8]

In Dickens's novels young women meant to be lovable tend to be small, pretty, timid, fluttering and often suffering at the hands of their official protectors, like Little Nell and Florence Dombey. Ruth Pinch (in *Martin Chuzzlewit*) is a good housekeeper and cook, has been a governess, and sings delightfully for her brother and his friend, but the symptoms of her reciprocated love are blushes, tears and a 'foolish, panting, frightened little heart'. Rose Maylie (in *Oliver Twist*) has no character at all beyond being virtuous and self-sacrificing. Little Em'ly, bold as a child on the beach, becomes another blank victim. Dora has more life, because Dickens can't resist exaggerating her silliness so that she becomes a figure of high comedy before the pathos sets in. There are more capable young women. Louisa Gradgrind (in *Hard Times*) is no fool, but still a victim, while Sissy Jupe keeps enough of her professional training in the circus to show more strength of character than anyone around her, a working child who sets the middle class to rights. The Marchioness (in *The Old Curiosity Shop*) is another of her type, servant, child of the workhouse, abused and starved, who arises from her basement kitchen, shows strength of character and floors her wicked employers; but Dickens pretty well abandoned her halfway through her history, perhaps because Little Nell had to hold centre stage or because he did not know how to develop the Marchioness. Polly Toodle, Paul Dombey's wet nurse, is also a young working woman whose instincts are surer than those of her employers. Where does Catherine Hogarth stand among these figures? Clearly, among the blank and blushing innocents, as a virtuous middle-class girl. She had no experience of anything but family life when he met her, and showed little evidence of being interested in anything outside the domestic world. Before their marriage he wrote to her to say how much he looked forward to exchanging solitude for fireside evenings in which her 'kind looks and gentle manner' would give him happiness, and assured her that her 'future advancement and happiness' was the mainspring of his labours.[9] Kind looks and gentle manner she doubtless had, and a wish to please – what she lacked was the strength of character needed to hold her own against her husband's powerful will. She was incapable of establishing and defending any values of her own, of making her own safe situation from which she should rule within the home, let alone taking up any other interest. So little of her personality appears in any eyewitness account of the Dickens household that it seems fair to say there was not much more there to describe, and that whatever she brought to the marriage as a twenty-year-old hardly had a chance to develop and mature in the regime set up and ruled over by a husband who seemed omnipresent and always knew himself to be right.[10]

Marriage was for him at least a solution to the problem of sex, and for the next twenty-two years they would share a large double bed. 'A winter's night has its delight,/Well warmed to bed we go,' wrote Dickens in a song for his opera this year, only to be told that any mention of bed was objectionable to the public. 'If the young ladies are especially horrified at the bare notion of anybody's going to bed,' he wrote, he would change it, but 'I will see them d——d before I make any further alteration.' He added, 'I am sure . . . we ought not to emasculate the very spirit of a song to suit boarding-schools.'[11] The bare notion of going to bed pleased him, as it should please a new husband. Catherine was pregnant in the first month of the marriage.

They were soon back in their newly furnished suite of rooms at Furnival's. She was young to be entering into the responsibilities of a wife in charge of her husband's domestic life – that is, insofar as Dickens allowed anyone to take charge of any aspect of his life. Her sixteen-year-old younger sister, Mary, was often with them, a trim and cheerful visitor who described Catherine as 'a most capital house-keeper . . . happy as the day is long'.[12] Happy and also dealing with the physical changes of pregnancy, and when she felt sick or unsteady Mary gave Charles companionship. *Pickwick* was not selling as briskly as hoped, and the project was struck by disaster at the end of April when Seymour, suffering from depression, shot himself. This could have been enough to sink the whole thing, especially when the replacement artist lacked the right touch. William Makepeace Thack-eray, who had skill and ambitions as an illustrator, came to see Dickens with his sketchbook and offered to take on the task, but he was turned down, and the commission went to Hablot K. Browne, a young artist and neighbour, with his studio in Furnival's Inn. Browne caught the spirit of the work perfectly, called himself 'Phiz' to fit 'Boz', and made his reputation alongside Dickens.

In May, Dickens agreed with Macrone that he would write a three-volume novel to be called 'Gabriel Vardon' – it became *Barnaby Rudge* – and delivered 'next November', for a payment of £200. The second volume of the *Sketches* was being prepared, and he still had his full-time job with the *Chronicle*. In June he was kept especially busy reporting a scandalous case in the law courts in which the Prime Minister, Lord Melbourne, was accused of adultery by the loutish jealous husband of Caroline Norton, the beautiful and gifted grand-daughter of Sheridan. The public was of course eagerly interested in this washing of the dirty linen of the upper classes, but Mr Norton failed to produce any evidence and lost his case. Dickens had to move nimbly between the roles of reporter and novelist, and in the same month he was inspired to carry *Pickwick* from its shaky start to popular success as he introduced the character of Sam Weller, Pickwick's cockney servant.

From this moment sales of the monthly numbers in their pale green wrappers rose steadily and soon spectacularly, and the critics vied with one another to praise it. The appearance of a fresh number of *Pickwick* soon became news, an event, something much more than literature. 'Boz has got the town by the ear,' a critic said, and he spoke

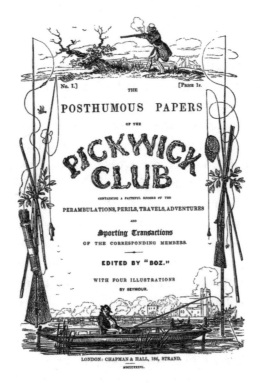

The Pickwick Papers as it first appeared, serialized in green-paper wrappers.

the truth.[13] Each number sold for a shilling and they were passed from hand to hand, and butchers' boys were seen reading them in the streets.[14] Judges and politicians, the middle classes and the rich, bought them, read them and applauded; and the ordinary people saw that he was on their side, and they loved him for it. He did not ask them to think but showed them what he wanted them to see and hear. The names of his characters became common currency: Jingle, Sam Weller, Snodgrass and Winkle, Mrs Leo Hunter the cultural hostess with her 'Ode on an expiring Frog', the political journalists Slurk and Pott, the drunken medical student Bob Sawyer. It was as though he was able to feed his story directly into the bloodstream of the nation, giving injections of laughter, pathos and melodrama, and making his readers feel he was a personal friend to each of them.

Dickens knew he had triumphed, and this sense of a personal link between himself and his public became the most essential element in his development as a writer.

He already had two publishers – Macrone for *Sketches* and Chapman & Hall for *Pickwick* – and in August 1836 he agreed to write a children's book for a third, Thomas Tegg, for £100. A children's book could be seen as a special case. Later in the same month, however, he entered into negotiations with a fourth, Richard Bentley, who had been pursuing him for some time. Bentley trumped Macrone with an offer of £400 for the copyright of his next novel. Dickens pushed him up to £500, and Bentley pushed Dickens up to promising two novels. Dickens then sold him the publishing rights in his opera, describing it as 'Boz's first play', which Bentley did indeed publish as a pamphlet. Dickens also agreed to become editor of a monthly magazine for Bentley, what was eventually called *Bentley's Miscellany*, to which he would contribute something of his own every month, for twenty guineas. This would bring him a further annual income of nearly £500.[15]

He now had arrangements with four different publishers, with all of whom he was for the moment on good terms. Macrone was just bringing out the second printing of the *Sketches*. At this point Dickens sensibly asked for time off from the *Chronicle* and was granted five weeks, since things were idle during the summer heat in London. He left with the suggestion that the *Chronicle* should run extracts from *Pickwick* while he was away.

He took Catherine to the village of Petersham in Surrey, between Richmond Park and the Thames, where they put up at the inn and enjoyed the quiet water meadows and leafy walks around Ham House. There they stayed into September, Catherine now halfway through her pregnancy. But even during this holiday he was often obliged to return to London, and rather than go to their empty rooms at Furnival's he took himself to his parents, currently lodging in Islington.[16] He was working on the opera with Hullah, and preparing for the opening of his farce, *The Strange Gentleman*, on 29 September at the St James's Theatre, with his friend John Pritt Harley, a well-loved comic actor, playing the lead.[17] It was a success, running for sixty nights, and boxes were offered to friends, family and publishers.

In November, Dickens signed his second agreement with Bentley. He also wrote to John Easthope at the *Chronicle* to tender his resignation; and he informed Macrone he wanted to withdraw from the agreement they had made on 9 May. Easthope was displeased at losing his brilliant reporter, and acrimonious letters were exchanged. The friendship with Macrone was also put under strain. He published the second series of *Sketches by Boz* in December, but things were not the same between them. Dickens was now committed to the following projects: he had to continue *Pickwick* in monthly instalments for another year; he had to provide a few more pieces for the *Sketches*; both his farce and his opera were being published and needed seeing through the press; he had promised a children's book, 'Solomon Bell the Raree Showman', by Christmas; he had to start preparing for his editorship of *Bentley's Miscellany*, which began in January and for which he must commission articles and also contribute a sixteen-page piece of his own every month; Chapman & Hall were hoping for a sequel to *Pickwick*; Macrone still wanted 'Gabriel Vardon'; and Bentley was expecting two novels.

Clearly, this was not a possible programme for one man. For the publishers it was maddening to find him reneging on a promise, as he did to Macrone, to Tegg and then to Bentley. One of the problems for him was that, as his fame grew and he was ever more in demand, he resented having made agreements for lower sums than he could now command. If Dickens is to be believed, each publisher started well and then turned into a villain; but the truth is that, while they were businessmen and drove hard bargains, Dickens was often demonstrably in the wrong in his dealings with them. He realized that selling copyrights had been a mistake: he was understandably aggrieved to think that all his hard work was making them rich while he was sweating and struggling, and he began to think of publishers as men who made profits from his work and failed to reward him as they should. Chapman & Hall kept on good terms with him largely by topping up what they had initially agreed with frequent extra payments. The book for children was quietly dropped. But by the middle of the following year, 1837, there were furious rows. His friend Macrone was now a 'blackguard' and a 'Robber'. Bentley was the next, becoming in due course an 'infernal, rich, plundering, thundering old Jew' – a quotation from his own dialogue in *Oliver Twist*.[18]

Meanwhile, Dickens sent Chapman & Hall an apology for late delivery of the monthly instalments of *Pickwick*, with a cry of joy over its ever growing success: 'If I were to live a hundred years, and write three novels in each, I should never be so proud of any of them, as I am of Pickwick, feeling as I do, that it has made its own way.'[19] He was beginning to plan the *Miscellany* for Bentley, and he had to tell Macrone he was withdrawing from writing 'Gabriel Vardon', and asked for his letter of agreement to be returned. He enforced his point by instructing his other publishers to refuse Macrone's advertisements for 'Gabriel Vardon'. Macrone gave way only when Dickens made over to him, for the low price of £100, the copyrights of both the first and second series of *Sketches by Boz* in December.[20] For the second series Dickens wrote a final piece, 'The Drunkard's Death', intended to finish the book 'with eclat'. It must be the worst in the series, a melodramatic tale of a drunkard given to 'wild debauch', imbiber of 'the slow, sure poison . . . that hurries its victims madly on to degradation and death'. When the drunkard's wife lies dying of a broken heart, he 'reeled from the tavern to her bedside in time to see her die'. His sons leave as soon as they can after this, but one night one returns home to the attic in an alley between Fleet Street and the Thames, pursued by the police for a capital crime, and – improbably, and unwisely – trusts his hated father to hide him. The drunkard betrays him and is cursed as the son goes to the gallows. Abandoned by his daughter, he takes himself to the Thames, plunges into the water, changes his mind, screams 'in agonies of terror', remembers the curse of his son and is carried away by the fierce tide to his death. Dickens in moralizing mood is not good company, and this is a feeble and overblown piece of prose, full of verbal and emotional clichés – a bit of early ham. But, as he told Bentley, he was 'Nothing but head and ears in work, and really half dead with fatigue.'[21]

The Village Coquettes opened on 6 December, with Hullah's music, and there were cheers for Boz at the curtain. But a young critic named

John Forster had something to say about the cheers and the piece: 'the libretto was totally unworthy of Boz,' he wrote, although 'the audience screamed for Boz!' He went on, 'Now we have a great respect and liking for Boz; the *Pickwick Papers* have made him, as our readers are very well aware, an especial favourite with us . . . Bad as the opera is . . . we feel assured that if Mr Braham [the producer] will make arrangements to parade the real living Boz every night after that opera, he will insure for it a certain attraction.'[22] Dickens wrote to Hullah about the review: 'It is *rather* depreciatory of the Opera, but . . . so well done that I cannot help laughing at it, for the life and soul of me.'[23] And it seems likely he thought Forster more right than wrong about *The Village Coquettes* because he later described it as the 'most unfortunate of all unfortunate pieces' and asked to have his name of Boz removed from the bills; and during the next year Forster became his best and most trusted friend.[24]

The *annus mirabilis* was coming to an end, with a bad story and a feeble libretto, but with a huge triumph for *Pickwick*, and a new novel ready in his head to start writing in January in tandem with further instalments of *Pickwick*. He was married, and the first baby was due in the first week of the new year. Over Christmas he dined with Ainsworth, danced quadrilles with the nieces of his publisher Edward Chapman in their home off the Strand, and invited Tom Beard to share in the family turkey. He also confessed to Beard that, whatever his disapproval of drunkenness in print, 'I arrived home at one oClock this morning dead drunk, & was put to bed by my loving missis.'[25] Catherine rose to the occasion well, and may even have felt a certain pleasure that, just for once, her ever busy and omnicompetent husband had put himself into a condition in which she could help, and take charge of him.

6

'Till death do us part'

1837–1839

Sometime in the evening or night of Thursday, 5 January, Catherine went into labour. Dickens was at home, and by the next morning both his mother and Mrs Hogarth had arrived to help and advise out of their considerable experience of childbirth; and with Mrs Hogarth came Catherine's sister Mary. In the morning Dickens found time to write to a colleague on the *Chronicle* to explain that he was 'chained to Mr Pickwick just now, and cannot get away', but hoped to be free on Tuesday.[1] Then, leaving Catherine in the care of the two mothers and the monthly nurse, and with the family doctor present or on the way, he and Mary went out together. They spent much of the day wandering happily from one second-hand furniture shop to another in search of a small table for the bedroom as a present for Catherine. At last a table was bought and they arrived back at Furnival's Inn, and soon after six in the evening Catherine gave birth to a son. The birth was a 'dreadful trial' to her, but the baby arrived safely, and the family could rejoice.[2] What Dickens chose to remember, when he looked back a year later, was that, since there was no room for Mary to sleep at Furnival's, he took her home to Brompton that night. It was too far for her to walk on a winter evening, which meant hiring a hackney cab, but he is likely to have walked back, taking the time to think about his work, and the happiness of the day which, being the festival of Twelfth Night, was a good birthday for his son. The following day Mary came to them again, and remained for most of the month, helping and cheering her sister and brother-in-law. A year later, when they no longer lived at Furnival's, he recalled this as a time of supreme happiness: 'I shall never be so happy again as in those Chambers . . . I would hire them to keep empty, if I could . . .'[3]

The baby – 'our boy', or 'the infant phenomenon' in his father's letters – was not christened for nearly a year, neither parent considering it a pressing matter or one of great religious significance, although Tom Beard was chosen to be godfather. For Dickens everything had to fall into place behind his work schedule, driven as he was to keep up the monthly instalments of *Pickwick* for Chapman & Hall, and preparing to embark on a new novel for Bentley, *Oliver Twist*, also scheduled to appear in monthly numbers starting in February in the *Miscellany*. The two serial stories would be running simultaneously for ten months, and Dickens would have to work like a juggler to keep both spinning. He said later that he was warned against serial publications – 'My friends told me it was a low, cheap form of publication, by which I should ruin all my rising hopes' – but whoever these friends were he triumphantly proved them wrong, and readers were as pleased with the pathos, horror and *grand guignol* of *Oliver* as with the comedy of *Pickwick*.[4]

Managing this double feat was an unprecedented and amazing achievement. Everything had to be planned in his head in advance. *Pickwick* had started as a series of loosely rambling episodes, but he was now introducing plot, with Pickwick accused of breach of promise, the dealings with lawyers, the trial and his imprisonment, all of which demanded more care in setting up each number; and *Oliver* was tightly plotted and shaped from the start. There was no going back to change or adjust once a number was printed; everything had to be right first time. How different this is from the way most great novelists work, allowing themselves time to reconsider, to change their minds, to go back, to cancel and rewrite. Each number of *Pickwick* and *Oliver* consisted of about 7,500 words, and in theory he simply divided every month, allotting a fortnight to each new section of each book. In practice this did not always work out as he hoped, and although he sometimes got ahead, there were many months when he only just managed to get his copy to the printer in time. He wrote in a small hand, with a quill pen and black (iron gall) ink at this stage – later he favoured bright blue – on rough sheets of grey, white or bluish paper, measuring about 9 x 7½ inches, that he'd fold and then tear in half before starting to write; he called these sheets 'slips'.[5] For *Oliver* he spaced the lines quite widely, fitting about twenty-five lines on each sheet where later he would cram forty-five. Something like ninety-five slips made up one monthly number. In the course of a day he might produce eleven or twelve slips, and if pushed up to twenty. He had also to arrange for the two illustrators – Browne for *Pickwick*, Cruikshank for *Oliver* – to see the copy to work from, more often than not deciding for them what would make the best picture. On top of this he was editing *Bentley's Miscellany*, which meant commissioning and dealing with other writers, and with the printers. The pressure was intense, but the results were gratifying: in February *Pickwick* sold 14,000 copies, and after the opening instalment of *Oliver* was reviewed in four papers, 1,000 extra copies had to be printed of the next number.

So far so good, but two weeks after giving birth Catherine was suffering from depression. She refused to eat, and only Dickens could persuade her to take anything. He himself had 'a violent attack of God knows what, in the head' and dosed himself with 'as much medicine as would be given to an ordinary-sized horse'. He told Bentley that, although he considered *Oliver* to be the best subject he had ever thought of, 'I really *cannot* write under these combined disadvantages', but at least he had finished this month's work.[6] Catherine had difficulty feeding the baby and gave up trying. A wet nurse was easily found to take over but, according to her sister, 'every time she sees her Baby she has a fit of crying and keeps constantly saying she is sure he will not care for her now she is not able to nurse him.' Mary sounds sympathetic but brisk in her letter, saying Catherine should forget what she had been through and remember that she has everything in the world to make her happy, including a husband who is 'kindness itself'. She goes on to talk proudly of his success: 'his time is so completely taken up that it is quite a favour for the Literary Gentlemen to get him to write for them.'[7]

Dickens wanted fresh air and exercise, and when the first number of *Oliver* was in print, with Cruikshank's illustration showing the small, starved hero asking the workhouse master for more gruel, he took Catherine, Mary and the baby with nurse or nurses to their honeymoon lodgings in Chalk for five weeks. Here he was able to write without interruption, although he had to return to London each week, either by steamer from Gravesend or else on the Dover coach. February, being short of days, was always a challenge for a writer working for monthly publication, but this time he had *Oliver* finished by the 10th and *Pickwick* by the 22nd. Then he was able to take the ladies to see the fortifications at Chatham and enjoy a 'snug little dinner at the Sun'. Catherine cheered up, and Tom Beard was invited to Chalk for the weekend, and to keep her and Mary company while Charles went out to dinner without them, invited by a contributor to the *Miscellany*, a literary lieutenant in the Marines living in the barracks in Chatham. Meanwhile he had made up his mind to leave Furnival's and instituted a search for a London house; and as soon as a suitable one was found in Doughty Street, between Gray's Inn and Mecklenburgh Square, he at once took a three-year lease at £80 a year. He asked Bentley for an advance of £100 to cover the cost of moving, and while the house was being prepared he and Catherine moved back to London, putting up for a few weeks in a rented house near Regent's Park. On the last day of March they moved into No. 48 Doughty Street.

The move was a mark of Dickens's confidence in his ability to maintain himself, with wife and child, at a new social level. The Doughty Street house was finer and larger than any he or his parents had ever lived in. It had twelve good rooms on three storeys, a basement and attics, and a small garden at the back, and it stood among similar handsome, solid, brick houses, all built at the turn of the century, in a wide and salubrious Bloomsbury street, gated at each end to keep out undesirables. Here he could live like a gentleman and work comfortably.[8]

At twenty-five he had achieved more than his father or any of his uncles, but he did not turn his back on his family. His parents were often at Doughty Street, and it became a second home for Frederick. Alfred, at fifteen, was being sent to learn engineering at Tamworth under the Stephensons, an apprenticeship certainly arranged by Henry Austin, who married Letitia this July. When Fanny also married a fellow musician, Henry Burnett, in September, the Dickens parents were left with only Augustus to look after. If Dickens had

Dickens drawn by Cruickshank at home in Doughty Street, 1837.

hopes their father would manage better with fewer responsibilities he was wrong, because John Dickens saw his son's success as an encouragement to expect more handouts. It also offered him the possibility of trading on his name. These activities verged on the criminal, but he never doubted that Charles would bail him out and protect him, if only to keep his own name unsullied, and about this he was right.

Just before the move to Doughty Street, Chapman & Hall sent Charles a cheque for £500, as a bonus above the usual payment for *Pickwick*, which had now been running for a year. Sales were still rising steadily – they reached 20,000 in May – and a week later they gave him a celebratory dinner. Bentley's idea for pleasing Dickens was to make sure he was elected to the Garrick Club, of which Bentley was a founder, a place where writers and actors gathered for convivial meals. At Dickens's request, Bentley also presented him with a complete set of his Standard Novels, bringing Jane Austen to the bookshelves of the study at Doughty Street, though not yet to the attention of their owner.[9] At the end of April, Dickens invited Bentley to dine in his new home. His fellow guests included the two fathers, John Dickens and George Hogarth, and two sisters, Fanny Dickens and Mary Hogarth. Bentley remembered that there was music after dinner, not from Fanny with her fine voice and classical repertoire but from Dickens himself, who sang his favourite patter song, 'The Dog's Meat Man', and gave his imitations of the best-known actors of the day. 'Dickens was in force,' wrote Bentley, and 'it was a right merry entertainment.' He said nothing about his hostess, but remembered that when he rose to leave at midnight his host pressed him to have another glass of brandy and water, which he was reluctant to take. Dickens then asked pretty Mary Hogarth to offer it to him, making it impossible for him to refuse.[10]

Now life delivered one of its cruel and arbitrary strokes, cutting across the expectations of everyone in the house. The following Saturday evening, Dickens took Catherine and Mary to the theatre. They returned home in good spirits, enjoyed some supper and a drink together, and went up to bed at one in the morning. A few moments later Dickens heard a cry from Mary's bedroom, and hurrying in found her still in her day clothes and visibly ill. Catherine came to see what was wrong. He said afterwards that they had no idea there was anything seriously the matter with her, but that they sent for medical assistance to be on the safe side. Whatever Dr Pickthorn said or did had no effect, yet still there seemed no cause for alarm. She was after all seventeen years old and until then had been in perfect health. Fourteen hours went by – bringing Mrs Hogarth, and possibly other doctors – before she 'sank under the attack and died – died in such a calm and gentle sleep, that although I had held her in my arms for some time before, when she was certainly living (for she swallowed a little brandy from my hand) I continued to support her lifeless form, long after her soul had fled to Heaven. This was about 3 o'Clock on the Sunday afternoon.'[11] 'Thank God she died in my arms, and the very last words she whispered were of me,' he told Beard.[12] Nothing more precise is known, except that no one was expecting her to die until the very last moments, and that 'the medical men imagine it was a disease of the heart.'[13] Still, it is curious that during the fourteen hours between her collapse and death no doctor was able to make any diagnosis, or to provide or even to suggest any form of care or treatment beyond allowing Dickens to administer brandy and hold the sick girl in his arms.

Before he laid her body down he was able to remove a ring from her finger and put it on one of his own, and there it stayed for the rest of his life.[14] Mrs Hogarth remained for a week 'in a state of total insensibility', except when she had to be forcibly restrained from going into the room where her child lay in her coffin. Catherine looked after her mother while she grieved herself for her much loved sister, and rose to the occasion as 'a fine-hearted and noble-minded girl', becoming 'so calm and cheerful that I wonder to see her'.[15] Dickens was unusually warm in his praise, and she maintained her calm even through the miscarriage she suffered during the next week. Possibly it was not entirely unwelcome to her.

Dickens himself was far from calm, and work was suddenly out of the question. In an unprecedented (and never repeated) action, he informed his two publishers that he was cancelling the *Pickwick* instalment for the end of May and *Oliver* for June. Rumours flew about that he had gone mad, or died, or been imprisoned for debt, and both publishers felt it necessary to put out notices explaining that this was not so, but that he was mourning the sudden death of a 'dear young relative to whom he was most affectionately attached and whose society has been for long the chief solace of his labours'. So went the notice in *Bentley's Miscellany*, pardonably exaggerating Mary's brief leading role in Dickens's life. He was obliged to ask them for money on account, possibly to deal with medical and funeral expenses for the Hogarths. He wrote an inscription for Mary's tombstone: 'Young, beautiful and good/God in His Mercy/numbered her with his angels/at the early age of seventeen'. He told Beard, with the hyperbole of fresh grief, that this sweet-natured but quite ordinary girl had been a paragon: 'so perfect a creature never breathed. I knew her inmost heart, and her real worth and values. She had not a fault.'[16] Every night she appeared in his dreams. He was at her funeral at Kensal Green on 13 May, and declared his wish to be buried in the same grave. In the shock and sadness of Mary's death, no one, not even Catherine, showed any surprise at his proposal.

Then he took Catherine out of London again, this time to a picturesque weather-boarded house known as Collins's Farm on the far side of Hampstead Heath.[17] Ainsworth and Beard visited them there; so did a new friend, John Forster, who came and stayed for several nights. Forster found Dickens distressed, trying to deal with feelings he could hardly manage. He needed attention, sympathy, distraction, and all this Forster gave him. Here was someone Dickens could talk to on equal terms, solid, clever and strong-minded, eager to be serviceable, and possessed of a tender heart. They had known one another slightly for six months, since Forster's put-down of *The Village Coquettes*, which had made Dickens laugh; but Forster dates their intimacy from these days in the spring of 1837 when Dickens, in the midst of his grief, opened his heart to him. On returning to London from Hampstead, Forster felt that 'I left him as much his friend, and as entirely in his confidence, as if I had known him for years.'[18]

Over their subsequent lifelong friendship Dickens sometimes mocked Forster and quarrelled furiously with him, but he was the only man to whom he confided his most private experiences and feelings, and he never ceased to trust him and rely on him. It was not a perfectly equal friendship, and Dickens sometimes took Forster for granted, and went through periods of coolness towards him, turning to another friend for a time; but when he was in real need of help it was always Forster to whom he went. And while Forster also had other friends to whom he was devoted – Macready, Bulwer, Browning, Carlyle – it was Dickens who became the sun and centre of his life, and on whom his happiness depended.

They were always at ease with one another, with no need to pose or pretend, and much in common. Each knew that the other had started with few advantages, from poor and undistinguished family backgrounds, and had a struggle to establish himself in a society in which money, rank and patronage often seemed to count for more than talent. Both had shown early promise and put in long, hard hours of work in order to make their way in the world against the odds. As writers too they both felt themselves to be on the side of the poor and oppressed, and believed that art could be used to attack injustice and cruelty, to mock the great and to insist on the human value of the lowest members of society. Forster was particularly eager to lay claim to the essential dignity of the writer and artist, and Dickens seemed born to vindicate this claim.

They were almost of an age, Forster born barely two months after Dickens, in April 1812. He was the son of a Newcastle butcher, his mother the daughter of 'a Gallowgate cow-keeper'. The Forsters were Unitarians, subscribing to that admirable and bracing type of Nonconformity that encouraged rational thinking, held that social ills were not willed by God but created by human action, and believed in democratic government. Forster was given his chance in life by an uncle, who made money as a cattle-dealer and paid for him to attend Newcastle Grammar School, where he showed outstanding ability and became captain of the school. He grew broad-shouldered and intense, with a thatch of dark hair. He read Byron and Scott and, like Dickens, became a passionate theatre-goer. At fourteen he drama-tized the story of Ali Baba, and at fifteen he wrote 'A Few Thoughts in Vindication of the Stage', expressing his view that it is 'where the human heart, upon the rack of the passions, confesses its slightest movements; where all masks, all disguises disappear, and truth, pure and incorruptible, shines in open day'. As a description of the stage it was a startling defence from a young Unitarian, given the view gen-erally held by Nonconformists, that the theatre was likely to corrupt. The next year he had his own play, on the subject of Charles I, put on at the Theatre Royal, Newcastle. It was given only one perform-ance, but it was a coup for a mere lad.

He had already been given a much better formal education than Dickens ever had, and his uncle then paid for him to go to Cam-bridge. After a month, finding that Unitarians could not get degrees, and that it was an expensive place, he turned his back on Cam-bridge and sensibly decided to go to London to read law at University College and the Inner Temple.[19] He was liked and respected by his teachers, and made his mark as 'a tall, ardent, noticeable young fellow', 'joyous, generous, sincere . . . the uncompromising advocate of all that was just, noble and good'. He dressed unfashionably but he was no puritan and had a taste for 'oysters, fog and grog', i.e., tobacco and alcohol.[20] In the year of the Reform Act, 1832, when he was twenty, he abandoned his legal studies, to the displeasure of his professor, and took up the precarious life of a man of letters. He found work reviewing for left-wing journals and embarked on biographical studies of the great figures of the English revolution, Cromwell, Vane, Pym, Hampden, Strafford. History, poetry, painting and the theatre all interested him, and he had a gift for making friends: with the essayist Charles Lamb; with Leigh Hunt, founding editor of the radical weekly the *Examiner*; with its current editor, Albany Fonblanque; with the novelist Bulwer and the young poet Browning, whose early work he reviewed; with Thomas Talfourd, radical barrister, playwright and MP; with the Irish artist Daniel Maclise, and the leading actor of the day, Macready. Lamb died in 1834; but all the others were introduced to Dickens by Forster during the first year of their friendship.

Forster had first noticed Dickens when he joined the *True Sun* in 1831 as drama critic, and saw one day, standing on the staircase at the office, 'a young man of my own age whose keen animation of look would have arrested attention anywhere, and whose name, upon enquiry, I then heard for the first time'.[21] No words were exchanged, but Forster kept this bright image in his mind. In 1834 he settled himself in a room in a lodging house at No. 58 Lincoln's Inn Fields, where he remained for twenty years, during which he gradually expanded into more rooms on the same floor and above, filling each one with his growing collection of books. Here he entertained modestly, giving breakfast parties, but there was a loneliness at the heart of his life; he no longer had much in common with his own family, and Newcastle was far away. He fell in love with a remarkable woman of letters, the poet Letitia Landon. Beautiful, prolific and compared by her admirers to Byron, she earned her own living publishing novels and reviews as well as volumes of verse; and she was ten years older than Forster. He proposed to her and was accepted, only to learn that scandalous stories were circulating of her liaisons with various men, some of them his own friends. When he felt he must ask her about what he had heard, she broke off the engagement, declaring that his suspicions were 'as dreadful as death'. Whether the stories were true or not, he was wounded and retreated into bachelor life.[22] The ethos of the time, and his own ambivalence about women, made intimacy with men altogether easier.

In 1835 he became the literary editor of the *Examiner*, and by the time he got to know Dickens he was a respected critic and becoming an influential figure in the London literary world. Dickens was a rising star whom Forster believed to be a genius, and was ready to serve that genius, while Dickens realized Forster could be an invaluable adviser and supporter. Each had something to gain from the friendship, but what counted still more was the strong spontaneous personal affection that rose up between them. They listened to one another, trusted one another and enjoyed one another's company. Dickens loved to expand his domestic circle, and Forster became the essential bachelor friend of the family, more fun than Beard, although he also remained close. Forster was courteous and friendly to Catherine and she responded and approved of him. When they noticed that his birthday coincided with the Dickenses' wedding anniversary, a ritual celebration was set up, involving a trip to Richmond for lunch at the Star and Garter on 2 April each year. And when the next Dickens child arrived, a little Mary, named inevitably for her dead aunt Mary Hogarth, Forster was invited to be her godfather.

This was one of those life-changing friendships that arises when two young men – or women – meet and each suddenly realizes a perfect soulmate has been found. The world changes for both, they are amazed at their good fortune, greedy for one another's company, delighted by the wit, generosity, perception and brilliance that flashes between them. It is like falling in love – it is in fact a form of falling in love, without the overt sexual element. Dickens and Forster both liked women well enough, but it was almost impossible for women to give them the sort of good companionship they craved. Some women were innocents, some predators, some disqualified in different ways. Young married women were likely to be perpetually pregnant, as Dickens was discovering. Catherine was pregnant again in the summer of 1837, and when he took her to Brighton he wrote complaining to Forster that 'unless I am joined by some male companion' he was 'unlikely to see anything but the Pavilion, the chain Pier, and the Sea'.[23] He was clearly hoping Forster would join them. The majority of women inevitably remained apart from the intellectual world in which men lived, and outside most of their activities and interests, and, since society was organized on this basis, men expected to spend a great deal of their leisure time with other men. Formal dinners and clubs excluded women, few women were brought up to ride or walk over long distances, and professional women were on the whole seen as a class apart from middle-class wives and mothers. Once Fanny Dickens married and became a mother, her career declined, gifted and musically educated as she was; and Forster's Letitia Landon earned herself a reputation that made him withdraw from her. But Forster and Dickens together could do whatever they liked, and so they did: they walked, they rode for miles out of town, they took lunch, they dined, they attended established clubs and set up new private clubs, they attended rehearsals in the theatre as well as official performances, they visited places that interested them, they called on friends, discussed business and enjoyed innumerable evenings out at chop-houses and inns. Among Dickens's surviving letters, there are a great many summoning Forster to ride with him or to come round and simply be with him: 'My Missis is going out today, and I want you to take some cold lamb and a bit of fish with me, *alone*. We can walk out both before and afterwards but I must *dine* at home on account of the Pickwick proofs.' 'I *ought* to dine in Bloomsbury Square tomorrow, but as I would much rather go with you for a ride . . . that's off . . . So engage the Osses.' 'As I have been sticking to it pretty hard all last week, I intend ordering a Oss to be at this door at 11 Oclock in the morning to convey me on a fifteen mile ride out, ditto in, and a Lunch on the Road. Can you spare the time to join me? We will return here to dinner at 5.' 'I could hug you and Talfourd too – I am so delighted to find that you are going to participate in my holiday. Come to me, and don't be later than 11. I think Richmond and Twickenham through the Park, out at Knightsbridge, and over Barnes Common, would make a beautiful ride.' 'You don't feel disposed, do you, to muffle yourself up, and start off with me for a good brisk walk over Hampstead Heath? I knows a good 'ous there where we can have a red hot chop for dinner, and a glass of good wine./All work and no play makes Jack a dull boy. I am as dull as a Codfish.'[24] And so on.

Pleasure apart, Forster's arrival in Dickens's life changed it profoundly. To begin with, he began immediately to ask Forster for advice and practical help in dealing with his publishers. The first problem was with Macrone, who owned the copyright of *Sketches by Boz* – he had paid £100 for them – and was now planning to republish them in monthly parts, reckoning they might sell as well as *Pickwick*. Dickens believed this would damage *Pickwick*. He was enraged and desperate to get back the copyright, for which Macrone now asked £2,000. When Chapman & Hall offered to buy the copyright for the sum asked, and to put out the *Sketches* themselves later, with illustrations by Cruikshank, Dickens at first turned to Forster for advice, but was so impatient that before Forster could answer he had agreed to Chapman & Hall's plan. There was a sad sequel: before the *Sketches* began to appear in November, Macrone fell ill and died. He was only twenty-eight, and his business had failed. Characteristically, Dickens forgot his rage against him and at once started a scheme to raise money for his widow and children.[25]

Forster was disconcerted by the Macrone dealings, but was ready to take on negotiations with Bentley, and from then on was involved in all Dickens's business with publishers. The result was that Dickens got back his copyrights after three years, had his salary for editing and contributing to the *Miscellany* raised, would be paid more than previously agreed for the long-planned next novel, 'Gabriel Vardon', now renamed *Barnaby Rudge*, and was promised bonuses for books that sold well. To Bentley, Forster was a bully who encouraged Dickens to be difficult and demanding, but the truth was that he spoke for Dickens and, when Dickens insisted on breaking contracts he had come to consider unfair, gave him support. Dickens's habit of reneging on contracts was not morally defensible as business practice – even his friends said so – but it has been argued that, since no one had foreseen his spectacularly rising sales, which meant his publishers made thousands out of his work while his rewards remained relatively modest, he had a case.[26] In these circumstances he felt entitled to insist on adjustments to the contracts, and Forster backed him. Chapman & Hall were prepared to be generous – later in the summer they gave Dickens another £2,000 bonus for *Pickwick* – with the result that Dickens regarded them as friends, while Bentley became 'the Robber'.

Dickens introduced Forster to Chapman & Hall, and soon Forster was acting as their chief literary adviser, where he continued until 1861 (and was succeeded by George Meredith). It was an arrangement that worked to everyone's benefit, the more so since Forster moved on from literary editor of the *Examiner* to editor, remaining there until 1856. And from the late 1830s on he acted as Dickens's 'right hand and cool shrewd head'. As has often been pointed out, he became effectively his literary agent before the job was invented – though he was unpaid. With his good business sense and stubbornness, he proved an extremely effective negotiator, adopting a high ground on behalf of his author, as for instance in October 1838, when he assured Bentley that Dickens was 'the greatest master of prose fiction in this or any other language'.[27] He read all his proofs, correcting and cutting when asked, and from 1838, as he recalled, 'There was nothing written by him ... which I did not see before the world did, either in manuscript or proof.'[28] Unlike a modern literary agent, he also felt free to review Dickens's books.

The July number of *Pickwick* was reviewed by Forster on its appearance, and gave him a chance to express his admiration for his new friend. It was the instalment in which Dickens described the Fleet Prison, where his hero is incarcerated for refusing to pay the breach-of-promise fine imposed on him by a corrupt judge. Every reader of *Pickwick* feels the change of tone and the great force of the account of prison life, and Forster was the first to do it justice: 'The truth and power with which it is made are beyond all praise – so certain, so penetrating, and so deeply-aimed, and yet, at the same time, so obvious and familiar, are the materials employed. Every point tells, and the reality of the whole is wonderful. We place the picture by the side of those of the greatest masters of this style of fiction in our language, and it rises in the comparison . . . We recognize in this fine writer a maturing excellence.'[29]

Forster's perceptiveness was especially acute in that he knew nothing, at this point, of Dickens's childhood experiences in the Marshalsea Prison. Dickens wrote at once to thank him: 'I feel your rich, deep appreciation of my intent and meaning more than the most glowing abstract praise that could possibly be lavished upon me. You know I have ever done so, for it was your feeling for me and mine for you that first brought us together, and I hope will keep us so, till death do us part. Your notices make me grateful but very proud; so have a care of them, or you will turn my head.'[30] Everyone is grateful for a good review, but the tone of Dickens's thanks is more than grateful, with its allusion to the marriage vow. They had been getting to know each other for only a few weeks, and this reads like a love letter. Seven months later another letter to Forster strikes much the same note: 'I know your sterling value, and look back with unmingled pleasure to every link which each ensuing week has added to the chain of our attachment. It shall go hard, I hope, 'ere [sic] anything but Death impairs the toughness of a bond now so firmly riveted.'[31] And in December 1839 he wrote to him of 'that feeling for you an attachment which no ties of blood or other relationship could ever awaken, and hoping to be to the end of my life your affectionate and chosen friend'.[32] Young men of the early nineteenth century might write to one another in florid terms, but to no one else did Dickens use such language – or at least no such letters survive – and they suggest how perfectly Forster filled a need for him that no one else, parents, sister, friend or wife, had done. Forster saw him as he wanted to be seen and listened to him as he wanted to be heard. He made it plain that he loved him and put him first, before even his own work. With him Dickens could most easily be himself, sharing his ideas, hopes, ambitions and unhappinesses. Few if any women did this for Dickens. In 1840, presenting Forster with a claret jug, he enclosed a note telling him, 'My heart is not an eloquent one on matters which touch it most, but suppose this claret jug the urn in which it lies, and believe that its warmest and truest blood is yours . . . let it add, to the wine we shall drink from it together, a flavor which the choicest vintage could never impart. Take it from my hand – filled to the brim and running over with truth and earnestness.'[33]

Forster's responses are lost – Dickens burnt all his correspondence in 1860 – but his attachment was absolute. When Dickens returned from six months' absence in America, in July 1842, he drove to Lincoln's Inn and, finding no one at home, guessed where Forster might be dining, told his driver to take him there and sent in a message to say that 'a gentleman wanted to speak to Mr Forster'. Dickens's own account of what happened next says everything about the intensity of his friend's feelings. Guessing it was Dickens, Forster came flying out of the house without stopping to pick up his hat, got into the carriage, pulled up the window and began to cry.[34]

7

Blackguards and Brigands

1837–1839

While Forster was making himself into an essential component of Dickens's working life, he did something equally important in his social life, opening it up and transforming it by introducing him into his own large and multi-talented circle of journalists, lawyers, novelists, poets, editors, actors and painters. Although Dickens had, for example, seen the actor Macready on stage many times, it was Forster who led him into the dressing room at Covent Garden in June 1837 and made them friends. Macready, twenty years older than Dickens, took an instant fatherly liking to him. Dickens responded with filial affection, and soon he was showing him his latest writing, discussing plays with him and attending performances regularly.

Here was a great man whose start in life had been a struggle like his own. Macready's father, an actor, had wanted to make his boy into a gentleman and sent him to Rugby School intending him to become a lawyer, but he was bankrupted, and at sixteen the young Macready had to leave school and earn his living on the stage. Rugby had inculcated him with the sense that he was a gentleman and he bitterly resented the low status of the acting profession. Falling in love with a child actress, he removed her from the stage and her family, and had her re-educated by his sister to become a suitable wife. By the time he and Dickens met they both had growing families. The wives – both Catherines – also made friends, and the two couples enjoyed spending time together. There were dinners, parties, expeditions and visits to the Macready home, first his house at Elstree in Hertfordshire and then at Clarence Terrace on Regent's Park, and Dickens was soon attending rehearsals and first nights as a matter of course. Often he took the latest number of the novel he was writing round to Macready and read passages aloud to him. Macready wrote down his honest opinion in his diary, more often than not praising the genius of Dickens, his humour or pathos, but sometimes expressing disappointment, although he was tactful enough not to mention this to Dickens. The friendship was unclouded by quarrels and lasted to the end of Dickens's life – Macready, although so much older, outlived him.

Macready and Forster were both members of the Shakespeare Club and Dickens was soon enrolled among its seventy or so members. They met on Saturday evenings at the Piazza Coffee House in Covent Garden for readings and discussions on cultural subjects, held a monthly dinner and occasionally organized a Shakespeare gala. Most of the friends he made here remained his friends for life, even though the club fizzled out in 1839.[1] The young Thackeray, artist and satirist, the poet Barry Cornwall, the playwright Douglas Jerrold, the literary lawyer and MP Thomas Talfourd, journalists Charles Knight and Samuel Laman Blanchard; and artists Daniel Maclise, Clarkson Stanfield, Frank Stone, Edwin and Tom Landseer, and George Cattermole. Dickens always felt comfortable with artists: none of them was rich, most had struggled to educate themselves, and all of them worked hard. Stanfield had started life as a child actor, been apprenticed to a coach painter, pressed into the Navy and sailed halfway round the world before he got work as a London scene painter and at last found his *métier* as a marine artist; he settled in Hampstead and was elected to the Royal Academy. He became Stanny to Dickens, who loved him dearly, and they enjoyed many jaunts, theatre trips and dinners together.[2] Frank Stone became another favourite, the son of a Manchester cotton-spinner; he had taught himself to paint and scraped a living with portraits and watercolours. Dickens nicknamed him 'Old Tone' or 'Pumpion', and became devoted to his children, whose mother Stone neglected for many years to marry. Maclise, just establishing himself as a painter of portraits and historical subjects, came of poor Irish parents. He shared Dickens's taste for low life and joined him for night-time rambles through rough parts of London, mixing with the criminal classes, keeping an eye out for pretty street girls and drinking more than was good for them. A bachelor, much admired by women for his good looks – he was tall and well built and wore his thick dark hair curling down his back –

Maclise got into scrapes with ladies. In the summer of 1837, as Dickens was getting to know him, he was in danger of being cited as a co-respondent in divorce proceedings when Lady Henrietta Sykes, previously Disraeli's mistress, was caught *in flagrante* with him. This was the *vie de Bohème* as it was played out in London: precarious earnings, irregular working hours, the pursuit of adventure and comradeship.

Forster also introduced Dickens to older, established writers. One was Leigh Hunt, famous for having been sent to prison for insulting the Prince Regent in his paper, the *Examiner*; now in his fifties, he had known Shelley, Byron and Keats, and was still renowned for his literary discernment, his essays and verse, his radical journalism and his personal charm. Another was Bulwer, landowner, Liberal politician, and prolific and successful novelist (*The Last Days of Pompeii*) and playwright (*Money*); he was estranged from his strong-minded wife, with whom he clashed furiously.

Then there was Thomas Talfourd, whom he had seen as a barrister in court while reporting the Norton v. Melbourne case. Although his name is hardly remembered now, Talfourd was an outstanding figure in his day, idealistic, hard-working and effective. The son of a brewer too poor to send him to university, he made his own way and by the late 1830s was MP for Reading, standing as a Liberal on the radical side of the party. He had protested against the Peterloo Massacre in 1819, supported universal male suffrage and the total abolition of slavery, steered through the bill giving divorced women custody of their young children, and was currently seeing through the 1842 Copyright Act that for the first time protected authors' earnings in England during their lifetimes and for a period after their death.[3] He also defended the publisher Moxon, who put out Shelley's *Queen Mab*, against the accusation of blasphemy.[4]

All this was congenial to Dickens, and to crown it Talfourd was also a playwright. His blank-verse drama *Ion* was given a hero who, on becoming King of Argos, declares himself a republican, disbands the army and makes the people promise never to re-establish the monarchy – after which he commits suicide, with the intention of leaving his people free. *Ion* carried a strong political charge and ran for a year in London, in 1836 and 1837, with Macready in the lead: this was the last year of the reign of the feeble William IV, when the monarchy was at a low ebb. It was revived many times and hailed as a masterpiece in America. Talfourd had a wide range of friends among writers and politicians, including Lord Melbourne and Lord Grey. He was generous and convivial, and he and his wife gave famously enjoyable dinner parties in their house in Russell Square, where Dickens became a favourite.

So great was Dickens's admiration for Talfourd that he made him the dedicatee of *The Pickwick Papers* when it appeared in volume form in November 1837. A dedication was a show of affection and respect, and also a gesture that cheered Dickens when he came to the end of a long book. He did not like parting with the characters whose voices and idiosyncrasies had filled his life for so many months, mourned for them when he reached the end, and said so at the conclusion of *Pickwick*: 'It is the fate of most men who mingle with the world and attain even the prime of life, to make many real friends, and lose them in the course of nature. It is the fate of all authors or chroniclers to create imaginary friends, and lose them in the course of art.'[5] It is also true that Dickens kept his characters alive in his imagination for the rest of his life.

※

The death of William IV in June and the accession to the throne of his niece, Princess Victoria, passed pretty well unnoticed by Dickens, hard at work on his two novels again. He took Forster on a tour of Newgate: a prison visit was a ritual to share with a friend. In July he made a rapid cross-Channel trip with Catherine and his illustrator Hablot Browne, visiting Ghent, Brussels and Antwerp. He had to be back in time for his sister Letitia's wedding to Henry Austin, and for dinner on 11 July at Macready's, where he met the philosopher and politician John Stuart Mill. Mill wrote to a friend that Dickens had a 'face of dingy blackguardism irradiated with genius' – a phrase cribbed from Carlyle's description of Camille Desmoulins, journalist of the French Revolution. 'Such a phenomenon does not often appear in a lady's drawing room,' he went on, perhaps a little shocked by Dickens's appearance and outspokenness, although Mill surely shared many of his social and political opinions.[6]

The blackguard meanwhile was writing to Bentley, telling him he hoped for much better terms, given the increased popularity of his works.[7] Bentley was ready to give bonuses when *Oliver* made the sales of the *Miscellany* soar, but not to relinquish the copyright of *Oliver*, as Dickens wished. According to Bentley, Dickens threatened to stop writing *Oliver*. Bentley gave way and a new agreement was signed, with Forster taking much of the blame for this hard bargaining. Wrangling continued throughout 1838. Dickens, however, agreed with Bentley to edit the memoirs of the famous clown Grimaldi for £300, just managing to squeeze the work into the three-month gap between finishing *Pickwick* in October 1837 and starting *Nicholas Nickleby* for Chapman & Hall in the new year. He also agreed to write a short book, *Sketches of Young Gentlemen*, for Chapman & Hall for £125. He started writing on 8 January and this too was done to time, despite the occasional disturbed night with one-year-old Charley, and it was published on 10 February. Forster also published this February a volume of biographies of revolutionary leaders of the English Civil War period, and Dickens found time to read one of them, and to write a letter appreciating its 'staunch and jolly' subject, and finding the whole biography 'glorious'.[8]

He had signed an agreement for *Nickleby* with Chapman & Hall in November, promising that the first number would be ready to appear at the end of March 1838. By 21 February the first chapter was written; on 28 February it appeared in print, and promised to be another success. The opening theme was the Yorkshire schools where unwanted boys, illegitimate, orphaned or otherwise out of favour with their guardians, could be dumped, and where they were kept with no holidays or breaks, ill-used and starved, without medical care, so that they pined, sickened and died in large numbers. Dickens had heard of such schools and knew they were a horror needing to be dealt with. He travelled to Yorkshire in February 1838 with Browne to see what they could find, pretending to be seeking a school for the son of a widowed friend. They were unable to visit any school, but talked to one headmaster with a bad record, and were warned by an honest Yorkshireman not to send a child to the school he was asked about – even a gutter in London would be better for the boy than such a school, he assured them, and repeated his warning emphatically.[9]

Dickens had already constructed in his mind one of his great comic characters, Mr Squeers, the headmaster of such a school, who advertises and comes to London to collect unwanted boys, colluding with those who are keen to be rid of them. What he does with Squeers and the situation might seem impossible but is in fact extraordinarily effective. He shows the cruelty and vileness of the school and the terror of the boys, starved, beaten, made to work and taught nothing, and at the same time he makes the appalling Squeers and his wife and monstrous son and daughter so funny that we can't help laughing at them. It would be like a joke in a concentration camp were it not shown through the eyes of the dashing hero, Nicholas Nickleby, who is strong enough to turn on Squeers and give him a beating, and good-hearted enough to rescue at any rate one of his victims, poor Smike, reduced to feebleness of mind and broken in health by the treatment he has received.

Nickleby makes a tremendous start, which is followed by a series of encounters between Nicholas and his sister, Kate, with other employers. Money is a running theme, and Kate is offered starvation wages – between five and seven shillings a week – by the London dressmaking establishment of Madame Mantalini and her high-spending, debt-ridden husband. She is also used, unpaid, by her financier uncle, to attract his aristocratic clients. Nicholas, paid five pounds a year as a schoolmaster, is offered ten times more – a pound a week – to write and act for Vincent Crummles's theatre troupe. By contrast, the MP Gregsbury, who has 'a tolerable command of sentences with no meaning in them' and who seeks a low-paid secretary to keep him informed of what he ought to know, offers only fifteen shillings a week.[10] Dickens stiffens his comedy with a strong economic backing.

Nickleby also excels in its descriptions of London life, as Forster pointed out in his review: 'We enter with him by night, through long double rows of brightly burning lamps, a noisy, bustling, crowded

scene, in which he shows us the rags of the squalid ballad-singer fluttering in the same rich light that shows the goldsmith's glittering
treasures, and where one thin sheet of brittle glass is the iron wall by
which vast profusions of wealth and food are guarded from starved
and pennyless men . . . At all times, and under every aspect, he gives
us to feel and see the great city as it absolutely is.' Forster gets this
right, praises the 'sparkling stream of vivacity or humour' in *Nickleby*
and was not afraid to point out some of its failures: the rambling
unplanned plot, the feebleness of several of the villains, to which
must be added the still greater feebleness of the benevolent characters
and the interminable and almost unreadable last quarter of the book,
where forced marriages, stolen wills, lost children found and sudden
deaths are all requisitioned from the crude traditions of melodrama.
Mrs Nickleby, whose confused stream of consciousness, and inattention to any attempt to interrupt it, was based, according to Dickens's
own word, on the conversation of his mother, is another of his great
comic creations, although even of her there is rather too much: he
always found it hard to let go of a character whose dialogue delighted
him. But the public was entertained, and had no objection to melodrama. After only eight instalments of *Nickleby* had appeared it began
to be dramatized, and was played in theatres all over England. It
reached the Theatre Royal in Newcastle in December 1838, as part of
a benefit for Mrs Ternan, a well-known actress, then seven months
pregnant with her third daughter, Ellen.

※

Dickens was under pressure all through 1838 with the renewed double
monthly tasks, now of *Oliver* and *Nickleby*. Forster said later that he
never knew him work so much after dinner or such late hours. There
was extra urgency because he had promised to complete *Oliver* for
publication in book form in September, months before the serial
publication was to end in March 1839. So he worked, and worked,
and although Doughty Street was a comfortable home, he had his
private worries there too. He loved his son Charley, 'the darling boy',
with passion, but was anxious about him when he could not be with

him. 'Don't leave him alone too much,' he wrote to Catherine from Yorkshire in February, as though he feared the precious boy might not be getting enough of her attention. On 6 March she gave birth to their second child, a daughter, Mary, always known as Mamie, or Mamey. Catherine was ill afterwards and he took her to Richmond to convalesce at the end of the month, leaving both children at home, the baby with the wet nurse. Forster came to join them on 2 April – the joint birthday and wedding anniversary – and it may have been after this that Dickens first spoke to him about his sense that he and Catherine were temperamentally unsuited to one another, amiable and compliant as she was; that they made one another uneasy, and that he saw trouble ahead.[11]

He could never stay in the same place for long. For June and July that year they agreed to take a house in Twickenham, in Ailsa Park Villas, Isleworth Road, close to the river, to enjoy the fresh air and to be out of town for the coronation.[12] There were regular boats between Hungerford Stairs and Twickenham, and in spite of his workload he immediately started inviting friends to come down: Forster, of course, and Beard, Mitton, Ainsworth, Talfourd, Hullah, Harley – even Bentley had an invitation. Thackeray came with Douglas Jerrold, whose stories he had just illustrated. There were visits to Hampton Court, rides by the river and games with balloons for Charley, now nicknamed the 'Snodgering Blee' by his loving father. Forster was made responsible for supplying the balloons and appointed President of the Balloon Club, and affectionately teased, Dickens concocting spoof letters to him from an imaginary female admirer.

Dickens noted that he finished his *Oliver* number on 7 July and started on the *Nickleby* number three days later, on 10 July; he spent Sunday correcting proofs instead of going to church. During these pleasant, crowded summer months he heard he was elected to the Athenaeum Club. He succeeded in getting his brother Fred work in a government office, as a clerk in the Treasury, by applying to the Patronage Secretary, Stanley. He wrote his will. He corresponded with the young and aspiring George Henry Lewes, telling him that 'I suppose like most authors I look over what I write with exceeding pleasure', that he felt each passage strongly while he wrote it, but that he had no idea how his ideas came to him – they came 'ready made to the point of the pen'.[13] His energy never flagged.

Back in Doughty Street in August, and now hopeless of finishing *Oliver* for book publication in September, he arranged to go to the Isle of Wight for a week's work and put it about that he was to be out of town for longer. In October he wrote the description of the murder of Nancy by her lover, the burglar Bill Sikes. He tried it out on Catherine, who was reduced to 'an unspeakable "*state*" ', he informed Forster with great satisfaction.[14] This was the germ of the readings he gave in 1869 and 1870, when he reduced whole audiences to unspeakable states, and himself to near-collapse: he read it for the last time on 8 March 1870, three months before his death. His confidence in *Oliver* grew as he advanced towards the end of the book, and he told Bentley, 'I am doing it with greater care, and I think with greater power than I have been able to bring to bear on anything yet.'[15] A review of his work in the *Edinburgh Review* gave him particular pleasure by praising him as the 'truest and most spirited delineator of English life since the days of Smollett and Fielding ... What Hogarth was in painting, such very nearly is Mr Dickens in prose fiction.'[16]

In *Pickwick*, an innocent middle-aged man is confronted with crooked lawyers and prison, and saved by his street-wise servant Sam Weller. *Oliver* set up a darker scene from the start, as the infant hero and his dying, unmarried mother, two innocents, are confronted with evil licensed by a state system meant to protect and help them. As a charity child, Oliver shows some spirit and gets into trouble that allows Dickens to give voice to a passionate indignation. Then, when he falls into the hands of a professional criminal, Fagin, who trains boys like the Artful Dodger to pick pockets, Dickens shows the mixture of terror and fascination that they produce in Oliver: they are kind to him, amuse him, feed him, shelter him and explain the world to him. Fagin and the Artful Dodger are the stars of the book, as every dramatization has made clear. The only thing that stops Oliver succumbing to their charm and being happily corrupted is that he has had a glimpse of another world, peaceful and orderly, where he might be given an education. He also unwittingly acquires an ally in

Nancy, the prostitute who pities Oliver and tries to protect him and help him get away from Fagin. Then Dickens tightens the tension and horror of the plot by making Nancy's lover Sikes a brutal burglar, and also an ally of Fagin.

It is melodrama, but with moments of real terror, as Oliver tries to escape the villains and they in turn are hunted to the death. Apart from the colourless virtuous characters, the chief failure of the book is Nancy, on whom Dickens lavished great care and whom he claimed to have modelled on a young woman he had known. He was proud of his portrait and said it was drawn from life, but he fails because he makes her behave like an actress in a bad play: she tears her hair and clothes, writhes, wrings her hands, sinks to her knees and contrives to lie down on a stone staircase in the street. She has visions of shrouds, coffins and blood, and is loaded with false theatrical speeches. 'I am that infamous creature,' she tells a would-be benefactress. 'The poorest women fall back, as I make my way along the crowded pavement ... the alley and the gutter were mine, as they will be my death-bed.' Again, 'Look before you, lady. Look at that dark water. How many times do you read of such as I who spring into the tide, and leave no living thing, to care for, or bewail them ... I shall come to that at last.'[17] Dickens must many times have observed prostitutes in the streets, yet he is creating a stereotype here, one he used again in later novels: the penitent woman who tears her hair and seeks the river to make an end of things. But Nancy's falsity could not spoil the success of *Oliver*, which rose to a fearful conclusion with her murder by Sikes and his subsequent grisly end. Fagin is hanged, and the Artful Dodger redeems the criminal classes with his great performance in the dock, cheeking the magistrate and making even the jailer grin.

❧

Oliver was finished and with the printers by the end of October, and Dickens had now only *Nickleby* to worry about. Restless as ever, he set off with Browne for a sightseeing trip to Leamington, Kenilworth, Warwick Castle and Stratford, and on into north Wales, leaving Forster to deal with the proofs of *Oliver*, and to keep Catherine cheerful with his visits. As so often happens after a period of intense work, Dickens became ill, and wrote home to say he had suffered such an ecstasy of pain in his side during the night that he felt half dead. He dosed himself with henbane, a violent and dangerous herb which acts as a sedative and pain-killer, and it did wonders for him. Forster decided to come to meet him in Liverpool – 'I trust you to see my dear Kate, and bring the latest intelligence of her & the darlings,' Dickens wrote to him.[18] Forster travelled up on the new Grand Junction Railway, and together they decided to cut short the trip and return to London to make sure *Oliver* went to press without any mistakes. This meant leaving Liverpool at three in the morning to arrive at Euston Square in the afternoon, but both felt it worth the effort. On 9 November *Oliver Twist* was published in three volumes. It sold well, and was read that winter by the young Queen Victoria, who found it 'excessively interesting'.[19] *Oliver* is the only one of Dickens's novels without a dedication, perhaps because he was too hard pressed to remember to make one: the obvious dedicatee was Forster, but he had to content himself with being Mamie's godfather.[20]

Having earned himself a little time off in November, Dickens finished a farce intended for Macready, *The Lamplighter*. Macready had to tell him it was not worth putting on, and Dickens accepted the verdict with good grace. He was able to see an early dramatization of *Nickleby* at the Adelphi Theatre, which caused him some groans. He also went to a demonstration of mesmerism, or magnetizing, by Dr John Elliotson, one of the founders of University College Hospital, London. Elliotson was denounced when the girls with whom he was working were found to be faking, and he resigned from the hospital, but he denied the charges against him and continued to practise medicine and mesmerism. Dickens believed in him, became a friend, employed him as his family doctor and was fascinated by mesmerism, so much so that he began to experiment with it himself three years later.

His chief problem during the autumn was the behaviour of his father, who had once again defaulted on a loan, leaving another Barrow brother-in-law, this time Edward, to pay £57. Dickens settled the debt, furious at the shame of it, and at the waste of his hard-earned money. He accepted that he must help his father with regular hand-outs, but he began to think of moving him out of London to keep him away from further temptation. December brought a great round of social activities, including the forming of the Trio Club with Forster and Ainsworth, which meant more dinners together. He dined with Elliotson on 27 December, Ainsworth on the 29th, Talfourd on the 30th and gave a dinner at home for New Year's Eve with Forster, Ainsworth and Cruikshank. Forster stayed at Doughty Street for several nights, so that little Charley, trotting confidently to the guest room on 4 January, 'was much disappointed to find you had not taken up your quarters there, permanently'.[21] Forster must have gone home to collect his present for Mamie's christening the next day at the new St Pancras Church. This was followed two days later by a long-planned 'gentle flare', which turned into a great gathering of family and friends, to celebrate both the christening and Charley's second birthday.

After a rapid visit with Ainsworth to Manchester, where they were offered a joint celebratory dinner, Dickens made the main business of January 1839 another fierce skirmish in his long battle with Bentley. The underlying cause was the impossibility of satisfying the two publishers he had engaged himself to, who were competing for his work. Chapman & Hall were also markedly more generous in their dealings with him than Bentley, who was inclined to stick to the terms already agreed. By now Dickens had decided he wanted to give up the editorship of the *Miscellany*, and to postpone the delivery of the promised next novel, *Barnaby Rudge*. He knew he needed a rest, he was angry with Bentley, and he decided that the best way forward was to send him a written blast of complaint. It is a mixture of rage and high-sounding rhetoric, and he submitted it to Forster, who may have added his own editorial touches. Part of it goes,

> the consciousness that my books are enriching everybody connected with them but myself, and that I, with such a popularity as I have acquired, am struggling in old toils, and wasting my energies in the very height and freshness of my fame, and the best part of my life, to fill the pockets of others, while for those who are nearest and dearest to me I can realise little more than a genteel subsistence: all this puts

me out of heart and spirits . . . I do most solemnly declare that morally, before God and man, I hold myself released from such hard
bargains as these, after I have done so much for those who drove
them. This net that has been wound about me, so chafes me, so exas-
perates and irritates my mind, that to break it at whatever cost . . . is
my constant impulse . . . and for the time I have mentioned – six
months from the conclusion of *Oliver* in the *Miscellany* – I wash my
hands of any fresh accumulation of labour . . .[22]

Bentley was ready to agree to much of what Dickens asked for, but
on condition that he set aside *Nickleby* for six months and took on no
other tasks. The condition was aimed at his rival publisher and was an
impossible one for Dickens to accept, because there was no question
of giving up *Nickleby* in mid-serialization. He accused Bentley of
'offensive impertinence'. Then he persuaded Ainsworth to take over
the editorship of the *Miscellany* and at once resigned from it himself.
All through February solicitors worked at yet another new agreement. It was the ninth, and it left Dickens with a good offer of
bonuses for *Oliver* and a commitment to deliver *Barnaby* to Bentley
on 1 January 1840. After these considerable concessions it was as well
for Bentley that he did not see Dickens's diary entry for his twenty-
seventh birthday on 7 February, with its smug cheerfulness: 'the end
of a most prosperous and happy year, for which and all other blessings I thank GOD with all my heart and soul'. There is something
Pepysian about this pious remark, coming on the heels of his cries of
woe and ferocious dealings with his publisher.[23]

※

With only one serial in hand now, there was time to attend to other
things. In March 1839 he travelled to Devon alone, having failed in
an attempt to persuade Forster to make the trip with him ('you
know how much you would lighten its weariness').[24] His intention
was to find a house in which to settle his parents and youngest
brother, Augustus. He had made up his mind to spend several hundred pounds on providing them with somewhere comfortable, but
far enough from London to keep his father out of mischief. With his

usual quickness he lighted on a cottage at once, a mile out of Exeter, 'a jewel of a place', with a respectable landlady, excellent parlour, beautiful little drawing room, noble garden, view of Exeter Cathedral, a thatched roof, cellars, coal holes, two or three bedrooms, etc., etc., and all exquisitely clean.[25] He took it immediately, stayed on to furnish it from local suppliers, and characteristically began to think how happily, if he were older, he himself might live there for many a year; only failing to consider that his parents were not choosing to live there but being told they must. Their opinion of the plan is not on record. He sent for his mother first, to deal with the curtains and prepare the house further, his father and brother to follow a few days later. His letters to Catherine were tender: 'To say how much I miss you, would be ridiculous. I miss the children in the morning too and their dear little voices which have sounds for you and me that we shall never forget.'[26] It looks as though their difficulties were no longer troubling him; and Catherine was pregnant again.

Having set up his parents, in May he took his own family to Elm Cottage at Petersham, a quiet village set between Richmond Park and the water meadows bordering the Thames. They stayed for four months, inviting the usual troops of friends to share their pleasures, the large garden with a swing, flowers and green leaves everywhere, glow worms jewelling the roads after dusk, the great tidal river. Dickens went to the races at Hampton several times, set up bowling, quoits and Battledore[27] to play with his friends, and caused amazement by getting up at six to plunge into the Thames and swim to Richmond Bridge before breakfast. He sometimes rode into town and back, even late in the evening, and now also had a carriage and groom to collect him when necessary. His fame can be judged by the fact that the local grandees wished to meet him, and on 1 July he dined at Little Strawberry Hill with the two ancient and learned Miss Berrys, Mary and Agnes, who had lived there since 1791, when their friend Horace Walpole had left them the house. They were historians and editors, they had known the salons of Paris before the Revolution and breathed another world; but what they made of Dickens, or he of them, is lost.

As he got on towards the end of *Nickleby* he began to turn over an idea for a new project to be carried out with Chapman & Hall the following year, that of a threepenny weekly magazine of occasional pieces and stories, which would be made up into volumes. He convinced himself that this would be less demanding than writing another novel as a serial, and it seemed to promise an attractive financial return. There was naturally much discussion with Forster. In July he also found that sending his father to Devon had not solved his problems. A letter with bad news from his mother made him 'sick at heart with both her and father too, and think this *is* too much', though he doesn't say what the trouble is. Then 'Alfred is instructed by his Papa that it's "all up"!!!'²⁸ His confidant was Mitton, who seems to have dealt with the problems for the moment.

Dickens was invited to speak at a celebratory dinner for Macready, after which Macready asked him to be godfather to his latest child. In agreeing, Dickens proposed that, in exchange, Macready should be godfather to the baby he and Catherine expected in the autumn, described as 'that last and final branch of a genteel small family of three'.²⁹ The letter makes clear that he wants to have no more than three children and sets up a mystery as to why, with his inquiring mind, and friends with medical knowledge, he appears to have done nothing to make sure that no more arrived.

From Petersham they went on almost at once, on 3 September, to Broadstairs, beside the sea in Kent, where they took another house and were joined by brother Fred for his holiday. Now Dickens's diary has the single word 'Work' every day until, on 20 September, he was able to write, 'Work./Finished Nickleby this day at 2 o'clock, and went over to Ramsgate with Fred and Kate to send the last little chapter to Bradbury & Evans in a parcel. Thank God that I have lived to get through it happily.'³⁰ Forster was due to come down, but Dickens decided to travel back to town himself to look over his proofs, so that they could dine together, go through the last number of *Nickleby* and take the boat in the morning, still together: 'beautiful passage. Kate and the dear children waiting for us at the pier.'³¹ After that it was swimming and sunshine from breakfast to dinner every day.

Nickleby was to be published in one volume in October. It was dedicated to Macready, and his favoured publishers, Chapman & Hall, were giving a celebratory dinner in the City on 5 October. Dickens said it was to be a quiet affair for one or two intimate friends, but in the event there were something like twenty guests and it turned into an occasion which Macready felt was 'too splendid'. The climax of the evening was the presentation of Maclise's portrait of Dickens, commissioned by Chapman & Hall and painted in the summer. The most attractive and the warmest of all the portraits, it shows him just turned away from the desk where he has been working, his eyes 'wonderfully beaming with intellect and running over with humour and cheerfulness', as Forster wrote later. He went on, 'there was that in the face as I first recollect it which no time could change . . . the quickness, the keenness, and practical power, the eager, restless, energetic outlook . . . Light and motion flashed from every part of it.'[32] This was Dickens as angel, with no sign of the blackguard.

To Bentley, Dickens did not appear as an angel. Bentley was expecting to receive the completed text of *Barnaby Rudge* in January, and was preparing to advertise it as a three-volume novel for 1840. But although Dickens told Cruikshank to expect chapters of the manuscript for illustration in October, and said he was getting on well with it, he soon put it aside again. His head was full of ideas for the weekly magazine he was proposing to edit for Chapman & Hall, to be called *Master Humphrey's Clock*. He was also, for good measure, scribbling some *Sketches of Young Couples*, also for Chapman & Hall; they would publish this anonymously, because he could not be seen to be breaking his agreement with Bentley to publish no other book.[33] So the tangle of his dealings with the rival publishers grew worse.

American publishers were adding to his distrust of the whole tribe. Across the Atlantic there was no legislation of any kind covering the rights of foreign authors, and publishers simply took what they wanted and did what they liked with it: for example, the Philadelphia firm of Carey, Lea & Blanchard had put out *Sketches by Boz* under several different titles in 1837, and incorporated part of *Oliver Twist* into one of the volumes, without asking permission or offering any payment to the author. In June 1837 they made their first contact

Engraving made from Maclise's portrait of 1839. When it was exhibited at the Royal Academy in 1840, Thackeray wrote in *Fraser's Magazine*: 'a looking-glass could not render a better facsimile. Here we have the real identical Dickens: the artist must have understood the inward Boz as well as the outward before he made this admirable representation of him . . . I think we may promise ourselves a brilliant future from this [countenance].'

with 'Mr Saml Dickens', as they called him, offering him a one-off payment of £25 for the parts of *Pickwick* they had been selling to the public since 1836 at large profit to themselves. In 1838 they sent Bentley £60 and Dickens £50 for advance proofs of *Oliver*, and tried to get proofs of *Nickleby*, because the acquisition of advance proofs put an American publisher into a stronger position against his rivals. Later they offered Dickens down payments of a little over £100 for advance proofs of *Master Humphrey's Clock* and *Barnaby Rudge*.[34] Dickens answered their letters politely, and for the moment accepted the situation he was helpless to change, but would challenge once he arrived in America.[35]

※

In the evening of 29 October 1839 a second Dickens daughter was born, named Kate for her mother, always known as Katey, and quite unlike her mother in her fiery disposition. Catherine was in labour for twelve hours, attended by a monthly nurse, by Dr Pickthorn and by her mother-in-law, who had come up from Devon, and to whom Dickens was paying five pounds for her services. He himself was suffering from one of his peculiarly lowering colds, declaring himself to be 'in such a sneezing, winking, weeping, watery state as to be quite unfit for public inspection'. But he was well enough to go house-hunting.[36] He had made up his mind that the house in Doughty Street was no longer big enough for the family's needs, and started looking at larger places around the southern end of Regent's Park; he also sent his mother to give her opinion of some of them. Speedy as ever, he found a suitable house within a week. It was No. 1 Devonshire Terrace, and he agreed to pay £800 for a twelve-year lease, with an annual rent of £160. Catherine's opinion does not seem to have been asked, and perhaps she hardly expected it to be, since six weeks' rest was usual for ladies after giving birth. In any case, her husband had chosen a very good house, large, light, airy and beautifully placed. Built in the 1770s, its main rooms were elegantly laid out on two floors, there were tall bow windows on the garden side, and the big walled garden was not overlooked by any other building. The park was across the road, and Portland Place and the West End a step away.[37]

Dickens was so eager to move that he offered many of the fittings he had put into Doughty Street to his landlord there, paid the rent to March when his lease expired and determined to be gone before Christmas. The new decade would be started in Devonshire Terrace, and he at once set about improving the house: installing mahogany doors, bookshelves, mantelpieces, great mirrors on the walls, thick carpets, white spring roller-blinds at every window, and the best available bathroom fittings. A dining table with five additional leaves was specially made for the columned dining room, and twelve leather chairs. The library became his study, its French windows opening on to a flight of steps down to the garden. There were nurseries in the attics, kitchens in the basement, cellars, a butler's pantry and a coach house in the mews at the end of the garden, in which Dickens presently installed a red-headed coachman called Topping.

The move was made in mid-December, when Catherine was back on her feet and Katey settled with her wet nurse. On the 16th Dickens told Bentley, who had indeed advertised *Barnaby Rudge*, thinking he was about to receive the completed manuscript, that he could not deliver it, and confessed that he had written only two chapters. The next day he described Bentley to Beard as 'the Burlington Street Brigand', promising 'war to the knife with no quarter on either side'. Beard was also asked to order cigars for him, 'a pound box of the unrivalled Cubas'.[38] The Dickens parents – 'relations from the country' as their son coolly described them – were at Devonshire Terrace for Christmas.[39] Chapman & Hall's printers, the businesslike William Bradbury and his partner Frederick Evans, a man as plump, cheerful and bespectacled as Mr Pickwick, sent round a gigantic turkey. On 2 January, Dickens wrote to them, 'The blessed bird made its appearance at breakfast yesterday, the other portions having furnished forth seven grills, one boil, and a cold lunch or two.'

Lucky not to have poisoned themselves, they embarked on the new decade. During the 1840s Dickens would be plagued with money problems and leave England to travel and live abroad for three long periods: to America, to Italy, and to Switzerland and

Paris. He would father five more unwanted sons. He would undergo surgery for a fistula in 1841, before chloroform was available, and insist on chloroform for Catherine in 1849 as she gave birth to their eighth child, Henry. He would see his sister Fanny die of tuberculosis and welcome his young sister-in-law Georgina Hogarth as a permanent member of his household. He would briefly edit a newspaper, change his publishers again, and embark on a long sequence of amateur theatrical productions. With his friend Miss Coutts he would set up an ambitious enterprise to help young prostitutes to start on new and better lives, establishing and organizing a Home for them in Shepherd's Bush. On top of this he would write two travel books; the first of his Christmas stories – the perennially popular *A Christmas Carol* – to be followed by more, all of which were dramatized; three full-scale novels, *Barnaby Rudge*, *Martin Chuzzlewit* and *Dombey and Son*. With *Dombey* he would at last reach a secure and comfortable financial position, and discover how much he enjoyed reading his own work aloud to friends, planting the idea of his later public readings. He would embark on *David Copperfield*, his own favourite among his novels. And he would appoint Forster to be his biographer.

Part Two

8

Killing Nell

1840–1841

As he approached his twenty-eighth birthday in February, Dickens knew himself to be famous, successful and tired. He needed and desired a rest, and he had made up his mind to keep 1840 free of the pressure of producing monthly instalments of another long novel. Instead, he intended to enjoy himself in a more leisurely way by editing *Master Humphrey's Clock*, the small miscellaneous weekly magazine. He planned to commission work from other writers and to contribute short stories and occasional essays himself; and to have pleasant dealings with his many artist friends about the fine illustrations that would adorn its pages. Chapman & Hall were to pay him £50 for each issue, plus half the profits, and he was confident that sales would be high. Copies would be distributed in Germany and America, and he expected to make something like £5,000 a year.

Things did not turn out as he hoped. The magazine, after selling 70,000 copies of the first number in April, failed to appeal to readers. Sales crashed. He saw that he must do something drastic to win them back, gave up the idea of a miscellany and realized he would have to be the sole contributor. The first thing to be done was to expand one slight story into a full-length serial, which meant he had to improvise from week to week a novel he had not even thought of in January. Instead of being free from the tyranny of writing serial fiction he found himself tied even more tightly to deadlines. He wrote to a friend lamenting that 'day and night the alarum is in my ears, warning me that I must not run down . . . I am more bound down by this Humphrey than I have ever been yet – Nickleby was nothing to it, nor Pickwick, nor Oliver – it demands my constant attention and obliges me to exert all the self-denial I possess.'[1]

Under this new strain his health suffered, and he was advised by his doctor to change his diet and take more exercise. In June he rented a house in Broadstairs, found it a propitious place for work and returned for another five weeks in September. Yet in London he crammed in as much as ever. He gave his time to good works, helping the unfortunate (Eliza Burgess, mentioned in the Prologue, was one) and encouraging poor aspirant writers, a carpenter and a young clerk, both of whom he advised patiently. Meanwhile his fame still grew. Maclise's portrait was shown at the Royal Academy, and engravings of it were in high demand. He made new friends, meeting at Lady Blessington's the brilliant and unconventional poet and essayist Walter Savage Landor, with whom he formed an immediate bond amid much joking and mutual admiration; and he travelled to Bath with Forster to visit him. At dinner with the politician Edward Stanley he first met Carlyle, who immediately produced a fine and florid description of him: 'clear blue intelligent eyes, eyebrows that he arches amazingly, large protrusive rather loose mouth – a face of the most extreme *mobility*, which he shuttles about, eyebrows, eyes, mouth and all, in a very singular manner while speaking, surmount this with a loose coil of common-coloured hair, and set it on a small compact figure, very small, and dressed rather *à la D'Orsay* than well'.[2] Mr and Mrs Carlyle became his friends. As to the colour of Dickens's eyes, they were reported variously as dark brown, dark glittering black, clear blue, 'not blue', distinct clear hazel, 'large effeminate eyes', clear grey, green-grey, dark slaty blue – with a little orange line surrounding the pupil – and even, by a cautious observer, as 'nondescript'.[3] Friends observed that he was short-sighted, but reluctant to be seen with spectacles.[4]

The aged Samuel Rogers, poet, art collector and retired banker, gave a dinner to introduce him to the three beautiful granddaughters of Sheridan: Lady Seymour and Lady Dufferin had succeeded in marrying into the aristocracy, while the third and cleverest, Caroline Norton, remained on the edge of society, estranged from her boorish husband, earning her living by writing, and touched with scandal, as Dickens knew from having reported the court case in which her name was linked with that of Lord Melbourne. Dickens was sympathetic, admiring and cautiously friendly.

Charles Dickens's grandmother worked as maid, then housekeeper, from 1781 to 1821, for John Crewe and his wife, Frances (*left and right above*), at their country seat, Crewe Hall (*above*), and their house in Mayfair. The Crewes' constant visitors were the brilliant politicians Charles James Fox (*left*) and Richard Brinsley Sheridan, promiscuous, hard-drinking, high-spending men: Crewe bailed out Fox, Sheridan had an affair with Mrs Crewe. The housekeeper's son, John Dickens, born 1785, grew up in this household. In 1805 he was given a job at the Navy Pay Office through the patronage of the Crewes and their friends.

In the first of these modest houses (*above left*) Charles Dickens was born in Portsmouth in 1812, the second child of John and Elizabeth Dickens. The family grew but the houses remained small: Ordnance Terrace, Chatham (*centre*), where they moved in 1817, and Bayham Street, Camden Town (*right*), into which they squeezed in 1822, by now with six children, a maid and a lodger.

In 1824 John Dickens was arrested for debt and held in the Marshalsea Prison. His wife and younger children moved in with him, leaving twelve-year-old Charles with a menial daytime job and lonely lodgings.

John Dickens saw himself as a gentleman of cultivated tastes, dressed smartly, borrowed money and ran up bills with his wine merchant. His wife Elizabeth's father also got into financial trouble, stealing from the Navy Pay Office for seven years until he was discovered and fled abroad.

Charles was put to work in a rat-infested warehouse on the Thames, below the Hungerford Market (*above*) now Charing Cross Station. His job was to cover and label pots of shoe blacking. He was bitter at being left without education, but he managed to live within his earnings, dividing the few coins he was paid into seven paper parcels each week to make sure he did not run out of money. After a time he persuaded his father to find him lodgings near the prison so that he could be close to his family. He observed the prisoners and thought about them as characters, and he also made up stories to amuse the little maid from the workhouse who still served the Dickenses.

Released from prison, John Dickens settled his family in The Polygon, a circle of houses in Somers Town, one of the new suburbs of North London, soon engulfed by more streets and sinking into shabbiness. It appears in *Bleak House* as the home of Harold Skimpole.

Charles's sister Fanny had gifts as a pianist and singer that won her prizes at the Royal Academy of Music, but her career was cut short and she died of tuberculosis in her thirties.

Charles loved his brother Fred, took him to live with him and found him a job, but Fred's scrounging and fecklessness became intolerable and he was cast aside and died penniless and alone.

Wellington Academy, where Charles had his second taste of education, was a low-grade private school at Mornington Crescent. He kept mice in his desk, learnt a bit of Latin and enjoyed boyish games. At fifteen he had to leave because of his father's renewed financial troubles, to become a smart office boy in a law firm.

At eighteen Charles had his portrait painted by his uncle Edward Barrow's wife Janet Ross, a professional artist. Dark curls, big eyes, carefully chosen clothes and a look that might be quizzical or apprehensive: he was about to fall in love with Maria Beadnell, who would torment him, and with the theatre, which grew into a lifelong obsession. He was also mastering shorthand to become a reporter.

The Adelphi Theatre on the Strand, where Dickens went almost nightly in the late 1820s and early 1830s to see the comic actor Charles Mathews perform his famous monopolylogues, studying his technique in order to become an actor. Later many adaptations of Dickens's books were played in the theatre.

In 1836 Dickens married Catherine Hogarth, daughter of a cultivated Scots family. Pleasant and docile, she could never match his energy or willpower.

In 1837 John Forster became Dickens's best friend and warmest admirer, advising and serving him in every way possible. In 1848 Dickens asked him to become his biographer, a task he fulfilled in the 1870s in his classic three-volume *Life*.

Catherine's younger sister Mary became part of the household, adored by Dickens. When she died suddenly at the age of seventeen, his grief was so intense that for the only time in his life he cancelled the next instalments of the two serials he was writing.

The house in Doughty Street was bought in 1837 with the money made from *Pickwick*. Here he wrote *Oliver Twist* and *Nicholas Nickleby*.

Forster introduced Dickens to William Macready, the leading tragic actor of the day, who became another close and lifelong friend.

The Irish artist Daniel Maclise, also introduced to Dickens by Forster, became a boon companion for some years, but later withdrew into gloomy reclusiveness.

Other friends included the comic actor John Pritt Harley, dressed to act in Dickens's farce *The Strange Gentleman* in 1836; the artist George Cruikshank, who illustrated Dickens's first book, *Sketches by Boz*, and *Oliver Twist*; and the artist Hablot Browne, who took the name 'Phiz' to go with Dickens's nom de plume 'Boz', illustrated *The Pickwick Papers* and worked with Dickens for twenty-three years.

A powerful, idealizing portrait of Dickens by Margaret Gillies, exhibited in 1844, engraved and since lost. Gillies was London-born in 1803, educated in Edinburgh and returned to London to earn her living as a painter. From the 1830s she lived with Dr Southwood Smith, the sanitary reformer and member of the royal commission on the employment of children, who had separated from his wife. Dickens knew him well, consulted him and trusted his advice. Gillies exhibited at the Royal Academy, and was interested in portraying 'true nobility, that of genius … to call out what is most beautiful and refined in our nature'. Other sitters were Harriet Martineau, Jeremy Bentham and Wordsworth.

He enthusiastically attended rehearsals and the first night of Talfourd's play *Glencoe*, with Macready in the leading role. In July he overcame his proclaimed disapproval of public executions to watch the hanging of Courvoisier, the valet who cut the throat of his master, the elderly Lord William Russell: Dickens had followed the trial closely and written two letters to the press objecting to the behaviour of the defending lawyer. He went with Catherine to Lichfield and Stratford early in the year, and in July took her with him to visit his parents in their Devon cottage, snatching a few days of holiday in Dawlish and Torquay. He gave a great celebration for the christening of their daughter Katey in August. 'Rather a noisy and uproarious day . . . not so much *comme il faut* as I could have wished,' observed Macready, who presented a gold watch and chain to his god-daughter, and a sovereign to her nurse. Between the ceremony and the dinner Dickens carried off as many of his friends as were willing for his idea of a treat, which was a tour of Coldbath Fields Prison. Catherine was now three months into another pregnancy.

Emotions ran high between him and Forster: in July, Dickens presented him with the claret jug which, he suggested, held his heart, and in August they had a row over the dinner table, no doubt fuelled by drink, but bad enough to make Catherine burst into tears and run from the room. It was quickly made up. Dickens had a temper and Forster could be pompous, but, as he put it, their 'hasty differences' were 'such only as such intimate friends are apt to fall into'.[5]

These were all distractions from the central business of the year, which was the story that had started as a few episodes and was being made into a novel, week by week, *The Old Curiosity Shop*. Against all the odds, it became the second-highest seller of all his books, surpassed only by *The Pickwick Papers*, another improvised tale. What sort of a story was it? A very odd one, a picaresque tale of a child who tries and fails to escape from her fate, with a supposed protector, her grandfather, addicted to gambling, and a grotesquely wicked pursuer, the dwarf Quilp, both putting her at risk and driving her towards her death. Nell herself has no character beyond sweetness, goodness and innocence, which endeared her to male readers; and Lord Jeffrey, the great Scottish judge, critic and sometime editor of the *Edinburgh Review*, even likened her to Cordelia, although the only resemblance is in their untimely deaths. At the age of thirteen, Nell effectively has to look after her grandfather, who has been corrupted by his fascination with money, rather as Dickens's maternal grandfather had been corrupted by money, and his father also, overspending, borrowing and failing to settle his debts; so this aspect of the story was quite close to home. And while there is very much more in the book than Nell, it is her death that made its fame. It was Forster who suggested that Dickens should kill her off: he seized the idea, and the slowly approaching death of Little Nell held readers in a state of excited anxiety on both sides of the Atlantic for many weeks. Letters came to Dickens imploring him to save her, and grave and normally equable men sobbed uncontrollably when they read that she was dead.

Dickens himself suffered as he wrote of Nell's decline, and shared his sufferings with his friends through November and December 1840. He told Forster, 'You can't imagine how exhausted I am today with yesterday's labours . . . All night I have been pursued by the child; and this morning I am unrefreshed and miserable. I don't know what to do with myself . . . I think the close of the story will be great.' Then, a few days later, 'The difficulty has been tremendous – the anguish unspeakable.'[6] To his illustrator, Cattermole, he wrote, 'I am breaking my heart over this story, and cannot bear to finish it.'[7] In January, Macready was told, 'I am slowly murdering that poor child, and grow wretched over it. It wrings my heart. Yet it must be.' A few days later it was Maclise who heard, 'If you knew what I have been suffering in the death of that child!'[8]

Another letter to Forster shows how Dickens used his suffering, deliberately summoning up painful feelings, in the cause of telling a better story: 'I shan't recover it for a long time. Nobody will miss her like I shall. It is such a very painful thing to me, that I really cannot express my sorrow . . . I have refused several invitations for this week and next, determining to go nowhere till I had done. *I am afraid of disturbing the state I have been trying to get into, and having to fetch it all back again.*'[9]

In such a state of mind he could not bear to be distracted or crossed, and there was a disconcerting episode when, as he was writing these chapters, Macready's three-year-old daughter, Joan, died suddenly. Dickens sent him an affectionate note, as a close but busy friend, while Forster, who was Joan's godfather and adored her, visited Macready daily, shared his grief, went to the funeral and gave way to intense sorrow himself. At this Dickens complained to Maclise about Forster's 'amazing display of grief': 'I vow to God that if you had seen Forster last night, you would have supposed our Dear Friend was dead himself.'[10] It looks as though he was jealous that Forster had turned his attention aside from the imaginary death they had dreamt up together to mourn the death of a real child, and in his jealousy raged against him. Little Nell must not be upstaged, even by Macready's dead daughter.

When Dickens reached Nell's death he chose not to describe it, but to let it happen offstage, in the village church where she and her grandfather had found shelter.[11] If he was torn to bits by his feelings, Victorian families, with their all too frequent experience of the deaths of children, responded in their thousands. Christianity told them they must accept and even be glad when a child went to heaven, but this hardly makes sense to a grieving parent. Macready put the case with stoic dignity, 'I have lost my child. There is no comfort for that sorrow; there is endurance – that is all.'[12] This seems right, and much truer than any suggestion that dead children turn into angels and proceed to enjoy themselves, but Dickens set out to palliate and soothe. Although he showed that Nell herself feared death, once she is dead he offers conventional words of comfort: 'Sorrow was dead indeed in her, but peace and perfect happiness were born; imaged in her tranquil beauty and profound repose.' His intention was 'to try and do something which might be read by people about whom Death had been, – with a softened feeling, and with consolation.'[13] With such readers in mind, he asked his illustrator to draw a tailpiece to the story, 'giving some notion of the etherealised spirit of the child'. Cattermole understood perfectly and showed her being lifted up to heaven by four angels, her eyes shut and a slight smile on her face.[14]

To modern readers, Little Nell herself is less interesting than her travels as she leaves London, walking through the edges of town where houses gave way to brickfields, past small Dissenting chapels and piles of oyster shells; and later through the Black Country, with its cinder-paths, blazing furnaces and roaring steam-engines, its miserable workers and starving children, which Dickens had seen for himself two years before; or taking refuge with stout Mrs Jarley who travels about with a hundred wide-eyed waxwork figures in her caravan, Mary Queen of Scots and Mr Pitt keeping company with a wife murderer and the wild boy of the woods. And there is a cast of remarkable characters, starting with Mr Quilp, the malevolent dwarf who hopes that Nell might become his second wife. Quilp delighted Dickens as Squeers did, by his sheer wickedness and energy, and is a pleasure to read about as he drinks boiling spirits from the saucepan, eats hard-boiled eggs with their shells, taunts and threatens his wife and mother-in-law, lusts after Nell, bites, pinches and plots evil like a pantomime villain.

Another section of the story is given to Dick Swiveller, a lanky, humorous clerk who keeps a notebook with the names of streets he has to avoid because he owes money to the shopkeepers. Like the young Dickens, Swiveller yearns after an unattainable girl for a while, is much given to quoting from popular poetry and coins special phrases of his own: alcohol is 'the rosy', sleep is 'the balmy', a single drink is a 'modest quencher' and a piece of bad news is 'a staggerer'. Working in a law office, he becomes aware that there is a small, half-starved girl-child kept locked in the basement, dressed in cast-off clothes, 'a small slipshod girl in a coarse apron and bib, which left nothing of her visible but her face and feet. She might as well have been dressed in a violin case.' She does all the work of the house and has no name. 'There never was such an old-fashioned child in her looks and manner. She must have been at work from her cradle.' First he pities her and then he becomes interested in her. 'She never went out, or came into the office, or had a clean face, or took off the coarse apron, or looked out of any one of the windows, or stood at the street door for a breath of air, or had any rest or enjoyment whatever. Nobody ever came to see her, nobody spoke of her, nobody cared about her.'[15] Dick's lawyer employer, Mr Brass, had said once that he believed she was 'a love-child', and a note in the manuscript suggests she was the daughter of his sister Sally Brass and Quilp. As Dickens adds, the name of love-child means anything but a child of love, and this little slavey is the embodiment of his dictum that 'the poor have no childhood. It must be bought and paid for.'[16] Dick privately teaches her to play cards, gives her food and drink, including 'purl', a cheering concoction of boiling hot beer with gin, sugar and ginger, grows fond of her and names her 'the Marchioness' in tribute to her extraordinary independence and dignity. She is thirteen, the same age as Nell, and has brains and character, but she is allowed only a small strand of the plot. Dickens may have worried that she would steal the limelight, and he cut short the tale of the poor clerk and the slavey, sketching in an adventure for them, and an improbably cheerful conclusion.[17]

❧

During the September visit to Broadstairs, while he was working hard on *The Old Curiosity Shop*, Dickens was observed by a clever young woman of nineteen, Eleanor Picken. She is a valuable witness because hers is the only written account of the impression he made on a young woman while he was still young himself. She published nothing until after his death, but she goes into enough detail to suggest she had kept notes at the time she knew him, and she says she drew on her diary; and her response to him is so fresh and frank that you are ready to trust what she says. It is also ambivalent. She remembered the days at Broadstairs as 'almost the brightest in my life', but she was worried by his changes of mood, and miserably upset when, having played games with her, flirted and teased her, he retreated into cold politeness and made it clear that he wanted to have nothing more to do with her. 'I had been so proud of the notice of so great a man, I had sunned myself in his smiles, that it was like an untimely frost,' she wrote wistfully.[18]

Eleanor had lost her father, a writer, as a child. She was well educated and had her own ambitions to write and to paint. She had been taken under the wing of the family of Charles Smithson, one of Dickens's lawyers, a partner of Mitton, after becoming unofficially engaged to a family connection of the Smithsons, who invited her to dinner to meet Mr and Mrs Dickens in the summer of 1840. He was already famous and she was excited to meet him, and ready to be awestruck. But she was not uncritical. While she admired his marvellous eyes and long hair, she did not like his taste in dress, the huge collar and vast expanse of waistcoat, and the boots with patent toes. She described him as sucking his tongue when he was thinking, dragging his fingers through his hair and comically raising one eyebrow before making a joke. She also said that he had a thickness in his speech, as if his tongue were slightly too large for his mouth, and she noticed the same thing in his brother Fred and their father. At the Smithsons' dinner Forster was a fellow guest, and Dickens let him hold forth while seeming preoccupied himself – this was perhaps when he sucked his tongue and ran his hand through his hair. Soon after this dinner he urged the Smithsons to take a house at Broadstairs, where he was going to be with his family in September. They did so, and Eleanor went with them. Mrs Smithson acted as chaperone, and her unmarried sister, Amelia Thompson, was also of the party. Although Amelia was ten years older than Eleanor, who described her as being 'of a certain age', they were good friends and went about together.

Eleanor found Mrs Dickens kindly and likeable. Her contribution to the fun of the family was making puns, the more outrageous the better, with an innocent expression, while Dickens tore his hair and pretended to writhe in agony. He was more complicated. Having looked forward with some excitement to spending her holiday close to the great man, Eleanor found that his moods changed without warning from day to day, now genial, now cold. His high spirits were contagious; his bad moods made her wonder how there could ever be any friendship with him. We know that he was producing weekly episodes of *The Old Curiosity Shop* that September, and that he usually worked from Tuesday to Friday, when he sent his copy to London, and corrected proofs of the previous number on Saturday to send with his comments to Forster on Sunday.[19] This meant he had to keep to a strict timetable, but Eleanor and Amelia were unaware of this, only that on one day he would initiate or join in games, and the next day walk past without a greeting, his eyes like 'danger-lamps'. She remembered that 'at these times I confess I was horribly afraid of him', although not too afraid to tell him later how much he had frightened her, and to observe that her confession amused him.

The games they played included Vingt-et-un – gambling with cards for small sums of money and cheating wildly to add to the fun – guessing games like Animal, Vegetable, Mineral, and charades. Dickens sometimes addressed the two young women in cod Elizabethan English, as 'charmer', 'fair enslaver', 'sweet lady', and asked them to dance with 'Wilt tread a measure with me?' After his brother Fred arrived to join them there was a memorable evening when the Dickens brothers, fooling about on the pier with Eleanor and Milly, decided that the four of them should dance a quadrille to music provided by Fred whistling and Charles playing on his pocket-comb. After the dance they walked to the end of the pier to watch the evening light fade as the tide came in. Eleanor tells her story well:

Dickens seemed suddenly to be possessed with the demon of mischief; he threw his arm around me and ran me down the inclined plane to the end of the jetty till we reached a tall post. He put his other arm round this, and exclaimed in theatrical tones that he intended to hold me there till 'the sad sea waves' should submerge us.

'Think of the emotion we shall create! Think of the road to celebrity which you are about to tread! No, not exactly to *tread*, but to flounder into!'

Here I implored him to let me go, and struggled hard to release myself.

'Let your mind dwell on the column in *The Times* wherein will be vividly described the pathetic fate of the lovely E. P., drowned by Dickens in a fit of dementia! Don't struggle, poor little bird; you are powerless in the claws of such a kite as this, child!'

. . . The tide was coming up rapidly and surged over my feet. I gave a loud shriek and tried to bring him back to common sense by reminding him that 'My dress, my best dress, my *only* silk dress, would be ruined.' Even this climax did not soften him: he still went on with his serio-comic nonsense, shaking with laughter all the time, and panting with his struggles to hold me.

'Mrs Dickens!' a frantic shriek this time, for now the waves rushed up to my knees; 'help me! make Mr Dickens let me go – the waves are up to my knees!'

The rest of the party had now arrived, and Mrs Dickens told him not to be so silly, and not to spoil Eleanor's dress. 'Dress!' cried Dickens . . . 'talk not to me of *dress*! When the pall of night is enshrouding us . . . when we already stand on the brink of the great mystery, shall our thoughts be of fleshly vanities?'

Eleanor finally succeeded in wrestling herself free. Her clothes were wet, and Mrs Smithson scolded her and thought her to blame. She may have had some reason. Clearly there was some chemistry between Eleanor and Dickens, and he must have felt that she enjoyed his attentions. She was after all the star of the evening, the chosen one, even if chosen as victim. But he was an aggressive admirer. On two occasions he rushed her under a waterfall, ruining the bonnet she was wearing each time, and he pulled her hair during games, a gesture both boyish and intimate. Quilp was in his mind, and his behaviour was Quilpish. But Eleanor was not a meek girl, and she also describes how she argued with him during games, and stood up for herself.

Eleanor Picken married her naval officer Edward Christian in 1842. She published two accounts of that September at Broadstairs, the first appearing a year after Dickens died, when she was fifty, and the second in the late 1880s, incorporating material about the Dickens parents that she had tactfully left out before. Evidently they had been in Broadstairs, and she described John Dickens as a good-looking man, 'rather an "old buck"' in his dress, and Elizabeth Dickens as agreeable and matter-of-fact, with no sign of Mrs Nickleby that she could see, in spite of Dickens's claim that his mother was the model for her. But she did love dancing, and her son seemed to disapprove of this, and looked 'as sulky as a bear' when she took to the dance floor with one or the other of her polite sons-in-law, Henry Austin or Henry Burnett. Both parents, Eleanor noticed, were ill at ease with Charles, and seemed to be in fear of offending him; and with reason, since at this time his father was being particularly troublesome about money.

Back in London, Eleanor went to lunch at Devonshire Terrace with the Smithsons, and found Dickens distant in manner. She called later to show them a portrait drawing she had made of Catherine, and while Catherine received Eleanor with great friendliness, he refused to see her or even to look at the picture. She was so upset that she left the house and did not call again. When they met again by chance at a ball, he was coldly polite, and Fred explained to her that he was 'odd sometimes'; this was in Broadstairs again, in 1842, after her marriage. Two things might help to explain why he turned against her. One was that she was ready to argue with him. Since his marriage he had been used to deference, while Eleanor describes herself defending Byron's verses when he criticized them, and standing up for herself generally. The other was that he may have noticed her diary keeping and objected to it. Dickens was the observer, and had no wish to be the observed. Whatever the reason for his change of attitude, she did not forget him, and eighteen years later she made one more attempt to speak to him, after a reading, described in Chapter 20.

Dickens's agonizing over the death of Little Nell did not hold him back from entertaining. There was an October feast, with many toasts, for all involved in the publication of *Master Humphrey's Clock*, designers, printers, publishers and woodcutters. There was a small party with charades on Christmas Eve, and a great New Year's Eve celebration, with dancing, more charades and 'frolics'. On Christmas Day he walked round the park 'at a posting rate' with Forster and Macready, fallings-out forgotten. Forster wrote to Dickens assuring him that *The Old Curiosity Shop* was his literary masterpiece, and the later numbers sold 100,000 a week. All this was good, but Dickens knew he must keep the magazine going for another year at least, and *Barnaby Rudge*, planned and started in 1839, began to appear on 13 February 1841, to run to December.

It was the least popular of his books at the time, and has remained so. Trying his hand at a historical novel, where Scott had been supreme and his friend Ainsworth successful, he was not on his own territory. The two most striking and memorable features of the story are Barnaby himself, the simple-minded hero with a pet raven, who wanders innocently through the mysteries of the plot; and the description of the Gordon Riots of 1780, when the London mob opened prisons, set fire to many buildings and caused mayhem. But the book is far too long for what it does, the villains are cardboard, the young women insipid, the plotting absurd, and Lord George Gordon himself barely characterized. Dickens moves into crude melodrama, as when Barnaby's father, the murderous Rudge, addresses himself with rhetorical questions, 'Do I fancy that I killed him? . . . Did I go home when I had done? . . . Did I stand before my wife, and tell her? . . . Did she go down upon her knees, and call on Heaven to witness that she and her unborn child renounced me from that hour . . .?'[20] Even Forster could not summon enthusiasm, and one reviewer wrote sadly of the 'man of genius winding himself up like a three years' clock'.[21]

Dickens knew he had to keep winding himself up to meet his obligations to Chapman & Hall. He owed them money, and his family was growing – a second son, Walter, was born the day after his own twenty-ninth birthday, on 8 February 1841. His habits were expensive, and Lord Jeffrey, visiting him in London in April, remarked on his giving 'rather too sumptuous a dinner for a man with a family, and only beginning to be rich'.[22] His brother Alfred could not get work, and Dickens was trying to find him a position in New Zealand. Their father was behaving outrageously, forging his signature on bills, which sometimes turned up at Chapman & Hall's offices as well as Devonshire Terrace. In March, enraged by this behaviour, Dickens put a notice in the London newspapers, disclaiming responsibility for promissory notes and saying he would not discharge any debts but his own and his wife's. He also did his best to persuade his father to move abroad, offering him a pension for himself, school fees for Augustus and an extra £40 a year for his mother should she wish to remain in England; but John Dickens refused to go.

In May, Dickens was invited to stand for parliament as the second Liberal candidate for Reading, where Talfourd was already an MP. He would have to pay his own expenses, it was expected that the Conservatives would win, and Talfourd had already decided not to stand; not surprisingly Dickens, though flattered by being asked, turned down the request. Still more flattering was the invitation to travel to Scotland to receive the Freedom of the City of Edinburgh in June. He left an unseasonably cold London to travel north with Catherine, to a warm and enthusiastic welcome. Crowds gathered round their hotel, and over 250 gentlemen attended the public dinner in his honour; the ladies were allowed into a gallery for the speeches after the meal. John Wilson, Professor of Moral Philosophy and formidable chief critic of *Blackwood's* under the name of Christopher North, praised his originality, compared him with Defoe and Fielding, and shrewdly pointed out as his one failure his inability to create women characters. Dickens replied gracefully, speaking of Little Nell – unmentioned by North – and saying that his intention had been to soften grief and 'put a garland of fresh flowers' on the subject of death. Speeches and toasts went on until midnight, Dickens speaking twice more. He kept Forster informed of the Edinburgh festivities and wished he were sharing in them; and he had to ask his publishers to send him a banknote for £50 to cover his expenses. Then, guided by their friend Angus Fletcher, the Scottish sculptor, he and Catherine set off on a short coach tour of the Highlands. The rain poured down, the winds blew, the cold was intense, the inns offered only beds of straw, and they narrowly missed being drowned fording a swollen river; and as they travelled, Dickens got on steadily with the next number of *Barnaby Rudge*.

Meanwhile in London an enterprising team had already dramatized *Barnaby*, although it was only half written, and put it on stage at the Lyceum, with the name part played by a young actress named Julia Fortescue. She was something of a hit. Maclise found her 'transcendent' and wrote to Dickens about her. Both had seen her in small parts in earlier adaptations of his novels, and Maclise teased him about his supposed interest in 'the wild attractions of her legs', her charm and beauty, her small waist, 'woman bust' and perfectly modulated voice. She played with such vivacity that Macready also went to see her, invited her to join his company at Drury Lane and rehearsed her in Shakespearean parts, including Juliet. He was disappointed in her progress, perhaps because she did not give her undivided attention to rehearsals. She had acquired a titled, and married, lover, Lord Gardner, Lord of the Bedchamber to the Queen and a favourite at court, and Julia was soon to bear him the first of five children. Macready did not allow her to play Juliet, and her professional career suffered from her personal situation, but several years later, in 1845 and again in 1848, she acted with Dickens's amateurs. He knew her well and was aware of her equivocal position, and how she was obliged to be secretive about it.[23]

Dickens and Maclise joked about women, and Maclise as a bachelor got plenty of teasing for his susceptibility and love-affairs. That August, when Dickens was at Broadstairs and Maclise was unwell in London, he urged him to come down for the good of his health and enjoy six weeks of sea air and rest, telling him he could eat and drink as he liked, get up when he liked and go to bed when he liked, and that, 'There are conveniences of all kinds at Margate (do you take me?) and I know where they live.'[24] The conveniences are prostitutes, and Dickens is telling Maclise he has located them in nearby Margate. It doesn't sound like a joke. Did Dickens go out and look for the Margate prostitutes simply to find out where they were for Maclise's sake? Or because he took an interest in seeing them and talking to them, for whatever mixture of reasons? Was he thinking of using their services himself? He had a reason for not wanting Catherine to become pregnant, in that he was planning a trip to America and a new pregnancy might prevent her going with him. His letter to Maclise continues 'in serious and sober earnestness' to urge him to come to Broadstairs, but whether Maclise did, and whether they went to Margate together, naturally remains unknown.

Dickens was unwell. He had been suffering from bilious attacks last-
ing for several days, and severe indigestion. He was also worried
about his professional future, fearing that he was burning himself out
and making himself too cheap. He knew that he had to have a break,
but how was it to be financed? In London in late August for a meeting with Chapman & Hall, he persuaded Forster, who was their
literary adviser as well as his personal agent, to present a further plan
to them, by which they would pay him to do nothing for a year and
then he would start to write a long novel in November 1842. He
would be paid for each monthly instalment, get three quarters of the
profits and retain half the copyright. *Master Humphrey's Clock* would
be closed down when *Barnaby* came to an end. However taken aback
the publishers were by this suggestion, they agreed to it. As Robert
Patten puts it, the agreement made between Dickens and Forster and
Chapman & Hall was 'a bold bet on one man's future creativity'.[25]
Dickens then raised the question of his wish to visit America, which
they declared themselves happy about. He told Forster he had made
up his mind to go. He persuaded Catherine to go with him and was
persuaded by Macready not to think of taking the children; and the
Macreadys offered to keep a close watch on them during their parents' absence. Now Devonshire Terrace had to be let and a smaller
house near the Macreadys found for the children, their nursemaids
and Fred, who would stay with them; and passages must be booked
for Dickens, Catherine and her maid Anne.

While all this was under way, Dickens became so ill that surgery
became necessary and urgent. He was suffering from an anal fistula.
The operation was carried out at home and, at that date, without anaesthetic.[26] It was performed by a specialist surgeon, Frederick Salmon, on
8 October, with entire success. Macready called that evening and suffered sympathetic agonies with his friend. A few days later he brought
Browning with him, and they found Dickens 'going on very comfortably'. The next day he was dictating letters to Catherine.

He was well set on the road to recovery, and intending to go to
Windsor to convalesce as soon as he was allowed to travel, when news
came of the sudden death of Catherine's brother George Hogarth. It
happened as unexpectedly as Mary Hogarth's, and upset Dickens as

much as Catherine, not because he knew George well but because he had been expecting to be buried beside Mary, and now felt he must give up that place to her brother. He was intensely distressed, told Forster that his love for Mary would never diminish, and that it felt like losing her for a second time.

Still, he reached the last words of *Barnaby* on 5 November, standing up to write, and two days later he and Catherine were installed at the White Hart in Windsor. After an alarming day of pains and twitches in his back and calves and a visit to the surgeon, he was soon himself again, and they returned home. On 8 December he told Lord Jeffrey, 'I am not at all tired with idleness . . . I have done nothing but walk, and lounge about, and read drowsily, all day long. – What do you think of my reading the Curiosity Shop, *all through*?'[27] He was well enough to go and sit to the Count D'Orsay for a portrait drawing in the morning, but not to dine, 'both because I want to hold on tight by my household Gods to the last, and on account of my health which I am afraid may suffer from too much dining'.[28] Both *The Old Curiosity Shop* and *Barnaby Rudge* were published, each in one volume, on 15 December. There were clothes to be made for America, letters of credit to be obtained, maps to be studied, introductions to be provided, packing to be done. Then only Christmas to be got through before they said goodbye to children and friends and took the train for Liverpool, to embark on the thoroughly up-to-date *Britannia*, the first Cunard wooden paddle-steamer to be built.

9

Conquering America

1842

Dickens was going to America to give himself a mental shake as well as a holiday from the pressure of constant writing. He knew he could be certain of a warm reception – enthusiasm for his work among American readers ran high – and he was confident that he would be able to gather enough material from his travels to make a book. He went also intending to raise the question of international copyright and the pirating of his books in America, which deprived him of the income on which he as a writer depended, with the idea that a change in the law might be brought about: hearing of his proposed visit, Lea & Blanchard reissued all his work in twenty parts and boldly invited him to visit them in Philadelphia.[1] But he had a more profound reason for making the long journey, and this was his desire to test out the hope that a better society was being established there, free of monarchy, aristocracy and worn-out conventions – to see 'the Republic of my imagination'.[2] The Americans, for their part, saw him specifically as 'The Great Republican of the Literary World', the English writer who was on their side, who believed in liberty and democracy, and who showed in his books that he cared about ordinary people and thought the poor more worthy of attention than the rich.[3] They prepared to give him an ecstatic welcome, and at the time of his arrival the *New York Herald* wrote: 'His mind is American – his soul is republican – his heart is democratic.'[4]

The *Britannia* would take them to Boston, and from there they would progress to New York, Washington and Baltimore and into the South, then as far west as St Louis, north through Ohio, across Lake Erie to Buffalo and Niagara Falls, and into Canada, before returning to New York for the return voyage in June. In all, they would be travelling more than 2,000 miles, sometimes through rough country, by railway, coach, canal and riverboat. It was a bold project. What he did not foresee was the American response to his fame, and how, after the first enjoyably triumphant week, the celebrity tour would become an irritating and exhausting ordeal, and pleasure would give way to resentment.

In his determination to get away he had booked their crossing in midwinter. They were to leave on 4 January and the *Britannia* was expected to reach Boston in two weeks. Devonshire Terrace was let, and the children were moved the short distance to Osnaburgh Street, where three nurses and a governess were to look after them, and their uncle Fred would also keep a close eye on things; and each day they were to go to the Macreadys. Charley was about to be five, Mamie three, Katey two and baby Walter not yet one, all of them too young to understand that their parents were to be away for an unimaginably long period of half a year. Farewell embraces made, Dickens, Catherine and her maid Anne took the Liverpool train on 2 January, accompanied by Forster. They had arranged to spend two comfortable nights at the Adelphi Hotel, and a small group was assembling in Liverpool to make their goodbyes, including the sculptor Angus Fletcher and Fanny Burnett, Dickens's sister, who came from Manchester. A preliminary visit of inspection to the *Britannia* dismayed Dickens when he saw the size of their stateroom. He complained that it was too small to admit their trunks, had bunk beds, and 'When the door is open, you can't turn round. When it's shut you can't put on a clean shirt, or take off a dirty one.'[5] Catherine took a more cheerful view, and remained on board while Dickens returned to the Adelphi for a farewell banquet of turtle, cold punch, hock, claret and champagne, after which the whole party escorted Dickens back to the ship, boarding it and 'indiscriminately shaking hands all around' before they left, as another passenger noted drily, only Dickens himself remaining composed.[6] Forster presented him with a pocket Shakespeare for his travels.

The Atlantic crossing turned out to be one of the worst the ship's officers had ever known. There were gales and high seas for much of the time, and it took eighteen days. Dickens and Catherine were both ill for most of the first week. On the tenth day the smokestack had to be lashed with chains to stop it being blown over and setting fire to the decks. All the lifeboats were smashed by the bad weather. Catherine wrote afterwards to her sister-in-law Fanny, 'I was nearly distracted with terror and don't know what I should have done had it not been for the great kindness and composure of my dear Charles.'[7] She developed toothache and a swollen face, but gallantly joined in games of whist in which all the players had to keep their tricks in their pockets and found themselves flung from their seats and rolling out of the saloon doors as the ship bucketed and plunged. When they approached Halifax in Nova Scotia they ran aground, and had to wait for the rising tide to release them from the rocks. But once they had put in to the harbour Dickens went ashore for oysters and cheered up, and as the *Britannia* continued south he stood on deck in the clear, frosty air, looking out eagerly as the coast of America gradually came in sight.

Boston, their first American city, seen under snow and in crisp, cold sunshine, delighted him, a place as bright and clean as a new toy, with its painted signboards in the streets, green blinds at every window, elegant white wooden houses, prim, varnished churches and chapels, and handsome public buildings. There were no beggars, and the city was run on admirable principles, with state-funded welfare institutions. Most of those who guided and befriended him were Harvard graduates, men of intellectual refinement and taste. Cornelius Felton, Professor of Greek, was firmly of the opinion that Dickens rivalled Shakespeare in his powers of invention, invited the Dickenses to dinner at once and became a friend for life. William H. Prescott, the historian, author of *The Conquest of Mexico*, gave another dinner for them. The poet Longfellow called, took Dickens out walking and found him 'a glorious fellow'. Charles Sumner, a young radical republican who went on to lead the anti-slavery movement in the Senate, showed him round the city. Some Bostonians had reservations about their famous visitor, finding him 'low-bred' or touched by 'rowdyism' — their word for vulgarity — with his coloured waistcoats and long hair, but then succumbed to his charm and acknowledged how clever he was — 'the *cleverest* man I ever met' wrote the author and politician Richard Dana, a respected Boston writer.[8]

A delegation from the 'Young Men of Boston', a group formed the previous November when his visit was announced, arrived at his hotel to invite him to a celebratory dinner on 1 February.[9] At the dinner he was welcomed as Boz, who could not be a stranger, and replied that he had dreamt for years of 'setting foot upon this shore, and breathing this pure air'. He laid great stress on his message as a writer who took for his subject 'the rejected ones whom the world has too long forgotten, and too often misused', and he said that letters from American readers about Nell, Oliver and Smike had encouraged him to come. After this he touched on the question of international copyright. This first time his remarks were politely ignored.[10]

So far so good. He was able to spend a day visiting factories at nearby Lowell and was much impressed by what he saw, especially the well-educated girl mill-workers, and he wrote to Forster, 'I have a book already.'[11] He also visited the Asylum for the Blind, the House of Industry for the Indigent, the School for Neglected Boys, the Reformatory for Juvenile Offenders and the prison, or House of Correction for the State, and found them models of their kind. But it was not long before he and Catherine began to wilt under the requests for autographs and letters inviting them to visit every part of the country, the deputations, the cheering crowds that gathered when he went out in the afternoon, the ladies who tried to snip bits off his fur coat and asked for locks of his hair. They were obliged to shake hands with many hundreds of people. Painters wanted to paint him, sculptors to sculpt him. He found the hotel rooms 'infernally hot', and he missed his usual long walks and rides. 'There never was a King or Emperor upon the Earth so cheered, and followed by crowds ... and waited on by public bodies and deputations of all kinds.'[12] America was gripped by hysteria. 'People *eat* him here,' wrote one sober Bostonian to his father in Washington.[13] Dickens now sensibly took on a secretary, George Putnam, an aspiring painter of his own age, to help him deal with the situation, and he proved efficient and congenial enough to be kept on for the rest of the trip.

When they left Boston on 5 February the entire management of their hotel was in the lobby to see them off, and twenty-five men who just happened to be there also insisted on shaking their hands.

Even so, Boston was more pleasure than pain, and it remained his favourite city. In Worcester, Springfield and Hartford they were again greeted with rapture, and at Hartford Dickens again raised the matter of international copyright. The dinner guests said nothing, but the local paper took the view that he should be pleased with his popularity and grateful for it too, and that it was mercenary to fuss about pirated copies. Much of the American press followed suit.

Catherine continued to have trouble with a swollen face, while managing to impress everyone with her straightforward and friendly disposition, but both were finding the demands of celebrity exhausting. They were obliged to spend two hours each day shaking hands with the hundreds who flocked to them wherever they were, determined not to miss their chance to meet the famous visitors. Dickens made up his mind to accept no more invitations after those already agreed for New York, although this was easier said than done. His good friend Felton came from Boston to travel with them by boat to New York, offering him just the sort of companionship he enjoyed. On the way he and Catherine were agreeably serenaded by the Yale students at New Haven, but also obliged to shake hands with another 500 strangers.

New York was preparing an extravaganza, a 'Boz Ball', for which 5,000 people had applied for tickets and 3,000 succeeded in obtaining them. It took place the day after their arrival, on the evening of 14 February, in the Park Theater, with its stage enlarged and turned into a ballroom decorated with medallions showing characters from Dickens's novels, and lit with hundreds of gaslights. When all the guests were assembled, Dickens appeared on the arm of a general in full-dress uniform, as the band played 'See the Conquering Hero Comes', followed by Catherine on the arm of the Mayor. They were cheered as they made a grand march twice round the ballroom. Actors then presented a series of tableaux from the novels, after which food was served. Dickens sent Maclise the Bill of Fare, which included 50,000 oysters, 10,000 sandwiches, 40 hams, 50 jellied turkeys, 12 Floating Swans, 350 quarts of jelly and blanc mange, and 300 quarts of ice cream. Then there was dancing: 'Heaven knows how we did it, for there was no room. And we continued dancing until, being no longer able even to stand, we slipped away quietly,' he told Forster. He was amused to read in a newspaper that he had never been in such society in England as he now enjoyed in New York.[14]

Four days later came the New York Dickens Dinner, at which Washington Irving spoke in his praise, and Dickens announced that he would accept no more invitations to public dinners or receptions, but would travel privately from now on. He also raised once more the subject of international copyright, and although there was support for what he said in the New York *Tribune*, the rest of the press remained hostile. He complained that he got little encouragement from American writers, although he did persuade twenty-five of them, headed by Washington Irving, to sign a petition for him to take to Congress. During the weeks they stayed in New York they saw Irving almost daily and made many visits to the theatre; and Dickens was led happily into a great many oyster cellars by Felton, who had a passion for them. He also made his rounds of the Lunatic Asylum, prisons, alms-houses, police stations and notorious rough districts, all carefully written up in his notes: but whereas he had admired the institutions in Boston, in New York he found most of them to be ill-managed, dismal or intolerable.[15] By 24 February he booked their return passage in June, by sailing ship this time, to avoid the horrors of their outward voyage on a steamer with its risk of fire. Both he and Catherine fell ill with sore throats and colds, and had to postpone their visit to Philadelphia, where he was to meet Edgar Allan Poe, who was a discerning admirer; Poe had sent him stories of his own, which impressed Dickens, and a favourable review of *The Old Curiosity Shop*.[16] He and Poe had two long conversations and parted on friendly terms; but Dickens was now 'sick and sore at heart' at the harsh treatment he was being given in the press over the copyright question, with accusations of ingratitude and greed.[17] From this point on he looked at America with an ever more disenchanted eye.

Delays in Atlantic mail ships meant that until now there had been no word of the children, but on 14 March there was at last news from

Osnaburgh Street, joyously read: Charley was attempting to write and Walter was weaned. Catherine had endured the long silence with perfect stoicism, and throughout the American trip she was at her very best, not only uncomplaining but always cheerful, charming and a good companion to her husband. Being his ally among strangers, with no children, friends, family or work to distract him, clearly changed the balance between them. Still more important, the simple fact of not being pregnant allowed her to be herself and to enjoy herself. The freedom from pregnancy is so striking that it raises the question as to whether it was chance (in which case, a chance that was never repeated), or a temporary after-effect of the surgery Dickens had undergone, or even whether they had a pact during the trip that they would avoid the possibility of her becoming pregnant. The affectionate delicacy of self-imposed abstinence by her husband could have pleased her more than satisfying his sexual needs. And he saw her in a better light too. He told Mitton later that she had 'proved herself an out and outer to travel' and even when he mocked her to Forster for her propensity to fall over and bruise herself or scrape skin off her legs, he added, 'she really has . . . made a *most admirable* traveller in every respect. She has never screamed or expressed alarm . . . has never given way to despondency or fatigue . . . has always accommodated herself, well and cheerfully, to everything; and has pleased me very much, and proved herself perfectly game.'[18] This is certainly one of the warmest testimonials Dickens ever wrote about Catherine. Even so, the tone is more what you might expect of a headmaster than a loving husband.

Neither of them had experienced anything like the way they were living now. For the first time since she had known him he was not under the pressure of one or several deadlines, forced regularly to his desk to produce a chapter or several chapters, to go through proofs, to deal with publishers and illustrators. He was not even thinking about a book. Nor did he have any of his friends to go out with, dining, walking, looking in on a club, drinking, theatre-going, taking night-time rambles through the streets, out till all hours. For the only time in their marriage Charles and Catherine were a couple facing the world with only the other to rely on, apart from the discreet services of maid and secretary. It may be that Catherine was able to be her best self only when the pressure of his all too distracting and absorbing work and masculine social life was removed and she felt she had a significant personal role in his life. She was twenty-seven that May, and she asked Fred Dickens to drink her health on her birthday, 19 May, in a letter written in April, signed 'Your truly attached sister KATE'.[19] Her birthday is not one that gets celebrated, or mentioned, elsewhere.

In Washington, Dickens had the bad luck to find a president who had not been elected but only taken over from the vice-presidency after the death of President Harrison a month into office in 1841. John Tyler was the tenth to hold the office, an undistinguished Virginian senator, now known as 'His Accidency' in political circles and backed by no party.[20] He received Dickens in a private audience, commented on his youthful appearance, and Dickens thought of returning the compliment, 'but he looked so jaded, that it stuck in my throat'.[21] The President was fifty-one, Dickens made a note of his gentlemanly manners and found he had nothing of interest to say or ask, and when an invitation to dinner at the White House arrived a few days later, Dickens declined on the grounds that he was leaving Washington before the date proposed. It is hard to imagine a modern writer snubbing the President of the United States in this way.

He was not much more impressed by what he heard at the Senate and the House of Representatives, 'no worse than ours, and no better' – faint praise from him.[22] But he sent a polite account to his Boston friend, Sumner, describing Senator Henry Clay as 'a fine fellow, who has won my heart', not surprisingly, over the international copyright question. Still, 'I have seen no place, yet, that I like so well as Boston . . . We are now in the regions of slavery, spittoons, and senators – all three are evils in all countries.'[23] He found the habit of spitting out gobs of chewed tobacco on the floor, common with American men, 'the most sickening, beastly, and abominable custom that ever civilization saw', and his descriptions of the results, seen everywhere on floors, stairs and carpets, are so vivid and disgusting that even reading them induces nausea.

There was worse. Going into slave-owning states so upset him for its blatant inhumanity that he decided to turn back after a short stay in Richmond, Virginia. From Baltimore he sent a great batch of letters to England on 22 March, to Maclise, Macready, Rogers, Talfourd, Fonblanque, Lady Holland, Lord Jeffrey, Mitton, brother Fred thanking him for his 'affectionate care of our dear darlings' and of course to Forster. It was at this point that he confessed, 'I don't like the country. I would not live here, on any consideration. It goes against the grain with me. It would with you. I think it impossible, utterly impossible, for any Englishman to live here, and be happy.'[24] Forster received what was effectively a running journal, written every few days; he knew that Dickens intended to use his letters as a basis for the book he planned to write and so kept them carefully. They were full of description and detail, and also intimate and affectionate; for example he sometimes wondered what Forster was doing ('perhaps you dine at the Crown-and-sceptre to-day, for it's Easter Monday – who knows! I wish you drank punch, dear Forster . . .'). He assured him that he constantly carried the pocket Shakespeare his friend had given him, 'an unspeakable source of delight that book is to me!', and said how much he regretted their old quarrels: 'Every little hasty word that has ever passed between us, rose up before me like a reproachful ghost . . . I seem to look back upon any miserable small interruption of our affectionate intercourse . . . with a sort of pity for myself as if I were another creature.'[25] Towards the end of the trip he wrote, 'I don't seem to have been half affectionate enough, but there *are* thoughts, you know, that lie too deep for words.'[26]

Late March and April saw them travelling along the Pennsylvania Canal through the Allegheny Mountains. He had much to say about the 'follies, vices, grievous disappointments' of America.[27] After a brief stop at Pittsburgh, a place of glass and gas works, foundries and heavy clouds of smoke, they spent five days in Cincinnati, 'a very beautiful city: I think the prettiest place I have seen here, except Boston. It has risen out of the forest like an Arabian-night city; is well laid out; ornamented in the suburbs with pretty villas . . . has smooth turf-plots and

well kept gardens.' There were drawbacks, for instance a temperance
festival in progress, naturally disapproved of by Dickens, and a party
given by a judge who introduced him 'to at least one hundred and fifty
first-rate bores, separately and singly . . . I really think my face has
acquired a fixed expression of sadness from the constant and unmitigated boring I endure.'[28] Each day it was getting harder for him to find
anything to admire or enjoy in America. At least in Pittsburgh Dickens had an 'extraordinary success in magnetizing Kate', first into
hysterics and then sleep, proudly reported to both Macready and Forster, who were told he intended to continue to treat her.

They proceeded to St Louis along the Mississippi, 'the beastliest
river in the world'.[29] In mid-April, Dickens made a dash into the prairie
('I would say to every man who can't see a prairie – go to Salisbury
plain') before they turned north again, hiring a private coach to take
them from Cincinnati to Lake Erie. The only road was a 'corduroy
road', made of logs, so rough that to the four of them inside the coach
it felt like 'going up a steep flight of stairs in an omnibus. Now the
coach flung us in a heap on its floor, and now crushed our heads
against its roof . . . Still, the day was beautiful, the air delicious, and
we were *alone*: with no tobacco spittle, or eternal prosy conversation
about dollars and politics . . . to bore us. We really enjoyed it . . .'[30]
They picnicked in the open air and slept in bug-infested log-houses.
The scale of the journey they were making is astonishing, and their
resilience admirable as they went on through wild terrain. Dickens
complained, in one of his grand generalizations, that the country
people in Ohio were 'invariably morose, sullen, clownish, and repulsive . . . destitute of humour, vivacity, or the capacity of enjoyment',
and that 'I have not heard a hearty laugh these six weeks, except my
own.' By contrast, he was moved by the plight of the native people,
known to him as the Wyandot Indians, the last tribe remaining in
Ohio, who were in the process of being persuaded to move west,
away from their own territory, on to land provided for them by a
'treaty'. He thought them 'a fine people, but degraded and broken
down'.[31] And they reminded him of home, because they looked like
the gypsies he had often seen at English race courses.

Arrived at Lake Erie, they took a steamship to Buffalo, where they found letters from home – 'oh! who or what can say with how much pleasure and unspeakable delight!'[32] Not only was there good news of the children, Forster had sent a letter signed by twelve British authors about international copyright, which Dickens had requested and which he immediately had copied by Putnam and forwarded to newspapers in Boston, New York and Washington. But although they were widely reprinted, and even found some support, they changed nothing, and international copyright was not sorted out until 1891, long after his death.

Canada lay ahead, but before that came Niagara Falls, where they stayed for ten days, until 4 May. Dickens responded to Niagara with intense emotion and was aroused to religious utterance: 'It would be hard for a man to stand nearer to God than he does there.' Dickens disliked and mocked displays of piety, but he maintained a reverential attitude towards the idea of God throughout his life. The sight of the great Falls led him to wish that Forster and Maclise had been with him to share 'the sensations of this time', and having mentioned God he was moved to think of death, and went on, 'what would I give if the dear girl whose ashes lie in Kensal-green, had lived to come so far along with us – but she has been here many times, I doubt not, since her sweet face faded from my earthly sight.'[33] Whether the Mary Hogarth who inhabited his imagination bore much relation to the real girl he had known, she remained a symbol he needed to hold on to, of the flawless and unattainable beloved. Did he actually believe her spirit wandered the world visiting selected beauty spots? It seems unlikely, any more than that he believed what he wrote by way of farewell to an American friend: 'Who that has ever reflected on the enormous and vast amount of leave-taking there is in this Life, can ever have doubted the existence of another!'[34] Precise and practical in doing good in his life, Dickens sometimes allowed himself to wander into feeble fancies when he approached spiritual matters.

In Canada they stopped briefly in Toronto – 'the wild and rabid to-ryism . . . is . . . *appalling*' – and took steamboats down the St Lawrence

River to Montreal and Quebec, passing great lumber rafts and noticing that the French population was characterized by red sashes on the boys and wide straw hats on the labouring women.[35] In Montreal he and Catherine joined in theatricals with the local British regimental officers and their wives; he threw himself enthusiastically into stage managing and acting, and she acted her part in the farce 'devilish well, I assure you'.[36]

All that remained was a last few days in New York, and a trip up the Hudson to see the Shakers, before they left America on 7 June. They were overjoyed at the prospect of getting home. After the miseries of the steamer on the way out, the *George Washington*, tall-masted and white-winged, carried them gallantly back to Liverpool in twenty-two days. Dickens entertained himself and fellow passengers by playing his accordion and organizing an all-male club whose members dined separately and dressed up as doctors, pretending to cure anyone who volunteered to be a patient.[37] They reached Liverpool on 29 June, and were in London that night.

They went first to the children. Charley told his mother that the reunion made him 'too glad', and he became ill, falling into convulsions so alarming that two doctors, one of them Elliotson, had to be summoned to attend to him during the night. He recovered and was none the worse for it, and the whole family was back in Devonshire Terrace on the last day of June. They had acquired a new member: fifteen-year-old Georgina, another Hogarth sister, blue-eyed, pretty, bright and scarcely out of the schoolroom. She was to have no further education but would join in caring for the Dickens children, rewarded by sharing in the life of the household, with its many pleasures and holidays. She idolized her brother-in-law, while he was delighted to have 'two pairs of petticoats' to go about with and made her his pet. No one could have guessed in 1842 the part she would play sixteen years later in the domestic life of her sister and brother-in-law.

⚜

Emotional reunions with Macready and Forster followed, and Forster organized a dinner at Greenwich to celebrate Dickens's return, for which he gathered twenty men. Edwin Landseer suggested they might have another welcoming dinner, 'with this difference – we will take some Women with us', but it did not materialize.[38] Dickens was already at work on his account of his travels, using his own letters claimed back from friends. He wrote fast: Forster gave a reading of the chapter about the outward crossing at a dinner on 19 July. In the same month Dickens also published a circular addressed to 'British Authors and Journals' about the copyright situation, stating his resolution to enter into no further negotiations of any kind with American publishers as long as there was no international copyright agreement, and to forgo any profits, a decision he stuck to for ten years.[39]

Dickens was briefly distracted when he heard that a London newspaper, the *Courier*, was folding, and suggested to Lady Holland that some leading Liberal politicians might acquire the premises and plant, and set up a new paper. He offered to write literary and political articles, saying he had 'perfect confidence that I could establish an organ for the party which would do good service'. It was a bold claim and a generous offer, but times were hard, the Liberal leaders did not share his confidence, and they were not prepared to put up any money.[40] He gave proof of his political commitment in a long and powerful letter to the *Morning Chronicle* supporting Lord Ashley's Mines and Collieries Bill, which sought to limit the employment of women and children underground.[41] England was in recession, and these were the 'Hungry Forties', bad for publishers and writers; but for the moment he put aside these matters, obliged to concentrate on writing about his American experiences.

August and September were spent at Broadstairs. There were visits from Maclise and Forster, sunshine and a regatta, but Dickens kept writing, with only occasional interruptions for bathing or dancing at the Tivoli Gardens, where Emma Picken, now Mrs Christian, appeared and danced with his brother Fred. Dickens mentioned her in a letter to Mitton, 'Emma Picken (as wos) and her husband are here, as you have heard.' The next sentence has been scratched out, and he goes on to say that 'Fred, I believe, has seen something of them.'[42] His writing made good progress: by 16 September he had reached Niagara, and the book was being printed in October. Longfellow came to stay at

Devonshire Terrace and Dickens entertained him with his specialities, taking him to Rochester, to visit London prisons, and to meet assorted tramps and thieves. The two men got on very well, and when *American Notes for General Circulation* was published on 19 October, Longfellow wrote an appreciative account of it to Sumner in Boston, saying it was 'jovial and good natured, and at times very severe. You will read it with delight, and for the most part approbation.'[43] Dickens and Forster went together to see Longfellow off at Bristol, and almost at once set off themselves, with Maclise and Stanfield, for Cornwall, where they hired an open carriage and took themselves to Land's End and St Michael's Mount, visited a tin mine, went to Truro, Bodmin and Tintagel, and marvelled at the height of the cliffs of north Cornwall. They all laughed a great deal, drank quantities of punch, enjoyed the ancient inns where they put up and judged the holiday a complete success.

Meanwhile Macaulay, who considered Dickens a man of genius and had asked to review *American Notes* for the *Edinburgh Review*, changed his mind on reading it and told the editor, 'I cannot praise it; and I will not cut it up.' He found 'some gleams of genius' but 'What is meant to be easy and sprightly is vulgar and flippant . . . what is meant to be fine is a great deal too fine for me, as in the description of the fall of Niagara.'[44] The reviews in England were mixed, but it sold well, going into four editions and making Dickens £1,000. In America, where it appeared in November, the sales were enormous: 50,000 copies selling in two days in New York and 3,000 in half an hour in Philadelphia.[45] The press was again divided, those who liked Boz praising his humour and humanity, while hostile papers treated him with contempt. The *New York Herald*, which had greeted him so warmly on his arrival in American, called the book the work of 'the most coarse, vulgar, impudent and superficial mind'.[46] Others accused him of hasty composition, egotism, coxcombry and cockneyism. Liberal Americans and abolitionists naturally liked his stance on slavery, and *American Notes* ends with two chapters in which he summarizes his impressions, one of them entirely devoted to slavery. In the final, general chapter he complained of the viciousness of the American press and the lack of moral sense among people who prized 'smartness' above goodness, and went on to itemize other defects of the Americans: he found them dull and lacking in humour, with poor manners; their diet was coarse and their eating habits graceless; they were short on personal cleanliness and their living conditions were insanitary. Behind these remarks is the condescension of the old world to the new, or so it must have seemed. Even Dickens's Boston friends saw that he would be unpopular. Dana, who thought Dickens a genius but no gentleman, wrote in his journal that 'His journey to America has been a Moscow expedition for his fame,' and Poe called it 'one of the most suicidal productions, ever deliberately published by an author, who had the least reputation to lose'.[47]

At the end of the year Dickens returned to fiction and embarked on a new serial novel, *Martin Chuzzlewit*. Its setting was England and its theme selfishness, but as he progressed he saw that he could use his American experiences further, and say more about the way he had been ill-used in America: not only their refusal to do anything about international copyright, but the publication in August of a crudely forged letter attributed to him in a New York newspaper,[48] and the rude reviews of *American Notes*. The more he thought about all this the fiercer grew his anger. When he came to write the American chapters of *Chuzzlewit*, he was avenging himself on everything he disliked about the way he had been treated, and pointing out, with savage humour, what he hated about America: corrupt newspapers, violence, slavery, spitting, boastfulness and self-righteousness, obsession with business and money, greedy, graceless eating, hypocrisy about supposed equality, the crude lionizing of visitors. He mocked their newspaper editors, their learned women and their congressmen through the figures of Mr Jefferson Brick, Mr La Fayette Kettle, Mrs Hominy and Congressman Elijah Pogram, and he parodied the overblown rhetoric of their speech and writing. Just one decent American appears, the generous Mr Bevan from Massachusetts, but he remains a shadowy figure. The satire is biting, funny and unfair, so much so that it lost him the friendship of Washington Irving.

His feelings about America remained angry, and two years later he warned Macready, who had been invited to lecture in New York, against the country. It was 'a low, coarse, and mean Nation' and 'driven by a herd of rascals'. 'Pah!' he finished his diatribe. 'I never knew what it was to feel disgust and contempt, 'till I travelled in America.'[49]

10

Setbacks

1843–1844

The return to fiction was a dismaying experience. *Martin Chuzzlewit* was planned as a big book to run as a serial for a year and a half and to have the same appeal as *Pickwick, Oliver, Nickleby* and *The Old Curiosity Shop*. The first monthly number appeared in December 1843, and it was soon clear that the public did not warm to it. Where *The Old Curiosity Shop* had reached sales of 100,000 each month, *Chuzzlewit* settled down to a fifth of that, never rising much above 20,000. The 1840s were a time of recession and severe hardship in England, and people did not have the money in their pockets to spend on stories, even stories by Dickens. His last two books, *Barnaby Rudge* and *American Notes*, had not increased his popularity. Worse, the new one got off to a poor start. Intended as a humorous chronicle of a family and mockery of people who boasted about their ancestors, Dickens had laboured to think up a droll name for the family, trying out his ideas on Forster – Sweezleden, Sweezleback, Sweezlewag, Chuzzletoe, Chuzzleboy and Chubblewig – but he managed only to be facetious in the opening chapter, and when modern Chuzzlewits are brought into the story, they are no more interesting than their forebears. The young hero Martin and his cousin Jonas are set up like toys programmed to run on course, one selfish, the other villainous, and Martin's grandfather is a mere mechanical device for activating an absurdly improbable and tedious plot.

The situation is partly saved by Pecksniff, a Chuzzlewit cousin who keeps his hand in his waistcoat as though ready to produce his heart for inspection, and who presides over much of the narrative, advancing his own interests by lying and keeping us entertained. Dickens's enjoyment in supplying him with his well-oiled voice is clear, as he relished creating Quilp and Squeers before him. Getting into his stride, he becomes inventive with minor characters like Mrs Todgers, in whose London lodging house Pecksniff goes to stay. Mrs Todgers is chronically anxious over the supply of gravy for the gentlemen's dinners: 'The gravy alone, is enough to add twenty years to one's age . . . The anxiety of that one item . . . keeps the mind continually upon the stretch. There is no such passion in human nature, as the passion for gravy among commercial gentlemen . . . a whole animal wouldn't yield – the amount of gravy they expect each day at dinner.'[1] She could have appeared in *Sketches by Boz*, and around her house Dickens creates a virtuoso piece of London scenery, consisting of byways, 'nothing that could reasonably be called a street', making it so hard to find that some people, invited to dinner there, go round and round until they give up and go home again. Her house boasts a roof terrace, decorated with dead plants in tea chests and rotten washing lines, from which you can see 'steeples, towers, belfries, shining vanes, and masts of ships: a very forest. Gables, house-tops, garret-windows, wilderness upon wilderness' – and the shadow of the Monument, making a long dark path over the rooftops.[2]

Mrs Todgers's boy Bailey is another lively character, an undersized, self-possessed lad who is petted by the lodgers, warns them against the fish ('Don't eat none of him!'), wears their cast-off clothes, which are several times too large for him, entertains Pecksniff's daughters by putting a lighted candle in his mouth, has himself shaved in advance of any whiskers appearing ('Go a tip-toe over the pimples!' he tells the barber), and is as worldly and knowing as an old roué. Mrs Todgers hits him and pulls his ears and hair regularly, and he leaves her for a new master, a City financier, who allows him more licence, for example to drive his horses at a gallop round St James's Square. Then, halfway through the book, Mrs Gamp, an ancient hard-drinking professional nurse, appears, and takes it over with her monologues, spoken in a language peculiar to herself, gorgeously mispronounced, much of it devoted to recounting conversations with her imaginary friend Mrs Harris. Dickens revived Mrs Gamp to make one of his public readings in the 1860s, and she and Mrs Harris have achieved a position quite independent of the book in which they first appeared. Like Pecksniff, they are so entertaining that the

failings of other parts of the book fade when they are speaking. The
same is true of the Anglo-Bengalee Disinterested Loan and Life Assurance Company, with its grand premises and lavish dinners, and its
porter whose red waistcoat is so impressive that it guarantees the
respectability, competence and funds of the company that employs
him, so that rival offices try to lure him away from the Anglo-Bengalee.
The satire on high finance is as good today as it was then. Long, confused and uneven as *Chuzzlewit* is, with the American scenes, some
sickly sentimentality and a showy murder thrown in, it also has these
scatterings of brilliance which suggest why Dickens felt it to be 'in a
hundred points immeasurably the best of my stories'.[3]

Yet even as he was meditating Mrs Gamp's first appearance he had
the dispiriting experience of going into the offices of his publishers
and hearing that they were thinking of reducing what they paid him.
A clause in their agreement allowed them to cut the payments from
£200 to £150 if sales of *Chuzzlewit* were not enough to repay the
advance – and they were not. Dickens was angry and hurt, and felt
unable to work for a week. He proudly insisted that they should cut
the payments at once, but he told Forster he felt 'rubbed in the ten-
derest part of my eyelids with bay-salt', and his immediate response
was to think of changing his publishers again.[4] Short of money, he
had to borrow from Mitton and instructed him to let one of his life-
insurance policies lapse. He asked Forster to sound out William
Bradbury and Frederick Evans, his printers, as to whether they might
like to become his publishers. They did not seem to be interested,
which was a relief for Forster, since he was Chapman & Hall's literary
adviser.

There was another year to go before *Chuzzlewit* could be finished,
but Dickens began to think of going away, giving himself another
break from novel writing, living cheaply abroad with his family and
telling his publishers he would make new arrangements whenever he
chose to return to England.[5] He told Forster he might write a book
while he was abroad and publish it in Paris. Another plan was to find
a patron, and he asked his friend Smithson, with whom he stayed in
Yorkshire in July, if he would advance him £3,000, but Smithson
was in no position to do so. Meanwhile American reviewers had seen

his account of their country as *Chuzzlewit* instalments appeared there, and were voicing their objections.

On top of this, the behaviour of his father presented him with what seemed an insoluble problem. John Dickens was perpetually applying to his son's friends and even his publishers for money, borrowing sums he could not possibly repay, which forced Dickens to pay on his behalf, and trying other financial dodges which were shaming to Dickens as he saw his name misused, and alarming because he never knew when the next parental demand on his income would turn up. This in spite of his father's pension from the Navy Pay Office, and his house paid for by Charles. He disliked the Devon cottage and had moved back to London, or at any rate to the south-east suburb of Lewisham, and, finding this inconveniently far from the centre of town, he wrote to Chapman & Hall inviting them to provide him with 'a free transit Ticket' on the Greenwich boat, which would allow him to spend 'two or three days a week at the Museum', now that he was a gentleman of leisure.[6] You have to admire such assurance and bravado. At this point Dickens was refusing to communicate with him directly, and wrote in despair to Mitton, who was dealing with him as best he could: 'I am amazed and confounded by the audacity of his ingratitude. He, and all of them, look upon me as a something to be plucked and torn to pieces for their advantage. They have no idea of, and no care for, my existence in any other light. My soul sickens at the thought of them.' His brother Alfred was still out of work, and Dickens was thinking of employing him as a secretary at a pound a week until a letter from his father, 'a threatening letter, before God! – to me!', made him change his mind. He asked Mitton to tell his father 'that his letter has disgusted me beyond expression'.[7]

At this time he was engaged in one of his most admirable charitable endeavours, raising funds for the children of Edward Elton, an actor in Macready's company, whose wife had died leaving him with six daughters and an eight-year-old son, and who was himself drowned at sea returning from an engagement in Hull. Dickens steamed into action, forming a committee, arranging a benefit, visiting the children and arranging for the eldest girl, Esther, to be given a place in a training college. Esther became a schoolteacher, as well as a virtual mother to her little sisters; one was helped to a musical career, one was found a position as a companion, one who was thought to be consumptive was sent to Nice, and the son became an actor like his father. Dickens remained active in helping them for many years. Few men with a multitude of demands on their time and money would be capable of keeping up such a level of commitment, goodness and generosity over so long a period. The Elton children were deeply grateful and in 1859 they sent a joint letter of thanks to the committee. In 1861 Dickens was still writing to Esther, a full, affectionate and even intimate letter, long after she was married and a mother.[8]

A further activity he took on was advising his friend Miss Coutts.[9] She asked him his view of the movement for 'Ragged Schools', set up in the poorest parts of London by volunteer teachers prepared to teach any who came, the homeless and starving, the disabled, even pupils who explained that their occasional absences were occasioned by prison sentences. Dickens's letter describing his visit to the Ragged School in Saffron Hill – where, incidentally, he had placed Fagin's house – is a masterpiece of descriptive writing and argument. He was shocked by what he saw, and also amused by the children's cheeky remarks about his white trousers and long hair. He praised the teachers as honest, good men, who 'try to reach the boys by kindness' but suggested that beginning with religious teaching was not the best way: 'To impress them, even with the idea of a God, when their own condition is so desolate, becomes a monstrous task,' and teaching such things as the Catechism was beside the point to children whose lives are 'one continued punishment'. He encouraged Miss Coutts to give her support, but wondered how many others would help: 'There is a kind of delicacy which is not at all shocked by the existence of such things, but is excessively shocked to know of them,' he warned her.[10] This was the beginning of his partnership with Miss Coutts in charitable work, which extended itself over the years – she seeking his advice and usually taking it, he making suggestions, researching on her behalf and giving up many hours of his time to it. Miss Coutts, who had inherited one of the largest fortunes in England and owned Coutts Bank, a house in Stratton Street and another in Highgate, was ready to give large sums of money to the causes she took up. She was also deeply and formally religious, but in spite of this she and Dickens, who now called himself a Unitarian, became devoted friends, and *Martin Chuzzlewit* was dedicated to her. He told Forster, 'She is a most excellent creature, I protest to God, and I have a most perfect affection and respect for her.'[11] She took an affectionate interest in his family, and her strong-minded companion, Miss Meredith, amused Dickens, and had given him a description of the nurse who was sent to look after her when she fell ill, from which came the idea for Mrs Gamp.

A family house in Broadstairs was taken again for August and September 1843, although Dickens was often obliged to be in London that summer, and hard at work. By the autumn he had fixed on his plan to go abroad and to make no writing commitments for the future. He was convinced that *Chuzzlewit* was good: 'That I feel my power now, more than I ever did. That I have greater confidence in myself than I ever had. That I *know*, if I have my health, I could sustain my place in the minds of thinking men, though fifty writers started up tomorrow.'[12] And he went on to blame reviewers, 'knaves and idiots', for the low sales, although friends were also disappointed, Jeffrey calling it 'grotesque and fantastical'; and even Forster delayed his review until the last number appeared.[13] But he also craved a proper rest in which to recharge his imagination. He disliked the idea of separation from Forster for a long time, but looked upon the plan 'as a matter of policy and duty'. The children would benefit from being in France, and the new baby – due in January – could be left in England with Catherine's mother.[14] By November he was talking of taking his 'menagerie' as far as Rome.

But now there was something else in his mind. In October, an idea had come to him for a short book to be sold at Christmas. By 24 October he had John Leech, a fine artist first introduced to him by Cruikshank, working on illustrations, and on 10 November he was discussing the cover and advertising with Forster.[15] He told his Boston friend Felton that he had composed it in his head, weeping and laughing and weeping again, as he walked about 'the black streets of London, fifteen and twenty miles, many a night when all the sober folks had gone to bed'.[16] Friedrich Engels, observing the slum housing, child labour, harsh employers, and overworked men and women in Manchester at this time, praised Carlyle as the only British writer who took account of the poor, and doubtless had not read anything by Dickens.[17] *A Christmas Carol* was Dickens's response to the condition of the working class in London, and his next Christmas book, *The Chimes*, followed up the subject. Carlyle, Engels and Dickens were all fired with anger and horror at the indifference of the rich to the fate of the poor, who had almost no access to education, no care in sickness, saw their young children set to work for ruthless factory-owners and could consider themselves lucky if they were only half starved. Dickens asked Chapman & Hall to publish his little book on commission, as a separate venture, and he insisted on fine, coloured binding and endpapers, and gold lettering on the front and spine; and that it should cost only five shillings.

It was published on 19 December and sold 6,000 copies in the few days before Christmas. Dickens presented copies to Jeffrey, Elliotson, Felton, Sydney Smith and his sister Letitia; he assured Macready it was the greatest success he had yet achieved. It went on selling into the spring of 1844, with seven editions by May. He had put into it his memories of Camden Town and the walk, or run, to work that Bob Cratchit does; and his sister Fanny's crippled son, now four, whom he had seen in Manchester in September, as Tiny Tim. From his own deep self he drew the understanding that a grown man may pity the child he had been, and learn from that pity, as Scrooge does. It was also his response to the Ragged School he had visited, and the Report of the Children's Employment Commission he had read a little earlier, which showed that children under seven were put to work, unprotected by any legal constraints, sometimes for ten to twelve hours a day, inspiring the scene in which the Spirit of Christmas Present shows Scrooge two stunted and wolfish children, calling them Ignorance and Want. When Scrooge asks, 'Have they no refuge or resource?' the Spirit answers him with his own words, 'Are there no prisons? Are there no workhouses?' The book went straight to the heart of the public and has remained lodged there ever since, with its mixture of horror, despair, hope and warmth, its message – a Christian message – that even the worst of sinners may repent and become a good man; and its insistence that good cheer, food and drink shared, gifts and even dancing are not merely frivolous pleasures but basic expressions of love and mutual support among all human beings.

Dickens was confident the book would bring him £1,000, allow him to pay off money he owed and leave him some in hand to take abroad. Again he was stunned with disappointment. The accounts for the *Carol* showed that almost all the profits were absorbed in the expenses of binding, special paper, coloured plates and advertising. At Christmas he was overdrawn on his Coutts account, something he desperately tried to avoid, given his personal friendship with Miss Coutts, and Mitton was asked for another loan. On the first 6,000 copies he made £137, and even at the end of 1844 the book had earned only £726. Worse, he took legal action against a pirated version of his story, sold for twopence on the day the second edition came out, and although he won the case the pirates, Messrs Lee and Haddock, declared themselves bankrupt, and Dickens had to pay £700 in costs and law charges. A third loan from Mitton was asked for, and received.

Dickens kept quiet about the financial disaster in order not to tarnish the success of his Christmas book. On the bright side, Tauchnitz, the Leipzig publisher who had been pirating English books on the Continent, had begun to deal fairly and was offering money for Dickens's work: his edition of the *Carol* was 'sanctioned by the Author'. In America it became his biggest seller, clocking up two million copies in a hundred years.[18] Dramatized versions were running in London in the new year; they have always been hugely successful, and many admirers of Dickens make a point of rereading it every year at Christmas.

At Christmas 1843 Dickens, for all his pressing problems, managed to maintain a high level of seasonal jollity. Macready was away acting in America, and Dickens and Forster appointed themselves chief entertainers at the children's party given by Mrs Macready on Boxing Day. Jane Carlyle described the occasion. 'Only think of the excellent D playing the *conjuror* for one whole hour – the best *conjuror* I ever saw – (and I have paid money to see several) – and Forster acting as his servant. This part of the entertainment concluded with a plum

pudding made out of raw flour, raw eggs – all the raw usual ingredients – boiled in a gentleman's hat – and tumbled out reeking – all in
one minute before the eyes of the astonished children and astonished
grown people!' A little later Dickens sank almost to his knees in an
unsuccessful effort to persuade Mrs Carlyle to waltz. Supper, crack-
ers and speeches were followed by a country dance into which
everyone was whirled, and at midnight Dickens bore off Thackeray
and Forster to 'finish the night' at Devonshire Terrace, and Mrs Carlyle reflected on how much more entertaining the 'little knot of
blackguardist literary people who felt ourselves above all rules, and
independent of the universe' were than those in aristocratic, conventional drawing rooms could possibly be.[19]

There was another conjuring show at Twelfth Night, for Charley's
seventh birthday, for which Dickens and Forster both dressed themselves in magicians' outfits, although by now Dickens was almost
floored by a cold: 'My chest is raw, my head dizzy, and my nose
incomprehensible.'[20] And there were always more family demands.
His youngest brother, Augustus, had reached the age of seventeen,
and Dickens busied himself trying to find him a job. His own new
baby was due, and Catherine was no longer the 'out and outer' she
had been in America: he complained of her being 'nervous and dull.
But her health is perfectly good, and I am sure she might rally, if she
would.'[21] Perhaps she was nervous of the coming ordeal, and not
happy about his plan to leave the baby with her mother when they
went abroad. On 15 January a third son, Francis, was born. She recovered quickly, but a month later Dickens wrote to his friend T. J.
Thompson, 'Kate is all right again; and so, they tell me, is the Baby.
But I decline (on principle) to look at the latter object.'[22]

At least he could get away from babies, nursemaids and wife, and
take on a role he enjoyed better, as glamorous visiting speaker. He
went north to address the Mechanics' Institute in Liverpool and the
Polytechnic in Birmingham. In Liverpool he saw his sister Fanny,
revisited the *Britannia* in dock and drank champagne on board; then
he got himself up in a 'magpie waistcoat' for his evening speech
before an audience of 1,300. He scored a triumph, and fell in love,
with Christiana Weller, a nineteen-year-old concert pianist who

performed at the reception. He invited himself to lunch with the surprised Weller family the next day and sent her some verses, joking that she shared a name with his Sam Weller and suggesting what he felt for her: 'I love her dear name which has won me some fame,/ But Great Heaven how gladly I'd change it.' He followed this up with a gift of two volumes of Tennyson – his own copies, given him by the poet – and told her father that 'she started out alone from the whole crowd the instant I saw her, and will remain there always in my sight.'[23] He also feared she would die young, her expression being so spiritual.

Smitten as he was, he went to an evening party given by Mr Yates, who ran the Institute, and stayed dancing until three in the morning, joining with forty couples in Sir Roger de Coverley. The next morning he was on the train to Birmingham, where he found the Town Hall decorated with artificial flowers arranged to form the words 'Welcome Dick' in gigantic letters. He retired to the inn where he was putting up, dined alone, 'took a pint of Champagne and a pint of Sherry . . . and was as hard as iron and as cool as a cucumber'.[24] The hall was crammed to the roof for his speech, which he thought the best he had ever given. He was on a high, and later that night he wrote a long letter to Thompson, boasting about the speech and confiding in him about Christiana: 'Good God what a madman I should seem, if the incredible feeling I have conceived for that girl could be made plain to anyone.'[25] His enthusiasm affected Thompson so strongly that he too found himself in love with Christiana, and since he was a rich widower he proceeded to woo her, keeping Dickens informed and strongly encouraged by him, since it allowed him to remain intimate with her, if only by proxy. He proposed that they should all go to Italy together for a 'gallant holiday', with books, boats and mules, and imagined himself growing a moustache and wearing a red sash for good measure. Thompson's courtship advancing only slowly, Dickens calmed down, and although he went to hear her play in London and spoke at her wedding the following year, once Christiana had become Mrs Thompson he turned against her and the whole Weller family.[26]

Chuzzlewit continued its course, and the plan was to go to Italy as soon as the last number appeared, at the end of June. A house was hired for them in Genoa by their Scottish friend Angus Fletcher, who was already in Italy and intended to join them there and work at his sculpture. Fletcher was instructed to have a water closet installed in the house. Dickens and Catherine took Italian lessons. In April he needed another loan from Mitton, and Devonshire Terrace was let from the end of May, so the whole family moved into No. 9 Osnaburgh Terrace. And on 1 June, after many preliminary discussions with Forster and with William Bradbury and Frederick Evans, an agreement was signed whereby they paid £2,000 into his account and he assigned to them a quarter share in everything he would write over the next eight years, without being formally committed to write anything, although it was expected that there would be another Christmas book for 1844. Their security was his remaining life-insurance policies. The deal was generous, and sensible. Dickens at last felt free, and Bradbury & Evans were going to do very well out of it. The villains, Chapman & Hall, were out of the picture as publishers of his new works – at least for the next fifteen years.[27]

II

Travels, Dreams and Visions

1844–1845

The last weeks in England were spent in a round of dinners, celebratory and farewell. Dickens also escaped for a few days' yachting with Fonblanque, editor of the *Examiner*, and visited Landor in Bath. For the long journey to Italy he had purchased a shabby old coach, 'about the size of your library', he told Forster. It needed to be at least that to hold the entire party, which included Georgina ('my little pet' to Dickens, and from now on indissolubly one of the family), the four children and baby Francis – reprieved from being left with Mrs Hogarth – their maid Anne, three junior nurses and maids, Roche, the French courier hired by Dickens, and a dog, the small white curly-haired Timber. Charley, who had been at day school in St John's Wood for six months, said goodbye to his teachers for a year.[1] On 30 June the last number of *Chuzzlewit* was out, and on 2 July they set off, taking their phaeton as far as Dover so that Forster and Fred could go with them for this first stage of the journey. Dickens disliked farewells, and his friends hated losing him and wanted to stay close for as long as possible.

They had two days in Paris, installed in the Hôtel Meurice in the rue de Rivoli. This was Dickens's first visit to the French capital, and he walked about the streets continuously, alone, and marvelling at everything: 'It is the most extraordinary place in the World ... almost every house, and every person I passed, seemed to be another leaf in the enormous book that stands wide open there.'[2] It was the beginning of an interest in France and a readiness to be delighted by most things French. On through Sens and Avallon to Chalons-sur-Saône, a beautiful summer journey, even if not ideally enjoyed in a coach packed with children and a dog with disordered bowels (as Dickens reported). There was some respite at Chalons, when the coach was loaded on to a barge that carried them to Lyons, where the

Saône joins the Rhone – another pause for sightseeing – and as far as Aix. Then by road to Marseilles and by sea to their destination, Genoa, on the Ligurian coast, which they reached in mid-July. From the boat, Genoa was a beautiful town, but, at close quarters, 'of all the mouldy, dreary, sleepy, dirty, lagging, halting, God-forsaken towns in the wide world, it surely must be the very uttermost super-lative. It seemed as if one had reached the end of all things.'[3]

Like many English visitors, they were amazed to find that the sky above Italy could be grey and cloudy even in summer, and it remained so for some time. The house Fletcher had found for them was also a severe disappointment. Dickens said the Villa Bagnerello looked like a pink jail, it was not in Genoa but several miles outside, at Albaro, and it was infested with fleas. Little Katey fell ill and would be nursed by no one but her father. But living was cheap, with excellent white wine at a penny farthing the pint, and he was not obliged to work, could breakfast at 9.30 and make punch with green lemons: 'I never knew what it was to be lazy before.'[4] The declaration is true and touching: not much leisure had been allowed into his life since the age of twelve. He found that he enjoyed swimming in the sea. He grew a moustache. He rode in and out of Genoa, and walked by day, until in August the heat made night the only time for walking. He found that his immedi-ate neighbour, Monsieur Allertz, was the French Consul at Genoa, a hospitable man of literary tastes, who gave splendid dinners, and introduced him to the French Romantic poet and diplomat Alphonse de Lamartine as he passed through Genoa on his way to Naples. Although at this date Dickens barely spoke French, Lamartine's wife was English, and the two men were ardent reformers with shared views about prison reform and copyright; they would meet again in Paris in 1847, and a third time in 1855. Other entertainment offered itself at the Teatro Carlo Felice, where he took a private box; the sea-son opened with a dramatization of Balzac's *Le Père Goriot*, and continued with Bellini's *La Sonnambula* and Verdi's new opera *I Lom-bardi*. He read Tennyson ('what a great creature he is!').[5] Yet he was restless, and when Fred came to spend his holidays with them, he trav-elled to Marseilles to meet him, and they visited Nice before taking the coastal road back into Italy together. Fred was also sporting a moustache, which may have decided Dickens to get rid of his; and, fond as he was of his brother, he was no substitute for his friends.[6] He told Maclise that 'Losing you and Forster is like losing my arms and legs; and dull and lame I am without you.'[7]

Palazzo Peschiere in Genoa, where Dickens lived with his family in 1844.

He set out to find somewhere better to live, and succeeded in renting the sixteenth-century Palazzo Peschiere, or 'Palace of the Fishponds', in the heart of Genoa but with spacious terraced gardens, and set on a height that gave it a view over the surrounding town, the harbour and the sea. They moved at the end of September. It was easily the most magnificent house he ever lived in, and he sent friends enthusiastic accounts of the fifty-foot-high ceiling to the great hall, the patterned stone floors, the frescoes, the bedrooms decorated with nymphs and satyrs, the balconies and terraces, the fountains and sculptures. Here he dreamt of a blue-robed, Madonna-like spirit whom he knew to be Mary Hogarth, and who, as he wept and stretched out his arms to her, asked him to form a wish and recommended the Roman Catholic faith to him. He woke with tears running down his face, roused Catherine to describe the dream and explained its causes to himself: he had been looking at an old altar in the bedroom and hearing convent bells. But in describing it to Forster he wondered whether he should regard it 'as a dream, or an actual Vision!'[8]

Dreams and visions are central in the Christmas book he started on now, *The Chimes*, in which a poor old man, Trotty Veck, is sent visions by the spirits of the bells in the church where he stands every day waiting for work, spirits described as goblins, phantoms or shadows. It is hardly read today, but it was written with red-hot feeling and meant to shame the cruel and canting rich of the 1840s. Like the *Carol*, it looked at the condition of the poor in England, but with a directly political message, attacking the complacency of political economists with Malthusian ideas, magistrates who sentenced suicidal young women to prison or transportation, and landowners who enforced the Game Laws and toasted 'The Health of the Labourer' at their agricultural dinners while allowing the labourers to starve. He knew what he was talking about: the magistrate he satirized was an acquaintance, and a smart political economist had attacked him in the *Westminster Review* for failing to inform readers of *A Christmas Carol* as to 'who went without turkey and punch in order that Bob Cratchit might get them'. In Trotty Veck's visions he sees his daughter and another young woman driven to prostitution and suicide by poverty, and the young man his daughter loves unjustly sentenced turning to crime; and although Dickens supplied a conventionally happy ending in which Trotty Veck wakes up and finds it was all a dream, readers could see that the visions were showing much of the truth of life for the poor. Modern readers may feel that he was more successful in his mockery of the powerful than in his presentation of the oppressed, but many tears were shed over them at the time.

Forster was so impressed when he read *The Chimes* that he made a secret approach to Napier, editor of the *Edinburgh Review*, telling him that it was 'in some essential points' the best thing Dickens had yet written, and asking to review it anonymously before publication. Napier agreed, and Forster wrote a eulogy, saying that 'Questions are here brought to view, which cannot be dismissed when the book is laid aside. Condition of England questions . . . Mighty theme for so slight an instrument! but the touch is exquisite, and the tone deeply true . . . Name this little tale what we will, it is a tragedy in effect.'[9] The piece was a puff, and there were smiles when its authorship got out. *The Chimes* did make something of a political uproar, as was intended, but in the long run it did not approach the popularity of the *Carol*, and Forster himself acknowledged later that it was 'not one of his [Dickens's] greater successes'.[10] Whether Dickens knew what Forster had done or not, the shared experience with *The Chimes* brought them still closer. While writing he had missed the streets of London, his usual thinking place, and he posted the first part of the story to Forster, telling him, 'I would give a hundred pounds (& think it cheap) to see you read it.'[11] Then it came to him that he could make a dash to London in late November, so that he *could* read it with Forster and other friends. The story was finished on 4 November, Dickens suffering from a cold so severe he could hardly see, and shedding tears over his own work.

On 21 November he set off northwards with his courier Roche. They went up the Simplon Pass by moonlight, saw the day break on the summit and sledged through snow dyed rosy red by the rising sun. Then Fribourg, Strasbourg, and a French diligence that got him uncomfortably to Paris in fifty hours. He made such good time that he arrived in England a day earlier than he had expected. He had asked Forster to book him a room in the familiar Piazza Coffee House in Covent Garden, to be near Lincoln's Inn, and on the evening of 30 November he walked into the public rooms, saw Forster and Maclise sitting by the fire and rushed into their arms. He had eight days in London, and the emotion was kept at a high level among the friends, all bachelors together for a few days, with much weeping, laughing, embracing and sitting up into the small hours.[12] Leech was invited to breakfast to be thanked for his illustrations, and Forster set up a tea party in his rooms for 3 December, at which Dickens read the whole story to a select group of guests – Carlyle, Maclise, Stanfield, a number of radical writers including Douglas Jerrold and the editor and essayist Laman Blanchard, and not forgetting brother Fred.[13]

Maclise sent Catherine a sketch of the scene, putting a radiant halo

over Dickens's head, and told her 'there was not a dry eye in the house
. . . shrieks of laughter . . . and floods of tears as a relief to them – I
do not think that there was ever such a triumphant hour for Charles.'[14]
And Dickens wrote to her, 'If you had seen Maclise last night – undis-
guisedly sobbing, and crying on the sofa, as I read – you would have
felt (as I did) what a thing it is to have Power.'[15] This first experience
of power as a reader of his own words was so intense and gratifying
that his old interest in performance began to stir in him again. He
gave a second reading, and he and Forster talked about putting on
plays. Meanwhile three separate dramatizations of *The Chimes* were
in preparation for Christmas runs in London.

If he was to reach Genoa for Christmas he had to be on his way
again, and on the evening of 8 December he set off. Paris was under
snow, and he lingered to spend a few days with Macready, about to
play Othello, Hamlet and Macbeth to the French. From Paris he
wrote a heartfelt letter to Forster, 'I would not recall an inch of the
way to or from you, if it had been twenty times as long and twenty
thousand times as wintry. It was worth any travel – anything! . . . I
swear I wouldn't have missed that week, that first night of our meeting, that one evening of the reading in your rooms, aye, and the
second reading too, for any easily stated or conceived consideration.'[16] The bond between them had been drawn tighter by the visit,
and once back in Genoa he moved the friendship into a new phase,
for the first time telling Forster something about his young life, with
a description of how he had hoped and planned to become an actor;
and over the next years he told him more, and gave him a written
account of the whole secret story of his childhood, his father's imprisonment and his work at the blacking factory; then suggested that
Forster should become his biographer. He was able to be intimate
with Forster as with no other man or woman, and so, scarcely into
middle age, he fixed on the idea that this was the one person he
trusted to write his life, and never wavered from that decision.

Just as he was writing the letter about his audition, Forster's brother
died suddenly, still in his thirties. Dickens wrote to comfort him. His
words read like a further consecration of their friendship. 'I feel the
distance between us now, indeed. I would to Heaven, my dearest

friend, that I could remind you in a manner more lively and affectionate than this dull sheet of paper can put on, that you have a Brother left.
One bound to you by ties as strong as Nature ever forged. By ties never
to be broken, weakened, changed in any way – but to be knotted tighter
up, if that be possible, until the same end comes to them as has come to
these . . . I read your heart as if I held it in my hand, this moment.'[17]

Meanwhile he had a new interest in Genoa. Among the friends they
had made there was a banker, Emile De La Rue, an English-speaking
Swiss from Geneva, married for ten years to an English wife, Augusta
née Granet.[18] They lived in a pretty, high-windowed and comfortable
apartment at the top of a Genoese palazzo, up many stairs and across
many landings lined with antique busts, and she appeared charming
and animated in society; but she was suffering from a nervous disorder
– tic douloureux, headaches, insomnia, occasional convulsions and
catalepsy – a list of ailments that sound very like those of the nineteenth-
century women who turned up a little later in the clinics of Dr Charcot
and Dr Freud and were described as suffering from hysteria. Just before
Dickens made his November dash to England, De La Rue mentioned
his wife's problems to him, and he responded. He may have said something about his doctor in London, Elliotson, who used mesmerism to
deal with cases of this kind, and gone on to say that he had some skill
in mesmerism himself. De La Rue was so impressed that, within days
of Dicken's return, he asked him to come over and try his powers on
Madame De La Rue. No doubt he was intrigued by the idea of the
famous writer attending his wife, and she was willing and pleased with
the attention. On 23 December, Dickens began the treatment. It was a
highly unusual situation, given that he had no medical training, but he
was eager to try what he could do, and the De La Rues were grateful.

Dickens was confident he could do something for Augusta De La
Rue and prepared to play the doctor. He believed in Elliotson, was
delighted with his own ability to send Catherine and Georgina into
trances, and felt that a real patient would give him the chance to do
good, and to justify his faith in mesmerism. At that time it was

thought of as being some sort of magnetic force, not yet explained or even understood, and Dickens would speculate as to whether the magnetism worked on the nervous system of the patient; but very little was known about the nervous system, and it was found later that the idea of a magnetic force had no basis in fact. It was nevertheless obvious, and remains true, that some people, not necessarily armed with any scientific qualifications, are able to produce behavioural changes in susceptible people. And there is no doubt that something did happen between Dickens and Augusta De La Rue, although it is hard to say what exactly it was.

His treatment consisted of putting her into sleep-like trances and then questioning her about her experiences or fantasies. Few of his notes survive, but he told her husband in one of the letters the two men exchanged during the treatment that she talked of being on a hillside, among a crowd of men and women, and suddenly seeing an absent brother, whom she named as Charles, leaning against a window, seeming sad. Dickens asked her what made him sad, and she said she would try to find out. Next Charles was walking up and down the room, looking out of a window at the sea, still very sad: she cried at this point. Dickens asked how he was dressed, and she replied 'in his uniform'. Then she said, 'He is thinking of me,' and after a pause explained that he believed himself forgotten, that her letters to him had miscarried. Then he was gone. She also talked of lying on the hillside and being hurt by stones rolled down by unseen people; and of a man haunting the place, dimly seen, whom she feared and did not dare to look at. Dickens decided this man was the bad spirit or phantom whom she had already mentioned on another occasion, and whom she feared greatly.

Freud might have interpreted all this, and a modern counsellor might ask about her past experiences. Was there in fact a brother called Charles? Where was he, and what was her relationship with him? When had she begun to suffer her symptoms? Did she grieve for her childlessness? What were her relations with her husband? If Dickens asked any questions of this kind, he left no record of them. He thought the treatment was going well when she began to sleep better in January, and told him that she had been 'pursued by myriads of bloody phantoms of the most frightful aspect; and that, after becoming paler, they had all *veiled their faces*'.[19] But there was still the evil spirit, or phantom, who gave her orders and was hostile to Dickens. She also talked about sensations of fire in her head, which cooled under his treatment, she said. And she told him she had suffered experiences too terrible to be described. They were like fevered dreams, she said, but they had really happened to her. Her account of her experience in the Trinità dei Monti Church in Rome sounds like a psychotic episode, something that seemed real and was more powerful than real experience, and more frightening. Such psychotic episodes can stay with patients for years, as this one clearly did, leaving her devastated, so much so that she even warned Dickens not to go to that particular church when he was in Rome.[20]

In fact he had already arranged to go to Rome, taking Catherine. They would be leaving Genoa on 19 January. The De La Rues would join them in Rome in March, and meanwhile he and Augusta De La Rue agreed to a plan whereby they would think of one another every day at 11 a.m., relying on being able to continue the treatment in this unusual way. They attempted the method, and there was an absurd episode when he thought he was mesmerizing her long-distance from the box of the coach on which he was travelling, only to find that Catherine, also seated on the box, and knowing nothing of the arrangement with Madame De La Rue, had gone into a trance. In Dickens's next letter to De La Rue he warned him that the 'devilish figure' of her fantasies was likely to drive her into madness, and speculated as to whether it had its origin in 'some great nerve or set of nerves on which her disease has preyed'; and this is when he also wondered if the disease was being cured by 'the inexplicable agency of the Magnetism'.[21]

Dickens himself was now so emotionally involved that in Rome, before the De La Rues arrived, he experienced night disturbances in which he woke up suddenly in the small hours in 'a state of indescribable horror and emotion'. He took this to be part of the battle between the evil phantom, doing its best to drive her to madness, and his own efforts to rescue her. 'I thought continually about her, both awake and asleep, on the nights of Monday, Tuesday, and Wednesday . . . I don't dream of her . . . but merely have an anxiety about her, and a sense of her being somehow a part of me, as I have when I am awake,' he wrote to De La Rue from Naples.[22] A modern therapist would be expected to guard himself against this degree of emotional involvement, but Augusta was sending him impatient letters, 'incoherent and unconnected . . . My mind misgives me that she must have had a bad attack, after this long interval.'[23] When the De La Rues were due to arrive in Rome in March, he rode out to meet them, and escorted them to the hotel in which both families were staying. Shortly afterwards De La Rue took Dickens into his wife's bedroom one night, where she was lying unconscious, having had a seizure, rolled into a tight ball. He said she had been in similar states for thirty hours at a time before, and untreatable; but Dickens, after taking up her long hair and tracing it to its roots gently to get at her head, was able to relax her into a peaceful sleep in half an hour.[24] On 19 March, Dickens noted in his diary, 'Madame DLR very ill in night. Up 'till four.'[25]

There were further night sessions. It did not occur to him that the situation might seem odd to anyone outside it. To Catherine, however, it was upsetting, and she made her objections known to what looked like an infatuation, or a *folie à trois*, in which he and the De La Rues were caught up together. She can hardly be blamed. She was pregnant once more, and must have hoped for some attention from her husband during their holiday together; but Dickens saw the pregnancy merely as 'a coming event, which I hadn't reckoned on . . . casting its shadow . . . in a very disconcerting manner' – this in a letter to a man friend.[26] He was fully taken up with his medical mission, and believed he was succeeding, by persuading Augusta that they were engaged in a struggle between the evil phantom intent on controlling her mind and himself, her good champion, offering her freedom and health. By encouraging her to see it as a story, a dramatic narrative, he no doubt hoped to give her something to hold on to, and that they could work on together.

She now told him about another disquieting symptom: that her phantoms threatened and beat her on the arm, leaving a physical soreness there.[27] The treatments were continued throughout their return journey to Genoa, 'sometimes under olive trees, sometimes in Vine-yards, sometimes in the travelling carriage, sometimes at wayside Inns during the mid-day halt'. If, as Catherine believed, there was an erotic element in all this for him, it was subsumed in his sense of mission. He saw himself as a rescuer, fighting for the good, and told Catherine later that he was simply following the intense pursuit of an idea that had taken possession of him, just as other ideas had done at different times.[28] And although he was obsessed, he was able to extricate himself calmly when other matters needed his attention.

They went through Perugia, Arezzo and Florence, where he made some visits, to the writer Thomas Trollope and to Lord Holland, British Minister to Tuscany; and arrived back at the Peschiere early in April. They found the children well and happy, and he urged Forster, who had suffered all winter from rheumatism in his knees, to come out to enjoy the roses and sunshine of the Italian spring, and to travel back with them in June. His thoughts turning to Devonshire Terrace, he asked Mitton to arrange for it to be repainted for their return, the hall and staircase 'a good green', a 'faint pink blush' to the ceiling of the sitting room, 'a little wreath of flowers to be painted round the lamp' and 'the paper must be blue and gold or purple and gold . . . I should wish it to be cheerful and gay.' It was to be 'a surprise for Mrs D.' Unluckily, Mrs D objected to the colour green so strongly when she heard of it that it was countermanded.[29]

He spent the last weeks before the return journey trying to teach De La Rue how to mesmerize his own wife, but without success. Dickens even went to stay with them while the preparations for departure were under way at the Peschiere. Augusta gave him presents – a purse, a pretty glass, some slippers – and just before he said his farewells she showed the intensity of her involvement by calling out to him that he must remember to magnetize her on 23 December next, at eleven in the morning, which would be the anniversary of their first session.[30] He wrote to De La Rue from Zurich, and again from Brussels, expressing his conviction that she had benefited to an almost 'miraculous' degree from the treatment – 'I believe it impossible to exaggerate the alteration of her Mind – where incalculably the greatest torment and the greatest danger used to lie.' Both De La Rues sent frequent letters, and Dickens did his best to tell Emile he should not feel inadequate for being unable to magnetize his own wife, and promised that if she fell ill again, he would come to her aid again. He urged them to visit England and said he would return to Genoa, in a long, emotional letter, recalling their travels together and 'our happy company. I can't forget anything connected with it. I live in the Past now, in sober sadness.'[31] In September he was addressing her as 'My dearest Madame De La Rue', and ending a long, affectionate letter with 'What would I give to see you . . .? I carry you about with me in the shape of a Purse; and though that pocket is in a very tender place – breast pocket – left hand side – I carry you about in tenderer places still, in your own image which will never fade or change to me, come what may.'[32]

Augusta De La Rue relapsed slowly into her previous state. By the end of 1845 Dickens was fully occupied with work he could not leave, but somehow in January 1846 both De La Rues were so convinced that he was about to visit them that they prepared for his imminent arrival, making up a room and having his favourite dish ready. They must have misunderstood something he said, or imagined the whole thing, since he neither came nor wrote to explain. They recovered from this, and she heard from him in April, when he excused himself by saying that Catherine was unwilling to revisit Genoa. The friendship survived; they kept up occasional exchanges of letters and met again in Switzerland in 1846, as we shall see. In 1853 he visited them briefly and offered to resume magnetizing; but now she refused, saying that it would be too painful to start and then stop again. He recommended Elliotson to her. She did not follow this up, having heard that he took insane patients: clearly she drew a distinct line between their condition and hers. Some correspondence continued, and in 1863, before a visit to England with her husband, Mme De La Rue described herself as 'a ruin now'. Such meetings as there were between Dickens and the De La Rues were friendly and uneventful. He remained interested in her, and her sufferings evidently continued, but she did not descend into madness, as they had feared, and continued to live her life as before, always supported and protected by her husband. The two men kept in touch, and Dickens never failed to send his love to her in his letters, although these were for the most part discussions of Italian politics and business. After 1866 there are no further known exchanges of letters, but Dickens went on thinking about the episode, and his account of it in a letter to Sheridan Le Fanu was made six months before his death. It ended, 'She is . . . a very brave woman, and has thoroughly considered her disorder. But her sufferings are unspeakable; and if you could write me a few lines giving her any such knowledge as she wants, you would do an action of equally unspeakable kindness.'[33] Le Fanu did not, and probably could not, respond to this appeal. Dickens was able to do nothing more. He had only months to live. De La Rue also died in 1870, and Augusta disappears from history at this point, still presumably tormented by cruel phantoms and still without any explanation for them. No account by her of her experiences with the phantoms, or with Dickens, has been found, and it is not possible to give a diagnosis of her mental problems now. It may also be questionable as to whether any qualified doctor would have served her much better than Dickens did at that time. He offered himself boldly to help her, armed only with his ability to hypnotize, his good will and his intense curiosity about aberrant human experience and behaviour. Whether the results justified his neglect of his wife and indifference to her jealousy is another matter.

A saintly wife might have put aside whatever dislike and disapproval she felt about his behaviour and the De La Rues' part in it. Catherine, pregnant, away from home, faced with her husband's obsession with his charming female patient, felt vulnerable and showed that she was cross with him. She may have remembered how she had been cross during their engagement, and how he reproached her sternly for it and warned her not to repeat the performance. If his behaviour rankled with her, hers also rankled with him, so much so that he still held it against her and reproached her with it eight years later.[34]

⁕

During his year in Italy, Dickens managed to cover most of the country's best-known cities, and, as he did in America, wrote descriptive letters to friends, chiefly Forster, intending to use them for a book, which he duly put together as *Pictures from Italy*. It was offered as a series of impressionistic essays, he kept away from politics and art criticism, and the best pages come from his sharp and idiosyncratic eye for detail. Vesuvius and Venice were the two sights that took hold of his imagination most forcibly. Arriving in Venice, he decided that nothing he had read or seen pictured began to do it justice. 'It is a thing you would shed tears to see,' he told Forster. 'I never saw the thing before that I should be afraid to describe . . . it is past all writing of or speaking of – almost past all thinking of.'[35] He dutifully invoked Shakespeare's Shylock and Desdemona, but he actually noticed the modern workers – how the carpenters in their shops 'tossed the light shaving straight upon the water, where it lay like weed, or ebbed away before me in a tangled heap' – and he had visions of a future when the whole place would be under water, and people would look down into the depths to try to see a stone of the old city.[36] Bologna, Ferrara, Modena and Milan were briefly visited on the same trip; Verona delighted him, Mantua he found stagnant and neglected, missing its glories altogether.

A second tour, made with Catherine to be in Rome for carnival and Easter, gave him more material. He described Carrara, where he was struck by the singing of the workers in the marble quarries, so good that they doubled as chorus in an act of Bellini's *Norma* given in the little opera house. Pisa's tower, smaller than he expected from his childhood picture book, made him feel, when he reached the top, as though he were on a ship that had heeled over in the ebb tide. He dwelt on Rome, the carnival festivities, and his dislike of Roman Catholicism, confirmed by visits to St Peter's and the elaborate Easter rituals. Ancient Rome – the Colosseum, the Forum, the triumphal arches and the stones of the Via Sacra – he saw as bearing the traces of the bloody gladiatorial spectacles put on by the emperors. He praised the industry of the modern Jews, observing that they were locked up each night at eight in their crowded ghetto. The Campagna pleased him best, and he walked many miles along the Appian Way, with its grass-grown ruins and mouldering arches, aqueducts, larks nested in the stones, and fierce herdsmen. And he gave a page to the guillotining of a man found guilty of murdering a German countess. As an opponent of public executions, and indeed of capital punishment, he felt obliged to go and wait for several hours to see a Roman one, and reported that when the criminal was finally brought the blade fell quickly, the head was put on a pole for display, and the guillotine, which he inspected, was dirty; also that the eyes in the severed head were turned up, and there seemed to be no neck left on the body. No one else, he complained, seemed affected by the 'ugly, careless, sickening spectacle' on which he lingered, before fixing it with his pen.[37]

Naples, Pompeii and Paestum followed, but the great set-piece is the ascent of Vesuvius, which Catherine and Georgina made with him. The weather conditions were such – snow had fallen and frozen to slippery ice over much of the volcano's surface – that they needed twenty-two guides, an armed guard and six horses for a party of six. They rode to the snow line, after which the ladies were carried in litters and Dickens walked with a stick, tumbling at every step. But the sky was clear and once the sun had set a great full moon appeared over the sea below, offering a sublime spectacle. The snow gave way to a region of cinders, ash, smoke and sulphur, since Vesuvius, unknown to them, was working itself towards another eruption, and here they all had to walk as best they could. When the party stopped near the summit, he insisted on crawling to the very edge of the crater and looking down into the boiling fires below, rejoining the others with his clothes alight in several places, giddy, singed, scorched and triumphant. The way down, sliding over sheets of smooth ice, was extremely dangerous, and two guides and a boy slipped and fell into the darkness. One guide and the boy were found, stunned and bloodied but alive, but the second guide failed to reappear. Catherine's and Georgina's clothes were torn to bits and his were burnt, but they survived, and were greeted with open-mouthed admiration by the Neapolitans for their foolhardy feat.

This is the high point of Dickens's narrative. He considered Naples and its famous bay inferior to Genoa. There is a perfunctory account of Florence, its palaces, piazzas, old bridges and shining Dome, but the prison, in a courtyard of the Palazzo Vecchio, gets a good paragraph, with its inner cells like ovens, while from the outer ones the merry, dirty, violent inmates begged through the bars, smoking and drinking and playing draughts. He ended with the wish that a noble people would be raised up from a country divided and misruled. All this was quickly put together once he was back in England. There were more bad reviews than good, but it made a modest profit for Dickens and his new publishers, Bradbury & Evans. Even on a travel book, his name mattered more than the judgement of the critics: published in May 1846, it went on selling gently and is still in print.

12

Crisis

1845–1846

The enormous coach carried the Dickens family home over the St Gotthard Pass, travelling between high snow walls, and using wooden logs as drags as it descended the north side, a fearful task for the four horses. Repairs were needed at the bottom, but within a week they were in Zurich and in another ten days in Brussels, where they were met by Forster, recovered from his rheumatic illness, and by Maclise and Jerrold. After a few sightseeing jaunts in Belgium, from which Dickens took a day off to write to the De La Rues, they were at Devonshire Terrace again on 5 July, in a chaos of unpacking. D'Orsay wrote at once, 'Voici, thank God, Devonshire Place ressuscité. Venez luncheonner demain à 1 heure et amenez notre brave ami Forster.'[1] Catherine settled down to await the birth of her sixth child in the autumn; she had reached her thirtieth birthday just before they left Italy. Georgina was now eighteen, and always ready to be a walking companion for her brother-in-law. Broadstairs was booked for August and September. Dickens had no large new project in mind, although he soon proposed an idea for a weekly periodical to Forster, to be called 'The Cricket', and made up in 'a vein of glowing, hearty, generous, mirthful, beaming reference in everything to Home, and Fireside'.[2]

Forster was discouraging, so Dickens enlisted him instead into putting on a play, and the two friends threw themselves into theatricals, choosing Ben Jonson's comedy *Every Man in His Humour* for their first attempt and persuading others to join them in the enterprise. 'Home, and Fireside' could not compete with the excitement of organizing public performances. For Dickens it was a way of dealing with his restlessness as well as fulfilling his old ambition to be a stage manager and actor. For this first attempt he recruited two of his brothers, Fred and Augustus, his publisher Frederick Evans, his friend Thompson, still hoping to marry Christiana Weller, and various *Punch* contributors including the artists John Leech and Frank Stone, Douglas Jerrold and one of the editors, Mark Lemon. A few friends – Maclise, Cruikshank, Stanfield – held out against all persuasion. A retired actress, Miss Fanny Kelly, allowed them to use her little theatre in which she gave lessons in the dramatic art and provided two of her pupils to play small female parts; but the leading lady was the beautiful professional actress Julia Fortescue, well known to Dickens for her performances in adaptations of *Oliver Twist*, *Barnaby Rudge*, *Chuzzlewit* and *The Chimes* – and the mother of two children by her married lover, Lord Gardner, something that was naturally never mentioned. The men all agreed to contribute their own modest expenses, Maclise consented to advise on costumes, and Stanfield painted the scenery. The theatre was full for the performance on 20 September, and the presence of both Tennyson and the Duke of Devonshire in the audience delighted Dickens. Two more performances were given in mid-November to privately invited audiences who paid generously for their places, all the proceeds going to charity, and Prince Albert attended one, as the President of a committee that would benefit.

Dickens continued to put on theatricals over the next twelve years with unabated enthusiasm, sometimes at home, more often in theatres before large audiences; and he was generally admired for his acting skills, said by many to equal those of a professional. But amateur theatricals are always more exciting to take part in than to watch, and it is not easy to know how good Dickens's productions really were. His celebrity meant that many people wanted to see them, from royalty to provincial citizens, and his powers of organization and energy in arranging tours meant that they did see them; those who talked of what they had seen mostly felt they had been present at a great occasion. Yet Forster himself suggested that the performances might not have been much better than the average amateur attempts. Jane Carlyle thought the acting of the first production 'nothing to speak of', Thomas Carlyle described 'poor little Dickens, all painted in black and red, and affecting the voice of a man of six feet', and Lord Melbourne was heard to bellow in an interval, 'I knew this play would be dull, but that it would be so damnably dull as this I did not suppose!' Even Macready, who was surprised to find Dickens so good an actor, was sardonic in his diary about the preparations and performance of *The Elder Brother* in January 1846: 'it is quite ludicrous the fuss which the actors make about this play,' he wrote, and he found it 'not well acted . . . the whole play was dull and dragging.'[3]

On the other hand, Mrs Cowden-Clarke, a clever, enthusiastic daughter of the music publisher Vincent Novello, asked Dickens if she might act with him in 1848, and wrote a glowing account of his efficiency as a manager, his genius as an actor and his 'indefatigable vivacity, cheeriness, and good humour' during rehearsals and performances.[4] Gifted men like John Leech and another artist, Augustus Egg, were pleased to join him.[5] So was Mark Lemon, the ebullient editor of *Punch*, who shared his enthusiasm for acting and wrote many farces himself.[6] Friendships were made and strengthened, he worked his actors hard and gave them a good time, and through them he raised large sums of money for good causes: many widows were helped, many orphans educated, some indigent writers supported and charitable institutions funded. There were theatricals in 1846, 1848, 1850, 1851, 1852 and 1857. Two comedies by Jonson, Shakespeare's *Merry Wives of Windsor* and various farces were done, Mrs Inchbald's *Animal Magnetism* and Charles Mathews's *Two in the Morning* as well as *Mr Nightingale's Diary*, written by Dickens and Lemon; also plays by friends, Bulwer's *Not So Bad as We Seem* and Wilkie Collins's *The Lighthouse* and *The Frozen Deep*. Dickens found acting, involving as it did the losing of himself in taking on another personality, intensely enjoyable, 'I hardly know for how many wild reasons,' he told Bulwer.[7] One, no doubt, was that being himself was more exhausting than impersonating a stage character, who would run on predictable tracks, whereas Dickens did not always know where he was going next.

In July, Bradbury & Evans threw a 'new notion' at him. It was nothing less than a project to set up a daily newspaper to rival *The Times*. Since Dickens himself had suggested such a thing three years earlier, he was immediately interested. It was to be a Liberal paper, and it had come about through Bradbury's friendship with another Derbyshire-born man, Joseph Paxton, the great gardener to the Duke of Devonshire at Chatsworth. Bradbury & Evans published Paxton's *Horticultural Register*, and when he found himself rich through investing in railways he urged them to become newspaper publishers as well. Consulting with Dickens, they found he was excited by the idea of editing the paper. Forster did not approve. Dickens wrote back justifying his interest by telling Forster that his own confidence in his future as a writer was wavering. With hindsight this seems absurd, yet he was seriously worried about the possibility of 'failing health or fading popularity', and these fears made the newspaper appointment attractive.[8] He had no capital to put into the project – he was still living from month to month financially – and when he was offered £1,000 a year to become editor he bargained for more, and got it. In November agreement was reached between him and Bradbury & Evans that he should become editor of the new *Daily News* for a salary of £2,000 a year. The paper was to be launched in January 1846.

Almost at once there was a hitch when one of the shareholders lost money and withdrew, at which Dickens took fright and said he would not proceed. Paxton, who had put in £25,000, persuaded Bradbury & Evans to increase their contribution to £22,500. Dickens changed his mind. Offices were taken in Fleet Street. He began hiring staff. Forster, Jerrold and Fonblanque were to write political leaders. His uncle John Barrow was sent at once to India to report on the Sikhs, who were breaking out of the Punjab to attack the British with a large and well-equipped army. His father-in-law, George Hogarth, was offered five guineas a week to write on music. The most unexpected appointment to anyone who knew of his relations with his own father was that of John Dickens, brought out of retirement to be in charge of the reporters. The man he had recently excoriated as a nightmare figure, casting a 'damnable Shadow', a drag-chain on his life, an outrageous villain who reneged on all his debts, was to be made into a responsible official, to be trusted to fix the terms on which reporters were hired, to deal with their copy and to contribute to the organization of the new paper. Even more surprisingly, John Dickens made a success of the job and became at the age of sixty a popular and respected figure in Fleet Street, where he arrived for work every evening about eight o'clock, full of fun, fond of a glass of grog and known as the father of Boz. And Boz himself claimed that there was not 'a more zealous, disinterested, or useful gentleman attached to the paper'.[9] Among all Dickens's reversals of opinion, this must be the most startling.

During the autumn of 1845 Dickens was also occupied in looking to his various charitable commitments, taking the trouble to meet Esther, the eldest of the Elton orphans, as she trained to be a teacher. He found in Esther Elton a 'quiet, unpretending, domestic heroism; of a most affecting and interesting kind', as he told Miss Coutts, and gave her name to Esther Summerson when he came to write *Bleak House* six years later.[10] Miss Coutts responded generously to his appeals, fortunately, since he was further involved in raising money for the widow and six children of his late protégé John Overs, and for the four children of Laman Blanchard, who had committed suicide in December. Miss Coutts, no doubt impressed by the extent of Dickens's charitable work, now offered to do something for him: she proposed to pay for Charley's education, clearly intending that he should get the very best available. Dickens accepted her offer, and assured her that Charley was 'a child of a very uncommon capacity indeed' and that 'his natural talent is quite remarkable'; but a few weeks later he cautioned her that he needed to be at a school close to home, as 'a strange kind of *fading* comes over him sometimes' when 'he is anxious at his book, or excited at his Play'. He added that he was 'not at all fearful for him, except as I know him to be very quick and sensitive'. Miss Coutts hoped Charley could be prepared for Eton.[11]

All the children were in Broadstairs in August and September, mostly in the care of their nurses while Dickens was busy in London, and Catherine resting before the arrival of their next child. He and Georgina attended the wedding of Christiana Weller to his friend Thomas Thompson in mid-October, Georgy as a bridesmaid, he to make a speech. Two weeks later Catherine gave birth to a fourth son, Alfred D'Orsay Tennyson, named for his two godfathers, the French Count and the English poet. Catherine suffered very much during the delivery but recovered quickly, Dickens noted. As for his feelings, for all the flamboyance of the names given to the baby, he told friends, 'I care for nothing but girls by the bye; but never mind me.'[12] Meanwhile the two girls were taught at home by governesses, Georgina started off the younger ones with their ABCs, and babies were cared for upstairs by their nurses, wet and dry. Mamie remembered that their father inspected every room in the house every morning, checking for tidiness and cleanliness.[13] Catherine's role in the household seems to have been almost entirely passive, her youth going by in perpetual pregnancies and her babies handed over at once to wet nurses, leaving her in a curious limbo. She took herself for two walks a day during each pregnancy, but she walked too slowly for her husband to join her.[14] There is no record of what she and Dickens talked about, and although she shared his enjoyment of the theatre he habitually went with his men friends. Georgina worshipped him, accompanied him on walks and made him laugh by mimicking their friends; and when she was not included in invitations he sometimes wrote asking that she might be.[15] Judging from his letters, there were not too many quiet evenings at home, and the marital bedroom was the only place where husband and wife were alone together.

※

The new Christmas story, *The Cricket on the Hearth: A Fairy Tale of Home*, was finished on 1 December, and Dickens went to see the Fleet Street offices on the same day. The *Daily News* was announced as being of 'Liberal Politics and thorough Independence' and promised City news, foreign coverage, scientific and business information on every topic connected with railways, and criticism of books and arts 'by some of the most distinguished names of this time'. Dickens found himself a secretary and subeditor, William Wills, a *Punch* contributor who had worked for *Chambers's Journal* in Edinburgh, a solid rather than a brilliant fellow, two years older than him, who would go on to become his indispensable right-hand man. And Dickens was off to Liverpool, looking for more support for the paper and appointing an agent there, leaving his father in charge of the office in his absence.

The Christmas period passed in preparations, partly for the performance of a second play, *The Elder Brother*, early in January, partly for the first day of publication of the *Daily News*, set for 21 January.[16] *The Times*, hostile to Dickens and seeing the *Daily News* as a rival, attacked his Christmas story as 'a twaddling manifestation of silliness', without damaging its sales. The first edition of *The Cricket*, 16,500 copies, sold out before the new year and it went on selling steadily through many reprints. The market for a Christmas book from Dickens had been created and the public now looked forward to getting one. If their quality declined, as it did – the review in *The Times* was not far from the mark – their sales increased, helped no doubt by the fact that no fewer than seventeen dramatizations of *The Cricket on the Hearth* were staged. Dickens threw an even larger than usual Twelfth Night party at Devonshire Terrace, with singing, dancing for the children, speeches, supper and a ball for the adults, who included Talfourd, Macready, Cruikshank, Landor, Forster, Stanfield, Marryat 'and a hundred more'.[17] They were celebrating Charley's ninth birthday, and Charley, according to his father, was busy writing a play in four acts with a hero named 'Boy'.[18]

⁂

The Times had a circulation of 25,000 copies and sold for sevenpence. As editor of the *Daily News*, which offered eight pages for fivepence, Dickens would need to establish his paper against that pre-eminent position, and to take readers from other dailies. It was a gamble, but at least it started at a moment favourable to newspaper sales. The first issue was to appear at a time of intense political excitement as the long-running battle against the hated Corn Laws, which put duty on imported corn and so kept the price of bread high in England and Ireland, came to a climax. On 22 January, Robert Peel, the Conservative Prime Minister, told the House of Commons that he had changed his mind about the Corn Laws. Peel, a man of exceptional intelligence and courage, was a new convert to Free Trade. His conversion split the Conservative Party, since the great landowning MPs were also farmers who depended on selling their corn at good prices, but Peel was determined to get his bill through against his own party. Dickens, hostile to the Conservatives, did not trust him and thought he was 'decidedly playing false', suggesting as much to his own leader writer.[19] But he saw the importance of what Peel was trying to do, and he prepared carefully for the Prime Minister's second great speech on 27 January, determined that his paper should distribute detailed reports of it all over the country. The speech lasted for three and a half hours, and John Dickens entered into the spirit of the occasion, writing to Peel to ask if he would supply copies of the documents used in his speech, and taking personal charge of carrying the paper reporting it to the West Country, with Augustus to help him. The editor of the *Western Times* was so impressed that he wrote, 'Mr Dickens is a gentleman of the most enviable stamina. Time seems to have made no impression on him whatever. He had left London in the morning, travelled here [to Exeter] by rail, thence to Plymouth by chaise, and back again, and favouring us with a call, announced his intention to go back to London that night – and kept his word. That is Boz's father.'[20]

If Boz's father had found his niche at last, Boz had not. On 30 January, nine days after taking up his position as editor, Dickens wrote to Forster telling him he was 'revolving plans in my mind for quitting the paper and going abroad again to write a new book in shilling numbers'.[21] It was not easy for him to admit that he had been in the wrong, and he extricated himself awkwardly. On the same day as his letter to Forster he wrote to Bradbury & Evans about his anxiety that the paper could be seen as corrupt through its one-sided presentation of railway news, since so many of its backers had money in the railways. He also complained about their interference in the appointment of a subeditor and other staff matters. He was entitled to raise these points, but it would have been fairer to mention his intention of leaving his post as he did so. Although the paper had sold 10,000 copies on the day after Peel's speech, sales fell sharply afterwards and settled at around 4,000. Macready noted in his diary his despair at how poorly the paper compared with *The Times*. Dickens contributed an article on Ragged Schools for the issue of 4 February, then dined out on that day and on the next, not quite the behaviour expected of the editor of a new paper with problems needing to be sorted out. After this he made a two-day birthday trip out of town, to his beloved Rochester, supported by Forster, Jerrold, Catherine and Georgina, staying at the Bull Inn and walking over Cobham Park, Chatham fortifications and Rochester Castle. While they were away he persuaded Forster to take over as editor, and when they got back to London he handed in his resignation.

He told Forster he was 'tired to death and quite worn out', and there is no doubt that he had found the pressure of work as editor too much. But within a week he was putting a brave face on things, writing to De La Rue, 'I am a gentleman again. I have handed over the Editing of the Paper (very laborious work indeed) to Forster; and am contemplating a New Book . . . The Daily News is a great success . . . but I am not quite trustful in . . . some of the people concerned in its mechanical and business management . . .'[22] He wrote to Wills, saying he missed him 'a great deal more than I miss the Paper', and to Evans, with complaints against Bradbury, accusing him of discourtesy to his father and interference in his arrangements with the staff, but insisting that he had no quarrel with him outside the newspaper.[23] He continued to supply copy for the paper, not only his Italian travel pieces but four long, well-argued articles on capital punishment, declaring his absolute opposition to it, which appeared during February.[24] He had been paid £300 by Bradbury & Evans at the end of December, to cover January and February, but on 5 March he wrote to them complaining that they had not paid him anything 'on account of the Newspaper' and that his account with Coutts Bank was therefore overdrawn, which he found embarrassing, given his friendship with Miss Coutts. The following day they paid another £300 into his account, and a further sum on 29 April.[25] But he had felt humiliated, although Miss Coutts is unlikely to have been aware of the details of his account. And he had also to face the knowledge that the editorship, which he had meant to relieve him of his fears of deteriorating health and fading popularity, had proved beyond his powers, and he was still floundering.

Later, Miss Coutts was one of the people to whom he admitted he had been wrong in taking the editorship: 'I have no doubt I made a mistake.'[26] For now, with vague thoughts of a new book in his head, he began night-time roaming around London. He decided that his best plan, financially and professionally, would be to rent out Devonshire Terrace again for another year and take the family to Switzerland, which he had thought attractive when they travelled through it on their return from Italy, and where he could live cheaply and write in peace. Meanwhile he kept up his social round in London. The usual celebration of Forster's birthday and the Dickenses' wedding anniversary took place in April in Richmond, with his 'two petticoats', Forster, Maclise, Stanfield and Macready, the last finding the party 'rather more tumultuous than I quite like'.[27] This was followed by a dinner party for the christening of little Alfred D'Orsay Tennyson Dickens later in the month. Both godfathers were present, and Dickens took the opportunity to suggest to Tennyson, still a bachelor, that he should join him in Switzerland and share a house there with the Dickens family. Tennyson might well have quailed at the thought of living with six young children, but the reason he gave the Brownings was not that: 'If I went, I should be entreating him [Dickens] to dismiss his sentimentality, & so we should quarrel & part, & never see one another any more. It was better to decline – & I have declined.'[28] Still, Tennyson remembered the invitation and later in the summer, touring with his publisher, he called on Dickens in Lausanne and was entertained with wine and many cigars.

Dickens sent a long letter to Augusta De La Rue telling her he had walked out of the editorship because of his objections to the business management of the paper, which was only partly true, and that he had ceased all contributions, which was not true; and that he expected the paper to fail, which did not happen. His letter is slightly disingenuous throughout. He was writing to impress and please a woman he was fond of, and did not want to tell her that the load of work had been too great, and that he was bruised, and felt he must leave London because, as he told Forster, 'I don't think I *could* shut out the paper sufficiently, here, to write well.'[29] He also assured her that he would like to go to Genoa again but that Catherine would not consider it – this was true – and that they would be going to Lausanne instead, which would allow him to 'run over' to Genoa; although in fact his intention was to move to Paris before Christmas. Meanwhile Charley's planned admission to King's College School had to be put off. Dickens told Miss Coutts he would have him taught in Lausanne and sent to school in England after Christmas, when he would be ten. Roche was hired again, and Devonshire Terrace let to Sir James Duke for a year from 1 June.[30] John Dickens was happily employed at the *Daily News*, solvent at last and no trouble to anyone.

⚘

Four days before leaving, Dickens took the first step in an enterprise that was to be a central part of his life for more than a decade, by sending Miss Coutts an outline of his idea for a charitable enterprise in which they might collaborate. Of the many striking letters Dickens wrote, this is one of the most astonishing, laying out over fourteen pages his plan for setting up an asylum for women and girls working the London streets as prostitutes. He avoided using the word 'prostitute' to spare Miss Coutts embarrassment, but it was of course what he meant, and she understood; and he launched into a preliminary consideration of the practical details of re-educating them into a different way of life. They were not drily listed, but set alongside a sympathetic consideration of the plight of the women. Reading the letter, you have the impression that he had been thinking through his ideas carefully for some time.[31] He began by insisting that every young woman they might help would have been living a life 'dreadful in its nature and consequences, and full of affliction, misery, and despair *to herself*. Never mind Society while she is at that pass. Society has used her ill and turned away from her, and she cannot be expected

to take much heed of its rights or wrongs. It is destructive to *herself*.'
He went on to say that he hoped it could be explained to each woman
who presented herself for their assistance 'that she is degraded and
fallen, but not lost, having this shelter; and that the means of Return
to Happiness are now about to be put into her own hands . . .' Women
might come straight from prison, where prostitutes were commonly
sent, but each one must choose for herself to come to the Asylum,
and want to be helped.

His idea was to begin with about thirty women, and he expected
they might fail with as many as half of them. His hope was that those
who stayed the course could be restored to society and even become
'Virtuous Wives'. He was especially interested in the possibility of
preparing them to emigrate to the colonies, Australia, South Africa
and Canada, and thought the government might give recognition
and aid to such a scheme. Failing government aid, he hoped that
'good people' might be found to take them into service. He invited
Miss Coutts to entrust him with 'any share in the supervision and
direction of the Institution . . . I need not say that I should enter on
such a task with my whole heart and soul.'[32] And although he was not
yet in a position to start on the scheme, he meant every word, and he
continued to write to Miss Coutts with further ideas and suggestions
from Switzerland.

On 29 May, Dickens dined with Forster, who accompanied the whole
family as far as Ramsgate the next day. This time the Dickens caravan
consisted of six children, Anne and two nurses, Roche the courier,
Dickens, Catherine and Georgina, and the same dog, Timber. At
Ramsgate they took the steamer to Ostend, then a river steamboat
up the Rhine, a voyage that must have taxed the vigilance of the
nurses. They reached Strasbourg on 7 June, went on by train to Basle,
and there fitted themselves into three coaches for the three-day drive
to Lausanne. On 11 June they were at the Hotel Gibbon and after an
intensive search for somewhere to live Dickens took Rosemont, a
house small enough to fit into the great hall of the Peschiere in Genoa,

Rosemont, the house above Lausanne taken by Dickens in 1846.

he observed, but delightfully placed on the slopes above Lac Léman. There were enough bedrooms for all of them and guests, a small study for him, with a balcony overlooking mountains and lake, and the garden was full of 'roses enough to smother the whole establishment of the *Daily News* in', he assured Forster, pressing him to come out and join him in reading and smoking in the many bowers scattered about the grounds.[33] No sooner had he arrived than he also began to plan to 'run over to you in England for a few days' in November, should his writing go well.[34] But he could not get going with his writing because the box holding his proper writing materials and the small bronze figures he liked to keep on his desk had not yet turned up. He managed only letters, and eleven chapters of a 'Life of Our Lord' intended for the older children, and not for publication. He became anxious that Bradbury & Evans, unsettled by their newspaper enterprise, might not be the best publishers for his proposed new book, and asked Forster to consider whether Chapman & Hall should be asked to take over again; and Forster managed to dissuade him from this idea.

On top of all this he wrote to Lord Morpeth, a Liberal peer whom he knew slightly, telling him he was ambitious for some public employment, and that he had hoped 'for years' to become a Police Magistrate, a position in which he might put his social knowledge – of the poor, of education and housing, of disease and vice, of prisons and criminals – to practical use. He believed Morpeth might be able to help him to such employment.[35] Forster was not consulted about this surprising idea, no doubt another by-product of Dickens's failure of confidence in his ability to return to novel writing, and nothing came of it.

On 28 June, however, fortified by the arrival of his box of writing materials, and a copy of *Tristram Shandy*, which he opened by chance at the words 'What a work it is likely to turn out! Let us begin it!', he wrote the first pages of the book that would establish him in a secure financial position for the first time in his life: *Dombey and Son*.[36] But he could not know this yet, and he remained nervous about whether he could write it, and jittery about being committed to produce his fourth annual Christmas story at the same time. The first instalment of *Dombey* was due to appear at the end of September. Unhappy letters went off to Forster. Beautiful as Switzerland was, it had a terrible drawback: he explained that he found himself afflicted by 'an extraordinary nervousness it would be hardly possible to describe' because there were no streets to walk through at the end of his day's work, and he felt the want of them badly.[37] Still, he wrote steadily to finish the first number in mid-July, putting off a trip to Chamonix to do so; he felt he had a strong and promising story in hand, and wrote at length to Forster about his ideas for its development. At the end of the month he sent him the first four chapters and outlined more of the plot, but added that he was suffering from 'queer and trembling legs' and could not sleep.[38]

The opening chapters, with the birth of Paul Dombey, the death of his mother, the appointment of a wet nurse – something Dickens knew a great deal about – and the setting up of the unhappy relationship between little Florence Dombey and her father in the great, sombre house somewhere 'between Portland Place and Bryanstone Square', and the other cheerful household in the City where Dombey's office boy Walter lives with his uncle Solomon Gills, maker of ships' instruments – all this is done with vigour and assurance, and Forster praised it highly. Dickens replied that he had 'not been quite myself . . . owing to the great heat', that the weather made it almost impossible to work, and that he was thinking of turning to the Christmas book because it would be a relief to get it out of the way.[39] Soon he was finding 'extraordinary difficulty in getting on fast', which he saw as the effect of his two years' freedom from writing. The lack of crowded streets remained a real problem, and London seemed to him like a magic lantern in the distance, without which the labour of writing day after day grew 'IMMENSE' (written in capitals).[40] His need to walk through streets at night was a tormenting 'mental phenomenon': 'I want them beyond description. I don't seem to be able to get rid of my spectres unless I can lose them in crowds.'[41]

He does not explain what he meant by his spectres, but the word is a reminder of Augusta De La Rue's 'phantoms', sometimes called 'spectres' by Dickens, the tormentors she saw in her fantasies.[42] The De La Rues were in Switzerland in August and Dickens managed to spend a day with them at Vevey, and surely talked with her of her troubled mental state, and as surely did not mention his own. Forster tried to cheer him by pointing out that there would be busy streets in Paris, where Dickens was moving in November, and that once there he could easily get over to London. But he was not to be comforted, and he found letters a poor substitute for Forster's presence. When he feared that he might not get the Christmas book written at all, he wrote, 'I would give the world to be on the spot to tell you this,' and added that he had thought of starting for London that very night.[43]

Some relief from his wretchedness came when he made up his mind to read the first number of *Dombey* to the new friends he had made in Lausanne, mostly among English residents. They included the Hon. Richard Watson, a landowner of liberal views who ran his estate of Rockingham Castle in Northamptonshire on enlightened lines with his cultivated wife Lavinia; also William de Cerjat, a Swiss gentleman who became a lifelong friend and correspondent, and Cerjat's brother-in-law William Haldimand, a rich and philanthropic expatriate. They were invited to a soirée in mid-September for a formal prepublication reading from the proofs, where he read for over an hour and delighted everyone present. His spirits lifted and he felt himself, briefly, inimitable again. In England, Bradbury & Evans were showing their mettle as publishers by preparing for publication of the first number with bill-stickers posting announcements of 'Mr Dickens's new work' in Exeter, Edinburgh, Glasgow, Coventry, Bath and London, salesmen distributing cards announcing terms for advertising in the forthcoming numbers, and a distribution of 3,000 red-and-black advertising show cards.[44] Dickens took himself to Geneva, hoping to throw off attacks of sickness, giddiness and a bloodshot eye, but still thinking of giving up the Christmas book, and telling Forster again, 'I would give any money that it were possible to consult with you.' The giddiness and headache continued, and Geneva's staid townscapes were useless. He continued to complain of 'the absence of streets'.[45] Catherine, who was again pregnant, went with him, and Georgina was soon summoned to join them: he was there for a week at the end of September and for another in late October. Afterwards, Forster concluded his friend had been 'gravely ill', and Dickens himself felt he had been 'in serious danger' when his spirits sank so low.[46]

Yet in Lausanne he did a second reading for local friends, which caused 'uproarious delight. I never saw or heard people laugh so,' he told Forster, and he was inspired with a new idea. He went on, ' I was thinking the other day that in these days of lecturings and readings, a great deal of money might possibly be made (if it were not infra dig) by one's having Readings of one's own books. It would be an *odd* thing. I think it would take immensely. What do you say?'[47] Forster did think it infra dig for a writer to become a paid performer, but once the idea had come to Dickens it never left him, and twelve years later he put it to the test and found it deeply satisfying. Not only did it 'take immensely', it gave him intense pleasure to stand up before an audience to act out his own imagined characters, and to find he could hold the house enthralled, laughing and crying by turns. And it did more than this, offering him the best proof of the admiration and love in which he was held by the public, nourishing his belief in himself, and helping to carry him through the pain and unhappiness that was by that time inescapable.

Another earlier plan he mentioned to Forster again was his ambition to found a periodical, a weekly, to be sold cheaply, with something of the *Spectator*'s current radicalism and something of the *Athenaeum*'s cultural distinction, as it was edited by Dilke, with Carlyle, Landor and Browning as contributors. Here again was an idea he would carry out later; for the moment Forster knew that the most important thing was to keep him on track with his writing, and he did his best from a distance to be adviser, encourager and nurse. When Dickens found his prose running into lines of blank verse as he struggled with his Christmas book, he told Forster, 'I *cannot* help it when I am much in earnest,' and asked him to 'knock out a word's brains here and there', which Forster duly did.[48]

Still more important than any of these exchanges was Dickens's confession to Forster that little Paul Dombey and Mrs Pipchin's establishment, where the children were underfed and unhappy, were based on his own experience: 'It is from life, and I was there – I don't suppose I was eight years old; but I remember it all as well, and certainly understood it as well, as I do now. We should be devilish sharp in what we do to children. I thought of that passage in my small life, at Geneva. Shall I leave you my life in MS when I die? There are some things in it that would touch you very much . . .'[49] Whether the spectres haunting Dickens were connected with the stirring up of unhappy childhood memories or not, his unburdening of himself to Forster helped and led on to his bringing the memories out, in the autobiographical narrative he wrote to show him and also in his next novel, *David Copperfield*. Paul Dombey, the sick child who has to endure whatever is imposed on him by his unfeeling father in the way of care and education – losing his nurse, lodged with the unkind Mrs Pipchin, sent to a school with lessons far beyond his capacity – is the immediate forerunner of little David, who also loses nurse and mother, is cruelly used by his stepfather, and is sent to a bad school and then out to work unsuited to his age or abilities.

Forster's unfailing sympathy and responsiveness was especially admirable since he was himself dealing with problems at the *Daily News*. He felt increasingly out of step with the proprietors, objected to the raising of the price in October and resigned the editorship in November. Dickens would leave for Paris with his family in mid-November, settle them in a rented house there and travel alone to London, staying at the Piazza Coffee House again, in mid-December; and Forster agreed to go to Paris in January for two weeks so that he and Dickens could explore the city together.

✻

Dickens sent an affectionate letter to Macready from Geneva in mid-October, telling him he was escaping there from a bad headache, thanking him for his kind words about the first two numbers of *Dombey*, which he had sent him in proof, and teasing him about his large family of eight children, with a rueful acknowledgement that he was as bad, since his seventh was expected in the spring. Macready was in the middle of a season at the Surrey Theatre in Blackfriars, playing in the great Shakespeare tragedies, *Hamlet*, *Lear*, *Othello* and *Macbeth*. His Lady Macbeth was Mrs Ternan, a hard-working and reliable middle-aged actress, once the beautiful Frances Jarman, and at present living in lodgings over a fire-engine manufactory in the Blackfriars Road with her old mother and her children. After playing with her one night he heard of the death of her husband, who had long been confined to a lunatic asylum in Bethnal Green. Macready thought of how he might help her and sent round a note offering to let her have ten pounds. Two days later she answered, 'accepting with much feeling my offer . . . and wishing it to be considered as a loan. I wrote to her, enclosing a cheque for the amount; but unwilling to hamper her with the sense of a debt, requested, if the surplus of her labours offered it, to transfer it as a gift from me to her little girl. Poor thing!' And the diary went on, 'Forster came into my room; all is not going well with him and the *Daily News*.'[50] Had Dickens been in England, Macready might well have applied to him for further help for the Ternans, knowing how generous he was in assisting families in distress; but he was altogether too far away, and too preoccupied. On 4 November Mrs Ternan visited Macready, bringing not the one little girl he expected but her three daughters, Fanny aged eleven, Maria nine, and seven-year-old Nelly. All had worked in the theatre from the age of two. In the course of the visit their mother gracefully recited Portia's speech on mercy – 'it blesseth him that gives and him that takes' – as an expression of gratitude to Macready for his goodness, and brought tears to his eyes. Then the family set off to do the best they could, and for the next five years they toured in Ireland and the north of England, living in lodgings on cold meat, bread and beer, making their own costumes, taking any parts they were offered and ready to learn four parts in a week if they had to. They were professionals but the mother insisted that her daughters should never forget that they were also ladies. They were clever and tough, and knew that you had sometimes to play trashy parts, and do your best to redeem them; and the theatre in which they worked, although it often fell short of what they hoped it might be, represented an ideal of culture and beauty to which they subscribed. They were modern young women, hard up and ambitious, and in another ten years they would become part of Dickens's world.

Meanwhile, Dickens, having tried and failed to put his ideas and energies into a newspaper intended to promote liberal ideas and serve the community in England, found his escape to Switzerland unhelpful as he returned to his real vocation as a novelist. The physical and mental crisis he went through, charted in his letters to Forster, was the most severe he had undergone, bringing him to the edge of a breakdown. He pulled himself through, helped and comforted by Forster's responses, and he began to open up memories he had so far kept hidden. Both the ordeal and the process of remembering would strengthen him and enrich his work over the next years.

13

Dombey, with Interruptions

1846–1848

Three carriages carried the family from Lausanne to Paris, children and nurses (and dog, no doubt) in one, adults in another. They left on 16 November, passed through the Jura in frost and fog, rose at five each morning and were on the road for nearly twelve hours each day, putting up at inns and reaching Paris four days later. They all piled into the Hôtel Brighton, Dickens immediately set about finding a house to rent, and within a week they were installed at No. 49 rue de Courcelles, close to the Champs Elysées and the rue du Faubourg St Honoré. It belonged to a French marquis, and Dickens complained that the doors and windows failed to close properly against the freezing weather, the bedrooms were as small as opera boxes, the drapery on the walls 'inscrutable', and the dining room absurdly painted to look like a grove of trees. He had already embarked on exploratory walks through the streets of Paris, and caught a glimpse of the King, Louis-Philippe, sitting far back in his carriage and protected by a throng of mounted guards and police who scanned the avenues suspiciously as they went forward. The King made a poor impression on him, and he decided that Paris was 'a wicked and detestable place, though wonderfully attractive'.[1] Soon he was planning dinner with Charles Sheridan, attaché to the Ambassador, at a famous restaurant in the Palais Royal, Les Trois Frères de Provence, and Forster agreed to come over for two weeks in January so that they could discover Paris together.[2] In a letter to Lord Jeffrey, Dickens told him that Forster was 'my right hand and cool shrewd head too', and he confessed to Forster just how close he had been to a breakdown in Switzerland.[3]

Dombey needed his attention, but as soon as he was installed in the rue de Courcelles a letter came from his father, giving him grim news of his sister Fanny's health. She had consumption – tuberculosis of the lung – and the doctor advised that neither she nor her husband should be told the truth, which suggested he did not expect her to recover. That evening Dickens was too upset to go with Catherine and Georgy to the theatre. A week later he was still unable to settle to work, disliking his study, unable to find a corner anywhere else in which to write, moving the furniture about, distracting himself by writing letters, grumbling about the French as lazy, unreliable and fit for nothing but soldiering, and taking Georgy out to see Paris by night.[4] But when he did get down to writing, he told Forster coolly, with none of the agonizing he had shown over the end of Little Nell, 'Paul, I shall slaughter at the end of number five,' and as soon as number four was done he took himself to London, the Piazza Coffee House in Covent Garden and Lincoln's Inn Fields again, for a week just before Christmas.[5]

He needed to be in London with Forster for the good of his soul as well as having many practical reasons for going. There were arrangements to be made for Fanny's care in her illness, making sure she was seen by the best doctors, and considering whether the Burnetts should be persuaded to move to London to be close to them. There was the publication of his new Christmas book, *The Battle of Life*, on 19 December, the story of a girl who gives up her lover to her sister, feebly sentimental, but it sold out its first printing of 24,000 copies before Christmas Day and made him £1,300 by the end of the year. The Keeleys were putting on a dramatized version at the Lyceum which Dickens had offered to supervise, and he gave a reading to the actors for which Forster lent his rooms; Dickens mocked his friend for his pains, and especially for providing seventy-six thick ham sandwiches for the company. Dickens found the Keeleys' production poor and did his best to liven it up. He also had business with publishers, consulting with Chapman & Hall about a cheap edition of his works, and this now went ahead.[6] Hurrying from one appointment to another he caught cold, so that 'I can hardly hold up my hand, and fight through from hour to hour', as he wrote to 'My dearest Kate', telling her he was impatient for a letter from her.[7]

Back in Paris just in time for Christmas, a letter went off to 'My Very Dear Forster', wishing him 'Many merry Christmases, many happy new years, unbroken friendship, great accumulation of cheerful recollections, affection on earth, and heaven at last, for all of us'. Forster had to hear about his cold too: 'I am going to take a jorum of hot rum and egg in bed immediately, and to cover myself up with all the blankets in the house. I have a sensation in my head as if it were "on edge".'[8] On the last day of 1846 he visited the morgue to look at the unidentified bodies laid out there. He went alone at dusk and saw an old man with a grey head in the otherwise empty place.[9]

The Battle of Life sold because there was a market for any Christmas book from Dickens, but the critics were merciless. When the reviews reached Dickens in January, he winced and told Forster he felt disposed to go to New Zealand, but at the same time he was on to the fifth number of *Dombey*: 'I am slaughtering a young and innocent victim – ' The deed done, he walked the streets of Paris all through the night before going to meet Forster in the morning.[10] The two friends packed their fortnight together with pleasures. They went to Versailles, St Cloud, the Louvre, the Conservatoire, to hear a lesson given, and the Bibliothèque Royale, where they saw Gutenberg's type and Racine's notes in his copy of Sophocles. They dined at the British Embassy, surveyed hospitals, prisons, the morgue again irresistible to Dickens, and went to every possible theatrical performance. They conversed with the playwright Scribe and took supper with Dumas. They talked with Gautier, with an ailing Chateaubriand, and with Lamartine, whom Dickens had met briefly in Genoa, and whose liberal politics he admired; and called on Victor Hugo in his apartment in the Place Royale. Hugo made a profound impression on both of them with his eloquence, and Forster observed that he addressed 'very charming flattery, in the best taste' to Dickens. Dickens thought he 'looked like the Genius he was', while his wife looked as if she might poison his breakfast any morning; and the daughter who appeared 'with hardly any drapery above the waist . . . I should suspect of carrying a sharp poignard in her stays, but for her not appearing to wear any'.[11] Having made his joke, he decided that 'Of all the literary men I saw, I liked Victor Hugo best.'[12]

The time he and Forster spent together in Paris developed his view of the people, and he began to see the virtues of the French, to forget his earlier outburst about their unreliability, and to be charmed by the people and the place. 'The general appreciation of, and respect for, Art, in its broadest and most universal sense, in Paris, is one of the finest national signs I know. They are 'specially intelligent people: and though there still lingers among them an odd mixture of refinement and coarseness, I believe them to be, in many high and great respects, the first people in the universe.'[13] This was the beginning of a real love for France, and the French reciprocated, with translations and imitations of his work, culminating ten years later in the publishers Hachette commissioning new translations of all the novels and stories, approved by Dickens.[14] Already in the 1840s his work was being translated into many other European languages, German, Italian, Dutch and even Russian, but with none did he have so close a relationship as with the French, whose language he learnt.[15] Forster said he had a poor accent but good written French. He signed off a letter to Forster 'Charles Dickens, Français naturalisé, et Citoyen de Paris', and in 1847 he began to write to D'Orsay in French, bold if simple and inaccurate: 'Ah Mon Dieu! Que les mois s'ecoulent avec une terrible rapidité! L'instant que je me trouve libre, je me trouve encore un forçat lié a la rame. N'importe! Courage Inimitable Boz! Vous l'aimiez assez-bien mon Brave, après tout!' Within two years he had mastered the language well enough for serious correspondence.[16]

※

Meanwhile he had his novel to write. It sold unexpectedly well from the opening number in October 1846, keeping Bradbury & Evans busy with reprints, and for the January number they began with 32,000 copies. The success was well deserved, because the book makes a tremendous start with the death of Mrs Dombey in childbed in the great sombre London house near Portland Place, her husband caring only for the newborn son, the fashionable doctors powerless, and her little daughter, Florence, weeping and holding on to her as 'clinging fast to that slight spar within her arms, the mother drifted out upon the dark and unknown sea that rolls round all the world'. The second chapter builds strongly on this with the hiring of a wet nurse to feed and care for baby Paul: Mr Dombey, jealous of the presence of an outsider and unhappy about handing his son to Polly Toodle, a motherly young woman with a husband working on the railways and many children of her own, insists that she give up her own name and be known as 'Richards' in his household, and does his best to remove any human feeling from the arrangement, telling her she need not become attached to the child, or the child to her. Reading this chapter makes you wonder about the wet nurses who came to work for the Dickens family year after year, and what sort of conversations Dickens may have held with them. And did his own small sons, passed from wet nurse to dry nurse to Georgina, sometimes seem uncertain whom they should attach themselves to?

Leaving this aside, the opening chapters of *Dombey and Son* are masterly in conception and writing. Polly Toodle is shown as a good, warm-hearted woman, 'quicker to feel, and much more constant to retain, all tenderness and pity, self-denial and devotion' than any man could be, writes Dickens. She alone comforts six-year-old Florence by telling her that her mother is in heaven and that she will see her there again.[17] But when she takes Florence home with her to Camden Town, the child is lost in the street and falls into the hands of an old woman who steals her clothes before sending her home, and Polly is held responsible and summarily dismissed. Little Paul's long decline begins when he loses the nurse who has been feeding him, and is hastened by his father's treatment, putting him into the care of the horrible Mrs Pipchin in Brighton for a year, and then sending him to a cramming school where he learns nothing, although he is a quick, sensitive and intelligent boy. He loves and relies on his sister above all others, and as he weakens and she grows, their father comes to hate the daughter he neglects. The telling of Paul's short life is a *tour de force*. At five, he questions his father about money and, receiving the answer that money can do anything, observes that it did not save his mother and cannot make him strong and well. He puts down Mrs Pipchin with his wit, hears the school clock talking and wonders whether his teacher, Cornelia Blimber, has any eyes behind her glinting spectacles. In fact he thinks like a small Dickens, which is partly what he is, as Dickens made clear to Forster when writing of

Mrs Pipchin's boarding house for children: it was 'from life, and I was there'.[18]

Forster prepared himself to hear the secrets of Dickens's early life, and the nation was held in thrall as he killed off this interesting child. Maclise protested privately about Florence, 'I'm never up to his young girls – he is so very fond of the age of "Nell" when they are most insipid,' but otherwise he found *Dombey* great, particularly admiring the presentation of London life.[19] Thackeray gave unmitigated praise to Dickens's blackly comic account of Paul's school at Brighton, where boys were force-fed the classics, and he found his death 'unsurpassed – it is stupendous'.[20] Sales fell off a little after Paul's death, but remained in the region of 30,000.

Dombey creates a world, draws in the reader and keeps its grip. The London he knew so well (and had missed so badly abroad) is set before us, from the grand residential streets to the northern edges of town, the modest dwellings and shops near the river in the City, and Camden Town. The energy and inventiveness are still there, although the near-perfection of the early chapters falls away sadly, and the idea proposed there – that Dombey and Son might become Dombey and Daughter – fails to deliver its promise. But he allowed himself plenty of room to elaborate on his comic characters, and the best of them are as sinister as they are funny. One is Major Bagstock, a retired Army officer bursting fatly out of his own skin, a flatterer and bully who fixes rewards and punishments for friends and enemies, and who introduces Dombey to his second wife, Edith. Another is Edith's mother, Mrs Skewton, the aged society lady who has to be assembled each day by her maid – with diamonds, short sleeves, rouge, curls, teeth and other juvenility – and taken apart at night, when 'the hair dropped off, the arched dark eyebrows changed to scanty tufts of grey; the pale lips shrunk, the skin became cadaverous and loose; an old, worn, yellow, nodding woman, with red eyes, alone remained ... huddled up, like a slovenly bundle, in a greasy flannel gown.'[21] She is one of Dickens's most splendidly disgusting creations, worthy of Swift.

Dombey himself is a construct of pride, obstinacy and cruelty in his dealings with his daughter. Florence's perfect submission and goodness have irritated readers, and indeed she has no character to speak of. Dickens shows that he does not quite know what to do with her by putting her into fairy-tale settings, allowing the Dombey house to fall into decay with extraordinary rapidity while her father is away on holiday, keys rusting in the locks, fungus appearing in the cellars, dust, spiders, moths, black beetles and rats taking up their abode in the walls, grass growing on the roof and fragments of mortar dropping down the chimneys – an unlikely situation in a splendid town house staffed by many servants. It is pure fantasy, but it allows Dickens to say, 'So Florence bloomed there like the king's fair daughter in the story.' She is in a fairy-tale again when she finds a safe retreat from her father's cruelty with good old Captain Cuttle, a retired sailor living in a ships' instrument shop, with a hook for a hand. Here Dickens acknowledges openly what he is doing with the words 'a wandering princess and a good monster in a story book might have sat by the fireside and talked as Captain Cuttle and poor Florence . . . and not have looked very much unlike them.'[22]

Florence does not inhabit the same world as her businessman father, although she is loved by his office boy, and Dickens tells the reader disappointingly little about the business of Dombey, or the reasons for its failure. He is more interested in describing Dombey's second marriage, to Edith, a young widow who agrees to become his wife while making it plain she does not care for him. She is following her mother's instructions to marry money, and Dickens underlines the point by giving her an unknown cousin Alice, who also sells herself, in her case as a prostitute. His intentions are serious, but undermined by his inability to present real women: Florence has to be a fairy princess; Edith is a leading lady in a *mélodrame*, Alice also. All Edith's behaviour is taken from the theatre, whether she is tearing the diamonds out of her 'rich black hair' and throwing them on the floor, trampling on her expensive bracelets, beating her hand against the marble mantelpiece until it bleeds, or puffing herself up as a sign of rage, inflating her nostrils, swelling her neck and dilating her whole form, like an angry toad (Dickens had been watching actresses carefully). Her face becomes that of a beautiful Medusa, looking on her husband to strike him dead. And when she is departing from the

Dombey house, she shrieks and crawls past Florence on the stairs 'like some lower animal'.

She leaves Dombey and runs off with his repellent office manager Carker in order to humiliate him. Dickens originally intended her to become Carker's mistress, but was talked out of this by his old and respected friend Jeffrey; instead he made the plot still more improbable by having her meet Carker in a distant part of France, Dijon, only to tell him she has no intention of having anything to do with him or ever seeing him again. Her scorn and bad temper make you doubt that any man could have contemplated sexual relations with her either in or outside marriage, and you can't help wondering how she handled the wedding night with Dombey. Dickens naturally excluded any allusions to sex, as the conventions of the time required, but the deeper reason was that he did not know how to write or think about it, at any rate in relation to adult women. There are moments when he apostrophizes Edith in the course of the narrative: 'Oh, Edith! It were well to die, indeed, at such a time! Better and happier far, perhaps, to die so, Edith, than to live on to the end!' He repeats the suggestion that it would be better to die than to be sexually disgraced in his next book, thinking of Little Em'ly, and in both cases it sounds like a piece of piety offered to a public that expected this sort of thing, either because he could not bring himself to write truthfully on this subject, or because he did not know how to.[23]

Carker, knowing himself to be pursued by a vengeful Dombey, hurries back to England and dies under a train. *Dombey* is often praised as the first great novel of the railway, and it makes good use of the building of the lines through Camden Town, which meant the demolition of rows of small houses with gardens, and changed the neighbourhood and patterns of life there, something he had observed closely.[24] Further on in the book trains are used as symbols, less successfully. When Dombey takes a train he feels it is 'a type of the triumphant monster, Death' because he is thinking of death that has taken his son. 'Away, with a shriek, and a roar, and a rattle' goes his train, giving 'glimpses of cottage-homes, of houses, mansions, rich estates, of husbandry and handicraft, of people, of old roads and paths that look deserted, small and insignificant as they are left behind: and so they do, and what else is there but such glimpses, in the track of the indomitable monster, Death!'[25] The prose becomes purple as Dickens enjoys himself with the image of the train as Death for two pages. Towards the end of the book he indulges himself again, as Carker is drawn to obsessive train watching, seeing the engines like fiery devils, roaring and dropping glowing coals, with two red eyes and a track of glare and smoke, until he falls to his death under one, and his mutilated fragments are cast into the air. Although Dickens himself thoroughly enjoyed travelling by train and made good use of the railways, their power to terrify was irresistible material for his fiction, and every reader remembers the death of Carker.

Another change to his original plan was to allow Walter – the office boy who loves Florence and is sent away by Dombey, and was originally meant to be corrupted and turn to the bad – to return as a hero. He has kept his love for her, and she greets him with the words 'Welcome to this stricken breast!' – she has taken over Edith's theatre talk. Her sisterly affection easily changes to something warmer, the young couple are married and a happy ending is allowed, in which Dombey, bankrupt, ill and alone, softens to his daughter at last, and becomes an improbably affectionate grandfather. Dickens said he wept continually over the manuscript as he approached the end. The judgement of one of Dickens's later friends, Wilkie Collins, was that no intelligent person could read 'the latter half of *Dombey* . . . without astonishment at the badness of it'. This is a harsh verdict but true: the disappointment is sharper because the early part of the book is so good and so full of promise, which is wasted in feeble plotting and over-writing. Another old friend, Ainsworth, described the later numbers of *Dombey* as 'infernally bad' and 'disgustingly bad'.[26]

Since then many critics have praised *Dombey* for its presentation of contemporary society, its concern for social problems, its exploration of relations between parent and child, and its suggested theme that the life of decency and affectionate feeling was becoming more difficult as society moved on.[27] You can argue about all these points: Mrs Pipchin and Mrs Skewton are both old and both strikingly lacking in decency or affectionate feeling, whereas young Susan Nipper and foolish Mr Toots are well endowed with both. Dickens introduces a homily against slum housing into a chapter otherwise given to a quarrel between Mr and Mrs Dombey, suggesting that they would have been better people had they devoted themselves to social problems rather than to private concerns; but this is a passing mention, peripheral to the book, which is essentially a story of private, domestic life. So much is the family the centre of interest that we are not even told what Dombey's business was, or the cause of its failure, other than his inattention. As Dickens finished the last chapters a huge gathering of Chartists, for whom he had considerable sympathy, was in London delivering a petition to parliament for extending the vote, but there is no hint of such contemporary issues in its pages.

✿

One look at the pressures on Dickens during the writing does something to explain the unevenness of the book, and causes astonishment that he got through it at all. In almost every month something happened to interrupt his work on *Dombey*, and he had to give up any idea of writing another Christmas book in 1847. There were family matters to begin with. Having let Devonshire Terrace until the end of June, he had to find another house to rent in London once they left Paris, and one in which Catherine could give birth in April in reasonable comfort. In February, just as Charley started as a boarder at his new school in London, he fell ill with scarlet fever, and Dickens and Catherine rushed over from Paris only to find they were not allowed to see him because of Catherine's pregnancy. They hovered anxiously, staying in a hotel in Euston while his Hogarth grandparents nursed Charley in their lodgings in Albany Street. Dickens busied himself with house hunting and finding furniture, and fell badly behind with writing the monthly number. 'My wretchedness, just now, is inconceivable,' he wrote to Georgy in Paris, where she remained in charge of the other six children.[28]

Charley recovered and was taken, thin and pale, to convalesce in Richmond, and only at the end of March were his younger sisters and brothers brought over to be reunited with their parents in a rented house at No. 1 Chester Square. It was close to their real home, between Albany Street and the park. Catherine had barely settled in before she gave birth to Sydney after an exceptionally painful labour, probably a breech delivery, so difficult that Dickens had to fetch a second doctor. She made a quick recovery, but three weeks later Dickens was attacked by a horse, a terrifying experience in which his sleeve was torn off and he feared the muscle of his arm was injured. It brought on a nervous seizure of the throat that required treatment and distressed him 'more fearfully than I could ever tell anybody', so that he could not write for several days.[29] He took himself to Brighton to get over it. After this all the children went down with whooping cough. They were settled in Broadstairs at the end of June, where they played on the beach, 'choking incessantly' according to their father.[30] So there were few months in which the writing of *Dombey* was not delayed or interrupted by domestic dramas and disasters; and always in the background was the worry of Fanny's progressive illness. In July he was able at last to move back to Devonshire Terrace and his familiar study.

Other distractions he took up voluntarily. In March his early publisher, William Hall, died, and he insisted on attending the funeral in Highgate, all that day thinking about how Hall had sold him the magazine in which his first piece had appeared in print fourteen years before – a knitting together of past and present that was important to him even when it meant losing a day's work. Then he undertook another theatrical enterprise, this time to raise money for Leigh Hunt, now in his sixties. Dickens appointed himself manager and took charge of casting, rehearsals, negotiating with theatres and organizing the company's travel. This occupied much of June and July: 'Between Dombey and Management, I am one half mad and the other half addled,' he complained.[31] Forster was busier than usual, having taken over the editorship of the *Examiner*, the liberal paper to which he had long contributed, and which he now enlarged and ran firmly and efficiently. And Dickens began to mull over an idea for an insurance scheme for writers, which would grow and require a great deal of organization and more fundraising theatricals in the next years.

In November he and Catherine visited their friends from Lausanne, the Watsons, in their home in Northamptonshire, Rockingham Castle. It was a spectacular place, set high above a ravine, built as a royal castle in the eleventh century and half destroyed in the Civil War, but it had retained its great hall, gatehouse and round towers, and been altered further over the centuries to make it into a private residence set round a courtyard. Watson had been an Army officer before inheriting the estate in the late 1830s, married his well-born wife and become a benevolent landlord, building a school and improving tenants' cottages. Cautious as Dickens was about the aristocracy, he was won over by the charm of both the Watsons, and Rockingham set his imagination to work. A few years later it became a partial model for Chesney Wold in *Bleak House*, the splendid but melancholy pile in which generations of titled Dedlocks lived luxurious and useless lives – a slightly equivocal tribute to the house of his friends which he nevertheless continued to enjoy visiting.

After this indulgence in high life he went on to Leeds to address the Mechanics' Institute on the subject of education, and praise their work, which included day and evening classes in chemistry, French, German, business studies, drawing and design; they had set up a good library, and attracted steadily increasing numbers of women students. An audience of several thousands had gathered to hear him, and when he appeared they rose to applaud 'the author of Little Nell', and clapped and cheered many times in the course of his speech, which was a passionate endorsement of the value of the educational work being done there. Although he had been 'half dead with cold on the chest and loss of voice', he told Forster he thought he had never spoken better.[32] After Christmas at home, he set off again, with Catherine, for Glasgow, where another educational institution for working men and women had invited him to speak, and where the same adoring and applauding crowds greeted him.

Catherine did not hear him speak because she had been taken ill on the train journey. She was suffering from an early miscarriage. Dickens made light of it to Georgy ('nothing to speak of'), but told his brother Alfred that she had become 'violently ill', he had been obliged to call two famous doctors, and they had forbidden anything but a direct return to London on the express train.[33] In this way he missed the intended meeting with Alfred and his wife and new baby, and also with their sick sister Fanny and her husband, Burnett. Once home in Devonshire Terrace, Catherine took to her bed for several days, evidently needing the rest.

In January 1848, thanking Thackeray for a letter of generous praise about *Dombey*, still unfinished, he told him, 'I am saving up the perusal of Vanity Fair until I shall have done Dombey,' and invited him to a dinner at the end of the month, to be followed by 'a prodigious country dance at about the small hours'.[34] One more distraction must be mentioned here. The letter he had written to Miss Coutts before leaving for Switzerland, with his scheme for helping prostitutes, led to the most absorbing and time-consuming project of the year, pushed forward with unflagging commitment and determination. Before the end of 1847, a year during which he wrote twelve episodes of *Dombey*, he had succeeded in establishing the Home for Homeless Women, funded by Miss Coutts and directed by himself. It required from him many visits, much interviewing of possible staff and assessing of possible inmates, many committee meetings and a very large amount of letter-writing. The next chapter will describe how he set about it.

⚇

The sales of each of the last three numbers of *Dombey*, in January, February and March 1848, were around 34,000, and people continued to buy back numbers for months afterwards. In 1847 he earned £3,800, and for the first time ever he had enough money in the bank to be able to invest. From now on he had no more serious financial worries – as Forster put it, 'from this date all embarrassments connected with money were brought to a close.'[35] It was a turning point in his life, curiously brought to him by the book that took as a central theme the powerlessness of money, whether to save life, to give health or to win love.

With the public so pleased and the earnings so good, he was naturally jubilant. He celebrated with Forster, Mark Lemon and John Leech by allowing himself a few days in Wiltshire, taking a day's gallop across Salisbury Plain and returning to London on the Great Western Railway. Then he gave a dinner for twelve men friends on the day before the last number appeared on 31 March. About this time he impregnated Catherine again: Sydney was one year old, and she had recovered from the miscarriage, but she must have felt weary of perpetual pregnancies and also fearful of the repeated ordeal of giving birth, without having any possibility of protecting herself. Between 1844 and January 1849 four sons were born, none of them desired by Dickens, although he warmed to each of them during their baby years, giving them absurd and affectionate pet names like Chickenstalker, Keeryleemoo, Skittles and Hoshen Peck or Ocean Spectre. The last of these sons of the forties would be Henry Fielding Dickens, and he would turn out to be the cleverest and ablest of all the children.

14

A Home

1847–1858

Dickens had been observing the women of the streets since he was a boy. They appear in *Sketches by Boz* and, however unrealistically, in Nancy in *Oliver Twist*, whose portrait was, he insisted, true, and based on what he had seen in actual life around him; also in *The Chimes*, and currently in *Dombey*, and there would be more.[1] In 1840 he had also made sure that Eliza Burgess, the servant girl accused of killing her baby, got a fair trial, and had succeeded not only in that but in helping her back to a respectable job and a decent future: his first known rescue of a young woman who might otherwise have faced a wretched fate. He was compassionate but not simple-minded, and he could be strictly realistic about prostitutes and men's experience of them and need for them: for example, he defended Samuel Rogers when he was publicly accused of corrupting girls who became prostitutes by saying they had certainly been willing partners, and commented in a letter, 'good God if such sins were to be visited upon all of us and to hunt us down through life, what man would escape!'[2] He expressed admiration of the French for recognizing the existence of the social evils and vices that the English refused to talk about.[3] In 1848 he told Emerson, in the course of frank masculine conversation among friends, that 'incontinence is so much the rule in England that if his own son were particularly chaste, he should be alarmed on his account, as if he could not be in good health.' Dickens was responding to Emerson's statement that educated young male Americans went virgin to their marriage beds, and agreeing with Carlyle that in Europe chastity in the male sex was 'as good as gone in our times'. Charley was still eleven years old when this exchange took place, but there is no reason to doubt Emerson's account of it, and Dickens was surely expressing his view that a healthy man needed sex and that there would be something odd about a young man who did not look for it where it was easily available.[4]

We have already seen how, in 1841, Dickens suggested to Maclise that they might inspect the prostitutes in Broadstairs, telling him he knew where they were to be found. He accepted that it was normal for men to make use of them; but at the same time he felt a huge pity for the women as the lowest and most helpless members of society, with no prospect other than deepening misery before them, and seemingly without any power to save themselves. If there was some inconsistency between his tolerance of the practice and his wish to rescue the practitioners, it may be that he reckoned he was unlikely to end prostitution single-handed, and that men would always find what they wanted in one way or another. The double standard troubled many thoughtful Victorians of both sexes, with its unjust loading of all the blame for prostitution on to the women, and its decree that any young woman who became pregnant outside marriage could never redeem herself from the disgrace. Mrs Gaskell, Gladstone and Thomas Hardy all said or did their bit at various times to combat such hypocrisy, and there were many private initiatives to help women who were its victims; but none was as bold, as original and as imaginative as Dickens's Home, which he insisted from the start must be a real home to the young women he set out to help, run on homely principles, and not a place where they had to expiate their sins.

Miss Coutts, good and generous and ready to follow where Dickens led, was prepared to fund the project, which would cost over £700 a year (more like £50,000 in the money of 2011), and she gave him almost free rein in setting it up. He needed to find a house large enough to take up to a dozen or so young women, sharing bedrooms, plus a matron and her assistant – his early plan to take thirty was given up as impractical. He decided that central London was unsuitable, but that it should not be too far out either, and in May 1847 he came upon a small, solid brick house near Shepherd's Bush, then still in the country, but well connected with central London by the Acton omnibus. The house was already named Urania Cottage but from the first he called it simply the Home, the idea that it should feel like a home rather than an institution being so important to him. He liked the fact that it stood in a country lane, with its own garden, and saw at once that the women could have their own small flowerbeds to cultivate. There was also a coach house and stables which could be made into a laundry, and it was surrounded by fields, which he presently persuaded Miss Coutts to buy, to be let out to the local milkman as grazing for his cows – and he could supply the girls in the Home with milk.

The lease was agreed in June and soon afterwards he started interviewing possible matrons, set builders to work putting the fabric of the house into good order, decorating and equipping it with shelves and fencing round the garden. Bedsteads and linen had to be bought, kitchen and laundry equipment, crockery and cutlery, books and a piano, all from good suppliers: Dickens paid for everything and sent the receipts to Miss Coutts. He loved planning, purchasing and fitting up rooms, his imagination was engrossed, and he gave his time and energy happily.

He does not seem to have discussed the project with Forster, who was aware of it but has little to say about it in his account of Dickens's life: there is one allusion to the plan and a promise that 'future mention will be made', but it is not.⁵ Dickens's chief allies and helpers were Augustus Tracey and George Chesterton, the governors of Tothill Fields and Coldbath Fields prisons respectively, both good friends already. He put them on to the committee alongside two clergymen who were prison chaplains and an archdeacon interested in emigration, to satisfy Miss Coutts's wish that the Home should be run on strict Church of England principles. Her personal physician, Dr Brown, was another committee member, and she also appointed Dr Kay-Shuttleworth, an educationalist with sound religious principles whom Dickens found a bore. He was happy with Christian prayers and precepts but did not care about denominations and was determined to avoid preaching, heavy moralizing and calls for penitence, taking the view that they would only alienate the inmates; but he had to give way when Miss Coutts dismissed a good young under-matron, Mrs Fisher, on discovering she was a Dissenter. He himself concentrated on finding sensible, tough, unshockable and kindly women to work with the inmates. He had to turn down applicants who were too innocent, and one who talked of the work at the Home as a 'horrible task', and on the whole his appointments were successful, the most remarkable of the matrons being Mrs Morson, the courageous young widow of a doctor, who was able to take on the job because she had parents who could look after her three small children while she worked. She stayed for five years, teaching, providing excellent food and cooking with her charges, mothering them so well that they wept when they parted from her; she worked closely with Dickens, sometimes visiting him at home, corresponded with Miss Coutts and referred to her charges as 'the family'. She was an outstanding woman, an unsung Victorian heroine, and she left only when she was snapped up by a second husband. She remained proud of the work she had done with Dickens.

His aim was to rescue two categories of young women: those who were already known to be prostitutes, and those likely to drift into it because they lacked family support, had fallen into bad company, could not get work, become thieves and pickpockets, or were simply starving and in some cases suicidal. They were to be offered places in the Home, with good food, an orderly life, training in reading, writing, sewing, domestic work, cooking and laundering, and prepared to emigrate to new lives in the colonies, Australia, Canada or South Africa. His plan was to interview each young woman recommended to him – mostly by prison governors, magistrates or the police, although there were also private recommendations – to question her about her life and form an opinion of her suitability. Once accepted she would be told that no one would ever mention her past to her and that even the matrons would not be informed about it, although he sometimes disclosed details to his favourite, Mrs Morson. Each young woman was advised not to talk further about her own history to anyone else, and there would be nothing punitive or penitential in her treatment. He had a horror of the 'almost insupportable extent' to which religion was pressed on women in refuges and asylums, and knew how the women dreaded it; and he insisted that the chaplain at the Home should be discreet and gentle, 'the least exacting of his order', who would understand that the inmates needed to be 'tempted to virtue', not frightened, dragged or driven.[6]

The words he wrote to be read to young women considering taking up a place offered at the Home were easy, direct and unabashedly intimate in their tone:

> If you have ever wished (I know you must have done so, sometimes) for a chance of rising out of your sad life, and having friends, a quiet home, means of being useful to yourself and others, peace of mind, self-respect, everything you have lost, pray read . . . attentively . . . I am going to offer you, not the chance but the certainty of all these blessings, if you will exert yourself to deserve them. And do not think that I write to you as if I felt myself very much above you, or wished to hurt your feelings by reminding you of the situation in which you are placed. God forbid! I mean nothing but kindness to you, and I write as if you were my sister.[7]

It would be hard to improve on this, and it is not surprising that many young women were moved to put themselves into his care.

It was expected that each of them would live at the Home for about a year before being given a supervised place on an emigrant ship, by which time she would be well nourished, healthy, better educated – able to read and write, for instance – and better able to manage her life. Dickens hoped they would find husbands, which is indeed what happened to many of them, although Miss Coutts had doubts about the morality of a fallen woman marrying. He and she also disagreed about the clothing supplied to the inmates, Miss Coutts favouring sober tints, Dickens insisting that they should have dresses in cheerful colours they would enjoy wearing. He prevailed, and he also encouraged some lightening of the reading matter provided, which he thought in danger of being grim and gloomy. In one of his many striking letters to Miss Coutts, who was as innocent as she was well intentioned, he suggested that 'All people who have led hazardous and forbidden lives are, in a certain sense, imaginative; and if their imaginations are not filled with good things, they will choke them, for themselves, with bad ones.'[8] Believing in the power of music, he arranged for his old friend John Hullah, now a distinguished teacher, to provide lessons in part singing; he was surely right about this, but Miss Coutts found it too expensive a luxury and ended the arrangement.

The conditions in which the women lived were not harsh but simple. They slept three or four to a bedroom, each with her own bed: one young woman cried at the sight of a good bed all to herself when she first saw it. They got up at six in the morning, and they made each other's beds, to discourage everyone from secreting alcohol. They had short prayers twice daily, before breakfast and in the evening. They were well fed, with breakfast, dinner at one and tea at six as their last meal of the day. There was schooling for two hours every morning, mostly reading, writing and simple arithmetic – not all of them could read or write – and free time before and after dinner and tea. There was reading aloud while they did their needlework, making and mending their own clothes. They had their own plots in the garden, which was otherwise maintained by Mr Bagster, the gardener. They did all the household tasks, which were rotated weekly: laundry, house cleaning, cooking, breadmaking and so on (and it is worth noting that the pupils in the early teacher-training colleges for women were also required to do the housework). They made soup for the poor, to give them the satisfaction of helping others. On Saturdays there was a grand house tidying and cleaning and everyone had a bath. On Sundays they went to church with the matrons, who would also take them out individually or in small groups on other days. None was allowed out on her own, or to have unsupervised visits, or private correspondence, for fear that old associates might try to draw her back to the life she had left behind her. A doctor came if anyone was ill, and they were taken to hospital for treatment if necessary. No one was accepted who was pregnant or had a child. They were given marks for good behaviour – punctuality, cleanliness – and could lose marks for bad behaviour; and the marks were worth money, so that they were able to accumulate some to use when they left. A Mr Duffy came to talk to them about emigration, what to expect and what problems they might face. The first three inmates left for Australia in January 1849, and twenty-seven more crossed the seas over the next five years.

Dickens expected failures, and there were girls who were bored by the ordered life at Shepherd's Bush and could not bear living so quietly. One told him frankly as he was leaving after a committee meeting that she wished she were going out too, preferably to the races. Another took up secretly with the local policeman. Two broke into the cellar with knives and got drunk on the beer stored there. One he described, after expelling her, as capable of corrupting a nunnery in a fortnight. Some were so used to stealing that they could not give it up. There were dramas and rows, girls who stirred up trouble, girls who ran away and girls who had to be expelled. But the majority did well. What was expected of them was realistic, and they felt their health and strength improving, and saw that they were being offered something they thought worth having at the end of their time. Jenny Hartley, who has written an outstandingly good and gripping book about the Home, has traced a number of them to Australia and Canada, found the records of their marriages and even located descendants.[9] She has also found a few records of the girls who were expelled, some of whom went back to prostitution, and some who died pathetic early deaths.

Dickens knew very well that he was only touching a huge social problem which had its roots in society's neglect of the housing and education of the poor, its tolerance of the grim conditions in which workhouse children were raised, its acceptance of the double standards and the miserable pay and treatment of the lowest grades of female domestic servants – and also perhaps in something ineradicable in the natures of men and women. In 1855, answering an inquiry from Lord Lyttelton about the presence of prostitutes in theatres, he wrote, 'It is always to be borne in mind that, in a great City, Prostitution *will be somewhere.*'[10] He advised Miss Coutts in further large schemes such as the building of better housing for the poor in Bethnal Green, and the Home continued its work for over a decade. Only when the circumstances of his life changed and made it impossible for him to continue his association with it did Miss Coutts allow it to run down; the fact that she soon did so may suggest that she had never been so devoted to the cause, or so confident of its success, as he was.

Other writers have taken up good causes, but Dickens gave more time and thought to his Home and his rescue plans for young prostitutes working the London streets than could have been reasonably expected of anyone, least of all a writer with a large family who was also, from 1850, editor of a weekly magazine. None of the young women he helped knew enough to understand who he was or appreciate how extraordinary it was that he should devote himself to helping them. In his letters he reports a few of their remarks, heard on his visits to the Home. A girl called Goldsborough answered his question about what sort of work she might do in the colonies with 'that she didn't suppose, Mr Dickerson, as she were a goin to set with her ands erfore her'.[11] Another complaining inmate volunteered 'Which blessed will be the day when justice is a-done in this ouse.'[12] A third, who had her marks for good behaviour taken away and was told she must earn them back, said to Dickens, 'Ho! But if she didn't have 'em giv' up at once, she could wish fur to go.' He grew fond of the cheeky ones and understood that the quiet routine of the Home was difficult for many of them, but he never hesitated to throw out those who made trouble. When they were expelled they were not allowed to keep their good clothes. Isabella Gordon was sent out crying, on a dark afternoon, with only an old shawl and half a crown. Outside, she leant against the house for a minute and then went out of the gate and slowly up the lane, wiping her wet face with her shawl. We know these details because Dickens was watching her and described what he saw. He was fascinated by them: yet he never wrote about them in his novels. Some returned to prostitution and stealing, like Mary Ann Church, turned out in 1852 for causing so much trouble, and Mary Ann Stonnell, who discharged herself and was soon in prison again. Another girl who was expelled died in a Shoreditch workhouse soon afterwards. Others did well, made the long voyages to the colonies and built decent lives for themselves, like Martha Goldsmith, who married a carpenter in Melbourne, and Rhena Pollard, who also married and had a large family in Canada. Louisa Cooper, after two years in the Home, went to the Cape and returned looking very respectable, engaged to be married to an English gardener, and bringing Dickens an ostrich egg as a present, 'the most hideous Ostrich's Egg ever laid – wrought all over with frightful devices, the most tasteful of which represents Queen Victoria (with her crown on) standing on the top of a Church, receiving professions of affection from a British Seaman'.[13]

No one in public life was aware of his work, and when he wrote an article about the Home for *Household Words* it was published anonymously. There may have been something lopsided about an enterprise that set out to save a few poor creatures out of the crowd, but that did not deter him, and he gave an extraordinary amount of time and energy to making a success of it, seeing it as a model for others to follow. His warmth and his concern for detail can be found in his letters to Mrs Morson. In July 1850 he asked her to 'Tell the girls who go tomorrow [to the Cape] . . . as my last message, that I hope they will do well, marry honest men and be happy.'[14] When Mrs Morson was to fetch a new inmate, he wrote to her, 'Will you send underclothing to Eliza Wilkin now living with her father at 18 Market Row Oxford Market – with money for her to get a warm bath – or two would be better, and instructions to her to do so, that she may be perfectly clean and wholesome; and make an appointment to call for her, say on Wednesday or Thursday next. She has a gown that will do for her to come in. I suppose you have not one ready? Bonnet and so forth, I suppose you had better send her, I think. She is a rather a short girl.'[15] He did what he did because he believed it was needed. If there was a providence in the fall of a sparrow, these girls were his sparrows, and he wanted to make them fly, not fall.

15

A Personal History

1848–1849

In 1848 Dickens allowed himself a nine-month break between books, and out of it came a new development in his friendship with Forster. A month after the final number of *Dombey* appeared, Forster published a book of his own, *The Life and Adventures of Oliver Goldsmith*, a biographical study of the eighteenth-century writer. It is a hefty volume, nearly 700 pages long, dedicated to Dickens with a sonnet in which Forster compared him to Goldsmith:

> O friend with heart as gentle for distress,
> As resolute with fine wise thoughts to bind
> The happiest to the unhappiest of our kind . . .

Dickens wrote at once to say the book was 'very great indeed' – adding slyly that it was also 'extremely large' – and a week later he sent a glowing commentary, 'having read it from the first page to the last with the greatest care and attention'. This was a considerable feat, because some of it is heavy-going, but he admired the vigorous picture of Goldsmith's times, and the presentation not only of Goldsmith's strength but also of his weakness, 'which is better still'. The praise was sweet, since Goldsmith had been a favourite of Dickens since his boyhood, and he added enough comment and argument to show he had engaged closely with the book. He went on to say how proud he was to be 'tenderly connected' with what Forster had done, and added, 'I desire no better for my fame, when my personal dustiness shall be past the control of my love of order, than such a biographer – and such a Critic!'[1]

In this way he appointed his own biographer, at the early age of thirty-six, and never afterwards wavered from his choice. They had their fallings out. Macready reports a quarrel in the autumn of 1847, and there were to be more, for Dickens could tease and impose on Forster, Forster could disapprove of Dickens's behaviour, and their political views diverged somewhat, but their friendship and trust in one other always restored itself. For the present, he found comfort in confiding in him: 'I am more at rest for having opened all my heart and mind to you,' he told him in a letter written this May in which he dwelt on 'the more than friendship which has grown between us'.[2] A year before, in the spring of 1847, Forster had been told by Charles Dilke, manager of the *Daily News* after Dickens left it, of his recollection of seeing Dickens as a child, working in a warehouse near the Strand, and of how Dilke had given the boy half a crown, received with a polite bow, while his father looked on. When Forster mentioned Dilke's story to Dickens, he was silent for several minutes. Realizing he had touched on something painful, Forster did not pursue the matter, but it led presently to Dickens telling him about the blacking factory and his father's imprisonment for debt. He said he had spoken to no one else of these things, but never forgotten them and silently contained the distress they had caused him over the years. Now Forster's sympathetic interest helped him to soften and look more objectively at the small boy he had been. Sometime later he decided to make a written account of those years, and gave it to Forster, who observed in his diary that there was 'No blotting, as when writing fiction, but straight on, as when writing an ordinary letter'. He added that Dickens enclosed a note saying that 'The description may make none of the impression on others that the reality made on him ... Highly probable that it may never see the light. No wish. Left to J. F. or others.'[3]

Unburdening himself of his hidden life led to further turning over of the past and the workings of memory in his mind. The Christmas story he wrote in 1848, *The Haunted Man*, took for its theme the importance of being able to remember even wrongs and sorrows suffered in the past, and suggests that it is only through our memories that we are able to feel for others, something already hinted at in *A Christmas Carol*, in which Scrooge pities the self he remembers.[4] And in 1849 he began on what became his own favourite among his novels, *David Copperfield*, a first-person narrative that draws on some experiences of his childhood and youth. But first he allowed himself a year off, between the finishing of *Dombey* and the first number of *David Copperfield*. He had learnt the value of a break from writing and he could now afford one.

🕮

The year was 1848, when revolutions broke out all over Europe, with uprisings in France, Prussia, all parts of Italy and the Austrian Empire. Only London remained quiet, although when the Chartists announced they were bringing their petition for the vote with six million signatures to London the government moved the Queen to the Isle of Wight and the Duke of Wellington was brought up to defend the capital against possible uprisings. But the Chartists were peaceful and there was no violence even when their petition was rejected by parliament. Dickens was not unsympathetic to their cause, but he made no public demonstration of support. However, he applauded the abdication of King Louis-Philippe in Paris, and the declaration of a republic, writing jubilantly to Forster, 'Vive la République! Vive le peuple! Plus de Royauté! . . . Faisons couler le sang pour la liberté, la justice, la cause populaire!', and signing himself CITOYEN CHARLES DICKENS.[5] His faith in the good sense of the French people took a jolt when they elected Louis-Napoleon, nephew of Napoleon Bonaparte, as President, and still more when he made himself Emperor, and imprisoned or drove into exile his republican opponents; but Dickens still found France irresistible.

He told Miss Coutts he was tempted by an offer to be returned as MP for one of the largest London boroughs, but that prudence, and the thought that it would be hard to write and earn while sitting in parliament, made him refuse it. He added, 'if I *did* come out in that way, what a frightful Radical you would think me!'[6] At the end of 1848 he wrote an article attacking a judge who, in trying a group of Chartists accused of planning violence, stated that the French Revolution of 1789 had been unnecessary and harmful, a 'mere struggle for political rights'. Dickens insisted that the judge was wrong, and that it had been a necessary struggle to overthrow a system of oppression.[7] And his republicanism led him to celebrate the bicentenary of the execution of Charles I in January 1849, privately, with his fiery friend Landor.[8]

Within his family circle one dark cloud overcast the year. Fanny, known to be ill with tuberculosis since 1846, had remained at home in Manchester working as a music teacher all through 1847 and into the early months of 1848. Dickens invited her husband, Burnett, to his *Dombey* dinner in March, asked him to sing and paid his train fare: he wanted to persuade him to bring his wife and two small boys to London, where Fanny would have the support of her family and the best doctors. Yet she struggled on through April until she became too weak to continue with her teaching. Dickens wrote urging her not to work – 'do, do, do decide to stop' – and sent money to help them, and they agreed to move at the end of the quarter, in late June.[9] By the time they were settled in a house in Hornsey, Fanny was pathetically weak and thin, and the doctor Dickens sent to her told him there was no hope. He saw for himself that she was dying, 'and not by very slow degrees' he told Mitton.[10] He described her calm resignation to the prospect of death, and said she did not regret working hard during her illness because it was in her nature to do so; and that she was distressed about her children, but not painfully so, because she believed she would see them again. In telling Forster this, Dickens confessed that he feared for his own children, in case they had the same dreaded disease in their blood.

Fanny lived on through July, when Dickens was away in Scotland with his theatrical troupe, keeping in touch as best he could through their father, who devoted himself to watching over her. Dickens sent her claret as a comfort, and once back in London was able to make daily visits for a while. But his children were in Broadstairs, he took Catherine, who was pregnant, to join them, and after a few more days in London he followed her. Patience, so necessary in caring for the sick, was not one of his virtues, and, being unable to save her, he did not know what else to do. He told Macready he almost wished the end would come, 'she lies so wasted and worn.'[11] John Dickens continued his vigil at the bedside of his eldest daughter and kept his son informed. She was now suffering frightful paroxysms in which she could hardly draw breath. On 1 September, Dickens returned to London to find her in just such a paroxysm, half suffocated, an appalling noise in her throat and an agonized expression on her face. He saw her sink into a sort of lethargy, but not sleep, and she died the next morning. She was thirty-eight. He had loved her, envied her early education and success as a singer, seen how marriage and motherhood constrained her so that she performed less and had to rely on teaching; and pitied her first son, a bright child born with a physical handicap, who now pined and soon also died, Dombey-like.[12]

Fanny and her husband were devout Dissenters and she had therefore asked to be buried in unconsecrated ground, and Dickens arranged the funeral according to her wishes, in the appropriate part of Highgate Cemetery, where Forster went with him on 8 September. Then he returned to Broadstairs for the rest of September, set to work on his Christmas story, and at the end of the month walked to London through his favourite Kentish territory, Maidstone, Paddock Wood, Rochester and Chatham. Another case of sickness greeted him in London with the news that Roche, his good courier during his travels in Italy, Switzerland and France, needed to be admitted to hospital, which Dickens arranged at once. He had heart disease, and not long to live.

In December came two more family events: the weddings of his brothers Augustus and Fred, neither much approved by Dickens. Augustus, just twenty-one years old, asked to have his reception at Devonshire Terrace, and Dickens agreed, but escaped after the wedding breakfast, 'as I think it probable that some of my very affectionate relations may hold on here, as long as there is anything to drink'.[13] Fred was intent on marrying Anna Weller, the younger sister of Christiana Thompson, and Dickens strongly disapproved of the marriage on the grounds of her young age, uncertain health and unstable temperament. Having reluctantly paid off some of Fred's debts, he kept away from the wedding, which took place in Malvern on 30 December, with John Dickens as the sole representative of Fred's family. It was reported that Fred appeared in a white satin waistcoat with velvet flowers and silver ornaments: he evidently shared his elder brother's taste for dressing up. Both marriages were disastrous, Fred's ending in divorce in 1859 and Augustus abandoning his wife Harriet in 1858, after she had become blind, and leaving for America with another woman.[14]

The year ended with *The Haunted Man* selling 18,000 copies on publication (although not many afterwards) and Dickens planning a jaunt with his friends, 'an outburst to some old cathedral city we don't know, and what do you say to Norwich and Stanfield-hall?' for the new year.[15] Stanfield Hall was the scene of a recent sensational murder, and the jaunt was to be fitted in before Catherine's confinement, expected in mid-January. Forster did not feel up to it, Dickens failed to enjoy himself much with Leech and Lemon, Stanfield Hall was a disappointment and Norwich dull, but Yarmouth caught his imagination, 'the strangest place in the wide world . . . I shall certainly try my hand at it,' he told Forster.[16] He was back in time for Charley's birthday party, performing conjuring tricks in a Chinese dress and a mask, and dancing the polka, which his daughters had been teaching him. The night before the party he had woken in the small hours, fearful that he had forgotten the polka step, and got up in the cold darkness to practise the dance by himself. At the party he told Forster about this nocturnal exercise and added gravely, 'Remember that for my Biography!'[17]

On 15 January, Catherine went into labour. It was again an awkward delivery, with the baby badly positioned. But Dickens had read about chloroform as an anaesthetic, found out the facts when in Edinburgh, where it was in regular use, and, with Catherine's agreement, arranged for a doctor from St Bartholomew's, trained to administer it, to be present at the delivery. There was strong opposition to its use among most London doctors, who said it would produce idiot children, impede labour and possibly kill the mother, but Dickens was fully justified: the baby was quickly extracted without any damage, while Catherine was spared pain and made a rapid recovery. Four years later chloroform was so well accepted that it was given to the Queen for the delivery of her child.

He had planned to call his boy Oliver Goldsmith, then changed his mind and made him Henry Fielding Dickens, as 'a kind of homage to the style of the novel he was about to write', he explained to Forster.[18] But in truth *David Copperfield* is great in a way that is peculiar to Dickens. It is not a robust comedy of social and sexual hypocrisy like *Tom Jones*, but odder, more precise and more painful. Attachment and loss, and the shaping of adult behaviour by early experience, are its central themes. The first fourteen chapters, covering David's early childhood, stand on their own as a work of genius. They show with a delicate intensity the pain of a child being separated from his mother, unkindly used by his stepfather, humiliated and punished without knowing why, sent to a boarding school run on a harsh and unjust system, helpless in the hands of people who don't like him. Many parts of this experience being common, many readers have responded to it. Dickens understands how slowly time passes for unhappy children. He shows how someone who offers love to a neglected child becomes all important, as Peggotty, his mother's servant, does for David: 'She did not replace my mother; no one could do that; but she came into a vacancy in my heart, which closed upon her, and I felt for her something I have never felt for any other human being.'[19]

He tells us that even very young children observe adults critically, and judge them, not only the ones they dislike but also ones they love, in David's case his mother, whose faults of vanity and pettishness he notices even before she betrays him by marrying a stepfather against whom she will fail to protect him. And in a justly famous scene he shows David grieving for his dead mother and also preening a little before his schoolfellows at having this important event in his life. Before Freud or any of the child experts arrived on the scene the voice of childhood was truly rendered by Dickens out of his own experience – and out of his imagination, since the earliest chapters of the book are purely imaginary. Suffolk was hardly known to him, and Blunderstone, the village where David was born, was plucked from 'Blundeston', seen on a signpost and not even visited.

This was his first book to be narrated in the first person. It was also only the second novel to give a voice to a child who is taken seriously as a narrator. Two years before he started to write *David Copperfield*, a great stir was caused by *Jane Eyre*, which opens with a child's narrative of cruel usage by her guardians and at school. Published under a male pseudonym, it was soon revealed as the work of an unknown Yorkshire woman, Charlotte Brontë. As far as is known, Dickens never read *Jane Eyre* – he makes no reference to it in any surviving letters – but Forster would certainly have done so, and it was he who suggested the use of a first-person narrative to Dickens: 'A suggestion that he should write it in the first person, by way of change, had been thrown out by me, which he took at once very gravely; and this, with other things, though as yet not dreaming of any public use of his own personal and private recollections, conspired to bring about that resolve.'[20] That two writers should have within a few years made the voice of an ill-used child central to a novel is a remarkable coincidence. To Charlotte Brontë the idea had come spontaneously, and if Dickens was influenced by her, either directly or indirectly through Forster, it was a happy cross-fertilization between two great writers. There is little resemblance beyond this, the tone of her early chapters being passionate and angry, of Dickens's sorrowful, almost elegiac, culminating in the child David being shown his mother dead, with his baby brother in her arms, and seeing her in his mind as the mother of his own infancy, and the little creature as himself, 'hushed for ever on her bosom'. For Dickens the change to a first-person narrative was liberating and enriching: where Oliver, Nell and even Paul Dombey were the brilliant products of high artifice, David is a fully imagined, living child.[21]

Dickens's techniques are all his own. In the early chapters, and in moments of high intensity, David moves between past and present tense in telling his own story, carrying the reader with a 'Let me see . . .', a 'Now I am . . .' or a 'We are . . .' In this way, talking of his childhood home, he writes, 'Here is a long passage – what an enormous perspective I make of it!' 'Now I am in the garden at the back . . .' 'We are playing in the winter twilight, dancing about the parlour . . . I watch [my mother] winding her bright curls round her fingers . . .' And as he describes his mother taking him through a lesson, with his stepfather and his sister in the same room, 'I trip over a word. Mr

Murdstone looks up. I trip over another word. Miss Murdstone looks up. I redden, tumble over half-a-dozen words, and stop. I think my mother would show me the book if she dared, but she does not dare, and she says softly: "Oh, Davy, Davy!" "Now, Clara," says Mr Murdstone, "be firm with the boy."' And here he is leaving home: 'See, how our house and church are lessening in the distance; how the grave beneath the tree is blotted out by intervening objects . . .'[22]

His descriptions are so finely accurate that he seems to be watching something taking place before his eyes as he writes (and he may have been, as Thomas Hardy saw pictures in his mind when writing his poems). For example, when Peggotty is describing his mother's last days and death to him: 'Here Peggotty stopped, and softly beat upon my hand a little while,' and later again, 'Another silence followed . . . and another gentle beating on my hand.'[23] This is wonderfully observed of someone who finds it hard to express herself and needs to search for the right words, unconsciously beating with her fingers as she does so. Another instance: when he makes David, worn out from his walk from London to Dover, and facing his formidable aunt Betsey at last as she stands in the front garden armed with her gardening knife, simply put out one finger and touch her. Anyone who has lived with a timid child recognizes that gesture, and doubtless Dickens had observed his younger brothers and sisters, and his own children, doing just that; and here he plucks it from his memory and makes perfect use of it.

The detail is astonishing, and the establishment of the theme of the whole book – the education and development of a man from childhood, through suffering to happy maturity – is done with tenderness and humour. David is not the young Charles Dickens, although he is lent some of his experiences at the blacking factory. He transfers the callousness of his real parents to David's sadistic stepfather, Mr Murdstone, and makes John and Elizabeth Dickens into the charming Micawbers, with whom he lodges while working at the factory. They, to a degree, counter the poverty and loneliness he has been consigned to, with the denial of education, comfort or hope, and offer him affection and respect. Micawber speaks with the voice of John Dickens, in torrents of elaborate speech, always hoping something will turn up, mood-swinging from elation to despair as financial disaster looms; and he offers David the dictum Charles was actually given by his father, 'Annual income twenty pounds, annual expenditure nineteen nineteen six, result happiness. Annual income twenty pounds, annual expenditure twenty pounds ought and six, result misery.'[24] A large and unforgettable character, he is glorious in his incompetence and absurdity, and always well intentioned; and Mrs Micawber is as absurd in her way, and also without a shred of blame for David's unhappiness. Having divided his father in two, and cleared both parents of blame, he adds another interesting touch by making both Mr and Mrs Micawber appear oblivious of the fact that David is a child. They talk to him and treat him as a fellow adult and an equal – something that might suggest an explanation for the way in which the Dickens parents had treated their son, expecting him to deal with pawnbrokers, work in a factory and manage entirely on his own. His quick intelligence and clear capacity to carry out whatever was demanded of him had allowed them to forget that he was a child; but he did not forget how they had behaved, and used it.

The transposition of Mr and Mrs Dickens to the Micawbers is exceptional, however, and almost all the characters David encounters as he grows up are supplied by Dickens's imagination. Peggotty's family of Yarmouth fishermen, living in an inverted boat on the sands, with Ham and Little Em'ly, a blue-eyed orphan brought up by her uncle Peggotty, have no known models. Nor has Steerforth, David's older schoolfriend, a Byronic figure irresistible to him. Even as David sees him behaving badly, he worships him for his charm; this is the nearest approach Dickens made to showing romantic homosexual love, and it is frankly done. When they meet again as young adults Steerforth takes David home to meet his mother and her companion, Rosa Dartle, and she appears as the most interesting woman in the book, with her scarred lip and biting intelligence. David is too innocent to understand her or her exchanges with Steer-forth, whom she finds as attractive as David does, but for whom she refuses to be 'a doll', whereas David is happy to be called 'Daisy' by him. When Steerforth, who has met the Peggotty family through David, speaks of them as 'that sort of people', meaning they are less

sensitive than those of higher social class, Rosa responds with 'Really!
. . . I don't know, now, when I have been better pleased than to hear
that. It's so consoling! It's such a delight to know that, when they suffer, they don't feel . . .'[25] While David in his innocence misreads the
exchange and thinks Steerforth is joking and teasing her to get a rise,
Rosa's sarcasm is her way of rebuking his callous view. David is
wrong, and his friend is about to lay waste to the lives of the Peggotty family, carelessly, to amuse himself. But David will always find
excuses for Steerforth, and always remember how he would think of
him after going to bed at school: '[I] raised myself, I recollect, to look
at him where he lay in the moonlight, with his handsome face turned
up, and his head reclining easily on his arm . . .'[26]

David's aunt Betsey is another formidable independent woman,
not the type usually admired by Dickens, and he gives her her due in
her good works and good sense, and especially in her care of her protégé Mr Dick, whom she has saved from a lunatic asylum. Mr Dick,
who has difficulty in thinking coherently, takes David out with him
to fly his kite, and David is happy with him, and believes that the kite
lifts his mind out of its confusion as it rises in the sky. Very possibly
it does, and certainly Dickens believed in the beneficial effects of
games and imaginative play for everyone. Further on in the book,
Dickens mocks his own taste for child-brides when he makes David
fall in love with the adorably pretty and near-imbecile Dora Spen-
low, and marry her. His love for her is intense, and believable, since
she is another version of his mother, and there are scenes of rueful
comedy as they struggle to keep house, and he comes to realize he has
made a mistake he must live with. We know from his notes that, as
author, he found it hard to make up his mind whether to let her live
or to kill her off, partly perhaps because he drew on his memories of
Maria Beadnell when writing about her. In the chapters involving
Dora he several times reverts to the present tense, underlining the
link with the chapters about his mother, where he did the same. So
the book binds past to present and present to past.

Inevitably in a work of this length, written in monthly instalments with no choice to rethink and revise, there are weaknesses.
The chapters set in Canterbury – the old schoolmaster Dr Strong

with *his* child-bride, wrongly suspected of infidelity, and the Wickfield family, lawyer father and virtuous daughter, Agnes, who loves
David selflessly – are thin stuff, although Wickfield's evil clerk Uriah
Heep, red-haired, red-eyed and clammy of hand, is entertaining, one
of Dickens's monsters with a leitmotiv, continually declaring himself
to be 'umble'. The big drama of the plot comes when Steerforth
seduces Little Em'ly and takes her away to Italy on his yacht, her
uncle sets off to search for her, and Steerforth is drowned in a storm.
Here again the links are made between past and present, when David
is reminded by the sight of Steerforth's drowned body of how he
looked as a sleeping schoolboy. But Em'ly is characterless, and the
prostitute Martha who helps to find her speaks in the dismal clichés
of melodrama: 'Oh, the river! . . . I know that I belong to it . . . I
can't keep away from it . . . It's the only thing in all the world that I
am fit for, or that's fit for me. Oh, the dreadful river!' Or, again, she
urges Mr Peggotty and David to 'Stamp upon me, kill me! You
can't believe – why should you? – a syllable that comes out of my
lips . . .'[27] The young women at Shepherd's Bush whom Dickens
knew so well did not talk like this, and yet he could not resist giving Martha the same stage language he had given to Nancy in *Oliver
Twist*. Agnes Wickfield, promoted to heroine, is calm, efficient and
sexless, and as lifeless as Em'ly; and, as John Gross has remarked,
David's literary success has to be taken on trust, and 'after the splen-
dour of the childhood scenes one is grateful, on the whole, not to be
told anything about books written with Agnes at his side as an ever-
present inspiration, "pointing upwards".'[28] But even these weak
points are not enough to spoil the achievement of the whole book.
David Copperfield is a masterpiece built on Dickens's ability to dig into
his own experience, transform it and give it the power of myth.

It ran in its green-paper wrappers, with the Phiz illustrations
which became an integral part of it, from May 1849 to November
1850. Dora and Steerforth were killed off, Heep sent to prison, the
Micawbers, Em'ly and her uncle Peggotty to Australia, taking
Martha with them; and David became a famous author, happily
married to a second wife. It sold less well than *Dombey*, but went on
to become his best-known book all over the world. Tolstoy particu-

larly admired it, and it has always been turned to for comfort by those who have suffered in childhood from loss or unhappiness, unkind or unjust treatment.

As he wrote, he was conscious of how far he had surpassed any expectations he could have had himself as a child. His books had made him a man of substance who could live as he chose. His household was efficiently run by an adoring sister-in-law, and he could provide summers at Broadstairs for his thriving brood of eight children, governesses for his daughters and superior schools for his sons: Charley was to go to Eton in January 1850. He could take himself to Paris or go walking in his beloved Kentish countryside whenever he felt the urge. He could very publicly raise money for good causes while indulging his passion for acting and directing, and discreetly and privately devote himself to his work at the Home in Shepherd's Bush. Miss Coutts, the wealthiest woman in the country, friend of royalty, listened to his recommendations for good works, funded them and was a devoted personal friend, intent on ensuring that his eldest son should have every advantage in life, from outsize birthday cakes to the finest education money could buy. And he was still married to the wife of his youth, and still called her 'My Dearest Kate' in his letters.

Delivering the monthly numbers on time was not as troublesome as it had been with *Dombey*, and he was able to keep part of each month free: 'If it be only half an hour's sitting alone in the morning, in my leisure part of the month, and half an hour's look at pen ink and paper, it seems to keep me in the train. And with so much before me, and the necessity always present to me of doing my best and sustaining my reputation at its highest point, I feel it better and wiser to keep near my oar.' This was to Richard Watson, who had suggested they all return to Switzerland for the summer.[29] Instead Dickens took a villa at Bonchurch on the Isle of Wight, where Thackeray saw him arriving on 23 July and noted, with a touch of envy, 'I met on the pier as I was running for dear life, the great Dickens with his wife his children his Miss Hogarth all looking abominably coarse vulgar and happy.'[30]

Friends were summoned to share in the pleasures of the villa with its private bathing and waterfall made into a shower bath, and Dickens gave one of his displays of conjuring tricks, which he described as being, in one case, the product of 'nine years' seclusion in the mines of Russia', and in another acquired for 5,000 guineas 'from a Chinese Mandarin, who died of grief immediately after parting with the secret'.[31] You can see what fun he could be as a father. After this Bonchurch let him down. He developed a cold which turned into an obstinate cough and he began to feel weak; a doctor examined him with a stethoscope, and recommended rubbings of the chest of a particular kind used against tuberculosis. No doubt the memory of Fanny's suffering and the fear that he might be going the same way came to him. He had a bilious attack, his legs trembled, he had no energy to walk, or to read, or even to brush his hair, and he became convinced that he would die if he remained for much longer on the Isle of Wight – all this he told Forster by letter. Suddenly his symptoms disappeared, but then Leech, who was with them in Bonchurch, was knocked over by a large wave and became so ill that Dickens had to treat him with magnetism. This done, with good effect, he hurried away to a hotel in Broadstairs to write the next number of *David Copperfield*, and was not back in London until mid-October. In November he was invited by the Watsons to Rockingham, and enjoyed being a guest in their fine and ancient castle with keep, portcullis and all modern conveniences, twenty-six servants, and a beautiful and well-run estate. He told Forster it was 'a very pleasant spectacle, even to a conscientious republican like yourself or me'.[32]

Two annoyances involved him with lawyers during the autumn. One he brought on himself by drawing a character in *Copperfield* too closely from life, with Miss Mowcher, a dwarf and beauty specialist who is shown doing Steerforth's hair, and preparing to help him in his seduction of Em'ly. Mrs Seymour Hill, a close neighbour of Dickens, herself a dwarf and a chiropodist, wrote objecting to his portrayal of her as Miss Mowcher, which was understandably causing her distress, professional and personal. Dickens at once wrote back admitting he had taken some characteristics from Mrs Hill, and that he had meant Mrs Mowcher to be badly behaved, but that he would now change the plot and make her into a good character. He made the same assurances to her lawyer, whom she had already consulted, and did what he had promised, transforming Miss Mowcher into a doughty fighter for virtue in later chapters. The other legal battle involved a rascally Englishman, Thomas Powell, who published a hostile and worthless biography of Dickens in America. When Dickens wrote exposing Powell's past as a thief and forger who had escaped justice in England by having himself committed to a lunatic asylum and then fled the country, Powell threatened to sue him for libel. The Americans relished the attack on Dickens and the quarrel rumbled on.

In December he took Charley to be interviewed at Eton, where he was due to start in January. He was found to be well up on Virgil and Herodotus, and intelligent, although in need of a little extra coaching in writing Latin verses on the Horatian model. Dickens was 'inexpressibly delighted' by the way his son went through the ordeal of the interview with a strange schoolmaster, and reported proudly to Miss Coutts on his success. Otherwise the end of the year was given to dealing with visits to the Home, on 21 December and Boxing Day. At Christmas he resigned for the second time from the Garrick Club, giving no reason.[33] There were the usual family jollities, and some dining out and pantomime-going with Mark Lemon and Stanny – Clarkson Stanfield, the marine painter and one of his dearest old friends. Catherine was pregnant again, the baby expected in August 1850.

16

Fathers and Sons
1850–1851

On the second Saturday in January 1850, a week after Charley's thirteenth birthday, his sisters and brothers set up a great wailing at Devonshire Terrace as he left home for Eton, accompanied by his father. Dickens was suffering from a cold that made him feel his head had swollen to an enormous size, but he managed to dine with Charley's tutor, a classical scholar and clergyman, while Charley ate by himself in a large empty hall. It was a glum start for him, no other boys having yet arrived – a little like David's introduction to Mr Creakle's school – but he took it well and as soon as they appeared he began to make friends, proved popular and learnt to turn out Latin verses with the best of them. A few days into term Dickens heard of the death of his friend and mentor Lord Jeffrey, whose last letter to him, written a week before, had warned him against Eton: 'what is most surely learned there is the habit of wasteful expense, and, in ordinary natures, a shame and contempt for plebeian parents.'[1] Jeffreys had added tactfully that he expected Dickens's son to resist these effects, and Dickens threw himself into the Eton experiment, arranging swimming lessons for Charley so that the boy could row on the river as he wished, and descending on him from time to time with picnics to treat his friends; but he must have remembered his own sardonic description of a well-born and fashionable London clergyman who had been 'celebrated at Eton for his hopeless stupidity', and he was never entirely convinced that this was the right sort of education for his boy.[2]

January was also the month in which he wrote of Little Em'ly's fall, wickedly seduced by Steerforth. He told Forster he hoped he would be remembered through her 'for many years to come', as indeed he was.[3] He was busy as ever visiting the Home, where other less glamorous Em'lys were being saved from disgrace, and at the same time he was setting up his new periodical, fixing on its name, *Household Words*, in February. His friend Wills from the *Daily News* was appointed assistant editor in daily charge, Forster became a salaried adviser, and letters went out to many possible contributors. Mrs Gaskell was one of the first approached, already known to him through Forster, who had placed her first novel, *Mary Barton*, with Chapman & Hall. It was one of the earliest to be centred on the lives of industrial workers, and Dickens told her there was no other writer he was keener to enlist, explaining that the aim of the journal was 'the raising up of those that are down, and the general improvement of our social condition'.[4] He warned her that everything in *Household Words* appeared anonymously, but she was pleased to become a regular contributor, and two thirds of her stories and articles were from now on published by Dickens, including the Cranford series and *North and South*. They also shared a concern for the fate of young women who fell into prostitution, and she asked, and received, his advice in helping a protégée to emigrate. A touch of flirtatiousness surfaces in some of his letters to her – 'Dear Scheherazade', 'I receive you, ever, (if Mr G will allow me to say so) with open arms', 'O what a lazy woman you are, and where IS that article!' – and she teased him for his grand style of life at Devonshire Terrace, and held her own against his editorial pressures, while he confided to Wills, 'Mrs Gaskell, fearful – fearful. If I were Mr G. O Heaven how I would beat her!'[5]

He was also much engaged with his brother-in-law Henry Austin, now Secretary of the Board of Health, and determined to give coverage to the unspeakable housing conditions of the London poor, which had led to recent cholera epidemics and many deaths. Dickens agreed to address the newly formed Metropolitan Sanitary Association in February, and gave them a sharp speech. Over the next years he would also advise Miss Coutts about building decent housing for the poor in Bethnal Green, and he was practical and fierce in his protests against what he saw as criminal neglect and complacency in local and national government. In the autumn of 1854 he ran a series of articles on public-health issues in *Household Words*, calling for more funds and more powers to act for the local boards set up to deal with health issues, and going into the urgent problems of sewerage in London. People must be amused, but it was no good amusing them if they were dying of preventable illnesses.

He established the office of *Household Words* in a house at No. 16 Wellington Street, in what was then, and still is, theatre land. It was old territory for him, familiar from his childhood, Wellington Street running from Covent Garden south across the Strand and on to Waterloo Bridge. He was again knitting together disparate pieces of his experience, and from the start he used Wellington Street as much more than an office. When it was being fitted up, he asked Evans to have gas put in upstairs, to make the rooms comfortable, and it became a means to escape into bachelor life, somewhere he could dress and dine before going to a box at the Adelphi or the Lyceum without having to return to Devonshire Terrace. In April 1851 he told Wills he wanted to make himself two good rooms at Wellington

No. 16 Wellington Street, Dickens's office and pied-à-terre from 1850 to 1859, when he moved to No. 26, still standing.

Street to live in during the summer when necessary, and he had two iron bedsteads put in to use during the period of the Great Exhibition, intending to let out Devonshire Terrace while the family was at Broadstairs. Sometimes he talked of his 'gypsy tent' and joked about boiling a kettle on a cord hanging from three sticks and eating stolen fowls, but the reality was that men friends were invited for dinner as well as drinks, and presently he had the upstairs rooms properly furnished, and later installed a housekeeper, making it into an informal second residence in which he could comfortably stay overnight.[6] He found Wellington Street so congenial that when he closed *Household Words* in 1859 and started a new periodical, he simply moved from No. 16 to the bigger No. 26 and set up the same arrangement on a larger scale, with five rooms for his own use upstairs, to which he brought some of the furniture from the family home. Taking the two houses together, Wellington Street was his other home for eighteen years, longer than any other. Accounts of his entertaining there, over which he sometimes presided in a velvet smoking coat, suggest that there was a high consumption of iced gin punch and hot brandy punch, much smoking of cigars, and delicious food brought in from Fortnum's – pickled salmon, pigeon pie, cold meats and hot asparagus – oysters from Maiden Lane and sometimes a baked leg of mutton stuffed with veal and oysters, a dish of his own invention.

※

Household Words, out every Wednesday for twopence, went well from its launch in March 1850, and was soon selling around 40,000 copies a week. Bradbury & Evans had a quarter share in it, Forster an eighth and Dickens a half, and he paid himself a steady £40 a month, contributing something like a hundred stories and articles in the first three years. He set out to raise standards of journalism in the crowded field of periodical publication and, by winning educated readers and speaking to their consciences, to exert some influence on public matters; and to this end he himself wrote on many social issues – housing, sanitation, education, accidents in factories, workhouses, and in defence of the right of the poor to enjoy Sundays as they chose. He

ran several pieces describing the work of the Metropolitan Police
detectives, a body of men he presented as preternaturally observant
and discreet, and unfailingly efficient, who enjoyed disguising themselves to pursue suspects; he entertained a group of them at
Wellington Street, and became friendly with Chief Inspector Field,
who worked in retirement as a private inquiry agent.[7] As well as these
factual articles he contributed purely entertaining ones, including 'A
Child's Dream of a Star', a piece about death and children that made
a great appeal to the readers of 1850. He even launched himself into
art criticism, attacking Millais's *Christ in the House of His Parents* as
'mean, odious, repulsive, and revolting'.[8] The article is ridiculous as
well as offensive about the whole Pre-Raphaelite movement, but
Dickens had convinced himself in a manic moment that he could take
on any subject.

Until October 1850 he was also writing *David Copperfield*, and
remained confident in the book even though it continued to sell less
well than *Dombey*. There was a moment of annoyance in February when
he had to change the character of Miss Mowcher. Then in May he was
'Still undecided about Dora, but MUST decide today,' as he told Forster: and, having decided to kill her, he allowed himself to go to the
Derby with a hamper from Fortnum's. In August, when Catherine
gave birth to a daughter, she was named Dora in honour of his dead
heroine. By then the other children were installed at Broadstairs,
where Dickens had taken Fort House for two months. He wanted to
be close to the sea as he finished his book, and there he wrote the great
storm scene, eight hours on one day and six and a half the next, feeling completely knocked over by it; and did indeed come to the end,
with a wistful feeling that he was sending some part of himself 'into
the Shadowy World'.[9] He told D'Orsay how much he liked working
at Broadstairs, 'cette Ile desolée de Thanet. Je l'aime, néanmoins par-
cequ'elle est tranquille et je puis penser et rêver ici, comme un géant.'[10]

After this the giant took another year-long break before the next
book. He was now sure of his position and his earning powers. In
April 1852 the *Economist* pronounced that 'the works of Dickens . . .
are [as] sure to be sold and read as the bread which is baked is sure to
be sold and eaten.'[11] As novelist, crusading editor and public figure he

was loved by the aspiring poor, listened to by the middle classes and found amusing by their betters. He could invite whom he wished to the large and lavish dinners he gave at Devonshire Terrace, Catherine presiding alongside him, and in the early fifties his social circle expanded in interesting directions. Lord John Russell, Prime Minister from 1846 to 1852 and leader of the Liberal Party, initiated a friendship that meant a good deal to both of them. Dickens was invited to dine by Russell, later dedicated *A Tale of Two Cities* to him, and sought his patronage when trying to get his son Frank into the Foreign Office.[12] Richard and Lavinia Watson, the friends made in Switzerland, continued to send pressing invitations to come to Rockingham Castle, and there he met Mrs Watson's cousin Mary Boyle, a cheerful forty-year-old who wrote novels, delighted in amateur theatricals and quickly established a friendship with him; if it meant more to her than to him there was real warmth on both sides, and they enjoyed mock-flirtatious exchanges.[13] The naturalist Richard Owen, Hunterian Professor of Comparative Anatomy and Physiology and a member of the Royal Commission on Public Health in 1847, wrote articles for *Household Words* and became an admirer, describing Dickens as 'a handsome man, but much more – there is real goodness and genius in every mark in his face'.[14] Austen Layard, renowned excavator of Nineveh, whom Dickens first met at Miss Coutts's, was now a Liberal MP, and the two met to discuss social and political questions. The chemist Michael Faraday readily agreed to Dickens's request to allow his lectures to be used as a basis for articles in *Household Words*. Lady Eastlake, writer and friend of the Carlyles, and wife of Sir Charles Eastlake, the first director of the National Gallery, declared how much she enjoyed the company of Dickens at dinner, and they corresponded. Bulwer grew steadily closer: he was, after Dickens, the most successful novelist of their time, enormously prolific, and two of his plays, *The Lady of Lyons* and *Money*, ran for decades. An aristocrat and landowner, he joined with Dickens in founding the Guild of Literature and Art, meant to replace the Royal Literary Fund, whose charitable donations were handed out by condescending patrons, whereas their new insurance scheme was planned to allow writers to help themselves.[15] Over the next decade Bulwer, Forster and Dickens gave much time and energy to promoting this scheme, and put on more plays to raise money for it.

These were some of the great and the good who became part of the pattern of Dickens's life in the fifties. A different kind of friend appeared in 1851 in the shape of Wilkie Collins, introduced to him by the artist Augustus Egg. Twelve years younger than Dickens, Collins was the son of a successful artist and just making his way as a writer of fiction. He had read for the Bar, but only at his parents' insistence, and he was a dedicated Bohemian. Dickens saw that he was gifted, a good journalist and a striking storyteller, and found his way of life, easy and unconventional in its dealings with women, interesting. The two men shared a taste for brightly coloured clothes. Collins might appear in a camel-hair suit with broad-striped pink shirt and red tie, and even in sober colours his physical appearance was odd, with his big head and small body, a cast in one eye and a tendency to tics and fidgets. His best biographer says he made 'a more or less conscious decision to be not quite a gentleman'.[16] Wilkie hero-worshipped Dickens, who had risen so high that he did not need to worry any longer about whether he was a gentleman or not. He became Dickens's chosen companion for many of his escapes and jaunts. In this he replaced Maclise, but he did not replace Forster as the most trusted friend, and Forster continued to receive confidences that were never made to Collins.

Solid success did not keep Dickens from restlessness, and the desire for flight from London overcame him regularly. In June 1850 he persuaded Maclise to go to Paris with him, but they found the heat too much, and Maclise was unable to share Dickens's enthusiasm for visits to the morgue. On returning they heard of the untimely death of the great political leader Robert Peel, and Dickens lamented his loss to the country: he had changed his view of the man but not of parliament, and remarked that Peel could 'ill be spared from among the great dust-heap of imbeciles and dandies that there is no machinery for sifting, down in Westminster'.[17] In February 1851, as he set off for Paris again, this time to do some research for *Household Words*, he told Bulwer, 'London is a vile place . . . I have never taken kindly to it since I lived abroad. Whenever I come back from the Country, now, and see that great heavy canopy lowering over the housetops,

I wonder what on earth I do there, except on obligation.'[18] The prospect of the Great Exhibition, due to open in May 1851, made him want to get out of town to avoid the many thousands of visitors, and he failed to be cheered by the signs of progress it brought, the railway companies running hundreds of special trains to bring in country people, many of them given their first sight of London. He forced himself to visit the Exhibition, found it a muddle and told Wills he had always had an instinctive feeling against it.[19]

But it was not only London and the Great Exhibition that depressed him. There was also the feeling that he had too many sons needing to be educated and launched into the world, boys he found noisy and difficult to communicate with, boys who seemed to be inheriting the worst characteristics of both sides of the family – indolence, passivity and carelessness with money. He disciplined them hard at home, insisting on tidiness and punctuality, gave them tasks and inspected their clothes, which led to 'mingled feelings of dislike and resentment' and whispers of 'slavery' and 'degradation'.[20] Then there was the problem of his brother Fred, always in debt and asking for money, following in their father's footsteps.

The year of the Exhibition also brought the end of the lease on Devonshire Terrace and sent him house hunting, in Highgate and around Regent's Park. He looked only in North London, and offered £2,700 for a large house called Balmoral on the Regent's Canal.[21] In the midst of his unsuccessful bidding Catherine fell ill and needed his attention. She was suffering from migraine-type headaches that made her wretched. Dickens told his brother-in-law Austin that she had been unwell at intervals for three or four years, 'with a tendency of blood to the head, and alarming confusion and nervousness at times'.[22] This is the first known mention of such an illness, but she seemed so unwell now that he suggested a water cure at Malvern, recommended by Bulwer, who had benefited from the treatment. Dickens handled the situation with great care and gentleness, renting a comfortable house in Malvern for her while she took the cure, going with her to settle her in and preparing to stay with her for most of the time she remained there. Georgina was also with her. At the same time Charley was sent home from Eton with influenza. Dickens was also heavily engaged in preparing theatricals. There was to be a royal command performance of a comedy written especially by Bulwer, *Not So Bad as We Seem*, intended to raise money for the Guild, and Dickens was engaged in writing a farce, which he had to lay aside.

Hurrying back to London for a rehearsal and a committee meeting at the Home, he heard that his father was dangerously ill and about to undergo surgery on his bladder. The Dickens parents were no longer living in Lewisham but lodging in Keppel Street, between Gower Street and Russell Square, in the house of a Dr Davey, to whom Dickens had sent his father for medical advice. The Daveys had become friends as well as landlords, and it was Davey who called the surgeon and alerted Dickens. He arrived at his father's bedside almost as the surgery took place: 'He bore it with astonishing fortitude, and I saw him directly afterwards – his room, a slaughter house of blood. He was wonderfully cheerful and strong-hearted.'[23] Dickens went out to collect some medicine, and then to Devonshire Terrace, where he found the children happy and played with baby Dora, and wrote reassuringly to 'My Dearest Kate' saying he hoped to return to Malvern the following day, which he did.

Three days later he was in London again, to more bad news of his father's condition. He was at the bedside at eleven at night on 30 March and saw that John Dickens was unable to recognize anybody. The Daveys' house was now crowded with members and connections of the family: Alfred, who had travelled down from his railway job in Yorkshire, Augustus, Letitia and Henry Austin with Mrs Austin senior, Fred's Weller sisters-in-law, the widow of Dickens's old friend Charles Smithson, and Amelia Thompson. Dickens stayed beside his father until he died at about five thirty in the morning: 'I remained there until he died – O so quietly . . . I hardly know what to do,' he told Forster.[24] But he did know exactly what to do, and as his father died he took his mother in his arms and they wept bitterly together. This was the description given by Mrs Davey, who said that he behaved throughout with great tenderness and told his mother that she could rely upon him for the future. It was necessary reassurance, since his father's effects were valued at under £40. Dickens immediately paid whatever his father owed, and his mother stayed with Letitia while he found her a house of her own, in Ampthill Square, close to Somers Town, where they had all lived together thirty years before.

He put notices of his father's death in the *Daily News*, the *Morning Post* and *The Times*. He was too distressed to sleep and was up for three nights, much of them spent walking the streets. On the 2nd of April, his wedding anniversary and Forster's birthday, the two men drank Catherine's health together, 'with loud acclamations' he told her.[25] The next day he wrote to Forster asking him to accompany him to Highgate Cemetery to choose the ground for his father's grave. Forster had dashed to Bulwer's place at Knebworth for rehearsals and returned to go with him, and on the day of the funeral the two went together again in the morning to Highgate, before both taking the train to Malvern to be with Catherine. The shuttling to and fro continued, and the rehearsals. There were a few kindly obituary notices for John Dickens in the papers. Dickens remembered to book Fort House at Broadstairs for the summer, from mid-May to the end of October.

A week later he was in London to preside at the dinner of the General Theatrical Fund, calling at Devonshire Terrace first to see the children in the care of their nurses, and playing with Dora, now nine months old. She seemed perfectly well when he left her for the dinner, but even as he was making his speech she suffered a convulsion and died quite suddenly. A messenger was sent to the dinner; Forster was called out and decided to let Dickens finish his speech before telling him what had happened. Forster then travelled to Malvern again, taking a letter from Dickens, to tell Catherine. Another Highgate funeral had to be planned and carried out, and Catherine brought to London and comforted.

Meanwhile the royal command performance of *Not So Bad as We Seem* was due on 16 May, to be given at the London home of the Duke of Devonshire, necessitating rehearsals, dinners, fitting of costumes, consideration of questions of etiquette concerning the royal party, and special white satin playbills to be made for them with gold and silver fringes. Bulwer's estranged and angry wife threatened to turn up in the audience dressed as an orange girl in order to distribute a rude memoir of her husband, and Dickens alerted his friend Chief Inspector Field of the Metropolitan Police detectives to look out for her on the night and

Dickens took a lease on Tavistock House in 1851, intending to keep it for life.

deal tactfully with her if necessary. All went well, and the Queen found the play 'full of cleverness, though rather too long' – no doubt a standard royal complaint – but she found the acting of Dickens, 'the celebrated author', admirable, and enjoyed the '*select* supper with the Duke' afterwards.[26] Her presence did what was wanted, giving a boost to the Guild and encouraging contributions to its funds.

After this busy and distressing time the Dickens family could at last get to Broadstairs, although with many returns to London. Dickens went to the Derby with Wills, visited Charley at Eton, attended the Duke of Devonshire's supper and ball for the cast of the play, and a banquet given by Talfourd in belated honour of *Copperfield*, to which Thackeray and Tennyson both came. There were more theatricals, with the first performance of the farce he and Mark Lemon had concocted together, *Mr Nightingale's Diary*, which gave them both the chance to appear in many different disguises and to ad-lib to their heart's content, Dickens wildly impersonating Mrs Gamp and Sam Weller at different moments. It was a big success with the public in London and the provincial towns to which they took it, and allowed him to prove once and for all that he could rival the man who had first inspired him, Charles Mathews, master of the monopolylogues.

In July he finally acquired another large London house with a garden, Tavistock House in Tavistock Square, for £1,500. It was in very poor condition and needed a great deal of work before the family could move in. His friend, the impoverished artist Frank Stone, had lived in it with his family, and Dickens now lent them Devonshire Terrace. He took a fifty-year lease on Tavistock House, saying he intended it to last out his life, and sent in an army of workmen.[27] Back in Broadstairs, he invited Forster for three sunny weeks in September, then in October Stone came down with Augustus Egg.

Egg had been in love with Georgina for some time and now proposed to her. He was a handsome and sweet-natured man, a good friend of Dickens and a successful painter who could well afford to support a wife, but although she liked him she turned him down. Dickens told Miss Coutts later that he asked himself 'Whether it is, or is not a pity that she is all she is to me and mine instead of brightening up a good little man's house', but Georgina, after nine years with the Dickens family, was too much in thrall to his charm and energy to consider any alternative to her position in his life.[28] She was still his pet at twenty-four, but she was a pet with a steely centre, and in the organization of the household her voice was second only to his, and poor ailing Catherine let her rule. Georgy's adoration flattered him and he flattered her in return, saying she was intellectually far superior to Egg, and that her capacities were greater than those of 'five out of six' men.[29] With him she travelled, entertained and was entertained, enjoying an enviable way of life at the side of a great man. The children loved their aunt, but she and Catherine were both regularly required to be at Dickens's side when he was away from home, leaving the little ones with nurses and governesses and, as the boys grew older, away at boarding school. Georgy cannot have seen much to envy in Catherine's position: even now she was pregnant yet again, with a tenth child, due in March 1852.

17

Children at Work

1852–1854

For the next five years Dickens packed so much activity into his life that it is hard to believe there is only one man writing novels, articles and letters, producing *A Child's History of England*, editing, organizing his children's education, advising Miss Coutts on good works, agitating on questions of political reform, public health, housing and sewerage, travelling, acting, making speeches, raising money and working off his excess energy in his customary twelve-mile walks. At home, a tenth and last child was born, and Dickens put on ambitious plays for Charley's birthday at Twelfth Night. All the children had parts, and in 1854 five-year-old Henry Fielding Dickens played in *Tom Thumb*, causing Thackeray to fall off his chair with laughter. The other Home at Shepherd's Bush was often visited and supervised with meticulous care; he took a close interest in individual young women, and corresponded with Miss Coutts about them and about the many problems of administration. In Wellington Street he presided over *Household Words* with a sharp editorial eye, chivvying Wills with detailed advice by post when away, contributing articles of his own and writing a short novel, *Hard Times*, in weekly instalments to boost circulation in 1854. He travelled about with his theatrical troupe to raise money for the Guild of Literature and Art. When Forster was ill, as he often was, he visited him and read aloud to cheer him. With his newer friends Wilkie Collins and Augustus Egg as travelling companions he revisited Switzerland and Italy. He made occasional dashes to Paris on the twelve-hour South-Eastern railway service, and one long stay there *en famille*. He mourned for three of his men friends, struck down unexpectedly during these years, all in their fifties: Richard Watson, dedicatee of *Copperfield*; the beautiful, Byronic D'Orsay, driven to Paris by his debts; and

Talfourd, the ever hospitable playwright and stalwart liberal judge. Also Macready's wife Catherine, succumbing to the tuberculosis that ravaged her children as well; she was a close friend of Catherine Dickens, who must have missed her badly.

A daguerreotype taken in 1852 shows Dickens clean-shaven, but he made occasional experiments with a moustache and by the summer of 1854 he had settled for one. In 1856 he added a beard, and the fresh-faced Dickens disappeared forever, to the sorrow of Forster, who had invited Frith to paint his portrait just too late to catch him, and of many others too, who thought the bristles hid the beauty of his mouth. His complexion was becoming weather-beaten, his frame lean as ever, his walking habits as vigorous, his pace still a steady four miles an hour.[1] From 1853 the family spent most of their summer holidays in Boulogne, which replaced Broadstairs in his affection. And in December 1853 he read from his Christmas books in Birmingham to audiences of nearly 6,000, and told Wills afterwards that he was ready to consider paid readings. After the last reading on 30 December, Wills wrote, 'If D does turn Reader, he will make another fortune. He will never offer to do so, of course. But if they *will* have him he will do it, he told me today.'[2] The idea was firmly implanted, although the first paid public reading was not to be until 1858.

Between 1852 and 1857 Dickens wrote three novels which addressed themselves to the condition of England, novels that have endured as accounts of mid-nineteenth-century life and as extraordinary works of art, poetic, innovative, irradiated with anger and dark humour, peopled by lawyers, financiers, aristocrats, bricklayers, circus performers, soldiers, factory-owners, imprisoned debtors and their jailers, child labourers, musicians and dancers, aesthetes, thieves, detectives, committee women, and wives jealous, fierce, tender and battered. There was less laughter than in the earlier books, and more reckoning of accounts, as a man in his forties might think right.

The first of these novels was *Bleak House*. His earliest ideas for the story had been 'hovering in a ghostly way' about him since February 1851, but that year, with its deaths, house moving and fund-raising, allowed him no time to settle to a new book, although he was intermittently writing and sometimes dictating to Georgina his *Child's*

History of England.[3] Any thought of starting serious work had to be postponed until they got into Tavistock House, which did not happen until mid-November. Then, within days of sitting down in his new study, he told his publisher Evans there would be a first number of his next novel ready for March 1852. The opening chapters were written in December, and they established at once that the personal themes of *David Copperfield*, attachment and loss, love and friendship, had been left behind for broader and more sombre ones. The scene was set with fog over London and mud underfoot:

> London. Michaelmas Term lately over, and the Lord Chancellor sitting in Lincoln's Inn Hall. Implacable November weather. As much mud in the streets, as if the waters had but newly retired from the face of the earth, and it would not be wonderful to meet a Megalosaurus, fifty feet long or so, waddling like an elephantine lizard up Holborn Hill. Smoke lowering down from chimney-pots, making a soft black drizzle, with flakes of soot in it as big as full-grown snow-flakes – gone into mourning, one might imagine, for the death of the sun . . . Fog everywhere. Fog up the river, where it flows among green aits and meadows; fog down the river, where it rolls defiled among the tiers of shipping, and the waterside pollutions of a great (and dirty) city. Fog on the Essex marshes, fog on the Kentish heights.[4]

Spreading his fog, and throwing in a dinosaur for good measure, Dickens makes this the most powerful beginning of all his novels, as he rolls out the dark, dirty English earth and sky to set the theme of the book. It will take on the worst aspects of the legal system – its inhumanity, sloth, corruption and obstruction – as a basis for a larger matter, the bad governance of society as a whole; and it will show the physical sickness of London – its toxic water, rotten housing, bursting graveyards and festering sewerage – as part of the effects of that bad governance. There will be almost none of the high-spirited comedy of the early novels: most of the jokes in *Bleak House* are edged with horror.

Dickens is writing as a poet, taking as much delight in delineating wickedness and dark places as goodness and beauty. His imagination, always bold, now offers scenes as odd and inspired as Shakespeare's,

Dickens leased No. 1 Devonshire Terrace, York Gate, Regent's Park, in December 1839 for twelve years – years of hard work and lavish entertaining, during which five more sons were born.

More friends: T. N. Talfourd (*left*), liberal lawyer, politician, playwright; Dickens dedicated *The Pickwick Papers* to him. Count D'Orsay, artist and dandy, living beyond his means with Lady Blessington, mother of his divorced wife.

The aged poet Samuel Rogers gave breakfasts at which good conversation was required, to which Dickens went alone.

Miss Coutts, shy, good and spectacularly rich, became a true friend, seeking and taking Dickens's advice on her charitable spending.

Dickens chose to cross the Atlantic in January 1842 on the earliest wooden Cunard paddle steamer. The weather was so bad and the experience so terrifying that the return was made by sailing ship.

Daniel Maclise painted five-year-old Charley, Mamie, Katey and baby Walter for Dickens and Catherine when they went to America for six months, leaving them in the care of nurses and the Macreadys.

Maclise's triple profile drawing of Charles, Catherine and Georgina fixes the domestic situation at Devonshire Terrace: husband in charge, submissive wife, little pet – little, but strong-minded.

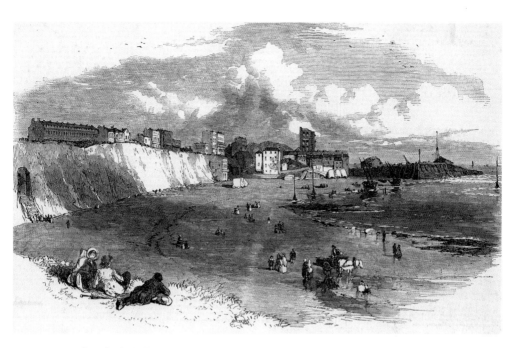

Many family holidays were taken at Broadstairs on the Kentish coast, which Dickens described to D'Orsay oddly as 'cette Ile désolée de Thanet', where he could think and dream 'comme un géant'.

Dickens travelled from Genoa to London in midwinter 1844 to read his Christmas story *The Chimes*, attacking the callousness of the rich towards the desperate poor, to a group of friends in Forster's rooms: these were the Hungry Forties. Maclise gave him a halo.

'About Paris! I am charmed with the place,' wrote Dickens in 1847. In the fifties and sixties he stayed at the Hôtel Meurice in the rue de Rivoli (*above*) and considered the French to be 'the finest people in the universe'.

He knew Lamartine (*left*), poet and liberal statesman, who headed the government in 1848, and Victor Hugo, who received him with 'infinite courtesy and grace'.

Boulogne became his favourite resort in the 1850s: 'best mixture of town and country (with sea air …) I ever saw; everything cheap, everything good'. He admired the honest and industrious people and the young women going barefoot 'with legs of bright mahogany, walking like Juno'. He rented several houses over the years, and sent four of his sons to boarding school here.

William Wills was always in England to hold the fort at the office from which they put out the magazine *Household Words* each week. He was the perfect assistant, devoted, diligent, a little dull, but discreet.

Wilkie Collins, novelist and Bohemian, met Dickens in 1851 and became a favourite companion in 'festive *diableries*'. They collaborated on stories and plays.

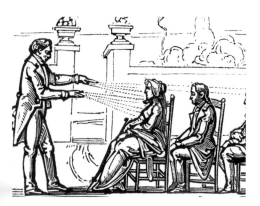

Dickens became obsessed with mesmerism, which he learnt about from his London doctor, Elliotson, and practised himself, on Catherine, on friends and on a sick woman he met in Genoa, Augusta De La Rue, wife of a banker. It was an intense emotional experience for all, arousing Catherine's jealousy without curing Madame De La Rue.

'What a great creature he is,' wrote Dickens of Tennyson, reading his poetry in 1844, and again in 1859 of the *Idylls*, 'they are all wonderfully fine – chivalric, imaginative, passionate.'

Another of Dickens's obsessions was with prisons and the treatment of society's rejects. He visited them wherever he went and was friends with prison governors in London. When he and Miss Coutts set up their Home for Homeless women, he sought advice from Tracey, Governor of Tothill Fields Prison – the picture above, made in 1862, shows women prisoners there working under the 'Silent' system, which Dickens disliked – and from Chesterton, Governor of Coldbath Fields Prison. A view of its men's dormitory in 1857 is shown below.

Dickens was a passionate supporter of the efforts made in the industrial towns of England to offer education to the workers, and he visited them often to speak. This is Birmingham Town Hall, where he appeared from the 1840s to the end of his life. He was loved in these places because the people believed he was on their side and spoke for them.

Lord John Russell, later Earl Russell, born 1792, educated Edinburgh, travelled abroad, loved France, toured English manufacturing cities 1811, entered parliament 1813, introduced the Reform Act of 1832, prime minister 1846–52. Dickens reported his early speeches, and knew him personally from 1846. Russell wrote to him praising *Bleak House*, invited him to dinner regularly and held him in affection. *A Tale of Two Cities* was dedicated to him.

Three more artists especially loved by Dickens: Frank Stone ('Old Tone'), Manchester-born 1800, self-taught, unconventional marital set-up. Clarkson Stanfield, son of an actor, went to sea, became a scene painter then marine artist, *Little Dorrit* dedicated to him. John Leech, Londoner, radical, worked for *Punch*, illustrated *A Christmas Carol*, family holidays with the Dickenses.

Dickens looking solid and confident, as he had reason to be in 1850 when this photograph was taken by the young French photographer Henri Claudet. He was engaged in writing *David Copperfield*, his favourite book. He launched his weekly magazine *Household Words* successfully. He gave much time to running the Home for Homeless Women. His son Charley started at Eton and a third daughter, Dora, was born. But Catherine was not well, and early in 1851 his father (*inset*) died, and Dickens, who had been so angry with him, now wept in his mother's arms and walked the streets for three nights grieving. Forster went with him to the funeral at Highgate Cemetery.

like half-crazed Miss Flite, whose madness tells the truth, and who keeps linnets and goldfinches caged in her window, giving them names, Hope, Joy, Youth, Ruin, Despair and Madness. The horribly respectable solicitor Vholes, given to entangling his victims like a snake, is shown giving 'one gasp as if he had swallowed the last morsel of his client'. The Smallweed family, worshippers of the god of Compound Interest, vicious in pursuit of money, despisers of story-books, fairy-tales, dolls and games, are seen at home meanly doling out stale crusts and drops from the bottoms of used teacups for the supper of their child servant, Charley. She has left her small brother and baby sister locked in a room to keep them safe while she is out working, and she is their sole support. Such things were imagined by Dickens: their factual counterpart can be found in Henry Mayhew's *London Labour and the London Poor*, published in the 1840s.

The second chapter of *Bleak House* sets the plot in motion, as Lady Dedlock, a society beauty married to an elderly landowner, faints when she catches sight of the handwriting on a legal document brought by the family lawyer, Mr Tulkinghorn. His curiosity is aroused and he decides to find out why she fainted. Mr Tulkinghorn dislikes women, seeing them as creatures who have secrets and interfere in his relations with his aristocratic male clients, and he is pleased to have a reason to hunt her down. This will be a mystery story, a whodunnit, as well as an account of English society. Dickens believed in entertaining his readers, and giving them a good plot was a way to do it. For him, popularity and high art were not at odds, and *Bleak House* is one of the first detective stories in the language, with a classic three-suspect murder at the climax. It is also a nineteenth-century fairy-tale or pantomime, with good and evil spirits, reversals, discoveries of lost parents and children, comedy and pathos, violent and tragic deaths and triumphs of love.

The third chapter introduces a narrator, Esther, and moves for the first time into the past tense. Throughout the book the author's narrative remains in the present, while Esther's account of her experiences is threaded in the past tense, varying the perspective. Esther is self-deprecating and anxious to be loved because she has grown up without parents and been told that she is the child of a sinful mother;

happily, when her gloomy female guardian dies, she comes into the care of a benevolent cousin, Mr Jarndyce of Bleak House, who is also taking in two other orphaned cousins, Richard and Ada. They are all wards of Chancery, and its victims too, since the case of Jarndyce v. Jarndyce has been running in the Chancery court for decades, wrecking lives as it goes. The kindly Mr Jarndyce has turned his back on the case and advises them to do the same; Esther becomes his housekeeper at Bleak House, and loves Ada and Richard like a sister.

Readers from Charlotte Brontë on have been irritated by Esther's tone, always the cheerful little woman and nobly forgetful of self. There were probably more women of her type about in the mid-nineteenth century than now, self-sacrificing to the point of masochism because of the way they had been reared and trained. But she is not stupid, and she can make trenchant remarks. When Miss Flite talks of honours given to good people, it is Esther who observes that 'it was not the custom in England to confer titles on men distinguished by peaceful services ... unless occasionally, when they consisted of the accumulation of some very large amount of money.'[5] There is a small link with life in that, as suggested in Chapter 12, Dickens took her name from Esther Elton, the orphaned girl he helped from 1843 on, who impressed him so strongly with her 'quiet, unpretending, domestic heroism; of a most affecting and interesting kind'. Her having been her father's housekeeper, her devotion to her younger sisters and brother and what he called 'her self-denial in a hundred ways' – all indicate that she was in his mind as he created the character of Esther Summerson.[6]

In Honoria, Lady Dedlock, and her sister, there may also be an allusion to the beautiful Sheridan sisters, brought up in society but without any fortune, marrying into the aristocracy in the case of Henrietta and Jane, and in Caroline's case involved in a scandal. It is situation, not character, he is using here, and Lady Dedlock is defined by her situation, shown as hardly more than a face, a figure and a haughty manner over the secret that threatens her with scandal. Other borrowings from life are well known: the detective Mr Bucket modelled on his friend Chief Inspector Field, and the French lady's maid Hortense on a notorious Frenchwoman, Mrs Manning, whom

Dickens saw hanged. Mr Boythorn, drawn from Walter Savage Landor, appears like him as a good-hearted blusterer, and pleased everyone who knew him. But Leigh Hunt, his family and friends were distressed by the portrait of the aesthete Skimpole, charming of speech and then revealed as a cold-hearted sponger, and although Dickens protested he had not meant to portray him, he was not believed, and the harm was done.

Bleak House contains few happy families and many single people, broken relationships and children orphaned or divided from parents. Esther, Ada, Richard, Charley Neckett and her siblings, Phil Squod, Guster and Jo have all lost their parents. Jarndyce, Boythorn, Krook, George Rouncewell, Gridley and Tulkinghorn are bachelors, and Skimpole, who has a wife and children, scarcely allows them to impinge on his life. Miss Flite is a spinster. Sir Leicester and Lady Dedlock are seemingly childless, and Lady Dedlock prefers death to the social stigma of being revealed as the mother of an illegitimate child. The Snagsbys are childless, although Mrs Snagsby suspects her husband of having fathered the street boy Jo. Mrs Jellyby has a family she neglects and a husband she reduces to bankruptcy. And so on. The Smallweeds are a close family, joined by mutual dislike and mistrust. Only the Bagnets present a warm and united group, the father an Army man, the mother indomitable, the son and daughters good and well behaved.

Child workers always caught Dickens's attention, and in this book there are several: Jo, the ignorant and solitary boy who sweeps crossings; Charley, a 'very little girl' who claims to be over thirteen, lives alone with her younger brother and baby sister, and goes out to earn their keep by washing for the Smallweed family and others. Guster, a slavey who came from the workhouse and has fits, is now over twenty, but has clearly grown up working for her employers; and Phil Squod, a crippled and disfigured adult who doesn't know his own age, describes how he started his working life at the age of eight, assisting a tinker. They are all reminders of what Dickens wrote in the proof of *The Old Curiosity Shop*, 'the poor have no childhood. It must be bought and paid for.'[7] His imagined children stand in parallel to the real girls he was currently interviewing for the Home at Shepherd's

Bush, most of them half starved, detached from any families they ever had, some from the workhouse, some from prison, needle-women, dressmakers or artificial-flower makers, casual or reluctant prostitutes: in the letter to Miss Coutts in which he discussed details of several of them, he told her, 'I have been so busy, leading up to the great turning idea of the *Bleak House* story, that I have lived this last week or ten days in a perpetual scald and boil.'[8]

In the book, Caddy Jellyby has been forced to work for her mother and denied a natural, cheerful childhood; and Esther, although kindly treated at her boarding school and happy enough there, works as a pupil teacher and trains herself to put the service of others before her own desires always. Each shows courage and ingenuity, and goodness too. Guster gives her supper to Jo, Squod helps to nurse him. Caddy, once escaped from her mother and married, looks after her prepos-terously selfish father-in-law and helps her dancing-master husband; Esther is loved by the girls she teaches. Charley remains as good as ever when she is promoted by Mr Jarndyce to become Esther's maid; only poor Jo, always moved on and too starved and neglected to fight for his life, gives up and dies. He became the most admired and popu-lar figure in the book, taken to the hearts of all the readers who were moved to read of the deaths of children. Dickens has Jo repeating the first few words of the Lord's Prayer on his deathbed. They mean nothing to him, but he likes 'Our Father' – 'yes, that's wery good, sir' – and feels for the hand of the doctor beside him as he says them. Some find this a sentimental presentation, but when it comes to Dickens's outburst of rage and sorrow that follows Jo's death there is no doubt that it is linked to a reality well known to him, and he is writing from head as well as heart: 'Dead, my lords and gentlemen. Dead, Right Reverends and Wrong Reverends of every order. Dead, men and women, born with Heavenly compassion in your hearts. And dying thus around us every day.'[9] There is no talk of angels here, or suffering turning to happiness for Jo.

The theme of the book does not need to be tied to a precise year, but the time is stated as being just before the railways arrived in the mid-1830s. This sets Esther's birth at about 1815, so that her soldier father would have fought at Waterloo, her mother would have been born in the later 1790s and Sir Leicester Dedlock in 1775, which makes a convincing timeline for each of them.[10] The story it tells is mostly grim, although peopled by comic and curious characters. There are survivors, and promises of happiness for a few, but many are left dead, or damaged.[11] *Bleak House* was ignored in the chief critical reviews, the *Edinburgh*, the *Quarterly* and the *Saturday*; and where it was noticed, although many critics allowed that Dickens was popular and possessed of genius, they also expressed disappointment that he had abandoned humour for the grotesque and contemptible, and that it was ill constructed. Even Forster, while praising its structure and declaring that 'novels as Mr Dickens writes them rise to the dignity of poems', found much of the book 'too real to be pleasant'.[12] Readers may have moments of impatience when tension slackens and the strain of keeping all the different strands going is felt, but soon the breadth and richness of Dickens's conception grows clear again, and his superabundance is felt not as a weakness but as a strength.

Forster said that, while Dickens pretended to be indifferent to criticism, he was hurt by it, and 'believed himself to be entitled to higher tribute than he was always in the habit of receiving'.[13] With *Bleak House* the public took no notice of the critics, and the monthly sales surprised Dickens and his publishers, fluctuating between 34,000 and 43,000. The editor of the *International Monthly Magazine* in America offered $2,000 to Bradbury & Evans for advance sheets and was told that Dickens had no new book in mind, after which *Harper's* sent their man straight to him and he agreed to let them have advance proofs for $1,728 (£360).[14] *Dombey* and *Copperfield* had both sold very well in America and Dickens had made nothing from them, so although there was still no prospect even of an international copyright agrement, he was negotiating again.[15] Sales in America rose to 118,000 copies monthly and became a valuable medium for advertising, leading to assertions in the press that Dickens was 'a literary Croesus'. In fact he made about £11,000 in all from *Bleak House*. Robert Patten puts it memorably: 'This return was not made from an expensive edition with elaborate binding and inflated price; it came from thousands upon thousands of individuals, putting down their shillings month after month in exchange for another thirty-two pages of tightly-packed letter-press – nearly 20,000 words – and two illustrations.'[16] Dickens spoke to the people, and the people responded, and saw that *Bleak House* is among the greatest of his books.

⁂

The writing took him from the winter of 1851/2 until the autumn of 1853, through his fortieth and forty-first birthdays. As the first episode appeared in March, Catherine gave birth to their seventh son, Edward, named for Bulwer but known in the family as Plorn. Shortly before his birth Dickens wrote to a friend that 'I begin to count the children incorrectly, they are so many; and to find fresh ones coming down to dinner in a perfect procession, when I thought there were no more' – a lovely joke, although he complained to Miss Coutts after the birth of Plorn that 'on the whole I could have dispensed with him' in a letter that was chiefly about plans to build model dwellings for the poor in the East End.[17] But Plorn became the spoilt baby of the family, sometimes referred to as 'the J. B. in W.' by his father – the Jolliest Boy in the World.

The other jolly boy, Charley, was enjoying Eton and was popular with his schoolfellows. Dickens had adored him from the start, believing that 'he takes arter his father' and that he was 'a child of very uncommon capacity indeed', although in need of encouragement.[18] He visited him at Eton, taking the train to Slough or Windsor, with hampers from Fortnum & Mason for a summer water party one July, and a more modest picnic of sandwiches and beer the next. But after two years he became dissatisfied with his progress and told Miss Coutts that while 'Eton would like to keep Charley making Latin verses for another five years', it did not seem to him 'rational in such a case'.[19] He decided to remove him as soon as he could, although he was only sixteen, and asked him to decide on a career. When Charley said he would like to become an Army officer, which Miss Coutts would certainly have funded by buying him a commission, his father talked him out of the idea at once, with great firmness, and persuaded him that a career in business would be the thing. Charley had little option but to agree, and he was promptly removed from Eton and packed off to Leipzig to learn German and start acquiring commercial skills. After nine months there his German teacher told Dickens that the dear boy had learnt the language pretty well but advised against commercial school, because severe discipline would not suit him, and besides he showed little interest in becoming a merchant. The hapless Charley, keen to please his father but with no interest at all in commerce, went home to be lectured further. Dickens reported to Miss Coutts that he suffered from 'lassitude of character, a very serious thing in a man' and that he had 'less fixed purpose and energy than I could have supposed possible in my son'.[20] He tried telling him about his own hard-working youth, and was dismayed by Charley's response, which was to wonder at his father and show no inclination to emulate his habits.

Dickens sent him back to Germany, where he produced some literary translations which pleased his teachers, and suggest he had aptitude in that direction. Once home again, his father tried to set up commercial training for him in Birmingham. The friend consulted there said Charley would do better to learn business in London, where the tone of commerce was higher, and he would have the advantage of living at home, which was not what Dickens had in mind. But for a while he allowed him to lend a hand in the office of *Household Words* and to join happily in family theatricals. Miss Coutts had a contact at Barings Bank, and after Charley had served a spell at a broker's he was offered a position by Barings, at £50 a year. He was now eighteen, a cheerful boy with good manners, and without ambition or drive. Three years later, at twenty-one, he would have the moral strength to defy his father, but he never learnt how to make money.

※

The girls were no problem, and in 1853 Katey, who showed a talent for drawing, began to attend art classes at Bedford College, recently established for women's education in Regent's Park. She seems to have been well taught and she became an accomplished painter, the only one of the Dickens children to follow their father into the arts.

Walter was being prepared for the Indian Army, Dickens having no objection to the military as a career, except for Charley, and as long as it was abroad. He solved the problem of the younger boys' education when he noticed a boarding school for English boys in Boulogne, run by two English clergymen, one of whom had been a master at Eton. The fees were only £40 a year. The boys had to speak French and studied the usual subjects, with fencing, dancing and German as extras. They were given two months vacation in summer, and none at Christmas unless the parents wished to see them then. It meant that they could be away from home for nearly ten months of the year. Frank and Alfred started together, aged nine and seven, in 1853. To be living an institutional life for such long stretches of time, away from mother, aunt and sisters, may have felt punitive to them, and possibly to their mother too. You wonder whether Dickens thought of them when he said in a public speech how much he disliked 'cheap distant schools, where neglected children pine from year to year'.[21] It was not how Charley and Walter had been treated.

They were kept there for five or six years, and in 1856 they even remained away from home over Christmas and until July 1857. Frank developed a stammer, bad enough for it to stand in his way later when he was considered for jobs. Neither Frank nor Alfred seems to have learnt much or been inspired with ambition to excel at anything. Dickens thought of putting them both in for Army cadetships, and settled for Alfred following Walter into the Indian Army. At fourteen Frank had the idea of becoming a doctor and was sent to school in Hamburg, perhaps because German medical training was good, but once there he changed his mind, did not want to stay in Germany, and was sent back to Boulogne for another year. Sydney started at the Boulogne school at eight and left at thirteen to go into the Navy at his own desire, and Henry also started at eight. He was the only one to record his opinion of the school, which he had found 'rather sad and forlorn' and did not look back on with any pleasure. The boys dined on tin plates and the food was unappetizing; and he thought poorly of the method of teaching French.

Dickens had not wanted more than three children, and he preferred daughters to sons, but he became interested in each baby as it appeared and felt concern, if not exactly love, for the six younger sons. When he said he found it hard to show his feelings for them, perhaps he meant it was hard to have the feelings he was expected to have for so many unwanted offspring; and in the press of writing, and running a magazine, and putting on plays, and looking after the Home in Shepherd's Bush, there was not much time or energy left over for them.

※

Education was a central topic of the novel he wrote in 1854, *Hard Times*, which ran weekly in *Household Words* between April and August. It was intended to boost the circulation and succeeded in doubling it, although Dickens found it difficult to fit his ideas into the space available in the magazine and badly missed the elbow-room given by monthly numbers. It had been agreed that it would be the length of just five numbers of *Bleak House*, and the texture of the narrative is noticeably cramped and prosaic after the expansiveness and poetry of *Bleak House*. Yet Ruskin thought it in several respects the greatest book Dickens had yet written and pronounced that 'his view was finally the right one, grossly and sharply told'.[22] The 'grossly and sharply' indicate his reservations about Dickens's method, and *Hard Times* is close to parable or fable and underlines its points simplistically: the cramming schoolmaster is called M'Choakumchild, the Utilitarian MP for Coketown, Thomas Gradgrind, is a hardware merchant living in a house called Stone Lodge, and the name of the rich and grasping mill-owner is Bounderby. The chief message of the book concerns the bad effects of an education that confines itself to purely factual and practical matters learnt by rote, ignoring the importance of imagination, sensibility, humour, games, poetry, entertainment and fun. M'Choakumchild presides over a dismal class where the pupils who can memorize facts get all the rewards, and this fun-free educational path is imposed by Mr Gradgrind on his children, who are brought up to respect facts and ignore feelings. He names two of his sons after his idols, Adam Smith and Malthus Gradgrind – reminding us that Dickens's sons were called after poets, essayists and novelists – Walter Landor, Alfred D'Orsay Tennyson, Sydney Smith, Henry Fielding and Edward Bulwer Lytton Dickens.

Hard Times is set in a working community, in and around Coketown, an industrial town populated by mill-workers, and based on Preston in Lancashire, where Dickens went early in 1854 to observe a long-running strike. His picture of the workers is partly perfunctory and partly sentimentalized, centred on the good worker Stephen Blackpool, who is ostracized for refusing to join a union and, caught between bad employers and bad mates, comes to grief. Gradgrind's favourite child, his daughter Louisa, marries the ludicrous Bounderby without love because she has been brought up not to acknowledge the existence of such a feeling. The marriage is made just plausible because the one person she does love helplessly is her brother, Tom, who will benefit, she hopes, from Bounderby's patronage. Tom predictably turns into a thief and a liar, and among his other crimes gets Blackpool accused of stealing the money he himself has taken from Bounderby. As for Louisa, like Edith Dombey she leaves her detested husband and turns from a promising human being into the standard Dickens endangered beauty: she 'strikes herself with both hands upon her bosom' and asks her father, 'What have you done, O father, what have you done with the garden that should have bloomed once in this great wilderness here?' It is left to Sissy (Cecilia) Jupe, a circus girl taken in by the Gradgrinds, to cheer and comfort them with her generous warmth and to rise to a moral authority possessed by none of them. All things good and seemly come from Sissy and nothing but failure from the Gradgrind system; the moral is pressed home hard and the plot seems to have been worked out with a slide rule.

Yet the message of the book is delivered with an originality that goes some way towards redeeming these weaknesses. It is spoken by the circus master Sleary, a fat, seedy man who travels around entertaining the poor with tightrope walkers, clowns, performing dogs and horses. Sleary tells Gradgrind that it is not good to be always working and learning, and that something else is needed in life: 'people must be amused.' The boldness of setting up Sleary and the circus people as exemplary figures who keep the best human values alive is a stroke that no one but Dickens could carry off, and it startles the reader, the more so because Sleary speaks with a lisp, and his dictum comes out as 'people mutht be amuthed.' What on earth? you ask yourself for a moment. Then you understand that even a man with a lisp can speak a truth. Dickens was ahead of his time in showing that people with handicaps could be likeable, intelligent and perceptive, and Sleary is there to remind everyone, the virtuous and the zealous, the comfortable, conventional middle classes and the parents ambitious for their children, that the world is various, and that the imagination is as important as the multiplication table, and more important than business or banking. You can't help wondering whether Charley read *Hard Times*, and, if so, what he thought of it. Dickens dedicated it to Carlyle, yet it was the only one of his novels he did not provide with a preface for the reprint, which suggests he was not quite satisfied with it. It was parodied, though not dramatized, translated into French and Russian, and has found some passionate critical defenders; but it is among the least popular of his books, perhaps because it cuts too narrow and formal a path, and fails to take note of its own message that people must be amused.

As the 1850s went by Dickens gave himself as fully as ever to editing and writing for *Household Words*, and to good works and theatricals, which were a branch of good works. What was changing was his domestic life and his relations with the Hogarths, his in-laws, and the two Hogarth daughters who shared his home, Catherine and Georgina. His energy and inventive powers did not flag, but there was a shift in his inner life, as though he were preparing himself, only half consciously, for a metamorphosis into a different creature.

18

Little Dorrit and Friends

1853–1857

Dickens's dissatisfaction with his marriage grumbled and sputtered below the surface. Catherine must have felt it and Georgy can't have missed it. Although he boasted of the size and beauty of the new baby born in 1852 – Edward, known as Plorn – he was oppressed by having so many sons needing care, education and guidance, and suspicious that they might have inherited the passivity of their mother or even the 'imbecility' of his in-laws.[1] Catherine was still in her thirties – she would not be forty until 1855 – so there was no guarantee that Plorn was the last. When they were apart he still wrote affectionately to her, 'I shall be very happy to be at home again myself and to embrace you – for of course I miss you *very much*.'[2] Yet he felt the need to get away, and in the autumn of 1853 he set off with two bachelor friends, Wilkie Collins and Augustus Egg, to revisit Switzerland and Italy. Chamonix, the Mer de Glace and a cloudless ascent of the Simplon pleased him, but from Naples he wrote home, to Georgy and Catherine separately, complaining of having received no letters at all for five days, and from Rome he lamented the lack of any from Forster or Wills, which suggests he was finding the trip rather dull.

The oddest letter to come out of it was one he wrote to Catherine in December, after he had seen the De La Rues in Genoa and recalled how jealous she had been of his intimacy with Madame in 1845. It begins with a striking piece of self-analysis as he told her that 'the intense pursuit of any idea that takes complete possession of me, is one of the qualities that makes me different – sometimes for good; sometimes I dare say for evil – from other men. Whatever made you unhappy in the Genoa time had no other root, beginning, middle or end, than whatever has made you proud and honoured in your married life, and given you station better than rank, and surrounded you

with many enviable things.'³ The graceless reminder at the end of the
benefits he has conferred on her leads on to a reproach that her attitude towards the De La Rues 'is not a good one, is not an amiable
one, a generous one – is not worthy of you at all', and a suggestion
that she should write them a cordial letter. He says he will never ask
her whether she has done so, and it would be 'valueless and contemptible' if she did it only because he asked, but it would place her
'on a far better station' in her own eyes if she did. This piece of moral
blackmail gives a chill glimpse into his conduct of their marriage at
this stage. Catherine, cowed, wrote the required letter. Four years
later Dickens had so far forgotten what a husband should be, and
what the amiable and generous behaviour he had urged on Catherine
was, that he wrote mockingly of her to De La Rue, telling him she
had been 'excruciatingly jealous of, and has obtained positive proofs
of my being on the most confidential terms with, at least Fifteen
Thousand Women . . . since we left Genoa'.⁴ It is not a pretty letter,
but by then what mattered most to him was that he should be seen to
be in the right.

His friendship with Forster was also going through a cooler patch.
Dickens sometimes allowed himself the licence to be brutally frank,
as when, after hearing Forster give a lecture of two and a half hours
on the seventeenth-century statesman Strafford, he sent him a critical
letter, telling him he had talked down to his audience, 'like a schoolmaster teaching very young children, which I think a London
audience would undoubtedly be resentful of'; and that, like most
biographers, he was too ready to invest his subject with all the virtues. He advised him to cut half an hour out of the lecture. Apart
from that, he said, it was excellent. Forster was wounded; Dickens
apologized and was forgiven.⁵ Forster, as editor of the *Examiner*, was
moving the paper away from radicalism and towards solid middle-
class values, which were not so congenial to Dickens, and which he
would later satirize in *Our Mutual Friend*. Yet Dickens was also capable of sweetness and sensitivity, as when Forster was bedridden with
rheumatic gout, and he went and sat beside his bed for a long evening,
reading aloud the whole of Goldsmith's *She Stoops to Conquer*. Both
men enjoyed the reading intensely.⁶ Forster was often ill: he had

bronchial trouble, he had rheumatic pains, he drank too much, ate heartily and failed to walk off the effects as Dickens did. Dickens also exercised on the water, rowing himself from Oxford to Reading in June 1855, 'through miles upon miles of water lilies, lying on the water close together, like a fairy pavement', a solitary day he described to Miss Coutts later.[7]

Only to Forster could Dickens show his unhappiness and yearnings, telling him things he seems to have discussed with no one else – not Macready, not his artist friends Maclise, Stanfield, Stone, Leech and Egg, not Collins, Wills or Miss Coutts, or Lavinia Watson, with all of whom he was in friendly contact. And even with Forster Dickens did not always find intimacy easy. He used circuitous ways of telling him about his problems, telling him that his situation resembled David Copperfield's during his marriage to Dora, 'the so happy and yet so unhappy existence which seeks its realities in unrealities, and finds its dangerous comfort in a perpetual escape from the disappointment of heart around it'.[8] In September, after finishing *Hard Times*, he wrote to Forster saying he thought of going away by himself for six months, to the Pyrenees perhaps: '*Restlessness*, you will say. Whatever it is, it is always driving me, and I cannot help it. I have rested nine or ten weeks, and sometimes feel as if it had been a year – though I had the strangest nervous miseries before I stopped. If I couldn't walk fast and far, I should just explode and perish.'[9]

This was from Boulogne, where the family was installed from June to October. Dickens had sent Georgy in the spring to choose a house, showing his increasing reliance on her judgement and readiness to use her as a surrogate as he had never allowed Catherine to be. The villa she chose, the 'Villa du camp de droite', was named for an old military camp close by and now active again, with French troops putting up a city of tents and huts on the clifftops between Boulogne and Calais: paths were made impassable, trumpets sounded and soldiers swarmed, but Dickens took all this in his stride and kept working and taking his walks. The reason for the military activity was war: in March 1854 the British and French had declared war as allies against the Russians. Their object was to prevent Russia from seizing the European parts of the Ottoman Empire: Britain feared for her route to India, and France under Louis-Napoleon was eager to avenge the first Napoleon's defeat at Moscow in 1812. There was enthusiasm for the fight in both countries after so many years of peace, and the allies were confident of an easy victory. Their plan was to take naval control of the Baltic and send a force to the Crimea to destroy the Russian shipyards at Sebastopol. Tens of thousands of men were to embark from Calais in British ships.

Dickens put up flags on the villa, and in September wrote cheerful letters about the visit of the French Emperor and the Prince Consort, who came to review the troops. Walking alone on the clifftops, his path crossed with that of the two leaders, followed by seventy brilliantly uniformed staff, all on horseback. Dickens described to Forster how he doffed his broad-brimmed felt hat, and the Emperor, who had met him at D'Orsay's and Miss Coutts's in London, pulled off his cocked hat in return, Albert following suit.[10] Dickens disapproved of both Albert, 'a perfectly commonplace man', and Napoleon III, 'the French usurper', but he appreciated the picturesque moment.[11]

The allies had misjudged their capacities and the war was to last two years, bringing the deaths of many thousands and driving Dickens to the angriest political outbursts of his life. He admired the courage of the soldiers and decided to support the war in principle, but at the same time he was appalled at the seeming indifference of the authorities to the 10,000 deaths in London from cholera in 1854, 'an infinitely larger number of English people than are likely to be slain in the whole Russian War'.[12] 'The absorption of the English mind in the War, is – to me – a melancholy thing. Every other subject of popular solicitude and sympathy goes down before it. I fear I clearly see that for years to come, domestic Reforms are shaken to the root; every miserable Red Tapist flourishes the war over every protester against his humbug.'[13] He mocked the bungling of the Prime Minister, Lord Aberdeen, in managing the conduct of the war, as Sebastopol remained in Russian hands, winter set in and the English troops died of disease, bitter cold and lack of medical care. This was when Florence Nightingale became a heroine, and William Howard Russell the first reporter from the front to supply immediate accounts of what was happening. The British political establishment and the military commanders both showed themselves to be incompetent. Dickens raged, and fed his anger into the novel he began to plan early in 1855, calling it 'Nobody's Fault' in bitter mockery of the government.

Throughout 1855 he wrote strongly expressed political letters to friends. He said that the rottenness of the political system made England like France before the Revolution, and that it might go the same way, given that an 'enormous black cloud of poverty' hung over every town, parliament was silent, and the aristocracy idle.[14] When Austen Layard, now a Liberal MP, formed the Association for Administrative Reform in May 1855, Dickens joined and addressed it, taking up Layard's complaint that merit and efficiency were passed over in public appointments in favour of 'party and family influences' and making this a running theme in his book. A series of articles in *Household Words* gave his views of the government, although he was careful to explain that he had no intention of entering politics himself: 'literature is my profession – it is at once my business and my pleasure, and I shall never pass beyond it.'[15] The Association for Administrative Reform fizzled out, but Dickens continued to fulminate in private, telling Forster in September that 'representative government is become altogether a failure with us, that the English gentilities and subserviences render the people unfit for it, and that the whole thing has broken down'.[16]

A few days later he wrote to Macready of 'flunkeyism, toadyism, letting the most contemptible Lords come in for all manner of places', and went on, 'I have no present political faith or hope – not a grain.' He added that he was now hammering away at 'Nobody's Fault', 'blowing off steam which would otherwise blow me up', and found relief from his dark political thoughts only in strenuous exercise.[17] The satirical parts of the book took on the great political families whose sons were given employment as by right, seats in parliament and well-paid positions as civil servants in government departments. Dickens calls them the Tite Barnacles and the Stiltstalkings, and has fun at their expense, showing the young ones idling in the great Circumlocution Office and Lord Decimus Barnacle himself dispensing patronage at a carefully arranged dinner, where he is encouraged by sycophantic fellow guests to tell his only joke. It involves lengthy reminiscences about a pear tree at Eton and pairs in parliament, and he takes much pleasure in boring everyone with it. In the glow of satisfaction this gives him he offers a senior position to his hostess's son, a young man described by his own wife as 'almost an idiot', but made acceptable through his access to the fortune of his millionaire stepfather. It is a devastating piece of mockery, it angered the men Dickens was ridiculing, and some of the bad reviews the book received later were a closing of ranks with the class under attack.

※

Laying out his dark vision of England absorbed Dickens for two and a half years, from early in 1855 until June 1857. He gives a striking account of the process of gestation in his letters, first of the scattered ideas and impressions that lead to 'writing and planning and making notes over an immense number of little bits of paper, and they turn out to be illegible'. After this comes the sensation that the story was a physical force, 'breaking out all round me' and also controlling him, so that he had to go off 'down the railroad to humour it'. Lavinia Watson was told in May of his 'walking about the country by day – prowling about into the strangest places in London by night – sitting down to do an immensity – getting up after doing nothing . . . tearing my hair (which I can't afford to do) – and on the whole astonished at my own condition, though I am used to it'. He told Miss Coutts that he had got himself into 'a state of restlessness impossible to be described – impossible to be imagined – wearing and tearing to be experienced . . . I get up and go down a railroad – come back again, and register a vow to go out of town instantly, and begin at the feet of the Pyrenees . . . get up and walk about my room all day – wander about London till midnight – make engagements and am too distraught to keep them.' Two weeks later his symptoms were still bad, but 'I am actually at work and in the middle of No. One', meaning the first four chapters of what he still called 'Nobody's Fault'.[18]

The quiet concentration found necessary by other writers was not a feature of Dickens's working life.[19] Throughout the months in which he laboured to take hold of his ideas and get started on the book, rival preoccupation of all kinds took his time and attention. There was *Household Words* to edit and write for, and his engagement with Layard's Association for Administrative Reform: addressing it at a public meeting, he energetically attacked Lord Palmerston (who had followed Aberdeen as Prime Minister), together with the House of Commons, likening them to a run-down theatrical company. He was busy with the Home in Shepherd's Bush, and engaged in trying to rescue another unfortunate young woman. When his early love, Maria Beadnell, wrote to him he was roused to intense emotion and made plans to meet her. He prepared, for his own amusement, a long reading-out of *David Copperfield*, which he did not then use until the 1860s. He embarked on the process of buying a house in Kent, after an all-male celebration of his birthday at a Gravesend inn, when he walked to Rochester through the snow and noticed as he went over Gad's Hill a sign saying there was a freehold to be sold there. It was 'the spot and the very house . . . literally "a dream of my childhood"', he told Wills, and instructed him to pursue the possibility of buying it.[20] Since he had already planned a trip to Paris with Collins, stopping at Boulogne to take Frank and Alfred out to dinner, he went ahead with that and left Wills to proceed. Collins fell ill, Dickens was so preoccupied and uncertain of his moves that he told Forster he might travel on from Paris to Bordeaux, and had further thoughts of moving to the Pyrenees in the summer. Once again he compared himself to David Copperfield, saying he was 'altogether in a dishevelled state of mind . . . Why is it that as with poor David, a sense comes always crushing on me now, when I fall into low spirits, as of one happiness I have missed in life, and one friend and companion I have never made?'[21]

There were more of these complaints to come, but instead of going to Bordeaux he took on the production of Collins's melodrama *The Lighthouse*, to be performed in Tavistock House at midsummer, with himself in the leading part, and followed by a farce largely improvised by himself and Mark Lemon – all major distractions involving weeks of work. In May he decided he would spend six months in Paris the following winter and made the first move to find accommodation for himself and family. How could anyone do all this and at the same time be gearing himself up to write a long novel? Dickens kept going by taking on too much. He knew no other way to live, and no day went by in which he did not stretch himself, physically, socially and emotionally.

When the school holidays came in July, he rented a house in Folkestone, took eight of the children there – Charley was working in London – and set up his writing routine, five hours' work every morning from nine to two, after which he walked alone until five o'clock in the afternoon. He complained of the boys being noisy, but not for long, because Walter left on 1 August for his Indian Army training school and eight-year-old Sydney went with Alfred and Frank on 1 September to boarding school in Boulogne, leaving only Mamie, Katey and the two youngest boys.

※

At this point, in September 1855, Dickens changed the title of the book from 'Nobody's Fault', his political joke, to the simple, childish-sounding *Little Dorrit*, the name used by one of his characters, Amy Dorrit, the daughter of William Dorrit, a debtor held in the Marshalsea Prison in Southwark. The story is set even further back than *Bleak House*, in the 1820s, when he was a boy.[22] William Dorrit has been in the Marshalsea debtors' prison for many years, but 1824 was the year of John Dickens's imprisonment there. Starting from this secret source of inspiration, Dickens's imagination led him to create Dorrit's youngest child, Little Dorrit, brought up in the Marshalsea, undernourished and thinly dressed, but with a persistent goodness that shines out over the shabby world through which she moves, and to which she contributes her practical skills, her hard work and her kindness to those more unfortunate than herself.

Although she is twenty-two years old in the main part of the story, she looks like a child, pale faced, small and thin, and she is a natural successor to the working children who appeared in *Bleak House*. But she is more than this: she threads a strand of poetry through the book, able to walk through the night-time streets unmolested, comforting, helping and allowing dignity to the brain-damaged and hairless Maggy and to Old Nandy from the workhouse, good to her ungrateful elder brother and sister, and making unannounced midnight appearances. Early in the story, when the forty-year-old Arthur Clennam is reviewing his wasted life and hopeless future by a dying fire, late at night in his lodging, asking himself what his situation is now but a descent to the grave, the door is softly opened 'and these spoken words startled him and came as if they were an answer: "Little Dorrit"'. It is a magical moment, and it is neither theatrical nor sentimental.[23] She acts as parent to her father, never complaining of his bad behaviour, let alone raging, as Dickens had so often done at his father. She has something of Cordelia, who comforted her father by telling him they might sing together in prison. Dickens knew his Shakespeare, and was no more tied to realism than Shakespeare. Little Dorrit is the wise child who redeems a sorry world.

Little Dorrit is the third in Dickens's condition-of-England novels, and returns to the broad sweep of *Bleak House*. The centre of the story is again London, an almost unredeemedly gloomy London, with its 'deadly sewer', once a fine, fresh river, running through it, its overworked people denied natural beauty, its melancholy streets 'gloomy, close, and stale', its broken old houses on whose steps sit 'light children nursing heavy children', and smart, cheap new houses with absurdly got-up footmen and grooms lounging outside. The 'crooked and descending streets' below St Paul's, between Cheapside and the river, lead down among warehouses and wharves through narrow alleys to the foul river and 'Found Drowned' bills. Everything offends the senses. The houses of the rich smell dismally of 'yesterday's soup and coach-horses'. The clothes of the poor are greasy. Old Nandy in his pauper's uniform smells of all the other workhouse men. Mrs Flora Finching, once pretty and lovable, now middle aged, eats too much, weighs too much, talks too much and smells of lavender water and brandy. On Sunday evening the church bells sound 'as if the Plague were in the city and the dead-carts were going round'. Dickens dislikes so much of what he sees, hears and smells – partly the London of his childhood, partly London in the 1850s – that his jokes are almost all uncomfortable or bitter.

He maps out a great London patchwork around the river, St Paul's and Cheapside, Barbican, Holborn and the Gray's Inn Road; the Borough, Southwark Bridge with its three narrow cast-iron arches, built in 1819, where Little Dorrit goes to be quiet and sit looking at the water beneath; Covent Garden and Pentonville; Richmond and Hampton Court; Cavendish Square and Park Lane; and Westminster, where the government offices are. And he takes his cast from all these places – the workhouse, the prison, the theatre, the government offices, the crammed dwellings of the poor in Bleeding Heart Yard, Mayfair mansions, grace-and-favour residences and suburban villas. They are woven together in an elaborately constructed plot, some of it over-elaborate and strained at the seams. The pantomime villain Rigaud who hails from a Marseilles prison fails to convince at any point, and is more memorable for being given the first cigarette to appear in Dickens's fiction than anything else.[24] Many of the characters are sent on travels through France, to the Alps, Venice and Rome, but London and especially the Marshalsea and its surroundings are the heart of the book.[25]

The question of money also runs through it: how to make it, how to lose it, how to manage without it; when is it real, and when notional? Perennial questions. The Dorrit family is raised from prison and debt to great wealth, investments are made and lost, the financier Merdle maintains the lifestyle appropriate to his vast fortune through his beautiful cold wife and his terrifyingly superior butler, without ever enjoying himself. Mrs Merdle has perfected a conversational style in which she expresses her preference for a simple life – 'A more primitive state of society would be delicious to me' and 'I am pastoral to a degree, by nature' – but is bound by Society, she explains, to respect its values, which are neither primitive nor pastoral. Politicians, bankers, bishops and lawyers are all eager to attend the dinners given by the Merdles. Mr Casby, a landlord with the look of a benevolent patriarch, squeezes his poor tenants mercilessly through his rent collector. The amateur artist Henry Gowan, cousin to the Barnacles, condescends to marry the daughter of the middle-class Meagles and to overspend the generous allowance they give her while despising them as social inferiors. Arthur Clennam, the unheroic hero, has been brought up by a ferociously pious mother whose creed is 'Smite Thou my debtors, Lord, wither them, crush them.' He discovers that his real mother, who died young, had been a poor singer training for the stage, and so dedicated to the world of art and imagination despised by his foster mother. Clennam is no businessman, and has to learn through adversity and loss where he may put his trust: not in business, not in government departments, not in religion, but only in the faithful human heart.

Mrs Merdle keeps a pet parrot who punctuates her talk with screams and screeches of sardonic-sounding laughter, like an alter ego signalling her real meaning to the listener. Flora Finching, once Clennam's sweetheart, now a widow with romantic delusions and an inability to talk coherently, is given speeches of baroque intricacy and absurdity, wonderfully funny until they become rather too much of a good thing. The wittiest and saddest scene in the book is the one in which William Dorrit, in prison, entertains his old friend Nandy from the workhouse and his new friend and benefactor, Arthur Clennam, to tea. Dorrit condescends to Nandy and apologizes for him behind his hand. 'Union, poor old fellow. Out for the day,' he explains to Clennam, who has just sent Dorrit ten pounds, without which there would have been no tea. Making Nandy sit on the windowsill to take his tea, Dorrit gives a running commentary on his defects to Clennam, saying his hearing and his legs are going, his memory is weak, and that he 'rusts in the life he leads' – a description equally applicable to himself. And after Nandy has left, gently escorted by Little Dorrit, Dorrit remarks on his being 'A melancholy sight . . . though one has the consolation of knowing that he doesn't feel it himself. The poor old fellow is a dismal wreck. Spirit broken and gone – pulverized – crushed out of him, sir, completely!' Dorrit is so cheered by being in a position to condescend that he goes to his prison window like royalty, and when other inmates of the prison look up 'his recognition of their salutes just stopped short of a blessing.'[26]

The scene comes to mind again later when, after Mr Dorrit has left the Marshalsea Prison and is travelling grandly abroad, rich and well dressed, and attending a magnificent dinner party in Rome, he falters, becomes confused and asks who is on the lock and where the turnkey is, begs for alms and reveals himself as what he was for so long, the Father of the Marshalsea. It is a highly dramatic scene, but it comes across as true and tragic, faultlessly done. Dorrit is dying, and naturally reverts to the place where he had spent twenty-five years of his life. If occasionally the narrative wears thin or grows confused, it also offers some of the best moments in all Dickens's writing – for instance when Mr Merdle, on a sinister errand, borrows a pen-knife with a tortoiseshell handle from his daughter-in-law Fanny, who watches him from her balcony as he goes on his way. It is a hot evening and she is pregnant and bored: 'Waters of vexation filled her eyes; and they had the effect of making the famous Mr Merdle, in going down the street, appear to leap, and waltz, and gyrate, as if he were possessed of several Devils.'[27] As indeed he is.

The last number of *Little Dorrit* appeared in June 1857. A few weeks before, Dickens had revisited the site of the Marshalsea. He described the visit in his preface to the bound edition, saying he had not been there since it was closed, and that he found some houses which preserved the great block of the former prison. He talked to a small boy in the street outside, and, pointing to the window of the room where, he says, Little Dorrit was born and her father lived, he asked the boy if he knew the name of the present tenant. The boy replied, ' "Tom Pythick." I asked him who was Tom Pythick? and he said, "Joe Pythick's Uncle." ' It's a wonderful story, and much better than the readers of the introduction knew. The boy's confident naming of the Pythicks is set against Dickens's imagined Dorrits. The real link with the place, his father's imprisonment in 1824, is left out, as is the small boy who used to visit him there.[28] The memory of John Dickens remained powerful in his mind, and his own relationship with him, made up of exasperation, love and rage; and it may be that Amy Dorrit, who forgives her corrupt father even when he behaves cruelly and shamefully towards her, overlooks all his failings and gives him unconditional love and support, becomes a way of dealing with the anger he had felt against his father and that he wished to set entirely aside after his death. If she is, to a degree, an emblematic figure, she may be seen as his own perfected, ideal self, the child who is never angry with his flawed father.

He was forty-five when he finished *Little Dorrit*, his eleventh novel, in May 1857. It ends with a wedding between a hero in his forties with a sad history, Arthur Clennam, and Little Dorrit, young enough to be his daughter – indeed, 'He took her in his arms, as if she had been his daughter.' The final sentence of the book describes them leaving the church to take up 'a modest life of usefulness and happiness', and is beautifully thought through: 'They went quietly down into the roaring streets, inseparable and blessed; and as they passed along in sunshine and shade, the noisy and the eager, and the arrogant and the froward and the vain, fretted and chafed, and made their usual uproar.'[29]

For him there was no such happiness, no inseparable beloved, no blessing on his life. There were duties and preoccupations, with his children's careers and education, with the running of the Home in Shepherd's Bush and the editing of *Household Words*; and there were always new plans to be made, a new house, a trip abroad, a play to put on. By good chance the house he wanted to buy at Gad's Hill belonged to a contributor to *Household Words*, the writer Eliza Lynn Linton, who had inherited it from her father. It was inspected and negotiated for, and sold to him in March 1856 for £1,700.

Other distractions in his life during the *Little Dorrit* period were two women who caught his imagination in different ways. The first was Caroline Maynard, calling herself Mrs Thompson, whose younger brother Frederick wrote to Dickens in the autumn of 1854, asking for advice and help. She had paid for him to be articled to an architect when she was the mistress of a gentleman, but after nine years with him his business failed and he abandoned her. She had a small child and no income, and she turned to prostitution. Her brother, unable to continue his training, lived with her in a small house in Bute Street, off the Brompton Road – the same house in which she received her clients – and he was in despair, himself earning a pittance only as a draughtsman, and wanting to rescue her from her way of life. She was in her thirties, and when Dickens first saw her he described her as 'rather small, and young-looking; but pretty, and gentle, and has a very good head'.[30] This was to Miss Coutts, whom he consulted about how they might be able to help her. He said how strongly he had been impressed by the brother's story: 'his perception of his sister's disgrace, and undiminished admiration for her, and the confidence he has grown up in, of her being something good, and never to be mentioned without tenderness and deference – is a romance at once so astonishing and yet so intelligible as I never had the boldness to think of.'[31] At once Dickens saw the situation as it might be used in fiction, even if a fiction he would never write.

Dickens called on her at Bute Street in December, when she told him she would willingly go to South Africa as long as she could take her child. He wanted Miss Coutts to meet her and after his return from Paris he arranged for a meeting at the Home in February 1855. There was no question of her becoming an inmate, since the Home did not take mothers with children; besides which, said Dickens, 'her manner, character and experiences, are altogether different.'[32] Miss Coutts had meanwhile sent another adviser, a clergyman, to visit Caroline, and he observed that she was well dressed, kept a maid and seemed 'by no means destitute'. He felt she had been softened by a life of luxury and would not be able to maintain herself by needlework, or face the life of an emigrant to the Cape or Australia, and noted that her father had been a drunkard, her mother was a nurse in the Kensington Workhouse, and her younger sister 'a milliner alas! of damaged reputation'. She was not after all so different from the girls at the Home.[33] The suggestion that she might emigrate was not pursued.

When the clergyman called on her again he learnt that her mother had died, and this time he suggested Miss Coutts might consult with Dickens again about how best to help her. In March, Dickens invited both brother and sister to visit him at Devonshire Terrace, putting the question 'What am I to do?' to Miss Coutts before their visit. Miss Coutts evidently suggested some course of action that Caroline could not accept, and Dickens wrote to Coutts again, saying, 'There is, of course, an end to it,' adding that he believed Mrs Thompson to be perfectly truthful and that 'she will recover herself somehow yet.'

But it looks as though Miss Coutts changed her mind and did set her up as a lodging-house keeper, presumably in a part of London where she was a stranger and could pass as a widow.[34] To disappear and transform yourself into a different person was something to interest Dickens the novelist, but nothing more is heard of her until the following May (1856), when he told Miss Coutts he had seen her, and that her letting of lodgings had not succeeded well enough for her to continue with it. She had given notice that she was leaving the house, and she would sell her furniture and use the money to emigrate with her little girl and her brother to Canada, where Dickens was confident she would find work as a housekeeper or some similar honest occupation. He did what he could to ease their journey by contacting the Canada Railway, and after this their story goes blank. Caroline Maynard, or Thompson, goes down in history as having stirred his imagination and kept his interest for over eighteen months. She had been persistent in seeking his help and in trying to remake her life in London, and she raised her own fare to Canada. She had also shown him another sort of prostitute from the girls at the Home and the bedraggled, ill-spoken creatures portrayed in his books. He noted that she could even do accounts.

Just as he was involving himself in helping Caroline Maynard, he had a letter from another woman. It came out of the blue and with over-powering effect. This time it was Maria Beadnell, the beloved of his youth, now a married woman, who wrote to him. Almost certainly he had not seen her since she jilted him in 1833.[35] He had kept in desultory contact with her father and knew of her marriage in 1845, when he was in Italy, and that she was now Mrs Winter, but the arrival of her letter, 'so busy and pleasant', with its news that she had two children, led him into a rhapsodic reply. 'Believe me, you cannot more tenderly remember our old days and our old friends than I do . . . Your letter is more touching to me from its good and gentle association with the state of Spring in which I was either much more wise or much more foolish than I am now' – and so on.[36] He told her he was about to leave for Paris – this was the trip with Collins – and offered to bring back anything she wanted for her daughters; and he added that Mrs Dickens would call and arrange a meeting between the two couples. In fact he said nothing to Catherine. Five days later he wrote another long letter to Maria from Paris, telling her he 'got the heartache again' from seeing her handwriting, and recalling the blue gloves she had worn and he had matched for her. It begins to sound like a love letter. 'Whatever of fancy, romance, energy, passion, aspiration and determination belong to me, I never have separated and never shall separate from the hard hearted little woman – you – whom it is nothing to say I would have died for . . . that I began to fight my way out of poverty and obscurity, with one perpetual idea of you . . . I have never been so good a man since, as I was when you made me wretchedly happy.' He even suggests her reaction to reading about Dora in *David Copperfield*: 'How dearly that boy must have loved me, and how vividly this man remembers it!'[37]

The excitement was rising in both of them. A third letter, written on his return home, assured her that 'No one but myself has the slightest knowledge of my correspondence, I may add in this place. I could be nowhere addressed with stricter privacy or in more absolute confidence than at my own house.' She had given him a version of the reasons for the end of their early love, no doubt obedience to her parents, and in return he told her that 'the wasted tenderness of those hard years' left him with a habit of suppression which made him chary of showing affection, even to his own children. He suggested they might once again enjoy a mutual confidence 'in perfect innocence and good faith . . . between ourselves alone. All that you propose, I accept with my whole heart.' She boldly suggested meeting in the streets, somewhere near St Paul's. That might be dangerous, he replied, because he could be recognized, and he proposed instead that she should call at Devonshire Terrace between three and four on Sunday, asking for Catherine, who would infallibly be out. The stage was set for a secret romance and a revival of a love on which they both looked fondly back. She warned him she was 'toothless, fat, old, and ugly', to which he replied, 'You are always the same in my remembrance.'[38]

The meeting took place. He saw an overweight woman, no longer pretty, who talked foolishly and too much. The edifice he had built up in his mind tumbled, and he beat an immediate retreat. There was, however, a dinner with their two spouses, which allowed him perhaps to compare the appetites and girths of Maria and Catherine and brood on their resemblances. Still, he showed himself at his best in writing a charming letter to Maria's daughter Ella, telling her about his new pet raven ('he will peck little holes in your legs if you like') and his own three-year-old, 'the Baby', Plorn, who was in bed with the measles and a large cart and two horses, a Noah's Ark with all the animals and people, a military camp with four cannons, a box of bricks, a clown and four crusts of buttered toast – a perfect letter for a child.[39]

A child was one thing, but from now on he made excuses not to meet Maria. He sent her theatre tickets and failed to turn up for the show himself. He explained that he must wander about 'in my own wild way', and that he held his inventive capacity 'on the stern condition that it must master my whole life . . . and sometimes for months together, put everything else away from me'.[40] He informed her he was going to be out of town for several Sundays in succession. When her baby died in June, he wrote to commiserate and added with dreadful firmness, 'It is better that I should not come to see you. I feel quite sure of that, and will think of you instead.'[41] Steely Dickens, armoured against his mistake.

Worse, as he thought of her in her latest incarnation, he created Flora Finching and gave her a leading part in *Little Dorrit*, overweight, greedy, a drinker and garrulous to match, absurd in her unstoppable and only half-comprehensible conversation, and given to arch reminders to her old lover of the distant past. Poor Mrs Winter was silly no doubt, but not so stupid as to fail to recognize herself when she read *Little Dorrit*. Although Flora was at any rate shown as a kind-hearted woman, this was a good deal crueller than what he did to Hunt with Skimpole. Writing to a reader who appreciated the character, he said, 'It came into my head that we have all had our Floras (mine is living, and extremely fat), and that it was a half serious half ridiculous truth which has never been told.'[42] While he was still writing *Little Dorrit*, he sent Maria copies of eleven of his books, each inscribed 'In remembrance of old times', and replied in a friendly way to her letter of thanks, explaining again how busy he was and how few letters he had time to write. She had paid for the double disillusionment she had inflicted on him, but she might have reflected that she had also been his muse and inspired two of his most memorable female characters.

19

Wayward and Unsettled

1855–1857

In October 1855 Dickens and Georgina travelled to Paris and found, with some difficulty, an apartment – 'a Doll's house' – on two floors at No. 49 Champs Elysées, into which they moved. During their first night there 'my little right hand', as he put it, woke him with her restlessness, telling him the place was dirty and that she could not sleep for the smell of her room. Georgina was no longer a girl – she was twenty-eight – and effectively the woman in charge of the Dickens household, and he at once ordered a thorough cleaning. Once it was done, the place was 'exquisitely cheerful and vivacious . . . and with a moving panorama outside, which is Paris in itself'.[1] Paris delighted him. A bright, wicked and wanton place he had called it in the 1840s, not altogether disapprovingly, and since then he had come to admire the intelligence of its inhabitants, and their mixture of refinement and coarseness. Now he relished the many pleasures he found in the miles of streets to walk, the sophistication of the people, the theatres and the opera, the seductive restaurants with their mirrors, red-velvet upholstery and attentive waiters, the 'tact and taste in trifles' shown in the displays in the shops.[2] He had told Miss Coutts that his intention was to give his daughters, Mamie now seventeen, and Katey just sixteen, some Parisian polish: they were to have dancing lessons, art classes, language coaching and wardrobes of French clothes. Catherine was coming on with the girls and the little ones from Boulogne, where she must have lingered to see her three boarding-school boys, and soon they were all settled in the Champs Elysées.

Dickens's command of the language had improved so much that he could now understand everything said at the theatre 'with perfect ease and satisfaction', and he boasted to Georgy, during his February trip with Collins, of receiving 'many compliments on my angelic manner of speaking the celestial language'.[3] Better still, *Chuzzlewit* was currently being serialized in a Paris paper, and it was extremely agreeable to be well known and well liked, to be greeted in shops with 'Ah! C'est l'ecrivain celebre! Monsieur porte une nomme [*sic*] très distinguée. Mais! Je suis honoré et interessé de voir Monsieur Dick-in' (his version). Not only this, they knew and loved his characters, 'Cette Madame Tojair (Todgers) Ah! Qu'elle est drole, et precisement comme une dame que je connais à Calais.'[4]

He worked hard in the flat on the Champs Elysées, and he walked, in a spell of frosty January weather, round the walls of Paris from the Barrière de l'Etoile to the river, and the next day along the river to the Bastille, under a sky of Italian blue.[5] There was a great deal of celebratory marching with bands through the centre, because the war in the Crimea was coming to an end and a peace conference would begin in Paris in February. Henry, aged six, remembered being put in a képi – the French soldier's hat – and held up to shout '*Vive l'Empereur!*' at a regimental review. Dickens permitted Ary Scheffer, a well-known artist, to embark on painting his portrait, but found it unrecognizable. He was pleased to meet Lamartine again, who, despite his own reduced circumstances, had asked to see him and spoke warmly to him of his work and his excellent French; and to renew his acquaintance with the playwright Scribe, and marvel at Scribe's wife, who, although mother of a grown-up son, was still a beauty and had kept 'the figure of five-and-twenty'.[6] The singer and friend of Turgenev, Pauline Viardot, invited him to dinner to meet George Sand, but since he hardly knew her work there was no meeting of minds. He summed her up as 'Chubby, matronly, swarthy, black-eyed' and 'with nothing of the blue-stocking about her, except a little final way of settling all your opinions with hers', and he was not encouraged by the meeting to read her work.[7] The great publishing firm of Hachette approached him with a proposal for a complete edition of his novels, with new translations, and this was happily negotiated over some excellent dinners with editors, translators and booksellers. Mamie and Katey enjoyed themselves, coached in Italian by Daniel Manin, the exiled Venetian patriot, and spending a good deal of time with Thackeray's daughters, Annie and Minnie, who were in Paris with their grandparents while their father lectured in America.

The Emperor Napoleon III who now ruled over France might be a 'cold-blooded scoundrel', but the French people and their way of life remained intensely congenial.[8] Dickens had after all first met Louis-Napoleon at the house of his dear friend D'Orsay, whom he admired so much that he made him godfather to his son Alfred.[9] D'Orsay's total disregard of convention, the fact that he was separated from his wife and seemingly the lover of his stepmother, his perpetually unpaid debts – all this had been brushed aside by Dickens, captivated by his chic, his brilliance as a portraitist, his wit and charm in society, his French *savoir-vivre*. D'Orsay and his fellow French looked at life differently from the English, and Dickens saw that there was something to be said for their point of view. And, although he detested the Emperor's assumption of absolute power, the political situation in England struck him as almost equally dismal, and led him to believe that 'Representative Institutions' had failed there for lack of an educated people to support them.[10]

In May 1856 he had a fierce disagreement with Miss Coutts's companion, Mrs Brown, on the subject of the French. When she spoke against them, he praised their openness about social problems, telling her that a leading difference between them and the English was that 'in England people dismiss the mention of social evils and vices which do nevertheless exist among them; and that in France people do not dismiss the mention of the same things but habitually recognise their existence.' Mrs Brown cried out, 'Don't say that!' and Dickens insisted, 'Oh but I must say it, you know, when according to our national vanity and prejudice, you disparage an unquestionably great nation.' At which Mrs Brown burst into tears.[11] A few months later he wrote to Forster grumbling about the constraints placed on English novelists compared with the French – he named Balzac and Sand – who were able to write freely and realistically, while 'the hero of an English book' was 'always uninteresting – too good'. Dickens went on to tell Forster that 'this same unnatural young gentleman (if to be decent is to be necessarily unnatural), whom you meet in those others books and in mine, *must* be presented to you in that unnatural aspect

, by reason of your morality, and is not to have, I will not say any of the indecencies you like, but not even any of the experiences, trials, perplexities, and confusions inseparable from the making or unmaking of all men!'[12] It was a comprehensive complaint about the circumstances in which he worked as a writer, and which he felt unable to challenge in his novels.[13]

Congenial as he found life in Paris, he was obliged to make frequent trips to London. When Dr Brown, husband of Miss Coutts's companion and a trustee of the Home, died at the end of October 1855, he went unhesitatingly to organize the funeral, putting aside his dislike of elaborate mourning ceremonies. He told Wills that his respect and admiration for Miss Coutts, 'so isolated in the midst of her goodness and wealth', made him determined to ease her distress at losing one of her few intimates, and he took the greatest pains to give help and comfort to her as well as to Mrs Brown.[14] While in London he observed that Charley was well 'but rather too spotty', and that the Hogarths, installed in Tavistock House to care for their grandson, were not looking after the place as they should. He complained to them, and spent the last night of his visit in his bachelor rooms in Wellington Street, drinking with Wills, to whom he wrote afterwards, 'I am impatient to know how the Gin Punch succeeded with you. It is the most wonderful beverage in the world, and I think ought to be laid on at high pressure by the Board of Health. After sleeping only two hours on the H[ousehold]W[ords] sofa, I arose yesterday morning like a dewy flower.'[15]

He was in England again in December, visiting another widow, Lavinia Watson, at Rockingham, and giving readings in Peterborough, Sheffield and Manchester. Letters to 'My Dearest Catherine' described the freezing weather in England – he told her he saw people 'actually sobbing and crying with the cold' at Euston Station – and a cheerful dinner with Frederick Evans, his publisher, with Forster also of the party, to celebrate the appearance of the first number of *Little Dorrit*. Back in Paris just in time for Christmas, he found all seven of his sons gathered for the festivities, and informed Wills that he was 'in one of his fits of depression – rather uncommon with him'.[16] Walter had become deaf, and was sent to the Parisian Deaf and

Dumb Institution, where they restored his hearing efficiently in three months. Friends came to stay from England: in March, Wilkie Collins dined with them every day and persuaded Dickens to try the student restaurants on the Left Bank; then Macready, the lonely widower. There were more trips to London for Dickens in February, March and May. He kept up the monthly instalments of *Little Dorrit* without strain, and was rewarded by sales even better than those of *Bleak House*, producing the best financial returns of his career. The first number in November 1855 sold 35,000 copies, after which sales rose to 40,000 and scarcely dipped below 30,000 through the twenty numbers, so that he made more from the serial sales than he had for any previous book, £600 a month.[17]

There were two great events in March 1856. One was the finalization of the purchase of Gad's Hill. The other was Forster's announcement that, having taken a senior civil service appointment and resigned his editorial chair at the *Examiner*, he was getting married. His bride was to be Elizabeth Colburn, the 37-year-old widow of a rich publisher, and in possession of a considerable income – a most suitable wife. Dickens was thunderstruck by his 44-year-old bachelor friend's decision, and there may have been a twinge of jealousy, a fear that he would lose his pre-eminent place with him, and also a sense of the irony of his embarking on matrimony even as Dickens was chafing against it. Forster had heard a good deal of his restlessness and dissatisfaction at home, and in April 1856 he had another letter from Dickens recalling 'The old days – the old days! Shall I ever, I wonder, get the frame of mind back as it used to be then? Something of it, perhaps – but never quite as it used to be. I find that the skeleton in my domestic closet is becoming a pretty big one.'[18] Both knew that the skeleton was his unhappiness with Catherine. The following week he described to Collins how he had taken her, with Georgina, Mamie and Katey, to dine at his favourite Paris restaurant, the Trois Frères in the Palais Royal, where, he reported, 'Mrs Dickens nearly killed herself . . .'[19] Catherine had grown fat, and no doubt ate more than she should, but the savagery of the remark must have shaken Collins, who was fond of her. In the same letter Dickens described his own visit to a Parisian ballroom where he looked over the prostitutes gathered there, all 'wicked and coldly calculating, or haggard and wretched in their worn beauty', one of whom, with 'nobler qualities in her forehead', took his eye. He said he intended to go out looking for her the following night: 'I have a fancy that I should like to know more about her. Never shall, I suppose.'

He left Paris at the end of April and chose to stay in Dover while Tavistock House was thoroughly cleaned after the departure of the Hogarths. 'I cannot bear the contemplation of their imbecility any more. (I think my constitution is already undermined by the sight of Hogarth at breakfast.)'[20] What's more, they left his house dirty, he told other correspondents. He had turned against not only Catherine but the whole Hogarth clan, with the one exception of Georgina, whose character he had formed since she was fifteen, and who gave him her unconditional adoration. To her he could complain even of her parents, and pass on an unkind description of Catherine in a book by Harriet Beecher Stowe, who accorded her the single word 'large'.[21] His own family gave him trouble too, another begging letter coming from his brother Fred, to which he replied, 'I have already done more for you than most dispassionate persons would consider right or reasonable in itself. But, considered with any fair reference to the great expenses I have sustained for other relations, it becomes little else than monstrous. The possibility of your having any further assistance from me, is absolutely and finally past.'[22] A touch of unreformed Scrooge here. Fred's behaviour was too strong a reminder of their father's in his worst days, and called for severity. Dickens was earning well but his expenses were somewhere between £8,000 and £9,000 a year.[23]

May was spent in London. *Dorrit* continued to occupy him each month, and he made his regular visits to the Home in Shepherd's Bush. He invited himself to the top of St Paul's to see the firework display for the end of the Crimean War, taking with him just one friend, Mark Lemon. In June the whole family was back in France for the summer, Boulogne again. In 1856 more months were spent in

France than in England, and Boulogne always pleased him, with its mix of town and country, its sea air, excellent hotels, food and drink, its industrious and honest people, the men sporting red nightcaps, the fishermen's wives walking like so many goddesses on their bare feet, beautiful legs brown as mahogany showing below their short working skirts. Collins came to stay, and Mary Boyle, and Jerrold, and life passed as agreeably as usual until they were driven back to England by an epidemic of diphtheria at the end of August; the three schoolboys, Alfred, Francis and Sydney, had to leave too, and were kept in England until mid-September, when they travelled back on their own by boat from London.

Forster's wedding to his Elizabeth took place in the outer London suburb of Upper Norwood on 24 September. It seems extraordinary that Dickens was not present at the ceremony, and that there are no surviving letters from him on the subject; but if the friendship touched a low point here, or Forster kept some letters to himself, there are friendly fragments written up to early September, and he wrote a very happy letter to Dickens in mid-October, and heard back from him.[24] The honeymoon was in the Lake District and lasted for two months, during which Forster continued to read the proofs of *Dorrit*; and as soon as they were back in London he showed Dickens over the house he had just taken in Montagu Square. The new Mrs Forster was childless, sweet-natured and intelligent, struck up a friendship with Jane Carlyle, and was perfectly prepared to allow Forster to make all the decisions about their life, the spending of what had been her money, where and how they lived and what company they kept. All was well on that front, and relations continued much as usual, with dinners together and Dickens consulting Forster as usual and even writing affectionate notes to Elizabeth.

※

Apart from the progress of *Little Dorrit*, Dickens's major preoccupation was now the preparations for a play to be performed at Tavistock House on Charley's twentieth birthday, Twelfth Night, in January 1857. It was to be another melodrama written by Collins, who first mentioned it to him early in 1856, and they had resolved to put it on together. It was called *The Frozen Deep*, and the inspiration came from Sir John Franklin's expedition of 1845 to find the North-West Passage, which had ended in tragedy and disputes about the final fates of the men, since there was some evidence that they had turned to cannibalism.[25] *The Frozen Deep* kept away from such grisly questions, was entirely fictional and stuck to human emotions, and Dickens immediately saw himself in the role of the sacrificial hero Richard Wardour, one of a group of polar explorers that includes the man who has won the heart of Clara, the woman he loves, away from him. The first act shows the women in England worrying about the three-year absence of the men. Clara fears that her rejected lover Wardour, known for his temper, may attack the man she is now engaged to, and Clara's old nurse, who has second sight, warns her that she sees blood on the snow – the second sight was Dickens's suggestion. At the end of the play Wardour, who has struggled against jealousy and murderous impulses, sacrifices his life to rescue his rival, and his noble death is witnessed by the women who have travelled to Newfoundland to meet the explorers.

From the first Dickens was intent on throwing himself into the part of a man who overcomes his own wickedness and ends by making the supreme sacrifice. As early as June 1856 he began to grow his beard in preparation for playing Wardour. He told Miss Coutts that the play was 'extremely clever and interesting – very serious and very curious' and became strongly emotionally involved in the whole process of putting it on.[26] In truth the plot is preposterous and the writing hardly better, but Victorian taste was broad and Dickens's performance, by all accounts outstanding – and perhaps simply his presence made up for its defects. When it was revived in the commercial theatre in 1866, it flopped. And, whatever the faults or merits of *The Frozen Deep*, its importance is that it precipitated a dramatic and irreversible change in Dickens's life. A few friends may have seen this coming, but not one could have guessed how far it would take him.

He was determined to make everything perfect. There was to be a chamber orchestra conducted by Francesco Berger, a young musician

Charley had made friends with in Leipzig, now living in London, who composed incidental music for the play. For the scenery he co-opted and bullied his painter friends. There was casting to be done, there were revisions to be made, stage effects to be thought out. A farce to follow the main play must be chosen. In October he memorized all his lines for *The Frozen Deep* during one twenty-mile walk through Finchley, Neasden and Willesden. His beard had grown impressively, giving him a rakish look.[27]

Catherine went to stay with the Macready family while Tavistock House was filled with joiners, Dickens became his own architect, and a wooden structure was put up behind the wall of the schoolroom that allowed a thirty-foot-long stage to be constructed. Stanfield, now reputed to be one of the finest marine painters in England, had been ill but could not refuse Dickens, and came up with a masterly arctic seascape. The device for producing snow throughout the second act needed much careful adjustment, and there was also a sunset effect, done with gas and red lights. There were formal rehearsals every Monday and Friday evening which gave the younger members of the cast – Mamie, Katey and Charley – a lesson in punctuality, order and perseverance, or so Dickens believed. The boys at school in Boulogne were not being brought home for Christmas this year.[28]

Forster, returning from his honeymoon in the Lake District in November, asked to read the play and made some criticisms. He particularly disliked the business with second sight, but, although his advice was not taken, he agreed to speak the verse prologue in rhyming couplets written by Dickens. The demand for places in the audience was so great that, before the opening on 6 January, Dickens reported that they expected ninety-three 'and at least ten will neither hear nor see'.[29] Seating the audience was more of a problem than it had been because the new fashion for crinolines seriously increased the girth of every woman. An extra performance was agreed on, making four in all, still with audiences packed in tight as could be managed. On play days, Dickens dined at three with Mark Lemon, on steak and stout, at the Cock in Fleet Street; and he gave detailed instructions for the serving of refreshments and supper at home, gin punch to be kept on ice under the table all evening and 'given only to myself, or Mr Lemon', and a good supply of Champagne all over the table.[30] He told a friend that he derived a strange feeling out of the play, 'like writing a book in company. A satisfaction of a most singular kind, which has no exact parallel in my life.'[31] Impersonating his own characters was something he had always done in the course of writing, but to do it in public was no doubt more demanding, and Wardour had to struggle between extremes of emotion, from the desire to murder to the resolve to save his enemy at the cost of his own life. After one performance he fainted as he sat by the kitchen fire.[32]

Critics from several papers including *The Times* were invited to *The Frozen Deep*, came, and wrote glowing notices. Georgina was praised for her 'refined vivacity', Mamie for her 'dramatic instinct' and Katey for her 'fascinating simplicity', but Dickens was the star and was declared the equal of any professional actor. Thackeray, who was there, remarked, 'If that man would go upon the stage he would make his £20,000 a year.'[33] All too quickly the four performances were over. Dickens reported to his Swiss friend Cerjat, 'It has been the talk of all London for these three weeks. And now it is a mere chaos of scaffolding, ladders, beams, canvass, paint pots, sawdust, artificial snow, gas pipes, and ghastliness. I have taken such pains with it for these ten weeks . . . that I feel, now, shipwrecked.'[34] Breaking up the theatre was an agony. He sent Berger a set of diamond shirt studs to thank him for his work. 'O reaction, reaction!' he groaned to Collins. Then in February he heard rumours that the Queen wished to see the play. Might it live again?

There were other distractions. Dickens was still intent on reforming or breaking the Royal Literary Fund, but getting no further with doing so, while the plans he, Bulwer and Forster had made for the Guild of Literature and Art matured. His brother Fred wrote protesting at his refusal to spare £30 and his unfeeling treatment: 'The World fancy from your writings that you are the most Tolerant of Men – let them individually come under your lash – (if one is to judge from your behaviour to your own flesh & blood) & God help them! –' and so it went on, yet ended 'Yrs affectionately . . . Many happy returns of the day'.[35] Dickens's forty-fifth birthday was celebrated with a dinner at home, and a few days later he went with Wills to his house at Gad's Hill to take formal possession. The house, solidly built about 1780, consisted of two floors of four rooms each, an attic, and servants' quarters and kitchen in the basement; there were gardens and a hayfield, and it stood on the hilltop associated with Falstaff, above Rochester and with fine views over the Kentish countryside. It needed a great deal of work to be made comfortable, but its value to him was in something greater than bricks, mortar and plumbing: it was the fulfilment of his childhood ambition, and another proof that the vulnerable small boy of 1820 could achieve whatever he set out to do.

His first plan was to use it as a summer residence and let it out to tenants in winter. He bought furniture here and there – a mahogany dining table, quantities of chairs, beds, bedding, marble washstands – and asked his brother-in-law Henry Austin to supervise the building work he wanted done.[36] He told Macready he hoped that buying Gad's was 'the best thing I could do for the boys – particularly Charley, who will now be able to have country air and change all through the fine weather; the railway enabling him to go up for business, and come down for dinner'.[37] The idea was that the house should be ready to receive friends on 19 May, when they would celebrate Catherine's forty-second birthday with a housewarming party. This is the only time her birthday is mentioned in his known letters, and it was the last they spent together.

Walter had his sixteenth birthday, passed his examinations well and was preparing for India, where, in May, the Mutiny broke out: he was due to sail in July. Dickens and Collins went to Brighton for a freezing weekend in March. In April he was approaching the end of *Dorrit*, but found time to read two stories, 'The Sad Fortunes of the Reverend Amos Barton' and 'Mr Gilfil's Love Story', in *Blackwood's Magazine* by an anonymous author, and recommend them to Forster: 'They are the best things I have seen since I began my course.'[38] They were George Eliot's first venture into fiction and, along with a third story, were later published as a book, *Scenes of Clerical Life*. Also in *Blackwood's* was an unfavourable review of *Dorrit* which upset him, appearing just before he began on the last section of the book. He was accused of bad construction, of making an unsuccessful attempt to write on social questions, and of giving 'twaddle' to William Dorrit to speak. He had broken an old resolution not to read attacks and told Forster he was 'sufficiently put out by it to be angry with myself being such a fool'.[39] A month later, on 9 May, the book was finished. Proofs of the last number were sent to Stanfield, to whom it was dedicated, with a tender letter saying it was 'a little record importing that we loved one another'.[40] Stanfield was in his sixties, they had known one another for twenty years, and all the sweetness of Dickens's character is in these words to his old friend.

A good deal of June was spent at Gad's Hill, where it was soon evident that neither the water supply nor the drains could cope with the new demands made on them. This meant troops of workmen tramping about the garden, boring holes, installing pumps, making new cesspools and digging up flowerbeds in order to lay pipes beneath the ground; then, after replacing everything, being forced to dig it all up again as further problems presented themselves. Only when they had bored to 217 feet in August did they find a sufficient spring of water, and this had to be pumped up daily by a horse. Dickens declared that when the first glassful was drunk at the surface, it would have cost £200.[41] Hans Christian Andersen, invited in April by Dickens to visit, arrived in June and remained for five weeks, largely outstaying his welcome. Dickens started by liking him well enough, but his eccentricities and difficulties with the English language exasperated Georgina, Katey and especially Charley, who was horrified to be asked to shave him one morning. Andersen got on best with Catherine, who was patient and gentle, and whom he saw as the embodiment of Agnes from *David Copperfield*. Miss Coutts and Mrs Brown came to Gad's to meet him, warned by Dickens that 'he speaks no language but his own Danish, and is suspected of not even knowing that.' They took him for a walk and lay on the grass while he made daisy chains, and afterwards suggested he should move on from Gad's Hill to stay with them in Stratton Street, an invitation he accepted, to the relief of his host.[42]

The timing of Andersen's visit was unfortunate because it coincided with Dickens being caught up in a new whirl of activity when he heard on 8 June of the death of his friend Douglas Jerrold, and immediately set about schemes to raise money for his widow and children. Here was his chance to revive *The Frozen Deep* and, knowing that the Queen was eager to see it, to arrange a performance for her. When she said she wanted it to be at Buckingham Palace, Dickens demurred on the grounds that it would put his daughters in a difficult social position at Court, and she allowed herself to be persuaded to come instead to the Gallery of Illustration in Regent Street, where further performances for the public were to be staged. On 4 July she brought a large party, including King Leopold of Belgium and her son-in-law Prince Frederick of Prussia, to a performance which she found 'intensely dramatic . . . touching . . . moving', as she wrote in her diary. In the interval between *The Frozen Deep* and the farce she sent for Dickens to congratulate him, and he sent back a message to say he felt it inappropriate to meet her dressed as he was to play the farce. A second request met with the same refusal, a considerable breach of etiquette, since a royal request was considered a command. But Dickens was pleased with himself for sticking to his point, and the Queen had the sense not to hold it against him. Her secretary sent a letter conveying her fulsome praise for the piece, the acting and the moral message, and assured him, 'Unofficially I may tell you – everything went off as well as possible.'[43]

Dickens also decided to give two paid public readings – the first ever – of *A Christmas Carol* at St Martin's Hall in Long Acre, for the Jerrold fund. They were greeted with tumultuous enthusiasm by an audience of 2,000. Another two public performances of *The Frozen Deep* followed. Meanwhile the Boulogne schoolboys came home for the holidays, their first at Gad's Hill, and saw Walter before he sailed for India. He wept as he said goodbye to his mother, sisters and younger brothers. Dickens and Charley went to Southampton to see him on board the *Indus*, and he was 'cut up for a minute or so when I bade him good bye, but recovered directly, and conducted himself like a Man'.[44] It was quite usual for boys of sixteen and younger to be sent off to serve in the Army and Navy, and after years of boarding school it may have seemed not much worse, but for the fact that India was half the world away.

Dickens too recovered directly, to deal with drains, rehearsals, another performance, another reading in Manchester and his plan, eagerly put forward, to create some new rooms at the Home. 'I know my plan is a good one – because it is mine!' he joked to Miss Coutts, but as so often the joke was meant seriously.[45] Now there were builders' estimates to be considered at Shepherd's Bush. Meanwhile the *Edinburgh Review* printed an attack on *Little Dorrit*, accusing Dickens of unfairness in his presentation of the English civil service, and of a failure to understand the administrative system in his satirical depiction of the Circumlocution Office.[46] Other objections were made which were open to rebuttal, and Dickens at once set about answering the attack, with great force and effect, writing half his article before one of his readings and finishing it the next morning, before another performance of *The Frozen Deep*. He could take on anything and everything, it seemed, rather than leave himself time to reflect on his dissatisfaction with his life, and what he might do about it.

A pressing request to take *The Frozen Deep* to Manchester now had to be considered. On 25 July he assured Miss Coutts that he was not going to do so, but a week later, after another visit to Manchester, and realizing that more money was needed for the Jerrold fund, he changed his mind. Francesco Berger was told to prepare for two performances at the Free Trade Hall in Manchester on 21 and 22 August. For this, given that the hall seated an audience of 4,000, it would be necessary to employ trained actresses, since the voices of the Dickens and Hogarth girls could not fill the space. It was not easy to find professional actresses to take over their parts at such short notice. Dickens was turned down by Emmeline Montague, and none had been found when he went to read in Manchester on 3 August.[47] On 8 August the final London performance took place, leaving him so tired that he kept to his bed all the next day, and wrote to Frank Stone asking him to take over his part in the farce, *Uncle John*, in Manchester. Catherine was now also ill in bed. On 12 August he booked twenty-three rooms for the whole troupe in a Manchester hotel and the next day he told a friend he would be rehearsing with the 'professional ladies' at the Gallery on Tuesday and Wednesday, the 18th and 19th. Mrs Ternan and two of her daughters had been found and recommended by Alfred Wigan of the Olympic Theatre, a friend of Dickens since he played in his farce *The Strange Gentleman* in 1836. Mrs Ternan, known for her grace, elegance and intelligence as a young actress in the 1820s, had had a long career and was still playing leading parts alongside her old friend Macready, as well as Charles Kemble and Samuel Phelps at Sadler's Wells, and her three daughters had been brought up to act from childhood. She and her two younger daughters, Maria and Ellen, had agreed to play in the farce as well as in *The Frozen Deep*, and were ready to learn their lines in the few days available.

Dickens remembered that he had seen Maria act as a child, and he took to both sisters and their mother immediately. The name 'Ternan' he pronounced Ter*nan*, with the emphasis on the second syllable, and the youngest daughter was always Nelly to him.[48] He rehearsed them at the Gallery on 18 August, and the same day wrote to Stone saying he no longer wanted him to take over his part in *Uncle John* but would play it himself. Dark-eyed Maria had seen *The Frozen Deep* performed at the Gallery, and she was to take the major part of Clara; Nelly, fair and blue-eyed, would play opposite Dickens in *Uncle John*.[49] After reassuring Miss Coutts in a last-minute note that his daughters were not to be subjected to the ordeal of appearing in the Free Trade Hall, he set off on 20 August for Manchester with a large family party, including Catherine, recovered from her illness, and his cast, musicians and technicians.

He was in such good spirits that he had everyone playing games on the train. There was no corridor, and conundrums were passed on sticks and umbrellas through the windows from carriage to carriage, with much laughter and shouting against the wind.[50] His elation continued, and in Manchester he gave his finest performances yet, reducing Maria Ternan to sobs of grief as she knelt over him while he died on stage, her tears dropping straight into his mouth and soaking into his beard.[51] Her mother and sister comforted her, everyone weeping and emotions running high, before they dressed for the farce.

Back at Gad's Hill, he wrote to Mrs Brown to say he had heard from Walter, whose ship had reached the Mediterranean, and with this news he included an account of his own unsettled state of mind: 'I feel as if the scaling of all the Mountains in Switzerland, or the doing of any wild thing until I dropped, would be but a slight relief.'⁵² The next day Collins was informed of his 'grim despair and restlessness', with a suggestion that they go away together to give themselves a subject for a travel piece in *Household Words*, and because he wanted to 'escape from myself. For, when I *do* start up and stare myself seedily in the face . . . my blankness is inconceivable – indescribable – my misery, amazing.'⁵³ In truth, he had found out that Mrs Ternan and all three of her daughters were going to be in Doncaster in mid-September, to perform at the theatre during race week, and he at once booked rooms at the Angel Hotel there for himself and Collins. Miss Coutts received a long account of Maria Ternan's performance at Manchester, her 'womanly tenderness' and 'genuine and feeling heart'.⁵⁴ With Forster he exchanged letters, answering his request for 'some confidences as in the old time' with a bleak announcement that

> Poor Catherine and I are not made for each other, and there is no help for it. It is not only that she makes me uneasy and unhappy, but that I make her so too – and much more so. She is exactly what you know in the way of being amiable and complying, but we are strangely ill-assorted for the bond there is between us. God knows she would have been a thousand times happier if she had married another kind of man, and that her avoidance of this destiny would have been at least equally good for us both. I am often cut to the heart by thinking what a pity it is, for her own sake, that I ever fell in her way; and if I were sick or disabled to-morrow, I know how sorry she would be, and how deeply grieved myself, to think how we had lost each other. But exactly the same incompatibility would arise, the moment I was well again; and nothing on earth could make her understand me, or suit us to each other. Her temperament will not go with mine. It mattered not so much when we had only ourselves to consider, but reasons have been growing since which make it all but hopeless that we should even try to struggle on. What is now befalling me I have seen steadily coming, ever since the days you remember when Mary was born; and I know too well that you cannot, and no one can, help me.⁵⁵

In his next letter he wrote of the 'wayward and unsettled feeling which is part (I suppose) of the tenure on which one holds an imaginative life, and which I have, as you ought to know well, often only kept down by riding over it like a dragoon'. He went on to say he felt it would be better for Catherine as well as himself if 'something might be done', impossible as that seemed; and he conceded that there was blame on his side as well as hers. At the end of the letter he asked Forster, 'What do you think of my paying for this place [Gad's Hill], by reviving that old idea of some Readings from my books. I am very strongly tempted. Think of it.'[56]

Part Three

20

Stormy Weather
1857–1859

Dickens's meeting with the Ternan family in August 1857, a small professional encounter hastily set up, led to changes in every aspect of his life: the wing of a butterfly flapped, and a whole weather system was unsettled. The storm blew up, and broke with his separation from Catherine. In the wake of this, friendships were severed, publishers dismissed, and *Household Words* ceased publication, to be replaced by a new weekly, with Dickens now proprietor as well as editor, and run from a larger office. He parted with his best illustrator, Hablot Browne. There were no more large-scale amateur theatricals. There were no more family holidays. His charitable work with Miss Coutts came to an end. His connection with the Home at Shepherd's Bush, over which he had presided with dedication for a decade, ceased in the spring of 1858, after which, lacking his involvement, the little community ran down, and by the early 1860s no more young women were taken in. In 1851, when he had purchased a fifty-year lease on Tavistock House, his intention had been to make it his home for the rest of his life, but now he lost interest in it, and in 1860 he sold it.[1]

Another great change was brought about by his decision to take up a second career as a professional reader. It was something he had thought of for several years, but a contributory reason for his decision to proceed with it was, at any rate as he explained it to Collins, his belief that the work involved would distract him from the pain of unsatisfied love – the Doncaster unhappiness, he called it.[2] The readings also gave him the extra income he needed in order to finance a growing number of dependants, the Ternans among them; and the constant travel required as he toured the provinces gave him a sort of freedom, making it hard for anyone to know whether he was at his rooms in the office in Wellington Street, or travelling to a reading, or at Gad's Hill, or somewhere quite different. His relations with the public changed somewhat too, because the Dickens heard at the readings was not quite the same as Dickens read on the page. He made his scripts from only a few of his novels and stories, dramatizing them with much redrafting, condensing and cutting, and many divergences from the originals, and the result was something simpler and inevitably cruder – highlights of comedy and pathos.[3] The readings were of the greatest importance to him, not only because they brought in much needed money but because they gave him reassurance that he was loved. A huge and loyal public turned out to hear him almost everywhere he went, giving him 'a roaring sea of response', cheering him, nourishing his spirit and protecting him from his detractors and critics.[4] It was a comfort he was to need badly.

He was always able to sparkle, charm and command admiration, but he aged in appearance now and began to look older than his years. The keen and lustrous eyes were sinking in their sockets and losing their brilliance, lines appeared across his brow and his cheeks were cut across by diagonal furrows. His hair thinned, his beard grizzled: some photographs show this clearly, others suggest he may have had them touched up on occasion. He remained an indefatigable editor, always assisted by Wills, and he continued to write both journalism and novels; and the core of his being, the creative machine that threw up ideas, visions and characters, persisted in its work. There was another venture into historical romance, *A Tale of Two Cities*, a popular treatment of the French Revolution, with a self-sacrificing hero closely resembling Wardour, the role he so much relished in *The Frozen Deep*. After this came a return to his highest form with *Great Expectations*. It is an almost perfect novel, in part like a ballad, drawn out of early memories and dreams, full of monsters, terrors and puzzles to be solved. This was followed by *Our Mutual Friend*, a bulging bag of grotesques in which sharp working girls are seen to be cleverer than their fathers, and greedy middle-class Londoners are mocked and reviled at their mahogany dining tables. Through both books corruption and violence are woven, and in both the river runs through the narrative, shining, dark and dangerous, 'stretching away to the great ocean, Death', as Lizzie Hexham sees it.[5] And through these years bad health wore away Dickens's strength, neuralgia, rheumatic pains, unspecified but unpleasant and persistent symptoms he associated with a bachelor life, trouble with his teeth and dental plates, piles. Then first his left foot, and then his right, took to swelling intermittently, becoming so painful that during each attack he became unable to take himself on the great walks that were an essential part and pleasure of his life.[6] Presently his hand too was affected. The decline was resisted, denied, fought against, but not to be stayed.

❦

What did Dickens hope for when he went to Doncaster to meet the Ternans? To revive some of the intense emotion of the Manchester performances, to make closer bonds of friendship with the family, and something more: he wanted Nelly, small, graceful and pretty as she was. She was eighteen years old. He thought he might have her, as his letters to Wills make clear. Hearing from Wills that young Jerrold had accused him of vanity in his charitable work, Dickens replied from Doncaster that he took no notice, adding, 'I wish I was as good a boy in all things as I hope I have been, and mean to be, in this,' and then, 'But Lord bless you, the strongest parts of your present correspondent's heart are made up of weaknesses. And he just come to be here at all (if you knew it) along of his Richard Wardour! Guess *that* riddle, Mr Wills! —'[7] The words tell us he has an urgent need to confess to someone what is happening and what he is feeling, but finds it so difficult that he makes himself into a boy, talks of himself in the third person and uses a funny voice. A further letter to Wills tells more: 'I am going to take the little – riddle – into the country this morning' and 'I *think* I shall leave here on Tuesday, but I cannot positively say. Collins and I part company tomorrow . . . I did intend to return home tomorrow, but have no idea now of doing that.' He is expecting more from his little riddle. Reassuring Wills that he will nevertheless deliver his copy for *Household Words* as promised, he uses a favourite phrase, 'So let the riddle and the riddler go their own wild way, and no harm come of it!'[8]

It sounds as though he hoped to carry off Nelly Ternan, and with her mother's consent. Collins, living an easy life with a mistress, could well have encouraged him. Dickens may also have thought of another friend, the actress Julia Fortescue, who for many years had a married lover, Lord Gardner, and how in 1856 he had heard at last of their being married and living 'quietly and very happily'.[9] But if Dickens believed he could set up a similar arrangement for himself he failed to make the right approach at Doncaster; and Mrs Ternan would have known more than he did about the drawbacks of Fortescue's position: she had put on a brave face while Gardner lived almost entirely apart from her among his aristocratic sporting friends, lost her stage career and endured a lonely life, bringing up their children mostly on her own.

Whatever took place at Doncaster, there was no seduction. He met and was impressed by the lively and ambitious eldest Ternan girl, Fanny, observed the closeness of the three sisters and declared his interest in helping all of them. Instantly, it seems, they became his dream family, the clever, pretty, poor, hard-working, fatherless sisters brought up in the theatre, where he was at ease and at home; and they could not fail to see the advantages of having such a friend as Dickens, or to feel his charm. At the same time Mrs Ternan could point out how young and pure her daughters were, how well brought up, how unsullied in spite of working in the theatre: she had seen to that. Friendship was established at any rate, and with that he returned to Tavistock House, excited and tormented. There, on 11 October, he instructed Catherine's maid Anne to have a partition put up, making a separation between his wife's bedroom and a dressing room where he would now sleep alone in a single bed. He was making clear to his wife – and inevitably to the rest of the household – that he was rejecting the proximity of her body in the marriage bed. It was his way of breaking a sexual habit that had been reduced to a humiliating form of relief, with no residue of tenderness. And now, in the ardour of his new love for Nelly, he wanted to be pure as a boy again.

Pure as a boy was impossible. Instead, the darkest part of his character was summoned up. He was ready to be cruel to his defenceless wife. A raging anger broke out at any opposition to his wishes. He used lies as weapons of attack and defence. His displays of self-righteousness were shocking. He was determined to be in the right about everything. He must have known he was not, but he had lost his judgement. The spectacle of a man famous for his goodness and his attachment to domestic virtues suddenly losing his moral compass is dismaying.

It would have been easier as well as pleasanter for him had Nelly fallen into his arms instead of requiring him to play out a charade of platonic friendship: a naughty girl could have made him happy. As it was, she remained unattainable, although elated by his attentions, and he yearned for her and suffered. And even as he was having his separate bedroom set up in October, he was writing to Buckstone, the theatre manager, expressing pleasure at his employing Nelly, urging him to give her more work (which Buckstone did, for two years) and enclosing an open cheque for £50, obviously intended for her.[10] In the theatre world he could count on understanding and tolerance, and he was establishing himself in the role of patron. Then there was a letter to De La Rue, blackening Catherine's character, saying she was unable to get on with her children, insanely jealous besides and incapable of happiness.[11] The atmosphere at Tavistock House was grim for everyone, and on another October night, unable to bear it, he walked from there to Gad's Hill, a good thirty miles. He got right away when he could, in December reading in the old way in Birmingham, Coventry and Chatham.

In December he also sent Henry, eight years old, to join his elder brothers at the school in Boulogne, where they were to remain over Christmas.[12] With four boys out of the way, five-year-old Plorn was the only child at home with his parents, his aunt Georgy, his big sisters and Charley. Miss Coutts and Mrs Brown were invited early in December to hear a reading of the Christmas story Dickens had written for *Household Words* with Collins, *The Perils of Certain English Prisoners*. It was meant as a tribute to the spirit of English soldiers and women who had suffered in the Mutiny in India, but set in the Caribbean and made into an encounter with pirates. Part boys' adventure story and part sentimental business about a common soldier who falls in love with the sister of an officer, it is poor stuff. There were no

Christmas parties and no celebration of Charley's twenty-first birthday in January.

You want to avert your eyes from a good deal of what happened
during the next year, 1858. His daughter Katey said, decades later,
that there was misery at home and that he behaved like a madman,
although at the time she found it impossible to protest. She saw her
mother humiliated, ordered to call on the Ternan family at Park Cottage, and urged her to refuse, to no effect, and Catherine went.[13]
There is another story of an engraved bracelet Dickens had made for
Nelly being wrongly delivered to Catherine. Meanwhile he was
absorbed in romantic dreams. He wrote semi-confessional letters to
admiring women friends – one to Lady Duff Gordon, saying, 'What
am I doing? Tearing myself – My usual occupation, at most times . . .
Nothing would satisfy me at this present writing, but the having to
go up a tremendous mountain, magic spell in one hand and sword in
the other, to find the girl of my heart (whom I never did find) surrounded by fifty Dragons – kill them all – and bear her off, triumphant.
I might finish the story in the usual way, by settling down and living
happily ever afterwards – Perhaps; I am not sure even of that.' Something similar went to Mrs Watson, about wanting to rescue a princess
he adores and wishing he had been born in the days of Ogres and
Dragon-guarded Castles; and to her he also boasted of his night walk
to Gad's, 'my celebrated feat', saying 'I had been very much put-out;
and thought, "After all, it would be better to be up and doing something, than lying here."'[14]

His inner turmoil did not keep him from all good works, and in
February he raised money for the Great Ormond Street Children's
Hospital with a speech so powerful that a building fund was started,
for which he also did a reading in April. In March he made his last
known visit to the Home in Shepherd's Bush, went to Edinburgh to
read and argued with Forster as to whether he should do paid public
readings. Forster saw public performance as a lesser pursuit than
writing, and also questioned whether it was quite gentlemanly. Dickens had no fears on either count, and insisted that many people
already believed he was paid for his charitable readings. In any case,
he had made up his mind. He told Collins that 'The Doncaster

unhappiness remains so strong upon me that I can't write, and (waking!) can't rest, one minute. I have never known a moment's peace or content since the last night of *The Frozen Deep*. I do suppose that there never was a man so seized and rended by one Spirit,' and he believed that by doing public readings, 'the mere physical effort and change . . . would be good, as another means of bearing it'.[15] By the Doncaster unhappiness he meant his failure to seduce Nelly, and when he told Forster his mind was made up to do the readings, he reverted to the domestic situation, telling him, 'It is all despairingly over . . . A dismal failure has to be borne, and there an end.'[16] After this he asked Forster to act for him in negotiations with Catherine over a legal separation. He knew he could rely on him, and that whatever Forster felt about the readings, or about the marriage, nothing could change his love for Dickens or his willingness to serve him.

※

The paid readings began on 29 April, at St Martin's Hall, with *The Cricket on the Hearth*, and Dickens was greeted 'with a roar of cheering which might have been heard at Charing Cross'.[17] He began by saying he saw readings as a way of strengthening what he felt to be almost a personal friendship with his readers, and with that he was cheered again, and so it went on; and it was reported that hundreds had been turned away from the box office. He was after all the nation's entertainer and known as the friend of the people. On 1 May he spoke briefly at the Royal Academy banquet, on 6 May he gave a second reading, and on 8 May he spoke for the Artists' Benevolent Fund. On 9 May he wrote to Miss Coutts to tell her that he and Catherine were virtually separated, that the marriage had been 'for years and years as miserable a one as ever was made', and that he had moved out of Tavistock House into his office rooms 'to leave her Mother free to do what she can at home, towards the getting of her away to some happier mode of existence if possible'. He said the children did not love her, and that her sister Georgina had observed this estrangement, as had her dead sister Mary, so many years ago. The letter ends with further accusations against Catherine of 'weaknesses and jealousies', adding that 'her mind has, at times, been certainly confused besides.'[18]

On Monday, 10 May, Dickens talked to Charley about the impending separation. Charley was taken by surprise and, not wanting to argue face to face – he must have remembered the arguments about his own future at Eton – he chose to write from his office at Barings to say that he had decided, clearly against his father's wishes, to live with his mother. He explained that it was not that he did not love his father but that he felt it his duty to be with her. Dickens later told others that he had suggested this plan, but Charley's letter makes it plain that it was not so. It was Charley's own idea, and his finest hour, making him a credit to Eton and to Miss Coutts. Later in the year, when his father suggested they might take a holiday in Ireland together, Charley did not take up the offer.

On this same 10 May, Georgina left for Gad's Hill, having made clear to her sister that she did not intend to support her in any way. She would have taken Plorn with her, and it is likely that Mamie and Katey went too. Georgy was prudently removing herself from the field of battle, and from the rest of her own family, who could be expected to be shocked by her preference for staying with her sister's unkind husband. They were indeed so outraged that they accused her of sexually supplanting Catherine, which was not the case.[19] She loved Dickens, whose petted companion she had been for half her life, and was also shrewd enough to see that she would be better off staying with him than leaving for a dull and impecunious life as an unmarried daughter living with her parents. For his part, he loved her for her devotion to him, and was intensely grateful to her for taking his side and continuing to act as housekeeper. Dickens announced that his eldest daughter, Mary, would be in charge of his domestic arrangements, but it was Georgy – Miss Hogarth – who ran things.

On 19 May, Catherine wrote to Miss Coutts as she prepared to leave Tavistock House, empty of all her children but Charley, and to go with her mother: 'I have now – God help me – only one course to pursue. One day though not now I may be able to tell you how hardly I have been used.'[20] Hers was a very quiet statement. Miss Coutts sent a message to Dickens asking him to call. Instead he wrote by return, 'How far I love and honour you, you know in part, though you can never fully know. But nothing on earth – no, not even you, can move me from the resolution I have taken.' He added, 'If you have seen Mrs Dickens in company with her wicked mother, I cannot enter – no, not even with you – upon any question that was discussed in that woman's presence.'[21] The wickedness of Mrs Hogarth lay in her alleging that the reason for the separation was Dickens's involvement with Nelly Ternan, and in casting doubt on Georgy's virtue for good measure.

Mark Lemon, as a close family friend, had agreed to act for Catherine, and, after another reading by Dickens on 20 May, negotiations began. Forster, Dickens and his lawyer Frederic Ouvry, who had taken over most of his legal business in 1856, reached a preliminary agreement with Lemon that Catherine should have £400 a year and a carriage.[22] Dickens moved back into Tavistock House, where he composed a letter about the separation – it is discussed below – which he sent to his manager Arthur Smith, authorizing him to show it 'to anyone who wishes to do me right'. Smith and his brother Albert were both at the heart of the theatrical world, good friends who could be relied on to support and if necessary protect Dickens. After another reading Dickens wrote to Ouvry about his mother-in-law and sister-in-law Helen, accusing them of 'smashing slanders' against him, but exonerating Catherine herself: 'She has a great tenderness for me, and I sincerely believe would be glad to show it. I would not therefore add to her pain by a hair's breadth.'[23]

On 27 May his Coutts account shows a payment of four guineas to 'N'. By now gossip was circulating round London. Annie Thackeray wrote to a friend, 'Papa says the story is that Charley met his Father & Miss whatever the actress' name out walking on Hampstead Heath. But I dont believe a word of the scandal.'[24] And when Thackeray heard talk at the Garrick that Dickens was having an affair with Georgina he contradicted it, saying it was with an actress. Dickens wrote to him to deny everything. The two men fell out further over another dispute at the Garrick Club, where Dickens's brash young friend Edmund Yates had insulted Thackeray, and the friendship between the two great novelists came to an end. The news of Dickens's separation reached as far as Germany, where Marian Evans (George Eliot) and George Henry Lewes heard it, and perhaps disapproved less than others, being themselves an adulterous couple.

More readings – with packed audiences – and on 1 June Dickens spoke for the Playground and General Recreation Society. After this he decided to publish a 'Personal' statement in the press. Forster did his best to get him to give up such a bad idea, but he was stubborn, even sending a copy of the statement to Catherine with a note saying he hoped all unkindness was over between them. The statement was cloudy, alluding to domestic troubles of long standing and now dealt with by an amicable arrangement, and to the wicked spreading of abominably false rumours involving 'innocent persons dear to my heart'. It must have been incomprehensible to the public in general, and although *The Times* printed it, and Dickens himself put it into *Household Words*, *Punch* refused it. This was enough to make Dickens break furiously with the proprietors of *Punch*, who were also his publishers, Bradbury and Evans, and to quarrel with its editor, his old and dear friend and fellow actor in so many theatricals, Mark Lemon.[25]

The quarrel was so fierce on his side that he insisted on his older children breaking off their long-established friendships with the Lemon and Evans children. Mamie's and Katey's friendships with Annie and Minnie Thackeray also became difficult, and even after Dickens had forced Mrs Hogarth and her daughter Helen to sign reluctant retractions of what they had said about his relations with Ternan – and with Georgina – he decreed that the children should not speak to their grandmother or aunt again. A letter to Charley warned him that he forbade them 'to utter one word to their grandmother or to Helen Hogarth. If they are ever brought into the presence of either of these two, I charge them immediately to leave their mother's house and come back to me.'[26]

On 8 June he wrote to Yates, from Gad's, where he had retreated: 'If you could know how much I have felt within this last month, and what a sense of Wrong has been upon me, and what a strain and struggle I have lived under, you would see that my heart is so jagged and rent and out of shape, that it does not this day leave me hand

enough to shape these words.'[27] On 9 June the statement appeared in
Household Words, on 10 June he read 'Little Dombey', his tightly condensed version of the life of Paul Dombey, to a weeping and cheering
audience. On 12 July he resigned from the committee of the Garrick
Club, and at the beginning of August set off on a provincial tour.
Meanwhile Arthur Smith had given a copy of the letter Dickens had
entrusted him with to the London correspondent of the New York
Tribune, and on 16 August it appeared in print in New York, and was
soon copied in the English papers. Harsher than the letter published
in *The Times*, it presented the marriage as having been unhappy for
many years, and Georgina Hogarth as responsible for long prevent-
ing a separation by her care for the children and her goodness. 'She
has remonstrated, reasoned, suffered and toiled, again and again to
prevent a separation between Mrs Dickens and me.' It went on to say
Mrs Dickens herself had often suggested a separation, 'that her always
increasing estrangement made a mental disorder under which she
sometimes labours – more, that she felt herself unfit for the life she
had to lead as my wife and that she would be better far away.' These
remarks sound like ones made during a quarrel, when Catherine can
well be imagined saying something along the lines of 'If things are so
bad . . .' or 'If you dislike me so much – it might be better if we were
to separate.' They are the sort of words a miserable wife might use,
hoping to bring her husband to treat her more kindly. The letter goes
on to boast of Dickens's generosity in making the terms of the separation and adds a further testimony to Georgina, named as having 'a
higher claim on his affection, respect and gratitude than anybody in
the world'. Then it speaks of how 'Two wicked persons who should
have spoken very differently of me . . . have . . . coupled with this
separation the name of a young lady for whom I have a great attachment and regard. I will not repeat her name – I honour it too much.
Upon my soul and honour, there is not on this earth a more virtuous
and spotless creature than this young lady. I know her to be as innocent and pure, and as good as my own dear daughters.' This was of
course Nelly. Finally, he says his children 'are perfectly certain that I
would not deceive them, and the confidence among us is without
fear'.[28]

Dickens said he had not authorized the publication of this shameful document but, given his instructions to Arthur Smith, it was a feeble defence. Ouvry told him it was 'unfortunate'. Elizabeth Barrett Browning, appalled, wrote, 'what a crime, for a man to use his genius as a cudgel against his near kin, even against the woman he promised to protect tenderly with life and heart – taking advantage of his hold with the public to turn public opinion against her. I call it dreadful.'[29] Thackeray and Mrs Gaskell were among those who felt that publicizing his domestic problems was about as bad as the separation itself. Nelly, working in Manchester at this time, was given a review so disapproving that it suggests her part in the scandal was known and had made her unwelcome to the theatre critic there.

Dickens began his first provincial tour of eighty-five readings at the beginning of August, taking in Scotland and Ireland (and leaving Georgina to make arrangements for the boys to visit their mother, who found them 'good and affectionate' but was saddened by their not being allowed to remain with her as long as she wished).[30] In Ireland he was amused to read that he had 'a bright blue eye', and less pleased with the comment that 'although only forty-six I look like an old man'.[31] And when Miss Coutts sent him a letter saying she had been visited by Catherine with some of the children, home for their summer holidays, he replied with another attack on Catherine, saying,

> ... since we spoke of her before, she has caused me unspeakable agony of mind; and I must plainly put before you what I know to be true ... She does not – and she never did – care for the children: and the children do not – and they never did – care for her. The little play that is acted in your Drawing-room is not the truth, and the less the children play it, the better for themselves ... O Miss Coutts do I not know that the weak hand that never could help or serve my name in the least, has struck at it – in conjunction with the wickedest people, whom I have loaded with benefits! I want to communicate with her no more. I want to forgive and forget her ... From Walter away in India, to little Plornish at Gad's Hill there is a grim knowledge among them ... that what I now write, is the plain bare fact. She has always disconcerted them; they have always disconcerted her; and she is glad to be rid of them, and they are glad to be rid of her.[32]

Catherine must have said something indiscreet, and Dickens, like a furious child, picked up the sharpest weapon to hand to discredit her with Miss Coutts: his claim that she was play-acting her love for her children, and that they did not love her. It was a ludicrous charge, belied by enough evidence to make his assertion unlikely to impress Miss Coutts.

The world was now divided for Dickens between those who supported him through the separation, or at least said nothing, and his enemies, who had failed him. In this situation the applause and praise received at readings became increasingly important as balm to his wounds, allowing him to believe in his own goodness. Having specialized in being a good man for so long and been known as such to the public, he was intent on keeping his good reputation: hence the public statements putting others in the wrong. But he could not entirely hide the truth from others or from himself. A villain does well to have a certain blitheness, which Dickens depicted in his early novels, where Squeers, Fagin, Mantalini and Quilp all make you laugh; but from *Dombey* on bad behaviour becomes serious and heavy-handed, as in Carker, Murdstone, Tulkinghorn, Rigaud, Fledgeby and Headstone. Even Steerforth is not funny, and Dickens was naturally quite unable to make jokes about his own situation as a man who puts away his wife and then finds the girl he loves unwilling to accommodate him. To Mary Boyle, whose affection he cherished, and who wrote to him in September with delicate inquiries, he justified his behaviour by saying he had made his public statements only to protect the innocent. Writing to her again in December, he added this: 'Constituted to do the work that is in me, I am a man full of passion and energy, and my own wild way that I must go, is often – at the best – wild enough. But vengeance and hatred have never had a place in my breast.'[33] You can feel sorry for him as he struggles, but it is impossible to like what he did, or on occasion to believe what he said.

People who had known him earlier were curious to see him in his new incarnation as a reader. In November 1858, when he was reading in Southampton, Eleanor Christian, the young woman he had flirted with in Broadstairs in 1840, and long since married and middle aged, came to hear him read *A Christmas Carol* on his second night there. She fancied he had 'withered and dwindled into a smaller man', but he read admirably, and she was eager to speak to him after the event. She went round, only to be told he had already left, through a window. Evidently he was not always happy to meet his public.

Katey, looking back years later, remembered something that adds to the picture of this time: she said that her father would scarcely speak to her for nearly two years after the separation, his reason being that she made occasional visits to her mother. At the same time, she added, he sometimes asked her about her mother.[34]

※

Before setting out on his tour he had arranged for Fanny Ternan to travel to Florence to study opera singing. He wrote various letters of introduction for her: to the wife of the English Minister at Florence, Lady Normanby; to Mrs Thomas Trollope, also resident in Florence; to friends in Genoa, the Consul there and De La Rue. Mrs Ternan was to travel out with Fanny to act as her chaperone, even though this left Maria and Nelly on their own in London. Dickens insisted that Park Cottage, their modest rented home in Islington, was unhealthy, and accordingly they moved to rooms in the heart of town, in Berners Street, off Oxford Street. Two pretty actresses living unchaperoned attracted some attention, and Dickens was appalled to hear from them that they were being pestered by a policeman, whom he suspected of being 'suborned to find out all about their domesticity by some "Swell". If so, there can be no doubt that the man ought to be dismissed.'[35] But, while he might instruct Wills to complain, and tell him there would be a 'most prodigious uproar' if the circumstances were stated in *The Times*, he knew very well that he depended on concealment, not publicity, in this case. So did Wills, and no more was heard of the policeman.

While this was going on his brother Fred was sued for divorce by his wife, who cited adultery, Fred responding that it was condoned. His youngest brother, Augustus, had meanwhile also deserted his wife and would soon leave for America with another woman. The

Hogarth family observed these happenings with sardonic satisfaction. Forster was overseeing the ending of the partnership with Bradbury & Evans, which had become 'as messy, and as decisive, a break as the one with Catherine'. Robert Patten, whose words these are, believes that Dickens construed their refusal to print his personal statement in *Punch* as a criticism of himself and of his image of the happy hearth, 'which for Dickens and his public seemed almost to constitute a new myth of the Golden Age'.[36] If this is right, Dickens was defending a myth which he knew very well had been desecrated by his own behaviour. The moral complications were such that, once again, he dealt with them through anger. Bradbury and Evans were both villains, to be cast out of his life for good.

⁂

Dickens's account with Coutts for December shows that he gave Nelly a Christmas present, 'C.D.E.T. £10'. The year ended, and 1859 began, with several readings in London of *A Christmas Carol*. After hearing him read this and the trial scene in *Pickwick*, Forster more than made up for his earlier disapproval with praise: 'You read in a masterly way last night, indeed. I was immensely moved altogether by your execution of both pieces of reading.'[37] Then he had to go into battle again on hearing that Dickens was thinking of letting Tavistock House to the Ternan family. Forster and his wife both felt that Dickens should remain there with his daughters 'to give the girls some society', and he wrote firmly advising him against the other plan: 'I entertain no doubt whatever that such a step would *most decidedly be very damaging indeed*. With you I say, it is not a matter of reasoning so much as of feeling: and I would not have you at this moment do such a thing for 8,000, far less 800 pounds. Do not laugh at this. I feel it very strongly.'[38] Wills too advised categorically against letting to the Ternans. Both men saw that such a move would give credence to the accusations of the Hogarth family and lead to more scandal, damaging to Dickens himself, to his family and to the Ternans. This time Dickens allowed himself to be persuaded. He had another argument with Forster over the naming of his new weekly magazine. Dickens wanted to call it 'Household Harmony'. Either he believed he could still represent the myth of the happy hearth with the reading public, or he was in denial about his own recent behaviour. Forster suggested the words might raise a few eyebrows in view of the recent events in the Dickens household. Dickens accepted Forster's judgement and gave in again. The magazine would be called *All the Year Round*, and Dickens would be its publisher, proprietor and editor.

21

Secrets, Mysteries and Lies

1859–1861

The portrait of Dickens painted by William Frith in January 1859 shows a man with angry eyes staring out as though to defy the world. It is not what you expect, knowing that artist and subject became friends, and reading Frith's description of going to Dickens's study, where he was starting work on *A Tale of Two Cities*, to watch him from a corner as he muttered, grimaced and walked about the room, pulling his beard. Neither was the beard what the commissioner of the portrait had wanted: Forster had been waiting since 1854 for his portrait of Dickens in hope of seeing a clean-shaven face again, but he had to give up after five years, and asked Frith to go ahead. And although there was affable conversation during the sittings, Frith saw something else in his face, and Dickens himself acknowledged rue-fully that he had done well when he was presented with the finished portrait. It was hated by Georgina. When it was shown at the Royal Academy, Landseer observed, 'I wish he looked less eager and busy, and not so much out of himself, or beyond himself. I should like to catch him asleep and quiet now and then.'[1]

He had survived the public part of his troubles and was taking up a new life – or, rather, several new lives. Dickens the public reader was preparing carefully adapted scripts from his novels and stories, with which he would soon travel all over the country, criss-crossing it by train; he was also already being urged to read in America, but as yet refused to commit himself, saying that a long absence would be 'particularly painful to me'.[2] Then there was Dickens the journalist, calling himself 'The Uncommercial Traveller', a first-rate reporter for his own magazine, travelling to places as far as Anglesey, Liverpool and Cornwall for stories. Dickens the country squire became a familiar figure in Kent as he walked his dogs and continued to improve the house at Gad's Hill – extending the grounds, giving work to local people and well liked in the village as 'a man as shifted a good deal of money in the place'; he was also known to be kindly and generous to the poor.[3] For the winter of 1859 he let Gad's to a tenant, but from then on kept it for himself throughout the year. Yet another Dickens, now magazine proprietor as well as editor, presided over No. 26 Wellington Street and surrounded himself with clever young men, aspiring writers who were eager to learn from him and ready to flatter: Edmund Yates, George Sala (both from theatrical families), Percy Fitzgerald, an Irish lawyer with a fluent pen, and John Hollingshead, a largely self-taught journalist who later became a theatre manager. Dickens gave them work, corrected and improved their copy, was a good friend to them and dined them well, making a great performance of the preparation of his gin punch, like 'a comic conjuror, with a little of the pride of one who had made a great discovery for the benefit of humanity'.[4]

At home, he struggled to steer his sons into careers. The example of their uncle Fred was not encouraging: early in 1862 Fred was imprisoned in the Queen's Bench Prison, having divorced, refused to pay alimony, fled abroad and returned bankrupt.[5] Alfred was being prepared at Wimbledon to take Army exams, which he failed in 1862. Frank was found a job in the City in 1860 but performed poorly and was taken to work at *All the Year Round* instead: his father got him a reader's ticket for the British Museum and sent him to lodge with the Stone family in London. Overcoming his objections to patronage, Dickens sought help from Lord John Russell and Lord Clarence Paget in getting a naval cadetship for Sydney in 1860. He also needed to give his daughters some social life, which was not always easy, given that there was a question mark over the respectability of their aunt Georgina; and that Wilkie Collins's brother Charles wanted to marry Katey, while Wilkie himself was living with Caroline Graves, a woman who already had an illegitimate child, of whose existence Katey and Mamie were supposed to be unaware, and whom they were certainly not allowed to meet. Secrets and lies threaded through the family's social arrangements.

Another of the secrets was of course that Dickens was the patron and protector of the Ternan girls and maintained his close interest in their careers and living conditions, as though they were a second set of daughters. In March 1859 their housing was sorted out when Fanny, back from Florence, and Maria, described as 'spinsters of 31 Berners Street', purchased the lease of No. 2 Houghton Place, Ampthill Square, a large house in the Mornington Crescent area. There is nothing in writing to prove that Dickens paid for it, but the circumstantial evidence is persuasive, and a year later, when Nelly reached the age of twenty-one and could own property, her sisters sold the house on to her. All three girls were working in the spring of 1859, Fanny singing in the popular French opera *Fra Diavolo*, Maria and Nelly both appearing in light plays and farces at the Haymarket; all the same, from May 1859 Dickens's accounts at Coutts Bank show many payments to 'HP Trust', 'HP', 'HPN' – standing, no doubt, for Houghton Place Trust, Houghton Place and Houghton Place Nelly.[6] And in August 1859 Nelly made her last appearance on stage, at the Haymarket, in a play by Charles Mathews the younger. She was cast as Mrs Gatherwool to Mathews's Gatherwool, the play was appropriately named *Out of Sight, Out of Mind*, and with it she ended her career. Whether this was by choice, or because she was offered no more work, or because Dickens preferred her not to work, remains obscure.[7]

As for Dickens the novelist, he gave his imagination a shake, turned away from chastising London's financiers, civil servants, politicians and lawyers and produced, at high speed and in weekly instalments, two novels in the two and a half years between 1859 and the summer of 1861. The first, *A Tale of Two Cities*, was an adventure story set in the second half of the eighteenth century.[8] It was inspired by Carlyle's study of the French Revolution and researched under Carlyle's guidance, and the central character, Sydney Carton, was a new departure for Dickens, a hard-drinking lawyer who rises to heroism, giving his life to save that of his rival in love. His other inspiration came, as he admitted, from Wardour in *The Frozen Deep*, but Carton is given more panache, and goes to a more thrilling death. It was to be serialized in *All the Year Round* from the first number at the end of April 1859, to give his magazine a cracking start, while Bradbury & Evans continued *Household Words* without him.[9]

He had not taken on a weekly serial since *Hard Times* in 1854, and this one was to be almost twice as long. He found it hard to begin, and a strain to fit his material into short weekly episodes, but it did its job of launching *All the Year Round* as he had hoped. Wills reported a print run of 100,000 after the first week, and in six weeks they were in profit.[10] There was no shortage of eager readers for *A Tale of Two Cities*, then or later: it is on record that in 1968 it far outsold all other Dickens novels in the US, and it remains a favourite with many English readers.[11] But his move away from social commentary did not make him any more popular with English reviewers, and he was either ignored or attacked, for lack of humour and a plot hard to follow. Forster was almost alone in praising *A Tale of Two Cities*.

It is true that the plot is too long drawn out and elaborate, working through the histories of three French families from the 1750s to the 1790s, linked by crime and cruelty; and that the horrific depiction of the *ancien régime* is somewhat mechanical in its horrors, the characters like emblematic puppets representing good and evil – virtuous doctor, perfect daughter and wife, wicked marquis, vengeful woman of the people. One of the best scenes is a spy trial in London, with an English crowd demonstrating its eagerness for the accused to be hanged, drawn and quartered before their eyes. Dickens also rises with verve to Paris in the Terror, with its tides of violence, street dancing, denunciations and settling of scores at summary trials. The climax of the action is preposterous and deeply sentimental, but the tension is so built up that Carton's famous last words before the guillotine – 'It is a far, far better thing that I do, than I have ever done . . .' – make their effect on all but the most determinedly stony hearts. This is Dickens the showman, amusing his people and drawing their tears.

'It has greatly moved and excited me in the doing,' he told Collins, 'and Heaven knows I have done my best and have believed in it.'[12] It took John Sutherland to show the anachronism in allowing Carton to use chloroform in the prison rescue scene decades before its use was known. Sutherland's clever essay should be reprinted with every new edition, because it adds to the entertainment, and *A Tale of Two Cities* was intended as entertainment.[13] The horrors, thrills and gallant self-sacrifice all have something of the popular theatre about them, and indeed it was quickly staged at the Lyceum by its French manager, Madame Céleste, a dancer herself; and the Carmagnole danced by bloody-handed revolutionaries in Paris was danced again to the applause of the British bourgeoisie in the stalls. Dickens also put the book out in monthly parts, with illustrations, but it was the last of his novels to be illustrated by 'Phiz', i.e., Hablot Browne. Although Browne had worked with him since *The Pickwick Papers*, he is said not to have taken Dickens's side over the domestic split, and there was no more work for him and not much further contact between the two men after 1859.[14]

※

Great Expectations, begun in October 1860 and published weekly from December to June 1861, is something altogether different. It did not come from research or the theatre but out of a deep place in Dickens's imagination which he never chose to explain, and perhaps never could, and it is all the better for that. It was also written more tightly than he originally intended, because he gave up his plan for twenty monthly numbers in order to run it weekly in *All the Year Round*, a task he found more difficult but carried off pretty well to perfection. It is a great book, delicate and frightening, funny, sorrowful, mysterious.

It is placed, like so many of his books, in the period of his own childhood and youth, and set in home territory for him, the Kentish marshlands and Rochester, and the London of the law courts, Newgate Prison, the Inns of Court, Soho, the Temple and the river. His hero walks one night from Rochester to London just as Dickens walked from Tavistock House to Gad's Hill; but, as already suggested, *Great Expectations* is not a realistic account of how the world was but a visionary novel, close to ballad or folktale. The orphan boy, with dead parents and siblings in the graveyard in the marsh, has a cruel elder sister who treats him like a male Cinderella. He encounters monsters – Magwitch, Orlick, Miss Havisham, Jaggers and the nameless man with a closed eye and a file – and he can't tell which threatens and which favours him. His innocence becomes tarnished by money and what it seems to promise. He neglects the good spirits who protect him – Joe the blacksmith and Biddy the simple schoolteacher – and is lured by Estella, a Belle Dame sans Merci.

The story begins in terror, the primal terror of the figure who rises up in the near-darkness to harm you, feared by all children. Pip is further terrified by the threat of being killed and eaten unless he performs the task he is given, which is to steal food and a file for his attacker, who is, we realize, an escaped convict. The guilt Pip feels for taking food from his home for the man on the marsh upsets him further, and he would like to confess to Joe, his only adult friend, but does not dare. He is then given two lessons in goodness, one from the recaptured convict, who tells the soldiers that he himself stole the food – this is to make sure Pip does not get into trouble – and the other from Joe, who tells the convict he is welcome to the food, as a fellow creature in need.

Pip's life is changed and controlled by mysterious forces, which first put him in contact with the rich, eccentric Miss Havisham and her adopted daughter, Estella, and then raise him from poverty as an apprentice blacksmith to unexplained riches and 'great expectations'. Pip is well intentioned and intelligent but passive, and he does not think of using the education he is given to take up a profession or make something of himself, but simply accepts that being a gentleman means a life of idleness. In charge of his affairs is the lawyer Mr Jaggers, a dark man with large hands and head, bristling eyebrows, a chin marked by the black dots of his beard, and a characteristic smell of the scented soap he uses to wash his hands. He tells Pip nothing about the source of his expectations, but from his first appearance he is seen to be the most powerful figure in Pip's world. He is feared by the criminal community, knows everyone's business and controls people as though they were his puppets; his scented hand-washing is to get rid of the dirty business he handles. His offices in Little Britain are decorated with casts of the faces of hanged men and, as Pip finds when he is summoned there, it is close to the meat market, Smithfield, 'all asmear with filth and fat and blood and foam, [which] seemed to stick to me' as well as 'the great black dome of Saint Paul's bulging at me from behind a grim stone building which a bystander said was Newgate Prison'.[15] This is the heart of London, a very dirty place.

Pip is the narrator, but Jaggers is the other pole of the book, connected to almost everyone in Pip's world – Miss Havisham and her relatives, the convict Magwitch and his associates, Estella and her real mother – and the plot depends on Pip's apprehensions of them being different from Jaggers's. Between Pip and Jaggers stands his clerk, Mr Wemmick, who has two separate natures, severity and tight lips at the office, playfulness and gentleness at home. Wemmick replaces Joe as the good spirit in Pip's life in London, this time a sophisticated and clever good spirit. He also does duty for Dickens's wish to have something droll – his word – in the book, because Wemmick invites Pip to share his private idyll, taking him to see the tiny fortified and moated house he has built for himself and his old, deaf father, 'The Aged P.', in the south-eastern suburb of Walworth – a miniature urban Strawberry Hill – and showing off his drawbridge, flagpole, fountain and garden in which he keeps a pig, rabbits and hens, and grows cucumbers, confident that Pip will appreciate them and never mention them to Jaggers. Another inspired touch of drollery is Trabbs's boy, Trabbs being the Rochester tailor who makes fine clothes for Pip when he comes into money: it is Trabbs's boy who mocks him mercilessly for his new grandeur and later, as it turns out, saves his life, expecting no thanks for either service.

Pip's narrative is full of mysteries, not all of which are explained: for instance, his two visions of Miss Havisham hanging from a beam. Nor can he, or we, ever be sure how mad Miss Havisham is. She seems mad enough when he first sees her, fixed in her distress at being jilted on her wedding day, yet she decides things for herself, gives orders to Jaggers and others, controls her money even though she chooses to let her house decay, and lives a life that is fantastical but deliberately so. She knows how to turn her adopted daughter into an

General mems: 1

General mems: 2

Dickens's working notes for *Great Expectations* from the manuscript
(transcription opposite).

instrument of revenge on the male sex, and she teases the relations who flatter her in the hope of an inheritance. She also changes, becoming remorseful as the story proceeds, and repenting of what she has done to Estella and to Pip. By the end she has almost restored herself to sanity, while Pip meditates on her 'diseased mind' and 'the vanity of sorrow' that has cursed her and all of them. Dickens leaves her case for us to observe without attaching labels or reaching after fact and reason, and by allowing this uncertainty he gives the portrait its truth.

Another unfathomable Kentish character, Orlick, morose and

Miss Havisham and Pip, and the money for
Herbert. So Herbert made a partner in Clarriker's
 Compeyson. How brought in?
 Estella, Magwitch's daughter
  Orlick – and Pip's entrapment – & escape
  To the flight
   Start
    Pursuit
     Both overboard
    Struggle – [deleted words]
    together. Compeyson
    drowned – Magwitch rescued
    by Pip. And
      taken—
Then:
 Magwitch tried, found guilty, & left for
    <u>Death</u>
  Dies presently, in Newgate
  Property confiscated to the Crown.
 Herbert goes abroad –
  Pip perhaps to follow.
 Pip arrested when too ill to be moved – lies in
 the chambers in Fever. Ministering Angel <u>Joe</u>
 Recovered again, Pip goes humbly down to
 the old marsh Village, to propose to Biddy.
 Finds – Biddy married to Joe

So goes abroad to Herbert (happily married to
Clara Barley), and becomes his clerk.
 The one good thing he did in his
 prosperity, the only thing that endures
 and bears good fruit

dangerous as a dog, works at the smithy. He batters Pip's shrewish sister to the floor in a fit of rage, leaving her brain damaged and speechless. No one can prove he did it, and Dickens introduces a black joke by making her, in her disabled condition, fix on Orlick as her favourite and insist on seeing him regularly. He remains a threat to everyone, and his plan to kill Pip would be horrific were it not weakened by being made theatrical. Orlick lures Pip with a fake message, ties him up, then pauses to boast lengthily of his wicked acts and intentions – he is going to throw his body into the lime kiln – and his rhetoric ensures a delay long enough to allow the rescue party to arrive, in time-honoured thriller style. Again, he goes free, but continues his aggressions until he is imprisoned, not villain enough, it seems, to be provided with a violent end like Sikes or Quilp.

Just as Dickens always felt himself a child of Rochester and the Kentish countryside, so Pip, even when he becomes a Londoner, living in chambers in Barnard's Inn and then the Temple, remains tied to the marshes, Rochester and the river, and his observations of the landscape run through the book. At the start, in the bitter cold of winter, he thinks what it might be like to die on the marsh if you were on the run: 'A man would die tonight of lying out on the marshes, I thought. And then I looked at the stars, and considered how awful it would be for a man to turn his face up to them as he froze to death, and see no help or pity in all the glittering multitude.'[16] He describes the white marsh-mist that veils the dykes, mounds, gates and scattered cattle, and carries the booming sound of the cannon from the prison ship, anchored off the coast. A red moon over the marsh lights him to his appointment with Orlick. And in summer, when the white sails of the ships on the Medway move up and down on the tide, he sees how 'the light struck aslant, afar off, upon a cloud or sail or green hill-side or water-line',[17] and its beauty makes him dream of what he most desires. In London he has feverish and futurist nightmares as the story works to its grim conclusion, and in his dreams he is a brick in a wall from which he cannot escape, and then 'a steel beam of a vast engine, clashing and whirling over a gulf'. He begs to have the engine stopped 'and my part in it hammered off'.[18]

When Dickens told Forster he was going to write another story in the first person, he added an assurance that it would be nothing like *David Copperfield*, and of course it is not. David's story is of a middle-class boy who overcomes cruel neglect by his own effort, becomes a successful writer, is allowed by fate to marry the girl he loves and then to lose her when she turns out to have been a mistake, and ends with a perfect wife and family. Not only is Pip quite a different sort of boy with a family background from the lowest, labouring level of society, his story is one of failure, failure to understand what is happening to him, failure to win the girl he loves, failure to save his benefactor, failure to make anything of himself. He just redeems himself morally, and that is enough, after all he has seen. It is

enough for the reader too. His statement of what he feels for the
indifferent Estella is the most powerful expression of obsessive love
for a woman in Dickens: 'when I loved Estella with the love of a
man, I loved her simply because I found her irresistible. Once for all;
I knew to my sorrow, often and often, if not always, that I loved her
against reason, against promise, against peace, against hope, against
happiness, against all discouragement that could be.'[19] Nothing
needs to be added to this, but Bulwer, in a foolish moment, wanted
Pip to be given a happy ending with Estella and suggested to Dickens that he should set aside his bleak final vision and write a cheerful
one. Amazingly, Dickens accepted Bulwer's advice and rewrote,
adding a chapter with a conventional variant and publishing it. Forster was told too late to object, but he was not pleased and thought it
marred the book. He wisely kept a copy of the original ending to be
compared with the substitute, and published it in the third volume of
his *Life of Dickens*. Few critics since have disagreed with Forster,
although the happy ending appears in every standard edition of *Great
Expectations*.

Both books were written while Dickens was having trouble with his
health. In June 1859 he told Collins, 'The "cold" is pretty much in the
old stage. So I have made up my mind to think no more of it, and to
go (in a general way) the way of all flesh.'[20] This may be interpreted
to mean that his love for Nelly – the "cold" – remained unconsum-
mated, and he looked elsewhere for sex. Not long afterwards he
wrote to his doctor, Frank Beard, 'My bachelor state has engendered
a small malady on which I want to see you. I am at Gad's Hill for the
summer, but have come up this morning on purpose.'[21] Beard prescribed medicines which irritated his skin and did not entirely cure his
ailment.[22] He told both Collins and Forster that he could not get quite
well, and that he thought only the sea would restore him, and he
would go to Broadstairs. He wrote again to Collins, 'Perhaps a tumble
into the sea might — but I suppose there is no nitrate of Silver in the

Ocean?'[23] As silver nitrate was used against gonorrhoea in the nine-teenth century, it may be that this was his trouble, a miserable and humiliating business.[24]

He was still unwell in the freezing new year of 1860, still taking medicine and seeing Beard. In March he had other ailments, a pain in his face, in June rheumatism in his back, so bad he was doubled up. They cleared up, but in December, as *Great Expectations* began its weekly publication, he was 'not quite well again, and being doc-tored', and he chose to stay at Wellington Street all through January 1861, refusing invitations and needing Beard's attentions every few days. 'I should like to be inspected – though I hope I can offer no new attractions,' he told him at the end of the month, and at last this par-ticular problem was dealt with.[25] In May he was able to enjoy hiring a steamer on the Thames for a day out with friends and family, from Blackwall to Southend and back, and gave the impression he had no cares.[26] Then he took himself to Dover alone to work on the last chapters of *Great Expectations* and breathe the sea air, again suffering from neuralgic pains in the face. He told Macready they had 'troubled me a good deal, and the work has been pretty close. But I hope that the book is a good book, and I have no doubt of very soon throwing off the little damage it has done to me.'[27] He did, and after this there were no more major problems with his health until 1865.

✿

His Hogarth in-laws remained unforgiven enemies, along with his former publishers Bradbury and Evans, and Catherine – 'my Angel wife' as he called her sardonically to Wills in a letter complaining of the financial demands made on him.[28] He and Miss Coutts avoided an outright quarrel, but there very few meetings with her and Mrs Brown, and little contact except when Miss Coutts wrote pressing him to be reconciled with Catherine, and he declined, as happened in April 1860, and again in February 1864.[29] Lemon, to whom he had been so close, was estranged and they met no more. Thackeray was also entirely lost, and in December 1859 he became a formidable rival editor of the newly founded *Cornhill*, specializing, like *All the Year*

Round, in running high-quality fiction serials. Maclise had withdrawn into reclusiveness by the mid-1850s and did not reappear in his life. In the autumn of 1859 his old friend Frank Stone died, leaving Dickens to grieve, to arrange his burial in Highgate and to help his children, to which he applied himself with his usual generosity. The end of theatricals meant he saw less of friends who had taken part as actors or designers, such as Leech and Stanfield, although Leech brought his family to stay at Gad's in the summer of 1861, and Stanny came to dine at Wellington Street.

Tom Beard, one of his oldest family friends, remained solid, whatever he thought of the separation. Charles Kent, a journalist and poet who had been writing favourable reviews of his work since 1848 and who held him in reverence, was promoted to a closer relationship, and began to be invited to Gad's. Mary Boyle, his old acting partner, continued to adore him, and they exchanged cheery letters from time to time, and Mrs Watson of Rockingham was also loyal, although there were not many meetings with either. With Bulwer, Dickens was on excellent terms, and since he had suffered his own marital disaster he was sympathetic, even inviting Dickens to bring Georgina and Mamie with him to stay at Knebworth. Macready, now living in Cheltenham, remained affectionate and uncensorious. His granddaughter said later that he took the Nelly Ternan affair quite calmly as he knew that Dickens was not the celibate type, and that he quite approved of his separation from his wife. He was perturbed only when, as he thought, Dickens was conducting the affair with insufficient discretion, and risking a public scandal.[30] Macready delighted Dickens by marrying again, in March 1860, Cecilia Spencer, a young woman of twenty-three to his sixty-seven, and his bride was soon pregnant.

Forster and Dickens had reversed roles: Forster was now the married man, rich and with a devoted wife, and Dickens the wayward 'bachelor' with hidden problems. Since Forster's love was always greater than any disapproval he felt for whatever Dickens did, or planned to do, his friendship remained unwavering, the only drawback being that he was obliged to be away from London a good deal, now that he had a government job inspecting asylums. Dickens still consulted him about his work and sent him proofs when possible, and the Forsters came to Gad's Hill for weekends. Proofs were also sent to Miss Ellen Ternan in Mornington Crescent, not only for her entertainment but her comments, because he valued her 'intuitive sense and discretion'. [31] So they discussed his writing in a way that must have been flattering to Nelly, and delightful for him. Francesco Berger, when very old, is said to have recalled musical Sunday evenings at Ampthill Square with Dickens and Nelly singing duets, but this often repeated and perfectly plausible story turns out to be a fabrication. [32]

Dickens's spirits rose and fell markedly. In May 1860 he entertained James Fields – the American publisher he had first met in Boston, and who was now eager to persuade him to visit the US again – at Tavistock House. He liked Fields, who became a worshipper, and was charmed by his young second wife, Annie, whom he was meeting for the first time. She noted in her diary, 'A shadow has fallen on that house, making Dickens seem rather the man of labor and of sorrowful thought than the soul of gaiety we find in all he writes.' [33] Shortly after this Charley left for Hong Kong to become a tea buyer, and in July Katey married Wilkie's brother Charles Collins, thirty-two to her twenty, a good-natured man but a semi-invalid, who was giving up art to try to write. Dickens blamed himself for Katey's decision, knowing she was marrying without love and to get away from home, but he put on a showy wedding at Gad's, with a special train to bring guests from London to Higham Station. Catherine was not invited, a piece of brutality in which Georgina, Mamie and Katey were all complicit. Katey left for her honeymoon wearing black, and the guests were entertained with games in the garden and taken to see Rochester Castle and Chatham before they departed. That evening Mamie found her father weeping into her sister's wedding dress, and he told her how much he blamed himself for the marriage. [34]

Days after the wedding he heard of the serious illness of his one respectable and hard-working brother, Alfred, travelled north to be with him and arrived to find he had died, like their sister Fanny, of tuberculosis of the lung. His widow, Helen, left with five young children, became his responsibility, and he brought them first to

Gad's, then found them a nearby farmhouse before settling them in a house in London and ensuring that the boys got an education. At the same time he was doing his best for his mother, who had reached 'the strangest state of mind from senile decay . . . her desire to be got up in sables like a female Hamlet, illumines the dreary scene with a ghastly absurdity that is the chief relief I can find in it.'[35] At least he was able to give her into the care of Helen, installing them all in a house together. He was now maintaining three households of women in North London: his wife in Gloucester Crescent, the Ternans, a few streets south in Houghton Place, and his mother in Grafton Terrace, Kentish Town, with Helen and her children. The sale of the lease of Tavistock House for 2,000 guineas in 1860 gave him some extra funds, and he took a town house for the season each year, to please Mamie and Georgina. In 1861 it was at Hanover Terrace, Regent's Park, within walking distance of all the other North London houses in which his dependants lived. Furniture was moved from Tavistock House to Gad's and to Wellington Street, where Dickens enjoyed showing off his 'five very good rooms' to friends who dined with him there; and where he had bedrooms for Georgy and Mamie should they ever need them.

In September 1860 he performed a ritual act, ridding himself of the past by burning thousands of letters accumulated over the years on a bonfire at Gad's Hill. His appointed biographer, Forster, was not consulted.[36] Eleven-year-old Henry Dickens, who lent a hand with the bonfire, remembered roasting onions in the hot ashes.[37] It was a good summer for him because he persuaded his father to let him leave the school in Boulogne and go to Rochester Grammar School instead.

Dickens's amusement for October was the sensational Road-Hill House murder in Somerset, much reported in the press, concerning a large and apparently respectable family and the discovery of the three-year-old son dead, suffocated and stabbed, in an outside privy. He had no doubt the murder had been committed by the child's nursemaid and his father together, after the child woke up and found them in bed together, at their 'blissful proceedings' as Dickens put it, and they feared he would tell his mother. He relished the idea of such scandalous goings-on, damaging as they were to the sacred image of middle-class domestic respectability: for a moment he could look at the world with the cynicism of a Quilp or a Jaggers. But, although his belief that the father of the family was the murderer delighted him, it was not taken up by the prosecution.[38]

His chief worry in the autumn was the falling circulation of *All the Year Round*, and it was this that decided him to change his plans for *Great Expectations* and make it a shorter book suitable for division into weekly parts, in the hope of boosting sales of the magazine. It started on 1 December 1860, and in the same month Chapman & Hall published the first volume of his *Uncommercial Traveller* pieces, which sold out and reprinted twice. The winter of 1860/61 was the coldest for many years, and this was when Dickens was unwell. He returned to London on Boxing Day, leaving Georgina to cope at Gad's while he settled at Wellington Street, seeing his doctor, going out with Collins and to theatres in the evening, and writing. As the weather improved he took his long walks again, discovering the new Millbank Road beside the river, with factories and railway work along it, and the 'strangest beginnings and ends of wealthy streets pushing themselves into the very Thames. When I was a rower on that river it was all broken ground and ditch, with here and there a public house or two, and old mill, and a tall chimney.'[39] He enjoyed contrasting the old urban landscape with the new, and looking back to youthful jaunts and river outings on a very different river.

⁂

Charley arrived home from China in February 1861, having seen Walter in Calcutta, and went to his mother's just as Dickens moved to the Hanover Terrace house rented for the season. As well as being immersed in writing *Great Expectations*, he was preparing six readings to be given in London in March and April; and when he had done them, to great applause, and finished writing his book, he tried to be lazy at Gad's. His sons Frank and Alfred both remembered rowing him on the Medway from Rochester to Maidstone, Dickens acting as cox, teasing and laughing with them, a river trip that must have given them a rare moment of shared enjoyment; and there were other expeditions on the Thames.[40] But he found that the younger boys at home for the holidays disturbed him, and he had new readings, from *Copperfield* and *Nickleby*, to prepare for an autumn tour. Then the plans for the tour were thrown askew by the death of his manager Arthur Smith, and after that his brother-in-law and old friend Henry Austin also died, leaving his sister Letitia another widow dependant on him. He invited her to Gad's, paid for the funeral, offered her money and set about vigorously applying for a pension for her through Lord Shaftesbury, citing the services Austin had given to public health. It took many letters and much insistence before he succeeded.

The last family event of 1861 was Charley's wedding. The bride, Bessie Evans, daughter of Dickens's onetime publisher, had been his sweetheart from childhood, and there was nothing surprising about the marriage, but Dickens chose to be outraged, having cast Evans into outer darkness. He tried to stop friends from attending the wedding, or entering the Evans house; and he blamed Catherine, who was of course at the wedding, and was indeed fond of the bride. He spoke ill of Bessie and warned Charley against going into partnership with his brother-in-law, young Frederick Evans, in a paper-making company, advice Charley, understandably enough, chose to ignore. His father was in any case embarked on a colossal reading tour, and on the day of the wedding he was somewhere between Brighton and Newcastle-on-Tyne and on his way to Scotland, impersonating Mr Micawber and Wackford Squeers in front of enraptured audiences. His Squeers, according to one observer, 'impresses us with the belief that he enjoys being a brute and is not an actor being brutal'.[41]

In 1862 the Russian novelist Dostoevsky, an admirer of Dickens's work – he had read *Pickwick Papers* and *David Copperfield* in prison – visited him at Wellington Street. Years later he wrote in a letter to a friend a remarkable account of what Dickens said in the course of their conversation about writing. Dostoevsky introduced Dickens's words with his own:

The person he [the writer] sees most of, most often, actually every day, is himself. When it comes to a question of why a man does something else, it's the author's own actions which make him understand, or fail to understand, the sources of human action. Dickens told me the same thing when I met him at the office of his magazine . . . in 1862. He told me that all the good simple people in his novels, Little Nell, even the holy simpletons like Barnaby Rudge, are what he wanted to have been, and his villains were what he was (or rather, what he found in himself), his cruelty, his attacks of causeless enmity towards those who were helpless and looked to him for comfort, his shrinking from those whom he ought to love, being used up in what he wrote. There were two people in him, he told me: one who feels as he ought to feel and one who feels the opposite. From the one who feels the opposite I make my evil characters, from the one who feels as a man ought to feel I try to live my life. Only two people? I asked.[42]

This is an amazing report, and if Dostoevsky remembered correctly it must be Dickens's most profound statement about his inner life and his awareness of his own cruelty and bad behaviour. It is as though with Dostoevsky he could drop the appearance of perfect virtue he felt he had to keep up before the English public. It also suggests that he was aware of drawing his evil characters from a part of himself that he disapproved of and yet could not control. Dostoevsky's Dickens reminds us of Eleanor Picken's, now one sort of man, now another, the mood-swinging, the charm turning to aggression, the fun that gets out of hand.

Whatever Dickens felt about how he ought to feel, he was guided by no one but himself at this time. What little can be gleaned about his relations with the Ternans is that in September 1859 he wrote to his friend Régnier at the Comédie-Française to tell him that Fanny Ternan, 'uncommonly clever and accomplished . . . as good and diligent as she is *spirituelle*', would be in Paris with her mother in October.[43] This was followed up by cheques for £50 to Mrs F. E. Ternan in Paris in October, and '£50 E. Ternan's Bill', so perhaps Nelly went to Paris to join her mother and sister. If Fanny had hoped to find work in Paris she was disappointed, but on her return she was engaged by the Eastern Opera House in the Mile End Road in London, and later joined the London Grand Opera Company, touring with them as Prima Donna. Maria was at the Lyceum acting with Madame Céleste and Mrs Keeley, both friends of Dickens, and Dickens went to see her perform more than once, but in February 1861 the Lyceum closed. The Census of April 1861 showed all the Ternans at Houghton Place with a seventeen-year-old servant, Jane, Mrs Ternan described as an 'annuitant', Fanny (25) a vocalist, Maria (23) an actress, and Ellen (22) without occupation.

Nelly's character remains clouded. A petted youngest daughter and little sister, she was now set apart, free of any necessity to earn her own living, but facing decisions that would determine her future. The words Dickens gave the adult Pip in *Great Expectations* to describe his feelings for Estella insisted that 'I did not . . . invest her with any attributes save those she possessed.'[44] If Dickens felt himself to be equally clear-sighted about Nelly's motivation in their dealings, he also, like Pip, appears to have 'loved her simply because I found her irresistible'. He makes Pip tell Estella, 'You are part of my existence, part of myself. You have been in every line I have ever read . . . You have been the graceful embodiment of every graceful fancy that my mind has ever become acquainted with . . . to the last hour of my life, you cannot choose but remain a part of my character, part of the little good in me, part of the evil.'[45] These are memorable statements of obsessive love.

In June 1861 Maria was acting at Rochester with the Windsor Strollers and in July she joined Fanny in the north, taking contralto parts with the touring opera company. In September Dickens wrote to Webster, manager of the Adelphi, asking him to give work to Maria and mentioning her mother at Houghton Place, but Webster did not oblige, and in December Maria was in Rochester again. It was depressing for Dickens, who tried so hard to help them, and still more for Fanny and Maria, both gifted and ready to take on anything, but unable to break through to real success. Perhaps they were not quite good enough. Perhaps their association with Dickens proved to be a disservice. While they struggled on, Nelly's life took a dramatic new direction.

22

The Bebelle Life

1862–1865

Over the next three years Dickens divided his life between England and France, crossing the Channel at least sixty-eight times, at a rough reckoning, and only occasionally giving a reason for his journey. He had his fiftieth birthday in February 1862. Ten years earlier, reaching forty, he had spent 1852 writing *Bleak House*, and his youngest child had been born. In 1862 he wrote little more than a very short story for the Christmas number of his magazine. It was called 'His Boots', and it was about an Englishman, a middle-aged grandfather (as Dickens was), with a temper and unforgiving to those who cross him, who goes to France, stays in a northern garrison town, interests himself in an illegitimate and virtually abandoned baby girl known as Bebelle, and ultimately takes her back to England as his adopted child. The story is well told, tender and touching, but it is not a major piece. Clearly Dickens had other things than writing on his mind in 1862.

One was the reading tour he had begun in the autumn of 1861, which had been interrupted by the death of Prince Albert in mid-December. He took it up again in Birmingham on 30 December and continued through January. 'Success attends me everywhere, Thank God,' he wrote to his sister Letitia, 'and the great crowds I see every night all seem to regard me with affection as a personal friend.'[1] So he pursued a triumphant way through Leamington, Cheltenham, Plymouth, Torquay and Exeter, stopping in Cheltenham with the Macreadys – he aged and infirm, but with a new and blooming young wife visibly preparing to present him with another child, and indeed she bore him a stout son in May. Then he returned north for what he described as an 'absolutely dazzling' close to the tour at Manchester and Liverpool.[2]

Personal success was one thing, family life another, and two letters to

Georgina in January show his exasperation, first with Alfred's widow, Helen, bothering him at his office – would Georgy make it clear to her that she must negotiate with her, or with Mamie? – and then with Georgy herself, for sewing the wrong buttons on his coloured shirts. You hear the voice of a man who expects to be looked after efficiently and get a glimpse of his dictatorial mode.[3] Another thing he disliked was having to exchange Gad's for the 'nastiest little house in London' in order to give Georgy and Mamie their promised 'season'.[4] It was in Hyde Park Gate in Kensington, on the wrong side of the park for Dickens, and he told Forster it stifled and darkened his powers of invention, but he was stuck there until the end of May. He made a point of spending two days and nights of every week at Wellington Street.

There were more readings in London through March and April, still mostly *Copperfield* and *Nickleby*, and he was able to boast to Forster of the money he was earning: 'Think of £190 a night!'[5] There was *All the Year Round* to occupy him, and much of his correspondence relates to articles commissioned and magazine business discussed with Wills. In other letters there are terse comments on public affairs. He refused to run anything about the proposed memorial to Prince Albert in his magazine, regarding him as a perfectly commonplace man and his son, the Prince of Wales, as 'a poor dull idle fellow'.[6] And he was cynical about the attitude of the Northern states to slavery in the American Civil War, which was bringing depression to England. It was also postponing any possibility of an American tour.

In April he went to see Charles Fechter, an actor who had made his career in France and was now putting on spectacular performances in London, as a Hamlet unlike any seen before, and as Ruy Blas in Victor Hugo's play, both admired by Dickens. Edmund Yates was working with Fechter's company, and Dickens wrote to Yates:

> I wish Fechter would take among his young ladies, Miss Maria Ternan. Not because I have a great friendship for her and know her to be one of the best and bravest of little spirits and most virtuous of girls (for that would have nothing to do with it), but because I have acted with her, and believe her to have more aptitude in a minute than all the other people of her standing on the stage in a month. A lady besides, and pretty, and of a good figure, and always painstaking and

perfect to the letter. Also (but this has never had a chance) a wonderful mimic. Whatever he showed her, she would do. When I first knew her, I looked her in the eyes one morning in Manchester, and she took the whole Frozen Deep out of one look and six words.[7]

Few recommendations come better than this, although it did Maria no good, as Fechter's company was about to be disbanded. But it tells us what Dickens saw in her – her courage, her professional quickness and conscientiousness, her good looks and her perfectly ladylike presence – and it says something about how Mrs Ternan had brought up her daughters, to pass as ladies even though they were working women. Only now Nelly was no longer a working woman.

There is no certainty about where she was or what she was doing in 1862, 1863, 1864 and until June 1865, when she appears on a train carrying passengers from the cross-Channel boat from France in which she was travelling with Dickens and her mother. Otherwise it is only from Dickens's letters that it is possible to conjecture that she was in France. But since we know he was her protector and closely concerned with her welfare, it is not a very bold assumption to make, given how much can be gleaned from his letters. Georgina's role has something to tell us too, because it was at the time he made two trips to France in the summer of 1862 that she declared herself ill. A healthy 34-year-old, she suddenly seemed to be going into a decline, unable to run the house or perform her usual duties. Dickens was anxious enough to call in two doctors, Frank Beard and Dr Elliotson, and she was diagnosed as having 'degeneration of the heart' and said to be in need of rest. He then offered to take her, with Mamie, to Paris for two months – only not until mid-October. This promise of a treat and a rest was enough to start her recovery, although she still spoke at times of feeling weak and of pains in the left breast. Once comfortably installed in Paris, and Dickens and Mamie in attendance, her heart regenerated itself spontaneously, and by the end of the two-month visit she was 'almost quite well'. Back at Gad's in 1863 she soon resumed her normal life. In fact she suffered no further illnesses and lived to be ninety. Degeneration of the heart had clearly been a misdiagnosis, and her biographer suggests politely that there may have been a psychosomatic element to her illness in 1862.[8] It had certainly frightened Dickens, which was no doubt what was intended.

There could have been a reason for Georgina putting on this performance. She may have feared that Dickens was going to make a further readjustment to his life – even perhaps to set up house with Nelly Ternan and to father more children – which would leave her without her pre-eminent place as his housekeeper, helper and best friend. Macready had after all just become a father again, in his sixties, with his new young wife. Georgina needed to be reassured, and Dickens evidently succeeded in reassuring her, by showing he was ready to take her to Paris, as in the old days, and by explaining the situation he was in regarding Nelly, and to some degree including her in it. It would help to explain Georgina's behaviour, now and later. There is no proof that it was Nelly who took Dickens to France the summer of 1862, or that the reason for her being in France was that she was pregnant, but it would make sense of Georgina's behaviour.

The story might go like this: as long as Nelly had resisted being his mistress, and Dickens was suffering from his bachelor ailment, there had been no danger of pregnancy, but, once cured, he pursued his suit and succeeded in becoming her lover. Mrs Ternan, who had already accepted his financial and professional help for her daughters, by then saw that the great Charles Dickens, so friendly and so generous, was not to be cast aside, and that given his difficult marital situation it might not be wholly wrong for Nelly to give him what he desired so ardently and needed so badly. Or maybe Nelly simply succumbed. Dickens was a great performer who knew how to please his audience. He was famous for his energy and he took his physical pleasures seriously, eating and drinking, walking, dancing, travelling, singing. He had fathered ten children on his wife in twenty years (leaving aside miscarriages), and he believed that sexual activity was necessary to a healthy man. He wanted his own blissful proceedings, and it seems he got them, and with them their consequences.

Scandal must be avoided, and a pregnant Nelly had to be hidden. Where better than France? The railway lines in northern France were extended in 1861 to make good links between the coast and Paris, a line from Boulogne passing through Amiens and another from Dunkirk passing through Arras. Nelly could be settled somewhere in that region to await the birth of her child and then easily moved to Paris, where there were good doctors and the anonymity of city, while everyone considered the future. In 1862 Dickens was in France in June, in July, probably in August, possibly in September, certainly in October, telling Collins he was suffering from 'miserable anxieties' and writing to Forster of being 'unspeakably wretched' with an 'unsettled fluctuating distress'.[9] He was seriously considering a reading tour in Australia as a way of making money.

In early October he told Collins he was working on his story, describing it as an evocation of a fortified French town; then he told Mrs Brown it was put into his head by seeing a French sailor acting as nurse to his captain's baby girl.[10] As it turned out, the centre of the story is the illegitimate baby, adopted by a secretive and shame-faced Englishman who is slowly drawn to love the child and redeemed by his good action. 'God will bless you in the happiness of the protected child now with you,' a Frenchwoman tells him as he leaves France for England with the child 'of no one'. In the critic John Bowen's account of the story and the time at which it was composed, he writes that 'although we can never be certain what occurred during these months, we can be sure that in France in the autumn of 1862, Dickens was thinking about the fate of illegitimate children, about sudden death, adoption, fatherhood and reconciliation by telling himself, and us, a story in which a middle-aged Englishman, estranged from his family, creates a happy ending for an illegitimate child in France.'[11]

But nothing was simple or straightforward. In September Georgina complained of feeling weak, and he took her to Dover for a rest. On 16 October he set off for France again, not going as far as Paris. Georgy crossed the Channel two days later with Mamie and her dog Mrs Bouncer, muzzled as required by French law. They installed themselves in a small, elegant apartment in the Faubourg St Honoré, not far from where the whole family had stayed in the winter of 1846, and they were visited in November by Bulwer, and by Wills, who brought Dickens 'cash for the enclosed cheque, in Gold'. In mid-December he departed for two days in London, leaving Georgy and Mamie on their own for nearly a week, and spending the other days only he knew where. On 18 December he wrote to Wills with another urgent request: 'I want a £50 note for a special purpose. Will you send me one by return of post?'[12] It sounds like money for Nelly, or for a doctor and a nurse. He returned to Gad's for Christmas with Georgy and Mamie, and at this point made his decision against the Australian reading tour. He told Forster he needed the money, 'with all the hands upon my skirts that I cannot fail to feel and see there, whenever I look around. It is a struggle of no common sort, as you will suppose, you who know the circumstances of the struggler.'[13] But there were more important considerations even than the money.

In mid-January 1863 he was back in France without the ladies. He remained there until mid-February. Before arriving in Paris he told Joseph Olliffe, an Irish friend who was physician to the Embassy, that he would be visiting a sick friend, and wrote again on arrival to say how he was suffering and that 'some unstringing of the nerves – coupled with an anxiety not to be mentioned here – holds sleep from me.'[14] Other friends and acquaintances were given different stories of long trips planned to Genoa or to Switzerland, but to Wilkie Collins he wrote only that he was 'unsettled and made uncertain by "circumstances over which —" &c &c&c' [*sic*].[15] He said he was leaving Paris for a week for an undisclosed destination – which could have been another district of Paris – and was officially back in Paris on 29 January and preparing to read about the death of little Dombey to his French admirers, feeling 'as though I could not muster spirits and composure enough to get through the child's death'.[16] Possibly Nelly's child had been born, and was frail.

In January he also attended a performance of Gounod's opera *Faust*, which shows the innocent Marguerite seduced with the help of a present of jewels, and he told both Georgina and Macready he had been badly upset by it. 'I could hardly bear the thing, it affected me so, and sounded in my ears so like a mournful echo of things that lie in my own heart,' he wrote to Georgina. He went on, 'But, as a certain Frenchman said, "No weakness, Danton!" So I leave off.'[17] This is the closest thing to a confession, and defies any interpretation other than that he was talking of himself and Nelly. Again, describing the stage presentation of Marguerite's loss of innocence to

Macready, who had known the Ternans for years, he wrote again, 'I couldn't bear it, and gave in completely.'[18] It can't have helped that, in the opera, Marguerite gives birth to a child who dies, is ostracized and accused of infanticide, and dies herself.

On 4 February he sent his manservant John back to England and embarked on some travelling alone, visiting both Arras and Amiens. He was in France again in March for 'some rather anxious business' that detained him '4 or 5 days'. In April he wrote of a 'hasty summons to attend upon a sick friend' and a 'rush across the Channel'. These journeys had to be fitted round readings in London, three in March, four at the end of April, five in May and three in June 1863, the month of Maria Ternan's wedding in London (she was marrying a well-to-do Oxford brewer, Rowland Taylor). Then in August he wrote of 'evaporating for a fortnight' in northern France, and again in November.[19] And so it went on, a pattern of activity that suggests he was always ready to go when sent for, and that he also set aside longer periods to be spent in France. This year he wrote some 'Uncommercial Traveller' pieces, and in the autumn he started on a full-length novel, *Our Mutual Friend*.[20] He also embarked on his 'Mrs Lirriper' stories, which appeared at Christmas 1863 and in 1864 and are again centred on an illegitimate birth. Mrs Lirriper, a London lodging-house keeper, takes pity on a young woman, abandoned by her lover, who dies in childbirth; she brings up the baby boy and some years later takes him to France, where he meets his penitent and dying father in Sens.

There seem to have been fewer trips to France for Dickens in 1864, when he was writing *Our Mutual Friend*, which started as a monthly serial in April for Chapman & Hall. Still, in February his bank account notes 'HBD [i.e., Her Birth Day] £3', a small present for 3 March, and a week later he set off for France again. In June he told one correspondent that he was bound for Belgium, but wrote to Wills that he was working desperately hard to get away, going in the direction of Paris for his 'Mysterious Disappearance'. He added, 'I seem to have a sort of inspiration that may blend the undiminished attractions of Mrs Lirriper with those of the Bebelle life in Paris.'[21] His remark could indicate that Nelly and the child were in Paris. Dickens was away for ten days. In November there was another week or ten days in France. In March 1865 it was 'HBD £3' again.

A great many questions hang in the air, unanswered and mostly unanswerable. If there was a child, neither birth date nor death date is known, not too surprisingly, since the Paris records were burnt in 1871. An American scholar, Robert Garnett, has constructed an account that puts a birth in late January to early February 1863, and the death of the baby soon after, in April. The birth date looks plausible, suggesting as it does that the child was conceived in April or May 1862. The death date seems wrong, because the absence of both Mrs Ternan and Nelly from Maria's wedding in June 1863 tells us that, in such a close family, there must have been a compelling reason for staying away. Besides, there were the many further visits to France by Dickens.

Here is another piece of evidence. Dickens wrote a letter in 1867 in which he spoke about Nelly in answer to a request from his friend Mrs Elliot, who was curious about the relationship and what she called the 'magic circle' inhabited by Nelly with Dickens; she boldly asked to be introduced to Nelly. Mrs Elliot was a strong-minded and somewhat raffish heiress with a history of divorce and dubious marriage, a friend of Wilkie Collins too; she acted briefly in *The Frozen Deep* in London, and she had ambitions as a writer. Dickens liked her, but he rebuffed her firmly over the matter of meeting Nelly. He told her that the magic circle was a circle of one only, and that 'it would be inexpressibly painful to N to think that you knew the history . . . She would not believe that you could see her with my eyes, or know her with my mind. Such a presentation is impossible. It would distress her for the rest of her life. I thank you none the less, but it is quite out of the question. If she could bear that, she could not have the pride and self-reliance which (mingled with the gentlest nature) has borne her, alone, through so much.'[22] Pride, self-reliance, a shrinking from exposure and a gentle nature that has carried her through 'so much' alone is Nelly's character, according to Dickens. What, if not the birth and loss of a child, could have made such demands on her pride and self-reliance, and required her to bear a great deal alone?

From Nelly herself there is only negative evidence: that, with the support of her sisters, she went to extraordinary lengths to conceal her relationship with Dickens after his death, with a bold lie about her age and by destroying his letters, which would surely have demonstrated the innocence of the relationship had it been non-sexual. It is from Dickens's own children that more positive evidence comes. His daughter Katey said that Nelly had borne a son to Dickens.[23] This she told privately to Bernard Shaw in the 1890s and, after Nelly's death, to her friend Gladys Storey with the intention that Storey should write and publish a book based on what she told her, as indeed she did. Miss Storey then noted that Henry Dickens confirmed what Katey had said: the child had been a boy, who had died early.[24]

If there was a child – an eighth son for Dickens – when did he die? After Dickens's widely spaced visits to France in 1864 things changed again and in the early months of 1865 he made at least four visits, and this despite his own recurrent illness, with a gouty foot so painful and swollen that it was sometimes difficult for him to walk. He was working hard to keep up the instalments of *Our Mutual Friend*, and he told Forster he was close to breakdown, but he was in France in January, in March, at the end of April and again at the end of May.[25] Such frequent trips could be an indication that the child was ill, and if he died in May, it would explain why the last of these visits ended with Nelly and Mrs Ternan travelling back to England with Dickens in June. The 9th of June 1865 is the first date on which Nelly can be definitely located again after three years of uncertainty, because it was when the 'tidal train' carrying them to Charing Cross in London hit a bridge with loosened plates and fell into the river below, at Staplehurst in Kent.

Dickens, Mrs Ternan and Nelly were alone in a first-class carriage near the front and escaped the worst, but Nelly thought they were all about to be killed and said, 'Let us join hands and die friends' – a remark that might suggest they were not at this moment on very friendly terms.[26] She had injuries to her arm and neck, and had to be extracted from the train, losing a good deal of her jewellery in the process, and then discreetly and hastily removed from the scene with her mother, before anyone could become aware that they had been travelling with Dickens. He, shaken as he was, went to help other passengers with his brandy flask and his comforting and practical presence, while the Ternans returned to Houghton Place. If Nelly was already distressed by the death of her child, she now had two traumas to recover from. She was ill for weeks and remained delicate. Dickens had his trusted manservant John take 'Miss Ellen' delicious food to tempt her appetite: 'tomorrow morning, a little basket of fresh fruit, a jar of clotted cream from Tuckers, and a chicken, a pair of pigeons, or some nice little bird. Also on Wednesday morning, and on Friday morning, take her some other things of the same sort – making a little variety each day.'[27] He also began to call her 'The Patient' in his letters to Wills: and patient she was obliged to be.

In an earlier book, *The Invisible Woman*, I suggested that the Staplehurst crash was a moment of reckoning for Dickens and for Ternan. Even with Nelly injured Dickens put his determination to protect his reputation before his wish to look after her. Both of them were obliged to have an innocent version of their relationship which could be used by friends and family, and this was that he was a friendly uncle or quasi-godfather who took an interest in her education. I suggested that Fanny and Maria must have tried to believe this in order to square their own consciences over any suspicion that the help they received from him was paid for by their sister's sexual favours. And whether or not Nelly had indeed borne and lost a child in France, and whether she was angry with Dickens for letting her go through a long ordeal with little support from him, the crash brought home to her the helplessness and humiliation of her position. It made clear to her and her sisters that, whether she was guilty or innocent, and whatever these terms meant, she was obliged to live her life in the gap between what could be said and what really happened – to be invisible.

For many years anyone who suggested publicly that there might have been a sexual affair between Dickens and Nelly Ternan was held to be a despicable scandal-monger by his admirers, although, curiously, his ill-treatment of Catherine did not worry them much. The Dickens family understandably wished to protect his reputation, and adultery was something for the law courts, unmentionable in decent society. When in 1935 Thomas Wright published a biography of Dickens that revealed a good deal about Ternan, he was attacked; and when Gladys Storey's *Dickens and Daughter*, an account of her conversations with Katey Perugini, was being prepared for publication in 1939, the first printer refused to go ahead because he found her mention of Dickens's separation and Ternan's role in it objectionable, and seems to have feared it might be actionable, even though all those involved were dead. Then a serious Dickens scholar, an American, Ada Nisbet, published her groundbreaking research in *Dickens and Ellen Ternan* in 1952, giving passages from Dickens's letters that had been omitted from Georgina and Mamie's edition; she also included material from an edition of letters to Wills that had been inked over, but was now retrieved by infra-red photography. Things changed after this. Two scholarly and thorough Dickens experts, K. J. Fielding and Edgar Johnson, writing in the early 1950s, both accepted that there had been a sexual love-affair between Dickens and Ternan. Felix Aylmer's 1959 *Dickens Incognito*, half brilliant research and half off track, contributed further information. The *Pilgrim Edition* of the letters revealed more details over the years. Manuscript notes by Gladys Storey that turned up after her death in 1978 added to what she had published earlier, and much of what Wright had said found confirmation. Philip Collins, a scrupulous and deeply knowledgeable Dickens scholar, cited Gladys Storey's account in his *Dickens: Interviews and Recollections* (1981), saying he found it 'substantially correct, and of great interest', while acknowledging that others still rejected the idea that Ternan was Dickens's mistress. He himself plainly believed that she was, since he wrote of Dickens 'contravening the *mores* of his age by sleeping with Ellen Ternan'.[28]

Things changed again. In 1990, the year in which I published *The Invisible Woman*, an account of Nelly Ternan's life, Peter Ackroyd wrote in his biography of Dickens that 'it seems almost inconceivable that theirs was in any sense a "consummated" affair.' Michael Slater's *Charles Dickens* (2009) correctly insisted that there is no proof that it was, and pretty well left it at that. Both were impressed by an unpublished manuscript written by the late Katharine Longley, a carefully researched piece of work written to assert Nelly's innocence.[29] I knew and liked Miss Longley, learnt from her and studied her manuscript, but her arguments did not convince me; rather, they inclined me to believe the evidence of Dickens's two children and Gladys Storey's notes, Dickens's own letters and the sequence of events described in this chapter – that he was Nelly's lover, and that she bore him a child who died. Even without documentary proof, and with uncertainties remaining, the sum of evidence from many different sources cannot easily be written off.

※

After this long excursion into Bebelle country, there is some catching up to be done, and gaps to be filled in. In March 1863 Dickens's one-time travelling companion, the artist Augustus Egg, who had proposed to Georgina, died in Algiers, where he had gone for his health. A sorrowing Dickens sat down and compiled a list of five other participants in *The Frozen Deep* who had died since 1858. Five months later Mrs Hogarth, his detested mother-in-law, died, eliciting a few impersonal lines to Catherine along with his authorization to the Kensal Green Cemetery Company to open the grave in which Mary Hogarth was laid, and where he had once hoped to join her; he did not offer a word of sympathy.[30] A few weeks later, in September, his own mother died – 'Her condition was frightful,' he told Wills – and he saw her buried at Highgate. On Christmas Eve 1863 Thackeray died in his sleep. Although he and Dickens had exchanged friendly words a week before at the Athenaeum, they had been effectively estranged since 1858. Dickens was at the funeral at Kensal Green and wrote a memorial piece for the *Cornhill*, praising Thackeray's character warmly, although he said nothing about his writing. His article appeared in February, the same month he heard of the death of his son Walter in India.

Walter had got into debt and Dickens was angry with him and had not been in contact for many months. There had been a note from Walter to Mamie in the autumn to say he was ill, and another at Christmas telling her he was now so ill that he was about to be sent home on sick leave; but before he could be embarked he died, of an aneurism, on the last day of 1863. Miss Coutts took the opportunity

of Walter's death to write to Dickens, again urging a reconciliation
with Catherine. His reply said that 'a page in my life which once had
writing on it, has become absolutely blank, and that it is not in my
power to pretend that it has a solitary word upon it.'[31] He neither
spoke nor wrote to Catherine about the death of their child, but paid
off Walter's debts and hardened his heart.[32]

Francis and Alfred, in their late teens, both disappointed him. In
October, Francis failed to get into the Foreign Office after coming sec-
ond in a competitive examination, despite having been nominated by
Lord John Russell and coached by a senior civil servant. His stammer
may have stood in his way, but Dickens found his failure 'unaccount-
able' and applied to Lord Brougham to get him a place in the Registrar's
Office in London. When this too proved impossible, Francis agreed to
go to India to join the Bengal Mounted Police and left for India in
December 1863, expecting to see his brother Walter. At the same time
Alfred's preparations to take the Army examinations for Woolwich
were thought by his teachers so unlikely to succeed that Dickens
decided to put him into a firm in the City, and when he failed to do
well there he was persuaded to go to Australia. In May 1865, as Dickens
left for France, Alfred sailed for Australia to become manager of a
sheep station in New South Wales. He saw neither of his parents again.

※

Professionally things were better, as we have seen. After two years
with no novel planned, at the end of August 1863, returning from
France, Dickens told Forster he had an idea for a new story that would
make a twenty-number novel, and by October he declared himself
fairly confident of it, and it became *Our Mutual Friend*.[33] He also did
good among his own friends that autumn, reconciling Forster and
Macready after a long estrangement brought about by Forster's disapproval of Macready's remarriage. In February 1864 he complained of
some of his private correspondence being published, destroyed a further batch of letters received, declared he would write 'as short letters
as I possibly can' in future and visibly carried out his intention.[34] There
were no readings in 1864. He took a house at Gloucester Place, Hyde

Park Gardens, until June, and refurbished his rooms at Wellington Street, choosing handsome new carpets for them. In March, after his visit to France, he wrote to Forster praising his new biography of the seventeenth-century statesman Sir John Eliot, and arranged for it to be prominently reviewed in *All the Year Round*. He told Forster he was working very slowly on his novel and wanted to have five instalments ready before the first number appeared on 30 April. On 23 April he celebrated Shakespeare's birthday 'in peace and quiet', going to Stratford for the day with Forster, Robert Browning and Wilkie Collins.[35] In the autumn another dear friend, the artist John Leech, not yet fifty, died, and Dickens went grimly to the funeral at Kensal Green, remembering their cheerful family holidays together, their walking club, their theatricals and Leech's much admired illustrations for the Christmas books. Then came the death of Joseph Paxton in June 1865, with whom he had set up the *Daily News*.

A new friend appeared to fill some of these losses: Charles Fechter, who in January 1863 became manager of the Lyceum Theatre, just opposite the Wellington Street office. Fechter was partly English, partly German, his education had been largely in France, French was his first language, and he had started his career in the theatre in Paris in the 1840s, becoming a star, but a quarrelsome one. Dickens had admired his acting in Paris, and when he moved to London in 1860 he made a point of seeing him again. He gave a thrilling and much praised Hamlet, his naturalism breaking with all the traditions, and a great Iago. His English was accented but good; his nerves made him vomit before each performance. He was famous for his bad temper, he borrowed money and was generally unreliable, yet Dickens took to him strongly, praising him for being 'a capital fellow and an Anti-Humbug'.[36] During the summer of 1864 he said Fechter usually came to Gad's on Sundays when he was there, and by 1865 he described him as 'a very intimate friend' and proposed him for membership of the Athenaeum.[37] Not surprisingly, the Athenaeum turned him down, but the Garrick Club welcomed him. English gentlemen's clubs were centres of intrigue, gossip and quarrels, and when Wills was blackballed by the Garrick and Dickens resigned – it was his fourth resignation – Fechter loyally followed suit.

Fechter never fitted into English society, entertaining in his dressing gown and sending guests to fetch their food from the kitchen. He was married to a French actress, became the lover of another, Carlotta Leclerq, whom he abandoned later for a third, and this Gallic *sans-gêne* had its appeal for Dickens, as D'Orsay's flouting of respectability had done, perhaps because it allowed him to become someone different himself when he was with them. Fechter made his own mark upon Gad's Hill when, in January 1865, he was inspired to give Dickens a perfect present: a great box full of all the parts needed to build a two-storey wooden Swiss chalet. Dickens had it put up at once. Set well away from the house, in the wilderness reached only through a tunnel he had built under the road, it gave him an airy upstairs writing room – 'a most delightful summer atelier' – hung with mirrors and full of light and birdsong.[38] Here he could escape from people, letters, anxieties, troubles, and work uninterrupted.

The chalet given to Dickens by Fechter in 1865 – a perfect present.

23

Wise Daughters

1864–1866

From the autumn of 1863 until the autumn of 1865, Dickens was writing *Our Mutual Friend*. It was to be his last completed novel. He did no readings during the two years it took, and although they were years of stress the book he made was an ambitious and powerful piece of work, full of sardonic humour and offering his final judgement on the society in which he lived. He had been hailed as a young writer for his echoing of Hogarth, and in this late work there is still a Hogarthian vigour and precision in his drawing of scenes and characters, no smoothing over of rough places, physical or moral deformities but rather a relish for them. He chose not to run it in *All the Year Round* but serialized it in twenty monthly numbers in green-paper wrappers in the old way. He also signed a contract with Chapman & Hall that raised for the first time the possibility that he might not live to finish a work, in which case Forster would negotiate compensation to the publishers. All being well, Dickens would be paid in three instalments: £2,500 on publication of the first number, and again at the sixth, then £1,000 at the end, a grand total of £6,000.[1] Knowing himself to be less energetic than he had been, he decided to have five instalments written before the first number appeared in April 1864. There were times when he became anxious about keeping up the pace, and in July, telling Forster he had been unwell and was still out of sorts, he complained that he had 'a very mountain to climb before I shall see the open country of my work'.[2] It did not help to find that sales were lower than those for any of his recent books. The starting monthly print order of 40,000 fell until, for the final number, only 19,000 copies needed to be stitched into paper covers;[3] but it attracted more advertising than any serial yet, making £2,750 to be shared equally between publishers and author. And the book has endured.

Our Mutual Friend offers us his last look at London, the London of the 1860s, 'a black shrill city, combining the qualities of a smoky house and a scolding wife; such a gritty city; such a hopeless city, with no rent in the leaden canopy of its sky'.[4] A city too in which people starve to death in the streets every week; and in which the middle classes are shown as corrupt, complacent, lazy, greedy and dishonest, more interested in the pursuit of shares than the pursuit of love. Among the rich and would-be rich he mocks are the Lammles, a confidence man and woman who marry, each under the delusion that the other has money; Veneering, a corrupt businessman going into parliament; and Podsnap, an insurance broker convinced of the superiority of the British over all other nations and set on ignoring any aspect of life that might trouble his complacency. Their good friend Lady Tippins, widow of 'a man knighted by George III in mistake for somebody else' and invited to raise the tone at the Lammles' wedding, makes private observations to herself in the church: 'Bride; five and forty if a day, thirty shillings a yard, veil fifteen pounds, pocket-handkerchief a present. Bridesmaids; kept down for fear of outshining bride, consequently not girls . . . Mrs Veneering; never saw such velvet, say two thousand pounds as she stands, absolute jeweller's window, father must have been a pawnbroker, or how could these people do it?'[5] We are into the comic world of Oscar Wilde or Noel Coward with this nasty, witty old woman's inner monologue.

Other characters inhabit the new London that is spreading haphazardly around the old: 'that district of the flat country tending to the Thames, where Kent and Surrey meet, and where the railways still bestride the market-gardens that will soon die under them . . . a toy neighbourhood taken in blocks out of a box by a child of particularly incoherent mind . . . here, another unfinished street already in ruins; there, a church; here, an immense new warehouse; there, a dilapidated old country villa; then, a medley of black ditch, sparkling cucumber-frame, rank field, richly cultivated kitchen-garden, brick viaduct, arch-spanned canal . . . As if the child had given the table a kick and gone to sleep.'[6] There is always a lot of mess and dirt in Dickens's London. Waste paper blows through the streets, and much of the plot relates to the great dust heaps piled up in Camden Town, rubbish that is worth a fortune once it has been sorted, making its owner into a 'Golden Dustman'. Dickens had published a description of the real dust heaps in *Household Words* in 1850,[7] and some critics have seized on them as symbols in the book; although, as John Carey points out, if they are meant to suggest that money is dirt, and that the accumulation of money is bad, this hardly fits with Dickens's view of money, which he valued and worked hard to earn.[8] The thing itself always fascinated Dickens more than whatever it might symbolize or represent.

Something that had not changed much since the 1830s when he first wrote about it was the condition of City clerks, travelling to work from northern suburbs through a 'suburban Sahara' of dust heaps, dog fights, rubbish heaps, bones, tiles and burning bricks.[9] They came further now, but were still likely to live in small and inconvenient houses and to have to share them with lodgers in order to keep up with the rent: in Holloway, Reginald Wilfer's family lets out the best rooms in the house to a lodger. The Wilfers are usually short of candles and low on food, often with nothing more than an old piece of Dutch cheese for supper, and when they have something better they fry it up over an open fire. The grown-up daughters share a room furnished with an upturned box and a small piece of glass for a dressing table, and they do not stand on ceremony, Bella coming downstairs in bare feet, with her hairbrush in her hand, to talk to her father. Dickens knows exactly how they live, perhaps with an echo of the Ternan household as he had seen it at Park Cottage.

His characters, like Dickens himself, leave town in order to feel better. They go to Blackheath or Greenwich, or along the Thames towards Hampton and further west – Staines, Chertsey, Walton, Kingston, where there are trees and green fields – as far as Oxfordshire: we remember Dickens's solitary boat trip when he rowed himself from Oxford to Reading in June 1855. Yet even out there the Thames has its sinister side, since people can drown or be drowned as easily as in town; and there are many drownings and near-drownings in *Our Mutual Friend*. Violence and danger threaten many of the characters, and Lizzie Hexam, who is attached to the

Thames from having grown up alongside it at Limehouse, also sees it as 'the great black river with its dreary shores . . . stretching away to the great ocean, Death'.[10]

In town, we are taken into the shops and workrooms of lesser London trades: Mr Venus, the taxidermist in his shadowy cluttered rooms; Fanny Cleaver, the dolls' dressmaker, so crippled she can hardly walk and her shoulders are uneven as she sits at her work bench where she cuts and glues fabrics, looking at first sight like 'a child – a dwarf – a girl – a something –' She calls herself Jenny Wren and she has a sharp tongue, a 'queer but not ugly little face, with its bright grey eyes' and a mass of golden hair.[11] She is our old friend the child worker, already well established in her profession at twelve or thirteen. The dolls' dressmaker upset some nineteenth-century readers who, like Podsnap, preferred not to acknowledge the existence of the deformed and disabled. Henry James, who gave *Our Mutual Friend* a ferociously bad review, particularly objected to Jenny as 'a poor little dwarf' put in to arouse 'cheap merriment and very cheap pathos . . . Like all Dickens's pathetic characters, she is a little monster; she is deformed, unhealthy, unnatural; she belongs to the troop of hunchbacks, imbeciles, and precocious children who have carried on the sentimental business in all Mr Dickens's novels.'[12] James did not trouble himself to remember Jenny as Dickens actually wrote her – as a young woman who has made a trade for herself, works at it hard and imaginatively, maintains herself, looks after her drunken father and is a staunch friend. She may have sentimental ideas about angels who comfort her when she is in pain, but that is a small defect to set against her virtues. James probably disliked Sloppy too, the workhouse boy presumed to be an idiot because he is ungainly, has a small head to his long body and has never been taught anything. Dickens, who had seen enough to know that ugliness and ignorance don't necessarily denote lack of intelligence, shows how Sloppy, given training, proper food and kindness, learns the trade of cabinet-maker.

Jenny is a girl who is wiser than her father, and another is her friend Lizzie Hexam, daughter of a Thames waterman who lives by robbing the corpses of the drowned. With a criminal father, no

mother and no education, she manages to be intelligent and prin-
cipled, brings up her younger brother, Charlie, and sends him away
to be given an education that will allow him to live a respectable life.
She is a needlewoman and has a job as keeper of the stockroom of a
seamen's outfitter, and we are shown that she is enterprising and
brave as well as lovely to look at. Some of this may stretch our belief,
and her inner life remains closed to us. Dickens can draw poor, ambitious young men like her brother and his schoolmaster Bradley
Headstone, but he can't get into the mind of Lizzie, and he gives her
nothing but conventional ideas and feelings. He describes her beautifully, seen by her admirer through a small window, sitting on the
floor by the brazier, 'with her face leaning on her hand. There was a
kind of film or flicker on her face, which at first he took to be the fit-
ful fire-light, but on a second look he saw that she was weeping . . . It
was a little window of but four pieces of glass, and was not curtained
. . . he looked long and steadily at her. A deep rich piece of colour,
with the brown flush of her cheek and the shining lustre of her
hair . . .'[13] Lizzie is like a Pre-Raphaelite painting, and Eugene, the
idle barrister who falls in love with her, is like a Du Maurier hero:
interesting types, each with a wonderful surface, but we are not
shown beyond the surface into the complex creature within. Their
story culminates in a breaking of the class barriers that divide them,
but only after he has been reduced to permanent invalidity, and she
must become more nurse than lover.[14]

Dickens does better with Bella Wilfer, in spite of making her part
of a plot that involves her in a series of unbelievable predicaments.
We can believe that she longs to escape from poverty in suburban
Holloway as much as the Ternan girls longed to escape from suburban Islington, but the crude course in moral improvement Bella is
put through is feeble stuff. When she declares, 'I want to be something so much worthier than the doll in the doll's house,'[15] we prick
up our ears, as Ibsen did, so that it is a let-down to find her settling
into life as a devoted married doll with her nose in the cookery
book, a baby to keep her busy and never questioning the husband
she has made into an idol. The best part of Bella is when she is shown
with her father, letting her feelings and her behaviour rip. She is his

favourite, he calls her 'my pet' and 'the lovely woman', and they keep up their flirtation throughout the book, enacting the ageing man's dream of a young girl who devotes herself to making him happy. Bella is always hugging her father, arranging and rearranging his hair and smothering him with *her* hair. She ties his napkin on for him and pins him to the door, holding his ears while she kisses him all over his face. They go on secret expeditions together, one of them to Greenwich, which he calls 'the happiest day he had ever known in his life'.[16] She gives him money to buy new clothes, is in his confidence about his unsatisfactory relations with his wife – her mother – and offers him a quiet corner to escape to in her house when she is married. Contemporary critics, mostly middle-aged men, found Bella irresistibly charming. As you read the scenes between her and her father, it is tempting to see Dickens with Nelly, or with his daughter Katey, or with an amalgam of the two; only Reginald Wilfer is no stand-in for him, and it would have taken courage for either Nelly or Katey to smother the great Charles Dickens in her hair, or to take hold of his ears while she kissed him. His account of Bella suggests that he would have enjoyed it if they had.

Bella and her father lighten a book that in other parts is grim, dark and violent. It is also sometimes tedious. The weakness of the plotting is a serious fault, and there is far too much of the good Boffins who have inherited the dust heaps, and one-legged Silas Wegg, and of John Harmon's fake identities.[17] But the jealous agony and rage of the schoolteacher Bradley Headstone, tightly controlled and repressed until he is driven to murder, is powerfully done. As Edmund Wilson, a fairer American critic than Henry James, pointed out, Dickens for the first time drew a murderer with a complex character in Bradley, and one who was a respectable member of society.[18] The scope of Dickens's observation is prodigious, and his satirical bite as sharp as a fresh razor. And as well as the Veneerings' horrible circle, he works some decent middle-class people into the story: those who run a hospital for children in the East End; and a hard-working clergyman, 'expensively educated and wretchedly paid', looking after a poor parish with the help of his intelligent wife 'worn by anxiety' and desperately overburdened with six children.[19] Dickens said he was 'sick of the church', but he recognized plain goodness and self-lessness, and what it exacted from those who practised it.[20]

You take away with you from *Our Mutual Friend* the river, tidal, dark and powerful, the cheerless townscapes of London, the skies, the clocks striking through the night, the littered streets and gritty London churchyards, a whole physical world. What is missing is the good new London, the works of the engineer Bazalgette that were started in the 1860s, the Thames Embankment 'rising high and dry . . . on the Middlesex shore, from Westminster Bridge to Blackfriars. A really fine work, and really getting on. Moreover, a great system of drainage. Another really fine work, and likewise really getting on.'[21] This was how Dickens described the building of the Embankment and the construction of the sewers in a letter to his Swiss friend Cerjat, written shortly after he had completed the book, and it makes you regret that he did not work some of those great enterprises into it. The moral climate of his London is sour and nasty, redeemed here and there only by private courage and virtue.

Another noticeable feature of the novel is the large number of characters who experience bodily distress or difficulty – Jenny hardly able to walk, one-legged Wegg, Eugene nearly dead for months after Bradley's attack, Betty Higden struggling to die in the open air, the wicked money-man Fledgeby whipped till he bleeds and then peppered. Their pains are a reminder that Dickens was often in pain himself, and that from February 1865 he was suffering intermittently from a foot so swollen he could not wear a normal boot, and so tender it often made it impossible for him to take the exercise on which he depended when he was working. It also gave him nights of 'sleepless agony', and he must have feared what it threatened for his future.[22] 'If I couldn't walk fast and far, I should just explode and perish,' he had told Forster more than a decade ago.[23]

❧

Still, the book was finished on 2 September 1865, and Dickens took a few days in Paris and Boulogne: it seems unlikely that Nelly went with him, given their previous cross-Channel journey and perhaps too their sorrowful memories of France. He told Forster that he had to have a special boot made 'on an Otranto scale' for his sore foot, and that he could not bear anything on it after four or five in the afternoon, when he had to sit down with his leg up on another chair. While in Paris he also suffered from sunstroke, badly enough to take to his bed and call in a doctor, but in Boulogne he managed a little walking by the sea.[24] On his return he wrote a Christmas piece for *All the Year Round* in the form of a monologue by a cheapjack, a tinker with a horse-drawn van. It was called 'Doctor Marigold's Prescriptions'[25] and, with its mixture of comical speech and pathos, was plainly written primarily for him to perform at his readings. Doctor Marigold describes the death of his beloved small daughter, his adoption of another little girl who is deaf and dumb, and how he teaches her to communicate and sends her to a school where she is well educated; she leaves him to marry and goes to China, but at the end he welcomes back her child, the third little girl in the story, who can hear and speak. It is skilfully constructed and deeply sentimental, Dickens hamming it up, and it went down well with audiences, and sold.

This autumn three of Dickens's sons were far away, Frank in India, Alfred in Australia and Sydney at sea. Charley was in London, trying to run his paper business with small success, and Henry and Plorn were still boys and based at home. Dickens now decided that sixteen-year-old Henry, who was doing well at school in Wimbledon, should be entered for the Indian civil service examination, but Henry had other ideas and in September he told his father he had no desire to become a civil servant and wanted to try for Cambridge. Dickens responded by writing to his headmaster to say he could not afford to send a son to university unless there was a real hope of his doing well there, and asking what he thought of Henry's abilities. The headmaster's opinion was favourable, and Henry was allowed to stay on at school for another three years, and given extra coaching in various subjects, mathematics and fencing, among others. His father taught him shorthand, though not very successfully, because the dictations he improvised for him to take down were so funny they both fell about laughing. Henry was an ambitious and intelligent boy; he worked hard and in 1868 was accepted by Trinity Hall, a Cambridge law college, and went on to win an exhibition. Dickens was almost as incredulous at the success of this aberrant son as he was proud of his achievement; and Henry went on to become a conventionally successful and distinguished member of English society.

The Christmas of 1865 was celebrated with a house party at Gad's Hill. Georgina and Mamie were in charge of the domestic arrangements, and Henry and Plorn were at home. Dickens arrived from London on 23 December and stayed for five days. Of the family, Katey and Charles Collins were there, and Charley, now forgiven for his marriage, with his wife Bessie and their babies, including 'Master Charles Dickens, Junior'. Monsieur and Madame Fechter were also invited, with their son Paul. Henry Chorley, a bibulous bachelor, old friend of the family, contributor to *All the Year Round* and critic – he had reviewed *Our Mutual Friend* favourably in October – was there.[26] Also Dickens's protégé and current illustrator, Marcus Stone, whose father Frank had been dear to Dickens. A surprise guest was seventeen-year-old Edward Dickenson, whose life Dickens had saved at Staplehurst: Dickens had pulled him out of a heap of broken metal where he was jammed upside down, then taken him to Charing Cross Hospital, where he had visited him during the five weeks he was there. Henry kept everyone busy with billiard contests, there were walks for the energetic, and the usual games – Dumb Crambo, Proverbs, Forfeits, whist, pool. The food was lavish, with cigars for the men, champagne and other wines, and Dickens's specially prepared gin punch. On Christmas Day Higham neighbours were invited, a Mr and Mrs Malleson with their daughter, and there was an unexpected arrival, Will Morgan, son of an American sea captain, another of Dickens's old friends. The great Christmas dinner culminated as usual in a flaming pudding, after which he proposed the toast in the words of Tiny Tim, 'God bless us every one'. After this there was dancing from nine until two in the morning.[27] Henry's account of the festivities does not say whether his father was able to dance this year, and on 29 December he was back at the office making up the next number of *All the Year Round* and proposing to visit Wills, who was ill, in his house in Regent's Park Terrace, Camden Town – a little too close to Catherine's house round the corner to be perfectly comfortable for Dickens.

On the other side of London, at Waltham Cross in Essex, another novelist, Anthony Trollope, gave a Christmas ball at his country house, and among the guests were Fanny and Nelly Ternan, who could now count two famous novelists among their friends. However delicate the state of Nelly's health, or her sadness, she was ready to make a good appearance at the Trollopes' ball in a girlish dress of pale green silk with an overskirt of matching tarlatan, a fine muslin, trimmed with white lace and dewdrops, and with scarlet geraniums and white heather in her hair.[28] Nelly's invitation to the Trollopes' ball had come through Fanny, who had been taken on in the spring of 1865 to give music lessons to their thirteen-year-old niece, Bice, daughter of Anthony's brother Thomas.[29] The Thomas Trollopes lived in Florence, where Bice's mother had died, and her uncle Anthony had travelled out to bring the child back to stay at Waltham House with him and his wife Rose and their boys: they were good-hearted people. Throughout the summer of 1865, while Nelly was leaving France and recovering from the rail accident, Fanny had travelled to Waltham every other weekend to teach Bice. She cheered Bice up so well and made such a friend of her that when Thomas Trollope came to fetch her back to Italy in the autumn she and Fanny agreed to write to one another. Thomas Trollope had met Fanny seven years before when she was in Florence to study singing, armed with an introduction from Dickens; and now she made herself well liked by all the Trollopes, who appreciated her for what she was, a gifted, agreeable and lively woman.

All three Ternan daughters had now given up their acting and singing careers. Fanny was teaching, Maria was in Oxford with her brewer husband, and Nelly was pursuing her own mysterious life. In December 1865, however, their mother announced her intention of returning to the stage, to appear in a double bill with Fechter's company. Dickens was greatly interested in the production and was at a rehearsal just before Christmas: she was already word perfect while Fechter had not yet begun to learn his lines.[30] One play was an adaptation of Scott's romantic tragedy *The Bride of Lammermoor*, the other a translation of Dumas's popular melodrama *The Corsican Brothers*. The Ternan sisters were at the Lyceum together on the opening night on 11 January 1866 to see their mother perform, and Dickens was without doubt in the audience too, and later reported that the show was 'an immense success'. It ran until June, when Mrs Ternan retired from the stage.

When Nelly let out Houghton Place in October, providing herself with a small income, Fanny and her mother found lodgings nearby in Mornington Crescent, and in January Maria and Nelly went together to St Leonard's-on-Sea on the Sussex coast, saying they needed sea air for their health. Meanwhile Dickens rented two cottages in Slough, at that time a quiet country village, where he thought he could go unrecognized by the country people and install Nelly discreetly. He used a false name – Charles Tringham – under which he paid the rates; his tobacconist in Covent Garden was a Mrs Tringham, which probably amused him. He believed that in a different place, with a different name, he could be a different person, and his life became more like a novel with a plot too complicated to be followed easily. When Mrs Elliot wrote pestering him again about Nelly, he told her, 'As to my romance it belongs to my life and probably will only die out of the same with the proprietor.'[31] He refused an invitation to speak in public on 3 March on account of 'an annual engagement', and celebrated Nelly's twenty-seventh birthday with her, possibly in Sussex, possibly in Slough, but much more likely at Verrey's, one of his favourite restaurants, in Regent Street.

His doctor, Frank Beard, had told him in February that he had a degeneration of the functions of the heart, which hardly surprised him, since he felt himself lacking in 'buoyancy and hopefulness'.[32] Still, to please Georgina and Mamie he rented a London house as usual, this time in what he called 'Tyburnia', at No. 6 Southwick Place, Hyde Park, as a base until June; and, regardless of his health problems, he prepared to set off for a new series of readings.

Maria Taylor now told her husband she needed to travel south, since she was suffering from rheumatism, and Oxford was damp; and she took herself to Florence. In May, Thomas Trollope invited Fanny to come out to be Bice's governess, and she too was soon in Florence.

Fanny had not been idle, and had written a novel, *Aunt Margaret's Trouble*, which she showed to Dickens. He was enthusiastic about it and prepared to run it in *All the Year Round*, but anonymously, and paid for out of his private funds, so that even in the office no one should know what he paid for it. It was dedicated to 'E. L. T.' – Ellen Lawless Ternan – and began to appear in July. In the same month Thomas Trollope, relieved to have his household put in order and his daughter cheered up by an efficient and good-natured woman, proposed marriage to Fanny Ternan and was accepted. There was to be a wedding in Paris in October, with Maria, Nelly and Mrs Ternan all present, and Bice was to be sent, to her considerable indignation, to boarding school in England: Fanny could be tough. Dickens wrote to Thomas Trollope to congratulate him warmly, saying he had foreseen the match, but he did not attend the wedding.

Fanny was thirty-one, her husband fifty-six, and both had reason to be pleased. He had acquired an affectionate and hard-working companion and she had taken a crucial upward step socially, her husband being a gentleman by birth and education, albeit a poor gentleman who had to earn his living as a writer. And now Fanny, who had achieved exactly what a young woman hoped to do by marrying into a rank of society higher than she was born into, began to worry about Nelly's position. Was her friendship with Dickens safe, or was he putting her reputation at risk? The fact was she could do nothing except preach caution to Nelly. That Dickens was now her publisher and patron, already commissioning a second novel, for which he paid her the extraordinarily large sum of 500 guineas for three years' copyright, made it just about impossible for her to raise objections to whatever was going on between E. L. T. and the editor of *All the Year Round*.[33] Her letters to Bice read curiously as she talks about Nelly as though she were living the life of a conventional young girl, with her mother in attendance and devoted to her pet dog; she passes on Nelly's silly jokes about the dog, and sends her love.

In the intersecting circles of Ternans, Trollopes, Dickenses, Hogarths, Forsters, Collinses, Elliots, Wills and Dickens's new readings manager, George Dolby, it is impossible to be sure how much anyone knew about Nelly. Forster, Wills, Dolby and Georgina were pretty well in the know, although not entirely; Katey, Charley and Henry were aware of Nelly's existence. To Wills, Nelly was 'the Patient'; to Dolby, she became 'Madame'. We have seen how Dickens fielded questions from Mrs Elliot, a friend of both Wilkie Collins and Thomas Trollope. He was so much on his guard that he did not even tell Wilkie Collins the name of the author of *Aunt Margaret's Trouble*. Soon he was warning Mrs Elliot to be careful what she said to the Thomas Trollopes: 'Of course you will be very strictly on your guard, if you see Tom Trollope, or his wife, or both – to make no reference to me which either can piece into anything. She is infinitely sharper than the serpent's tooth. Mind that.'[34] It looks as though Fanny had a double role for him: as a writer he published and as someone who could not be trusted with information about his life with Nelly. And it makes you wonder how he and Nelly talked about Fanny together, or he and Thomas Trollope, when they met, as they did; and whether the 500 guineas Dickens paid for *Mabel's Progress*, duly serialized from April 1867, was meant to keep Fanny quiet.

Years after Dickens's death Nelly said that she had begun to feel remorse about her relations with him at some stage during their association, and that her remorse had made them both miserable.[35] It may have been a fluctuating remorse, since she was clearly eager to go to America with him, and she made sure she was back from Italy to welcome him on his return. One perpetual worry must have been the fear of becoming pregnant again, and Fanny, protective and practical, and now a knowledgeable married woman, could have urged Nelly to try to avoid further sexual relations with Dickens. There is no way of knowing, but whatever went on between Dickens and Nelly, anxiety, remorse, reluctance and guilt are all spoilers of joy.

With the publication of *Our Mutual Friend* in November 1865 his best work was almost done. A warning of mortality came in that same month when his fellow novelist, contributor and sometime friend, Elizabeth Gaskell, died suddenly, aged only fifty-five, just before completing her novel *Wives and Daughters*.[36] Over the next years he willed himself to produce a few more articles and some effortful stories, and with a last summoning of creative energy he planned and wrote a good part of another novel. He also kept up a bruising programme of activities. He was rarely in the same place for more than a few days at a time, and said of himself, 'I am here, there, everywhere and (principally) nowhere.'[37] World events had their effect on him, the end of the American Civil War in 1865 bringing renewed invitations to cross the Atlantic to entertain a public eager to hear him and ready to pay generously for the privilege. He needed the money, but 1865 was also the year in which the trouble with his foot began to make things more difficult for him: it seems clear to modern medical opinion that it was gout, but he would not accept the diagnosis, and found doctors who agreed with his denial. From now on he appears as a man assailed, proud and obstinate, not merely keeping going by strength of will but forcing the pace, at the cost of increasingly distressing symptoms. Nelly remained his darling, but she was not always easy and he was not always well. His son Henry remembered his 'heavy moods of deep depression, of intense nervous irritability, when he was silent and oppressed'.[38] Yet he never allowed himself to sink into permanent gloom, and even now there are many more accounts of his charm and conviviality than of his low moments. He was the inimitable still, and would be to the end, with his own trick of putting aside agony and exhaustion and reappearing suddenly, like a clown from behind the curtain, full of energy, amazing everyone with his good humour and laughter, and his determination to get on with the chief work of his life.

24

The Chief

1866–1868

In 1866 a new figure appeared in Dickens's life who did a good deal to cheer him. This was George Dolby, a big man, full of energy, optimism and know-how, and talkative, with a stammer he bravely disregarded. He was thirty-five, just married, a theatre manager out of work and keen to take on the running of Dickens's next reading tour. He was sent by Chappell, the music publishers who were setting up the tour, and he won Dickens's confidence at once, and quickly became a friend.[1] Through Dolby's eyes we see again how irresistibly charming Dickens could be, how funny, how energetic, even when suffering from hideous pain and difficulty in getting about. He became a hero to Dolby, who revered him, called him 'Chief', and over the next four years saw him in every mood, from wild high spirits as he demonstrated how to dance a hornpipe in a moving railway carriage, to tears of remorse after he had shouted angrily at his tour manager for being too cautious. Dolby's Dickens is the boys' Dickens, the Pickwickian Dickens, at ease with his male companions and masculine pleasures. They laughed and joked together like boys, and enjoyed the small rituals of travel, the 'artful sandwich' favoured by Dickens (French roll, butter, parsley, hard-boiled egg and anchovy), the mixing of the gin punch, the coffee made on a spirit lamp, the game of cribbage. Dolby took in his stride being treated to a prison visit in Stirling during a rare free hour, and accepted that whenever there was a circus running nearby it had to be seen. For his part, Dolby showed off by standing on his head, which was a big, solid one. He perfectly understood that Dickens's favourite restorative between the two parts of his reading every night consisted of 'A dozen oysters and a little champagne'.[2] He observed that his Chief always took a draught of brandy an hour into each train journey, followed by sherry later, and the two of them smoked cigars steadily throughout each trip.[3] Dickens said Dolby was 'as tender as a woman and as watchful as a doctor'.[4] He served him to the end of his life, Dickens trusted him with his secrets, and Dolby never betrayed his trust.[5] He said that Dickens had given him 'the brightest chapter of my life'.

Dolby needed to be resilient, because over the next four years he was with Dickens for many months of continuous travel. The first tour they did together lasted for three months in the spring of 1866, covering Scotland, the north, Birmingham and Clifton. A four-month tour starting in January 1867 added Ireland, Wales, Hereford and more northern cities. The American tour, from December 1867 to March 1868, took in Boston, New York, Philadelphia, Washington and other towns in the eastern states. After this there was the farewell tour, during which they travelled all over the British Isles from October 1868 until April 1869, when it had to be cut short; and then there were the last London readings in 1870. During this time Dolby was in charge of the complex arrangements necessary for such tours, saw how his Chief prepared and worked, endured long train journeys with him and nights in different hotels – Dickens refused to stay with friends – and performances in public halls of all kinds, some vast, many inconvenient, in which Dolby sorted out the technical problems and Dickens stood up alone to entertain audiences, usually worked up to a high pitch of expectation and enthusiasm but just occasionally not. There was no question but that he wanted to do the readings, but his own accounts of his health sometimes make distressing reading.

Yet he went on. Readings brought in much better money than book sales, and he was desperate to earn, feeling he was in a trap from which he had to escape by earning – the trap of having been born with the wrong parents, supplied with the wrong brothers, married to the wrong wife, father of the wrong sons, with the result that he was surrounded by dependants. He had 'my wife's income to pay – a very expensive position to hold – and my boys with a curse of limpness on them. You don't know what it is to look round the table and see reflected from every seat at it (where they sit) some horribly well remembered expression of inadaptability to anything.'[6] Even his son-in-law was unable to earn a living. There were needy sisters-in-law and orphaned nephews and nieces. There was Georgina's future to think of, and his daughters'. There was Nelly, who had given up her life to him.

If money was the basic reason for the reading tours, something else kept him always eager to continue with them. Whatever the physical and emotional strain, his audiences nourished his spirit. Even when he was worn out, the contact with the people who came to hear him was precious to him. Their response confirmed to him that he was a star, the great man who was also the people's friend; they came to worship and adore, queuing up to hear him, applauding him with shouts and cheers. From them he felt how much love he could command; and he had power over them, the power of the great actor he felt himself to be, an almost hypnotic power. They laughed when he wanted them to laugh, trembled and shed tears when he meant them to tremble or shed tears. The readings left him elated as well as exhausted. Even Frank Beard, his doctor, thought the occasional reading likely to do him more good than harm.[7]

The readings were never taken directly from his books, but rather from scripts he had adapted carefully to allow him to impersonate his favourite characters and offer highlights of the narrative. Of the novels only *Pickwick*, *Nickleby*, *Dombey*, *Chuzzlewit* and *Copperfield* figured at all, and they were filleted, reworked and reshaped, brought much closer to simple dramas, with the emphasis always on humour and pathos. Mr Micawber, the wooing and death of Dora, the flight of Little Em'ly and the drowning of Steerforth, were condensed into a narrative that stood for 'David Copperfield'. From *Pickwick* he made 'The Trial' (Bardell and Pickwick) and 'Mr Bob Sawyer's Party'. *Chuzzlewit* was 'Mrs Gamp'. Some listeners felt this as a loss, but for most it was a supreme experience to hear Dickens himself speak for his characters. Half of the readings were made from Christmas stories, *A Christmas Carol* always a favourite. For the 1866 tour he added the newly written 'Doctor Marigold', which gave him the voice of the cheapjack who loses his daughters, with many opportunities to play on the heartstrings. The success of the tour was beyond anything he or the organizers had imagined, with thousands turned away in some towns, and immense takings.

Annie Thackeray remembered how she responded to a London reading:

> We sat in the front, a little to the right of the platform; the great Hall was somewhat dimly lighted, considering the crowds assembled there. The slight figure (as he appeared to me) stood alone quietly facing the long rows of people. He seemed holding the great audience in some mysterious way from the empty stage. Quite immediately the story began. Copperfield and Steerforth, Yarmouth and the fishermen and Peggotty, and then the rising storm, all was there before us ... The lights shone from the fisherman's home; then after laughter terror fell, the storm rose; finally, we were all breathlessly watching from the shore, and (this I remember most vividly of all) a great wave seemed to fall splashing on to the platform from overhead, carrying away everything before it, and the boat and the figure of Steerforth in his red sailor's cap fighting for his life by the mast. Some one called out; was it Mr Dickens himself who threw up his arm?[8]

The triumph was paid for with pains in foot, hand, heart and left eye, nervous seizures, sleeplessness and, as he told Forster, depression at the end of each tour. While he was travelling in 1866 Jane Carlyle died suddenly, another old friend gone. The Bayswater house was given up that June and he resumed his slightly more normal life, divided between Wellington Street, Gad's Hill and wherever Nelly was – for the moment in Slough, where he figured as Mr Tringham. Some letters that summer were headed 'Eton' and 'Windsor', and explained that he was walking, or waiting for a train. In July he started running Fanny Ternan's novel *Aunt Margaret's Trouble* in *All the Year Round*, keeping its authorship strictly secret, and wrote to Thomas Trollope to say how pleased he was that she was in Florence with him; and at the end of July Fanny and Trollope announced their forthcoming marriage. In August there was a cricket match at Gad's, in September Dickens was 'seized in a most distressing manner' in the heart or the nervous system, and Beard was applied to for medicine against pains in the

stomach and chest.⁹ Dolby was invited for a weekend and congrat-
ulated on the birth of a daughter.¹⁰ In October news came from
America of the death of Augustus, Dickens's youngest brother, the
third of his siblings to die from tuberculosis of the lung. Augustus
left, beside a widow in England whom Dickens was already helping, a mistress and several children in Chicago, and he feared they
would 'bring upon me a host of disagreeables', and arranged to
give the eldest son, Bertram, an allowance of £50 a year during his
own lifetime.¹¹

During October he worked on four 'railway stories' for the Christmas number of *All the Year Round*. One was 'Main Line. The Boy at
Mugby', a humorous tribute to the horrors of the refreshment room
at Rugby Station, another a ghost story, 'The Signalman'. At the end
of the month Fanny and Thomas Trollope were married in Paris; the
wedding was attended by Maria, who came from Florence with
them, and her husband Rowland Taylor, from Oxford, and also by
Mrs Ternan and Nelly. Dickens wrote warmly to the bridegroom.
Immediately after this his manservant of many years, John Thompson, was found to be stealing from the cash box at the office.
Thompson seemed unaware of the gravity of his crime and turned
down Dickens's offer to get him a job as a waiter at the Reform Club
with 'Oh I couldn't do that, Sir.'¹² Bearing in mind the fact that
Thompson knew all about Nelly, Dickens then set him up in a small
business.¹³ He was replaced at Wellington Street by a housekeeper, a
young woman with a child, Ellen Hedderley: Dickens asked Georgina to tell her 'there is no objection to her child, and she will have a
good sitting room at the bottom of the house, three bright airy rooms
adjoining each other at the top, coals and candles, and a guinea a
week.'¹⁴ As you would expect, he was a decent and kindly employer.
He took on a new man, Henry Scott, as his valet. Later in November
he met Dolby to make plans for the next reading tour, to start in
January 1867. In December he told a friend he would be away in
Buckinghamshire on a three-day visit from the 17th, which sounds
like Nelly's Christmas celebration. At Gad's Hill he set up a programme of races for the local people on Boxing Day, relishing his
role as benevolent squire. While the rush of so many disparate events

and activities may be hard for us to follow, his grip on everything that mattered to him remained firm.

The year 1867 began with a resumption of hard work and travel, thirty-six readings between 15 January and the end of March: Portsmouth, London, Liverpool, Chester, Wolverhampton, Leicester, London, Leeds, Manchester, Bath, London, Birmingham, Liverpool, Manchester, Glasgow, Edinburgh, York, Bradford, Newcastle, Wakefield, London, Dublin, Belfast, Dublin, London, Cambridge, Norwich. A commercial traveller could hardly have matched his hours on the railways. Already in February he described himself as suffering from piles, sleeplessness, faintness and soreness of whole body, but he continued with the tour as planned.[15] In March he was shuttling between visits to Nelly in Slough and readings in Ireland and Norwich. In April he had a break in the readings between the 12th and the 25th, spending a good deal of that time with Nelly, who was unwell; on the 20th he took Wills to Slough with him to see her, and on their return to London he let his attention wander for a moment and left in a cab his 'small black bag or Tourist's Knapsack' containing a book and a bundle of manuscripts.[16]

Another lapse of attention meant he also lost his private pocket diary later in the year, in America. He was worried about this and it was not returned to him; and because it was recovered and in due course recognized as what it was, we are very much better informed about where he was and what he was doing in 1867 than we should otherwise have been.[17] The diary offers a page per month, and the names of the towns in which he gave readings are written in full, just as Forster, Wills, Dolby, Macready, Wilkie, Stanfield, Fechter and Charley and Sydney Dickens have their names spelt out. But other entries are abbreviated, sometimes to single capital letters: 'G. H.' for Gad's Hill, 'Sl' for Slough, 'Off.' for his Wellington Street office, 'Peck:m' for Peckham, 'Ga.' for Georgina, 'M' either for Maria Ternan or her mother, and 'N' for Nelly: thus he writes '(N. ill latter part of this month)' at the foot of the page for April, 'N walks', 'N there too' one evening at the Lyceum, 'Long wait for N at house' in June.

The diary allows us to confirm what we already know – that in May, for instance, he was reading in the north of England on Wednesday the 1st and on Thursday the 2nd – and then tells us what we should otherwise not have known – that he was at Slough on Friday the 3rd. On 3 May Dickens was with N and M, and on Saturday, 4 May, he went into town with N and M, did some work at the office and then went to Gad's that evening, hung pictures there on Sunday morning, returned to the office, dined at the Athenaeum and was back in Slough that night. On Tuesday, 7 May, he noted an evening walk, still in Slough, and on 8 May he took the train from Windsor, N no doubt walking with him to the station. He then went to the office and in the evening read in Croydon, 'Copperfield' and 'The Trial' from *Pickwick*. On that day he also wrote to Georgina telling her he could not get down to Gad's before Monday, 'being fairly overwhelmed by arrears of work' (which was not the whole truth of course). He added that he was sending his new valet Scott to Gad's with his laundry, and asked her to send him back some clean clothes.[18]

The next day he dined at the Athenaeum and went on to the Lyceum, Fechter's theatre '(N there too)'. On 10 May he was at the office and dined at Verrey's with N and M, returning to Slough again for the next three nights. His diary entry for 13 May notes 'To Pad.', and his letters show that he went to the Great Western Hotel in Conduit Street, where he occasionally put up, preparatory to giving his last reading of the tour in London, 'Dombey' and 'Bob Sawyer's Party'. He was back in Slough for Wednesday the 15th and Thursday the 16th. On the 17th he took the train from Windsor, Nelly again walking across the fields with him to the station. On 18 May Georgina arrived in London and he took her to dinner and the Royalty Theatre in the evening; and on the same day his dearly loved friend Stanfield, the marine painter, died, as he noted the following day in his diary. On 20 May his office housekeeper Ellen was ill, so he moved into the Great Western Hotel again, after dining with Forster and Georgy. During the next few days he saw his doctor, Frank Beard, and also Wilkie Collins and Dolby. His letters show he was wrestling with the question of whether to go to America, telling Forster 'you have no idea how heavily the anxiety of it sits upon my soul. But the prize looks so large!'[19] He was at Slough again on the 24th and the 25th, at Stanfield's funeral on the 27th, then at Gad's for the remaining days of May, finding his sailor son Sydney on leave there.

This may be more detail than one normally wants about anyone's life, but it has the value of showing clearly how Dickens divided his time between his various commitments, and how large a proportion of it was devoted to Nelly. It also suggests that balancing her claims and Georgina's was not always easy.

In June, with the readings over, the diary shows him looking at houses with Nelly in the south-eastern suburb of Peckham, and notes that she kept him waiting on the day they had planned to move into a temporary place: evidence that she was not always at his bidding (this is 'at P. Long wait for N at house' on 22 June). Other entries show that he took his work with him and got on with it there: 'working there Tuesday ... [26 June] at P. (tem:) Finish Silverman, in Linden'. 'George Silverman' was a story he wrote for the *Atlantic Monthly*, 'tem' was the temporary house they rented, and 'Linden' stood for Linden Grove, in the hamlet of Nunhead, where the house they settled on for a more permanent residence stood. It was large and comfortable, built as one of a group of houses meant for middle-class families, well equipped with bedrooms and bathrooms, possessing a good garden and stables, and looking out over open fields. The pleasant situation was not Dickens's only reason for persuading Nelly to look at houses there: it was also close to the new station opened at Peckham Rye in 1865, which gave easy access both to Waterloo and to Gad's Hill, the nearby station at Higham being on the London, Dover & Chatham line. Either the house was already named Windsor Lodge or they agreed that it should be: what could be more respectable? They must have laughed together sometimes about their invented identities, as the rates on Windsor Lodge were paid at first under the name 'Frances Turnham', which evolved into 'Thomas Turnham', 'Thomas Tringham' and then 'Charles Tringham'. They needed to agree on what the two servants would call them and on how letters were to be addressed to Nelly; and to discourage friendly and curious neighbours who might notice the comings and goings of Mr Turnham – or was it Tringham?[20] – and remark on his resemblance to the writer Charles Dickens.[21]

The writing he did that summer, whether at Peckham, Wellington Street or Gad's, was sad stuff. 'George Silverman's Explanation' is the narrative of a man, born to miserably poor parents in Preston, orphaned very young, who grows up with a sense of his own unworthiness that prevents him making friends, although he achieves a university degree and becomes a clergyman and teacher. He even rejects the affection of a girl he loves. It reads like a theoretical case history and gives no real sense of Silverman's inner or outer life, or of those around him. The satire on the speech and behaviour of the Nonconformist sect who help him as a boy is tedious, and the portrait of the aristocratic woman who gives him a living, makes use of him, and turns against him, fails to shock because it lacks credibility. Although some critics have struggled to find psychological interest in it, it is one of his failures.[22] He also produced some slight stories for children, 'Holiday Romance', for the American market.[23] Further, he collaborated with Wilkie Collins on a crudely melodramatic tale, *No Thoroughfare*, intended to be adapted by Collins for the stage as a vehicle for Fechter, who would play the murderous villain of the piece. All these works show diminished power and poor judgement and are read today only because they are by Dickens: but they brought in money, and he kept going.

In August he travelled to Liverpool with Dolby to see him aboard ship for Boston, where he was to investigate what might be expected of a reading tour, and also to sound out the possibility of Nelly's going to America with them. Dickens was using a stick for his lameness, and in Liverpool his left foot swelled so badly that on returning to London he went straight to a specialist, who diagnosed an inflamed bunion and insisted he must rest.[24] For several days he lay on the downstairs sofa at Wellington Street. When he was a little better he wrote to Dolby, 'Madame sends you her regard, and hopes to meet you when you come home. She is very anxious for your report, and is ready to commit herself to the Atlantic, under your care. To which I always add: "*If* I go, my dear, *if* I go."'[25] These are wonderfully revealing sentences, telling us that Dickens spoke of Nelly as 'Madame' to Dolby, a reminder of her French years and an acknowledgement of her status in his life. They also show that she was so eager to go to America that she was ready to make the crossing even under the care of Mr Dolby. What is not clear is what persona she would have been given in the US, since she could hardly be Mrs Dolby – or Mrs Tringham. The most interesting thing of all is that this is the only occasion on which we hear the voice of Dickens speaking to Nelly, his 'my dear' slightly jokey, and slightly admonitory too: '*If* I go, my dear, *if* I go.' She is pushing him, and he is making his position clear.[26] But how could any of them ever have expected to make such a plan work?

The diary shows that there were two cricket matches at Gad's Hill in August. The Forsters were there for the first on the 13th and the 14th, and there was another on the 29th. Dickens also began work with Collins on the Christmas number of *All the Year Round*. On 2

George Dolby and 'The Chief' – Dolby cheered and cared for Dickens, and managed his later reading tours, with love and loyalty.

September, hearing that there were rumours of his being unwell, he wrote to *The Times* asserting, 'I was never better in my life,' and repeating it in a second letter to the *Sunday Gazette*.[27] He knew that reports of ill health might jeopardize the American tour. Meanwhile Dolby was on his way back to England, and at the end of the month there was a tripartite meeting – Dolby, Forster and Dickens – to decide on whether to go ahead with the American plan. Forster, like Wills, was strongly opposed to his going, Dolby was in favour. Dickens made up his mind to go and sent a telegram on 30 September to say he would go. It was followed by a letter to his friend and publisher in Boston, James Fields, telling him that Dolby, who was returning to America almost at once, was 'charged with a certain delicate mission from me, which he will explain to you by word of mouth', and on the same day he wrote to Mrs Fields declining her invitation to stay with them in Boston. Although James Fields was informed of Nelly's existence, and at some stage passed on what he was told to his wife, it would have been out of the question for Dickens to take Nelly into their respectable household.[28] Dolby sailed again on 12 October, charged with talking further with Fields as to whether he thought it possible for Nelly to travel with Dickens in America.

Nelly let her sister Fanny know that she planned to come to Florence with their mother at the end of the month.[29] She told Dickens she was going to Italy, but both of them still hoped she might yet follow him to America. His diary entries for October show him at Peckham from the 1st to the 3rd, dining in London at Verrey's on the 2nd with Nelly and Dolby. He was at Peckham again from the 7th to the 10th, and from the 15th to the 17th. On the 16th he wrote to Dolby, 'It may be a relief to you when you get this, to know that I am quite prepared for your great Atlantic-cable message being adverse . . . I think it so likely that Fields may see shadows of danger which we in our hopeful encouragement of one another may have made light of, that I think the message far more likely to be No than Yes. I shall try to make up my mind to it, and to be myself when we meet.' The 'to be myself' suggests how sharp the disappointment would be, even though he was prepared for it. On the 18th N and M were at his office.

He was at Peckham again from the 20th to the 25th, with a farewell dinner at Verrey's on the 25th (the diary entry, which read 'Dine Verreys N', was enclosed in a double-lined box). After this Nelly set off for Florence with her mother, arriving there at the end of the month.

Dickens arranged for Forster to have 'a general and ample Power of Attorney to act for me in all things' during his absence.[30] He gave dinner to Forster and Macready at Wellington Street on the 28th, dined with Percy Fitzgerald on the 29th and Wilkie Collins on the 30th, and went to Drury Lane on 1 November. A committee that included Fechter, Wilkie Collins, Charles Kent, the editor of the *Daily Telegraph* and Bulwer had been busy setting up a public farewell banquet for him before he set off for America. It was fixed for 2 November, with sponsors sought and tickets sold to the general public, making it a curious mixture of grandees, friends and fans to be gathered together in the London Freemasons' Hall. The venue was decorated for the occasion with laurel leaves and the titles of Dickens's books in gilded lettering, and music was provided by the band of the Grenadier Guards. About 450 men attended, and a hundred ladies were allowed to watch from the gallery, Georgina, Mamie and Katey among them. They did not miss much, because according to one report the waiters were drunk, the soup cold, the ice cream warm; and there were scrambles for greasy fragments of tepid dishes.[31] Among the notables present were the Lord Chief Justice, the Lord Mayor of London and the President of the Royal Academy. Gladstone expressed doubts as to whether dining was the best way to show admiration for Dickens and both he and Disraeli declined invitations; other friends confined themselves to messages of support, among them Carlyle, Tennyson, Browning, Ruskin, Frith, Arnold, Lord Shaftesbury and Lord John Russell. Forster disapproved of the way the dinner was organized, and was prevented from attending by an attack of bronchitis.[32] Dickens, almost overcome with emotion, and obliged to deal with a newly wired dental plate, spoke well as he always did, and was repeatedly cheered; and there were many more speeches and toasts, so that it was nearly midnight when he emerged into Great Queen Street, where a further crowd had gathered to cheer him yet again.

Among the letters wishing him well for the journey was one from Catherine, to which he replied, thanking her with something approaching warmth: 'I am glad to receive your letter, and to accept and reciprocate your good wishes. Severe hard work lies before me; but that is not a new thing in my life, and I am content to go my way and do it. Affectionately yours –'[33]

A week later he was seen off aboard the *Cuba* in Liverpool by Georgina, Mamie, Katey, Charley, Wills, Wilkie and Charles Collins, Charles Kent, Arthur Chappell and Edmund Yates. He travelled with his valet Scott and his reading equipment, and took most of his meals in his cabin during the ten-day Atlantic crossing, nursing the painful foot. He had left Wills with instructions for communicating with Nelly. 'If she needs any help will come to you, or if she changes her address, you will immediately let me know if she changes. Until then it will be Villa Trollope, a Ricorboli, Firenze, Italy . . . On the day after my arrival out I will send you a short Telegram at the office. Please copy its exact words, (as they will have a special meaning for her), and post them to her as above by the very next post after receiving my telegram. And also let Gad's Hill know – and let Forster know – what the telegram is.' A further note says that Forster 'knows Nelly as you do, and will do anything for her if you want anything done'. Nelly would understand that if the telegram read 'all well' it meant she was to set off for America, but if 'safe and well' she was not to come. He knew she was in Florence and they must have discussed how she might travel to America, but on 21 November, two days after reaching Boston, he wrote to Wills 'After this present mail, I shall address Nelly's letters to your care, for I do not quite know where she will be. But she will write to you, and instruct you where to forward them. In any interval between your receipt of one or more, and my Dear Girl's so writing to you, keep them by you.'[34]

The next day he sent a coded telegram to Wills: 'Safe and well expect good letter full of hope'. Fields, sympathetic as he was to Dickens's difficulties in his private life, had made it clear there could be no Madame on the tour. Nelly remained at the Villa Ricorboli throughout the winter, sewing shirts for Garibaldi's soldiers, turning down an invitation to spend Christmas in Rome, and another to join her sisters and brother-in-law Tom Trollope on a trip to Vesuvius. She was still there in March on her twenty-ninth birthday.

※

Boston was Dickens's favourite American city, and he made a good start in a comfortable hotel with a large suite adorned with flowers by Mrs Fields herself. His foot improved and the clear, frosty weather allowed him to take eight-mile walks with her husband. Both were flattered by the intimacy he offered, and he confided in James Fields his unhappiness in having so many children by an uncongenial wife. He enjoyed a few quiet dinners with old friends, Longfellow, Charles Norton, Emerson, but it was understood that he needed time alone. He was impatient for the first reading on 2 December, knowing how much lay ahead and how high expectations were. On 22 November the young Henry James wrote to his brother, 'Dickens has arrived for his readings. It is impossible to get tickets. At 7 o'clock A.M. on the first day of the sale there were two or three hundred at the office, and at 9, when I strolled up, nearly a thousand. So I don't expect to hear him.'[35] James did in fact hear what he later described as the 'hard charmless readings', but his verdict was not the public's, and from the first Dickens almost always commanded full houses and ecstatic applause.[36] People knew that this was *the* event that must be caught now or never, and they were ready to come for miles and through all weather to hear the great man. Sometimes he was showered with bouquets and buttonholes, and always cheered. Dolby had to battle with speculators who bought blocks of tickets, and he was regularly and unfairly blamed in the press for the problems produced. He kept his head and acted as firmly as he could, and the sales were spectacular. In the first few days they made a profit of £1,000 and at the end of the tour the final sum was a dizzying £20,000.[37]

The first New York readings coincided with heavy snow storms. The audiences turned up just the same, but Dickens was struck down with one of his terrible colds in the head. He tried 'allopathy, homeopathy, cold things, warm things, sweet things, bitter things, stimulants, narcotics, all with the same result. Nothing will touch it.'[38] It turned into what he described as 'American catarrh' and kept its hold on him for the rest of the tour, made worse by the constant travelling in overheated and unventilated trains. In January he told Forster he had 'no chance of being rid of the American catarrh until I embark for England. It is very distressing. It likewise happens, not seldom, that I am so dead beat when I come off that they lay me down on a sofa after I have been washed and dressed, and I lie there, extremely faint, for quarter of an hour. In that time I rally and come right.'[39] The decision was made to cut down the ambitious original plan, which was to take the tour as far as Chicago and the west as well as to Canada and Nova Scotia, and to remain in the east throughout. He found it increasingly hard to sleep. Dolby describes going anxiously into his room during the night and each time finding him awake, although protesting he was perfectly cheerful; but Dickens told Georgy, 'I can scarcely exaggerate what I sometimes undergo from sleeplessness.'[40] He could not get up in the mornings, and presently had to be prescribed sedatives.

At the end of March he told Forster, 'I am nearly used up . . . if I had engaged to go on into May, I think I must have broken down.'[41] During the later stages of the tour his lameness was so bad that Dolby had to help him across the platform to his reading desk and off at the end. His appetite diminished until he was eating almost nothing. He described his regime himself: 'I cannot eat (to anything like the necessary extent) and have established this system. At 7 in the morning, in bed, a tumbler of new cream and two tablespoonsful of rum. At 12, a sherry cobbler and a biscuit. At 3 (dinner time) a pint of champagne. At five minutes to 8, an egg beaten up with a glass of sherry. Between the parts [of the reading], the strongest beef tea that can be made, drunk hot. At a quarter past 10, soup, and any little thing to drink that I can fancy. I do not eat more than half a pound of solid food in the whole four-and-twenty hours, if so much.'[42] In spite of this, no reading once announced was cancelled. In all he delivered seventy-six.

There was very little sightseeing. On his birthday in February he met the President, Andrew Johnson, and commented on his look of courage, watchfulness and strength of purpose, but gave no account of their conversation; and when Johnson was impeached shortly afterwards, Dickens was chiefly concerned that it might damage the receipts for the readings. It didn't, and Johnson was acquitted. In Baltimore he visited a model prison, where he was delighted to see prisoners working at their trades in communal workshops, paid for their work and altogether humanely treated, better than in any English prison he knew. In March he took Dolby and the rest of his team to Niagara for a two days' break: the sun came out to cheer them all, making rainbows in the falling water, the spray and over the landscape – an effect that was better than Turner's finest watercolours, he told Forster.[43] Dolby's efficiency and companionship pleased him so much that, when a telegram came announcing the birth of a son to Mrs Dolby at home in Herefordshire, Dickens arranged through Wills for a pony, together with all its trappings and panniers, to be delivered to the Dolby household, and for a photograph of it to be sent to Dolby; and Dickens agreed to stand as godfather to the boy.[44]

The day after his reading in Portland, a twelve-year-old girl who had not been able to attend, and who happened to be travelling on the same train, contrived to slip into an empty seat next to him. She was a spirited child and soon engaged him in conversation. She told him she had read almost all his books, some of them six times, adding, 'Of course I do skip some of the very dull parts once in a while; not the short dull parts but the long ones.' Dickens found her irresistible, pressed her on which were the dull bits and made notes of what she said, laughing all the time. They held hands, he put his arm round her waist, and she gazed at his face, 'deeply lined, with sparkling eyes and an amused, waggish smile that curled the corners of his mouth under his grizzled moustache'. She told him that *David Copperfield* was her favourite, and he said it was his too. He asked her if she had minded missing his reading very much and, in telling him how much she had, tears came into her eyes, and to her astonishment she saw tears in his eyes too. Her flattery enchanted him and they talked all the way to Boston, where she remembered her mother was somewhere on the train and Dickens went with her to find her and introduce himself. The child's name was Kate Douglas Wiggin.

Dickens lying on the grass with his theatrical group – Charley, Katey, Georgina and Mamie all visible – in the summer of 1857. He had grown his beard the year before in preparation for taking the lead as the self-sacrificing hero in Wilkie Collins's 'Romantic Drama' *The Frozen Deep*.

Frith's 1859 portrait of Dickens shows him in a state of excited misery, parted from Catherine, in love with Nelly Ternan, obliged to protect his own reputation from attack, and unwell – all of which doubtless contributed to the ferocity of his expression.

Catherine Dickens had no defence against her husband when he publicly proclaimed her alleged failings to justify his behaviour, but she kept her dignity.

Georgina Hogarth chose to remain with Dickens, adding spice to the scandal and earning his profound gratitude.

Mrs Ternan, a respected actress, played leading roles opposite Macready and Kemble. She brought up her daughters to earn their living on the stage from childhood, but money was always short. Dickens was impressed and entranced by them: Maria (*left*), Fanny (*right*) and Nelly (*centre*).

Nelly looks like a child in this photograph, with a ribbon in her tightly curled golden hair, short sleeves and an uncertain expression. She did not take to the stage as readily as her elder sisters, she was never much of a performer, and in August 1859 she gave up her career as an actress. In March 1860, when she was twenty-one, she became the owner of a large house in Mornington Crescent, No. 2 Houghton Place, Ampthill Square. Soon after this she disappears from the scene and Dickens begins to make many mysterious journeys to France.

The train crash at Staplehurst, where Dickens helped the injured while Nelly, who was hurt, was spirited away.

Dickens bought Gad's Hill House in 1856 and made it into his country residence, extending and improving it, buying more land, acting the village squire, and entertaining friends.

Dickens loved France because literature was respected there, and he made many friends among French writers, often dining with Eugène Scribe, author of 300 comedies, and corresponding with Alexandre Dumas père in French, offering to be his '"guide à Londres" (faute de mieux)' in 1851.

Céline Céleste, dancer, actress, born in Paris, made her name in US, in England from 1830. Theatre manager Benjamin Webster was her lover and business partner; both worked with the Ternans and with Dickens, who relished her production of *A Tale of Two Cities*.

Charles Fechter's acting career was established in Paris, where Dickens first saw him. He gave a great Hamlet in London in 1860, and by 1865 Dickens described him as a very intimate friend, often at Gad's Hill, 'a capital fellow and Anti-Humbug'.

'Whenever I am at Paris, I am dragged by invisible forces into their Morgue.' It was an obsession he described without trying to explain. This illustration to an *Uncommercial Traveller* piece of 1860 catches the 'neat and pleasant little woman' with her child described by him, and charmingly suggests Dickens, middle aged, courteous. As he told it, he was taken faint, and went off to have a brandy and a dip in the floating swimming bath in the Seine.

Dickens reading the murder of Nancy by Sikes to an audience eager to be horrified. It excited and exhausted him, and he loved doing it. 'I wanted to leave behind me the recollection of something very passionate and dramatic, done with simple means, if the art would justify the theme,' he told Forster.

Katey Dickens, 'Lucifer Box' as her father called her for her fiery nature, was a loving daughter, but clear-sighted, and she determined to give posterity the truth about him as best she could.

Nelly, Dickens's 'magic circle of one', was, he said, gentle, proud and self-reliant, had much to bear alone, and would be distressed if her history were known.

Charley Dickens (*left*) never became the businessman his father tried to make him: well mannered and impractical, he left his family penniless. Henry (*right*), the only son to prosper, persuaded his father to let him go to Cambridge and became a lawyer.

The old lion, grizzled, ravaged, fierce, not giving up. He disliked being photographed but he put up with it, sitting at his desk, quill pen in hand – inimitable as ever.

Cartoon showing Dickens crossing the Channel for Paris with books under both arms, published in *L'Eclipse* in 1868, drawn by the French artist André Gill – he took the pseudonym in homage to Gillray – from a photograph by John Watkins.

'The British Lion in America', an American cartoon of 1867, elaborates on a photograph by Jeremiah Gurney and shows Dickens wearing a flashy jacket and a lot of jewellery, and with a wine glass.

Dickens and Kate Wiggin walked hand in hand along the platform as far as the carriage sent to meet him before saying goodbye. This was the year Louisa May Alcott published *Little Women*, the novel that established New England girls as modern heroines, and Kate Wiggin was in the same mould. She grew up to become a successful writer herself, produced her own bestseller, *Rebecca of Sunnybrook Farm*, and in 1912 published her account of the meeting with Dickens.[45]

With Wills he exchanged letters every few days about the business of the magazine, and in each of his went one for Nelly, to be forwarded. The letters have disappeared, but the few words to Wills that went with them are eloquent: 'Enclosed is another letter for my dear girl'; 'My spirits flutter woefully towards a certain place at which you dined one day not long before I left, with the present writer and a third (most drearily missed) person'; 'I would give £3,000 down (and think it cheap) if you could forward *me*, for four and twenty hours only, instead of the letter'; 'Another letter for my Darling, enclosed'; 'You will have seen too (I hope) my dear Patient, and will have achieved in so doing what I would joyfully give a Thousand Guineas to achieve myself at this present moment!'; 'Toujours from the same to the same'; 'One last letter enclosed.'[46] Wills also received a small box from Niagara, addressed by Dickens to himself, which he was told to put in his bedroom at Wellington Street – a present for someone unnamed, no doubt Nelly. It was probably Wills who paid the rates on Windsor Lodge in January 1868, on behalf of Charles Tringham. Wills was also asked to handle cheques, one for £250 in November, another for £1,000 on 10 January, and a third on 2 March for £1,100, in all likelihood to be passed on to Nelly, a generous amount to cover her travel and living expenses.[47]

The tour ended with more readings in Boston and New York. In April, Boston was almost blotted out in 'a ceaseless whirl of snow and wind', and Annie Fields found Dickens's Copperfield reading 'a tragedy last night – less vigor but great tragic power came out of it . . . I should hardly have known it for the same reading and reader.' A week later she was in New York to hear him again, and this time he called for punch ingredients afterwards, his spirits rising rapidly, and the rest of the evening was given to drinking, laughing and singing comic songs.

'We did not separate until 12, and felt the next morning (as he said) as if we had had a regular orgy.'[48] This was on 15 April, and on the 18th he was due to address the New York press at a banquet given in his honour. As he dressed for it his foot was so swollen and sore that he and Dolby agreed there was no question of getting a boot on. Dolby went out to find a gout-stocking to put over the bandages and finally managed to borrow one from an obliging English gentleman. Arriving an hour late, and in great pain, Dickens had to be helped up the stairs of Delmonico's, but by nine o'clock he was able to rise and deliver a speech that gave the assembly everything they wanted. He reminded them that he had started as a newspaper reporter himself, and praised the changes he had seen in America since his first visit. He spoke of the politeness and the sweet-tempered reception he had received this time, and promised to have his present praise printed as an appendix in every reprint of his two books about America (meaning *American Notes* and *Martin Chuzzlewit*).[49] In a rousing finish he told them that the people of England and America were essentially one, that it rested with them to uphold the great Anglo-Saxon race and all its achievements, that both had striven for freedom and that it was inconceivable that they should ever go to war against one another – a cue for rapturous cheers and applause as he hobbled off.

There was still the ordeal of the last reading, and there were farewells to make. Dolby narrowly escaped being arrested by the US tax men as they embarked on 23 April. During their last few moments in America, they had a glimpse of Anthony Trollope arriving in New York. Three days into the voyage the bad foot was much improved, Dickens was able to leave his cabin to exercise on the deck, and his appetite returned. On 1 May they were in Liverpool, the next morning on the train that arrived at 3 p.m. at Euston. Dolby ends his account of the great American tour by describing his Chief walking away alone with his small bag. He was making a magical disappearance, because he did not arrive at Gad's Hill until 9 May. Since Nelly had left Florence for England on 24 April, it seems likely that Mr Tringham and Madame spent the week together at Windsor Lodge, entertaining one another with travellers' tales, walking and perhaps riding together, and taking pleasure in the English spring.

'Things look like work again'

1868–1869

Returning to Gad's Hill on 9 May, Dickens was greeted with flags and welcoming villagers. Almost at once he began to prepare for the 'Farewell Tour' he would be starting in October with Dolby. He also arranged a passage to Australia for sixteen-year-old Plorn. A shy boy with no idea of what he wanted to do in life, he had been taken out of school at fifteen and was currently at an agricultural college in Cirencester. Dickens wrote to Alfred, now farming in Australia, telling him to expect his younger brother at the end of the year, adding that Plorn could ride, do a little carpentering and make a horse shoe, but admitting it was not possible to know whether he would take to life in the bush.[1] He gave Alfred other news of family and friends: that Katey's husband Charles Collins was seriously ill with asthma and brain disease, that Wills had suffered a hunting accident that forced him to give up work, that Wilkie Collins and Fechter were both ill and even Henry, in his last year at school and due to go up to Cambridge in the autumn, had damaged his knee and was in bed – 'all the rest of us being in a flourishing condition' he added drily. Soon there was worse, as Charley's paper business failed, leaving him bankrupt and with personal debts of £1,000 and five children to support.

Charley was always given special treatment, and Dickens took him on to the staff of *All the Year Round*, contriving to convince himself that he was a good man of business and subeditor; and although the loss of Wills was serious, he sacked Henry Morley, who had been with him since joining the staff of *Household Words* in 1851, to make way for Charley. Dickens wrote Morley a friendly letter of explanation, saying he hoped he would continue to contribute, but Morley chose not to, and lost a small steady income. He went on to an academic career and later in life gave interestingly mixed testimonials to his onetime employer, describing him as a man possessed of 'great genius, but not a trained and cultivated reason', lacking in sound literary taste, but always remembered with affection as someone he had worked with happily through 'nineteen years of goodwill'.[2]

At the end of May, Dickens spent three days in Paris seeing Fechter and contributing to the preparations for the opening of *L'Abîme*, the French version of *No Thoroughfare*, in which Fechter was to star. The French critics had reservations about the play, 'un mélodrame assez vulgaire', but Paris was thrilled to welcome the great Dickens, audiences were pleased, and it gave Fechter a success. In July, Longfellow and his daughter arrived at Gad's for a visit, and Dickens had two postilions dressed up in old-fashioned red jackets to go with the carriage along the Dover Road to see the sights of Kent: 'it was like a holiday ride in England fifty years ago,' Dickens said, much taken with his idea of a heritage tour.[3] He put on the same show for other visitors, American and English, the Fieldses, Bulwer, Layard, the Tennents and Lady Molesworth.[4] The Nortons came to Gad's in August, Mrs Norton looking about with a sharp eye, declaring 'the house itself not in any respect pretty', and Dickens an excellent host, although he made it clear he must work in his study each morning. She got a glance at the study, which was also his bedroom, observed its perfect neatness and the 'brilliant bit of Oriental covering' on his bed, another present from Fechter. Gad's was his delight, and during the summer he began negotiations to buy the freehold of the meadow and arable adjoining it, twenty-eight acres of land, for which he agreed to pay £2,500.

In September, Plorn was taken to Portsmouth by Henry. 'He went away, poor dear fellow, as well as could possibly be expected. He was pale, and had been crying, and (Harry said) had broken down in the railway carriage after leaving Higham station; but only for a short time.'[5] Georgina gave him a parting present of cigars. Dickens also wept at parting but reminded him in a letter of how he himself had to 'win my food' at a younger age, recommended him to say his prayers and hoped that he would be able to say in after life 'that you had a kind father'.[6] To Dolby he wrote complaining of the costs and charges of 'these boys': 'Why was I ever a father? Why was *my* father ever a father!'⁷ To others, he spoke of his grief at parting with Plorn, but it is hard not to see in this something of the 'this hurts me more than it hurts you' of a severe and unrelenting schoolmaster. Then, after taking advice, he allowed Henry £250 a year and ordered what he supposed to be necessary supplies for his room in Trinity Hall: three dozen sherry, two dozen port, three dozen light claret and six bottles of brandy.

Ten days after Henry left for Cambridge on 10 October, news came of the death of Dickens's brother Fred in County Durham. They had hardly been in touch since 1858, although Fred had turned up in Canterbury in the autumn of 1861 asking for a free pass for an acquaintance to one of Dickens's events, and early in 1865 Dickens wrote to him to express his hope that he was doing well, while not offering any help.⁸ Fred had been in prison, and bankrupt; and he died in grim poverty, living on 'a penny bun and a glass of ginger beer' for his breakfast and otherwise mostly cold gin, according to George Sala, and not able even to afford to smoke. Fred had shared in much of Dickens's early married life, looking after the children during the first American trip and joining them for holidays in Italy as well as in Broadstairs; but when Dickens cast someone off he did not relent. He asked Dolby to go to Darlington, where Fred had died, and then wrote to the doctor who had looked after him, saying he had been his favourite when he was a child; but he did not go to the funeral, sending Charley as his representative.⁹

Katey's situation troubled Dickens, because Charles Collins was an invalid and it was not much of a marriage; and Dickens showed his disappointment and disapproval of Charles, which led to strained relations with Wilkie, and the two men seeing less of one another. The only children officially at home now were Henry, during the Cambridge vacations, and Mamie, who was increasingly away visiting friends. Even before Plorn's ship had put to sea – it was delayed by adverse weather – Dickens wrote buoyantly to Dolby, 'Things in general look like work again,' and fixed dinner with him at Verrey's on 1 October. He wanted to look forward, to be making plans for the future, and to talk about the new reading he had prepared, taken from *Oliver Twist*, 'Sikes and Nancy', giving the murder of Nancy by Bill Sikes – 'very horrible, but very dramatic'.[10] It was meant to be sensational, and he was pleased to have made something so powerful, as he told Forster when writing to him for advice on whether he should perform it in public or not.[11] Forster was against, and so was Dolby, but Dickens was also consulting with Chappells, who were putting up the money, and they suggested a trial reading. This was arranged for November, when the new tour was already under way, to be given in London, with oysters and champagne served to the select audience afterwards. Dickens wrote to Fields boasting about how horrible it was, and, after hearing it, Forster was even more strongly against further public performances. One critic said he had felt an irresistible desire to scream, and a physician warned of the danger of contagious hysteria in the audience, but an actress encouraged Dickens by telling him the public had been 'looking out for a sensation these last fifty years, and now they have got it'.[12] Dickens had every intention of going ahead and told Forster, 'I wanted to leave behind me the recollection of something very passionate and dramatic, done with simple means, if the art would justify the theme.'[13]

He went on to give the murder reading twenty-eight times between January 1869 and March 1870, and the effect was just as he had hoped, exciting and horrifying his audiences. It had its effect on him too, raising his pulse and prostrating him for a while at the end of the reading. Yet he was determined to keep giving it. He wanted the excitement and the public wanted to be horrified; and it was an argument with Dolby, who tried to persuade him to cut down on 'Sikes and Nancy' in favour of quieter readings, that led him to shout angrily and then burst into tears. Philip Collins, who wrote so well about Dickens, tells us he himself tried reading 'Sikes and Nancy' to audiences and found it more than enjoyable: 'anyone who has enough talent to perform this Reading at all competently, must find it exhilarating. The satisfaction must have been immensely stronger for Dickens than for me.'[14] Collins also quotes Edmund Wilson's remark that 'Dickens had a strain of the ham in him, and, in the desperation of his later life, he gave in to the old ham and let him rip.' He did not need the words written down even: the son of his old illustrator, Hablot Browne, described him throwing away his book for 'Sikes and Nancy'.[15]

The immediate effect of each reading, or performance, of the murder was to reduce him to a condition in which he found it difficult to get off stage, and once he had been helped to the sofa he had to lie down, unable to speak for some minutes – this was Dolby's account. He recovered with the help of a glass of champagne and would then go blithely back on stage for the next reading; but later in the evening the shock to his nerves recurred, 'either in the form of greater hilarity or a desire to be once more on the platform, or in a craving to do the work over again'. Here, as in so many other aspects of his life – in his dealings with his sons, in his complicated domestic arrangements – there were opposing forces at work. The Sikes readings were a strain on his physical and nervous system, as he came to realize, but they were also an experience he found irresistibly exciting and elating.

The new tour had started on 6 October in London, and there were eighteen readings scheduled for London, Manchester, Brighton and Liverpool, taking them through November, when there was a pause for the period of the election, which brought Disraeli's resignation and the return of Gladstone as Prime Minister. During the pause Dickens took up his London street walks again, going as far as Limehouse and Stepney, visiting the poorest and most miserable homes where sick people lay untended and the children had the pinched faces that came from three generations of undernourishment. While he was in this part of the East End he noticed a newly established hospital for sick children, set up by a young doctor and his wife, and was greatly impressed by the place and those who worked in it, including the nurses, who were paid only one pound a month and could have earned more elsewhere. Much of the sickness dealt with came from chronic malnutrition and filthy living conditions, and many young patients were invited back for meals after being discharged, simply in order to keep them healthy. His description of the living conditions in the area and of the East London Children's Hospital's commitment to its patients appeared in *All the Year Round* just before Christmas, and brought many offers of support for the hospital. His persistence in walking through parts of the East End regarded as no-go areas by the middle classes, and his journalist's skill in describing what he saw and alerting others who might do something to help there, confirmed his reputation as the friend of the people, and his belief that working through his writing was more effective than any political action.

In December he gave ten more readings in Scotland and Ireland. Soon, as Dolby wrote, 'we found ourselves going on in the same way and leading the same life we had led so often before, and it was at times difficult to imagine we had ever had any cessation of it.'[16] This meant that Dickens's health showed signs of breaking down again as it had in America, with severe pains affecting his right foot. He did not let it slow him down. On 21 December he was at the office, on the 22nd he did a London reading, on Christmas Eve he was with Forster at the funeral of his sister, returning to his house party at Gad's that evening and terrifying his guest, Austen Layard, in the bedroom next to his, from which Layard heard him rehearsing the Sikes and Nancy reading. On Christmas Day he wrote letters and on Boxing Day he refused an invitation, saying he had a previous engagement – possibly to visit Nelly, who was staying in Worthing. He was in London again on New Year's Day. Having noticed that Georgina was in low spirits, he suggested she should go with him to Ireland for ten days while he read in Dublin and Belfast: Dolby's account omits to mention that she joined them, no doubt out of tact.[17] Just before they set off Dickens wrote to his Swiss friend Cerjat saying that if his daughter Mary were to marry (which he did not expect) he would sell Gad's Hill 'and go genteelly vagabondizing over the face of the earth' – with whom, if anyone, he does not say.[18] A few days later he was paying out the £2,500 for the land around Gad's Hill.[19]

After the Irish readings came the West Country ones, then the Midlands. The readings in Scotland had to be postponed when the pain in his foot was so excruciating that he could not stand on it, and he became 'so faint while dressing that I was within an ace of Gone'.[20] With rest, and a sofa installed on the train taking him north, he got through two readings in Edinburgh and two in Glasgow, giving the

Sikes murder at all of them, and again in London on his return; he told Georgina he was no longer taking champagne during the readings, but only brandy and water.[21] In March he celebrated Nelly's birthday with her and Wills in London. Soon after this he read in Hull, where he went into Dixon's shop in Whitefriargate and, in the course of buying six pairs of ladies' silk stockings, asked the young assistant what he liked doing in the evenings, to which the assistant replied that he liked the theatre and dramatic readings, but could not get a ticket for today's reading; a few questions showed that he had a good knowledge of the work of Dickens. Only when he found a card inscribed 'Please Admit Bearer' pressed into his hand did the young man realize he was talking to Dickens himself; but he remained baffled as to why the great writer should be buying ladies' stockings.[22]

From York, Dickens had to hurry south for the funeral of Sir James Tennent, the dedicatee of *Our Mutual Friend*, only eight years older than him, whose death upset him badly. Then back on the road, East Anglia, Manchester again, Sheffield, Birmingham and Liverpool, where a great banquet was given in his honour and had him on his feet again with a speech of thanks to the 650 guests and as many spectators in the gallery, with the band of the police force in the vestibule and the band of the Orphans Asylum in the gallery, flags, flowers, a silver-gilt fountain dispensing rose water, the Chancellor of the Exchequer, the Master of Trinity College, Cambridge, and Lord Houghton (Richard Monckton Milnes as was) all speaking before him. More readings in Liverpool, then on to Leeds: and here, since he was sleeping badly and his foot was 'growling' again, he and Dolby agreed to take a coach to the pretty town of Chester for two days' rest before continuing the tour.

In Chester on 18 April Dickens had a stroke. He did not describe it as such, telling Dolby only that he had suffered a very bad night, but from Blackburn, where they arrived the next day, he wrote to Frank Beard describing his symptoms: giddiness, uncertainty of footing especially on the left side and an extreme indisposition to raise his hands to his head. To his friend Norton, who had been at Liverpool, he wrote saying, 'I am half dead with travelling every day, and reading afterwards.'[23] To Georgina he wrote, 'My weakness and deadness

are *on the left side*, and if I don't look at anything I try to touch with
my left hand, I don't know where it is.'[24] The following day he began
to feel more like himself, read *A Christmas Carol* and 'Bob Sawyer's
Party', travelled on to Bolton for the next reading, and wrote again
to Georgina and to Forster to say he was better and expected to be
able to continue the tour. But when Frank Beard caught up with him
in Preston and examined him, he said there were to be no more readings. Dolby had to cancel the rest, while Beard took Dickens back to
London to consult Sir Thomas Watson, who confirmed Beard's view
that the patient had been on the brink of paralysis of the left side and
apoplexy, meaning a haemorrhage of the brain.

Dickens explained to all concerned that he had become ill from the
'constant Express travelling' and that the doctors had made him give
up the tour as a precautionary measure, to stop him from becoming
ill. At the same time he told Ouvry he wished to make a new draft of
his will, set about it at once and signed it on 12 May.[25] He was kept
busy by the magazine, now without experienced assistants. He
reviewed Forster's biography of Walter Savage Landor himself, at
length and with great warmth, when it appeared in July. In August
he started running Fanny Trollope's novel *Veronica*, a risqué story of
a girl seduced by a man old enough to be her father. Knowing that
Fechter was preparing to travel to America, he wrote a glowing
account of his theatrical career for the *Atlantic Monthly*. His son Sydney wrote from his ship with an abject confession that he had run up
debts and asking his father to settle them: it was an old familiar story,
the debts were paid, Dickens was angry. Another unwelcome business was sorting the mass of papers left to him by his friend Chauncey
Townshend, who had died while he was in America, leaving a will
appointing him literary executor and asking him to publish a book
giving an account of his religious opinions. It was a dismal waste of
his time and energy, but he carried out the assignment honourably
enough, telling Townshend's lawyers privately that 'it would be preposterous to pretend it [the book he compiled] is worth anything.'[26]

The arrival of James and Annie Fields in England in May for a
prolonged European holiday raised his spirits and inspired him to
feats of hospitality. First he took a suite for himself in the St James's

Hotel in Piccadilly in order to show them the sights of London, Windsor and Richmond. Then, with Dolby also of the party, and Sol Eytinge, an American painter, he took them to Shadwell, in the East End, under police protection, and they were able to go into an opium den, where they watched and listened to the mutterings of an old woman dealer. After this the whole party was invited to spend a week at Gad's Hill in early June, with many walks, games of croquet and bowls in the garden, charades in the evening, elaborately planned lobster picnics in the woods, drives through hop gardens and orchards, visits to Rochester, where they all climbed to the battlements of the castle, and to Canterbury, where Dickens dismissed the cathedral verger and gave his guests his own guided tour. There was a visit to Chatham and another to Cobham Woods, and the week culminated in a great dinner, with dancing in the drawing room afterwards that continued until first light.[27] The Fieldses were back at Gad's in October, when they met Henry, in high favour since winning a college scholarship at the end of his first year, and both his sisters were there again. After dinner Mamie played Scotch reels on the piano, and Dickens could not resist getting to his feet and leading Katey in a dance. 'I never saw anything prettier; Katie with her muslin kerchief as in the old time and the double white hollyhocks in her hair & her quaint graceful little figure and he, light and lithe as a boy of 20 – those two take great delight in each other.' So wrote Annie Fields in her diary, seeing him rejuvenated as he showed off with his daughter, a glimpse of a man who had already been near death and had only nine months left to live, but who could still look like a boy absorbed in the pleasure of dancing with a beloved girl.[28]

The Fieldses were not introduced to Nelly during their stay in England, but Dickens spoke of her to James Fields, telling him that 'when he was ill in his reading only Nelly observed that he staggered and his eye failed, only she dared tell him' – a remark that indicates her presence at readings earlier in the year, possibly in the north.[29] There was a cricket match at Gad's in August, at which, according to Katey, Nelly was present, staying as a guest in the house, and taking part in the cricket too. No doubt she was presented as a friend of the family – and why not? A genuine friendship began to grow up between her and Georgy and Mamie.[30] In September, when Dickens was going to speak to the Birmingham and Midland Institute, an educational body he had supported from its beginning sixteen years earlier, he told Dolby, 'I have a notion . . . of supplementing the speechmaking with a small N excursion next Day to Stratford, or Kenilworth, or both, or somewhere else, in a jovial way.'[31] Mr Ryland, the Birmingham organizer, was told that Dickens wouldn't be staying with him, since he would be with his secretary, Mr Dolby, and they must be away early next morning; and Nelly and Dickens were able to make a short cultural jaunt together, and pay their homage to Shakespeare, or Amy Robsart, or both.[32]

Dolby knew Nelly well enough to approach Dickens through her: in November, for instance, Dickens wrote to him from Wellington Street, 'In answer to your enquiry to N – I do not *think* I shall be here until Wed. in the ordinary course. But I can be in town on Tuesday at from 5 to 6, and will dine at the Posts with you, if you like.'[33] And Dolby gave his own interesting account of how Dickens divided his time, saying the early days of the week were devoted to business, 'Mr Dickens, on these days, taking up his residence at the office in London, returning to Gad's with his guests, as a rule, on Friday, and remaining there until the following Monday' – leaving the middle of the week open, with a neat space for the Tringham life at Peckham.[34]

※

For several years Lord and Lady Russell had made a habit of inviting Dickens to a summer dinner at Pembroke Lodge, their house in Richmond Park, and this year he agreed to stay overnight. Two accounts of the evening were given, one by the Russells' granddaughter, who was charmed by the great man. She noticed his frilled shirt and diamond studs, his white hair and his abstemiousness: 'At dinner he ate and drank very little. Champagne did not circulate at Pembroke Lodge, nor was it the fashion in those days to have whiskey-and-sodas; but there was port and madeira, and we sat for some time over the wine. Mr Dickens drank madeira sparingly.'[35] Dickens's own account,

given to Dolby, is rather different. He told him that, knowing Lord
Russell's 'very temperate habits', he had packed a bottle of Ballard's
punch in his portmanteau, intending to mix himself a drink in his
room at bedtime. He went without a servant, expecting to do his
own unpacking, and was embarrassed to find that the valet who laid
out his dress suit had also arranged his bottle of punch on the mantel-
shelf, with a tumbler, wine glass and corkscrew beside it. 'At this
spectacle he was troubled in spirit,' he told Dolby. Worse followed.
At half past ten, the hour at which the Russells normally went to
bed, as Dickens stood up to wish them goodnight, they both started
laughing and Lady Russell said, 'Don't be in a hurry, the *tray* will be
here in a minute.' And in came a servant with all the materials for
making punch.[36] Dickens told Dolby the story against himself with
good humour; but packing a private bottle and planning a secret
drink does suggest that his need for alcohol had become a serious
dependence.

✿

In August he began to turn over an idea for a new novel, a murder
mystery and a love story, much of it set in Rochester, where the
cathedral was put to some sinister usage. This was the chief occupation of the autumn. In October he found a title, *The Mystery of Edwin
Drood*, and was able to read some of it to James Fields, who had been
with him when he visited the Shadwell opium den described in the
opening pages; and at the end of the month he read the whole of the
first number to the Forsters. Charles Collins asked if he might illustrate it and was invited to design the cover. Dickens was pleased with
what he did, and happy for him to provide the illustrations, but Collins let him down, declaring himself too ill. Dickens turned to Luke
Fildes, who had been recommended by Millais; the young artist was
jubilant to have been given the job, which he did well.

Dickens's own health was so troublesome that he told Georgina he
was giving up tea and coffee in the morning, and asked her to prepare
'Homeopathic Cocoa boiled with milk' for his breakfast instead.[37] He
kept at his writing, and also managed to deliver two public lectures

during the autumn; while Dolby noticed 'a slow but steady change working in him, and had serious doubts whether he would be able to get through the twelve Readings announced' for the next year, as Dickens insisted there must be, to say a last farewell to his London public.[38] He kept his eye on the future, even if only in joking with Thomas Trollope, who pressed Dickens to visit him in Italy, about how he was going to cross all the passes of the Alps, 'and I am also "going" up the Nile to the Second Cataract, and I am "going" to Jerusalem, and to India, and likewise to Australia. My only dimness of perception in this wise, is, that I don't know when . . . But whenever (if ever) I change "going" into "coming", I shall come to see you.'[39] And on 13 December he signed a contract for *Drood*, to be published by Chapman & Hall in twelve numbers, starting in March 1870, and put out in green-paper covers. Chapman paid £7,500 for the right to all profits on the first 25,000 copies, and after that equal shares for publisher and author, and two American publishers vied for the rights, which finally went to Harper's for £1,000. He was now committed up to the spring of 1871.[40]

At Gad's Hill he entertained a great deal, the Fieldses again, Forster, the playwright and novelist Charles Reade, his journalist friend Charles Kent, his solicitor Ouvry. Dolby describes an all-male gathering there with Fechter, his American theatre manager Palmer and Webster of the Adelphi – madeira to drink, gambling on the billiards and a Bohemian atmosphere, but this was unusual. Dickens's pride in the place was great: he had his house boy Isaac put into page's livery, and he was always making more improvements, ordering the construction of a large conservatory, another gauge for the future, for which the insurance alone cost £600. He was amused to hear that Wills in retirement was perfectly happy in his idle life, settled in a country house in Hertfordshire: idleness was not an option for Dickens. He kept an eye on public affairs, worrying about the situation in Ireland and the Fenians, who gathered in large numbers for a protest meeting in London. He expressed his indignation against Mrs Beecher Stowe, who had published a book called *Lady Byron Vindicated*, writing to John Murray to tell him of how he had visited Byron's daughter Ada years before, and how 'She little thought, in speaking to me of her father, that the Ghoules were even then growing their nails for his grave.'[41] Perhaps he foresaw a *Mrs Dickens Vindicated*.

In December, Fechter departed for America after a farewell dinner at Gad's, leaving his wife and son in England and taking his mistress with him as his leading lady. He also took Dickens's valet Scott, who knew America, an arrangement Dickens must have made out of the goodness of his heart. At Christmas there was a small family gathering: Georgina, his two daughters, Henry, who had passed his Little Go examination[42] with all honours, Charles Collins, and Charley and Bessie with a grandchild, or so he told Macready, although by now there were four grandchildren.[43] To Dolby he wrote saying this Christmas was one of great pain and misery to him, and contrasted it sadly with the one they had spent together in America. Then, as he said pathetically, he had the use of his legs, but this year he was confined to his bed the whole day, getting up only in the evening to join the party in the drawing room after dinner.[44] Yet by New Year's Eve he was well enough to go to London, and to read the second number of *Drood* aloud to the Forsters.

26

Pickswick, Pecknicks, Pickwicks

1870

No one can imagine their own death, even when they know it is approaching. Dickens rejected and defied his illness with a spirit that would not flinch or budge. At the same time he sensed danger and set about putting order into his affairs – family matters, money, copyrights. His days were now packed with business meetings, readings, public and private, office work to do with the magazine, discussions with illustrators, plans for more improvements at Gad's, the rebuilding of the staircase, changes to the garden and the new conservatory. Then there were speeches to deliver, dinners and receptions, his daughters' amateur theatricals in which they involved him, social obligations to insistent friends, to politicians and even to royalty – and woven through all this, the writing of his novel *The Mystery of Edwin Drood*. He did not pause until the day he fell unconscious to the ground.

Keeping to his practice of renting a London house to allow Mamie to enjoy herself, he took another in Bayswater, at No. 5 Hyde Park Place, close to Marble Arch, belonging to the Liberal politician Milner Gibson, who had served in Lord Russell's last government. He told Dolby he liked the view over the park, where he could see people enjoying themselves, and that he also enjoyed the rattling of early morning wagons taking produce from Paddington to the markets, even when he was woken by it, because it showed that an important part of the world was already at work. In the same way, he added, he liked sleeping at the office, Wellington Street being one in which 'when the last cab had gone "off", the first market cart came "on".'[1]

There were five London readings in January, one of them a special matinee on the 21st to allow theatre people to hear 'Sikes'. Dickens wrote to Wills afterwards, saying he had decided it had been 'madness ever to do it continuously. My ordinary pulse is 72, and it runs up under this effort to 112. Besides which, it takes me ten or twelve minutes to get my wind back at all: I being in the meantime like the man who lost the fight.' He went on to say he hoped Wills would come to hear it, and told him he would be doing it twice in February and once in March. Meanwhile he had something wrong with his right thumb – it must have been gout again, which travels about – and he could not write plainly. He ended the letter, 'The patient [i.e., Nelly] was in attendance and missed you. I was charged with all manner of good and kind remembrance.'[2] His bad thumb obliged him to put off a dinner with Gladstone.

His father-in-law, George Hogarth, now eighty-six, was still working as a journalist, a respected figure and well liked for his good nature and unassuming ways. In January he fell down the stairs at the office of the *Illustrated London News* and died as a result of the fall in February, nursed to the end by Catherine's married sister, Helen Roney, who lived close to her. Dickens, thirty years younger than his father-in-law, had not spoken to him for over a decade, and he made no sign to the Hogarth family, who can hardly have expected it, but all the obituaries pointed out the relationship between the two men, and Georgina used black-bordered paper for her correspondence as a token of mourning for her father.

Although he did not choose to remember Mr Hogarth, ceremonies and courtesies were important to Dickens. He spent his fifty-eighth birthday with the Forsters, who gave a dinner to which Georgy came, and Katey with her husband. He wrote to Macready to congratulate him on reaching his seventy-seventh on 3 March. On the same day Nelly's birthday lunch was held, this year at Blanchard's in Regent Street, with Wills and one other guest, probably Dolby: one wonders how much any of the participants enjoyed these occasions. On Sunday, 6 March, Dickens dined with George Eliot and Lewes, who found his conversation energetic and entertaining, although they thought he looked 'dreadfully shattered'. On the 8th he gave a reading: the sentimental 'Boots at the Holly-tree Inn', next the Sikes murder, for the last time, sending his pulse racing, and finally the comic 'Bob Sawyer's Party'. The next day, overcoming his lack of enthusiasm for royalty, he went to Buckingham Palace for an afternoon interview with the Queen, who had 'signified in a note that she wished "to make my acquaintance"'.[3]

What made him soften? He had shown some photographs of the American Civil War to Arthur Helps, a man of literary tastes and talent who was Clerk to the Privy Council and a courtier, and Helps had mentioned them to the Queen, who asked to see them, and then expressed a wish to meet Dickens. From his point of view, he may have wanted to do something for Mamie, who had social ambitions and could be received at court once he had been.[4] Etiquette demanded that he remain standing throughout his conversation with the Queen, and she also stood, leaning on a sofa. It was not a sprightly exchange. She regretted she had never heard him read and he explained firmly that the readings were over – although in truth there was a last one yet to be given – and that he did not give private readings. They talked of his American trip, the Queen mentioned a supposed discourtesy shown by the Americans to her son Prince Arthur on a visit, and Dickens assured her that the royal family was popular across the Atlantic. She asked him if he could account for the fact that it was no longer possible to find good servants in England, and he suggested the educational system might be unhelpful. She talked of the rising price of food.

She then presented him with a copy of the book she had written, *Leaves from the Journal of Our Life in the Highlands*. He can hardly have forgotten how he had chided Wills for allowing praise of this royal work to appear in his magazine: 'I would not have had that reference made to the Queen's preposterous book (I have read it) for any money. I blush to join the Shameful lick-spittle Chorus. It is amazing to me, knowing my opinions on such matters, that you *could* have passed it.'[5] Now he naturally accepted the preposterous book with grace. The Queen expressed a wish to be given copies of his works, and was promised a specially bound set. Dickens then left, to meet Dolby as agreed in the Burlington Arcade, and the two went off arm in arm to dine at the Blue Posts in Cork Street.

There was another dinner with Dolby on 12 March, when Dickens entertained him with the Chappell brothers to thank them for

organizing the readings.[6] Three days later, on the 15th, he gave his
final reading at St James's Hall. It was an occasion of high emotion for
reader and public. Crowds were turned away at the door as an audience of 2,000 gathered inside, many paying only a shilling for a seat,
and when he came on to the platform they rose to their feet to cheer
him. He gave them *A Christmas Carol* and 'The Trial of Pickwick'.
Forster was in the audience and thought he had never read so well,
with delicacy and the quiet sadness of farewell. Dolby was backstage,
ready to support him as necessary. Charley was in the front row on
the orders of Frank Beard, in case his father should falter: 'you must
run up and catch him and bring him off with me, or, by Heaven, he'll
die before them all.'[7] He did not falter, although he could not say
'Pickwick', making it Pickswick, Pecknicks or Pickwicks. At the end
the audience called him back several times until he spoke some farewell words, telling them to expect his new novel's first instalment in
two weeks, and then, 'from these garish lights I vanish now for ever-
more, with a heartfelt, grateful, respectful, affectionate farewell.'
'The brief hush of silence as he moved from the platform; and the
prolonged tumult of sound that followed suddenly, stayed him, and
again for another moment brought him back; will not be forgotten
by any present,' wrote John Forster.[8]

The bond with Forster was as strong as it had ever been, and he
read each number of *Edwin Drood* aloud at his house in Palace Gate as
he finished it, and talked over the plot with him. On 21 March, ten
days before the first number was published, he read the fourth, and
afterwards confided to his friend that, as he walked along Oxford
Street earlier, he had once again been unable to read the right side of
the names written on the shop fronts. At the end of the month he
wrote to him describing a recurrence of severe haemorrhage from his
piles which left him shaken: the laudanum he took to help him sleep
would have caused constipation, making the piles worse. Still, he was
not deterred from leading his active life. On 28 March he signed an
agreement with Frederic Chapman and Henry Trollope, son of
Anthony and a new partner in Chapman & Hall, covering the copyright of all his books, which was shared equally between himself and
the publishers. He celebrated Forster's birthday with him on 2 April.

On 5 April he spoke at the dinner of the Newsvendors' Benevolent and Provident Institution, warming them up with jokes and urging them to contribute more to their own pension fund. On 6 April he put on court dress and attended a levee at the palace. The next day he held a large reception at Hyde Park Place, at which the violinist Joachim and the pianist Charles Hallé both performed, as well as solo and group singers. He had done nothing so ambitious in the way of entertainment since the days at Tavistock House.

In April, Charley formally took over from Wills at *All the Year Round*. Then, on 2 June, Dickens added a codicil to his will giving Charley the whole of his own share and interest in the magazine, with all its stock and effects.[9] In this way he did the best he could to look after the future of his beloved first-born son, in whom he had once placed such hopes: he would not – could not – now give up on him, in spite of his failures and bankruptcy. Henry continued to do well at Cambridge and could be relied on to make his own way. In May he wrote to his fourth son, Alfred, expressing his 'unbounded faith' in his future in Australia, but doubting whether Plorn was taking to life there, and mentioning Sydney's debts: 'I fear Sydney is much too far gone for recovery, and I begin to wish that he were honestly dead.'[10] Words so chill they are hard to believe, with which Sydney was cast off as Walter had been when he got into debt, and brother Fred when he became too troublesome, and Catherine when she opposed his will. Once Dickens had drawn a line he was pitiless.

The conflicting elements in his character produced many puzzles and surprises. Why was Charley forgiven for failure and restored to favour, Walter and Sydney not? Because Charley was the child of his youth and first success, perhaps. But all his sons baffled him, and their incapacity frightened him: he saw them as a long line of versions of himself that had come out badly. He resented the fact that they had grown up in comfort and with no conception of the poverty he had worked his way out of, and so he cast them off; yet he was a man whose tenderness of heart showed itself time and time again in his dealings with the poor, the dispossessed, the needy, other people's children. Again, the lover who longed to take Nelly to America with him could not think of living permanently with her in England, not only because of the inevitable scandal, but also because he was attached to his life at Gad's Hill, calmly presided over by Georgina, who served him and limited the demands she made on him. There was another life he valued too, with Dolby and at the office, where he could enjoy being a bachelor, dining well, theatre-going and drinking late with men friends. He grumbled about Forster, his dullness, his surrender to middle-class values and conventions, but he could not manage without him, and the words he had written to him in 1838 – that nothing but death should impair 'the toughness of a bond now so firmly riveted' – remained true to the end. In his writing too there were conflicts, a touch of ham certainly, but alongside it the dazzling jokes, the Shakespearean characterization, the delicacy and profundity of imagination, the weirdness and brilliance of his descriptive powers.

***

The Mystery of Edwin Drood sold well from the start, outstripping *Our Mutual Friend* by 10,000 and reaching 50,000 a number. Dickens, sending pages of manuscript to the printer, put in a note to tell him, 'The safety of my precious child is my sole care,' an unexpected image from this most masculine of writers who had never before described his work as his child.[11] *Drood* has fascinated readers because it is a murder story left unfinished and unsolved, with touches of exoticism, opium, mesmerism, Thuggee practices,[12] all new departures for him. It also contains haunting and melancholy descriptions of Rochester, the city of his childhood, beautifully rendered; but the mystery is a slight one, the villain less interesting than he promises to be at first, the comedy only moderately funny, the charm a little forced, and the language reads at times like a parody of earlier work. There is a nicely done bad child who throws stones and pronounces cathedral 'KIN-FREE-DER-EL', which Dickens may have heard and appreciated in the streets of Rochester; and what was finished – twenty-two chapters, making half of what was intended – is perfectly readable.

Drood has to be seen in three ways. First, as the unfinished mystery which has received extraordinary attention just because it is a puzzle left by Dickens and offers itself for endless ingenious speculation by those who enjoy thinking up solutions. Secondly, as half a novel which cannot be regarded as a major work, and which has divided opinion sharply even among Dickens's warmest admirers, from Chesterton's hailing it as the creation of a dying magician making 'his last splendid and staggering appearance' to Gissing's and Shaw's dismissal of it as trivial and of no account. And thirdly, as the achievement of a man who is dying and refusing to die, who would not allow illness and failing powers to keep him from exerting his imagination, or to prevent him from writing: and as such it is an astonishing and heroic enterprise.

Until the end of May he was officially based at Hyde Park Place, but often at Wellington Street, and sometimes he escaped to Gad's, and without doubt to be with Nelly too. Early in February he tells a friend he has been away in the country for two days, in mid-April he says he has been 'working hard out of town' over a weekend, and later in the month he mentions 'a long country walk' at Gad's Hill – any or all of these might mean time with her.[13] The death of Maclise brought sorrow although they had scarcely been in touch for years, and he spoke tenderly of him at the Royal Academy dinner on 30 April. It was his last speech and made a great impression. On 2 May he and Mamie dined with his old friend Lavinia Watson and her children, on a visit to London from Rockingham. After this he told one correspondent he was going out of town 'to get a breath of fresh air' for two days, and another, 'I have been (and still am), in attendance on a sick friend at some distance,' which sounds like Peckham again.[14]

On 7 May he read aloud the fifth episode of *Drood* at Forster's. Now the pain in his foot was stirring again and he began to be 'dead-lame' and had to take more laudanum at night. Ouvry was asked to come to his office to transact business and other engagements were cancelled, including his attendance at the State Ball at Buckingham

Palace on the 17th, to which Mamie went without him. He managed
to dine with the American Ambassador, Motley, and with Disraeli,
and took breakfast with Gladstone.[15] On 22 May, Forster dined with
him at Hyde Park Place. He had news of the death of another once
dear friend, Mark Lemon, and sent Charley to represent him at the
funeral. Then on 24 May he somehow got himself to dinner with
Lord and Lady Houghton, she being the granddaughter of the Lady
Crewe for whom his grandmother had worked as housekeeper: he
was invited there to meet the Prince of Wales, who particularly
wished to be introduced to him, together with Leopold II, King of
Belgium. Dickens was at the dinner and in reasonably good form, but
he was unable to go upstairs to the drawing room afterwards.[16]

He was also kept busy by his daughters, giving advice and assistance to an amateur group with whom they were putting on a play at
the Kensington house of a rich builder, Charles Freake, whose children were their friends. Dickens went there for some rehearsals, and
indeed Katey said she was with him constantly in town about this
time.[17] There was another dinner with the indefatigably hospitable
Lady Molesworth. One guest recalled him as bubbling over with fun,
but the young Lady Jeune, who had her only meeting with him at
Lady Molesworth's dinner table, remembered sitting between him
and Bulwer, aware that 'the noise and fatigue of the dinner seemed to
distress him [Dickens] very much.'[18] Worse, his lameness was making
it more difficult for him to work at his novel: 'Deprivation of my
usual walks is a very serious matter to me, as I cannot work unless I
have my constant exercise.'[19]

So on 25 May he took himself to Gad's Hill, 'obliged to fly for a
time from the dinings and other engagements of this London Season,
and to take refuge here to get myself into my usual gymnastic condition' – but 'circuitously, to get a little change of air on the road'.[20] He
remained there until 2 June, sending Fechter a rhapsodic description
of the improvements to the house and garden: the conservatory was
finished, the rebuilt main staircase had been gilded and brightly
painted, and the garden was being managed by a new gardener who
had improved the gravel paths and installed forcing houses for melons
and cucumbers as well as flowers.[21]

View of the house at Gad's Hill from the garden at the back, showing the conservatory (*right*) Dickens had built.

He was still resting at Gad's when the Hyde Park Place house was officially given up, on the last day of May. Then, on Thursday, 2 June, he was back in London, at Wellington Street, where Dolby, making his weekly visit to the office, found him immersed in business and looking strained – depressed, and even tearful, he noted. They had their lunch together, talked of Dolby visiting Gad's to see the improvements, shook hands, said 'next week, then' and parted. That evening he went to the Freakes' mansion in the Cromwell Road to join his daughters at their theatrical entertainment and acquitted himself well as stage manager, although Charles Collins found him sitting alone behind the scenes afterwards, apparently thinking he was at home – which home, you have to ask.[22] It was a hot night and he went back to Wellington Street to sleep. There Charley found him in the morning, so absorbed in working on *Drood* that he did not answer when spoken to. He remained seemingly oblivious of the presence of his son, and even when he turned in his direction appeared to look through him. So Charley left him without any farewells.

Forster was away in Cornwall, working. Dickens was back at Gad's in the evening, where Georgina was expecting him. He ordered four more boxes of his usual cigars and, for his painful foot, a 'voltaic band', a type of electric chain that had become a fashionable all-purpose cure, recommended to him by the actress Mrs Bancroft and supplied by Isaac Pulvermacher, Medical Battery Maker.[23] Both his daughters came down on Sunday, and after Georgina and Mamie had gone to bed that night he sat up talking with Katey. 'The lamps in the conservatory were turned down, but the windows that led into it were still open. It was a very warm, quiet night, and there was not a breath of air: the sweet scent of the flowers came in . . . and my father and I might have been the only creatures alive in the place . . .' So Katey sets the scene for her great talk with her father in which she asked his advice – should she take up an offer to go on the stage? He warned her against the idea, telling her she was pretty and might do well, but that she was too sensitive. 'Although there are nice people on the stage, there are some who would make your hair stand on end. You are clever enough to do something else.' As they talked on he said he wished he had been 'a better father – a better man' and told her things he had never discussed with her before, no doubt concerning the separation from her mother and his relations with Nelly. He also expressed a doubt as to whether he would live to finish *Drood* – 'because you know, my dear child, I have not been strong lately'. He spoke, she said, 'as though his life was over and there was nothing left'.[24]

Katey and Mamie were leaving for town together the next morning. When they came down their father was already working in his chalet in the wilderness – he had ordered his breakfast for 7.30 because he had so much to do, he told the maid – and since he disliked partings they did not think of disturbing him. But, as they sat in the porch waiting for the carriage to take them to the station, Katey felt she wanted to see him again. She hurried through the tunnel under the road to the wilderness, then up the steps to the upper room of the chalet in which he worked. When he saw her he pushed his chair away from the writing table and took her into his arms to kiss her, holding her in an embrace she would never forget.

In the afternoon he walked into Rochester with his dogs and posted his letters. He also went down into the cellar with a notebook in which he entered details of the casks kept there, heading it 'Details of Contents of Casks in the Cellar – an account being kept on a slate in the cellar of what is drawn daily from each cask – and added together in this Book at the end of every week beginning 6th June 1870'. On the first page he made seven entries for sherry, brandy, rum and Scotch whisky, giving the number of gallons and when purchased, e.g., 'Cask Very Fine Scotch Whiskey 30 gallons – came in 1st January 1869'. On page 2 he noted that three quarts of sherry had been used in the previous week, and on page 3 that a pint each of old pale brandy and dark brandy had been drawn. On page 5 he wrote that two gallons of his 'Very Fine Scotch Whiskey', stored in casks and stone jars, had been used in London.[25]

On Tuesday he worked at *Drood* again and wrote more letters, one to Luke Fildes telling him he would be at Gad's from Saturday, 11 June – i.e., not before then – until the following Tuesday or Wednesday, and inviting him down for the next weekend. After lunch he and Georgy went in the carriage to Cobham Woods, where he got out in order to walk home alone; later he hung Chinese lanterns in the conservatory, and they both admired them in the evening. He had his breakfast served early again, at 7.30, on Wednesday, 8 June, and one of the maids left to be married that morning. A few letters written that day said he would be in the office in London on Thursday, and during the morning he looked in at the Falstaff Inn opposite to cash a cheque from the landlord, Mr Trood, as he often did, on this occasion for £22.[26]

After this Georgina was the only person known to have seen him until after six in the evening. In the servants' hall below stairs there was the cook Catherine, the maid Emma, and the young house boy Isaac Armitage, and somewhere about outside were the groom George Butler, the new gardener Mr Brunt and some under-gardeners, local boys who would go home in the evening. Georgina said that Dickens came to the house in the middle of the day for an hour's rest and to smoke a cigar, and then went back to work in the chalet, contrary to his usual habit, returning to the house in the late afternoon to write letters and entering the dining room at six, looking unwell. He sat down and she asked him if he felt ill and he replied, 'Yes, very ill; I have been very ill for the last hour.' On her saying she would send for a doctor, he said no, he would go on with the dinner, and go afterwards to London. He made an effort to struggle against the fit that was coming on him, and talked incoherently and soon very indistinctly. Georgina gave several versions of what happened, and she told Forster that he mentioned a sale at a neighbour's house and something about Macready before stating his intention of going to London immediately. In another version, when she suggested calling the doctor, he said no, complaining of toothache, holding his jaw, and asking to have the window shut, which she did.[27] In every version she gave their final exchange, her 'Come and lie down', and his reply, 'Yes, on the ground', as he collapsed on the floor and lost consciousness.[28] Haunting last words. Now at last the core of his being, the creative machine that had persisted in throwing up ideas, visions and characters for thirty-six years, was stilled.

Forster, who like everyone else took his account from Georgina, describes her as trying to get him on to a sofa, but there was no sofa in the dining room. She said she got the servants from below, where they always remained unless sent for, to bring a sofa from the drawing room, on to which he was lifted. Yet Steele, the local doctor who was summoned by Isaac, the house boy, stated with certainty that Dickens was on the floor when he arrived and that it was he who asked for the sofa to be brought into the dining room and he who lifted him on to it; and later he would point out the exact place where he had found Dickens lying. We all know that memories of such events are likely to be uncertain and unreliable: for instance, Isaac said later that he had gone to fetch the doctor on the pony Noggs, although that particular pony had been put down a year before.

There is another possible version of the events of Wednesday, 8 June. In this, Dickens left for Higham Station after he had cashed the cheque with Mr Trood and made the familiar journey by train and cab to Peckham. At Windsor Lodge he gave Nelly her housekeeping

money. Sometime soon after this he collapsed. Nelly, with the help
of her maids, of the good-natured caretaker of the church opposite –
sworn to secrecy – and of a hackney cabman, got the unconscious man
into a big two-horse brougham supplied by the local job-master, used
to driving Nelly and Dickens, and drove with him to Gad's Hill. She
knew that Dickens's reputation, and her own, depended on her action,
and one of her two maids could have sent a telegram to Georgina warning her to expect them, while the other could have gone with her to
help. The journey must have taken several hours, but the roads were
empty because the railway handled all the traffic now: Dickens had just
written in *Drood* of 'high roads, of which there will shortly be not
one in England'. Getting an inert or semi-conscious man into Gad's
Hill would be a problem, but it was managed, and the dining room
was where he would be expected to be at this time of day, between
six and seven o'clock. It seems a wild and improbable story, but not
an entirely impossible one, given what we know of Dickens's habits.
It is supported by the fact that Georgina, a careful and efficient person, wrote to their solicitor Ouvry in a letter dated 'Thursday' to say
she found £6.6s.3d. in the pockets of his suit after his death. Given
that he had cashed a cheque for £22 on the morning of 8 June, where
did the £15.13s.9d. go?[29]

Yet Georgina's account, even with its slight variants, carries
conviction; and in any case, sometime after six o'clock in the evening
the two versions become one again. Nelly returned to Peckham. Dr
Steele arrived, had a sofa brought into the dining room and the
patient lifted on to it. He saw that he was past help and held out no
hopes of recovery but went through some palliative medical procedures and said he should be kept warm. Katey and Mamie, summoned
by telegram, arrived about midnight. 'Directly we entered the house
I could hear my father's deep breathing. All through the night we
watched him, taking it in turns to place hot bricks at his feet, which
were so cold,' wrote Katey.[30] Frank Beard had come with them. He
was no more hopeful than Steele, and Steele left. Beard stayed, and in
the morning Charley arrived. The London specialist they sent for
came and said there had been a brain haemorrhage, and everyone
understood there could be no good outcome. Mary Boyle appeared,

was seen by Charley and Georgina, and went away again. Nelly arrived, or returned, in the afternoon, and remained.[31] A long day went by. Soon after six in the evening Dickens gave a sigh, a tear appeared in his right eye and ran down his cheek, and he stopped breathing.

Henry arrived from Cambridge two hours later, distraught at having been told of his father's death by a railway porter. Dickens's sister Letitia Austin arrived. During the night, Mamie cut a piece of hair from her father's 'beautiful, dead head'.[32] Red geraniums and blue lobelias were brought into the dining room and banked around the body, and the windows left uncurtained to let in the sunlight. In the morning Katey went to London to tell her mother what had happened. The Queen, unaware of Dickens's marital situation, or politely following correct usage, had sent Catherine a telegram from Balmoral. Millais came to draw Dickens's dead face, already bound up by the undertakers, and the sculptor Thomas Woolner took a cast.

Dolby, reading of the death in the newspaper, went straight to Gad's Hill. He was kindly received by 'Miss Dickens and Miss Hogarth', who told him of Dickens's final moments. They asked if he would like to see the body, 'but I could not bear to do so. I wanted to think of him as I had seen him last. I went away from the house, and out on to the Rochester road. It was a bright morning in June, one of the days he had loved; on such a day we had trodden that road together many and many a time. But never again, we two, along that white and dusty way, with the flowering hedges over against us, and the sweet bare sky and the sun above us. We had taken our last walk together.'[33]

※

The funeral arrangements were troublesome and involved more than one change of plan. Charley and Charles Collins, knowing that Dickens had expressed a wish to be buried in the part of Kent he loved so well, began by approaching the vicar of the church of St Peter and St Paul in the nearby quiet village of Shorne, and it was agreed that he should be buried in the churchyard there, on the east side.[34] Then a pressing request was brought to Gad's from the Dean and Chapter at Rochester Cathedral that Dickens should be buried there – not outside as he had wanted, which was impossible, but in the St Mary's Chapel. Shorne was cancelled, Rochester agreed to, and a grave was dug.[35] At the same time Dean Stanley at Westminster Abbey wrote to a literary friend, Frederick Locker-Lampson, to say he was 'prepared to receive any communication from the family respecting the burial', but had heard nothing and felt it would be inappropriate to take the initiative himself. Locker-Lampson said he forwarded Stanley's note to Charley Dickens, but it failed to reach him. Meanwhile Forster was on his way from Cornwall, from which Georgina had summoned him by telegram. He arrived at Gad's on Saturday morning and was able to see Dickens in the still open coffin and to kiss his peaceful face.

On Monday *The Times* ran an editorial calling for Dickens to be buried in Westminster Abbey. This galvanized Forster and Charley, and at eleven o'clock they were in London to see Dean Stanley. The violence of Forster's grief was such that at first he was hardly able to speak. When he recovered his calm, he said, 'I imagine the article in *The Times* must have been written with your concurrence.' No, said the Dean, although he had given it to be understood privately that he would consent to burial in the Abbey should it be requested, and he added that now the article in *The Times* had appeared no further application was needed. Forster then explained to the Dean the conditions insisted on by Dickens in his will: that there should be three plain mourning coaches only, no funeral pomp of any kind and no public announcement of the time or place of his burial. The Dean agreed, but pointed out the difficulties of preserving secrecy. He said they must bring the body to the Abbey that night after the public had left the place, that the grave would have to be dug during the night, and the few mourners must be there at nine the next morning before the usual service at ten. Most of this was agreed to.

> Accordingly at six o'clock that evening I told the clerk of the works to prepare the grave. We went into the Abbey and by the dim light chose a spot near Thackeray's bust, and surrounded on various sides by Handel, Cumberland and Sheridan.[36] It was fortunate that such a

place remained vacant. I left him to make the grave, and retired to bed. At midnight there came a thundering knock at the door. My servant went to open it. It was a messenger from the *Daily Telegraph*, announcing that the body had been moved from Rochester, and that therefore the probability was that it was going to be buried in Westminster Abbey, and they wished to know at what time. My servant answered that I had gone to bed and could not possibly be disturbed.[37]

In fact the body in its oak coffin was carried in a special train from Higham early the next morning, 14 June, to Charing Cross. The family travelled on the same train and they were met by a plain hearse and three coaches. There are slightly varying accounts of who was present, but there were certainly the four children still in England, Charley, Mamie, Katey and Henry; also Letitia Austin, Georgina, Charley's wife Bessie and Dickens's nephew Edmund, Alfred's son; Forster, both the Collins brothers, Frank Beard and probably Ouvry.[38] Catherine Dickens was not invited. It is unlikely that Nelly was there although just possible that she took herself to the Abbey. George Sala gave the number of mourners as fourteen, 'with perhaps as many strangers who accidentally chanced to be present, gathered round the grave to take a last look at the coffin' – which suggests he was there himself.[39]

The great bell was tolled and the Dean and canons met the mourners and the coffin, carried through the cloisters into the nave. The doors were closed. There was no singing and no eulogy, just quiet organ music as a background to the reading of the burial service.

'Man that is born of woman hath but a short time to live, and is full of misery. He cometh up, and is cut down, like a flower; he fleeth as it were a shadow, and never continueth in one stay.' Forster wrote afterwards, 'The solemnity had not lost by the simplicity. Nothing so grand or touching could have accompanied it, as the stillness and silence of the vast Cathedral.'

⚜

A friend in America found words that expressed what everyone felt. 'Dickens was so full of life that it did not seem possible he could die,' wrote Longfellow, and went on, 'I never knew an author's death to cause such general mourning. It is no exaggeration to say that this whole country is stricken with grief.'[40] So America mourned with England. In London, at the Abbey, where the grave was left open for two days for the public to see the coffin lying five feet below the stone floor of Poets' Corner, thousands filed past, bringing the heart-felt, useless notes they had written for him, and offerings of flowers that filled up and overflowed the grave. In his will he had expressed his wish to have no memorial. Instead, he said, 'I rest my claims to the remembrance of my country upon my published works, and to the remembrance of my friends upon their experience of me.' Nothing could have been better. He was, and he continued to be, a national treasure, an institution, a part of what makes England England; and he continues to be read all over the world.

The unadorned gravestone in Westminster Abbey: Dickens wanted nothing but his name.

27

The Remembrance of My Friends
1870–1939

Forster grieved, beyond comfort. He went to Carlyle after the funeral, in tears and 'weeping every word', then illness overcame him and he retreated to his bed.[1] On 22 June he wrote to Charles Norton, 'I have not been able, nor shall be, to have speech on these matters with anyone. And to you for the present I will only further say that nothing in future can, to me, ever again be as it was. The duties of life remain while life remains, but for me the joy of it is gone for ever more.'[2] His duty was plain to him, and in October, while still obliged to continue his work for the Lunacy Commission, he started on his *Life of Charles Dickens*.

Of Dickens's 'young men' – not so young now – Sala wrote to Yates on 27 June, 'To me he was *everything* . . . In him I have lost all that I most highly reverenced and loved; and we are neither of us at an age, dear Edmund, to be able to replace such losses.'[3] He expressed a hope that Forster would write a biography, and meanwhile produced his own instant one, its best pages describing Dickens the London walker.[4]

The women closest to Dickens soon scattered. Mrs Tringham was seen no more at Windsor Lodge and the last rates were paid in July. Georgina gave her the pen Dickens had been writing with in his last days, and Forster transacted with her whatever financial business needed to be taken care of. She now had freedom and enough money to do as she pleased, and she went first to her sister Maria in Oxford, then to lodgings in Kensington, before taking the train for Paris with a maid at the end of August. If she hoped to visit friends, and the grave of a child, she was unlucky in her timing, because the Germans, at war with the French, were advancing on Paris as she arrived, and she had to leave quickly. Back in England she set off again by sea for

Italy, to spend the winter with the Trollopes at Villa Ricorboli, as she had done three years before. Thomas Trollope described a gay season in Florence, with Hans von Bülow offering evenings of Beethoven, Schubert and Schumann, and sightseeing trips into the Tuscan maremma. There was some gossip: a Florentine friend wrote to Browning explaining that Mrs Trollope had been highly paid by Dickens for her novels because she was Miss Ternan's sister, to which he replied, 'the relationship between Mrs T. and "Miss T." never crossed my mind.'⁵ Whatever conversations took place that winter between Mr T., Mrs T. and Miss T. about the man who had been a friend to all of them, they were not recorded.

In the spring of 1871 Nelly returned to Oxford, slim and youthful-looking in her black clothes. Her sister Maria organized parties and she made an impression on the undergraduates she met, as a well-read, high-spirited girl who enjoyed poetry and horse riding, had suffered a mysterious bereavement and was delicate. In the autumn she returned to Italy, and in December Mrs Annie Fields in Boston heard 'quite accidentally' that 'N. T.' was in Rome 'with Mrs Tilton', a friend of the Trollopes living in the Barberini Palace. By now Mrs Fields had been told a good deal about Nelly by her husband, and she wrote, 'I feel the bond there is between us. She must feel it too. I wonder if we shall ever meet.'⁶ Mysteriously she added, 'Where is Dickens. [*sic*]'

Georgina, Mamie and Katey returned to Gad's Hill from the Abbey together, Katey leaving her husband to look after himself in London.⁷ Dickens had decreed that the house should be sold. The contents of the library went to Charley, all his manuscripts to Forster, and his private papers and jewellery to Georgina, along with enough capital for her to live on comfortably. Georgy busied herself sending mementos to friends, saw that all the servants were given the small legacies he had left them, and went to Wellington Street to go through his personal papers there. In July the pictures were sold at Christie's, and at the end of the month Katey returned to her sick husband, and Georgy and Mamie left for a rented place at Weybridge, to be out of the way for the sale of furniture and wine at Gad's on 1 August, followed by the auction of the house.

To Georgina's horror, Charley made a successful bid for Gad's Hill. She complained that his presence at the auction deterred other bidders and kept the price down to £8,600, so that the sale put less into the total estate than it should have done. She did not want to see him at Gad's where she had lived with his father, especially considering that Charley had been the only one of the children to defy him over the separation, and had married in the face of Dickens's strongly expressed disapproval. For him to take over his father's place seemed wrong to her, but he was not prepared to be dictated to by Gina, as he called her, who was only ten years older than him. He had to take out a mortgage and sell his father's library, and she was angry again when he sold the chalet in which Dickens had worked, to be exhibited to the public. This she managed to prevent, and it was given to Lord Darnley and kept in Cobham Park.[8]

Georgina settled in London, in a house in Gloucester Terrace, Hyde Park, in the same district where she had lived with Dickens only six months before. She was forty-three, the age Catherine had been at the time of the separation, and she became the unofficial widow, religiously observing the anniversaries of Dickens's birth and death, choosing to spend Christmas alone to remember him, guarding his reputation and never doubting that the best part of her life was behind her. 'Nothing will ever fill up that empty place,' she told Annie Fields, 'nor will life ever again have any *real* interest for me.'[9] The Dickens children needed her care no longer, but she felt responsible for providing a home for Mamie, who, at thirty-three, came and went as she pleased, and for Henry during his university vacations. When Frank returned on leave from the Bengal Mounted Police, Georgy found him 'affectionate and pleased to see us . . . but I don't think he cares much about anyone'.[10] He speculated with his inheritance, lost most of it, chose not to return to India and was soon destitute. Georgy, his sisters and Henry helped him and he was found a job with the North West Mounted Police, sent to Canada and never seen again by any of them. He did not return to England and, like several of his brothers, died suddenly, of heart failure, in Moline, Illinois, in 1886, aged only forty-two. His funeral was paid for by the people of Moline.

Catherine Dickens told her daughter-in-law Bessie, Charley's wife, that she had already lived twelve years of widowhood and felt there was now nobody nearer to Dickens than she was.[11] She asked her daughters and sister to visit her at Gloucester Crescent, and she and Georgina spoke to one another for the first time since 1858. After this Katey was a frequent visitor, Mamie and Georgina occasional callers. Catherine needed comforting in 1872 when Sydney died at sea, only twenty-five years old, and always an affectionate son to her. Charley was devoted to his mother, and she was often at Gad's Hill, enjoying the company of her grandchildren; her grandson Charles Walter recalled later that people came to Gad's from all over the world 'to visit the home of my grandfather', and she may have felt some pride in her status then.[12] Two more daughters were born to Charley and Bessie during their years there, and the family was well liked in the neighbourhood.

Charles Collins died of cancer in 1873. The marriage had not been a success and Katey was too sensible to pretend to grieve for long. She was working hard at her painting, she had several admirers, and within six months of his death she married another fellow artist, Carlo Perugini, with whom she was happy.[13] Even the loss of their only child in infancy did not darken their days permanently. They lived a hard-working and sociable life among their artistic and literary friends and, although they never made much money, by the late 1870s Katey had established herself as a painter, and her pictures were accepted by the Royal Academy.

Forster was at Katey's wedding to Perugini, and gave her a generous gift of £150. He had spent the years since 1870 on his biography of Dickens, the three volumes appearing in the autumns of 1872, 1873 and 1874, and arousing intense interest. Earl Russell wrote to Forster of his delight and pain in reading, adding, 'I shall have fresh grief when he dies in your volumes.'[14] The revelations about Dickens's childhood, Forster's memories of over thirty years and his quotations from intimate letters gave his work an authority no one else's could have matched. On page after page he brought Dickens alive with 'the passionate fullness of his nature', his energy, charm and brilliance and also his anger and obsessiveness. He presented a genius but not a saint, and he suggested that the same forces that had driven him to achieve so much also drove him to break up his life – that the young Dickens's sense that his will could achieve everything he set out to do meant that, in the later years, the same strength of will became the agent of his own destruction. He said nothing about Nelly – he had her to consider as well as the family – but at the end of the third volume he set discretion aside enough to print Dickens's will, with its defiant naming of Ellen Lawless Ternan first among the legatees. It is a great book, as readable today as it was when it was first published, and it bears no sign that he was struggling with illness as he wrote it. His duty lovingly done, he lived less than another two years.

Forster died on 1 February 1876, at home in Palace Gate, Kensington, round the corner from St Mary Abbot's Church in which, on the day before, 31 January 1876, Nelly was married, in a white dress and with flowers in her hair, to one of the undergraduates she had met at Oxford in 1870. George Wharton Robinson, son of a gentleman, brought up by a widowed mother, had been in love with her for five years, in the course of which he had graduated and become a clergyman. He was twelve years younger than Nelly, but he didn't know it because she had reinvented herself, and she was now in her twenties. Her mother was dead, her sisters colluded with her, and she had learnt deception from a master. George was persuaded to become a schoolteacher and after a honeymoon in Italy they took over the running of a boys' school in Margate. She recovered from her delicate health and became a robust young matron. They had two children, Geoffrey, born in 1879, the adored son who filled the place of the son she had lost, and a daughter, Gladys, in 1884. Nelly helped in the school, organized concerts and plays with the pupils, and also entertainments in the town, put on to raise money for charitable purposes. She made a particular feature of her readings, a large number of them from Dickens.

She read *A Christmas Carol*, she read 'Our Housekeeping' from *David Copperfield*, she impersonated Mrs Jarley of the waxworks from *The Old Curiosity Shop*, she read from *A Tale of Two Cities*, from *Nicholas Nickleby*, from *Bleak House*, and more. This was her secret celebration of her old lover, and it went with her friendship with Georgina and Mamie, which was close enough for her to have written an elegy for the death of Mamie's dog, the famous Mrs Bouncer beloved of Dickens, in 1874. Both visited her in Margate and were introduced to friends. For Nelly's birthday in 1882 Mamie gave her a 'Charles Dickens Birthday Book' compiled by herself, inscribed 'to Nelly Robinson with the Editor's love and best wishes for March 3rd, 1882'.[15] Like her sisters, Georgina and Mamie tacitly accepted Nelly's new age (reduced in the 1881 census to twenty-eight, fourteen years less than her real age of forty-two). For her part, Nelly put it about that she had been a god-daughter of Dickens and a mere child when she knew him. She must have had nerves of steel in case Mamie or Georgina let drop any remark that undermined her story, but it was in all their interests to protect his reputation, and Georgina may well have appointed herself as the best person to watch Nelly and keep her from saying or doing anything to endanger it. Although Nelly's husband and children gave her the strongest reason for keeping silent about the past, she sometimes dropped hints – that she had been at the Staplehurst accident for instance – and she undoubtedly had letters in her possession that would have been worth a small fortune had she chosen to put them on the market.

Whatever mixture of watchdog and friendship there was in Georgina, she became genuinely and enduringly attached to Nelly and her children. In the summer of 1882, when she was holidaying in Boulogne with her nephew Henry's family, Nelly was also there with three-year-old Geoffrey, and he played on the sands with little Enid, Hal, Gerald and Olive Dickens. Nelly wrote their names into her 'Charles Dickens Birthday Book', and Mrs Henry Dickens later said she had been introduced to Mrs Robinson by Georgina.[16]

❦

Henry had married in 1878 and he prospered as a lawyer. Also in 1878 Charley fell ill, worn out with the effort of keeping up his income and commuting between Kent and London. He had never learnt to be the businessman his father had tried so hard to make him, and he had to sell Gad's Hill, move into the office in Wellington Street and farm out six of the seven children among relatives. In 1879 Catherine

Dickens died. During her last illness she gave her carefully stored letters from Dickens to Katey, asking that they should be preserved as evidence that he had once loved her. Katey kept them for twenty years before deciding to hand them over to the British Museum in 1899, with an embargo on their being shown before 1925.

In the year of Catherine's death the first of a four-volume edition of Dickens's letters, collected and edited by Georgina and Mamie, was published. Georgina wrote a biographical introduction to each year's letters without mentioning the separation between Dickens and Catherine or the turmoil and complications in his life. It was an achievement to put the letters together, and another kind of achievement to simplify the story behind them. Like Forster's biography, the letters were widely reviewed, read and admired. The last volume came out in 1882. Mamie's devotion to her father's memory was as great as her aunt's. Towards the end of her life she wrote, 'My love for my father has never been touched or approached by any other love. I hold him in my heart of hearts as a man apart from all other men, as one apart from all other beings.'[17] This did not keep her close to the rest of the family. By the 1880s Georgina decided she preferred to live alone, Mamie being so erratic and inconsiderate. Mamie moved to Manchester, where she attached herself to a clergyman and his wife, doing good works and, Georgina feared, drinking too much. Georgina and Katey disapproved of the clergyman and made occasional trips north to keep an eye on Mamie.[18]

Wills died in 1880. He wrote no memoir but he talked of the past with family and friends, and left letters from Dickens containing many references to Nelly. They were carefully gone through before being published in 1912, some wholly rejected, others cut or inked over.[19] Wills was friendly with Eliza Lynn Linton, who had been a contributor to the magazines and known Dickens well, and Wills may have been partly responsible for remarks in her memoirs, in which she wrote of Dickens having a secret history, of loving 'deeply, passionately, madly' and being 'tricked and betrayed' by someone 'cleverer, more astute, less straight than himself'. A straightforward woman herself, although reduced here to dropping hints, she said further that 'no one could move him; and his nearest and dearest friends were as unwilling to face as they were unable to deflect the passionate pride which suffered neither counsel nor rebuke.'[20] A different view of Dickens was given by Dolby in his charming *Charles Dickens as I Knew Him* of 1885, which entirely omitted his friendship with Madame, and indeed her existence. Leaving out the women in Dickens's life made appreciation easier. In 1887 Thomas Trollope published his memoirs, with no mention of his own wife's stage career or of his sister-in-law Nelly, but with a glowing tribute to Dickens: 'Of the general charm of his manner I despair of giving any idea to those who have not seen or known him . . . His laugh was brimful of enjoyment . . . He was a *hearty* man, a large-hearted man that is to say. He was perhaps the largest-hearted man I ever knew.'[21]

Charley went to America in October 1887 and had a success giving his father's readings from *Pickwick* and 'Dr Marigold'. 'I don't profess to like the idea of Charley's reading his Father's books, and I *cannot* believe it is anything remarkable,' wrote Georgina to Annie Fields.[22] On returning to England he gave up editing *All the Year Round*, went to work for the publishing house of Macmillan and served them well, writing biographical introductions to new editions of his father's works. In 1893 he closed down *All the Year Round*, which had run for thirty-five years. He wrote various affectionate reminiscences of his father, describing his eager restless energy, his enjoyment of singing and dancing, his skill as an actor, his liking for toasted cheese at the end of a meal, how he played games as though his life depended on his success, how comfortable he made Gad's Hill, and how he refused to allow advancing age to limit his activities.

The 1880s saw the deaths of Carlyle, a very ancient Macready and Wilkie Collins, who was looked after by Frank Beard following a stroke; and early in the 1890s the two Beard brothers, Tom and Frank, both died. The ranks of those who had known Dickens were thinning, and none of these men left any formal account of him, although he appears in Macready's diaries, published in 1912, and Carlyle had earlier expressed his love for 'the good, the gentle, high-gifted, ever-friendly, noble Dickens – every inch of him an Honest Man'.[23]

For some years the Robinsons' school in Margate flourished. Anthony Trollope came to give the prizes one year, and Georgina Hogarth another, alongside a local clergyman, William Benham. Benham, a middle-aged man with literary and theatrical tastes and a great love for the work of Dickens, had exchanged brief letters with him in 1866, and also got himself into the Abbey for the funeral. He was active in many spheres: chairman of the Margate School Board, raiser of money for charities, restorer of the church, lecturer on church history as well as on Dickens, regular preacher at Canterbury Cathedral and friend of the Archbishop. Benham and Mrs Robinson worked together to raise money for good causes, giving readings and putting on concerts. This led to private conversations in which he pressed her on her friendship with Dickens, and somehow persuaded her to reveal part of the truth. According to Benham she said Dickens had set her up in the house in Ampthill Square and visited her two or three times a week, that she came to feel remorse about the relationship, and that her remorse had made them both unhappy. If this was all she said, it was a sharply abbreviated account of their twelve years. She said too that she now loathed the thought of their intimacy, which was no doubt what was expected of a woman telling her priest about an unsanctified sexual relationship.

In 1886 George Robinson became ill or had a breakdown – it is hard not to think this was connected with Nelly's indiscretions – and the school was given up. The family moved into lodgings in London, where he did some teaching, and the children were sent to boarding school. They were living in Sutherland Avenue in Maida Vale in 1892 when Thomas Trollope died, and after this Nelly helped her sister Fanny write a life of his mother, the earlier Frances Trollope, and also translated a travel book about Zermatt into English; they were both well done.[24] Money was short, and in the mid-1890s the Robinsons moved to the country, near Reading (in 1897 she read *A Christmas Carol* in aid of poor relief at Tilehurst village hall). The next year Geoffrey, who had been prepared for the Army, got his commission and was posted to Malta. Later he served in Nigeria and Ireland.

In 1893 Dickens's last remaining sibling, Letitia Austin, died, aged eighty-four, a quiet and amiable old lady, leaving no written record of herself or her brother. Also in 1893 Benham met Thomas Wright, an established writer, who had announced he was doing research for a new biography of Dickens, and told him what he had gleaned from Nelly. Hearing of Wright's intentions, Sala wrote an article in the *Manchester Evening News* objecting, on the grounds that Forster's life said all that was needed except for 'circumstances connected with the later years of the illustrious novelist which should not and must not be revealed for fifty years to come at the very least'.[25] Georgina wrote to Wright asking him not to proceed with his life of Dickens. A collector of Dickens material, W. R. Hughes, told Wright he had been offered Dickens's letters to Nelly by a private vendor and refused to buy them, saying they could not have been acquired honestly and advising the vendor to burn them.[26] The letters were much talked about but nobody appears to have seen them. In 1895 Sala's autobiography mentioned the 'secret' and said that hardly anyone living knew of it now that Collins and Yates were dead. He should have known he was wrong. In 1897 Katey Perugini, who had been corresponding with Bernard Shaw about her mother's letters, wrote of *other* letters 'in which the real man *is* revealed, minus his Sunday clothes and all shams, and with his heart and soul burning like jewels in a dark place! I say there *may* be such letters and they may be one day given to the world' – although she had been assured that they had been burnt.[27] Katey doubted they had, but since the letters have never been found they must have been destroyed: bad for us, because his letters to Nelly would have explained a good many things and given us a clearer view of him, but Dickens would have approved. If he had had his way, no one would have seen any of his letters.

Nelly could have done with the money. All three Ternan sisters grew poorer as they aged. Fanny Trollope published her last novel in 1892, the year her husband died, leaving very little. Maria, who had long since left her husband and taken up an adventurous life as a painter, writer and foreign correspondent in Italy, retired to England in 1898, and by 1900 she was living with Fanny in Southsea, a district of Portsmouth. In 1901 Nelly sold the Houghton Place house in Ampthill Square that Dickens had given her, over Fanny's protests. Maria died in 1904, nursed by Fanny to the end, of cancer, which would kill both her sisters. The Robinsons moved to Southsea to be close to Fanny and kept their heads just above water by taking private pupils. Nelly was operated on for cancer in 1907 and recovered. Georgina Hogarth was a faithful correspondent, writing to Nelly and to her daughter Gladys.

Money was also short with most of Dickens's children now. Income from his books had been divided among them but it dried up as they came out of copyright.[28] Katey and Carlo Perugini depended mostly on what they could earn by selling their pictures, and there were years when it was very little. In 1896 Charley and Mamie both died in their fifties, and Charley's widow was left penniless, with five unmarried daughters; her son had been disowned by the family, allegedly for marrying a bar maid called Ella Dare, and was never mentioned again, although he lived until 1923. Bessie Dickens was given a Civil List pension of £100 a year, and when she died in 1908 the remaining four unmarried daughters were allowed to share it, giving them £25 a year apiece. Plorn, in Australia, went from failure to failure, first with the sheep station he bought, then as an MP, elected on his name, and after that in business. His wife left him and he took to gambling and asking for handouts, which Henry sent and got no thanks for, and he died in 1902, aged fifty, leaving unpaid debts. In 1900, incidentally, Dolby the faithful died in a paupers' hospital, the Fulham Infirmary, in London.[29] Georgina's income was steadily reduced as she lived on through her eighties, and she had to sell letters and memorabilia to keep going, although Henry was always there to support her when necessary.

Henry was the only one to prosper. He made a clear success of his legal career and brought up his seven children to follow in his industrious footsteps. He took a great interest in Dickensian institutions as they were established, first the all-male Boz Club in 1900, then the Dickens Fellowship in 1902, and then the Dickens's Birthplace Museum, which was established in the Portsmouth house in which Dickens was born when it was purchased in 1903. In 1904 he did readings from his father's work, and continued over the years to raise money for charitable causes in this way.[30] The *Dickensian* periodical magazine was founded in 1905 and, like the

Fellowship and the two museums (but not the Boz Club), it is still flourishing.

Nelly was widowed in 1910 – the year Canon Benham also died – and moved in with her sister Fanny. In the same year Alfred Dickens returned to England from Australia, having lost whatever money he made in business there, intending to lecture on his father's life and work. In 1911 Ethel Dickens, one of Charley's daughters who had been earning her living running a typing agency in Wellington Street, collapsed with exhaustion and made a public appeal for money, saying she and her unmarried sisters were destitute. The *Daily Telegraph* took up the story and a Christmas Fund was organized, aiming to raise £10,000 for their relief. Other members of the Dickens family were outraged by Ethel's cheek but the response was remarkable: £2,500 coming in from the United States, gifts from royalty, rich and poor proving how much the name of Dickens still meant to the public; and a trust fund was established for Charley's daughters. Alfred went to New York to speak in the centenary year, 1912, and there he dropped dead on 2 January – yet another Dickens son with a weak heart; his funeral, like his brother Frank's, was paid for by his American hosts. Celebrations in London were postponed, although in Portsmouth free teas for 1,000 children were given on Dickens's birthday. In America, Kate Wiggin published her account of the conversation she had struck up with Dickens when she was twelve and sat down next to him on a train in 1868.[31]

⚜

The friendship between Georgina and Nelly was important to both of them and strongly maintained. In 1913 Geoffrey was in Southsea with his mother when Fanny Trollope died, and Georgina, herself recovering from surgery, wrote to him:

> My dear Geoff, I must send a few words of sympathy to *you* as I know well what a loss you have sustained in the death of your Aunt . . . I am very thankful that you have been able to be with your dear Mother at this time of deepest sorrow to her – she tells me that you have been of the greatest help and comfort to her – God knows she must need both

help and comfort! I hope you may be able to stay on with her for a little while longer – I don't expect or wish her to make the effort of writing to me – But I shall be grateful if you will send me a note in a few days just to tell me how she is – and if she has as yet made any plans for the future.

I should have liked to have sent some flowers as a form of my affectionate remembrance of dear Fanny. But I have not heard where – or when – the funeral was to be – and I fear that the time must be past! If it is *not* so, (although I can't help hoping that the saddest of all days for your poor dear Mother is over) would you, dear Boy, be so very kind as to buy some flowers *from me* and place them on her coffin – and let me know later on what you paid for them. I won't write any more – I have not been very well – and my head is not very strong – and my writing is bad – but you will give my dearest love to your Mother and to Gladys and your dear self from your very affectionate old friend Georgina Hogarth.[32]

An eloquent letter for a woman of eighty-six, and it shows how close the bonds were between the two women who had shared their lives with Dickens, and shared his time and attention, fifty years before. Nelly died six months later, in April 1914, cared for by Geoffrey, who registered her age as sixty-five.[33] Mother and son loved one another dearly, yet he had no idea of her real age or her early life, that she and her sisters had been actresses, or of her years with Dickens. He would find out none of these things until the 1920s, because he re-enlisted on 5 August 1914, fought a tough war and continued to serve in the Army with Dunsterforce in Persia until 1920. Only on his return did he go through his mother's and aunt Fanny's papers and begin to understand how they had deceived everyone.

Georgina lived to be ninety-one, dying in April 1917, cared for by Henry and his wife. Katey's husband died at Christmas 1918, a great sorrow for her. Henry and Katey were now the only Dickens children left alive. They were also the most intelligent. Katey, called 'Lucifer Box' as a child by her father for her tendency to fire up, had been the last of his wanted children, and Henry was the son who surprised and delighted him at the end of his life. It was Katey who was most intent on speaking out about their father. When in the

1890s she told Bernard Shaw what she knew of her parents' separation, she said she wished someone would correct the prevailing view of Dickens as 'a joyous, jocose gentleman walking about the world with a plum pudding and a bowl of punch'.[34] In the 1920s, regretting that she had not written a proper account of him, conscious that she knew more about him than anyone else living, and that neither Nelly nor Georgina needed to be considered any longer, she decided to do something. Lucifer Box went into action.

She asked a young woman friend, Gladys Storey, known to her since 1910, to take down what she had to say about her parents, and from 1923 Miss Storey made notes of their conversations. If there was not much method in their procedure, what Miss Storey put down makes good sense. Katey spoke out as no one had done before, mixing love and anger, but clear in what she said. One of her objects was to do justice to her mother and to atone for her own failure to give her support at the time of the separation; but she also loved her father and was not out to blacken his name, only to tell the truth as far as she was able. Sometimes she went too far for Miss Storey, who wrote down her remark 'My father was not a gentleman – he was too mixed to be a gentleman' in her notes, but did not quote it when she came to write her book.[35]

Katey died in May 1929, and it took Miss Storey a decade to shape her material into a narrative, *Dickens and Daughter*. It was published in 1939, five years after Thomas Wright's *Life of Charles Dickens* had horrified his admirers with its revelations about the affair with Nelly. But he had not known Dickens, and this was the voice of Dickens's daughter. *Dickens and Daughter* was furiously attacked, although the attackers were somewhat discouraged when Bernard Shaw wrote to *The Times Literary Supplement* to say that Mrs Perugini had told him everything in the book forty years before. He accepted the truth of Miss Storey's account, and she passed on another piece of information to him: that Nelly lived her later life in fear of her children learning of her association with Dickens.[36]

Katey had been old enough to be a clear-eyed observer of the break-up of her parents' marriage. 'Ah! We were *all* very wicked not to take her part,' she said. 'Harry does not take this view, but he was only a boy at the time, and does not realize the grief it was to our mother, after having all her children, to go away and leave us. My mother never rebuked me. I never saw her in a temper. We like to think of our great geniuses as great characters – but we can't.' Of her mother, she said, 'My poor mother was afraid of my father. She was never allowed to express an opinion – never allowed to say what she felt.'[37] She praised her mother for her 'dignified and nobler course of silence' when her husband was making public statements.[38] She also said, 'My father was like a madman when my mother left home, this affair brought out all that was worst – all that was weakest in him. He did not care a damn what happened to any of us. Nothing could surpass the misery and unhappiness of our home.'[39]

'I know things about my father's character that no one else ever knew; he was not a good man, but he was not a fast man, but he was wonderful!' she said, her buts acknowledging the difficulty of making a definitive moral judgement on him.[40] Miss Storey described a day when she said dramatically, '"I loved my father better than any man in the world – in a different way of course . . . I loved him for his faults." Rising from her chair and walking towards the door, she added: "My father was a wicked man – a very wicked man." And left the room.'[41] She also reported Katey saying he did not understand women, and suggesting that any marriage he made would have been a failure.[42]

Everything she said about Nelly sounds credible, the 'small fair-haired rather pretty actress' who flattered her father and, while not a good actress, 'had brains, which she used to educate herself, to bring her mind more on a level with his own. Who could blame her? He had the world at his feet. She was a young girl of eighteen, elated and proud to be noticed by him.'[43] She said Dickens made a settlement on Nelly and kept an establishment with two servants for her at Peckham. She mentioned the son of Nelly and Dickens who had died in infancy.[44] The existence of the son was confirmed to Miss Storey by Henry Dickens, who told her 'there was a boy but it died', and also that Nelly's son Geoffrey had come to him to ask if it was true that his mother was Dickens's mistress 'and he had to admit it'.[45] The discoveries Geoffrey made about his mother, and the realization that she and his aunts had deceived him to the end of their lives, horrified and wounded him. He destroyed papers, told his sister not to talk to anyone about their mother and remained silent himself. He died in 1959, leaving no children, a sorrowful man.

Henry never wrote or spoke in public of these matters. His reminiscences of his father, which appeared in 1928, were outspoken about other things: his father's moods of depression and irritability, and the resentment of his brothers at the strict discipline imposed on them at home.[46] He also mentioned his father's 'strongly radical political views' and his laughing suggestion, mentioned earlier, that, 'his sympathies being so much with the French, he ought to have been born a Frenchman.'[47] A French Dickens defies the conventional view of him as an English national treasure, and he is that, but he is also something much wider. The whole world knows Dickens, his London and his characters. 'All his characters are my personal friends,' said Tolstoy, who kept his portrait hanging in his study and declared him to be the greatest novelist of the nineteenth century.

He left a trail like a meteor, and everyone finds their own version of Charles Dickens. The child-victim, the irrepressibly ambitious young man, the reporter, the demonic worker, the tireless walker. The radical, the protector of orphans, helper of the needy, man of good works, the republican. The hater and the lover of America. The giver of parties, the magician, the traveller. The satirist, the surrealist, the mesmerist. The angry son, the good friend, the bad husband, the quarreller, the sentimentalist, the secret lover, the despairing father. The Francophile, the player of games, the lover of circuses, the maker of punch, the country squire, the editor, the Chief, the smoker, the drinker, the dancer of reels and hornpipes, the actor, the ham. Too mixed to be a gentleman – but wonderful. The irreplaceable and unrepeatable Boz. The brilliance in the room. The inimitable. And, above and beyond every other description, simply the great, hard-working writer, who set nineteenth-century London before our eyes and who noticed and celebrated the small people living on the margins of society – the Artful Dodger, Smike, the Marchioness, Nell, Barnaby, Micawber, Mr Dick, Jo the crossing sweeper, Phil Squod, Miss Flite, Sissy Jupe, Charley, Amy Dorrit, Nandy, hairless

Maggie, Sloppy, Jenny Wren the dolls' dressmaker. After he had been writing for long hours at Wellington Street, he would sometimes ask his office boy to bring him a bucket of cold water and put his head into it, and his hands. Then he would dry his head with a towel, and go on writing.

Notes

Abbreviations

AYR	*All the Year Round*
Catherine D	Catherine Dickens
D	Charles Dickens
F	John Forster
GH	Georgina Hogarth
HW	*Household Words*
P	*The Pilgrim Edition of the Letters of Charles Dickens* (details for each volume can be found in the Select Bibliography)

Prologue: The Inimitable 1840

1. Dickens's words from his account written many years later, 'Some Recollections of Mortality', *AYR*, 16 May 1863. Other information from the report on the trial at the Old Bailey printed in *The Times*, 10 Mar. 1840.
2. D to F, [?15 Jan. 1840], *P*, II, p. 9. Taken from Forster's *Life of Charles Dickens*, I (London, 1872), Chapter 13.
3. There is a small discrepancy, however: in a letter written at the time he says he could not sleep on the night after the inquest, but in the 1863 account he says he dreamt of the face of the accused girl. 'Some Recollections of Mortality', *AYR*, 16 May 1863.

   Magdalen Asylums were well intentioned but not pleasant, and Dickens later formed a poor opinion of them when he saw a good many young women who emerged from their care during the 1850s, after he had set up the Home for Homeless Women. He thought they were too punitive in their attitudes, and did not feed the young women properly.

4. D to Richard Monckton Milnes, 1 Feb. 1840, *P*, II, p. 16.

5. D to F, [?Jan. 1840], *P*, II, p. 15; D to Mrs Macready, 13 Nov. 1840, *P*, II, p. 150.

6. Louis Prévost, a linguist who later worked at the British Museum. There are several payments to him from Dickens.

7. This is John Overs, to whom Dickens devotes a great deal of time and trouble over the years, advising him, helping him to place articles and finding him employment. Overs died at the age of thirty-six in 1844, leaving a wife and six children, whom Dickens continued to assist.

8. D to Catherine D, 1 Mar. 1840, *P*, II, p. 36; D to Thomas Beard, 1 June 1840, *P*, II, p. 77.

9. So his daughter Katey said: Gladys Storey, *Dickens and Daughter* (London, 1939), p. 223.

10. 'A Walk in the Workhouse', *HW*, 25 May 1850.

11. D to Jacob Bell, 12 May 1850, *P*, VI, p. 99.

12. Walter Bagehot in *National Review*, Oct. 1858.

13. He used the name in printed correspondence in *Bentley's Miscellany*, which he edited in 1837 and 1838, and during this period his old school-master sent him a silver snuff box inscribed 'To the inimitable Boz', 'Boz' being the name by which he first signed himself in print. With this encouragement, he began to refer to himself as 'the inimitable'.

14. Annie Thackeray, given in Philip Collins (ed.), *Dickens: Interviews and Recollections*, II (London, 1981), p. 177.

Part One

1 The Sins of the Fathers 1784–1822

1. Having been No. 13 Mile End Terrace, then No. 387 Mile End Terrace and then No. 396 Commercial Road, the property is now No. 393 Old Commercial Road.

2. John Dickens had met Huffam when first working in London. He had an official position as 'Rigger to His Majesty's Navy', having come to

official attention by rigging a privateer to fight against the French. The extra *h* in 'Huffham' was a mistake.

3. See article on ancestry of Dickens in the *Dickensian* [1949], based on research by A. T. Butler and Arthur Campling, assembled by Ralph Straus.

4. See Gladys Storey's *Dickens and Daughter* (London, 1939), pp. 33–4. But since Annabella Crewe was not born until 1814 and would hardly have memories before 1819, she cannot have remembered old Mrs Dickens complaining about her son. Perhaps she was passing on what she had been told by others.

5. His book collection was taken over by his son Charles in Chatham – see below.

6. Information about Frances Crewe from Eric Salmon's article in the *DNB*, and from Linda Kelly's *Richard Brinsley Sheridan* (London, 1997).

7. D reporting to F on his father's 'characteristic letter', written to Catherine Dickens, and other remarks by him, [?30 Sept. 1844], *P*, IV, p. 197.

8. An imagined episode could bring together Sheridan, aged thirty-three, with the housekeeper, aged thirty-nine, in a Crewe Hall back bedroom, and account for John Dickens's inheriting Sheridan's disastrous inability to live within his income, and Charles Dickens's passion for the theatre. Too good to be true, of course.

9. A private memorandum among Gladstone's papers after reading the Northcote–Trevelyan Report of 1853 goes: 'The old-established political families habitually batten on the public patronage – their sons legitimate and illegitimate, their relatives and dependents of every degree, are provided for by the score.'

10. The announcement read: 'On Friday, at Mile-end-Terrace, the lady of John Dickens Esq., a son.'

11. The source is her granddaughter Katey, given by Gladys Storey in *Dickens and Daughter*, p. 25.

12. No. 16 Hawke Street was, according to Gladys Storey in *Dickens and Daughter*, p. 40, a tiny house built without a front garden on a 'squalid little street'. Dickens told Forster that he remembered tottering about the front garden with his sister Fanny, with something to eat in his hand, watched by a nurse through the basement window: but it

cannot have been the first home, which he left long before he could walk, so perhaps it was the back garden of Hawke Street, or Wish Street. His other Portsmouth memory was of being taken to see the soldiers exercising.

13. *Mansfield Park* was written between 1811 and 1813 and published in 1814, so the Portsmouth she describes, which she knew from her brothers being at the naval school, is very much the place in which Dickens was born.

14. Forster, *The Life of Charles Dickens*, I (London, 1872), Chapter 1.

15. She died in 1893.

16. Forster, *Life*, I, Chapter 1 – he dates Dickens telling him this five years before the writing of *David Copperfield*, hence 1844. Dickens must have formed the phrases in his mind and kept them. In a speech given in 1864 Dickens talks about an old lady who 'ruled the world with a birch' and put him off print. But, by his own account, his mother taught him to read.

17. Quoted in Philip Collins, *Dickens: Interviews and Recollections*, I (London, 1981), p. 2, taken from Robert Langton's *The Childhood and Youth of Dickens*, first published in 1883.

18. The spasms of pain are likely to have been caused by a kidney stone, according to 'The Medical History of Charles Dickens' in Dr W. H. Bowen, *Charles Dickens and His Family* (Cambridge, 1956). His reading position is described in Gladys Storey's *Dickens and Daughter*, p. 44, presumably described by Dickens to his daughter Katey.

19. D to F, 24 Sept. 1857, recalling his childhood in Chatham, *P*, VIII, p. 452 and fn. 5.

20. In 1883 Alderman John Tribe, son of the old landlord of the Mitre Inn, said he had once possessed a note from his childhood friend Charles, written on John Dickens's card, saying 'Master and Miss Dickens will be pleased to have the company of Master and Miss Tribe to spend the Evening on . . .' *P*, I, p. 1.

21. Forster, *Life*, I, Chapter 7, quoting from a letter Dickens wrote to the press in 1838, after being attacked for editing Grimaldi's *Memoirs* without having seen him perform.

22. D to Mary Howitt, 7 Sept. 1859, *P*, IX, p. 119.

23. D to Cerjat, 7 July 1858, *P*, VIII, p. 598.

24. The stories of the recitation and of the snuff are from Forster's *Life*, I, Chapter 1, and would have been told him by Dickens himself.
25. A version of her appears in *The Old Curiosity Shop*, where she has no name until she is called 'the Marchioness' by Dick Swiveller.
26. D to F, [?27–8 Sept. 1857], *P*, VIII, p. 455.
27. A collection of essays by Oliver Goldsmith.

2 *A London Education 1822–1827*

1. Walking was the way all but the rich got about. 'We used to run to the doors and windows to look at a cab, it was such a rare sight': this is Dickens reminiscing about life in Camden Town and thereabouts in the 1820s, before the coming of the railways, in 'An Unsettled Neighbourhood', *HW*, 11 Nov. 1854.
2. Gladys Storey, *Dickens and Daughter* (London, 1939), p. 44 – she gives Harriet Ellen as her name.
3. See D to T. C. Barrow, 31 Mar. 1836, in which he recalls the visits he made and the affectionate relationship established. *P*, I, p. 144.
4. John Forster, *The Life of Charles Dickens*, I (London, 1872), Chapter 1.
5. He had the watch before her death, because he talks about having it in his pocket when he was at the blacking warehouse in his account of that time. Forster, *Life*, I, Chapter 2.
6. For his godfather's tip and for his getting lost, see 'Gone Astray', *HW*, 13 Aug. 1853.
7. My italics, from Forster, quoting Dickens's words, in his *Life*, I, Chapter 1.
8. The house was demolished in the late nineteenth century. Maples was built on the site, to be succeeded by the new University College Hospital.
9. Forster, *Life*, I, Chapter 2. Mr Micawber appears in *David Copperfield*, the novel Dickens wrote in the late forties, parts of which draw on his own experience; and Micawber is loosely based on John Dickens in that he cannot keep out of debt, that he moves quickly from despair to cheerfulness, and that he expresses himself in elaborate turns of phrase.
10. Ibid.
11. Ibid.

12. Ibid., Chapter 3.
13. William Dickens inherited £500 from his mother, who had already given him £750. John Dickens got £450.
14. Chandos Street is now called Chandos Place.
15. Forster, *Life*, I, beginning of Chapter 2.
16. Ibid.
17. See Michael Allen's arguments in the 'The Dickens Family in London 1824–1827', *Dickensian* (1983), p. 3, where Allen believes that Dickens went on working at Warren's until Mar. or Apr. 1825, i.e., for over a year. In the *Dickensian* (2010), pp. 5–30, he suggests a quite different timetable: that Charles started working at the blacking factory in Sept. 1823, moved to Chandos Street in Jan. 1824 – the same month his father was arrested – and left work in Sept. 1824. His arguments are based on impressive research but not conclusive.
18. Forster, *Life*, I, Chapter 2.
19. Ibid.
20. Ibid.
21. Ibid.
22. Dickens altered his intended finish to *Great Expectations* on a plea from Bulwer to let Pip and Estella be united in a happy ending, which seems a mistake, but even in the second version the tone of the narrative is not joyous or triumphant. See Chapter 21 below.

3 Becoming Boz 1827–1834

1. Richard Newnham, the retired tailor of Chatham who lent money to John Dickens, died in June and left £50 worth of shares to Letitia, in trust until her marriage.
2. Skimpole, based on Leigh Hunt, appears in *Bleak House* as the prototype of the artistic man who professes unworldliness, never pays tradesmen and expects his friends to settle his debts and keep him supplied with money. His house at The Polygon is semi-derelict but he lives in a room furnished with beautiful objects, flowers, fruit, etc., as Esther sees when Mr Jarndyce takes her to visit him.

    The Polygon also appears in Chapter 52 of *The Pickwick Papers*, when Mr Pickwick's solicitor's clerk, arriving at Gray's Inn just before ten o'clock, says he heard the clocks strike half past nine as he walked through Somers Town: 'It went the half hour as I came through the Polygon.'

The Polygon's most famous inhabitants had been William Godwin and his wife Mary Wollstonecraft, who died there in 1797 giving birth to their daughter, Mary, who grew up to marry Shelley. In the 1830s, when the Dickenses were there, the theatrical painter Samuel De Wilde and the engraver Scriven also lived there. The Dickenses left just before the coming of the railways running to their great stations close by at Euston (opened in 1838), King's Cross and St Pancras, when the air grew filthy and Somers Town descended into grim squalor. The Polygon was demolished in the 1890s and replaced by flats for railway workers, now also gone.

3. In Chapter 30 of *The Pickwick Papers* he describes 'office lads in their first surtouts, who feel a befitting contempt for boys at day-schools . . . and think there's nothing like "life"'.

4. In *The Pickwick Papers* he makes the 'salaried clerk' in the law office go 'half price to the Adelphi Theatre at least three times a week'.

5. See 'The Streets – Morning', first published in the *Evening Chronicle*, 21 July 1835, 'Sketches of London No. 17'.

6. The girls are from 'The Prisoners' Van', first published in *Bell's Life in London*, 29 Nov. 1835, now Chapter 12 of the section 'Characters' in the Oxford Illustrated *Sketches by Boz* (Oxford, 1957; my edition 1987). The boy on trial is from 'Criminal Courts', first published as 'The Old Bailey' in the *Morning Chronicle*, 23 Oct. 1833. Dickens returned to the court in *Great Expectations* in 1860.

7. George Lear left an account of Dickens at Ellis & Blackmore and suggests another clerk, Potter, certainly acted in the little theatre in Catherine Street, off the Strand, and possibly Dickens too.

8. From 'Private Theatres', first published in the *Evening Chronicle*, 11 Aug. 1835.

9. 'Gin Shops' first published 19 Feb. 1835 in the *Evening Chronicle*; and 'Miss Evans and the Eagle' first published 4 Oct. 1835 in *Bell's London Chronicle*, a weekly journal.

10. 'A Christmas Dinner' (originally called 'Christmas Festivities') appeared in *Bell's Life in London* on 27 Dec. 1835. Jolly grandpapa goes to buy the

turkey, grandmamma makes the pudding, all the accessible members of the family are invited, quarrels are made up, there is kissing under the mistletoe, blind man's bluff, songs are sung, wine and ale drunk and everyone is happy.

11. John Forster, *The Life of Charles Dickens*, III (London, 1874), Chapter 14, 'Personal Characteristics'. He also took Forster to the markets 'from Aldgate to Bow' on Christmas Eve.

12. Norfolk Street became Cleveland Street, as it is today.

13. He gave his Buckingham Street rooms, where he lodged in 1834, to young David Copperfield, and the habit of plunging into the Roman bath.

14. D to John Kolle, [?Aug. 1832], *P*, I, p. 9.

15. See *David Copperfield*, Chapters 38 and 43. Dickens remembered his shorthand, which was Gurney's, well enough to teach it to his son Henry forty years later.

16. 'Doctors' Commons' in *Sketches by Boz* first appeared in the *Morning Chronicle*, 11 Oct. 1836, and drew on a case on which Dickens reported on 18 Nov. 1830. The courts were moved in 1857, the buildings demolished later.

17. 'Shabby-genteel People' first published 5 Nov. 1834 in the *Morning Chronicle*.

18. Dickens's later love, Nelly Ternan, was also a third and petted daughter. Alfred Beadnell died in India in Aug. 1839, and his father sent Dickens letters relating to the death, receiving in return a long and curious letter of condolence: 'He spoke of returning to England where at best he could have been with you but for a time. He is now with you always. The air about us has been said to be thick with guardian angels, and I believe it, in my soul. The meeting with you to which he now looks forward is darkened by no thought of separation. The idea of death, which would seem to have been frequently present to him, is past – and he is happy.' D to G. Beadnell, 19 Dec. 1839, *P*, I, p. 619.

19. 'City of London Churches', *AYR*, 5 May 1860, reprinted in *The Uncommercial Traveller*. Michael Slater suggests the church was St Michael Queenhithe, which stood on what is now Huggin Hill, not far from the Beadnells' house in Lombard Street, and has since disappeared.

20. Gerald Grubb gives a persuasive account of Dickens's start as a parliamentary reporter in the *Dickensian* [1940], pp. 211–18, which relies

partly on the information Dickens gave himself to a German scholar, Dr Kunzel, in 1838, and also on his statement to Wilkie Collins that he made his start in the gallery 'at about eighteen'. Grubb also cites Samuel Carter Hall, who said Dickens at fourteen was bringing in 'penny-a-line stuff' to the *British Press*, where his father worked, in 1826.

21. From 'A Parliamentary Sketch', published in finished form in Dec. 1836 in *Sketches by Boz: Second Series* and based on two earlier pieces published in 1835. A portrait of a foolish MP, Cornelius Brook Dingwall, appears in a story called 'Sentiment' published in *Bell's Weekly Magazine* in 1834: 'He had a great idea of his own abilities, which must have been a great comfort to him, as nobody else had.'

22. D to F, [?15 Sept. 1844], *P*, IV, p. 194.

23. D to Lord Stanley, 8 Feb. 1836, *P*, I, pp. 126–7. Dickens told his American friends, the Fieldses, about this incident, and it is also mentioned by Forster in *Life*, I, Chapter 4.

24. According to Charles Kent, *Charles Dickens as a Reader* (London, 1872; reprinted with an introduction by Philip Collins, Farnborough, 1971).

25. D to Thomas Beard, 2 Feb. 1833, *P*, I, p. 15. Fn. gives Mrs Dickens's invitation, mentioning 'Quadrilles/8 o'clock'.

26. D to Maria Beadnell, 18 Mar. 1833, *P*, I, p. 17.

27. D to Maria Beadnell, 16 May 1833, *P*, I, p. 25.

28. D to Mrs Winter, 22 Feb. 1855, *P*, VII, p. 545.

29. D to Maria Beadnell, 19 May 1833, *P*, I, p. 29.

30. D to Mrs Winter, 22 Feb. 1855, *P*, VII, p. 543.

31. D to F, letter of 1845, cited in Forster's *Life*, II, Chapter 9.

32. D to F, 30–31 Dec. 1844, *P*, IV, p. 245.

33. Macready's diary for 5 Dec. 1838, given in Philip Collins (ed.), *Dickens: Interviews and Recollections*, I (London, 1981), p. 29.

34. Charles Kent, *Charles Dickens as a Reader*, p. 263.

35. Henry Rowley Bishop (1786–1855) was the composer, the American John Payne (1791–1852) the librettist. The story of a Sicilian peasant girl and a duke was immensely popular, and 'Home, Sweet Home' became one of the best known of all English songs.

36. *Amateurs and Actors* was a musical farce by Richard Brinsley Peake, who wrote much of Charles Mathews's material. The best character in it – and the most original – is the Charity Boy, always hungry, ill-used,

Geoffry Muffincap; he does not know who his parents are and calls himself a Norphan. He is hired as a servant for 18*d.* a week, his earnings all being taken by the master of the workhouse.

37. His own account in the 1847 preface to the cheap edition of *The Pickwick Papers*.

38. D to Henry Kolle, 3 Dec. 1833, *P*, I, p. 32. He described delivering the piece, 'A Dinner at Poplar Walk', to Johnson's Court in his introduction to the cheap edition of *Pickwick* in 1847.

39. Ibid.

40. It was usual for publishers to sell books from their premises.

41. The title of the story was changed when it was collected in *Sketches by Boz* (First Series) to 'Mr Minns and His Cousin'. One of the guests at the dinner is given an obsessive desire to tell stories about Sheridan, 'that truly great and illustrious man', but is prevented.

42. The novel could have been *Oliver Twist*.

4 *The Journalist 1834–1836*

1. It was George Stephenson's project and began to be built in the summer of 1836, a passenger railway running from Blackwall on the north bank of the Thames through the East End, with stations at Poplar, West India Dock, Limehouse, Stepney and Shadwell, terminating at the Minories. Part of it was built on a brick viaduct, part through a cutting, and it used cable haulage. It opened in July 1840. It is hard not to think that Dickens would have gone to look at it, especially since Austin became his brother-in-law in 1837. What Austin saw of the housing of the poor during the construction of the railway gave him his great interest in improving housing, and especially sanitation, which he shared with Dickens.

   Dickens did travel on it in 1848, describing it in 'The Chinese Junk' in the *Examiner*, 24 June 1848: 'You may take a ticket, through and back, for a matter of eighteen pence . . . The flying dream of tiles and chimney pots, backs of squalid houses, frowzy pieces of waste ground, narrow courts and streets, swamps, ditches, masts of ships, gardens of dock-weed, and unwholesome little bowers of scarlet beans, whirls away in half a score of minutes.'

The railway did not succeed and was overtaken by other lines. Although a few trains were still running up to 1951, all traces of it have now disappeared. See Nick Catford's admirable account of it on http://www.disused-stations.org.uk/p/poplar/index.shtml.

2. 1 July 1834, Hansard, from which the account of what was said in parliament given in this paragraph is derived.

3. Poulett Scrope, Thomas Attwood, Sir Henry Willoughby are the three speakers mentioned here. The quality of the arguments used against the amendments to the Poor Law is impressive. The debates, recorded in Hansard, can be read online.

4. One example: about 1860, Joseph Arch's father was dying, penniless after a life of labour. Arch took him in and his wife had to give up her charring to look after him. Arch asked parish guardians to give his wife 1s.6d. a week, 6d. less than she had earned, towards nursing his father. He was told that his father could go into the workhouse. He refused angrily, his father died in his home, and the Arches got into debt. See *Joseph Arch: The Story of His Life, Told by Himself* (1898).

5. The phrase is given by Forster in his *Life of Charles Dickens*, I (London, 1872), Chapter 4. The first piece to be signed 'Boz' was in the Aug. issue of the *Monthly* magazine.

6. D to Mitton and Thomas Beard, Nov., Dec. 1834, *P*, I, pp. 43–51.

7. Furnival's Inn was on the north side of Holborn, between Leather Lane and Brooke Street. It was demolished in 1906.

8. When Fred went out in the evening, Dickens would sometimes send for a friend to keep him company, as on 31 Dec. 1835 when he invited Mitton round, even though he was busy writing.

9. D to Thomas Beard, 16 Dec. 1834, *P*, I, p. 50; D to Henry Austin, 20 Dec. 1834, *P*, I, p. 51. The brandy could have come from his French employer.

10. D to Thomas Beard, 11 Jan. 1835, *P*, I, p. 53.

11. Dickens's view of the Hogarths' superior standing is suggested in a letter, D to Catherine Hogarth, [?June 1835], *P*, I, p. 67, in which he is asking her to be at the head of his breakfast table, and says, 'you might without difficulty head a more splendid one my dear girl, through life.'

12. Catherine Hogarth to her cousin, 11 Feb. 1835, Philip Collins (ed.), *Dickens: Interviews and Recollections*, I (London, 1981), p. 16.

13. D to Catherine Hogarth, [?June 1835], *P*, I, p. 64. In fact they were not able to marry until Apr. 1836.

14. D to Catherine Hogarth, [?late May 1835], *P*, I, p. 61. The letter suggests they have been engaged for three weeks. It was carried by Fred, and Dickens's warning seems to have been effective.

15. D to Catherine Hogarth, 4 Nov. 1835, *P*, I, pp. 86–7.

16. D to Catherine Hogarth, 1 Dec. and 16 Dec. 1835, *P*, I, pp. 100, 107. His experience in covering elections did nothing to encourage him to respect the political process: he saw violence, corruption and stupidity at work, which he would satirize in *Pickwick*.

17. D to Catherine Hogarth, 18 Dec. 1835, *P*, I, pp. 109–10.

18. D to Macrone, 27 and 29 Oct. 1835, *P*, I, pp. 83, 84.

19. D to Macrone, 7 Jan. 1836, *P*, I, p. 115.

5 *Four Publishers and a Wedding 1836*

1. D to Catherine Hogarth, [?21 or 22 Jan. 1836] and [?23 Jan. 1836], *P*, I, pp. 119, 120.

2. According to George Sala, a protégé of Dickens decades later, the woman Macrone treated so badly was his aunt Sophia, and her loan was never repaid.

3. Fletcher's bust of Dickens was exhibited at the RA, but Dickens thought it 'not like – *especially about the head.*'

4. See Chapter 3 above.

5. D to Catherine Hogarth, 11 Mar. 1836, *P*, I, p. 139.

6. D to Catherine Hogarth, [?20 Mar. 1836], *P*, I, pp. 140–41.

7. D to T. C. Barrow, 31 Mar. 1836, *P*, I, pp. 144–5.

8. He makes a joke of the difference between their rates of walking in a letter to his brother-in-law Austin, 7 Mar. 1844: 'I was coming to you yesterday, and brought Kate to walk half the way. She walked so impossibly slowly, that I was benighted at Covent Garden Market, and came back again.' *P*, IV, p. 64.

9. D to Catherine Hogarth, [?19 Nov. 1835], *P*, I, p. 95.

10. Lillian Nayder's biography of Catherine, *The Other Dickens* (Ithaca, NY, 2010), makes a brave attempt to establish her as a capable and intelligent woman, but essentially confirms the picture of a woman whose

capacities, whatever they might have been under different circumstances, were stifled in her marriage.

11. D to Hullah, 20 Sept. 1836, *P*, I, p. 175. Dickens won the argument, and the line remained in the Lord Chamberlain's copy and the published version.

12. Mary Scott Hogarth to her cousin Mary Hogarth, 15 May 1836, *P*, I, p. 689, in Appendix E.

13. 31 Dec. 1836, cited in Philip Collins (ed.), *Dickens: The Critical Heritage* (London, 1971), p. 10.

14. G. S. Lewes reported seeing the butchers' boys. Ibid., p. 64.

15. The agreement with Bentley for the novels was made 22 Aug. 1836, for editing the *Miscellany* on 4 Nov. 1836. Both agreements are given in *P*, I, p. 649.

16. Edward Street, north of the City Road, was the address, a long way for him to go.

17. John Pritt Harley, the son of a London draper, born 1786, apprenticed to another draper, worked as a law clerk and began to act in 1806, first as an amateur, then in companies in Kent and the north. From 1815 he worked in London, playing clowns in Shakespeare and farces, highly acclaimed and popular, and known as 'Fat Jack', being very thin. He acted with Macready at Covent Garden in 1838, joined Kean's company in 1850. He was taken ill during a performance and died a few hours later, penniless, in 1858.

18. It is Bill Sikes's description of Fagin in Chapter 13.

19. D to Chapman & Hall, 1 Nov. 1836, *P*, I, pp. 188–9.

20. D to Macrone's printer Hansard, [?1 Dec. 1836], *P*, I, p. 203 and fn. 1.

21. D to Bentley, 12 Dec. 1836, *P*, I, p. 211.

22. Forster's review appeared in the *Examiner*, a radical paper edited by Albany Fonblanque, already an admirer of Dickens's work, and to whom he had sent a 'Book of the Songs' in the opera.

23. D to Hullah, 11 Dec. 1836, *P*, I, p. 210.

24. D to Harley, 7 Apr. 1837, *P*, I, p. 246.

25. D to Thomas Beard, [?Dec. – close to Christmas – 1836], *P*, I, p. 217.

6 'Till Death Do Us Part' 1837–1839

1. D to J. P. Collier, 6 Jan. 1837, *P*, I, p. 220.
2. Mary uses the words 'dreadful trial' in describing her sister's feelings, which might mean the failure to breastfeed but seems more likely to refer to the birth. Mary Hogarth to her cousin Mary Scott Hogarth, 26 Jan. 1837, Philip Collins (ed.), *Dickens: Interviews and Recollections*, I (London, 1981), p. 17.
3. D's diary for 6 Jan. 1838, *P*, I, p. 630.
4. Dickens gives the warning in the preface to the 1848 edition of *Nicholas Nickleby*.
5. Only about forty-five pages of the manuscript of *The Pickwick Papers* have survived, and 480 – about two fifths – of the manuscript of *Oliver Twist*. They are the corrected first drafts sent to the printer.
6. D to Bentley, 24 Jan. 1837, *P*, I, p. 227.
7. Mary Hogarth to her cousin Mary Scott Hogarth, 26 Jan. 1837, Collins, *Interviews and Recollections*, I, p. 17.
8. The house is now the Charles Dickens Museum.
9. Bentley published his editions of Austen in 1833. Forster noted that Dickens had not read any Austen when writing *Nickleby*, and, according to a later friend, the poet Frederick Locker-Lampson, 'he did not unduly appreciate Miss Jane Austen's novels'. Collins, *Interviews and Recollections*, I, p. 117.
10. Bentley's recollection is given in *P*, I, p. 253, fn. 2.
11. Letter to unknown person, probably relation of Mary, June 1837, *P*, I, p. 268.
12. D to Thomas Beard, 17 May 1837, *P*, I, p. 259.
13. D to Richard Johns, 31 May 1837, *P*, I, p. 263.
14. D to Mrs Hogarth, 26 Oct. 1837, *P*, I, p. 323.
15. D to Richard Johns, 31 May 1837, *P*, I, p. 263; D to Thomas Beard, 17 May 1837, *P*, I, p. 260.
16. D to Thomas Beard, 12 May 1837, *P*, I, p. 258.
17. It is still standing, a private house behind walls, known as Wylds.
18. John Forster, *The Life of Charles Dickens*, I (London, 1872), Chapter 6.
19. Only those who subscribed to the 39 Articles of the Church of England could graduate.

20. Quotes from James A. Davies, *John Forster: A Literary Life* (New York, 1983), p. 9, and from Richard Renton, *John Forster and His Friendships* (London, 1912), p. 12.

21. Forster, *Life*, I, Chapter 4.

22. It is possible, although not certain, that she had engaged in several love-affairs and even borne children to her publisher, as well as having flings with Forster's friends Maclise and Bulwer. Her story ended tragically when she married the Governor of the Gold Coast in 1838, travelled with him to Africa and died there of poisoning, possibly suicide.

23. D to F, 3 Nov. 1837, *P*, I, p. 328.

24. D to F, [?26 July 1837], *P*, I, p. 287; D to F, [?Aug. 1837], *P*, I, p. 297; D to F, 24 Sept. 1837, *P*, I, p. 312; D to F, [?Oct. 1837], *P*, I, p. 317; D to F, 11 Jan. 1838, *P*, I, p. 353. This was their first visit to Jack Straw's Castle, according to Forster.

25. He put together a collection of entertaining pieces called *The Pic Nic Papers*. It was not easy to organize, and did not appear until 1841, but then provided £450 for Eliza Macrone and her two children. Macrone died in Sept. 1837, the *Sketches* were reissued from Nov. by Chapman & Hall in pink covers at one shilling a number.

26. Macready noted his disapproval in his diary: William Toynbee (ed.), *The Diaries of William Charles Macready*, II (London, 1912), pp. 45–6. For arguments on both sides see Robert L. Patten, *Charles Dickens and His Publishers* (Oxford, 1978), p. 85.

27. F to Bentley, 22 Oct. 1838, cited by Davies in *Forster*, from manuscripts in the Berg Collection, New York Public Library.

28. Forster, *Life*, I, p. 105.

29. Unsigned review in the *Examiner*, 2 July 1837. Auden said in his essay that Mr Pickwick ceases to be a god and becomes human at this point.

30. D to F, 2 July 1837, *P*, I, pp. 280–81. Dickens transposes the words of the marriage service, 'till death us do part'.

31. D to F, [?11 Feb. 1838], *P*, I, pp. 370–71.

32. D to F, [?6 Dec. 1839], *P*, I, p. 612.

33. D to F, 8 July 1840, *P*, II, p. 97.

34. D to J. Chapman, 3 Aug. 1842, *P*, III, p. 302. Dickens tells the story of his meeting with a 'most intimate friend' on his return from the US without naming him, but there can be no doubt about his identity.

7 Blackguards and Brigands 1837–1839

1. Galas had been held in 1827 and 1830, but in Dec. 1839 there was a row at the dinner when Forster, who wanted the proceedings to be dignified, told off some members for unseemly behaviour during a speech, leading to a mass exit and the demise of the club.

2. Clarkson Stanfield (1793–1867) was named for the abolitionist Thomas Clarkson, a friend of his father, who was a Catholic actor and author. Born in Sunderland, Clarkson kept to his father's religion. He was in the Navy at fifteen and served under Captain Charles Austen (younger brother of Jane Austen) for two years aboard the Sheerness guardship *Namur*. He took Turner to the lunch party Dickens gave to celebrate *Martin Chuzzlewit* in 1844. He painted particularly admired backdrops for Dickens's later amateur productions.

3. The Copyright Act ensured that every book published in the author's lifetime remained his property (in England at least) and for seven years after his death belonged to his heirs. Should the author die fewer than forty-two years after the first publication of a book, the heirs would be entitled to the copyright for forty-two years after his death.

4. Passages from *Queen Mab* were held to be blasphemous, the jury found against Moxon and he had to expunge them. This was in 1841. Moxon also published Lytton, Browning and Tennyson.

5. *The Pickwick Papers*, Chapter 56.

6. J. S. Mill in a letter, given by Philip Collins (ed.), *Dickens: Interviews and Recollections*, I (London, 1981), p. 18.

7. D to Bentley, 2 July 1837, *P*, I, pp. 282–3.

8. D to F, 11 Feb. 1838, *P*, I, p. 370.

9. Dickens wrote of this strongly worded warning from a Yorkshireman in his preface to the first cheap edition of 1848.

10. I have drawn on John Bowen's discussion of the economic theme in *Nickleby* in Chapter 4 of his excellent book *Other Dickens: Pickwick to Chuzzlewit* (Oxford, 2000).

11. Dickens recalls this time to Forster in a letter of 3 Sept. 1857: see Chapter 19, p. 285.

12. House and streets are long since gone.

13. D to G. H. Lewes, [?9 June 1838], *P*, I, p. 403.
14. D to F, 2 Oct. 1838, *P*, I, p. 439.
15. D to Bentley, 3 Oct. 1838, *P*, I, p. 439.
16. *Edinburgh Review*, 68 (Oct. 1838), pp. 75–97, anonymous but by Thomas Henry Lister, quoted in Philip Collins (ed.), *Dickens: The Critical Heritage* (London, 1971), p. 72.
17. *Oliver Twist*, Chapters 40, 46.
18. D to F, 2 Nov. 1838, *P*, I, p. 449.
19. As she noted in her diary for 30 Dec. 1838 and 1 and 3 Jan. 1839, cited by Kathleen Tillotson in her edition of *Oliver Twist* (Oxford, 1966), p. 400.
20. There was no dedication to Forster until 1858, when Dickens dedicated the complete Library Edition of his works to him.
21. D to F, 4 Jan. 1839, *P*, I, p. 491.
22. D to Bentley, text as given by F, 21 Jan. 1839, *P*, I, pp. 493–4.
23. The diary is given in *P*, I, p. 640. In Mar. 1838 Dickens mentions Pepys's Diary in an unpublished letter to the *Miscellany*, *P*, I, p. 382. He owned Braybrooke's five-volume edition.
24. D to F, 1 Mar. 1839, *P*, I, p. 515.
25. D to Catherine D, 5 Mar. 1839, *P*, I, p. 517, also letters to Forster and Mitton.
26. D to Catherine D, 5 Mar. 1839, *P*, I, p. 523.
27. Later known as badminton, a game played with shuttlecocks.
28. D to F, 11 July 1839, *P*, I, p. 560; D to Mitton, 26 July 1839, *P*, I, p. 570.
29. D to Macready, 26 July 1839, *P*, I, p. 571.
30. The diary is given in *P*, I, this entry p. 642.
31. D's diary for Sun., 22 Sept. 1839, *P*, I, p. 643.
32. John Forster, *The Life of Charles Dickens*, I (London, 1872), Chapter 6.
33. They were published on 10 Feb. 1840 and no one seems to have attributed them to Dickens at the time.
34. These exchanges described in Robert L. Patten, *Charles Dickens and His Publishers* (Oxford, 1978), pp. 95, 97, 110–11.
35. He raised the idea of a visit to the US in a letter to the American publisher Putnam in Aug. 1838, *P*, I, p. 431, and on 14 July 1839 wrote to Forster from Petersham mentioning his idea that he might go there to write 'a series of papers descriptive of the places and people'. *P*, I, p. 564.
36. D to W. Upcott, a book collector, 28 Oct. 1839, *P*, I, p. 594.

37. The house has long since been demolished, but there is a plaque commemorating Dickens's residence on the south side of the Marylebone Road.
38. D to Thomas Beard, 17 Dec. 1839, *P*, I, p. 619.
39. D to W. Upcott, 28 Dec. 1839, *P*, I, p. 623.

Part Two

8 Killing Nell 1840–1841

1. D to Landor, 26 July 1840, *P*, II, p. 106.
2. Carlyle to his brother John, 17 Mar. 1840, Charles Richard Sanders (ed.), *The Collected Letters of Thomas and Jane Welsh Carlyle*, XII (Durham, NC, and London, 1985), pp. 80–81. Count D'Orsay was famous as a dandy, more Regency than Victorian in his style.
3. See Philip Collins (ed.), *Dickens: Interviews and Recollections*, I (London, 1981), p. 74 and fn. Also Arthur S. Hearn in the *Dickensian* (1926), pp. 25–9. I have collected more variants.
4. Thomas Trollope in his memoirs, and Marcus Stone, on p. 50 of his MS memoir at the Charles Dickens Museum, adding that he saw him using a pince-nez. Percy Fitzgerald also describes 'the strained eyes, peering through the gold-rimmed glasses, always of strong power; the face bent down to the manuscript which lay on the table', quoted in Collins's introduction to his *Interviews and Recollections*, from 'Memories of Charles Dickens' (1913), p. 77.
5. F to D, 16 Jan. 1841, *P*, II, p. 187, fn. 4.
6. D to F, 3 Nov. 1840, *P*, II, p. 144; D to F, 12 Nov. 1840, *P*, II, p. 149.
7. D to Cattermole, 22 Dec. 1840, *P*, II, p. 172. George Cattermole (1800–1868) was an antiquarian painter, son of a Norfolk squire, friend of Forster. He married in 1839 a distant cousin of Dickens through his mother's family, and spent his honeymoon at Richmond that Aug., when Dickens lent him many books and also his pony carriage.
8. D to Macready, 6 Jan. 1841, *P*, II, p. 180; D to Maclise, 14 Jan. 1841, *P*, VII, p. 823.
9. D to F, [?8 Jan. 1841], *P*, II, pp. 181–2. The italics are mine.

10. D to Maclise, 27 Nov. 1840, *P*, II, pp. 158–9. He had the grace to ask Maclise to burn his cross letter, but it survived.

11. Cattermole's illustration shows her lying in a comfortable bed and looking surprisingly plump for a thirteen-year-old who is supposed to have wasted away.

12. 26 Nov. 1840, William Toynbee (ed.), *The Diaries of William Charles Macready*, II (London, 1912), pp. 100–101.

13. D to F, [?17 Jan. 1841], *P*, II, p. 188.

14. D to Cattermole, 14 Jan. 1841, *P*, II, p. 184.

15. Extracts from *The Old Curiosity Shop* are from Chapters 34, 34, 36.

16. A remark given to Nell's grandfather, written in the manuscript of *The Old Curiosity Shop*, but deleted in proof.

17. The Marchioness saves Dick's life by nursing him through illness, and her evidence against the Brasses foils their plot with Quilp. Dick sends the Marchioness to boarding school to be educated, after which they marry and settle in Hampstead. Macready's education of his young working wife may be thought of here, and it points forward to Eugene and Lizzie in *Our Mutual Friend*.

18. Eleanor Emma Picken, later Eleanor Christian, published 'Reminiscences of Charles Dickens from a Young Lady's Diary' in the *Englishwoman's Domestic Magazine*, 10 (1871), pp. 336–44, under the initials of her married name, E. E. C. Her second article, 'Recollections of Charles Dickens, His Family and Friends', appeared in *Temple Bar*, 82 (1888), pp. 481–506.

19. Elizabeth M. Brennan suggests this timetable in her critical edition of *The Old Curiosity Shop* (Oxford, 1997), p. l, n. 127.

20. *Barnaby Rudge*, Chapter 62.

21. In the *Tablet*, 23 Oct. 1841.

22. Lord Jeffrey to Cockburn, 4 May 1841, *P*, II, p. 260, fn. 3. Jeffrey, editor of the *Edinburgh Review* from 1803 to 1829, was one of the most powerful and respected critics in the land, and an early and fervent admirer of Dickens. This was their first meeting.

23. Lord Gardner's chief interests were hunting and shooting, and his place in society was assured since he had been Lord of the Bedchamber to both William IV and Queen Victoria, who was fond of him. Although he promised to marry Julia when his wife died, there is no record of the

marriage, but she claimed there was one, and the children were received into society. The sons could not inherit their father's title, but the youngest, Herbert, entered parliament as a Liberal in 1885 and had a distinguished career, serving in Gladstone's government. He was raised to the peerage as Lord Burghclere in 1895. Information from George Martelli, *Julia Fortescue, afterwards Lady Gardner, and Her Circle* (privately printed, 1959).

24. D to Maclise, 16 Aug. 1841, *P*, VII, p. 831. An extract and facsimile of this letter appeared in a Sotheby catalogue in July 1987 but the present whereabouts of the original is not known.

25. Robert L. Patten, *Charles Dickens and His Publishers* (Oxford, 1978), p. 127.

26. An anal fistula is usually caused by an abscess. What happens is that a hole in the rectum produces a new path for the contents of the bowel, opening somewhere near the anus. Symptoms are likely to be throbbing and constant pain, irritation of the skin round the anus, fever and pus or blood when passing stools and a general feeling of being unwell. The treatment is for the surgeon to cut open the fistula and scrape or flush it out. It is then laid open and flattened. The surgeon must take care not to damage the anal sphincter. It is likely to take one or two months to heal. Mercifully, it rarely recurs.

27. D to Jeffrey, [?8 Dec. 1841], *P*, II, p. 442.

28. D to D'Orsay, 13 Dec. 1841, *P*, II, p. 497.

9 Conquering America 1842

1. Robert L. Patten, *Charles Dickens and His Publishers* (Oxford, 1978), p. 128. Dickens wrote saying he would visit them, and did so, meeting Henry Carey, now retired. They gave Dickens copies of their editions of his books and other presents, and he bought more books from them, but in July 1842, after his return to England, he declared publicly that he would have no more dealings with American publishers. *P*, III, p. 259, fn. 3, and see below in this chapter.

2. As he told Macready later, 22 Mar. 1842, *P*, III, p. 156.

3. For example, he was toasted as such at the celebratory dinner at Hartford on 7 Feb. 1842, K. J. Fielding (ed.), *The Speeches of Charles Dickens: A Complete Edition* (Brighton, 1988), p. 24.

4. Given in preface to *P*, III, p. xii.

5. D to Fred Dickens, 3 Jan. 1842, *P*, III, p. 7.

6. Pierre Morand, a commercial traveller, was a fellow passenger from whose account of the voyage this is taken, *P*, III, p. 9, fn. 1.

7. Catherine D to Fanny Burnett, 30 Jan. 1842, *P*, III, p. 629.

8. Richard Dana's journal records initial hostility and later concedes that Dickens was impressive, *P*, III, pp. 38–9, fn. 1. W. W. Story mentioned the rowdyism, *P*, III, p. 51, fn. 2.

9. Among their members were James Russell Lowell and James T. Fields, both of whom became good friends of Dickens later.

10. Fielding, *The Speeches of Charles Dickens*, pp. 19–21.

11. D to F, [?4 Feb. 1842], *P*, III, p. 50.

12. D to Mitton, 31 Jan. 1842, *P*, III, p. 43.

13. William Wetmore Story, lawyer, sculptor, essayist and friend of Henry James, to his father Joseph Story, Judge of the US Supreme Court, 3 Feb. 1842, *P*, III, p. 51, fn. 2.

14. D to F, 17 Feb. 1842, *P*, III, pp. 71, 72; D to Maclise, 27 Feb. 1842, *P*, III, p. 94, fn. 9.

15. See D to F, 6 Mar. 1842, *P*, III, p. 101.

16. Poe had praised *The Old Curiosity Shop* for its 'chaste, vigorous, and glorious imagination'. Dickens later corresponded with Moxon about Poe, and may have spoken to other English publishers, but failed to find any for him. D to Poe, 27 Nov. 1842, *P*, III, pp. 384–5.

17. D to the Mayor of Boston, J. Chapman, 22 Feb. 1842, *P*, III, p. 76.

18. D to Mitton, 26 Apr. 1842, *P*, III, p. 212; D to F, 24 to 26 Apr. 1842, *P*, III, pp. 204–5.

19. Catherine D to Fred Dickens, 4 Apr. 1842, *P*, III, p. 189, fn. 4.

20. He is chiefly remembered for having fifteen children, the largest number of any President. He was a slave-owner on his tobacco plantation, and went on to support the secession of the Southern states in 1861, the year of his death.

21. D to David Colden, 10 Mar. 1842, *P*, III, p. 111.

22. D to Fonblanque, 12 [and ?21] Mar. 1842, *P*, III, p. 119.

23. D to Sumner, 13 Mar. 1842, *P*, III, p. 127.

24. D to F, 22 Mar. 1842, *P*, III, p. 135.

25. D to F, 28 Mar. 1842, *P*, III, p. 172; D to F, 22–3 Mar. 1842, *P*, III, p. 165.

26. D to F, 26 Apr. 1842, *P*, III, p. 211.

27. D to Macready, 1 Apr. 1842, *P*, III, pp. 173–6; D to F, 2 Apr. 1842, *P*, III, p. 180.

28. D to F, 15 Apr. 1842, *P*, III, pp. 193, 194.

29. Ibid., p. 193.

30. D to F, 24 Apr. 1842, *P*, III, p. 206.

31. Ibid., pp. 207–8.

32. D to F, 26 Apr. 1842, *P*, III, pp. 208–9.

33. Ibid., pp. 210, 211.

34. D to J. Chapman, 2 June 1842, *P*, III, p. 249.

35. D to F, 12 May 1842, *P*, III, p. 236; and Chapter 15 of *American Notes*.

36. D to F, 26 May 1842, *P*, III, p. 247.

37. See D to Felton, 31 July 1842, *P*, III, p. 293.

38. Landseer's letter to Maclise, 5 July 1842, given *P*, III, p. 264, fn. 3.

39. D's printed circular dated 7 July 1842, *P*, III, pp. 256–9, fn. 2, p. 258.

40. D to Lady Holland, 8 and 11 July 1842, *P*, III, pp. 262–3, 265–6.

41. D, signing his letter 'B' [for Boz?], to ed. of the *Morning Chronicle*, *P*, III, pp. 278–85.

42. D to Mitton, 21 Sept. 1841, *P*, III, p. 328.

43. Longfellow to Sumner, 16 Oct. 1842, *P*, III, p. 335, fn. 1.

44. Macaulay to Napier, 19 Oct. 1842, *P*, III, p. 289, fn. 2.

45. Figures given by Patten, *Dickens and His Publishers*, p. 131.

46. See *P*, III, p. 348, fn. 2.

47. Dana's journal cited *P*, III, p. 348, fn. 1. Poe in the *Southern Literary Messenger*, 9, 60 (Jan. 1843), *P*, III, p. 348, fn. 2.

48. On 11 August 1842 the *New York Evening Tattler* published a letter purporting to be from Dickens, addressed to the *Morning Chronicle* and dated 15 July 1842. Dickens was accused of ingratitude towards his hosts and 'unpardonable insolence' in criticizing the American people for their devotion to money-making. Appendix B, *P*, III, pp. 625–7.

49. D to Macready, 3 Jan. 1844, *P*, IV, p. 11.

10 *Setbacks 1843–1844*

1. *Martin Chuzzlewit*, Chapter 9.

2. Ibid.

3. D to F, 2 Nov. 1843, *P*, III, p. 590.

4. D to F, 28 June 1843, *P*, III, p. 516.

5. D to F, 1 Nov. 1843, *P*, III, p. 587.

6. John Dickens's letter to Chapman & Hall, 9 July 1843, *P*, III, p. 575, fn. 2.

7. D to Mitton, 28 Sept. 1843, *P*, III, pp. 575–6.

8. D to Esther Nash, 5 Mar. 1861, *P*, IX, pp. 388–90, and see fn. 2 on p. 390.

9. Angela Burdett-Coutts (1814–1906) was the youngest child of Sir Francis Burdett and Sophia Coutts, and inherited a fortune from her mother. She was always Miss Coutts to Dickens, since she did not become a baroness until after his death.

10. D to Coutts, 16 Sept. 1843, *P*, III, pp. 562–4.

11. D to F, 24 Sept. 1843, *P*, III, pp. 572–3.

12. D to F, 2 Nov. 1843, *P*, III, p. 590.

13. Jeffrey to D, 26 Dec. 1843, given in Philip Collins, (ed.) *Dickens: The Critical Heritage* (London, 1971), p. 148, which also prints Forster's very favourable review, pp. 184–6 (which said what Dickens himself believed, that it was his best book yet).

14. D to F, 2 Nov. 1843, *P*, III, pp. 590–91.

15. John Leech, London born (1817), Charterhouse and medical school at Barts, father bankrupted, became a professional artist and cartoonist for *Punch*. He shared radical views with Dickens, and his drawings of street children, published in 1840 with the satirical title 'Children of the Mobility', i.e., mob, or poor, are outstanding, and were admired by Dickens. The boy Ignorance and the girl Want, done for *A Christmas Carol*, are of their kind. Leech became a close friend, walking and holiday companion of Dickens, and he and his wife also shared holidays with the Dickens family.

16. D to Felton, 2 Jan. 1844, *P*, IV, p. 2.

17. Engels's great study of what he observed in Manchester, *The Condition of the Working Class in England*, was published in 1845.

18. Robert L. Patten, *Charles Dickens and His Publishers* (Oxford, 1978), p. 332.

19. Jane Carlyle to Jeannie Welsh [n.d. but after 26 Dec. 1843], given in *P*, III, pp. 613–14, fn. 4.

20. D to Mitton, 4 Jan. 1844, *P*, IV, p. 14.

21. D to Felton, 2 Jan. 1844, *P*, IV, p. 3.

22. D to T. J. Thompson, 15 Feb. 1844, *P*, IV, p. 46. T. J. Thompson was the wealthy brother-in-law of Dickens's solicitor Charles Smithson, partner of Mitton.

23. D to T. E. Weller, 1 Mar. 1844, *P*, IV, p. 58.

24. D to Fanny Burnett, 1 Mar. 1844, *P*, IV, p. 56.

25. D to T. J. Thompson, 28 Feb. 1844, *P*, IV, p. 55.

26. Christiana did not die young, but bore two famous daughters, both brought up in Genoa, Elizabeth born in 1846, who became a highly successful painter (as Elizabeth Butler), and Alice in 1847, who became the poet, Alice Meynell.

27. He would return to them again in 1859, for *A Tale of Two Cities*.

11 *Travels, Dreams and Visions 1844–1845*

1. The headmaster was Dr Joseph King, a friend of Macready, a remarkable teacher who started his boys on Homer and Virgil without rote grammar, and was assisted by his daughter Louisa. The school was at No. 9 Northwick Terrace, a fairly easy walk from Devonshire Terrace.

2. D to D'Orsay, 7 Aug. 1844, *P*, IV, pp. 166–7.

3. Ibid., p. 169.

4. Ibid., p. 170.

5. D to F, 6 Oct. 1844, *P*, IV, p. 199.

6. He was clean-shaven in Nov., as shown in Maclise's sketch.

7. D to Maclise, 22 July 1844, *P*, IV, p. 162.

8. D to F, [?30 Sept. 1844], *P*, IV, pp. 196–7.

9. F to Napier, 16 Nov. 1844, in the form of an addition to letter as a 'P.S. Very private', V & A Forster Collection, f. 686; *Edinburgh Review*, 81 (1845), pp. 181–9.

10. Forster's *The Life of Charles Dickens*, II (London, 1873), Chapter 6.

11. D to F, [?21 Oct. 1844], *P*, IV, p. 206.

12. Dickens told Miss Coutts he had only a very few days in town and was seeing no one, in a letter in which he asked her to help the children of his protégé John Overs, who had died leaving six young ones. He sent greetings to her companion, Miss Meredith, who was about to be married to Dr William Brown, and would be remaining as her close companion, friend and neighbour.

13. Dickens had known Jerrold slightly since the Shakespeare Club, and had asked him to contribute to *Bentley's Miscellany* in 1836. He was a friend of Stanfield, with whom he had served at sea as a boy, the son of an actor, apprenticed to a printer, and had educated himself, becoming a successful playwright in the 1830s, when *Black-Eyed Susan* ran for 300 nights. He turned to weekly journalism, ran his own papers and was a contributor to *Punch* from its start in 1841. Dickens admired him greatly, felt comfortable with him, and free to share his radical and anti-establishment ideas with him. Jerrold responded and by the 1840s had joined the inner circle of his friends.

14. Maclise to Catherine D, 8 Dec. 1844, *P*, IV, p. 234, fn. 6.

15. D to Catherine D, 2 Dec. 1844, *P*, IV, p. 235. He also wrote to his sister Fanny, 8 Dec. 1844, that he had written 'a decided Staggerer', and of the impression it had made on his friends and on the printers, who 'laughed and cried over it strangely'. He told her, 'When you come to the end of the 3rd part you had better send upstairs for a clean Pocket Handkerchief.' *P*, IV, p. 860 (in supplement).

16. D to F, [?13 Dec. 1844], *P*, IV, pp. 238–9.

17. D to F, 8 Jan. 1845, *P*, IV, pp. 246–7.

18. Granet is not an English-sounding name, but information about Augusta De La Rue is lacking.

19. Dickens gave this account to Sheridan Le Fanu, prolific writer of ghost and horror stories, 24 Nov. 1869, *P*, XII, p. 443. Le Fanu's *The Rose and the Key* appeared as a serial in *AYR* six months after the death of Dickens, in Jan. 1871.

20. Trinità dei Monti is the famous church at the top of the Spanish Steps in Rome. It has many side chapels with religious paintings and frescoes.

21. D to De La Rue, 27 Jan. 1845, *P*, IV, pp. 254–5.

22. D to De La Rue, 10 Feb. 1845, *P*, IV, p. 264.

23. D to De La Rue, 25 Feb. 1845, *P*, IV, p. 274.

24. Ibid.

25. D reminded Mme De La Rue of this in a letter of 17 Apr. 1846, *P*, IV, p. 535.

26. D to Lord Robertson, whom he had met in Edinburgh, 28 Apr. 1845, *P*, IV, p. 301.

27. He revealed this in a review of a book about ghosts by Catherine

Crowe, *The Night Side of Nature*, in the *Examiner*, 26 Feb. 1848, reprinted in Michael Slater (ed.), *The Dent Uniform Edition of Dickens's Journalism*, II (London, 1996), in which he speaks of a 'patient', and he drew De La Rue's attention to the review in a letter, *P*, V, p. 255.

28. D to Catherine D, 5 Dec. 1853, *P*, VII, p. 224.
29. D to Mitton, 14 Apr. 1845, *P*, IV, pp. 297–8, and 20 May 1845, *P*, IV, p. 312.
30. Dickens mentions the glass she gave him in a letter to her 27 Sept. 1845, saying he drank 'a bottle of old Sherry from it, in my dressing room' during an evening's performance, *P*, IV, p. 390. On 23 Dec. 1845 De La Rue noted that she felt the effect from eleven to half past, 'a most uncomfortable day I don't know whether D. mesmerized her on that day in London' – nor do we know. *P*, IV, p. 320, fn. 4.
31. D to De La Rue, 29 June 1845, *P*, IV, pp. 323–5.
32. D to Mme De La Rue, 27 Sept. 1845, *P*, IV, p. 391.
33. D to Le Fanu, 24 Nov. 1869, *P*, XII, p. 444.
34. See Chapter 18 below.
35. D to F, 12 Nov. 1844, *P*, IV, p. 217.
36. *Pictures from Italy*, 'An Italian Dream'.
37. *Pictures from Italy*, 'Rome'.

12 *Crisis 1845–1846*

1. D'Orsay to D, 6 July 1845, *P*, IV, p. 326 and fn. 3.
2. D to F, early July 1845, *P*, IV, p. 328.
3. Macready's diary for 2 and 3 Jan. 1846, William Toynbee (ed.), *The Diaries of William Charles Macready*, II (London, 1912), p. 318.
4. Mary Cowden-Clarke (1809–98), *Recollections of Writers* (1878), cited in Philip Collins (ed.), *Dickens: Interviews and Recollections*, I (London, 1981), pp. 90–96. A daughter of Vincent Novello, Italian-born music publisher, she was born in London and knew Leigh Hunt, the Lambs, Mary Shelley, Keats and Keats's schoolmaster John Clarke, whose son Charles Cowden-Clarke she married. She compiled a concordance to

Shakespeare and produced an edition of his plays. She persuaded Dickens to invite her to act with him as Mistress Quickly in *The Merry Wives of Windsor*. In 1856 the Cowden-Clarkes moved to Nice, then Genoa, where she died in 1898.

5. Augustus Egg (1816–63), London born, had an inheritance from his father and a good artistic training, and he specialized in literary and historical subjects with considerable success. He suffered from asthma but was a hard-working, sociable and generous bachelor, and he readily agreed to join in Dickens's theatricals and in the course of acting with Georgina formed an attachment to her.

6. Mark Lemon (1809–70) worked in a brewery and then a pub before becoming the spectacularly successful editor of *Punch* in 1841. He was as convivial as Dickens and also shared his humanitarian concerns, in 1843 publishing Thomas Hood's 'The Song of the Shirt', which tripled the circulation. Dickens first invited him to dinner in that year, and found that Lemon's passion for amateur theatricals was as great as his own. A close friendship was formed between the two men and their large families (Lemon had three sons and seven daughters).

7. D to Bulwer, 5 Jan. 1851, *P*, VI, p. 257.

8. D to F, [?1 or 2 Nov. 1845], *P*, IV, p. 423.

9. D to Evans, 26 Feb. 1846, *P*, IV, p. 506.

10. D to Coutts, 10 Sept. 1845, *P*, IV, pp. 374–5; also D to T. J. Serle, 23 Dec. 1845, *P*, IV, p. 454. For *Bleak House* see Chapter 17 below.

11. D to Coutts, 10 Sept. 1845, *P*, IV, p. 374; and D to Coutts, 1 Dec. 1845, *P*, IV, p. 442.

12. D to Mrs Milner Gibson, 28 Oct. 1845, *P*, IV, p. 418.

13. Mamie Dickens, *My Father as I Recall Him* (London, 1897), p. 16.

14. See Arthur A. Adrian, *Georgina Hogarth and the Dickens Circle* (Oxford, 1957), p. 15. He cites a letter to *The Times* from Lady Robertson Nicoll, 22 May 1943: 'My mother, when a girl, lived in Camden Square, and often used to see the Dickens family, then living in Devonshire Terrace. My grandmother used to relate laughingly that she always knew when a new Dickens baby was coming because Mrs Dickens would religiously take a walk twice a day, passing her window.' If this is true, she was not a bad walker, as it is a good mile from Devonshire Terrace to Camden Square.

15. Ibid., p. 14.

16. The play was Fletcher's *The Elder Brother*, 'Adapted for Modern Representation' by Forster and published by Bradbury & Evans. The rival brothers were played by Forster and Dickens.

17. The novelist Frederick Marryat wrote of 'a hundred more' in a letter given in *P*, IV, p. 466, fn. 2.

18. D to Coutts, 7 Jan. 1846, *P*, IV, pp. 466–7.

19. D to W. J. Fox, 23 Jan. 1846, *P*, IV, p. 479.

20. W. J. Carlton, 'John Dickens, Journalist', *Dickensian* (1957), p. 10.

21. D to F, 30 Jan. 1846, *P*, IV, p. 485.

22. D to De La Rue, 16 Feb. 1846, *P*, IV, p. 498.

23. D to Wills, 16 Feb. 1846, *P*, IV, p. 500; D to Evans, 24 Feb. 1846, *P*, IV, p. 503.

24. Philip Collins, in his *Dickens and Crime* (London, 1962; my edition 1994), p. 227, writes that Dickens addressed no other social question at such length as in these articles arguing the case against capital punishment; and that he changed his mind on the subject later.

25. D to Bradbury & Evans, 5 Mar. 1846, *P*, IV, p. 514. He was paid £722.5s.5d. on 29 Apr., rather a generous payment for his short editorship. He had received a payment from them on 31 Dec. 1845, £300 to cover the months of Jan. and Feb. 1846. On 6 Mar., they paid another £300 into his Coutts account.

26. D to Coutts, 22 Apr. 1846, *P*, IV, p. 539.

27. Macready, *Diaries*, II, p. 333.

28. R. B. Martin, *Tennyson* (Oxford, 1980), p. 302.

29. D to F, [?17–20 Apr. 1846], *P*, IV, p. 537.

30. Probably for £300, the rent paid for a year by the previous tenant.

31. D to Coutts, 26 May 1846, *P*, IV, pp. 552–6.

32. Ibid.

33. D to F, 13 or 14 June 1846, *P*, IV, p. 561.

34. D to F, [?22 June 1846], *P*, IV, p. 569.

35. D to Morpeth, 20 June 1846, *P*, IV, pp. 566–7. Lord Morpeth, seventh Earl of Carlisle, was Chief Secretary for Ireland 1835–41, a supporter of liberal causes and a poet. Either he failed to answer Dickens's letter or Dickens lost or destroyed his reply.

36. D to F, [?28 June 1846], *P*, IV, p. 573.

37. D to F, 5 July 1846, *P*, IV, p. 579.
38. D to F, 25–6 July 1846, *P*, IV, p. 592.
39. D to F, 7 Aug. and 9 and 10 Aug. 1846, *P*, IV, pp. 599, 600.
40. D to F, 30 Aug. 1846, *P*, IV, p. 612.
41. D to F, [?20 Sept. 1846], *P*, IV, p. 622.
42. D called them 'spectres' as an alternative to 'phantoms' in his letter to Sheridan Le Fanu about her case, 24 Nov. 1869, *P*, XII, p. 443.
43. D to F, 26 Sept. 1846, *P*, IV, p. 625.
44. Robert L. Patten, *Charles Dickens and His Publishers* (Oxford, 1978), p. 184.
45. D to F, 30 Sept. and 1 Oct., 3 Oct. 1846, *P*, IV, pp. 626, 627.
46. Forster, *The Life of Charles Dickens*, II (London, 1873), Chapter 13, 'Literary Labours at Lausanne'. D to F, 30 Nov. 1846, *P*, IV, p. 670. 'I may tell you, now it is all over. I don't know whether it was the hot summer, or the anxiety of the two new books coupled with D. N. [*Daily News*] remembrances and reminders, but I was in that state in Switzerland, when my spirits sunk so, I felt myself in serious danger.'
47. D to F, 11 Oct. 1846, *P*, IV, p. 631.
48. D to F, 13 Nov. 1846, *P*, IV, p. 656. The story was *The Battle of Life*, the fourth of the Christmas stories and possibly the worst.
49. D to F, 4 Nov. 1846, *P*, IV, p. 653.
50. Macready, *Diaries*, II, p. 347.

13 Dombey, with Interruptions 1846–1848

1. D to F, 30 Nov. 1846, *P*, IV, p. 669. Dickens went on 'there can be no better summary of it, after all, than Hogarth's unmentionable phrase' – which is 'French houses were gilt and bullshit', which is probably what Dickens wrote, according to the editors.
2. D to F, [?30 Nov. 1846], *P*, IV, p. 669. Charles Sheridan was the grandson of Richard Brinsley Sheridan, son of Thomas and brother of Caroline Norton, well known to Dickens. He died of tuberculosis a few months later, in May 1847, at the Embassy in Paris.
3. D to Jeffrey, 30 Nov. 1846, *P*, IV, p. 670.
4. D to F, 6 Dec. 1846, *P*, IV, p. 676.

5. Ibid.

6. The cheap edition put out all his existing titles in several different formats, as weekly numbers at a penny halfpenny, monthly parts at 7*d*., printed in double columns, and was intended for the very poor, 'to be hoarded on the humble shelf where there are few books', as he wrote in his prospectus. There were new frontispieces by well-known artists such as Leech, Browne, Stanfield, and new prefaces by Dickens. They went on sale in Mar. 1847. Sales were not as good as expected and by the end of 1848 Dickens acknowledged his disappointment, but they were kept going and in 1858 he did another cheap edition.

7. D to Catherine D, 19 Dec. 1846, *P*, IV, pp. 680–81.

8. D to F, 27 Dec. 1846, *P*, IV, pp. 685–6.

9. D to F, [?early Jan. 1847], *P*, V, p. 3.

10. D to Charles Sheridan, 7 Jan. 1847, *P*, V, p. 3.

11. Forster, *The Life of Charles Dickens*, II (London, 1873), Chapter 15. D to Countess of Blessington, 27 Jan. 1847, *P*, V, p. 15.

12. D to De La Rue, 24 Mar. 1847, *P*, V, p. 42.

13. Ibid.

14. Dickens provided an introductory note to 'the great French people, whom I sincerely love and honour', Robert L. Patten, *Charles Dickens and His Publishers* (Oxford, 1978), p. 257. He later told the French writer Paul Féval that his fondness for France began in 1847, when he observed, at the funeral of another writer, Frédéric Soulié, how widespread the respect for literature was there. Féval and Soulié were both writers of popular, sensational novels.

15. See R. H. Horne in *A New Spirit of the Age*, cited in Philip Collins (ed.), *Dickens: The Critical Heritage* (London, 1971), p. 202.

16. For Forster's remark, *Life*, II, Chapter 15, 'Three Months in Paris': 'He never spoke that language very well, his accent being somehow defective; but he practised himself into writing it with remarkable ease and fluency.' D to F, 10–11 Jan. 1847, *P*, V, p. 5; D to D'Orsay, 5 Apr. 1847, *P*, V, p. 53 ('Goodness! How horribly fast the months go by! The moment I am free I find myself a galley slave again. Courage Inimitable Boz! You loved him well enough, old fellow, after all!'). By 4 Aug. 1849, Dickens was able to write a well-expressed letter of

condolence in French to his friend Régnier on the death of his daughter.

17. *Dombey*, Chapter 3.
18. D to F, 4 Nov. 1846, *P*, IV, p. 653.
19. Maclise to F, 1843, V & A Forster Collection, 48.E.19.
20. Quoted in *P*, V, p. 227, fn. 1.
21. *Dombey*, Chapter 27.
22. Ibid., Chapter 49.
23. Ibid., Chapter 30.
24. For the little houses in Staggs's Gardens, with their runner beans, rabbits, hens and washing lines, and the railway lines that destroy the houses and transform the district with warehouses, taverns, lodging houses, improved stucco houses, clocks giving standardized railway time, and railway company buildings for the workers, see *Dombey*, Chapters 6 and 15.
25. *Dombey*, Chapter 20.
26. Wilkie Collins's remark was written into the margin of Forster's *Life*, noted by Frederic G. Kitton, *The Novels of Charles Dickens: A Bibliography and a Sketch* (London, 1897), pp. 109–10, and given by Patten in his *Charles Dickens and His Publishers*, pp. 207–8. Ainsworth's remarks in letters to friends are given *P*, V, p. 267, fn. 2.
27. Kathleen Tillotson, Humphry House, J. Hillis Miller and Stephen Marcus are among these critics.
28. D to GH, 9 Mar. 1847, *P*, V, p. 33.
29. Dickens told Miss Coutts about the attack, 16 and 23 May 1857, *P*, V, pp. 67, 70. He reverted to it fourteen years later in a letter to his sister Letitia, 25 Nov 1861, *P*, IX, p. 521.
30. D to M. Power, 2 July 1847, *P*, V, p. 111.
31. D to T. J. Thompson, 19 June 1847, *P*, V, p. 95.
32. D to Coutts, 27 Nov. 1847, *P*, V, p. 204; D to F, 2 Dec. 1847, *P*, V, p. 204.
33. D to GH, 30 Dec. 1847, *P*, V, p. 217; D to Alfred Dickens, 1 Jan. 1848, *P*, V, p. 221.
34. D to Thackeray, 9 Jan. 1848, *P*, V, p. 228. Dickens does not appear to have written to Thackeray about *Vanity Fair*, but he praised its 'treasures of mirth, wit and wisdom' when he spoke at a dinner for Thackeray in Oct. 1855, according to Forster's *Life of Charles Dickens*,

III (London, 1874), Chapter 2. Paul Féval, the French novelist who met Dickens in 1862 through Fechter, and later visited Gad's Hill, wrote in June 1870 that 'Dickens looked on *Vanity Fair* as an absolute masterpiece.' Philip Collins (ed.), *Dickens: Interviews and Recollections*, II (London, 1981), p. 293.

35. Forster, *Life*, II, Chapter 17.

14 *A Home 1847–1858*

1. Dickens's preface to the Library Edition of 1858 makes the point about Nancy.
2. D to John Overs, 27 Oct. 1840, *P*, II, pp. 140–41.
3. Interestingly in a letter to Georgina, D to GH, 5 May 1856, *P*, VIII, p. 110, in which he describes an argument with Miss Coutts's companion Mrs Brown about the morality of the French, which he defended so stoutly that she burst into tears – see Chapter 19 below.
4. *P*, V, p. 276, fn. 10, reporting Emerson's *Journals and Miscellaneous Notebooks 1847–1848*, M. M. Sealts (ed.), X (Cambridge, Mass., 1973), pp. 550–51.
5. Forster's *The Life of Charles Dickens*, II (London, 1873), Chapter 20.
6. D to Coutts, 3 Nov. 1847, *P*, V, pp. 182–3.
7. Dickens's Appeal, which he sent to Miss Coutts, 28 Oct. 1847, and which was printed as a leaflet, is given as Appendix D in *P*, V, p. 698.
8. D to Coutts, 15 Nov. 1848, *P*, V, p. 440. The lighter reading suggested by a matron, and approved by him, was the poetry of Wordsworth and Crabbe.
9. Jenny Hartley, *Charles Dickens and the House of Fallen Women* (London, 2008), a remarkable piece of research and writing. I have made use of some of her discoveries about the histories of the young women in this chapter.
10. D to Lord Lyttelton, 16 Aug. 1855, *P*, VII, p. 691. He went on, 'Something is gained when it is by itself, and is in a degree under the restraint of a sort of social opinion.'
11. D to Coutts, 23 May 1854, *P*, VII, pp. 335–6.
12. Ibid.
13. D to Coutts, 15 Nov. 1856, *P*, VII, p. 223.

14. D to Mrs Morson, 14 July 1850, *P*, XII, p. 625.
15. D to Mrs Morson, 31 Oct. 1852, *P*, XII, p. 644.

15 *A Personal History 1848–1849*

1. D to F, 14 and 22 Apr. 1848, *P*, V, pp. 279, 288–90.
2. D to F, 7 May 1848, the anniversary of Mary Hogarth's death, *P*, V, p. 299, and Forster's *The Life of Charles Dickens*, II (London, 1873), Chapter 20.
3. Forster says in the first chapter of his *Life*, from which the quotations are taken, that this was in Jan. 1849. It seems a long gap between the spoken and written account. Forster does occasionally misdate events in his book, and he may be mistaken here.

   In 1892 Charley Dickens stated, in his introduction to the Macmillan edition of *David Copperfield*, that his mother had told him that Dickens had read the account to her, telling her he intended to publish it as part of a planned autobiography, and that she had tried to persuade him not to, on the grounds that he had spoken harshly of his father and mother; and that he had accepted her advice and decided to make it into *David Copperfield*. Although this does not fit very well with Forster's dates and the writing of *David Copperfield*, there is no particular reason to doubt Charley's account.
4. *The Haunted Man* was the last of the five Christmas stories published as separate volumes. It is a slight improvement on its two immediate predecessors, but still not a successful piece of writing. The most interesting character in it is a terrifying and credible feral child.
5. D to F, 29 Feb. 1848, *P*, V, pp. 256–7. 'Long live the Republic! Long live the people! No more kings! Let's give our blood for liberty, for justice, for the cause of the people!'
6. D to Coutts, 24 May 1848, *P*, V, p. 317. This is the only source for his being offered the seat.
7. 'Judicial Special Pleading' appeared in the *Examiner*, 23 Dec. 1848, reprinted in Michael Slater (ed.), *The Dent Uniform Edition of Dickens's Journalism*, II (London, 1996), pp. 137–42. Dickens expanded his views on the Revolution of 1789 in *A Tale of Two Cities*.
8. See *P*, V, p. 481, fn. 4, giving Forster's letter to Leigh Hunt saying

Dickens had gone to Bath to celebrate Landor's seventy-fourth birthday and the bicentenary of the execution of Charles I.

9. D to Fanny Burnett, 3 May 1848, *P*, VII, pp. 886–7, and 9 May 1848, *P*, V, pp. 301–2.

10. D to Mitton, 1 July 1848, *P*, V, p. 358.

11. D to Macready, 4 Aug. 1848, *P*, V, p. 384.

12. Henry Burnett died, aged eight, in Jan. 1849.

13. D to Frank Stone, 5 Dec. 1848, *P*, V, p. 453. Augustus married Harriet Lovell, daughter of a deceased East India Company official.

14. Harriet Lovell was the daughter of Francis Lovell of Sloane Street, formerly Madras.

15. D to F, 31 Dec. 1848, *P*, V, p. 464.

16. D to Catherine D, 8 Jan. 1849, *P*, V, p. 471; D to F, 12 Jan. 1849, *P*, V, p. 474.

17. Forster's *Life*, II, Chapter 20.

18. D to F, late Jan. 1849, *P*, V, p. 483.

19. *David Copperfield*, Chapter 4.

20. Forster, *Life*, II, Chapter 20. Mrs Leavis assumed that Dickens had read *Jane Eyre* in her chapter on *David Copperfield* in *Dickens the Novelist*, but U. C. Knoepflmacher, in 'From Outrage to Rage: Dickens's Bruised Femininity', states, without giving a source, that 'Dickens denied having read *Jane Eyre* before he embarked on the story of David Copperfield', Joanne Shattock (ed.), *Dickens and Other Victorians: Essays in Honour of Philip Collins* (Basingstoke, 1988), p. 76. Philip Collins's *Dickens: Interviews and Recollections*, II (London, 1981), p. 289, gives a note by an unknown hand on Gad's Hill paper and thought to date from about 1860, which reads 'Dickens had not read *Jane Eyre* and said he never would as he disapproved of the whole school. [This apropos of Miss Hogarth saying it was an unhealthy book.]'

21. Charlotte Brontë read and liked *David Copperfield*, telling W. S. Williams, 13 Sept. 1849, 'I have read "DC"; it seems to me very good – admirable in some parts. You said it had affinity to "JE". It has, now and then – only what advantage has Dickens in his varied knowledge of men and things!' This was Brontë being modest, and surely the best parts of *David Copperfield* are the childhood, family and domestic scenes. T. J. Wise and J. A. Symington (eds.), *The Brontës: Their Lives,*

Friendships and Correspondence, III (originally pub. 1932; Oxford, 1980), p. 20.

22. The extracts from *David Copperfield* are from Chapters 2, 2, 2, 4, 10.

23. *David Copperfield*, Chapter 9.

24. Ibid., Chapter 12.

25. Ibid., Chapter 20. Later Dickens makes Rosa behave with coarse cruelty towards Em'ly, which seems to me to jar with the person shown in Chapter 20.

26. Ibid., Chapter 6.

27. Ibid., Chapter 46.

28. John Gross, *The Rise and Fall of the Man of Letters* (London, 1969), p. 31.

29. D to Richard Watson, 21 July 1849, *P*, V, p. 579.

30. Thackeray to Mrs Brookfield, 23 July 1849, Gordon N. Ray (ed.), *The Letters and Private Papers of William Makepeace Thackeray*, II (Oxford, 1945), p. 569.

31. See Appendix G to *P*, V, p. 706.

32. D to F, 30 Nov. 1849, *P*, V, p. 663.

33. Dickens's relations with the Garrick Club are hard to follow. He first joined in 1837, resigned in 1838, rejoined in Feb. 1844, resigned again in Dec. 1849, was a member again in 1854, resigned in the summer of 1858 over the Yates–Thackeray dispute, and resigned again in 1865 when Wills was blackballed.

16 Fathers and Sons 1850–1851

1. Jeffrey's letter dated 6 Jan. 1850 is given in *P*, V, p. 461, fn. 3.

2. In his essay of 1836, 'Sunday under Three Heads', reprinted in the Oxford Illustrated *The Uncommercial Traveller and Reprinted Pieces* (Oxford, 1958; my edition 1987), pp. 635–63.

3. D to F, 23 Jan. 1850, *P*, VI, p. 14.

4. D to Mrs Gaskell, 31 Jan. 1850, *P*, VI, pp. 21–2. *Mary Barton* was published in 1848 and was attacked in the Tory press.

5. D to Mrs Gaskell, 25 Nov. 1851, *P*, VI, p. 545; D to Mrs Gaskell, 13 Apr. 1853, *P*, VII, p. 62; D to Mrs Gaskell, 25 Feb. 1852, *P*, VI, p. 609; D to Wills, 11 Sept. 1855, *P*, VII, p. 700.

6. For the gypsy life, see D to Spencer Lyttelton, 20 May 1851, *P*, VI, p. 393.

7. 'A Detective Police Party' appeared in *HW* on 27 July 1850. Field was the inspiration for Inspector Bucket in *Bleak House*, and Dickens employed him to keep an eye on Bulwer's estranged wife Rosina when she threatened to cause trouble at one of their theatrical events. See Philip Collins, *Dickens and Crime* (London, 1962), for a good account of Dickens's relations with the police.

8. 'Old Lamps for New Ones' appeared in *HW*, 15 June 1850, and is reprinted in Michael Slater (ed.), *The Dent Uniform Edition of Dickens's Journalism*, II (London, 1996), pp. 242–8.

9. D to F, 21 Oct. 1850, *P*, VI, p. 195.

10. D to D'Orsay, 1 Oct. 1850, *P*, VI, p. 184: 'this desolate Isle of Thanet. But I like it because it is peaceful and I can think and dream here, like a giant' – Dickens's striking vision of himself and his imaginative power.

11. Quoted by Robert L. Patten, *Charles Dickens and His Publishers* (Oxford, 1978), p. 236, from the *Economist* of 3 Apr. 1852.

12. This was in July 1863 and proved unavailing. In 1865 Russell, again Prime Minister, offered him a place for a son, and Dickens replied he had none needing one.

13. Mary Boyle, born in 1810, was the daughter of a vice-admiral and granddaughter of an earl, and her elder sister was a maid of honour to Queen Adelaide. She had published two novels in the 1830s and a volume of poems in 1849. Dickens found her amusing, enjoyed acting with her and was fond of her, and probably impressed by her background, but he did not allow her to impose on him professionally. He took one piece she offered for *HW* and rewrote it substantially, and although he was gentle about it he seems to have made it plain that he wanted no more. She remained devoted to him to the end of his life, for example arranging deliveries of fresh flowers to him during his American tour of 1867–8.

14. See *P*, VI, p. 780, fn. 3, quoting Owen's private journal. Owen's attacks on Darwin proved disastrous to his own reputation.

15. Dickens had served on the committee of the Royal Literary Fund but disliked its proceedings and did not attend its dinners after 1841. The Guild also gave grants and built houses for needy writers on the Lytton Estate at Knebworth, but, despite the great efforts of Dickens, Forster and Bulwer, the scheme did not succeed.

16. See Catherine Peters's *The King of Inventors: A Life of Wilkie Collins* (London, 1991), p. 101.

17. D to Harriet Martineau, 3 July 1850, *P*, VI, p. 122.

18. D to Bulwer, 10 Feb. 1851, *P*, VI, p. 287. This Paris trip was made with Leech and Spencer Lyttelton, a raffish cousin of Mrs Watson.

19. D to Wills, 27 July 1851, *P*, VI, p. 448.

20. Henry F. Dickens, *Memories of My Father* (London, 1928), p. 26.

21. Balmoral House was close to Macclesfield Bridge crossing the canal, at the juncture of Avenue Road and Albert Road. It belonged to John Cheek, manufacturer. Dickens dealt through William Booth, an auctioneer, whose presumed son, another William Booth, reported that in 1911 a barge carrying gunpowder along the canal exploded, wrecking the house.

22. D to Henry Austin, 13 Mar. 1851, *P*, VI, p. 314.

23. D to Catherine D, 25 Mar. 1851, *P*, VI, p. 333. The death certificate stated that John Dickens had suffered a rupture of the urethra from old standing stricture and consequent mortification of the scrotum from the infiltration of urine. He was sixty-five.

24. D to F, 31 Mar. 1851, *P*, VI, p. 343.

25. D to Catherine D, 4 Apr. 1851, *P*, VI, p. 348.

26. Queen Victoria's journal entry is given *P*, VI, p. 386, fn. 4.

27. D to Augustus Tracey, 10 Oct. 1851, *P*, VI, p. 517. Tavistock House, built at the beginning of the nineteenth century, was demolished in 1901, and the offices of the British Medical Association built on the site.

28. D to Coutts, 25 Oct. 1853, *P*, VII, pp. 171–2. Dickens was writing from Milan, where he was travelling with Egg and Collins. Egg married in 1860 and died young in Algiers in 1863.

29. Ibid.

17 *Children at Work 1852–1854*

1. Young Marcus Stone, son of Frank Stone, first saw him when he was 'about forty' and remembers him thus: manuscript in library at Charles Dickens Museum, p. 49.

2. Wills's letter is quoted by Philip Collins in his *Dickens: The Public Readings* (Oxford, 1975), p. xx, and dated 30 Dec. 1853.

3. It was partly dictated and partly written in his own hand, and serialized at intervals in *HW* from Jan. 1851 to Dec. 1853. A slapdash but sometimes amusingly opinionated version of the nation's story told through the kings and queens, it ends in 1688 with the flight of the last bad Stuart – 'the Stuarts were a public nuisance altogether' – and welcomes the establishment of the Protestant religion in England. A final note hails Queen Victoria as 'very good, and much beloved'. In volume form it sold very badly.

4. The Megalosaurus was so named by William Buckland (1784–1856), geologist, palaeontologist and clergyman, in 1824 when he found the fossilized remains of a gigantic carnivorous lizard at Stonesfield in Oxfordshire and wrote the first full account of a fossil dinosaur.

5. Towards the end of Chapter 35. Esther is of course giving Dickens's view. Charlotte Brontë asked her publisher, 'Is the first number of "Bleak House" generally admired? I liked the Chancery part, but when it passes into the autobiographic form, and the young woman who announces that she is not "bright" begins her history, it seems to me too often weak and twaddling; an amiable nature is caricatured, not faithfully rendered, in Miss Esther Summerson.' T. J. Wise and J. A. Symington (eds.), *The Brontës: Their Lives, Friendships and Correspondence*, III (originally pub. 1932; Oxford, 1980), p. 322.

6. See *P*, IV, pp. 374–5, 454; *P*, III, p. 538, fn. 2; and more about Esther, *P*, III, *P*, IX.

7. The words were cancelled from the proof, presumably for reasons of space.

8. D to Coutts, 19 Nov. 1852, *P*, VI, p. 805.

9. Q. D. Leavis is the author of the chapter on *Bleak House* in *Dickens the Novelist* (London, 1970). This discussion is in Chapter 3 and on p. 137, and refers to Chapter 47 in *Bleak House*. She writes that the end of the chapter is 'not sentimental but ironical in effect and . . . in intention, since it is followed by the indignant and generous outburst with which Dickens ends the chapter'. But it does not strike me as ironical, and I can imagine Alan Woodcourt finishing the prayer silently for himself.

10. All the travel is by coach, and in Chapter 55 Dickens writes, 'Rail-roads shall soon traverse all this country, and with a rattle and a glare

the engine and train shall shoot like a meteor over the wide night-landscape, turning the moon paler; but, as yet, these things are non-existent in these parts, though not wholly unexpected.'

11. John Sutherland raises the question of the causes of the deaths of Captain Hawdon, Jo and Lady Dedlock in his *Who Betrays Elizabeth Bennet?* (Oxford, 1999), and gives well-argued and convincing answers. He suggests that Hawdon deliberately overdoses on opium, but that Dr Woodcourt testifies that it was unlikely to have been deliberate because he was in the habit of taking large doses, so avoiding a verdict of suicide and allowing him to be buried in consecrated ground. Lady Dedlock then also takes opium to finish her life close to his grave, after her long night walk, which would have exhausted and chilled but not killed her, and again Woodcourt avoids specifying the opium as the cause of death. As for Jo, Dr Sutherland agrees with Susan Shatto's view that he dies of pulmonary tuberculosis.

12. Unsigned review in the *Examiner*, 8 Oct. 1853, printed in Philip Collins (ed.), *Dickens: The Critical Heritage* (London, 1971), p. 290, and Forster's *The Life of Charles Dickens*, III (London, 1874), Chapter 1.

13. Forster, *Life*, III, Chapter 14.

14. Robert L. Patten, *Charles Dickens and His Publishers* (Oxford, 1978), p. 233.

15. For *Dombey* and *Copperfield* US sales see ibid., p. 209.

16. Ibid., p. 234.

17. D to Sheridan Muspratt, [?Feb. 1852], *P*, VI, p. 591 (Muspratt was a chemist, living in Liverpool, and married to an American actress, Susan, sister of Charlotte Cushman). D to Coutts, 16 Mar. 1852, *P*, VI, p. 627.

18. D to F, 30 June 1841, *P*, II, p. 313; D to Coutts, 10 Sept. 1845, *P*, IV, p. 373.

19. D to Coutts, 18 Apr. 1852, *P*, VI, p. 646.

20. D to Coutts, 14 Jan. 1854, *P*, VII, p. 245.

21. Dickens addressing the Warehousemen and Clerks' Schools in Nov. 1857, describing the sort of schools he disliked, K. J. Fielding (ed.), *The Speeches of Charles Dickens: A Complete Edition* (Brighton, 1988), p. 242.

22. *Unto this Last* in the *Cornhill Magazine*, 2 (Aug. 1860), p. 159, given in Collins, *The Critical Heritage*, p. 314.

18 *Little Dorrit and Friends 1853–1857*

1. Dickens uses the word 'imbecility' of Mrs Hogarth in 1854 and of the whole Hogarth family on 17 Apr. 1856, in a letter to Wills, *P*, VIII, p. 99.

2. D to Catherine D, 14 Nov. 1853, *P*, VII, p. 198.

3. D to Catherine D, 5 Dec. 1853, *P*, VII, p. 224.

4. D to De La Rue, 23 Oct. 1857, *P*, VIII, p. 472.

5. This was in May 1854.

6. D tells Cerjat about this 3 Jan. 1855, *P*, VII, p. 496, but the reading must have happened earlier, possibly in 1852, 1853 or 1854.

7. D to Coutts, 27 May 56, *P*, VIII, p. 125.

8. D to F, [?Jan.–17 June 1854], *P*, VII, p. 354.

9. D to F, 29 Sept. 1854, *P*, VII, p. 428.

10. D to F, 10 Sept. 1854, *P*, VII, p. 412.

11. Both characterizations made later, of Albert after his death and of Louis-Napoleon in 1865, but representing his consistently held views of them.

12. D to Mrs Watson, 1 Nov. 1854, *P*, VII, p. 454.

13. D to Cerjat, 3 Jan. 1855, *P*, VII, p. 495.

14. D to Cerjat, 'I fear that I see that for years to come, domestic Reforms are shaken to the root,' 3 Jan. 1855, *P*, VII, p. 495; D to Layard, 10 Apr. 1855, *P*, VII, p. 587; D to F, 27 Apr. 1855, *P*, VII, p. 599.

15. D to *Daily News*, 14 June 1855, p. 2, given in K. J. Fielding (ed.), *The Speeches of Charles Dickens: A Complete Edition* (Brighton, 1988), p. 199. Dickens made the same point in his speech to the Association on 27 June: that he did his public service through literature, and would not step outside that sphere of action.

16. D to F, 30 Sept. 1855, *P*, VII, p. 713.

17. D in Folkestone to Macready, 4 Oct. 1855, *P*, VII, pp. 714–16.

18. D to Wilkie Collins, 4 Mar. 1855, *P*, VII, p. 555; D to F, [?2–3 May 1855], *P*, VII, p. 608; D to Mrs Watson, 21 May 1855, *P*, VII, pp. 626–7; D to Coutts, 8 May 1855, *P*, VII, p. 613; D to Coutts, 24 May 1855, *P*, VII, p. 629. The manuscript, like those of all the later novels, is written in a much smaller and more closely packed hand, and much more heavily revised.

19. A comparison with the working conditions of his fellow novelist Flaubert, writing and rewriting *Madame Bovary* at the same time, immured in the silent retreat his father had provided for him in the Norman countryside, unencumbered by wife, children or any other personal or professional obligations, able to spend days over a single page, is instructive. Both novelists lived their characters' experience with them, grimacing as they wrote, but Flaubert could not endure interruptions and gave the world a perfectly considered, finished and polished piece of writing, while Dickens, who not only tolerated but often seemed to court distraction, pitted his prodigious inventive power against the demands of serialization and a tangled plot.

　　In spite of 'Madame Bovary, c'est moi' Flaubert presents his characters with godlike contempt, whereas Dickens mocked some and pitied some but approached them on the whole as fellow human beings.

20. D to Wills, 9 Feb. 1855, *P*, VII, p. 531.

21. D to F, 3 and [?4 Feb.] 1855, *P*, VII, p. 523.

22. Dickens starts the narrative 'thirty years ago', and repeats 'thirty years ago' at the beginning of Chapter 6, which introduces William Dorrit. On the next page we are told that he had entered the Marshalsea Prison 'long before'. We already know that Little Dorrit, encountered in Chapter 5, is twenty-two, and was born in the Marshalsea, which means her father must have begun his imprisonment about 1802. This places the main action of the story in the mid-1820s, the reign of George IV and the childhood of Dickens.

23. *Little Dorrit*, end of Book One, Chapter 13.

24. In the first chapter. Dickens started smoking cigarettes, recently introduced into France, in 1854. D to Wills, 21 Sept. 1854, *P*, VII, p. 418, asking him to send four bundles of them from his office to Boulogne.

25. Chapter 14, headed 'Little Dorrit's Party', has interesting preparatory notes: 'Out all night – *Woman in the street*. "If it really was a party now!" – *Burial Register for a pillow*. This was Little Dorrit's party <?after> The vice desertion, wretchedness of the great Capital. this was the party from which she went home.'

26. *Little Dorrit*, Book One, Chapter 31. Always a favourite scene of mine, and I was delighted to find that George Gissing, in his *Charles Dickens: A Critical Study* (London, 1898), writes of it, 'For delicacy of treatment,

for fineness of observation, this scene, I am inclined to think, is unequalled in all the novels.'

27. *Little Dorrit*, Book Two, Chapter 24.

28. D to F, 7 May 1857, *P*, VIII, p. 321, gives a slightly different account. The small boy he meets in Marshalsea Place is nursing a very big baby, tells Dickens about the history of the place, and calls the room's tenant Jack Pithick.

29. Sales of the one-volume edition of *Little Dorrit,* published in May 1857 at 21*s.*, were very good indeed: in eleven years it sold something like 85,000 copies.

30. D to Coutts, 11 Dec. 1854, *P*, VII, p. 482.

31. D to Coutts, 17 Nov. 1854, *P*, VII, pp. 468–9.

32. D to Coutts, 11 Dec. 1854, *P*, VII, p. 482. Maynard was her real name, but she was also known as Caroline Thompson, possibly taking the name of the father of her child, since Dickens sometimes referred to her as 'Mrs Thompson'.

33. Revd William Tennant to Coutts, 3 Feb. 1855, *P*, VII, pp. 918–19.

34. See *P*, VII, p. 917, fn. 2.

35. The *Pilgrim* editors refer to an account by Georgina of a visit to the Winters by Dickens with Catherine and herself in the year of her marriage, written in 1906, which fits so ill with his saying in his letter that 'four and twenty years vanished like a dream' that it seems unlikely. In 1845 he was abroad for the first six months, then busy with large-scale theatricals, the birth of his son Alfred (which would have kept Catherine at home for several weeks), writing his Christmas book and preparing to edit the *Daily News*. It would make a nonsense of his letters to Maria ten years later, in one of which he specifically says that 'the few opportunities that there have been of our seeing one another again, have died out' because he avoided them.

36. D to Mrs Winter, 10 Feb. 1855, *P*, VII, pp. 532–4.

37. D to Mrs Winter, 15 Feb. 1855, *P*, VII, pp. 538–9.

38. D to Mrs Winter, 22 Feb. 1855, *P*, VII, pp. 543–5.

39. D to Ella Winter, 13 Mar. 1855, *P*, VII, pp. 563–4.

40. D to Mrs Winter, 3 Apr. 1855, *P*, VII, p. 583.

41. D to Mrs Winter, 15 June 1855, *P*, VII, pp. 648–9.

42. D to Duke of Devonshire, 5 July 1856, *P*, VIII, p. 149.

19 *Wayward and Unsettled 1855–1857*

1. D to Wills, 21 Oct. 1855, *P*, VII, p. 724.
2. D to William Haldimand, 27 Nov. 1846, *P*, IV, p. 665, 'Paris is just what you know it – as bright, and as wicked, and as wanton, as ever.' Again in 1863 he found it 'immeasurably more wicked than ever', this time to Wilkie Collins, 29 Jan. 1863, *P*, X, p. 200. 'The time of the Regency seems restored, and Long live the Devil seems the social motto,' which suggests openly displayed sexual licence, hard drinking, greed and gambling.
3. D to GH, 16 Feb. 1855, *P*, VII, p. 540.
4. D to Wills, 24 Oct 1855, *P*, VII, p. 726. This is Dickens's (French translation: 'Ah! The famous writer! Monsieur bears a distinguished name ... I am honoured and interested to see Monsieur Dick-in' and 'That Madame Tojair (Todgers) ... How funny she is, and exactly like a lady I know in Calais'). A translation of *Chuzzlewit* was serialized in the *Moniteur* from Jan. to Oct. 1855.
5. D to F, 27 Jan. 1856, *P*, VIII, p. 37.
6. D to F, 24 Feb. 1856, *P*, VIII, p. 63. Dickens must have known that Lamartine, now poor and living quietly, had been one of the leaders of the revolution that established the Second Republic in France in 1848, had expected to be elected President and seen instead the rise of Louis-Napoleon and his own extinction as a political voice. He had nevertheless pushed forward the causes of the abolition of slavery and the death penalty. Dickens admired and liked him, but his example confirmed the wisdom of his own refusal as a writer to engage directly in politics.
7. D to F, 20 Jan. 1856, *P*, VIII, p. 33. But see below, D to F, 15 Aug. 1856.
8. D to F. O. Ward, 14 Jan. 1852, *P*, VII, p. 575. In Dec. 1851 a bloody *coup d'état* established Louis-Napoleon as President with dictatorial powers. Mass arrests of his opponents followed, and many were exiled without trial. In Nov. 1852 he declared himself Emperor, calling himself Napoleon III. Dickens did not live to see the end of his reign in Sept. 1870, when the French were defeated by the Prussians.
9. Dickens had met Louis-Napoleon at Miss Coutts's as well as at D'Orsay's in London in the 1840s, and always disliked him. But D'Orsay was the

son of a Napoleonic general, and when he moved to France in 1849 he hoped to be given a position by Louis-Napoleon. Dickens saw D'Orsay in Paris in 1850 and 1851, and early in 1852 he was appointed Directeur Générale des Beaux Arts, only to die in July of the same year.

10. D to Macready, 4 Oct. 1855, *P*, VII, pp. 715, 716. Dickens wrote more freely to Macready than to anyone else about his political despair.

11. D to GH, 5 May 1856, *P*, VIII, p. 110.

12. D to F, 15 Aug. 1856, *P*, VIII, p. 178. Forster prints it, and the *Pilgrim* editors reproduce it, with the word 'natural' in line 4 ('the hero of an English book is always uninteresting – too good – too natural, &c.') – but 'unnatural' makes better sense of the passage.

13. Things did not change until Hardy challenged 'the doll of English fiction' in *Far from the Madding Crowd* (1874) and *Tess of the D'Urbervilles* (1891) – both bowdlerized by editors who serialized the novels – and showed *Jude the Obscure*'s sexual and marital problems (in 1894). Disapproving English critics accused Hardy of writing like Flaubert, whose *Madame Bovary* was published in 1857.

14. Dr Brown died in Pau, in south-west France, in Oct., and his body had to be embalmed and taken back to England for the funeral in Nov. D to Wills, 28 Oct. 1855, *P*, VII, p. 728.

15. D to Wills, 10 Nov. 1855, *P*, VIII, p. 741.

16. D to Wills, 30 Dec. 1855, *P*, VII, p. 774.

17. See Robert L. Patten, *Charles Dickens and His Publishers* (Oxford, 1978), p. 251.

18. D to F, 13 Apr. 1856, *P*, VIII, p. 89.

19. D to Wilkie Collins, 22 Apr. 1856, *P*, VIII, p. 95.

20. D to Wills, 27 Apr. 1856, *P*, VIII, p. 99.

21. In *Sunny Memories of Foreign Lands* (1854). D to GH, 22 July 1854, *P*, VII, p. 377.

22. D to Fred Dickens, 12 Dec. 1856, *P*, VIII, p. 236.

23. Patten, *Dickens and His Publishers*, p. 240.

24. When the wedding was planned Dickens would have expected to be still in Boulogne, and was in London only because of the diphtheria epidemic there. On the other hand, crossing the Channel would not have kept him away from any occasion at which he wished to be present, so there must have been some problem or

disinclination, whether Forster's or his; or more likely the bride may have wanted a very quiet wedding, since she had a severe speech defect (mocked by Dickens to Georgina in a letter, 14 Nov. 1860, *P*, IX, p. 399). Eliza Crosbie (1819–94) was the daughter of a naval officer, her first husband, Henry Colburn, a publisher for whom Forster had edited Evelyn's diaries.

25. Dickens wrote two long articles in *HW* attacking the evidence given by Inuit hunters to Dr John Rae and ridiculing the idea that British explorers could have sunk to cannibalism. In 1997 the Inuit account seems to have been vindicated when the bodies of some of the men were found, and clear evidence of cannibalism discovered; but the matter is still disputed.

26. D to Coutts, 3 Oct. 1856, *P*, VIII, p. 199.

27. See the photograph of the acting group taken in Albert Smith's garden on 12 July 1857 (see third inset).

28. See D to Coutts, 10 July 1857, saying the boys were 'just home from Boulogne after a year's absence'. *P*, VIII, p. 372.

29. D to F, [?3–4 Jan. 1857], *P*, VIII, p. 251.

30. D's orders to his manservant John Thompson, given in *P*, VIII, p. 254, fn. 3.

31. D to Sir James Tennent, 9 Jan. 1857, *P*, VIII, p. 256.

32. D to Mary Boyle, 7 Feb. 1857, *P*, VIII, pp. 276–7.

33. See *P*, VIII, p. 261, fn. 4, quoting letter of William Howitt, 15 Jan. 1857.

34. D to Cerjat, 19 Jan. 1857, *P*, VIII, p. 265.

35. Fred's letter of 7 Feb. 1857, given in *P*, VIII, p. 277, fn. 3.

36. D to Henry Austin, 15 Feb. 1857, *P*, VIII, pp. 283–4.

37. D to Macready, 15 Mar. 1857, *P*, VIII, p. 302.

38. D to F, [?mid-Apr. 1857], *P*, VIII, p. 317. There is a mention of *Pickwick* in 'Amos Barton' which must have particularly pleased Dickens, where the gloomy evangelical clergyman 'thinks the immense sale of the "Pickwick Papers", recently completed, one of the strongest proofs of original sin'.

39. D to F, [?5 Apr. 1857], *P*, VIII, p. 309.

40. D to Stanfield, 20 May 1857, *P*, VIII, p. 328.

41. D to Mrs Brown, 28 Aug. 1857, *P*, VIII, p. 422.

42. Edna Healey, *Lady Unknown: The Life of Angela Burdett-Coutts* (London, 1978), pp. 135–6.

43. C. B. Phipps to D, 5 July 1857, *P*, VIII, p. 366, fn. 1.

44. D to Coutts, 20 July 1857, *P*, VIII, p. 381.

45. D to Coutts, 10 July 1857, *P*, VIII, p. 372.

46. 'The Licence of Modern Novelists' was published in the *Edinburgh Review*, 104 (July 1857), pp. 124–56, anonymously, but known to be the work of Fitzjames Stephen. Dickens published his reply, 'Curious Misprint in the Edinburgh Review' in *HW*, 16 (1 Aug. 1857), pp. 97–100. As Philip Collins points out in his *Critical Heritage* (London, 1971), p. 366, Stephen's brother Leslie commented that Fitzjames himself later expressed views about the English system of government and the need for reform that were not so different from those of Dickens. What Fitzjames Stephen found objectionable was the rough caricaturing of civil servants, which is what makes the comedy and the strength of the satire in *Little Dorrit*. Other critics complained of its being duller and darker than his earlier novels.

47. Emmeline Montague had acted with Dickens in his theatricals, and recalled his energy, his lavish way with gin punch, his irritability and restlessness. She found Mrs Dickens a delightful hostess.

48. So Katey told Gladys Storey, *Dickens and Daughter* (London, 1939), p. 127.

49. So Dickens told Mrs Watson later, 7 Dec. 1857, *P*, VIII, p. 488.

50. Francesco Berger described this in his *Reminiscences, Impressions, Anecdotes* (London, 1913).

51. D's description to Coutts, 5 Sept. 1857, *P*, VIII, pp. 432–4.

52. D to Mrs Brown, 28 Aug. 1857, *P*, VIII, p. 422.

53. D to Wilkie Collins, 29 Aug. 1857, *P*, VIII, p. 423.

54. D to Coutts, 5 Sept. 1857, *P*, VIII, pp. 432–3.

55. D to F, [?3 Sept. 1857], *P*, VIII, p. 430.

56. D to F, 5 Sept. 1857, *P*, VIII, p. 434.

Part Three

20 Stormy Weather 1857–1859

1. D told Henry Austin, who was putting the house in order for him, 'It is a life business (I hope)'. 26 Sept. 1851, *P*, VI, p. 494.

2. D to Wilkie Collins, 21 Mar. 1858, *P*, VIII, p. 536.

3. Philip Collins's *Dickens: The Public Readings* (Oxford, 1975) gives the texts. The reading from *Dombey and Son*, 'Little Dombey', is so condensed as to shock anyone who appreciates the original, and much the same is true of the reading from *David Copperfield*. They give one some sympathy with Forster's fear that this was a lower form of art.

4. Phrase from D to Macready, 31 Mar. 1863, *P*, X, p. 227.

5. In Chapter 6 of *Our Mutual Friend*. Dickens's first experience of the river also came from his childhood, when his father took him on the Navy yacht to Sheerness.

6. Everything about the nature of these attacks – their timing, their acute painfulness, the swelling that made it impossible for him to wear a shoe or boot, their moving from one foot to the other and later to a hand – indicates gout. Dickens strongly resisted and denied this diagnosis, perhaps because gout was associated with high consumption of alcohol. He always insisted it was caused by walking in the snow. When a summary of his symptoms over the last five years was submitted to a group of doctors recently they were unanimous in seeing gout as the reason for the pain in his feet and hand.

7. D to Wills, 19 Sept. 1857, *P*, VIII, p. 449.

8. D to Wills, 20 Sept. 1857, *P*, VIII, pp. 450–51.

9. D to Macready, 'a piece of news I have, that I think you will be pleased to hear. Lord Gardner has married Julia Fortescue, and they are living quietly and very happily.' 13 Dec. 1856, *P*, VIII, p. 238. It is not certain that any legal marriage took place.

10. D to Buckstone, 13 Oct. 1857, *P*, VIII, p. 466.

11. D to De La Rue, 23 Oct. 1857, *P*, VIII, pp. 471–2.

12. Una Pope-Hennessy, *Charles Dickens* (London, 1945), p. 176, no source given.

13. See Chapter 27 below for Katey's account of this to Gladys Storey, told in *Dickens and Daughter* (London, 1939), p. 96.

14. D to Lady Duff Gordon, 23 Jan. 1858, *P*, VIII, p. 508; D to Mrs Watson, 7 Dec. 1857, *P*, VIII, p. 488.

15. D to Wilkie Collins, 21 Mar. 1858, *P*, VIII, p. 536.

16. D to F, 27 Mar. 1858, *P*, VIII, p. 537, and 30 Mar. 1858, *P*, VIII, p. 539.

17. Account by Yates, given in K. J. Fielding (ed.), *The Speeches of Charles Dickens: A Complete Edition* (Brighton, 1988), p. 263.

18. D to Coutts, 9 May 1858, *P*, VIII, pp. 558–60. In Aug., Catherine's aunt Helen Thomson wrote to Mrs Stark, a family connection, telling her that Dickens had tried to get a doctor to say Catherine was of unsound mind, and that the doctor had refused, saying he considered her perfectly sound in mind. *P*, VIII, Appendix F, p. 746.

19. Lucinda Hawksley's *Katey: The Life and Loves of Dickens's Artist Daughter* (London, 2006) suggests that Georgina underwent a virginity test and that the certificate of virginity was among the family papers, although no one knows its present location. See p. 134 and fn.

20. Catherine's letter to Miss Coutts is given in *P*, VIII, p. 565, fn. 2. Catherine might have been better advised to stay at Tavistock House and force Dickens to move out. It would also have made it more difficult for him to keep the children.

21. D to Coutts, 19 May 1858, *P*, VIII, p. 565.

22. Dickens met Ouvry, a partner in Farrer's, in 1856, and began to use him in preference to Mitton for much of his business. The final settlement on Catherine gave her a house of her own and a respectable £600 a year.

23. D to Ouvry, 26 May 1858, *P*, VIII, p. 569.

24. Annie Thackeray to Amy Crowe, [n.d.], Gordon N. Ray, *Thackeray*, II (Oxford, 1958), p. 478, n. 46.

25. Bradbury & Evans, in a statement put out in May 1859, described Dickens's desire that they should publish his statement in *Punch*, a comic magazine, as expecting them 'to gratify an eccentric wish by a preposterous action'. See Appendix C in *P*, IX, [p. 565].

26. D to Charley, [?10–12 July 1858], *P*, VIII, p. 602.

27. D to Yates, 8 June 1858, *P*, VIII, p. 581.

28. See *P*, VIII, pp. 740–41.

29. Cited in *P*, VIII, p. 648, fn. 4.

30. Catherine D's letter quoted by Helen Thomson, Aug. 1858, *P*, VIII, p. 559, fn. 1. Henry and Alfred both spoke later of regular affectionate visits.

31. D to GH, 25 Aug. 1858, *P*, VIII, p. 637, and fn. 4.

32. D to Coutts, 23 Aug. 1858, *P*, VIII, p. 632.

33. D to Mary Boyle, 10 Sept. 1858, *P*, VIII, p. 656, and 9 Dec. 1858, *P*, VIII, p. 717.

34. Gladys Storey's notes of her conversations with Katey held between

1923 and her death in 1929, now lodged at Charles Dickens Museum. See Chapter 27 below.

35. D to Wills, 25 Oct. 1858, *P*, VIII, pp. 686–7.
36. Robert L. Patten, *Charles Dickens and His Publishers* (Oxford, 1978), p. 262.
37. F's letter given in *P*, IX, p. 10, fn. 2.
38. F to D, 14 Jan. 1859, *P*, IX, p. 11, fn. 5.

21   Secrets, Mysteries and Lies 1859–1861

1. Forster gives this comment in his *Life of Charles Dickens*, III (London, 1874), Chapter 9.
2. D to his tour manager Arthur Smith, 26 Jan. 1859, *P*, IX, p. 17.
3. William Richard Hughes, *A Week's Tramp in Dickens-Land* (London, 1891), p. 87.
4. John Hollingshead, *My Lifetime*, I (London, 1895), p. 97.
5. Fred was released from prison after three months, but from now on he sank into poverty, unrelieved by his elder brother, who had almost no more contact with him.
6. See *P*, IX, p. 11, fn. 1.
7. We do know, however, that her sister Maria took over her part.
8. Dickens put it out in monthly parts, with illustrations by Hablot Browne ('Phiz'), to appeal to his old public.
9. *HW* was closed in May.
10. D to F, 16 June 1859, *P*, IX, p. 78. Wills had naturally moved with Dickens and continued to be his chief assistant, and with a share in the profits. Chapman & Hall, which would publish the monthly parts, took some of the 100,000 copies, and some went to America, but it was still an impressive figure.
11. Robert L. Patten, *Charles Dickens and His Publishers* (Oxford, 1978), p. 332.
12. D to Wilkie Collins, 6 Oct. 1859, *P*, IX, p. 128.
13. John Sutherland's essay on *A Tale of Two Cities* adds considerably to the pleasure of reading the novel, and is found in his *Who Betrays Elizabeth Bennet?* (Oxford, 1999).
14. Patten, *Dickens and His Publishers*, p. 304.
15. *Great Expectations*, Chapter 20.

16. Ibid., Chapter 7.

17. Ibid., Chapter 15.

18. Ibid., Chapter 57.

19. Ibid., Chapter 29.

20. D to Wilkie Collins, 12 June 1859, *P*, IX, p. 76.

21. D to Frank Beard, 25 June 1859, *P*, IX, p. 84.

22. D to Frank Beard, 1 July – 'the new medicines have prevailed, and nearly thrown the enemy', and 6 Aug. 1859, *P*, IX, pp. 88, 103.

23. D to Wilkie Collins, 16 Aug. 1859, *P*, IX, p. 106.

24. That Dickens, who worked to save young women from becoming prostitutes, may have used prostitutes himself may be hard but not impossible to believe.

25. D to Frank Beard, 29 Jan. 1861, *P*, IX, p. 377.

26. According to Forster in his *Life*, III, Chapter 14.

27. D to Macready, 11 June 1861, *P*, IX, p. 424.

28. D to Wills, 11 Mar. 1861, *P*, IX, p. 391.

29. See D to Coutts, 8 Apr. 1860, *P*, IX, p. 233, in which he writes, 'I do not suppose myself blameless.' D to Coutts, 12 Feb. 1864, *P*, X, p. 356.

30. Mrs Puckle was the daughter of Macready's youngest son, Sir Neville Macready. Her remarks are printed in an article by Philip Collins, 'W. C. Macready and Dickens: Some Family Recollections' in *Dickens Studies*, 2, 2 (May 1966), p. 53.

31. D to Wills, 30 June 1859, *P*, IX, p. 87. The 'woman I trust' for an opinion on his proofs, mentioned by D to Bulwer, 15 May 1861, *P*, IX, p. 415, is surely Nelly.

32. Berger was supposedly reported by Andrew de Ternant in *Notes and Queries* in 1933, the year of Berger's death, aged ninety-nine. I have lately found that de Ternant was a notorious fabricator of stories, about Debussy among others, and regularly planted his inventions in *Notes and Queries*, which suggests this is another of his hoaxes.

33. Quoted in fn. 3 to D to Fields, 20 May 1860, *P*, IX, p. 256.

34. Katey is the source here, talking to Gladys Storey, *Dickens and Daughter* (London, 1939), p. 106.

35. D to Frances Dickinson, 19 Aug. 1860, *P*, IX, p. 287.

36. Katey was not present, as is sometimes said, but abroad on her honeymoon.

37. According to Storey, *Dickens and Daughter*, p. 107, and given in *P*, IX, p. 304, fn. 1.
38. So he told first Collins and then his Swiss friend Cerjat, 24 Oct. 1860, 1 Feb. 1861, *P*, IX, pp. 331, 383. Readers of Kate Summerscale's *The Suspicions of Mr Whicher* will know that a quite different solution emerged.
39. D to Cerjat, 1 Feb. 1861, *P*, IX, p. 383.
40. Philip Collins (ed.), *Dickens: Interviews and Recollections* (London, 1981), I, p. 156, cites Alfred's memory of the rowing trips in an interview given in Nov. 1910. Frank also recalled rowing him to Maidstone.
41. The observation was Kate Field's, made later in her *Pen Photographs of Charles Dickens's Readings* of 1868, and cited by Malcolm Andrews in his *Charles Dickens and His Performing Selves: Dickens and the Public Readings* (Oxford, 2006), p. 255.
42. Stephanie Harvey's translation of Dostoevsky's letter, dated 18 July O.S. 1878, in her article 'Dickens's Villains: A Confession and a Suggestion', *Dickensian* (2002), p. 233.
43. D to Régnier, 17 Sept. 1859, *P*, IX, p. 124.
44. *Great Expectations*, Chapter 29.
45. Ibid.

22 *The Bebelle Life 1862–1865*

1. D to Letitia Austin, 4 Jan. 1862, *P*, X, p. 4.
2. D to Thomas Beard, 1 Feb. 1862, *P*, X, p. 29.
3. D to GH, 24 and 28 Jan. 1862, *P*, X, pp. 22, 25.
4. D to Thomas Beard, 5 Apr. 1862, *P*, X, p. 66.
5. D to F, 8 Apr. 1862, *P*, X, p. 67.
6. D to Cerjat, 16 Mar. 1862, *P*, X, pp. 54–5.
7. D to Yates, 3 Apr. 1862, *P*, X, p. 64.
8. Arthur A. Adrian, *Georgina Hogarth and the Dickens Circle* (Oxford, 1957), pp. 76–81 and esp. p. 79.
9. D to Wilkie Collins, 20 Sept. 1862, *P*, X, p. 129; D to F, 5 Oct. 1862, *P*, X, p. 134.
10. D to Wilkie Collins, 8 Oct. 1862, *P*, X, p. 137; D to Mrs Brown, 21 Oct. 1862, *P*, X, p. 150.

11. I am much indebted to John Bowen's article 'Bebelle and "His Boots"': Dickens, Ellen Ternan and the Christmas Stories' in the *Dickensian* (2000), pp. 197–208, which discusses how Dickens's writing may be read in relation to his life at this time. He points out that Dickens introduces a character, M. Mutuel, who seems to be based on his Boulogne landlord; and that Langley, the central figure, has quarrelled with his daughter in England, who also had a child who has died. Dickens's contributions to the next two Christmas issues of *AYR*, 'Mrs Lirriper's Lodgings' (1863) and 'Mrs Lirriper's Legacy' (1864), were further concerned with an illegitimate birth, and then with a visit to France.

12. D to Wills, 18 Dec. 1862, *P*, X, p. 178.

13. D to F, 22 Oct. 1862, *P*, X, p. 148.

14. D to Olliffe, 18 Jan. 1863, *P*, X, p. 196. Sir Joseph Olliffe was a childhood friend of Maclise, who introduced Dickens to him. He studied medicine in Paris and married a rich English wife, and both admired Dickens's work and became friends whom he saw when in Paris.

15. D to Wilkie Collins, 20 Jan. 1863, *P*, X, p. 198.

16. D to Wilkie Collins, 20 Jan. and 29 Jan. 1863, *P*, X, pp. 198, 201.

17. D to GH, 1 Feb. 1863, *P*, X, p. 206. It was Danton himself who said this, on the scaffold.

18. D to Macready, 19 Feb. 1863, *P*, X, p. 215.

19. D to Ouvry, 17 Mar. 1863, *P*, X, p. 224; D to Leighton, 9 Apr. 1863, *P*, X, p. 230; D to Wilkie Collins, [?Aug. 1863], *P*, X, p. 281.

20. He had mentioned to Forster, 25 Aug. 1862, *P*, X, p. 120, a preliminary idea for a story about two strongly contrasted groups of people and an electric message, which was possibly the germ of *Our Mutual Friend* – although it lost the electric message, tantalizingly.

21. D to Mrs Nicholls, 26 June 1864, *P*, X, p. 408; D to Wills, 26 June 1864, *P*, X, p. 409.

22. D to Mrs Frances Elliot, 4 July 1866 [*recte* 1867], *P*, XI, p. 389.

23. Gladys Storey, *Dickens and Daughter* (London, 1939), p. 94. See Chapter 27 below.

24. When Storey's book was attacked, as it was, Bernard Shaw wrote to the *TLS* in 1939 to say that Mrs Perugini (Katey Dickens) had told him everything in it in the 1890s. For Henry Dickens's statement, see manuscript note by Gladys Storey in Charles Dickens Museum papers; David

Parker and Michael Slater's account of the Storey manuscripts in the *Dickensian* (1980), pp. 3–16, and see Chapter 27 below.

25. D to F, [?end May 1865 – F said the day before D left for France], *P*, XI, p. 48.

26. D to Mitton, 13 June 1865, *P*, XI, p. 56, giving a long account of the accident without naming his companions.

27. D to John Thompson, 25 June 1865, *P*, XI, p. 65.

28. Thomas Wright, *The Life of Charles Dickens* (London, 1935); Gladys Storey, *Dickens and Daughter* (London, 1939); Ada B. Nisbet, *Dickens and Ellen Ternan* (Berkeley, 1952); K. J. Fielding, *Charles Dickens* (London, 1953); Edgar Johnson, *Charles Dickens: His Tragedy and Triumph* (Boston, 1952). Philip Collins (ed.), *Dickens: Interviews and Recollections* (London, 1981), I, p. xxiv, for the quoted remark, and Philip Collins, *Dickens and Crime* (London, 1962; my edition 1994), p. 309, and see also pp. 312–13.

29. Miss Longley said she had approached the story without bias, but a note in her hand, dated 15 Mar. 1975, shows she was never impartial in her approach, since it reads, 'It was very important to my thesis – that Ellen Ternan was not in fact the mistress of Charles Dickens.' Manuscript note by Katharine M. Longley now in Pocket 13 of the Wright Papers at Charles Dickens Museum.

30. D to Catherine D, 6 Aug. 1863, *P*, X, p. 280. His authorization was necessary because he owned the plot in the cemetery.

31. D to Coutts, 12 Feb. 1864, *P*, X, p. 356.

32. See Nisbet, *Dickens and Ellen Ternan*, p. 41, quoting from the *Letters and Memoirs of Sir William Hardman* [Second Series, London, 1925, p. 148], which gives Sir William, a friend of Mrs Dickens, saying her grief over Walter was 'much enhanced by the fact that her husband had not taken any notice of the event to her, either by letter or otherwise. If anything were wanting to sink CD to the lowest depths of my esteem, *this* fills up the measure of his iniquity. As a writer, I admire him; as a man, I despise him.'

33. D to F, 30 Aug. 1863, *P*, X, p. 283; D to F, 12 Oct. 1863, *P*, X, p. 300.

34. D to R. J. Lane, 25 Feb. 1864, *P*, X, p. 363.

35. D to Frith, 13 Apr. 1864, *P*, X, p. 381.

36. D to R. B. Osborne, 1 June 1864, *P*, X, pp. 400–401.

37. D to Ouvry, 30 Apr. 1865, *P*, XI, p. 37.

38. D to Fechter, 21 July 1865, *P*, XI, p. 75. I am indebted to Catherine Peters's *The King of Inventors: A Life of Wilkie Collins* (London, 1991) for information about Fechter.

23 Wise Daughters 1864–1866

1. Robert L. Patten, *Charles Dickens and His Publishers* (Oxford, 1978), pp. 302–3.
2. D to F, 29 July 1864, *P*, X, p. 414.
3. Figures from Patten, *Dickens and His Publishers*, pp. 216, 308.
4. *Our Mutual Friend*, Book 1, Chapter 12.
5. Ibid., Book 1, Chapter 10.
6. Ibid., Book 2, Chapter 1.
7. The piece was by R. H. Horne and entitled 'Dust; or, Ugliness Redeemed'.
8. John Carey, *The Violent Effigy: A Study of Dickens's Imagination* (London, 1973), p. 111.
9. *Our Mutual Friend*, Book 1, Chapter 4.
10. Ibid., Book 1, Chapter 6.
11. Ibid., Book 2, Chapter 1.
12. James's review in the *Nation* (New York) appeared on 21 Dec. 1865. It is reprinted in Philip Collins (ed.), *Dickens: The Critical Heritage* (London, 1971), pp. 469–73.
13. *Our Mutual Friend*, Book 1, Chapter 13.
14. Possibly mirroring Dickens's fear of what his situation with Nelly was becoming.
15. *Our Mutual Friend*, Book 4, Chapter 5.
16. Ibid., Book 2, Chapter 8.
17. Dickens drew on plots of two plays of the 1830s by Sheridan Knowles, one about a young woman cured of being mercenary, the other about a young woman whose father steals from the bodies of drowned men.
18. Edmund Wilson, 'The Two Scrooges' in *The Wound and the Bow* (Cambridge, Mass., 1941; my edition London, 1961), p. 74.
19. *Our Mutual Friend*, Book 1, Chapter 9. The hospital for children pre-figures one described by Dickens in *AYR*, 19 Dec. 1868, after a visit, and to which he returned with James and Annie Fields in May 1869.

See Michael Slater (ed.), *The Dent Uniform Edition of Dickens's Journalism*, IV (London, 2000, with John Drew), pp. 352–64. The good clergyman Frank Milvey's wife Margaretta is shown as suffering from having too many children, like Amos Barton's wife Milly, who dies young and worn out with excessive childbearing, in George Eliot's *Scenes of Clerical Life*, admired by Dickens.

20. Henry James found the whole book 'lifeless, forced and mechanical' and all the characters unnatural, and suggested that Dickens failed as a novelist because he had no general understanding of human passions. He allowed that 'he is a great observer and a great humorist', but no philosopher. James was of course thinking through his ideas for the sort of novel he meant to write, and it made him harsh. Edmund Wilson on the other hand wrote in 1941 that 'Dickens has here distilled the mood of his later years, dramatized the tragic discrepancies of his character, delivered his final judgment on the whole Victorian exploit, in a fashion so impressive that we realize how little the distractions of this period had the power to direct him from the prime purpose of his life: the serious exercise of his art.'

21. D to Cerjat, 30 Nov. 1865, *P*, XI, p. 116. The sewers had been opened in Apr. 1865 and would be completed in 1875, and the first part of the Embankment was opened in July 1870, shortly after Dickens's death.

22. See D to Frank Beard, 21 Mar. 1865, *P*, XI, p. 28. It must have been the first onset of gout that was to torment him intermittently for the rest of his life. Gout is not life-threatening but often goes with high blood pressure and vascular disease.

23. D to F, [?29 Sept. 1854], *P*, VII, p. 429.

24. D to F, mid-Sept. 1865, *P*, XI, pp. 91–2; D to Yates, 13 Sept. 1865, *P*, XI, pp. 90–91.

25. This was entitled 'Doctor Marigold' when reprinted as a Christmas story.

26. Henry Chorley (1808–72) destroyed all his correspondence with Dickens. He was a close family friend. A journalist with the *Athenaeum* since 1830, he was especially knowledgeable about music and opera (he found Verdi vulgar, Schumann and Wagner decadent, but praised Mendelssohn). He became a heavy drinker, is thought to have been in love with Mamie. He left her £200 a year for life in his will, asked her

to send him branches from the cedar trees at Gad's and had himself buried with them when he died in 1872. (Information from the *DNB*, *Pilgrim Edition*, Arthur A. Adrian, *Georgina Hogarth and the Dickens Circle* (Oxford, 1957).)

27. Henry Dickens gave a brief account of this Christmas in the 'Gad's Hill Gazette', produced with his father's encouragement and for which he was given some training in typesetting. Mamie Dickens also wrote about Gad's Hill Christmases in general in her *My Father as I Recall Him* (London, 1897).

28. Fanny Ternan to Bice Trollope, 16 Feb. 1866, unpublished letter.

29. Bice is given the Italian pronunciation in two syllables, *Bee-chay*.

30. D to GH, 21 Dec. 1865, *P*, XI, p. 125.

31. D to Mrs Elliot, 2 Mar. 1866, *P*, XI, p. 166.

32. See D to GH, 9 Feb. 1866, *P*, XI, p. 155.

33. The draft agreement between the editors of *AYR* and the author of *Aunt Margaret's Trouble* is printed in *P*, XI, p. 536.

34. D to Mrs Elliot, 4 July 1866 [*recte* 1867], *P*, XI, p. 389. This is the same letter in which he told her about Nelly having had much to bear alone, discussed in Chapter 22 above.

35. See the author's *The Invisible Woman*.

36. No letter of condolence to William Gaskell is known, and the last known personal letter from Dickens to Mrs Gaskell was written in 1861.

37. Dickens refusing an invitation from Mrs Ellicott, wife of the Bishop of Gloucester, 2 Apr. 1867, *P*, XI, p. 348. He used almost the same phrase to Mrs Elliot in Mar. 1867.

38. Henry F. Dickens, *Memories of My Father* (London, 1928), pp. 14, 26.

24 The Chief 1866–1868

1. Dolby published in 1885 his memoir, *Charles Dickens as I Knew Him*, written from memory and 'copious notes', and described by Mamie Dickens as 'the best and truest picture of my father that has yet been written'. Dickens described his stammer to Georgina in a letter of 6 Mar. 1867, 'He has a rock ahead in his speech just now, which he can *not* get over. This is, Cambridge . . . Fifty times a day . . . he tries it –

Ca-a-a-a-and then Car-ar-ar, and then Caw-aw-aw-ar-o – and then shoots it out with a suddenness that seems to frighten and astonish him.' *P*, XI, p. 328.

2. So D wrote to Mamie, 14 Apr. 1866, *P*, XI, p. 184.

3. George Dolby, *Charles Dickens as I Knew Him* (London, 1885; my edition 1912), p. 11.

4. Remark given by Malcolm Andrews, *Charles Dickens and His Performing Selves: Dickens and the Public Readings* (Oxford, 2006), p. 150.

5. This is particularly to his credit because he ended his days penniless, in the workhouse, in 1900, and might have sold what he knew.

6. D to Wills, 6 June 1667, *P*, XI, p. 377. The remark suggests Dickens looking back, since at this date only Henry and Plorn were still at home, and there was nothing limp about Henry; but Charley was a frequent visitor. The letter, which strongly argues Dickens's case for going to America, is written on Nelly's monogrammed writing paper. Wills wrote round the top of the letter, 'This letter, so illustrative of one of the strong sides of C. D.'s character – powerful will – I think ought decidedly to be published in justice to Forster and myself who dissuaded him from America – which killed him eventually. – W. H. W.'

7. D to Macready, 23 Feb. 1866, telling him about Beard diagnosing 'great irritability of the heart', and that 'Rest is enjoined, but an occasional Reading rather encouraged than objected to.' *P*, XI, p. 163.

8. From *From the Porch* (1913), given in Philip Collins (ed.), *Dickens: Interviews and Recollections*, II (London, 1981), pp. 178–9. This was Lady Ritchie recalling her experience as Annie Thackeray in 1870.

9. D to F, [?6 Sept. 1866], *P*, XI, p. 243; D to Frank Beard, 6 Sept. 1866, *P*, XI, pp. 242–3.

10. D to Dolby, 4 Sept. 1866, *P*, XI, p. 239.

11. D to Wills, 21 Oct. 1866, *P*, XI, p. 257. For Dickens's payments see Arthur A. Adrian, *Georgina Hogarth and the Dickens Circle* (Oxford, 1957), p. 110, citing the *Dickensian* (1939), p. 145.

12. D to GH, 6 Nov. 1866, *P*, XI, p. 265. A sign that Thompson might be getting above himself is in the 1861 census, where he describes himself as a 'publisher', living with his wife, children and one servant at No. 26 Wellington Street, Strand.

13. According to Marcus Stone. 'Marcus Stone, R. A., and Charles

Dickens', *Dickensian* (1912), p. 216, gives Stone's statement, made to the *Morning Post*, 4 July 1912. Dickens may have felt it best to help Thompson, who knew much about his private arrangements with Nelly. Thompson's two daughters, Emily (born 1854) and Matilda Dorrit (born 1857), were both christened at St Martin-in-the-Fields. In the 1871 census he is listed as unemployed, sharing a house in Shoreditch with a new wife, Mary Anne, who works as a dressmaker, assisted by his younger daughter, a collar-dresser, and in partnership with two women doll-makers, Henrietta Adams, who lives with them, and Anna Watson, a visitor. The elder daughter, Emily, now worked as a servant in Hackney. Information from Nicholas P. C. Waloff, who suggests that the 'small business' in which Dickens set up Thompson could have been the dress- and doll-making carried out by the women.

14. D to GH, 5 Nov. 1866, *P*, XI, p. 263.
15. D to Mamie, 17 Feb. 1867, *P*, XI, p. 315; D to Frank Beard, 18 Feb. 1867, *P*, XI, p. 316; D to GH, 19 Feb. 1867, *P*, XI, p. 317.
16. D to Station Master, Paddington, 20 Apr. 1867, *P*, XI, p. 357. This is the 'Loss' marked in the diary. People lose things when they are tired or stressed. Whether the 'Tourist's Knapsack' was returned is not known.
17. He lost the diary, a very small notebook bound in leather, in America and it turned up in New York in 1922 from an unnamed private collector. It was bought by the Berg brothers, great collectors, and remained unexamined in their collection for twenty-one years until 1943, when the curator saw how interesting it was.
18. D to GH, 8 May 1867, *P*, XI, p. 364.
19. D to F, [?20–25 May 1867], *P*, XI, p. 372.
20. According to Gladys Storey's notes Katey talked of 'an establishment with two servants for her at Peckham' – see Chapter 27 below.
21. Philip Collins, always perceptive, believes Dickens 'must have felt a certain satisfaction in so ably playing his part in a really good mystery-plot of his own invention: not written, this time, but lived'. *Dickens and Crime* (London, 1962; my edition 1994), p. 316.
22. 'Silverman' was written for the American market and serialized in the *Atlantic Monthly*, Jan.–Mar. 1868, while he was in the US, and from Feb. 1868 in *AYR*.

23. They appeared in Ticknor & Fields children's magazine *Our Young Folks*, but not in volume form. The Americans paid the very large sum of £1,000 each for 'Silverman' and 'Holiday Romance'.

24. Sir Henry Thompson, a well-known surgeon, said the bunion was made worse by erysipelas, an inflammation characterized by red skin.

25. D to Dolby, 9 Aug. 1867, *P*, XI, p. 410.

26. Nelly was described by a friend, Helen Wickham, as sometimes making 'extraordinary scenes' when she did not get her way, in the 1890s. 'She could be quite a little spitfire.' Katharine M. Longley, to whom this description was given, in 'The Real Ellen Ternan', *Dickensian* (1985).

27. D to ed. of *The Times*, 2 Sept. 1867, *P*, XI, p. 416; D to ed. *Sunday Gazette*, 3 Sept. 1867, *P*, XI, p. 420.

28. James Fields, head of the publishers Ticknor & Fields, was five years younger than Dickens. He had heard him speak in Boston in 1842. In May 1860 he and his much younger (second) wife, Annie, visited Dickens in England, friendship was established, and Fields began to press Dickens to come to America to read. The four years' duration of the American Civil War, Apr. 1861 to Apr. 1865, obliged him to put the plan aside.

29. Fanny Trollope was aware of this plan by 8 Oct.

30. D to Ouvry, 20 Oct. 1867, *P*, XI, p. 458.

31. K. J. Fielding (ed.), *The Speeches of Charles Dickens: A Complete Edition* (Brighton, 1988), p. 370.

32. He barely mentions it in his *Life of Charles Dickens*, III (London, 1974), Chapter 13. See Adrian, *Georgina Hogarth and the Dickens Circle*, p. 103, for one account, and Fielding's *The Speeches of Charles Dickens*, pp. 368–74, for another.

33. D to Catherine D, 5 Nov. 1867, *P*, XI, p. 472.

34. Huntington MS, HM 18394.

35. Henry James to William James, 22 Nov. 1867, Leon Edel (ed.), *Henry James: Letters*, I (London, 1974), p. 81.

36. James's description from many years later, given by Collins, *Interviews and Recollections*, II, p. 297, from *The Notebooks of Henry James*. James also came face to face with Dickens at Norton's house, and found that 'the offered inscrutable mask was the great thing, the extremely hand-

some face, the face of symmetry yet of formidable character, as I at once recognised, and which met my dumb homage with a straight inscrutability, a merciless *military* eye'. This is from Henry James's *Notes of a Son and Brother* of 1914.

37. Worth something like fifty times as much today, i.e., close to a million. Precise conversion is not possible because it depends on whether you are using the retail price index, average earnings, per capita Gross Domestic Product, share of GDP or GDP deflator.

38. D to F, 5 Jan. 1868, *P*, XII, p. 5. He also told Forster, 3 Jan. 1868, *P*, XII, p. 2, 'My landlord invented for me a drink of brandy, rum and snow, called it a "Rocky Mountain Sneezer," and said it was to put down all less effectual sneezing; but it has not had the effect.'

39. D to F, 14–15 Jan. 1868, *P*, XII, pp. 14–15.

40. D to GH, 21 Jan. 1868, *P*, XII, p. 20.

41. D to F, 30–31 Mar. 1868, *P*, XII, p. 86.

42. Forster's *Life*, III, Chapter 15 and fn.

43. D to F, 13, 14 Mar. 1868, *P*, XII, p. 75.

44. Dolby, *Charles Dickens as I Knew Him*, p. 341. In July 1868 Dickens presented his godson with a massive silver bowl, plate, fork and spoon, at Marylebone Church. See D to Fields, 7 July 1868, *P*, XII, p. 150.

45. *A Child's Journey with Dickens* by Kate Douglas Wiggin (Boston and New York, 1912).

46. Only a few of the letters to Wills have survived, with many inked-over passages, later deciphered with infra-red photography. All are now printed in *P*, XI and *P*, XII.

47. These payments to Wills were noted by Edgar Johnson, *Charles Dickens: His Tragedy and Triumph* (Boston, 1952) – see notes xc–xci. He mentions another to 'Wills Trust' for £250 on 7 Nov. 1867. He writes that he found no other record showing how the sums were invested and that 'the reader may give these payments totalling £2,250 what significance he wishes.' The editors of the *Pilgrim Edition* mention only the £1,000, which is referred to in a letter to Georgina, saying it was 'probably intended for Nelly'. *P*, XII, p. 6, fn. 7.

48. Both these quotes from Annie Fields's diaries are taken here from Collins, *Interviews and Recollections*, II, pp. 320, 321, 322.

49. The promise was kept.

25 'Things look like work again' 1868–1869

1. D to Alfred Dickens, 16 May 1868, *P*, XII, p. 110.
2. D to Macready, 20 July 1868, *P*, XII, p. 378. D to Morley, 2 Oct. 1868, *P*, XII, p. 192. Morley went on to teach literature at University College, London. His views are given in Philip Collins (ed.), *Dickens: Interviews and Recollections*, II (London, 1981), p. 193.
3. Forster's *Life of Charles Dickens*, III (London, 1874), Chapter 8, quoting from D to Fields, 7 July 1868, *P*, XII, p. 149.
4. Lady Molesworth, *née* Andalusia Carstairs (1803–88), an Irish singer and actress who played at Drury Lane in the 1840s, was married and widowed before marrying Sir William Molesworth, Bart., and becoming a rich and enthusiastic lion-hunting hostess. Dickens was fond of her and enjoyed her dinners.
5. D to Mamie Dickens, 26 Sept. 1868, XII, p. 188.
6. D to Plorn Dickens, 26 Sept. 1868, *P*, XII, pp. 187–8.
7. D to Dolby, 25 Sept. 1868, *P*, XII, p. 187.
8. D to GH, 7 Nov. 61, *P*, IX, p. 500; D to P. Cunningham, 15 Feb. 1865, *P*, XI, p. 16.
9. D to Dr Hewison, 23 Oct. 1868, *P*, XII, p. 207.
10. D to Dolby, 29 Sept. 1868, *P*, XII, p. 190.
11. D to F, given in *Life*, III, Chapter 17, and [?10–15 Oct. 1868], *P*, XII, p. 203.
12. These quotes from George Dolby, *Charles Dickens as I Knew Him* (London, 1885; my edition 1912), p. 351.
13. Forster, *Life*, III, Chapter 17, and [?15 Nov. 1868], *P*, XII, p. 220.
14. Philip Collins, *Dickens and Crime* (London, 1962; my edition 1994), p. 269.
15. Edgar Browne, *Phiz and Dickens, as They Appeared to Edgar Browne* (London, 1913), p. 146.
16. Dolby, *Dickens as I Knew Him*, p. 347.
17. Dickens's friends accepted Georgina's part in his life, but she was not generally invited with him, and among neighbours in Kent and some of his American friends there was uneasiness about her position.
18. D to Cerjat, 4 Jan. 1869, *P*, XII, p. 267.

19. D to Ouvry, 12 Jan. 1869, *P*, XII, p. 273.

20. D to Dolby, 19 Feb. 1869, *P*, XII, p. 294.

21. D to GH, 26 Feb. 1869, *P*, XII, p. 299.

22. The young man, Edward Young, told his family about his meeting with Dickens, and an account of it was printed in his obituary in 1927. His granddaughter remembered him well and told me that he said they were black stockings, but it was not thought suitable to mention this in the obituary.

23. D to Frank Beard, 19 Apr. 1869, *P*, XII, p. 336; D to Norton, 20 Apr. 1869, *P*, XII, p. 337.

24. D to GH, 21 Apr. 1869, *P*, XII, p. 339.

25. This was his final will, appointing Forster and Georgina his executors, responsible for managing his personal estate and copyrights and holding the proceeds to be distributed equally among all his children when they should reach the age of twenty-one. All the children were over twenty-one when he died except Edward (Plorn), who was eighteen. He left £1,000 to 'Miss Ellen Lawless Ternan, late of Houghton Place, Ampthill Square', settled money on Georgina and on Mamie, and made Charley and Henry responsible for the capital that would provide their mother with an income for life. To Forster ('my dear and trusty friend') he left all his manuscripts and his watch, and to Georgina his private papers. To Charley he left his library, engravings and various knick-knacks. There were small bequests to servants. He wanted Gad's Hill to be sold as part of the estate.

26. D to W. J. Farrer, 15 Dec. 1869, *P*, XII, p. 451.

27. This is Dolby's account, *Charles Dickens as I Knew Him*, pp. 421–9.

28. Quoted by George Curry in *Charles Dickens and Annie Fields* (San Marino, Calif., 1988), reprinted from the *Huntington Library Quarterly*, 51 (Winter 1988), p. 48.

29. Diary of Annie Fields, quoted on p. 42 of ibid.

30. Katey told Gladys Storey about Nelly staying at Gad's, reported in *Dickens and Daughter* (London, 1939), p. 127. For Nelly's later friendship with Georgy and Mamie see Chapter 27 below.

31. D to Dolby, 11 Sept. 1869, *P*, XII, p. 408.

32. D to Arthur Ryland, 6 Sept. 1869, *P*, XII, p. 407.

33. D to Dolby, 27 Nov. 1869, *P*, XII, pp. 445–6.
34. Dolby, *Charles Dickens as I Knew Him*, p. 338.
35. Una Pope-Hennessy, *Charles Dickens* (London, 1945), p. 451, attributes this account to young Lord Ribblesdale, but Collins, *Interviews and Recollections*, II, p. 112, attributes it to Lord Russell's granddaughter Baroness Deichmann, *Impressions and Memories* (London, 1926), pp. 101–3, which must be right.
36. Dolby gives the story as Dickens told it to him on p. 432 of his *Charles Dickens as I Knew Him*.
37. D to GH, 12 Nov. 1869, *P*, XII, p. 439.
38. Dolby, *Charles Dickens as I Knew Him*, pp. 440–41. One of the lectures was given at the Crystal Palace to the crews of the Harvard and Oxford boats who raced against one another, and allowed Dickens to express his warm feelings about America again; the second, already mentioned, was to the Birmingham and Midland Institute, with which he had been long connected, and to which he returned for the last time in Jan. 1870.
39. D to Thomas Trollope, 4 Nov. 1869, *P*, XII, p. 434.
40. As with *Our Mutual Friend*, there was a clause in the contract covering repayment of the advance should he die before the book was finished, to be arranged with Forster.
41. D to John Murray, 19 Oct. 1869, *P*, XII, p. 426.
42. Or Responsions, an exam taken in the second year, no longer in existence.
43. D to Macready, 27 Dec. 1869, *P*, XII, p. 457.
44. Dolby, *Charles Dickens as I Knew Him*, p. 441. Georgina also says he was unable to walk that day, in her edition of his letters.

26 Pickswick, Pecknicks, Pickwicks 1870

1. George Dolby, *Charles Dickens as I Knew Him* (London, 1885; my edition 1912), pp. 452–3.
2. D to Wills, 23 Jan. 1870, *P*, XII, p. 470.
3. D to C. E. Norton, 11 Mar. 1870, *P*, XII, p. 488.
4. Mamie attended the Queen's ball on 17 May, without her father, who was not well enough. Forster's *The Life of Charles Dickens*, III (London, 1874), Chapter 20.

5. Dickens had given his opinion of the book to Wills in a letter from America, 25 Feb. 1868, *P*, XII, pp. 59–60, in which he chided him for putting words of praise into *AYR*.

6. On account of this he had to decline dinner with Sir Charles Dilke, grandson of the Charles Dilke who had given him half a crown when he was working at the blacking factory. D to Dilke, 27 Feb. 1870, *P*, XII, p. 483.

7. Given in Malcolm Andrews, *Charles Dickens and His Performing Selves: Dickens and the Public Readings* (Oxford, 2006), pp. 264–5.

8. Forster's *Life*, III, Chapter 20, gives Dickens's words and describes the scene. Others say he kissed his hand to the audience and had tears on his face.

9. The codicil appears at the end of his will, dated 2 June and witnessed by two of his assistants at Wellington Street, Holsworth and Walker. Wills retained his one eighth share in *AYR*, which Charley bought out after his father's death.

10. D to Alfred Dickens, 20 May 1870, *P*, XII, pp. 529–30.

11. D to George Clowes, 18 Feb. 1870, *P*, XII, p. 481. As far as I know this is the only time Dickens uses the formulation: compare Jane Austen with her 'sucking child' (*Sense and Sensibility*) and her 'darling child' (*Pride and Prejudice*).

12. The Thuggee were an Indian secret society that came to the attention of the British in the early nineteenth century and were largely put down by them. The Thuggee specialized in murdering and robbing travellers, strangling them with a cloth noose and disposing of the bodies rapidly.

13. D to S. Cartwright, 11 Apr. 1870, *P*, XII, p. 508; D to Charles Kent, 25 Apr. 1870, *P*, XII, p. 512; D to Arthur Helps, 26 Apr. 1870, *P*, XII, p. 513. When on 31 May he told Mrs Bancroft he had reached Gad's 'from town circuitously, to get a little change of air on the road', it was perhaps via Peckham. *P*, XII, p. 541.

14. D to Arthur Helps, 3 May 1870, *P*, XII, p. 519; D to Mrs Dallas, 2 May 1870, *P*, XII, p. 517.

15. Forster, *Life*, III, Chapter 20.

16. Lady Houghton was born in 1814 Annabella Hungerford Crewe, daughter of the second Baron Crewe and granddaughter of the first

Baron and Lady (Frances) Crewe, the famous beauty and Whig host-ess, who had employed Dickens's grandmother as housekeeper.

Dickens had described the Prince of Wales as 'a poor dull idle fellow' to Cerjat, 16 Mar. 1862, *P*, X, p. 55. He also complained to Macready, 31 Mar. 1863, at the time of the royal wedding, 'We really have been be-princed to the last point of human endurance; haven't we?' *P*, X, p. 227. Mamie insisted on her father taking her, with extreme reluctance, to the Prince's ball in the City in May 1863.

Leopold II of Belgium, Queen Victoria's first cousin, was the mon-ster who made himself a private colonial empire in the Congo, of land largely bought for him by Stanley, and was guilty of atrocities on a massive scale. He was responsible for the enslavement, mutilation and deaths of many thousands of people in Africa. He was also so disliked in Belgium that his funeral was booed. He was altogether a vile man, although Dickens is unlikely to have known this.

17. The play was a translation of a French drama, *The Prima Donna*, sug-gested by Dickens after he had seen one of his daughters acting in a country-house production of another play, written by Herman Meri-vale, a lawyer with dramatic ambitions, and also a contributor to *AYR*. Merivale was also involved in the production at the Freake house in Cromwell Road, and said Dickens stage managed well and showed no sign of illness beyond wearing a slipper on his bad foot and using a stick. His account is hard to square with what we know of Dickens's condition at this time, but Merivale insisted that he rose cheerfully to the dramatic occasion.

18. Lady Dorothy Nevil in her *Reminiscences* talked of the bubbling: see Philip Collins (ed.), *Dickens: Interviews and Recollections*, II (London, 1981), p. 350. Lady Jeune, later Lady St Helier, published her *Memories of Fifty Years* in 1909, and gives her memory of Dickens on p. 78. In-evitably with someone as famous as Dickens there are conflicting accounts of him.

19. D to Mrs Percy Fitzgerald, 26 May 1870, *P*, XII, pp. 534–5.

20. Ibid., p. 534; D to Mrs Bancroft, 31 May 1870, *P*, XII, p. 541.

21. D to Fechter, 27 May 1870, *P*, XII, p. 538.

22. According to Percy Fitzgerald, Collins, *Interviews and Recollections*, II, p. 353.

23. Pulvermacher (1815–84) was a Prussian who used Faraday's 1831 invention of the induction coil to make his electrical chains. He patented them in the US, came to London in 1859 and was successful in selling them, claiming that they cured all kinds of rheumatic, neuralgic, epileptic, paralytic and nervous complaints, as well as indigestion and spasms, and that 'Philosophers, divines, eminent physicians, in all parts of the world, recommend them.' He had a shop in Oxford Street and ended his days living on the heights of Hampstead, in Windmill House.

24. Katey wrote and spoke several accounts. See Collins, *Interviews and Recollections*, II, pp. 354–8, and Gladys Storey, *Dickens and Daughter* (London, 1939), pp. 133–4.

25. This is one of Dickens's last manuscripts, written in a small ruled book in blue printed wrappers, with the words 'Gad's Hill Cellar Casks' in his hand with an oval on the front. At the end of page 1 he added 'Besides which there are 5 Gallons in stone jars of the Whiskey to be used first – ' Page 4 is blank. I am grateful to David Clegg for sending me in September 2002 the sale catalogue of Jarndyce, No. 46 Great Russell Street, which prints these details. It is headed: 'Dickens's Last Project: Stocktaking the Cellar at Gad's Hill'.

26. William Richard Hughes, *A Week's Tramp in Dickens-Land* (London, 1891), p. 207: Hughes was told this by Trood himself, the landlord of the Falstaff Inn, who said he had been offered £24 for the cheque because of the signature, but turned it down.

27. This was the version given by Sala in his account of Dickens's death in the *Daily Telegraph*, reprinted in his short biography of 1870, *Charles Dickens*.

28. This is partly taken from Georgina's account in her edition of Dickens's letters, which gives a short narrative for each year and ends with her description of the last days. Also Arthur A. Adrian, *Georgina Hogarth and the Dickens Circle* (Oxford, 1957), pp. 136–7, crediting the obituary in *The Times* – which of course relied on Georgina's narrative – and Gladys Storey's in *Dickens and Daughter*. Storey, whose information came through Katey, says Dickens also mentioned Forster among his incoherent words. Forster, in his final chapter, says

dinner had been begun before Dickens showed signs of trouble and pain, and that the only coherent words he spoke were a wish for dinner to go on. Then he spoke incoherently and rose, and Georgina struggled to get him on to the sofa. There were clearly no servants in the room, and in any case the food was sent up in a dinner-lift.

29. The dogs, if they were about, would have recognized Nelly: see Dolby on how they never forgot anyone they had been introduced to, *Charles Dickens as I Knew Him*, p. 57.

    After *The Invisible Woman* was published I was sent information which suggested this different narrative for 8 June. I worked out a possible sequence of events and gave the arguments for and against in an appendix to the paperback edition, to which I refer interested readers. No more information has come to light since then and I accept that it seems an unlikely story, although not an impossible one, given what we know of Dickens's habits.

30. Katey's words to Gladys Storey, *Dickens and Daughter*, p. 136.

31. Nelly's daughter Gladys told Malcolm Morley that her mother told her she was present when Dickens died (*Dickensian*, 1960). Gladys Storey told Walter Dexter that Katey had told her Georgina sent for Nelly, Dexter to Le Comte de Suzannet, 22 Feb. 1939, letter in Charles Dickens Museum. Una Pope-Hennessy said that Gladys Storey told her that Katey said she fetched Nelly, and put this into her *Charles Dickens* (London, 1945), p. 464.

32. She sent a piece of the hair to Norton, Dec. 1873. Adrian, *Georgina Hogarth and the Dickens Circle*, p. 199.

33. These are the splendid last words of Dolby's *Charles Dickens as I Knew Him*.

34. Shorne Church was heavily restored a few years later and the village has expanded and changed.

35. GH to Ouvry, 18 June 1870, says expenses were incurred 'by the Cathedral people at Rochester in preparing the grave, tolling the bell, etc.'. Given by Arthur A. Adrian in 'Charles Dickens and Dean Stanley', *Dickensian* (1946), p. 156.

36. Richard Cumberland, eighteenth-century playwright, is little remembered now except as Sheridan caricatured him as Sir Fretful Plagiary in *The Critic*.

37. Dean Stanley's account is taken from Adrian, 'Charles Dickens and Dean Stanley', pp. 152–4.

38. Wilkie Collins said Charles Reade was there and wept on his shoulder, although no one else lists him. The absence of Tom Beard, one of the oldest friends, is surprising.

39. Sala's account is given in the *Dickensian* (1950), p. 116. George Sala (1828–96), son of an actress, worked closely with Dickens on *HW* and *AYR*. He also had a connection with the *Daily Telegraph*, which suggests he may have had something to do with the knocking on the Dean's door.

40. Longfellow to F, 12 June 1870, Forster, *Life*, III, Chapter 14.

27 The Remembrance of My Friends 1870–1939

1. Manuscript in the National Library of Scotland, Thomas Carlyle to John Carlyle, 15 June 1870, see the *Dickensian* (1970), p. 91.

2. F to Norton, 22 June 1870, Manuscript in the Houghton Library, Harvard, cited in James A. Davies, *John Forster: A Literary Life* (New York, 1983), p. 123.

3. Given in *P*, XII, p. 325, fn. 6, from J. A. McKenzie (ed.), *Letters of George Augustus Sala to Edmund Yates in the Edmund Yates Papers University of Queensland Library* (St Lucia, Qld, 1993), Victorian Fiction Research Guides nos. 19–20, p. 131. Sala had not seen Dickens since the Liverpool banquet in Apr. 1869. He wrote an obituary for the *Daily Telegraph* and then published a short, warm-hearted and ill-informed biography.

4. Sala knew nothing of Dickens's childhood or family background, saying he was born into 'a respectable middle-class family' and received 'a strictly middle-class education'. He also referred to the 'great shadow that fell across his hearth' and said he would avoid prying into secrets, which should not be inquired into for fifty years.

5. Browning to Isa Blagden, 19 Oct. 1870, after she had written to him suggesting that Fanny Trollope had been overpaid for her novels by Dickens because of his relationship with her sister. Edward C. McAleer (ed.), *Dearest Isa: Robert Browning's Letters to Isabella Blagden* (Austin, 1951), p. 349.

6. Annie Fields's diary for 6 Dec. 1871, quoted by George Curry in *Charles Dickens and Annie Fields* (San Marino, Calif., 1988), p. 60.

7. He was taken in by Leslie Stephen and his wife Minnie, Thackeray's younger daughter, who knew Katey of old, and had married Leslie Stephen in 1867.

8. With Ouvry's help Georgina bought back the chalet and gave it to Lord Darnley.

9. GH to Annie Fields, 1 Mar. 1871, Arthur A. Adrian, *Georgina Hogarth and the Dickens Circle* (Oxford, 1957), p. 181.

10. GH to Annie Fields, 17 Mar. 1871, ibid., p. 167.

11. Charley's wife Bessie wrote this to Alfred in Australia. From Alfred Tennyson Dickens's letter to G. W. Rusden, 11 Aug. 1870, MS State Library of Victoria, given in Philip Collins (ed.), *Dickens: Interviews and Recollections*, I (London, 1981), p. 156.

12. Charles W. Dickens in *Mumsey's Magazine*, 28, 6 (Sept. 1902).

13. Lucinda Hawksley, who discovered the record of a wedding in Sept. 1873, in a register office with no family present, records it in her biography *Katey: The Life and Loves of Dickens's Artist Daughter* (London, 2006), and suggests Katey may have feared wrongly that she was pregnant. The official wedding followed in June 1874.

14. Forster, *The Life of Charles Dickens*, III (London, 1874), Chapter 14.

15. Sydney Cockerell, a reliable witness, wrote in the *Sunday Times*, 22 Mar. 1953, after an article about Dickens, that he had met Mamie and Georgina at the Revd Robinson's – i.e., Nelly's husband, George Wharton Robinson – about 1880, when he was thirteen, living in Margate. He remembered Mrs Robinson as a close friend of his mother, and her reciting *A Christmas Carol* at parties.

16. Charles Dickens Museum, Storey Papers VIII, p. 89; also Suzannet Papers, Walter Dexter to Le Comte de Suzannet, 22 Feb. 1939, 'it is confirmed by Miss S that the children of Henry D and of E. T. used to play together on the sands at Boulogne'; also, 'Lady D[ickens] told me that Georgina Hogarth introduced Lady D to Ellen Ternan when she was Mrs Robinson.' Storey Papers VIII, p. 89.

17. These are the opening words of Mamie Dickens's *My Father as I Recall Him* (London, 1897).

18. For Mamie's alleged drinking, see Adrian, *Georgina Hogarth and the*

Dickens Circle, p. 241. He writes that Georgina grew worried about her erratic behaviour in the 1880s, and that she grew 'more and more unstable emotionally as she sought in changes of scene – in alcohol, even – some anodyne for the dissatisfaction which plagued her'.

19. In 1912 they were published as *Charles Dickens as Editor*, edited by R. C. Lehmann, heavily cut, but fortunately the originals survived and were preserved in the Huntington Library, and infra-red treatment revealed the inked-over passages, printed by Ada Nisbet in 1952.

20. Eliza Lynn Linton, *My Literary Life*, published posthumously in 1899. It sounds as though she had Nelly in mind.

21. Thomas Adolphus Trollope, *What I Remember*, II (London, 1887), p. 113.

22. GH to Annie Fields, 19 Jan. 1888, quoted in Adrian, *Georgina Hogarth and the Dickens Circle*, p. 246.

23. Carlyle to F, 11 June 1870, cited in Collins, *Interviews and Recollections*, I, p. 63.

24. Emile Yung's *Zermatt et la vallée de la Viège*, printed and published in Geneva by Thévoz; the English edition also printed in Geneva but published in London by J. R. Gotz in 1894.

25. In Sept. 1893, information from Katharine M. Longley's typescript, fn. 109 to Chapter 13.

26. According to Wright in *Thomas Wright of Olney. An Autobiography* (London, 1936). Wright also said that Charley had threatened to 'speak out' at various times, presumably about his father's liaison with Nelly.

27. Shaw recalled this in his letter to the *TLS* in 1939.

28. As mentioned in n. 3, Chapter 7, English copyright at this time was for forty-two years after publication or seven years after the death of the author, whichever was greater. This meant that *Copperfield* came out of copyright in 1892, *Great Expectations* in 1902 and *Drood* in 1912, the centenary year, after which there was nothing. An Anglo-French copyright agreement of 1852 established Dickens's rights in France, giving his widow a share for life, and his children for twenty years, i.e., until 1890. Whether there was any income from America, or from other countries, I have not been able to establish, but it seems unlikely.

29. In the *Dickensian* (2010), p. 75, Tony Williams quotes from a newspaper

cutting about Dolby's death, found by Michael Slater pasted into a copy of *Charles Dickens as I Knew Him*: 'a distant relative named Rycroft, who identified the body, said he thought the deceased had got so shabby that he had been ashamed lately to approach friends for help'. Also that the *New York Times* for 3 Nov. 1900, reporting his death, mentioned his admission to the Fulham Infirmary 'five years ago'. Dolby's book was reissued in 1912.

30. He had given a reading for working men as early as 1874, at the suggestion of his mother, who wrote to Plorn about the success of the occasion, 11 Dec. 1874, typescript of a letter at the Charles Dickens Museum.

31. She came to London in 1923 as a New York delegate to the Dickens Fellowship and died in England of pneumonia, aged sixty-six.

32. GH to Geoffrey Wharton Robinson, 17 Aug. 1913, manuscript in private possession.

33. Nelly left about £1,200, but curiously she had more money than she had realized, so that her will had to be resworn at £2,379.18s.11d.

34. Katey Perugini to Bernard Shaw, 19 Dec. 1897, quoted in Lucinda Hawkesley, *Katey*, p. 310.

35. After Storey's death in 1978 many of her handwritten notes were found and are now deposited in the Charles Dickens Museum. A good account of them by David Parker and Michael Slater appeared in the *Dickensian* (1980), pp. 3–16.

36. Storey to Shaw, 23 July 1939, British Library Add. MS 50546, f. 76.

37. All from *Dickens and Daughter* (London, 1939), p. 219.

38. Ibid., pp. 96, 98.

39. Ibid., p. 94.

40. Ibid., p. 134.

41. Ibid., p. 219.

42. Ibid., p. 134.

43. Ibid., p. 93.

44. Ibid., p. 94.

45. This is from the unpublished Storey papers that came to light after her death in 1978.

46. Henry F. Dickens, *Memories of My Father* (London, 1928), pp. 14, 26.

47. Ibid., p. 28.

Select Bibliography

Kathleen Tillotson, Graham Storey and others (eds.), *The Pilgrim Edition of the Letters of Charles Dickens*, 12 vols. (Oxford, 1965–2002)

Vol. I, 1820–1839, Madeline House and Graham Storey (1965)

Vol. II, 1840–1841, Madeline House and Graham Storey (1969)

Vol. III, 1842–1843, Madeline House, Graham Storey and Kathleen Tillotson (1974)

Vol. IV, 1844–1846, Kathleen Tillotson (1977)

Vol. V, 1847–1849, Graham Storey and K. J. Fielding (1981)

Vol. VI, 1850–1852, Graham Storey, Kathleen Tillotson and Nina Burgis (1988)

Vol. VII, 1853–1855, Graham Storey, Kathleen Tillotson and Angus Easson (1993)

Vol. VIII, 1856–1858, Graham Storey and Kathleen Tillotson (1995)

Vol. IX, 1859–1861, Graham Storey (1997)

Vol. X, 1862–1864, Graham Storey (1998)

Vol. XI, 1865–1867, Graham Storey (1999)

Vol. XII, 1868–1870, Graham Storey (2002)

The Dickensian 1905–2010

Ackroyd, Peter, *Dickens* (London, 1990)

Adrian, Arthur A., *Georgina Hogarth and the Dickens Circle* (Oxford, 1957)

Andrews, Malcolm, *Charles Dickens and His Performing Selves: Dickens and the Public Readings* (Oxford, 2006)

Aylmer, Felix, *Dickens Incognito* (London, 1959)

Bentley, Nicolas, Slater, Michael, and Burgis, Nina (eds.), *The Dickens Index* (Oxford, 1988)

Bodenheimer, Rosemarie, *Knowing Dickens* (Ithaca, NY, 2007)

Bowen, John, *Other Dickens: Pickwick to Chuzzlewit* (Oxford, 2000)

Carey, John, *The Violent Effigy: A Study of Dickens's Imagination* (London, 1973)

Chittick, Kathryn, *Dickens and the 1830s* (Cambridge, 1990)

Collins, Philip, *Dickens and Crime* (London, 1962)

— *Dickens and Education* (London, 1963)

— *Dickens: The Public Readings* (Oxford, 1975)

— (ed.) *Dickens: The Critical Heritage* (London, 1971)

— (ed.) *Dickens: Interviews and Recollections*, 2 vols. (London, 1981)

Davies, James A., *John Forster: A Literary Life* (New York, 1983)

Dolby, George, *Charles Dickens as I Knew Him* (London, 1885)

Fielding, K. J. (ed.), *The Speeches of Charles Dickens: A Complete Edition* (Brighton, 1988)

Fisher, Leona Weaver, *Lemon, Dickens, and 'Mr Nightingale's Diary': A Victorian Farce* (Victoria, BC, 1988)

Forster, John, *The Life of Charles Dickens*, 3 vols. (London, 1872, 1873, 1874)

— *Lives of the Statesmen of the Commonwealth of England* (London, 1840)

— *The Life and Adventures of Oliver Goldsmith* (London, 1848)

— *Walter Savage Landor: A Biography*, 2 vols. (London, 1869; my edition 1872)

Furneaux, Holly, *Queer Dickens* (Oxford, 2009)

Gissing, George, *Charles Dickens: A Critical Study* (London, 1898)

Hardy, Barbara, *The Moral Art of Dickens: Essays* (London, 1970; my edition 1985)

Hartley, Jenny, *Charles Dickens and the House of Fallen Women* (London, 2008)

Hawksley, Lucinda, *Katey: The Life and Loves of Dickens's Artist Daughter* (London, 2006)

House, Humphry, *The Dickens World* (Oxford, 1941)

Hughes, William Richard, *A Week's Tramp in Dickens-Land* (London, 1891)

Johnson, Edgar, *Charles Dickens: His Tragedy and Triumph* (Boston, Mass., 1952)

Leavis, F. R., and Leavis, Q. D., *Dickens the Novelist* (London, 1970)

Miller, J. Hillis, *Charles Dickens: The World of His Novels* (Cambridge, Mass., 1958)

Nisbet, Ada B., *Dickens and Ellen Ternan* (Berkeley, Calif., 1952)

Patten, Robert L., *Charles Dickens and His Publishers* (Oxford, 1978)

Pope-Hennessy, Una, *Charles Dickens* (London, 1945)

Renton, Richard, *John Forster and His Friendships* (London, 1912)

Schlicke, Paul, *Dickens and Popular Entertainment* (London, 1985)

— *Oxford Reader's Companion to Dickens* (Oxford, 1999)

Slater, Michael, *Charles Dickens* (New Haven, Conn., and London, 2009)

— (ed.) *The Dent Uniform Edition of Dickens's Journalism*, 4 vols. (London, 1994–2000)

   Vol. I, *Sketches by Boz and Other Early Papers 1833–1839* (1994)

   Vol. II, *'The Amusements of the People' and Other Papers, Reports, Essays and Reviews 1834–1851* (1996)

   Vol. III, *'Gone Astray' and Other Papers from Household Words 1851–1859* (1998)

   Vol. IV (with John Drew), *The Uncommercial Traveller and Other Papers 1859–1870* (2000)

Storey, Gladys, *Dickens and Daughter* (London, 1939)

Tillotson, Kathleen, and Butt, John, *Dickens at Work* (London, 1957)

Tomalin, Claire, *The Invisible Woman: The Story of Nelly Ternan and Charles Dickens* (London, 1990)

Toynbee, William (ed.), *The Diaries of William Charles Macready* (London, 1912)

Watts, Alan S., *Dickens at Gad's Hill* (Goring-on-Thames, 1989)

Wilson, Edmund, 'Dickens: The Two Scrooges' (lecture, 1939), then published in *The Wound and the Bow* (Cambridge, Mass., 1941; revised 1952)

❦

Bates, Alan, *A Directory of Stage Coach Services 1836* (New York, 1969)

Healey, Edna, *Lady Unknown: The Life of Angela Burdett-Coutts* (London, 1978)

O'Callaghan, P. P., *The Married Bachelor; or, Master and Man* (Dick's Standard Plays, 313 the Strand [n.d. but 1830s]), and Peake, Richard Brinsley, *Amateurs and Actors* (London, 1818), musical farce. Both plays put on by Dickens and family in Bentinck Street in 1833

Peters, Catherine, *The King of Inventors: A Life of Wilkie Collins* (London, 1991)

❦

There are innumerable editions of Dickens, Oxford World Classics and Penguin providing some of the best value, many with introductions of high quality. The Oxford Clarendon hardback critical editions of the novels are still far from a complete set and those already published are all out of print, a sad situation. *Oliver Twist*, Kathleen Tillotson (1966), *Little Dorrit*, Harvey Peter Sucksmith (1979), *David Copperfield*, Nina Burgis (1981), *The Old Curiosity Shop*, Elizabeth M. Brennan (1997), have all been of great assistance.

Acknowledgements

My first thanks go to the Clarendon Press at Oxford, and to the editors of *The Pilgrim Edition of the Letters of Charles Dickens*. The twelve volumes are an indispensible source for anyone attempting to follow the course of Dickens's life, and I am indebted to all its editors: Kathleen Tillotson, Madeline House, Angus Easson, Margaret Brown, Nina Burgis, K. J. Fielding and, in particular, to Graham Storey, who was a friend from my undergraduate days, and ever generous and helpful.

The Dickens House Museum has been particular supportive to me in my research, allowing me to work in their library, and I am grateful to the director, Florian Schweitzer, to the curator, Fiona Jenkins, and to all the staff for making me welcome and letting me come and go whenever I needed to. Thanks also to the Trustees of the wonderful Wisbech Museum, and to its curator David Wright and his assistant Robert Bell, for allowing me to examine the manuscript of *Great Expectations* and other Dickens material held there.

Thanks to the curators and staff of the National Art Library at the Victoria and Albert Museum for permission to examine manuscripts and proofs of novels by Dickens and other papers in the John Forster Collection. The London Library has been, as usual, an essential support in my research, both for supplying me with books and for giving me access to reference books on line. I am grateful also to the British Library, and to Cambridge University Library for so speedily providing me with a copy of the dramatized version of *Great Expectations*. Richard High at the Special Collections, Brotherton Library, Leeds University, kindly sent me a photocopy of a Dickens letter held there.

Warmest thanks to Tim Wright, who has lent me manuscript

letters by Georgina Hogarth and Mrs Wharton Robinson (Nelly), and given me a copy of her translation of *Zermatt and the Valley of the Viège*. Also to Benedict Nightingale, for lending me his copy of *Julia Fortescue, afterwards Lady Gardner, and Her Circle* by George Martelli, a privately printed and rare book.

I am grateful to Jenny Hartley for her *Charles Dickens and the House of Fallen Women*, which contains many discoveries and valuable insights I have drawn on.

Thanks to Jonathan Miller for giving me a wise and illuminating tutorial on mesmerism. Also to Dr Virginia Bearn for a helpful discussion about Dickens's health. Claire Sparrow gave me useful information about psychosis. Professor Ray Dolan, director of the Wellcome Trust Centre for Neuroimaging, generously gave time to consider Dickens's symptoms, consulted with medical colleagues and reported on their conclusions, as well as presenting me with a clear account of vascular disease and of gout.

With astounding generosity Roy Stanbrook, Harbour Master of the Lower District of the Port of London, sailed me in his beautiful yacht, the *Meteor*, down the Medway from Chatham to Sheerness and into the Thames estuary as far as Gravesend, so that I could experience something similar to Dickens's childhood voyages with his father, with whom he sometimes sailed in the Navy yacht from Chatham to the Pay Office at Sheerness and back, about 1820. Roy and his wife Ann were perfect hosts, and gave my husband and me an unforgettable June day on the water. My warmest thanks to them, and also to Helen Alexander, who introduced me to Roy.

Nicholas P. C. Waloff sent me fascinating information about his ancestor, Dickens's manservant, John Thompson, which he had researched himself, for which I am grateful.

Thanks to Dickens's descendants, Lucinda Hawksley, H. D. B. Hawksley and Mark Dickens, all of whom have been helpful to me.

Thanks to David Clegg for drawing my attention to the Jarndyce catalogue entry on Dickens's listing of the contents of his part of his cellar at Gad's Hill, one of his last pieces of writing, made on Monday, 6 June 1870, in a small ruled book.

Andrew Farmer has again drawn the maps, as he did for my books on Jane Austen, Samuel Pepys and Thomas Hardy: Dickens presents a particularly difficult task, and I am again indebted to him for his patience and delighted with his work.

I was especially pleased when my old friend Douglas Matthews agreed to make the index.

I have been unusually fortunate in my publishers. Tony Lacey has been my editor at Viking Penguin for almost a quarter of a century – since 1987 – and has given me support, advice and encouragement throughout these years. Over the same period I have also benefited from the knowledge and exemplary skills of my copy editor, Donna Poppy. This is the first of my books to be edited digitally, and Donna dealt with my refusal to make my corrections on-screen, explained the process and then transferred all my pencillings to her computer – a rare act of friendship.

The work of finding and dealing with illustrations was enthusiastically entered into by Tony Lacey, Ben Brusey, Donna Poppy and Claire Hamilton. Dinah Drazin once again laid out the picture sections with great skill, taking on the challenge of my wanting to cram in more than at first seemed possible.

Robert Sanders is the hero who fixed my old computer when it gave trouble and even managed to install WordPerfect into a new one, for which I am truly grateful.

Finally thanks to my husband for once again putting up with a distracted wife, and never failing in patience and kindness.

Index

Note: Works by Charles Dickens (CD) appear directly under title; works by others under author's name.

CLAIRE TOMALIN is the author of seven highly acclaimed biographies. *The Life and Death of Mary Wollstonecraft* won the Whitbread First Book Award. *The Invisible Woman: The Story of Nelly Ternan and Charles Dickens* carried off three prizes. *Jane Austen: A Life* was described by *The New York Times* as a book that 'radiates intelligence, wit and insight'. *Samuel Pepys: The Unequalled Self* was the 2002 Whitbread Book of the Year. *Thomas Hardy: A Time-Torn Man* was hailed by Melvyn Bragg as 'another triumph for a biographer who goes from strength to strength', and *Mrs Jordan's Profession* was praised by the late John Gross as 'compelling, shrewd in its judgements, exceptionally well written, and informed by a vivid sense of the past'.

She has three children and three grandchildren, and is married to the playwright and novelist Michael Frayn.